The Production of Knowledge

Whilst a great deal of progress has been made in recent decades, concerns persist about the course of the social sciences. Progress in these disciplines is hard to assess and core scientific goals such as discovery, transparency, reproducibility and cumulation remain frustratingly out of reach. Despite having technical acumen and an array of tools at their disposal, today's social scientists may be only slightly better equipped to vanquish error and construct an edifice of truth than their forbears – who conducted analyses with slide rules and wrote up results with typewriters. This volume considers the challenges facing the social sciences, as well as possible solutions. In doing so, we adopt a systemic view of the subject matter. What are the rules and norms governing behavior in the social sciences? What kinds of research, and which sorts of researcher, succeed and fail under the current system? In what ways does this incentive structure serve, or subvert, the goal of scientific progress?

Colin Elman is Professor of Political Science and Director of the Center for Qualitative and Multi-Method Inquiry in the Maxwell School, Syracuse University. He co-founded (with Diana Kapiszewski, Georgetown University) the Qualitative Data Repository.

John Gerring is Professor of Government at University of Texas at Austin. He serves as co-PI of *Varieties of Democracy* and the *Global Leadership Project*.

James Mahoney is the Gordon Fulcher Professor in Decision-Making at Northwestern University, where he holds appointments in Political Science and Sociology. He is Founding Director of the Comparative-Historical Social Science program at Northwestern.

Strategies for Social Inquiry

The Production of Knowledge

Editors
Colin Elman, *Maxwell School of Syracuse University*
John Gerring, *University of Texas at Austin*
James Mahoney, *Northwestern University*

Editorial Board
Bear Braumoeller, David Collier, Francesco Guala, Peter Hedström, Theodore Hopf, Uskali Maki, Rose McDermott, Charles Ragin, Theda Skocpol, Peter Spiegler, David Waldner, Lisa Wedeen, Christopher Winship

This book series presents texts on a wide range of issues bearing upon the practice of social inquiry. Strategies are construed broadly to embrace the full spectrum of approaches to analysis, as well as relevant issues in philosophy of social science.

Published Titles
John Boswell, Jack Corbett and R. A. W. Rhodes, *The Art and Craft of Comparison*
John Gerring, *Social Science Methodology: A Unified Framework, 2nd edition*
Michael Coppedge, *Democratization and Research Methods*
Thad Dunning, *Natural Experiments in the Social Sciences: A Design-Based Approach*
Carsten Q. Schneider and Claudius Wagemann, *Set-Theoretic Methods for the Social Sciences: A Guide to Qualitative Comparative Analysis*
Nicholas Weller and Jeb Barnes, *Finding Pathways: Mixed-Method Research for Studying Causal Mechanisms*
Andrew Bennett and Jeffrey T. Checkel, *Process Tracing: From Metaphor to Analytic Tool*
Diana Kapiszewski, Lauren M. MacLean and Benjamin L. Read, *Field Research in Political Science: Practices and Principles*
Peter Spiegler, *Behind the Model: A Constructive Critique of Economic Modeling*
James Mahoney and Kathleen Thelen, *Advances in Comparative-Historical Analysis*
Jason Seawright, *Multi-Method Social Science: Combining Qualitative and Quantitative Tools*
John Gerring, *Case Study Research: Principles and Practices, 2nd edition*

The Production of Knowledge

Enhancing Progress in Social Science

Edited by

Colin Elman
Maxwell School of Syracuse University

John Gerring
University of Texas at Austin

James Mahoney
Northwestern University

CAMBRIDGE
UNIVERSITY PRESS

University Printing House, Cambridge CB2 8BS, United Kingdom

One Liberty Plaza, 20th Floor, New York, NY 10006, USA

477 Williamstown Road, Port Melbourne, VIC 3207, Australia

314–321, 3rd Floor, Plot 3, Splendor Forum, Jasola District Centre, New Delhi – 110025, India

79 Anson Road, #06-04/06, Singapore 079906

Cambridge University Press is part of the University of Cambridge.

It furthers the University's mission by disseminating knowledge in the pursuit of education, learning, and research at the highest international levels of excellence.

www.cambridge.org
Information on this title: www.cambridge.org/9781108486774
DOI: 10.1017/9781108762519

© Cambridge University Press 2020

This publication is in copyright. Subject to statutory exception and to the provisions of relevant collective licensing agreements, no reproduction of any part may take place without the written permission of Cambridge University Press.

First published 2020

Printed in the United Kingdom by TJ International Ltd. Padstow Cornwall

A catalogue record for this publication is available from the British Library.

ISBN 978-1-108-48677-4 Hardback
ISBN 978-1-108-70828-9 Paperback

Cambridge University Press has no responsibility for the persistence or accuracy of URLs for external or third-party internet websites referred to in this publication and does not guarantee that any content on such websites is, or will remain, accurate or appropriate.

Contents

	Detailed Contents	page ix
	List of Figures	xiii
	List of Tables	xiv
	List of Contributors	xv
	Acknowledgments	xvii
1	Introduction John Gerring, James Mahoney and Colin Elman	1

Part I Discovery 15

2	Exploratory Research Richard Swedberg	17
3	Research Cycles Evan Lieberman	42

Part II Publishing 71

4	Peer Review Tim F. Liao	73
5	Length Limits John Gerring and Lee Cojocaru	98

Part III Transparency and Reproducibility 127

6	Transparency and Reproducibility: Conceptualizing the Problem Garret Christensen and Edward Miguel	129

7	Transparency and Reproducibility: Potential Solutions Garret Christensen and Edward Miguel	165
8	Making Research Data Accessible Diana Kapiszewski and Sebastian Karcher	197
9	Pre-registration and Results-Free Review in Observational and Qualitative Research Alan M. Jacobs	221

Part IV Appraisal 265

10	Replication for Quantitative Research Jeremy Freese and David Peterson	267
11	Measurement Replication in Qualitative and Quantitative Studies Dan Reiter	284
12	Reliability of Inference: Analogs of Replication in Qualitative Research Tasha Fairfield and Andrew Charman	301
13	Coordinating Reappraisals John Gerring	334
14	Comprehensive Appraisal John Gerring	354
15	Impact Metrics John Gerring, Sebastian Karcher and Brendan Apfeld	371

Part V Diversity 401

16	What's Wrong with Replicating the Old Boys' Networks? Dawn Langan Teele	403
17	Ideological Diversity Neil Gross and Christopher Robertson	432

Part VI Conclusions   457

18	Proposals John Gerring, James Mahoney and Colin Elman	459
	References	487
	Index	543

Detailed Contents

List of Figures		*page* xiii
List of Tables		xiv
List of Contributors		xv
Acknowledgments		xvii
1	**Introduction**	1
	A Systemic Approach	3
	Social Science as a Field of Endeavor	6
	Outline	8
	Conclusion	12

Part I Discovery 15

2	**Exploratory Research**	17
	The History of Exploratory Studies	19
	What, Exactly, is an Exploratory Study?	23
	The Informal Exploratory Study (Pre-Study)	32
	Afterthoughts on Exploratory Research	37
3	**Research Cycles**	42
	The Biomedical Research Cycle	45
	The (Near-)Absence of a Research Cycle in Contemporary Political Science	52
	Costs: The Crowding-Out of Discovery – Premature Experimentation	54
	Toward a Framework for a Research Cycle	59
	What Role for Registration/Pre-Analysis Plans?	65
	Conclusions and Recommendations	68

Part II Publishing 71

4	Peer Review	73
	The Standard Practice	75
	An Evaluation of the Standard Peer Review Practice	81
	The Proposed Alternatives	87
	Conclusion	95
5	Length Limits	98
	Survey	99
	Proposal 1: Clarity and Consistency	105
	Proposal 2: No (Tight) Limits	107
	Conclusions	124

Part III Transparency and Reproducibility 127

6	Transparency and Reproducibility: Conceptualizing the Problem	129
	A Model for Understanding the Issues	130
	Publication Bias	134
	Specification Searching	143
	Inability to Replicate Results	146
	Conclusion	164
7	Transparency and Reproducibility: Potential Solutions	165
	Improved Analytical Methods: Research Designs and Meta-Analysis	165
	Study Registration	172
	Pre-Analysis Plans	174
	Disclosure and Reporting Standards	184
	Open Data and Materials, and Their Use for Replication	189
	Future Directions and Conclusion	194
8	Making Research Data Accessible	197
	What are "Data"?	199
	Making Data *Meaningfully* Accessible	201
	Evolving Infrastructure for Data Accessibility	205
	Catalyzing Access to Research Data	213
	Conclusion	219
9	Pre-registration and Results-Free Review in Observational and Qualitative Research	221
	Skewed Social Knowledge	225
	Two Institutional Responses	236

Detailed Contents

	Criteria for Blind Selection	242
	Can Studies without Results be Evaluated?	257
	Conclusion	262

Part IV Appraisal 265

10 Replication for Quantitative Research 267
 The Meanings of Replication 269
 Is there a Replication Problem? 272
 How Do Replication Crises Happen? 274
 Can We Reduce False Positives? Should We? 277
 How Do We Promote More and Better Replication Work? 279
 Conclusion 282

11 Measurement Replication in Qualitative and Quantitative Studies 284
 Measurement Replication in Quantitative and Qualitative
  Approaches 286
 Measurement Errors Exposed by Replication Efforts 289
 Going Forward 299

12 Reliability of Inference: Analogs of Replication in Qualitative Research 301
 Analogs of Replication in Qualitative Research 303
 Same-Data Assessments of Inference in Qualitative Bayesianism 318
 Suggestions for Moving Forward 331

13 Coordinating Reappraisals 334
 Reappraisal Institute 335
 Reappraisal Directory 336
 Reappraisal Scorecard 337
 Support Infrastructure 346
 Recruitment and Bias 348
 Incentives to Replicate 351
 Anticipated Impact 352

14 Comprehensive Appraisal 354
 A Different Kind of Appraisal 355
 Individualized Appraisal versus Comprehensive Appraisal 362
 Conclusions 368

15 Impact Metrics 371
 Databases 373
 Objections 379

	Clarifications	386
	The Impact of Impact Metrics	388
	Conclusions	396

Part V Diversity 401

16	What's Wrong with Replicating the Old Boys' Networks?	403
	Women in the Academic Pipeline	405
	The Normative Construction of Disciplinary Centrality	412
	Market-Driven Compensation Structures	418
	Remedies for Gender Domination	423
17	Ideological Diversity	432
	The Politics of American Social Scientists	433
	Calls for Political Diversification	434
	Evaluating the Claims	442
	Toward a Sociology of Politics and Ideas	446
	Conclusion	455

Part VI Conclusions 457

18	Proposals	459
	Conflicting Imperatives: True versus New	459
	Principles	463
	Recommendations, Exhortations, Suggestions	465
	Metrics of Reform	480
	Challenges and Opportunities	483
	References	487
	Index	543

Figures

3.1	A research cycle heuristic	page 44
5.1	Impact, marginal effects	120
6.1	AER papers with data exempt from the data-sharing requirement	153
7.1	Studies in the AEA trial registry, May 2013 to October 2018	173
9.1	Expected learning conditional on $p(H)$, $p(E|H)$, and $p(E|\sim H)$	261
10.1	Publishing barriers and replication frequency	275
12.1	Reliability of inference	304
16.1	Women's representation among faculty and doctoral recipients, 1870–2015	406
16.2	Women's representation among undergraduates and doctoral recipients in the social sciences	408
16.3	Gender and authorships in various social science disciplines, 1950–2000	413
17.1	Party identification and education	445

Tables

2.1	Mentions of methods in top sociology journals (1895–2016)	page 21
2.2	Mentions of methods in all sociology journals (1895–2016)	21
2.3	The goals and methods of different types of exploratory studies	40
3.1	A criterial framework for assessing contributions in a political science research cycle	60
4.1	A summary of the six proposals	96
5.1	Political science journals	100
5.2	Sociology journals	103
5.3	Economics journals	116
5.4	Impact, marginal effects	120
6.1	Predictive value of research findings	133
6.2	Examples of recent meta-analyses in economics	141
6.3	Transparency policies at selected top economics and finance journals	149
7.1	Erroneous interpretations under "cherry-picking"	176
9.1	Use of qualitative evidence in 94 articles in 8 highly ranked political science journals (2015 and 2016)	230
9.2	Patterns of results in 94 qualitative and mixed-method articles in 8 highly ranked political science journals (2015–2016)	233
9.3	Potential prior unobservability in all observational empirical articles published in nine leading journals in 2015	246
13.1	Reappraisals	341
13.2	Corroboration	342
13.3	Validation Types	344
13.4	Validity of Original Hypothesis	345
13.5	Reappraisal Scorecard	347

Contributors

Brendan Apfeld Department of Government, University of Texas at Austin

Andrew Charman Department of Physics, University of California at Berkeley

Garret Christensen US Census Bureau

Lee Cojocaru Department of Political Science, Boston University

Colin Elman Department of Political Science, Syracuse University

Tasha Fairfield Department of International Development, London School of Economics

Jeremy Freese Department of Sociology, Stanford University

John Gerring Department of Government, University of Texas at Austin

Neil Gross Department of Sociology, Colby College

Alan M. Jacobs Department of Political Science, University of British Columbia

Diana Kapiszewski Department of Government, Georgetown University

Sebastian Karcher Qualitative Data Repository, Syracuse University

Tim F. Liao Department of Sociology, University of Illinois at Urbana-Champaign

Evan Lieberman Department of Political Science, Massachusetts Institute of Technology

James Mahoney Departments of Political Science and Sociology, Northwestern University

Edward Miguel Department of Economics, University of California at Berkeley

David Peterson Institute for Society and Genetics, University of California, Los Angeles

Dan Reiter Department of Political Science, Emory University

Christopher Robertson Department of Sociology, Northwestern University

Richard Swedberg Department of Sociology, Cornell University

Dawn Langan Teele Department of Political Science, University of Pennsylvania

Acknowledgments

Portions of this book were presented at the annual IQMR workshop in 2017 and 2018. For feedback we are grateful to Jamie Druckman, Kendra Koivu, Markus Kreuzer, Jay Seawright, Hillel Soifer, and Steven Wilson. For skilled research assistance, we thank Isabel Castillo and Rahardhika Utama.

Several chapters evolved from previously published articles: Chapter 3 (Lieberman 2016), Chapter 5 (Gerring and Cojocaru 2016) and Chapters 6–7 (Christensen and Miguel 2018).

1 Introduction

John Gerring, James Mahoney and Colin Elman

In recent years, methods of data collection in the social sciences have expanded in range and sophistication. New data sources (many of them hosted on the worldwide web) and data harvesting techniques (e.g., web crawlers) have been discovered, leading to big-data projects of a sort previously unimaginable (Steinert-Threlkeld 2018). One can now read and electronically code foreign newspapers, government reports, interviews and even archival material without leaving one's office. Techniques for measuring obscure or sensitive attitudes and activities, and developing scales for composite indices, have been refined (Bandalos 2018). Relationships among individuals can be probed with social network tools (Borgatti, Everett and Johnson 2018). The location of subjects and events can be tracked with GIS points and polygons (Steinberg and Steinberg 2005). Surveys can be implemented with less time and cost (especially when subjects are recruited through online platforms like M-Turk, Facebook or Crowdflower), most field sites are more accessible than ever and qualitative data of all sorts can be recorded in their original form (Kapiszewski, MacLean and Read 2015).

Methodological tools for data analysis have likewise undergone major changes. A revolution in thinking about causal inference has occurred (Morgan and Winship 2015). Quasi-experimental and experimental techniques are now brought to bear on topics previously regarded as purely observational (Druckman and Green 2011; Dunning 2012; Kagel and Roth 2016). Machine learning allows one to make inferences from huge quantities of data (King 2014). New frameworks promise to broaden our thinking about causal inference through causal graphs (Pearl and Mackenzie 2018), Bayesian probability (Fairfield and Charman 2020; Humphreys and Jacobs 2021) and set theory (Schneider and Wagemann 2012). Finally, specialized software (Python, R, SAS, Stan, Stata and so forth) facilitate all of these tasks of data collection and analysis.

Clearly, a great deal of progress has been made over the past several decades. Even so, nagging worries persist about the course of social science.

Progress in these disciplines is hard to assess and core scientific goals such as discovery, transparency, reproducibility and cumulation seem frustratingly out of reach. Despite their impressive technical acumen and the many tools at their disposal, today's social scientists may be only slightly better equipped to vanquish error and construct an edifice of truth than their forbears – who conducted analyses with slide rules and wrote up results with typewriters.

As an example, let us consider the problem of reproducibility. A key issue in the production of knowledge is the *re*production of knowledge. If a finding cannot be reproduced by someone else, it cannot be directly confirmed or disconfirmed. Worryingly, many published findings cannot be repeated – or, if repeated, cannot be reproduced. Publication biases, giving precedence to methods or results that are novel, accentuate this problem. Indeed, published results may have a *lower* probability of being true than unpublished results. Insofar as replication serves as a hallmark of science, social science is falling woefully short.[1]

Even if studies are replicated perfectly, one may doubt that knowledge in these disciplines would cumulate neatly into a progressive body of research – one that discards false theories and preserves true theories, reaching consensus on an issue and constructing a unified theoretical framework upon which new knowledge can grow. Instead, one often finds that old findings are forgotten (Gans 1992), and the same theories – many of them decades or centuries old – are recycled, without ever being decisively proven or disproved, to be joined by new theories, which enjoy their time in the sun and then a slow demise.[2] Social science follows fashion, and it is not entirely clear that this year's fashion brings us closer to the truth than last year's fashion.

Our purpose in this volume is to consider the challenges facing the social sciences, as well as possible solutions to those challenges. In doing so, we adopt a *systemic* view of the subject matter. Entire disciplines, with all of their moving parts, constitute our units of analysis. We begin this chapter by laying out the approach. Next, we consider the scope of the volume, which

---

[1] See Atmanspacher and Maasen (2016), Camerer et al. (2016), Chang and Li (2015), Dewald, Thursby and anderson (1986), Ioannidis (2005), Open Science Collaboration (2012, 2015). Although there is considerable ambiguity about what it means to replicate, or fail to replicate (Parts III–IV, this volume), we take it for granted that the problem is non-trivial.

[2] On problems of cumulation and reaching consensus in the social sciences, see Abbott (2001), Chernoff (2014), Cole (1994), Collins (1994), Geller and Vasquez (2005), Johnson (2003), Rule (1997), Simowitz (1998), Sjöblom (1977, 1997), Smith (2005, 2008). On the rise and fall of intellectual movements see Frickel and Gross (2005).

encompasses all of the social sciences. In the third section, we outline the contents of the volume. The final section offers a brief conclusion.

A Systemic Approach

Traditionally, social science methodology has focused on individual studies, i.e., how to conduct a study and how (ex post) to judge the adequacy of that study. This is what one finds, for the most part, in the pages of methods journals and textbooks and in methodology classes. We have learned an enormous amount from this finely honed approach. Indeed, many of the advances signaled at the outset of this chapter may be credited to it.

Even so, the current disorderly state of social science suggests that a piecemeal approach to scientific progress may not be entirely satisfactory. Truth and falsehood are often difficult to discern, even after the most vigilant peer review. Efforts to reduce error (the publication of studies whose findings are untrue) by raising the bar to publication inevitably edge out the most innovative work, which (almost by definition) is less likely to be regarded as true, in favor of work in established research traditions, where the payoff to scientific progress is lower. Replications of work already published are rare, and their results often ambiguous (findings may be supported to some degree or in some respects, but not in others, or the results hinge upon assumptions that cannot be tested). Finally, the bits and pieces of truth that we feel fairly confident about do not fall neatly into place within a larger theoretical scaffolding. Cumulation is not easy.

A study-centered approach to social science will not solve these larger problems. In response, we propose a broader approach, one that focuses on the system within which studies are produced and vetted.

This "system" is hard to bound, as it includes multiple organizations – departments, universities, journals, presses and professional associations – each of which enjoys some degree of independence but all of which interact in crucial ways, affecting each other's behavior. For present purposes, an academic system will be understood to include all of these interacting parts. It is at least as large as a discipline (e.g., economics) and in some respects transcends individual disciplines (which are in any case overlapping, as discussed below).

We do *not* consider the broader society within which social science is situated. This lies beyond the scope of the volume, though we readily acknowledge that social science is affected by pretty much everything that goes on in society. It is not a closed system.

A systemic framework is intended to complement – not replace – methodology's traditional focus on individual studies. One sits within the other, and neither makes sense without the other. Specifically, methodological advice with respect to conducting and appraising individual studies must be consistent with meta-level advice about how to conduct one's professional life.

Unfortunately, conflicts between these two levels are rampant in today's academy. For example, signals emanating from the community of methodologists suggest that scholars should seek, above all, to avoid Type-1 errors – falsely rejecting a true null hypothesis. At the same time, signals from the academy with respect to hiring, salary and promotion suggest that innovation and productivity are the principal keys to success (Whicker et al. 1993).

A systemic approach to social science brings these potential conflicts into view, forcing us to consider how they might be harmonized and how we might avoid the whack-a-mole dynamic that often ensues when a reform focuses on one scientific goal without considering the effect of that reform on other scientific goals – or when a reform focuses on one corner of the scientific universe without considering the effect of that reform on other corners.

An example of the latter is the current call for replication, intended (among other things) to combat publication bias in favor of studies that reject the null. While the number of replications has grown in recent years it is still miniscule. Nor is it clear that it will solve the problem of publication bias. Indeed, one recent study suggests that replication studies are also subject to a distinctive publication bias of their own – in favor of studies that disconfirm a published study (Berinsky et al. 2018). This sort of ping-pong game ("True"-"Not True") is not likely to lead to a broad consensus on the topic under investigation.

A systemic approach suggests that the shortcomings of social science are not the fault of insufficiently sophisticated methods. While a study-based methodology certainly has room for improvement, further refinements are probably insufficient to solve the core problems facing the social sciences today.

Nor do we believe that social science falls short because of irresponsible or poorly trained researchers. Granted, some individuals may have a poor grasp of the methods at their disposal and thus make suboptimal choices among them or reach interpretations unwarranted by the evidence at hand. A few individuals falsify data or misreport results. Nonetheless, we believe that most researchers pursue their craft in a reasonable and honest manner.

To the extent that social scientists fail to fulfil the ideals of a progressive science, we believe the blame lies primarily with institutions rather than with individuals.[3] It is not a product of a few bad apples. It is the product of a system with fundamental design flaws.

Institutional analysis is commonplace in the analysis of politics, economics and society (DiMaggio and Powell 1991; Hall and Taylor 1996; North 1986), and it seems reasonable to apply the same analytic lens to the community of scholars. If one wishes to understand the behavior of individuals (e.g., citizens, consumers or terrorists) or organizations (e.g., governments, political parties, interest groups, firms or schools), one must understand the official rules and informal norms that structure behavior within these contexts.

An academic discipline is one such context. A priori, there are good reasons to suppose that institutions structure the behavior of social scientists. Although *academe* is often described as an "individualistic" enterprise, the competitive struggles that characterize our work fit within a common template. Indeed, the structure of rewards – based primarily upon publication in top journals and presses – is nearly identical across fields and at various stages of one's career. Moreover, the search for truth (define it how you will) is necessarily a communal enterprise. The questions scholars ask are framed by a field's existing stock of knowledge, they are addressed using research techniques they hold in common and their answers are promulgated to and judged by peers (Merton 1973b). Academics is a highly professionalized and institutionalized field of endeavor.

What, then, are the rules and norms governing behavior in the social sciences? What kinds of research, and what sort of researcher, wins and loses under the current system? In what ways does this incentive structure serve – or subvert – the goal of scientific progress? A wealth of research on institutions has shown that formal rules and informal norms often persist even when they do not facilitate what most participants would regard as an optimal outcome. Institutions are sticky, even when inefficient (David 1985). This leads to our final question. Can institutions that govern the production of knowledge be altered so as to better serve the goals of science?

These are the questions animating the present volume. Thankfully, the systemic aspects of social science have begun to receive greater attention. Responsibilities that individual scholars owe their research communities are being spelled out in a clearer fashion, and conformity to those norms is more closely monitored. The infrastructure needed for scholars to deliver on these obligations is under development. Scholars are beginning to take more

---

[3] One might also blame the subject matter, an issue discussed in the next section.

seriously the ways in which sociological aspects of knowledge production can hinder progress in the social sciences, and they have begun to devise institutional responses to those problems. We seek to take stock of this work and to push it forward – with special focus on the communal context in which individual studies are generated, digested and disseminated.

Social Science as a Field of Endeavor

Problems in realizing scientific progress are not unique to social science (Laudan 1977). However, it seems fair to say that methodological obstacles are more profound in the context of the social sciences than in the context of the natural sciences. As an example, one might consider the so-called "replication crisis." Researchers in medicine, physics and chemistry often face obstacles in replicating each other's results. Nonetheless, attempts at replication occur on a regular basis in the natural sciences, while they are rare in the social sciences. Moreover, replications in the natural sciences usually manage, over time, to sort out the good from the bad, or merely ugly – which cannot be said with confidence of the social sciences.

In these respects, we take the traditional view that natural science disciplines are more consistently on track with expectations about scientific progress than social science disciplines. This justifies our focus on the latter, a perennial problem child within the family of sciences.

It is understandable to find confusion and ambiguity in research focused on the decisional behavior of human beings, where outcomes are subject to myriad causes and to contextual variation (including variation over time), where questions of theoretical interest cannot always be studied experimentally, where categories may depend on collective agreement for their meaning and where the results of any study are available to the subjects of interest and may shape their future behavior. Social science is hard. In this light, the non-progressive features of social science are endemic to the enterprise (Collins 1994; Hacking 1999; Winch 1958).

Nonetheless, to say that pathologies are intrinsic to social science does not mean that they are always present in equal degrees. The practice of social science has fundamentally transformed over the past half-century, suggesting a high degree of malleability and the possibility of improvement. That issues of knowledge production have received attention in recent years is testament to the willingness of social scientists to examine their own routines and credentials, and to consider possible reforms. It should be clear that the authors of this volume take the goal of science seriously and do not view it as incompatible with the "naturalistic" goals associated with biology, chemistry, engineering and physics. Indeed, we draw on the experience of those fields wherever relevant.

Social science is in some ways different and in some ways the same as natural science. We do not feel the need to stake out a precise position in this perennial debate. The important point is that this book is written by social scientists and for social scientists, and does not purport to reflect upon the production of knowledge in the natural sciences except by way of an occasional comparison or contrast.

Social science, for present purposes, includes the core fields of economics, political science and sociology along with their many offshoots – business, management, communications, demography, education, environmental policy, international relations, law, social work and so forth. Fields like psychology and public health sit astride the social/natural science divide, while other fields like cultural anthropology and history straddle the social science/humanities divide. These areas lie on the periphery of our concerns.

So delimited, the social sciences share a common subject – understanding social behavior in a scientific fashion. As such, these fields have a great deal in common. They share concepts and approaches, and encounter similar methodological obstacles (Gerring 2012b). Increasingly, academics form partnerships that stretch across disciplines and publish in journals that are not restricted to any single discipline. Their topics intermingle. Accordingly, economists, political scientists and sociologists who study the same subject usually have more to say to each other than to their colleagues studying other subjects. Disciplinary boundaries are increasingly hazy – except insofar as they govern academic institutions (e.g., PhD programs, departments, conferences and journals). From a sociology-of-science perspective it matters greatly whether one's field is economics, political science or sociology. From a methodological or substantive perspective, not so much.

That is why this book is formulated in an inclusive fashion, encompassing all the social sciences. Contributing authors hail from all three major social science fields. Although some chapters are centered on one or two of these disciplines, this is a matter of familiarity and logistics. It is hard to cover all disciplines with equal facility, especially within the confines of a single chapter. Authors naturally gravitate to what they know best, and this means that each chapter is likely to tilt toward the author's home turf. In any case, none of the issues discussed in this volume are discipline-specific; they pertain broadly to all the social sciences.

Outline

Having defined the scope of this project, we turn to its content – the production of knowledge. We divide this subject into five areas, corresponding to the five sections of the book: (a) discovery, (b) publishing, (c) transparency and reproducibility, (d) appraisal and (e) diversity.

Discovery

While most work on social science methodology focuses on the task of appraisal, one must not lose sight of the importance of discovery. For social science to progress, researchers must push upon the frontiers of what is known. Innovative work, work that takes risks and conceptualizes topics in new ways, must therefore be valorized and rewarded – and, if possible, taught.

In Chapter 2, Richard Swedberg focuses on exploratory research, which he defines as research aimed at the discovery of something new and important. Swedberg argues that exploratory research is at the heart of all good research, yet exploratory research is risky (because it is often unsuccessful) and undervalued in the social sciences. He distinguishes different kinds of exploratory studies and provides guidelines for their effective use going forward. In Chapter 3, Evan Lieberman contrasts the place of exploratory work within the broader research cycle in political science versus biomedical research. Whereas exploratory studies in the biomedical sciences are valued because of their substantively important role, these studies are assigned a marginal position in political science's more truncated research cycle. Lieberman identifies the source of the problem with the disproportionate attention allocated to research focused on the precise estimation of causal effects in political science.

Publishing

Publishing in a top journal or press has long been regarded as a hallmark of professional success in the academy, and there is no sign that is likely to change in the near future. Consequently, journals and presses perform a central gatekeeping function, and rules governing access to these venues are critical to scientific progress within a discipline.

In Chapter 4, Tim F. Liao draws on his own experience as a journal editor to critically evaluate the peer review system of journal publication. He identifies several major problems with peer review as currently practiced, ranging from unconstructive, slow and cranky reviews to systemic norms that privilege normal science over new developments and paradigmatic shifts. In response, Liao proposes six specific solutions, assessing the feasibility of each. In Chapter 5, John Gerring and Lee Cojocaru consider the consequences for social science of length limits – i.e., word or page limits – in scholarly journal publications. They summarize journal practices in political science and sociology, showing that length limits are pervasive though arbitrary (in partial contrast to economics). Gerring and Cojocaru argue that length limits bias research toward topics that can meet those limits and stand as an obstacle to knowledge production in the social sciences.

Transparency and Reproducibility

Transparency and reproducibility are core components of scientific progress. Without detailed information about the data and analysis employed in a study, it is impossible for other researchers to gauge its probable truth-value or to reproduce the result.

In Chapter 6, Garret Christensen and Edward Miguel frame the nature of the problem, presenting a simple model for estimating the likelihood that research findings are true under different assumptions. They then consider several specific issues: publication bias, specification searches and the inability to reproduce findings. Using empirical data, they show that these problems are pervasive in the social sciences across all disciplines. In Chapter 7, Christensen and Miguel turn to the question of solutions. They offer several plausible if partial solutions, including study registration, pre-analysis plans, improved statistical practices and better data sharing. They suggest these solutions provide grounds for optimism going forward. In Chapter 8, Kapiszewski and Karcher argue that the benefits that data sharing has the potential to bring will accrue more quickly if scholars make their research data *meaningfully* accessible – interpretable and analyzable by others, and shared via the increasingly sophisticated infrastructures being constructed for publishing and preserving research data. They also consider a series of steps that could and, they argue, should be taken in order to establish making research data accessible as a scholarly norm and encourage more social scientists to share their data. In Chapter 9, Alan M. Jacobs explores whether pre-registration and results-free review is a solution to a serious problem in the social sciences: published results often cannot be believed. In particular, Jacobs explores whether the practices of pre-registration and results-free review can inform observational research, especially qualitative research in the social sciences. He shows why and how benefits of these practices often can be realized – and should be realized – in observation and qualitative research.

Appraisal

Scientific progress depends upon replicating the results of previous studies. Without such replications, there is no way to verify the truth-value of findings, or to extend theories to new areas (i.e., new populations). However, individual replications, by themselves, are unlikely to secure scientific progress. Findings must also be integrated into a larger body of work (e.g., meta-analysis) and a broader theoretical framework (synthesis).

In Chapter 10, Jeremy Freese and David Peterson use the crisis concerning replication in social psychology as a springboard for discussing the challenges of replication in quantitative research more generally. They note that replication itself can mean different things: the use of the same procedures, the use of the same data and/or the reproduction of findings. Freese and Peterson see issues of replication as inherently complex and raising tradeoffs for researchers that defy simplistic one-size-fits-all solutions. In Chapter 11, Dan Reiter focuses on the specific area of measurement replication, which he shows is crucial to knowledge accumulation in both qualitative and quantitative research. Reiter uses measurement replication as a lens to consider three types of errors common in the social sciences – errors in fact, errors in interpretation and context and errors in consistency of application. He concludes with concrete suggestions for improving measurement replication in the future. In Chapter 12, Tasha Fairfield and Andrew Charman consider analogs of replication for qualitative research grounded in Bayesian reasoning. They show how Bayesianism directs these researchers to explore whether previous scholars may have overstated the weight of evidence in support of the advocated argument by failing to assess how likely that evidence would be if a rival hypothesis were true. They focus on practices of appraisal that can help qualitative scholars improve inferences, building more consensus and better promoting knowledge accumulation.

In Chapter 13, John Gerring offers a specific proposal to address some of the problems raised by the replication crisis: coordinating reappraisals at an institutional level. He defines reappraisals broadly to include a large range of follow-up studies. His specific proposal includes the creation of a reappraisal institute, an accompanying infrastructure to help oversee the creation and collection reappraisals, and a scorecard system to keep track of findings and agendas. In Chapter 14, Gerring considers how *comprehensive appraisal* – a systematic and encompassing approach to reviewing a research domain – could usefully complement our current system of individualized reviews. He argues that knowledge accumulation depends on appraisal as well as discovery, but that the former is currently marginalized in the social sciences. Gerring's proposal is a remedy designed to elevate this second moment of science – the moment appraisal. In Chapter 15, Gerring teams with Sebastian Karcher and Brendan Apfeld to consider another sort of appraisal: post-publication impact metrics. They argue that quantitative measures of scholarly impact, especially citation counts for publications using databases such as Google Scholar, offer a more objective assessment of impact than reputation, which is the tradition metric. Gerring, Karcher and Apfeld systemically compare the leading databases used for citation counts, calling attention to both the appeal of citation-based metrics as well as their shortcomings.

Diversity

Diversity matters for the production of knowledge because social science shapes and is shaped by broader society. If scholars systematically fail to address important problems that exist society, including those related to race, class and gender, the enterprise falls short in its basic mission to contribute knowledge that is useful for the creation of a better world. To achieve its potential, social science must include scholars who represent the needs and aspirations of the societies in which they live. Without an adequately diverse group of scholars, social science knowledge is likely to reflect the interests of certain social groups and not others.

In Chapter 16, Dawn Teele considers the ways in which academic institutions best fit the interests of men, especially white men. Focusing on political science, she shows how the discipline's canon is still defined by the scholarship of white men, who are not centrally concerned with questions of gender and race. Teele discusses the existence of a gendered division of labor across methodology, which leaves most women's work on the low-value qualitative side of things. She calls attention to the pay gap that exists between men and women as well as the ways in which co-authorship, parental leave and spousal hiring differentially benefit men. In Chapter 17, Neil Gross and Christopher Robertson discuss the pros and cons of institutions aimed at ideological diversification in the US academy, where professors are politically liberal in high numbers. They review arguments in favor of diversification, both old and new, but do not find convincing evidence to show that diversification would enhance research or teaching. Before wholesale institutional reform, Gross and Robertson call for more research on the question of whether knowledge production would look different in a liberal-oriented versus a conservative-oriented academy.

Conclusion

The topics addressed in this volume are wide-ranging. Even so, this book is not intended to offer a comprehensive portrayal of the production of knowledge. Many aspects of this topic are ignored or only briefly touched upon. We have nothing to say, for example, about the role of funding in social science (Lewis 2000), the autonomy of academic work from social and economic pressures (Lynd 1939), the organization of higher education (Lewis 2013), the institution of tenure and standards for tenure (Bless 1998) or career patterns and workplace environments (Altbach 2000; Blackburn and Havighurst 1979; Blackburn and Lawrence 1995). Needless to say, this is not a textbook in the sociology of knowledge (Fourcade 2009; Lamont 2009; Merton 1973b).

Instead, we hope to focus attention on areas of knowledge production that (a) are deemed to be problematic (from the perspective of the broad goal of scientific progress) and (b) are potentially reformable. To that end, we asked contributors to adopt a prescriptive stance, addressing the question *What's wrong and what can be done about it?* A short conclusion offers tentative proposals, drawn largely from the foregoing chapters.

Many of the issues vetted in this volume have been previously discussed, as suggested by the trail of citations and lengthy list of references. Some of them – e.g., replication, publication bias, file-drawer bias – have long histories.[4] The contribution of this volume is to bring them together in one place, and to provide a road forward.

We trust that the results of our labors will be of interest to practicing social scientists, even if they disagree with some of our conclusions or have additional ideas for reform that are not properly vetted in this book. The historical moment seems to be ripe for reform, perhaps even revolution – though we restrict ourselves to changes that we regard as incremental.

We interpret this favorable juncture as the product of three trends. First, methodological issues have risen to the forefront of the social science

---

[4] For early work see Glass et al. (1981), Greenwald (1975), Light and Pillemer (1984), Rosenthal (1978, 1979), Smith (1980).

disciplines. We now debate the choice of research designs or estimators with the same ferocity that we once debated substantive issues and theoretical paradigms. Second, the goal of scientific progress is now (perhaps more than ever before) widely shared. Finally, social scientists are generally interested in making their work relevant to practical problems and policy debates. In order to do that, we need to get our collective act together. Specifically, scholars who study a particular question need a mechanism for attaining consensus and communicating that consensus to the broader community. In order to speak truth to power, one must have a grasp of what the truth might be, and – since this is a probabilistic endeavor – an associated level of uncertainty.

Part I

Discovery

When one considers the crowning achievements of science, one thinks immediately of great discoveries – penicillin, pasteurization, the general theory of relativity and so forth. It is harder to identify "home runs" in social science. Even so, there are areas of apparent advance. We know a great deal more today about what factors influence elections, about the impact of social networks and about how to improve health outcomes through public policies than we did several decades ago. These are just a few examples of progress on vitally important topics in the social sciences.

How, then, did these discoveries occur? One is tempted to say that there are no rules for discovery, as discovery involves breaking with established rules. Surely, discovery is less rule-bound than testing. This may account for the absorption of social science methodology with the latter.

Even so, one cannot simply wash one's hands of the topic of discovery in the expectation that lightbulb moments are stochastic or innate. Surely, there is more than can be said about how to push forward the perimeter of knowledge – arriving at new hypotheses and, potentially, new findings.

In this section, authors approach this topic from a systemic perspective, in keeping with the framework of the volume. Chapter 2 focuses on exploratory research, understood as research where research questions are undeveloped, or hypotheses are highly speculative – where, in any case, there is high risk of coming up empty. Chapter 3 discusses the way in which knowledge evolves through the work of many scholars, all of whom shares an interest in a problem but each of which brings a different skill or expertise to the table. In this *research cycle*, some researchers perform a key role at the beginning, identifying a problem (a diagnosis, in medical terms), while others play a role further along in the process, perhaps at the stage of developing a full-fledged theory or in testing that theory.

2 Exploratory Research

Richard Swedberg

Exploratory research in social science can be defined in different ways, but its core, I believe, consists of an attempt to discover something new and interesting, by working your way through a research topic.[1] Doing this type of research is risky by definition, since it is not possible to know in advance if something novel will come out of the whole thing. And for an answer, you have to wait until you are well into the research process.

Looking at things from this perspective means that all good science is the result of exploratory research. The opposite is unfortunately not the case; all exploratory research, as most of us know from experience, does not result in something innovative. But again, this can only be found out at a point when you are deep into the research.

Exploratory research, as defined here, is the soul of good research. Without the ambition to say something new, research would come to a standstill. Non-exploratory research can by definition only result in repetition of what is already known. And apart from studies that aim at replication, this will not move science forward.

There does, however, exist a problem with defining exploratory research in this way: it becomes very broad and hard to handle. The notion that research should be conducted with the ambition to say something new is imperative, but it only carries you so far. When the term exploratory research is used in this sense, it also has a tendency to become synonymous with all that is regarded as good research – plus everything that has led to this result. This means a very huge literature, and one that already covers a host of different topics.

For this reason, the focus of this chapter will be narrowed down to one particular form of exploratory research, namely *the exploratory study*. It will be argued that there exists a neglected and mostly forgotten tradition in sociology

---

[1] For useful help and information, I thank Michela Betta, Alicia Eads (for the tables), Charles Crothers, Arlie Hochschild, Jennifer Platt, the editors of this book and the anonymous readers.

to use exploratory research to produce what is known as "exploratory studies," and that something can be learned from these studies also when it comes to exploratory research in general. In this type of literature, as will be shown, we find something that is very helpful, namely references to a number of concrete studies as well as to different ways of using exploratory studies that can all be inspected and scrutinized, for strengths and weaknesses.

As will be shown next in this chapter, exploratory studies have taken a number of different forms in sociology, depending on their goals and means. The two forms that have been the most common are the following: (1) a topic that has not been researched before, is given a first tentative analysis; and (2) an already existing topic is explored in order to produce new ideas and hypotheses, but without being able to properly verify these.

But exploratory studies, it will also be suggested, can take other forms as well, including *new forms*. You can, for example, make a first exploratory study of a topic yourself, in order to see if you want to devote a full study to it. Related to this, exploratory studies represent useful tools for students, especially when they plan their dissertation. Finally, there is also the case that if someone has a radically new idea that looks promising, it may be useful to test it provisionally, because if the idea were true the consequences would be huge (so-called high-risk ideas).

For the reasons just mentioned, exploratory studies deserve to be part of the general toolkit of the social scientist, something they are currently not. In fact, little is known today about the exploratory study, not only in sociology but also in the other social sciences. I have looked at around thirty textbooks in social science methods and found that none contains anything close to a full discussion and presentation of exploratory studies. A few mention the topic, but that is all (e.g., King, Keohane and Verba 1994; Lewis-Beck, Bryman and Liao 2004; Somekh and Lewin 2005; Gray et al. 2007; Box-Steffensmeier, Brady and Collier 2008; Della Porta and Keating 2008; Walters 2010; Gerring 2012a). The history of the exploratory study is similarly unknown (e.g., Platt 1996).

Just like the early, non-reflective form of a concept is known as a proto-concept, we may call today's version of the exploratory study a proto-method (Merton 1984:267). This means, among other things, that the exploratory study is currently not as evolved as it could be. It also means that the exploratory study can be considerably improved – and some suggestions for how this can be done will be made as well.

By way of approaching the topic of exploratory studies, the next section of this chapter will look at the history of this type of study. This will be followed by an argument for a new type of exploratory study that is especially helpful for theorizing empirical material at an early stage, and that has as a purpose to help the researcher to decide whether to conduct a full study or not. A typology of the different types of exploratory studies that are discussed in this chapter will also be introduced, centered around their goals and methods.[2]

The History of Exploratory Studies

There currently exists no information on how often exploratory studies have been used, nor when they made their first appearance. To my knowledge, there only exists one single work in the social sciences that is exclusively and explicitly devoted to exploratory research, including exploratory studies. This is a slim volume called *Exploratory Research in the Social Sciences* by sociologist Robert Stebbins, which appeared in 2001 in a series by SAGE on qualitative research methods (Stebbins 2001). In its 60 pages the author describes what is meant by exploration, what an explorer is, how to write up the result of exploration and the like.

Stebbins, however, has next to nothing to say about the history of exploratory studies or how common they are. His suggestion that you can trace their origin to *The Discovery of Grounded Theory* (1967) by Barney Glaser and Anselm Strauss does not seem to be correct. The term "exploratory study" can be found in social science writings already in the late 1920s.[3] This goes for economics as well as for psychology, political science and sociology.

It would seem that the very first time that the phrase "exploratory study" appeared in a sociology journal in the United States was in 1929 (Hankins 1929:452). A few years later several sociological monographs had been published that described themselves as exploratory studies (e.g. Angell 1936:271; Blumer 1933; Dollard 1937; Stouffer and Lazarsfeld 1937).

---

[2] No attempt will be made in this chapter to discuss the method of so-called exploratory data analysis. Developed in the 1970s by mathematician John Wilder Tukey (1977), "exploratory data analysis … consists of an approach to data analysis that allows the data themselves to reveal their underlying structure and that gives the researcher a 'feel' for the data. It relies heavily on graphs and displays to reach these goals" (Pampel 2004:359). For the use of exploratory data analysis, see also Healy and Moody (2014:113–117).

[3] An N-gram similarly shows that the terms "exploratory study" and "exploratory research" started to be used in books in English in the 1920s (N-gram for "English" from September 18, 2016). There exist no entries for "exploratory study" and "exploratory research" in *The Oxford English Dictionary*.

One of these early studies received quite a bit of attention, both from other sociologists and the general public. This was a volume called *Caste and Class in a Southern Town* (1937) by John Dollard. Drawing primarily on a number of life histories, the author analyzed the race relations in a small Southern town in a way that drew praise from such reviewers as W. E. B. Du Bois and Robert E. Park (Du Bois 1937; Park 1937).

Dollard described his work as an exploratory study and said that "the task of an exploratory study is to pick out the crude outline of the object later to be more exactly defined" (Dollard 1937:32). When his study was reissued in 1949, Dollard was careful to point out that an exploratory study is by definition not of very high scientific quality. He also presented a normative argument why it may be useful to conduct an exploratory study. When you analyze an urgent social problem, Dollard said, you cannot always wait till all the information on the topic is available.

I would not have the reader think that I believe this book to be a good example of scientific work in its best and terminal form. I see it rather as an exploratory work of science, of the fumbling and fiddling out of which more authoritative descriptions of reality will emerge. I wish I could be certain that we would have the time for a final scientific description of our society before we shall be called to account for its disastrous imperfections. (Dollard 1937: xiv)

Everett C. Hughes, who by this time had replaced Robert E. Park as the leader of the Chicago School, reviewed the new edition of Dollard's book for *The American Journal of Sociology*. In his view Dollard was wrong in equating good science with good methods; Hughes also criticized Dollard for not discussing the issue of whether the main topic had been properly understood and conceptualized. In the view of Hughes, "primitiveness of method probably does less damage than overrefinement of techniques applied to problems that have not been sharply defined and conceptualized" (Hughes 1949:208).

A few years after Dollard's book appeared, the first journal article in sociology that declared itself to be an exploratory study was published (Hayes 1942). The author, who is forgotten today, suggested that an exploratory study is based on research that is not representative in nature. For a sample to be representative, you need to use statistics. "The study is regarded as preliminary or exploratory because the instrument by which the data were obtained has not been refined and perfected; nor has a statistically reliable sample been obtained" (Hayes 1942:165).

Even if exploratory studies have not attracted much commentary during their existence, they have nonetheless been an important part of US sociology. The methods that have been most popular among sociologists are (in this

Exploratory Research

Table 2.1 Mentions of methods in top sociology journals (1895–2016)

	Title	Abstract	Text	Text
Survey	100	1,117	6,922	42%
Network	214	505	2,592	16%
Case study	59	137	1,489	9%
Experiment	81	208	2,579	16%
Participant observation	6	25	283	2%
Ethnography	7	27	508	3%
Exploratory study	4	8	276	2%
Any method mentioned				90%

Note: The number of all articles in JSTOR has been established through a search of "the."
Source: JSTOR October 15, 2016. The three journals are *American Journal of Sociology* (1895–2015), *American Sociological Review* (1936–2013) and *Social Forces* (1925–2012).

Table 2.2 Mentions of methods in all sociology journals (1895–2016)

	Title	Abstract	Text	Text
Survey	1,331	10,068	61,497	35%
Network	984	3,338	27,572	16%
Case study	806	1,761	15,130	9%
Experiment	464	1,545	20,216	12%
Participant observation	18	451	3,375	2%
Ethnography	141	374	6,373	4%
Exploratory study	131	159	2,648	2%
Any method mentioned				80%

Note: The number of all articles in JSTOR has been established through a search of "the."
Source: JSTOR October 15, 2016.

order): surveys (by a broad margin); networks, experiments and case studies; and ethnography, participant observation and exploratory studies. This goes for the three top journals in US sociology as well as for sociological journals in general (see Tables 2.1 and 2.2). Judging from JSTOR, it would also seem that more exploratory studies have been carried out in sociology than in either political science, psychology or economics. While you can find exploratory studies in the main journals of the professional associations of sociology, psychology and political science, this is not the case with economics.[4]

---

[4] If you include all of the economics journals in JSTOR, a different picture emerges; economics now looks more like the other social sciences.

By analyzing the exploratory studies that have been published in sociological journals, one can learn quite a bit about the way that this type of study has been seen by sociologists and for what purpose it has been used. What an analysis of this type does not reveal, however, is that several of the best-known studies in US sociology are exploratory studies, and that the authors of works in this genre include such prominent sociologists as Herbert Blumer, James Coleman, Alvin Gouldner, Arlie Hochschild, Marie Jahoda, Paul Lazarsfeld, Seymour Martin Lipset, Robert K. Merton and Samuel Stouffer. As examples of articles and books that are exploratory studies (according to explicit statements by their authors), one can mention such well-known works in sociology as Merton's study of locals and cosmopolitans (1949); *Voting* (1954) by Berelson, Lazarsfeld and McPhee; *Patterns of Industrial Democracy* (1954) by Gouldner; *Union Democracy* (1956) by Lipset, Trow and Coleman, and *The Managed Heart* (1983) and *Strangers in Their Own Land* (2016) by Arlie Hochschild. Some methodological innovations also have their origin in exploratory studies, such as snowball sampling.[5]

Most of the sociologists just mentioned were associated with the Department of Sociology at Columbia University and its Bureau of Applied Social Research (1944–), led by Paul Lazarsfeld. In fact, more than 30 studies that were either exploratory studies or pilot studies were produced under the auspices of the Bureau by C. Wright Mills, Hans Zetterberg, Kingsley Davis and other well-known sociologists (Barton 1984).[6] According to the standard work on the history of survey research in the United States, much of what was produced at the Bureau during the height of its existence can be characterized as "exploratory forays in pursuit of interesting ideas in theory and method, often conceived as work to be tested later by broader inquiry" (Converse 1987:286).

Since Columbia University was the leading department in sociology after World War II for something like 20 years, it would be helpful to know how

---

[5] According to Herbert Hyman, "The study [by Merton on *Time* readership from 1943] also yielded a methodological by-product, the procedure later named snowball sampling" (Hyman 1991:204; see also Handcock and Gile 2011). Merton had asked the readers of *Time* to name people they considered influential. See also Barton (1979), Converse (1987:286 ff.).

[6] It is common in modern sociology to distinguish between pilot studies and exploratory studies, with the former meaning an early run to test if some survey question or the like works well. Many sociologists in the recent past, however, have used the terms pilot study and exploratory study interchangeably, and roughly in the sense of an early but incomplete study of a certain phenomenon (e.g., Merton 1949:181, 194; Lipset and Bendix 1952:503; Hughes 1960:viii). It can be added that just as there exists next to no knowledge today of the use of exploratory studies in sociology, this is also the case with pilot studies (e.g., Platt 2011; see, e.g., van Teijlingen and Hundley 2001).

What, Exactly, is an Exploratory Study?

> This report is wholly of an exploratory nature. Its purpose is to develop ideas and techniques. Any resemblance between the figures in this report and in a real survey will be pure coincidence.
>
> – Robert K. Merton," TIME-Readership and the Influence Structure of Dover, N.J." (1943), p. i

It is an interesting fact that even if several of the key members of the Department of Sociology at Columbia University used exploratory studies, these were not mentioned in the important reader in research methods that Paul Lazarsfeld and Morris Rosenberg published in 1955, *The Language of Social Research*. Whatever the reason for this may have been, it helps to explain the semi-obscurity that surrounds the method of exploratory studies.

Another fact that has operated in the same direction is that the sociologists at Columbia University who used exploratory studies often mentioned this fact somewhere deep in the text. In such well-known studies as *Union Democracy* and *Patterns of Industrial Bureaucracy*, for example, the reader is not told that these works constitute exploratory studies until the very end of the book, in an appendix (Lipset, Trow and Coleman 1956:430; Gouldner 1954:247; see also Angell 1936:271; Hochschild 2016:247).[7] It is true that Merton begins his article on locals and cosmopolitans with the statement that "this is an exploratory study," but as far as I can tell this is an exception (Merton 1949:180).

It is possible to argue that using the expression "exploratory study" is of less importance than using the approach that comes with the term.[8] and this brings us to the question of trying to describe what characterizes an

---

[7] For more recent examples of the tendency to "hide" the fact that a study is of an exploratory nature somewhere in the text, see, e.g., Skocpol (1980:156). In a discussion of neo-Marxist theories of the state, Skocpol here argues that an "exploratory essay" can be useful. The reason she gives is that this type of study helps you to replace an empty discussion of theory with an exploration of the interface between theories and a concrete historical trajectory (in this case the New Deal).

[8] It is, for example, possible to see the studies by Erving Goffman as a kind of exploratory study. In *The Presentation of Self in Everyday Life* Goffman says, for example, that his analysis in this study constitutes "a guide worth testing in case-studies" (Goffman 1959:xii).

exploratory study. The way that this will be done is not by citing some definition or analyzing sample of articles from JSTOR, but by taking a good look at some of the studies that were produced at Columbia University. There are several advantages to this way of proceeding. First, while the exploratory study was not invented by the sociologists at Columbia University, it was used here by a number of researchers who were all in contact with one another. In this way, the exploratory study acquired a certain collective or general form. Also, given the high caliber of the work by people such as Merton, Lazarsfeld, Gouldner and so on, we would expect to find solid arguments in their studies about the advantages and disadvantages of using exploratory studies.

What, then, does an exploratory study look like, if we use as our model the kind of studies that were produced at Columbia University? According to a couple of studies, it was the empirical situation that made it necessary to use an exploratory approach. In their joint study from 1937, Lazarsfeld and Stouffer state that it was difficult for them to get good data on the effect of the Depression on the family (Lazarsfeld and Stouffer 1937). The reason for this was that by this time the most dramatic downturn in the business cycle was over. In this situation, they noted, an exploratory study would be useful.

In his study of nationalism in Nigeria, James Coleman advanced a similar argument as to why his study was exploratory in nature (Coleman 1958). The level of passions involved, he said, made it hard to get solid facts. The existing facts were often fragmentary and contradictory in nature (Coleman 1958:vi).

A general lack of knowledge about some topic that was important to study constituted another reason for using an exploratory study. There was a need to know more about some topic; and since very little information existed, the study had to be exploratory in nature. Merton, for example, used this argument in his study of medical students as well as in a study of the role of age among scientists (Merton 1957, 1973a).

There also existed another reason for carrying out an exploratory study, according to Merton et al. While some social phenomenon may already have been studied quite a bit, there is always a need for new and interesting hypotheses. Also in this case the researcher was justified in moving ahead, with less-than-stellar facts. But even if some new hypotheses were produced, they could not be verified. Or, in Merton's succinct formulation, this type of exploratory study was designed "to raise questions rather than to answer them" (Merton 1973a:507).

The language in hypothesis-generating exploratory studies typically contains a number of qualified formulations, which signal to the reader that the hypotheses are tentative in nature. Something "may" be true or "appear" to be the case; "there is some evidence that" something is true and so on (Merton 1949:193, 199, 206; see also, e.g., Merton 1973a:544, 556). According to one study, "words like 'few' or 'many in this article refer, of course, only to frequencies within the interview material and must be understood within the limitations of our unrepresentative sample" (Jahoda and Cook 1952:301, n.6).

One might think that the hypothesis-generating exploratory study would lose in value once its creative hypotheses had been proved or disproved by other studies. But this is not necessarily what has happened, and studies like *Union Democracy* and *Patterns of Industrial Democracy* are still read and cited today. The reason for this is that they address substantive issues in powerful and inspiring ways. In the case of the study by Lipset, Trow and Coleman, one can find many interesting ideas about democracy and the social structure of trade unions; in the case of Gouldner's study, one finds several creative insights about the use of formal versus informal rules in a factory.

If we now switch from the topic of what to study and why to the question of how to carry out an exploratory study, it is clear that people had different opinions. At one end of the spectrum, there are Stouffer and Lazarsfeld, who in *Research Memorandum on the Family in the Depression* (1937) laid down fairly rigorous rules for how to proceed when you gather data in an exploratory study. At the other end, there are those who advocated a more flexible approach, such as Merton (1949, 1957) and Gouldner (1954).

In primarily focusing on "the methodological difficulties" that come with exploratory studies, Stouffer and Lazarsfeld state that this type of study should have three general goals (Stouffer and Lazarsfeld 1937:27). These are: to *nullify*, to *verify* and to *clarify*. For this to be possible, the hypotheses must also be properly operationalized.

The plan has been [in this study] to state a hypothesis in rather general terms, discuss its theoretical implications, and then to restate it in operational facts so that facts to be collected can either verify it, nullify it, or at the least, clarify it. (Lazarsfeld and Stouffer 1937:3)

Stouffer and Lazarsfeld did not approve of the tendency of some sociologists to use "broad concepts" and argued that these should be eliminated (Lazarsfeld and Stouffer 1937:3). When they spoke of verification, they meant using statistical tools. And when they referred to the need for clarification, they were especially thinking of case studies.

It is clear that statistics constituted the only way to truly verify something for Stouffer and Lazarsfeld. Still, they were careful to point out that statistics has its limits. They ended their study with the following statement.

Some of us are extremely interested in helping push research more in the direction of verification. But that cause will not be served by an insistence on an exclusive technique which too often may yield trivial results where valid, and pretentious nonsense where invalid. (Stouffer and Lazarsfeld 1937:201)

The main target of Stouffer and Lazarsfeld, however, was not so much the lack of statistics in exploratory studies as the ways in which case studies were used. They noted that data of very poor quality was sometimes used in this type of study, especially in community studies. It was imperative, in their view, to always try to use high-quality data. The situation may be such that case studies are needed, but this is no reason for accepting low-quality data.

It is true that many exploratory studies made use of case studies (or a single case study), and also that authors sometimes failed to live up to the expectations of Stouffer and Lazarsfeld. What is not so obvious in hindsight, however, is why Stouffer and Lazarsfeld only discussed statistics and case studies. Maybe this was due to the fact that they wrote their rules for how to conduct exploratory studies well before the wave of exploratory studies at Columbia University had begun.

However the circumstances, besides case studies another method that was often used in exploratory studies was the interview. As a distinct method, the interview had its breakthrough among sociologists in the late 1930s, and it soon existed in many different forms (Platt 2002). Open-ended interviews or "exploratory interviews," as they were sometimes also called, were quite popular (e.g., Jahoda and Cook 1952:296–297; Lipset, Trow and Coleman 1956:vi–vii; Zuckerman 1972:169). The focused interview, another novelty at the time, was also seen as suitable for exploratory studies (e.g., Merton and Kendall 1946; Merton, Fiske and Kendall 1956:12–15; Merton 1987a:557–558).

But interviews were not the only other method that was used, besides case studies and statistics. Merton, for example, did not only use surveys, case studies and (focused) interviews in his exploratory studies, but also sociometric procedures and so-called sociological diaries (e.g., Merton, Reader and Kendall 1957:42–53). According to Merton, it was important to use several different methods in exploratory studies.

One can find a detailed discussion of what methods to use in exploratory studies in one of the most popular methods textbooks in sociology of the time – *Research Methods in Social Science* (1951, 1957) by Marie Jahoda and others. In order to carry out a study of this type, the reader is told, you may for example use the method of "the experience survey" (people with much experience of what is to be studied are interviewed) or the method of "'insight-stimulating' examples" (the focus is on selected and especially interesting instances of what you want to study; see Jahoda, Deutsch and Cook 1951, 1:32–47; Selltiz, Jahoda, Deutsch and Cook 1959:51–65). Marie Jahoda and one of her co-authors of this textbook also conducted an exploratory study of security clearance and related topics, in which such topics as jokes and "the social atmosphere" were probed for ideas and leads (Jahoda and Cook 1952:301, 312).

If Stouffer and Lazarsfeld could be found at one end of the spectrum, when it comes to rigor in handling methods in exploratory studies, Alvin Gouldner was at the other end. In his view, one of the great advantages of the exploratory study was precisely that it allowed you to ignore the demands for verification, and instead focus on developing new and interesting hypotheses.

In one of his exploratory studies, Gouldner and his co-author noted that "we have deliberately sought to devise and place ourselves within a 'context of discovery' rather than a 'context of proof'" (Gouldner and Peterson 1962:63). The reason for this stance, they said, was that existing statistical methods were not suitable for discovering and developing new ideas.

All of us are aware that social scientists today often face the choice of using elegant methods on trivial problems or, putting down fastidious inclinations, of confronting basic problems with available methods, even if they have to trim their statistical sail to do so. We are under no illusion [that the main problem discussed in this study] has been definitely solved. We have not found the Northwest Passage. Yet the effort reported on here may have given others a clearer glimpse of where and how to look for it. (Gouldner and Petersen 1962:65–66)

Gouldner writes similarly in *Patterns of Industrial Bureaucracy* that,

the objective of this study, then, is to identify some of the variables relating to bureaucratization, hypothetically accounting for its growth or contraction. No effort has been made to specify metrically or quantify these variables or their interrelations. Measurement, it would seem, first requires some degree of clarity about what is to be measured. (Gouldner 1954:17).

In summing up what has been said so far in this chapter on what constitutes an exploratory study, we can tentatively say the following. An exploratory study can essentially be carried out for two different purposes. The first is to increase the knowledge of a topic that is little known but needs to be better known. The second is to generate new and interesting hypotheses about a topic that is already known.

There also exists some variation when it comes to the means of how to carry out an exploratory study, as opposed to its goals. According to some sociologists, you must operationalize your concepts and use the facts to verify, nullify, clarify. You should use statistical evidence whenever possible; when this is not possible, you can use case studies but in a very careful way. Other sociologists, in contrast, were of the opinion that you can also use open-ended interviews, single case studies and many other methods, as long as these can help you to come up with new ideas and hypothesis.

It should be emphasized that studies with the purpose of generating new ideas were often very thorough, even if the data was not of the type that allowed for verification. When Merton, for example, carried out the exploratory study that resulted in the distinction between locals and cosmopolitans, he interviewed 116 people. *Patterns of Industrial Bureaucracy* by Gouldner was based on 174 interviews as well as a huge number of observations and documents.

It was not acceptable, in other words, to use just about any way to produce interesting results. A sociologist who wanted to carry out an exploratory study, in order to come up with some new hypotheses, should be able to justify why she used a certain method; she also had to gather quite a bit of material. A certain tension resulted from these two demands. On the one hand, the point of the exploratory research was to come up with new and exciting hypotheses. On the other hand, the only way you were allowed to do this was by following the rules of how to use a certain method, be it case studies, exploratory interviews and so on.

This tension was clearly present in the view of the single case study; it is still not clear what differentiates the (single) exploratory case study, on the one hand, from the explanatory or descriptive case study, on the other.[9] It was not this issue, however, that triggered the debate in the mid-1950s that led to the

---

[9] "The exploratory case study investigates distinct phenomena characterized by a lack of detailed preliminary research, especially formulated hypotheses that can be tested, and/or by a specific research environment that limits the choice of methodology" (Streb 2010). *Medical Innovation* by Coleman, Katz and Menzel fits this description. It was preceded by a pilot study but characterized as a non-representative "'case study'" (Coleman, Katz and Menzel 1966:17, 191). According to Streb, "the main reason for the controversy caused by exploratory case study is its intuitive approach, which is also its biggest advantage when phenomena are studied that are as yet unrecognized."

decline of exploratory studies at Columbia University. This was instead the use of significance tests (e.g., Selvin 1957:519–520).

Lazarsfeld and others at the Bureau of Applied Social Research took the position that you do not need to use significance tests in exploratory studies (e.g., Katz 1955; Kendall 1957:301 ff; Converse 1987:285–286). For a good example of the type of arguments that were advanced, the reader is referred to the methodological appendix that Coleman wrote for *Union Democracy*, in which he contrasts "exploratory studies" to "confirmatory studies" (Lipset, Trow and Coleman 1956:419–438; cf. Selvin 1957:519 n.3). This appendix is thoughtful and well worth reading today. Coleman notes, for example, that when you are interested in getting to understand the way that a social system works, it may be enough to study one case intensely, in contrast to when you want to describe and generalize from a population. "Statistical tests of hypotheses," he wrote, "seem to be of quite limited aid in building theoretical social science" (Lipset, Trow and Coleman 1956:432).

There also existed another argument why you could dispense with significance tests. According to Patricia Kendall, also associated with the Bureau of Applied Social Research, "at [an] early stage of thinking about [some problem] it would seem desirable to assemble a wide array of evidence, even if some of it is not conclusive" (Kendall 1957:302).

But Coleman and the other Columbia sociologists were sharply criticized for their views, and they can be said to have lost the debate, in the sense that their arguments for ignoring tests of significance were not heard after this time. Jim Davis, also a rigorous methodologist, argued that he was well aware that not using tests of significance was "the trademark" of people working at the Bureau of Applied Social Research (Davis 1958:445). In the view of Davis, however, this view was "dangerous"; "the net result is 'art', not 'science' " (Davis 1958:446). To what extent the disappearance of exploratory studies among the avant-garde of US sociology from around 1960 and onwards was caused by critique of this type is not clear. It would nonetheless seem that arguments of Davis' type helped to create the impression that exploratory studies are "unscientific" and therefore should be avoided.

While the discussion of significance tests among quantitatively oriented sociologists involved a number of sociologists and eventually resulted in a book (Morrison and Henkel 1970), the discussion of exploratory studies among qualitative sociologists was not very vigorous. They were basically uninterested in the method of the exploratory study, which they felt was a way of ignoring field work in sociology. Field work, in their view, was only seen as legitimate by quantitative sociologists if it was used in exploratory studies, while statistics had to be used in the main and definitive study.

As an example of this type of one can mention a critique from 1960 made by Everett C. Hughes.

Some place is given to less formal field observation [in survey research], but it is called "pilot study" or "exploratory study", and is considered preparatory to the main business of getting a questionnaire on the road. Its aim is to learn how to standardize the questions one wants to ask, not generally to learn what questions to ask. Great ingenuity is sometimes shown in such exploration and pretesting, but it is usually done with a certain impatience, since it delays the real work of 'administering' the questionnaire. Once the questionnaire is settled upon, any doubts about the questions must be explained away, since it is too expensive and disturbing to change anything at this point. (Hughes 1960:viii)

Herbert Blumer, another leading figure in qualitative sociology, was similarly critical of exploratory studies of the Columbia type (see also Glaser and Strauss 1967:259–262). Like Hughes, he felt that they were part of a trend to ignore fieldwork in sociology and replace it with statistics. Blumer also pointed out that it was impossible to get money for an exploratory study, since you would invariably be asked when you applied what your hypotheses were, what data you intended to use, and so on – all questions that could only be answered *after* the exploratory study (Blumer 1969:37).

In Blumer's view this led to a situation in which sociologists who used survey research and other statistically based methods ended up doing research without having much knowledge of what they were studying.

The scholar who lacks firsthand familiarity [with his topic] is highly unlikely to recognize that he is missing something. Not being aware of the knowledge that would come from firsthand acquaintance, he does not know that he is missing that knowledge. Since the sanctioned scheme of scientific inquiry is taken for granted as the correct means of treatment and analysis, he feels no need to be concerned with firsthand familiarity with that sphere of life. In this way, the established protocol of scientific inquiry becomes the unwitting substitute for a direct examination of the social world. (Blumer 1969:37–38)

While Blumer did not advocate the use of the Columbia version of exploratory studies, he did suggest that sociologists should engage in what he called "exploration" as part of their research. When you carry out a study, he said, you should begin by doing field work in the form of "exploration." Blumer described this part of the study as being broad and flexible, something that was very important at the outset of the research.

The phase of exploration should be followed by what Blumer called "inspection," which can be described as the analytical part of the inquiry. You now try to transform the result of the exploratory phase into something that is more general and conceptual in nature. The end result is a form of theory, which is firmly based on empirical material.

Blumer played a central role during the last decades of his life at the Department of Sociology at Berkeley; one of his students in exploratory studies was Arlie Hochschild, who recalls:

I learned "exploratory analysis" from Blumer whose course on social interaction I audited but didn't take. Interview "around" a subject he told us, in order to locate it. Blumer was carrying to Berkeley the "Chicago" tradition of ethnography. (Hochschild 2017)

Hochschild's first exploratory study appeared in the late 1960s, and today she is the best-known proponent of this type of work in contemporary sociology (Hochschild 1969). According to Hochschild, all of her most important studies are exploratory studies (Hochschild 2016:247), from *The Managed Heart* (1983) over *The Second Shift* (1989) and *Time-Bound* (1997) to *Strangers in Their Own Land* (2016).

In *Strangers in Their Own Land*, Hochschild describes her method in the following way.

This book is based on a kind of research sociologists describe as "exploratory" and "hypothesis generating". The goal of it is not to see how common or rare something is, or where one does and doesn't find it, or to study how the something comes and goes through time – although I draw on the research of others who address such questions. My goal has been to discover what that something actually is. (Hochschild 2016:247)

Hochschild's approach to exploratory studies in *Strangers in Their Own Land* differs on one interesting point from the way that exploratory studies were conducted at Columbia University. People like Coleman, Gouldner et al. were of the opinion that you can only generate hypotheses with the help of exploratory studies, but not test them, and that this should be clearly stated. The test would presumably be made in another study. In *Strangers in their Own Land* Hochschild both develops some ideas and tests these statistically (with the help of Rebecca Elliott and Mike Hout).

Whether this strategy of both suggesting and testing ideas in the very same study will be followed by other social scientists who are interested in exploratory studies remains to be seen. It does, however, represent a new and interesting way to carry out an exploratory study, and is from this perspective an innovation of sorts in the history of exploratory study. It will hopefully also help to obliterate the false impression that exploratory studies are qualitative in nature, while real studies are based on statistics.

The Informal Exploratory Study (Pre-Study)

The types of exploratory study that flourished after World War II still exist, even if they do not seem to be regarded as a very attractive option by modern social scientists. As already mentioned, current textbooks on methods do not discuss exploratory studies; students are not being taught how to carry them out. Still – and this is the theme of this section of the chapter – a case can be made for also using exploratory studies today.

Since the modern world is in a state of constant change, it happens quite often that a new topic needs to be understood and tentatively explored by social scientists. Among recent examples one can mention globalization, climate change and the intersection of biology and sociology. It is also clear that topics that are already well established are often in need of new and creative hypotheses. Without these, social science research will become lifeless and dull. Exploratory studies represent one antidote to this.

It should also be noted that the situation when it comes to methods is somewhat different today than what it was in the years after World War II. Many new methods have been introduced into sociology after the demise of the Columbia School, and old methods have been improved. The attitude toward what methods should be used has also changed in sociology. Mixed methods are, for example, becoming popular today, and ethnographic studies are increasingly being accepted. All of these changes make it imperative to raise the question of whether you do not also need to update the exploratory study.

With this purpose in mind, I would like to make an argument for a new type of exploratory study. Its main purpose is to unleash the full potential of exploratory studies to produce new ideas and hypotheses. Just as free will exists, so does free thinking, and what I shall call the informal exploratory study attempts to exploit precisely this feature to its fullest.

An important characteristic of this type of exploratory study is that it is not intended to be published. This may seem like a trivial statement. It is, however, precisely this feature that allows it to be more creative than the old type of exploratory study. The reason for this is that it allows the researcher to use any kind of method, as long as it has a positive result in terms of ideas.

The old type of exploratory study lost much of its appeal, as we have seen, by being attacked from two sides. On the one hand, statistically minded sociologists argued that significance tests must always be used or the result of the study must be discounted (e.g., Morrison and Henkel 1970). On the other hand, qualitative sociologists saw little use for exploratory studies (e.g., Everett C. Hughes, Herbert Blumer). They argued that more field work and less statistics were needed, and that exploratory studies filled no useful role.

Both of these critiques, however, lose much of their force if the exploratory study is not published. The reason for this is that both the demand to be more systematic and scientific, on the one hand, and that field work should hold a privileged position vis-à-vis statistics, on the other, now become irrelevant. What matters is not the method and how well it is used, but to come up with new ideas, however this is done.

But if an exploratory study is not going to be published, why should you conduct it in the first place? and, if you decide to do so, when should this be done? The purpose of this type of study, to repeat, is to maximize the chances of coming up with something new. And the time to use this type of study is *before* a full study has been decided on. This is the reason why it has also been called a *prestudy* (Swedberg 2014).

An informal exploratory study has primarily two purposes. One of these is to make the researcher know something about her topic before the design for the main study has been drawn up. The second is for the researcher to come up with new ideas. This can be accomplished in several ways. If a standard method is used, for example, a small sample is enough since the point is to get some knowledge and come up with new ideas, not to amass evidence. More importantly, any kind of "method" that may throw light on the topic can be used – be it in the form of guesses, dreams, sleeping on the matter, poetry or whatever else will trigger some new idea or insight about the topic.

By proceeding in this way, the researcher will have a chance to get to know the topic in a non-systematic but novel manner. She will also be in a better position to judge if she is on the trace of something really new and interesting than if she had not carried out the informal exploratory study. If this does seem to be the case, carrying out a full study may lead to some important results. The researcher now has some good reasons to investigate the topic for full force and according to the rules for verification. But if this is *not* the case – if nothing in the early study points to some novel ideas or insights being possible – it might be a good idea to cancel the project.

When you conduct research there is never a guarantee that the results will be worthwhile. This is the situation that all serious researchers face. To cite Max Weber in "Science as a Vocation": "The scientific worker has to take into his bargain the risk that enters into all scientific work: Does an 'idea' occur or does it not?'" (Weber 1946:136). By carrying out an informal exploratory study, however, it is possible to decide at an early stage if it might be worthwhile or not to engage in a full-scale study of some topic.

A few reservations are in place. First, note that while an informal exploratory study may maximize the chances of being creative, it only has the power to suggest ideas, never to prove them. For the latter, the use of solid methods is necessary, and this means that a full study according to the rules must be conducted.

There is also the fact that innovative ideas may develop during the course of a full study, whether it is preceded by an exploratory study or not. This is especially the case if the researcher has worked for a long time on a certain type of problem. The same is true if a study has been very long in gestation, such as *Union Democracy*, which Lipset worked on for several years before he was joined by Martin Trow and James Coleman (Lipset 1967). But again, and as Weber says, you never know when you will get an idea, and working hard is unfortunately no guarantee. "Ideas occur when they please, not when it pleases us" (Weber 1946:136).

Exactly how does the informal type of exploratory study maximize creativity in research? In addressing this question, which is central to the argument that is being made here, it may be helpful to briefly refer to the concept of *abduction* that was introduced by philosopher Charles Sanders Peirce (e.g., Chomsky 2009:35–38; Swedberg 2014:236–246). While this concept is well known in philosophy, it is less commonly used in the social sciences.

By abduction, Peirce means the invention of a scientific explanation. To come up with an explanation means adding something that is new to the factual situation. This cannot be accomplished either through induction or deduction but only through abduction. The abduction addresses an empirical issue but is not based on empirical facts. It is also not worth anything, according to Peirce, before it has been tested against facts according to current scientific practice.

"Abduction is the process of forming an explanatory hypothesis" (Peirce 1934:171). Note that Peirce uses the word "process" in this well-known quote. Even if it may feel like a "flash" when you have an idea for an explanation (abduction), it could not have happened without hard and imaginative work by a well-trained scientist. According to Peirce,

A[bduction] is that process in which the mind goes over all the fact of the case, absorbs them, digests them, sleeps over them, assimilates them, dreams of them, and finally is prompted to deliver them in a form, which, if it adds something to them, does so only because the addition serves to render intelligible what without it, is unintelligible. (Peirce 1906:4–5; 1934:181)

Drawing on Peirce's ideas, I suggest that a social scientist who wants to carry out an exploratory study can use just about anything to come up with an explanation. The main point is to develop a new idea. But how this is done, and if the method is reliable or not, or if result is verifiable or not, is irrelevant. In the passage just cited, Peirce mentions dreaming as one of the methods that can be used. Elsewhere he also says that scientists have much to learn from artists when it comes to making sharp observations (Peirce 1992:182).

By way of elaborating a bit on Peirce's last idea, let us for a moment imagine what may be called art-based exploratory research. Take, for example, the interview technique that has been developed by Svetlana Alexievich, who received the Nobel Prize in literature in 2015 (e.g., Knowles and Cole 2008; Barone and Eisner 2011). According to Alexievich, when you interview a person you should try to avoid the official version of things ("the script"). What is important is instead to help the person to find her own voice ("their own personal story"; e.g., Palattella 2016). By proceeding in this way, you may get a fresh and more accurate empirical account of what has happened.

There exist many other ways to increase the chances of perhaps making a discovery when you investigate something empirically. In trying to nail down the meaning of a phenomenon it may, for example, be useful to try to come up with associations or work with different metaphors and analogies. There also exist some other useful suggestions for how to develop new ideas in the appendix to *The Sociological Imagination* by C. Wright Mills, entitled "On Intellectual Craftmanship" (Mills 1959:195–226).

By proceeding in these and similar ways, what Merton calls serendipity may be triggered (Merton 1968b:158–162; Merton and Barber 2006). While the notion of serendipity is well known, Merton has also developed some other ways that facilitate the discovery of new things. One of these is to look for new problems, rather than for solutions to old ones ("problem-finding"). "It is often more difficult to find and to formulate a problem than to solve it" (Merton 1959:ix).

Another of Merton's suggestions for how to proceed is to specify exactly what you do not know. "Specified ignorance" is defined as "the express recognition of what is not yet known but needs to be known in order to lay the foundation for still more knowledge" (Merton 1987b:1). Furthermore, once you know what you are looking for, you will also want to locate the right type of material to study it. "Strategic research materials" consist of "strategic research sites, objects, or events that exhibit the phenomena to be explained or interpreted to such advantage, and in such accessible form that they enable the fruitful investigation of previously stubborn problems and the discovery of new problems for further inquiry" (Merton 1987b:1–2).

Peirce worked for many decades on his theory of abduction and broadened it well beyond its original meaning (e.g., Fann 1970; Douven 2011). Abduction eventually came to mean more or less anything novel that is part of a scientific theory. "Abduction," as Peirce put it, "must cover all the stages by which theories and concepts are engendered" (Peirce 1934:590).

This expanded notion of abduction also fits the informal exploratory study well. When you want to say something new, you may try to come up with a new explanation. But you can also innovate in many other ways (e.g., Gutzkow, Lamont and Mallard 2004). You can, for example, discover some new type of method or a new type of fact. Description can be of help here, also the ambition to find puzzles.

Peirce was of the opinion that the human mind has been formed through evolution in such a way that human beings have a good chance of figuring out the correct solution to certain scientific problems but not to others. Human beings, as he put it, have a tendency to guess right in certain cases. This capacity, he argued, is similar to the instinct of animals to build nests and to solve some other problems they face. Peirce ended his famous essay "Guessing" (1907) in the following way.

Our faculty of guessing corresponds to a bird's musical and aeronautic powers; that is, it is to us, as those are to them, the loftiest of our merely instinctive powers. I suppose that if one were sure of being able to discriminate between the intimations of this instinct and the self-flatteries of personal desire, one would always trust to the former. For I should not rate high either the wisdom or the courage of a fledgling bird, if, when the proper time had come, the little agnostic should hesitate long to take his leap from the nest on account of doubts about the theory of aerodynamics. (Peirce 1929:282)

Whether the capacity of human beings to invent new theories and ideas is biologically based or socially based is a much debated question. The main point to be made here, however, is a different one, namely that the way the human mind works is something that the social scientist needs to know more about, in order to be in a position to learn how to theorize better. Most of this type of knowledge, it should also be noted, comes today from cognitive science and not from social science.

Peirce's notion that human beings have some kind of instinct that allows them to think creatively is also interesting for other reasons. Some of these amount to an argument in favor of the informal exploratory study. This instinct may come easier into play, for example, if the social scientist is released from the demand to carry out a study according to the methodological rules. Her mind will then be allowed to wander more freely, while still dealing with facts.

Topics such as intuition, guessing, speculation, having hunches and so on now become important to know more about; this brings us back to cognitive science. Sometimes the results of studies in this field can be translated into practical knowledge and advice for how to do research in social science. It is, for example, clear that the social scientist – like the bird in Peirce's example – needs to develop confidence in his or her capacity to solve certain problems, even when she is not following the rules of existing methodologies. Weber said something similar when he pointed out that we do not need anatomical knowledge in order to know how to walk (Weber 2012:140).

Afterthoughts on Exploratory Research

An exploratory paper like this one has no place for "conclusions", but it does call for a few afterthoughts.
– Robert K. Merton, "Age, Aging, and Age Structure in Science" (1973), p. 559

It is clear that the old type of exploratory study, as used by Merton et al., did produce good results and therefore deserves to be seen as a valuable method in social science. The case is somewhat different with the informal exploratory study. This is a method that has still to prove its value. My own view is that it is promising and worth trying. Taking risks is necessary in science as elsewhere. But before saying anything more on this topic, I first want to make an argument for institutionalizing a minor version of the informal study already today.

This would be a kind of informal exploratory study for graduate students to conduct before they present their proposal for a doctoral dissertation.

Instead of graduate students pinning their hope on the lucky chance that their search for data on some topic will result in something interesting, a first informal exploration of their topic would augment their chances to produce an important dissertation. Exploration of this type, it can be added, could also include the use of many different models, to see if the initial ideas seem robust (Young and Holsteen 2015). By conducting a study of this type, they would also have a better empirical knowledge of their topic when they write their proposals.

It is also possible to use the informal exploratory study in courses in theorizing at the graduate level. I have done this myself for several years in graduate seminars. The basic idea is to teach students how to theorize by letting them work with empirical material in specially designed exercises, and the informal exploratory study allows them to do this. It is important that when the students carry out these exercises they do not need to follow the methods they use according to the rules. The reason for this is that in order to learn how to develop some theoretical ideas in confrontation with empirical data, the students need to focus most of their attention on the theoretical task. By being released from the task of putting together and/or analyzing a good data set according to the rules, the students can instead focus all of their energy on theorizing the material. In my view, this method works relatively well (for an account of how to teach such a course as well as for a course description, see Swedberg 2016).

So far in this chapter five different types of exploratory studies have been discussed: (1) a version of what may be called the standard exploratory study, which has as its goal to make a first inroad into an area that is currently little known; (2) a second version of the standard exploratory study, which has as its goal the development of new hypotheses for a topic that is already known; (3) the informal exploratory study that aims at maximizing the development of new ideas; (4) the informal exploratory study/pilot study for dissertations; and (5) exploratory studies used in student exercises, to learn theorizing.

This, however, does not exhaust the usefulness of the exploratory study, which is very flexible in nature and can take a number of different forms. There also exists, for example, an interesting type of exploratory study that has been developed by state agencies in various countries, including the United States. For a few decades the National Science Foundation, the Department of Defense and some other federal agencies have, for example, funded what they call high-risk exploratory research. The basic idea is to fund research that is potentially very innovative but where the chance of failure is high. This type of "transformative research" is defined by the NSF as follows.

Transformative research involves ideas, discoveries, or tools that radically change our understanding of an important existing scientific or engineering concept or educational practice or leads to the creation of a new paradigm or field of science, engineering, or education. Such research challenges current understanding or provides pathways to new frontiers. (NSF 2016a).

It was early realized at the NSF that the peer review process was not suitable for this kind of proposal, since it is inherently conservative in nature. Instead it was decided to assign the right to accept or reject this type of proposal to foundation officers (Rothenberg 2013; Wagner and Alexander 2013). An alternative would have been to assign the grants by chance, something that NSF chose not to do but which is the practice elsewhere.[10]

The first major program to fund transformative research at NSF was created in 1990, called Small Grants for Exploratory Research (SGER). In 2007 it was replaced by several different programs, most importantly by one called the Early-concept Grant for Exploratory Research (EAGER). A reward from the EAGER program can be up to a few hundred thousand dollars. It typically lasts for two years, and it does not require external review. According to the current instructions on the web page of NSF:

The EAGER funding mechanism can be used to support exploratory work in its early stages on untested, but potentially transformative, research ideas or approaches. This work could be considered especially "high risk-high payoff" in the sense that it involves radically different approaches, applies new expertise, or engages novel disciplinary or interdisciplinary perspectives. Exploratory proposals may also be submitted directly to an NSF program … The EAGER mechanism should not be used for projects that are appropriate for submission as "regular" (i.e., non-EAGER) NSF proposals. (NSF 2016b)

To what extent have NSF's programs for high-risk exploratory research been successful? According to the one evaluation I have been able to locate, NSF's Small Grants for Exploratory Research (SGER) was very successful during the 16 years of its existence (Wagner and Alexander 2013). Based on a

---

[10] In New Zealand, so-called Explorer Grants (for health-related research) are allocated at random. To be chosen a proposal will have to fulfill certain conditions, but from that point on it is chance that decides if the proposal will be funded or not (HRC 2016). I thank Lambros Roumbanis for telling me about this type of grant.

Table 2.3 The goals and methods of different types of exploratory studies

1. **The standard exploratory study (Type 1)**
   The goal is to explore a topic that is little known, and to produce a publishable work. A multi-method approach is helpful.

2. **The standard exploratory study (Type 2)**
   The goal is to develop new hypotheses and ideas about a topic, and to produce a publishable work. Standard methods should be used. The sample size should be substantive, even if statistically rigorous procedures are not possible.

3. **The informal exploratory study (Prestudy)**
   The goal is to develop new ideas, and any means whatsoever can be used. The size of the sample can be small to fair.

4. **The high risk exploratory study**
   The goal is to develop highly innovative ideas in cases where the risk of failure is also high. To be proven valuable the innovative idea should be evaluated with the help of standard methods.

5. **The pilot study or exploratory study used for a thesis proposal**
   The goal is to research a topic informally so that the general design for a dissertation will be more likely to result in important findings. Standard methods as well as unconventional methods can be used, and there is no requirement for a representative sample.

6. **The exploratory study used in student exercises**
   The goal is to allow students to theorize empirical problems without getting sidetracked by strict methodological requirements. Any method can be used, standard as well as non-conventional ones, and there is no requirement for a representative sample.

citation analysis, interviews with experts and a survey, it was concluded that more than 10 percent of the projects had resulted in transformative results.

To the earlier types of exploratory studies that have been discussed so far in this chapter, I therefore suggest that we add one more: *the high-risk exploratory study*. For this type of exploratory study to come into being, you need support from some institution that gives grants for social science research. The main idea, to repeat, is to look for very powerful ideas that may turn out to be very fruitful, but that may also lead nowhere. This is clearly going a step beyond the standard exploratory study as well as the informal exploratory study. Still, it seems that it would be a good idea to introduce this type of exploratory study in social science, since it would encourage social scientists to think big and to speculate (e.g., Lave and March 1993).

All in all, in this chapter six different types of exploratory studies have been distinguished. A brief summary of what these look like can be found in Table 2.3, in which an attempt has also been made to distinguish between the goals and methods that are used in each case.

Two final points need to be made before ending this chapter. The first is that as long as the social sciences continue to ignore the possibility of making exploratory studies, they will limit their capacity to produce new ideas and innovative research. The technique and knowledge for how to proceed in carrying out this type of studies is here, ready to be used.

In his chapter to this volume, Evan Lieberman (Chapter 3) makes a related point. He notes that in biomedical science there exists more of an interest in the early stages in the research cycle, and that this is also reflected in what is being published. In political science, in contrast, it is more common to focus squarely on the causal claim, and to disregard the processes of description, initial forms of explorations and the like. This means that the early stages of the research cycle tend to be ignored and devalued.

The second point that needs to be made before ending this chapter is that exploratory research should not be seen exclusively as a method. It is also very close to theory, especially to theorizing. As has been shown, one type of exploratory study has precisely as its purpose the generation of new ideas, another the testing of high-risk ideas and so on.

The ambition to carry out exploratory research, in the sense of trying to say something new through research, and not just repeat what is already known, also needs to be made explicit and discussed in the education of social scientists. Similarly, exploratory studies should be part of what is being taught and discussed in theory courses as well as methods courses in the social sciences.

3 Research Cycles

Evan Lieberman

A research cycle in a scientific discipline is constituted by researchers working at various stages of inquiry, from more tentative and exploratory investigations to the testing of more definitive and well-supported claims.[1] As a particular research area matures, scientists are less frequently surprised by new phenomena because core processes are well understood. They are more likely to focus their efforts on making precise estimates of causal effects, often through randomized experiments. And indeed, such a pattern is evident in biomedical research: Descriptive and correlational work is often published in the major biomedical research journals, although different criteria are used to assess their significance than are used to assess experimental research.

In this chapter, I consider the value of this model for political science. My motivation is a sense that political scientists may be paying disproportionate attention to studies that focus on the precise estimation of causal effects to the exclusion of other types of complementary research – so much so that the range of questions to which we can eventually apply sophisticated strategies for causal inference may become severely limited, curtailing our collective contributions to useful knowledge. Put another way, might we be able to answer a greater number of causal questions, with respect to a richer set of subject areas, if we created more intellectual space (particularly in leading, peer reviewed journals) for high-quality scholarship that does not make strictly causal claims – or that draws more tentative conclusions about causal relationships? Would scholars be more likely to accurately describe the nature of their contributions if they were not under pressure to report their findings as "causally well identified?"

---

[1] A previous version of this chapter was published as, "Can the Biomedical Research Cycle Be a Model for Political Science?" *Perspectives on Politics*, vol. 14, no. 4, 2016, pp. 1054–1066. (Reprinted with permission.) Thanks to David Collier, Colin Elman, Tulia Falletti, John Gerring, Kosuke Imai, Jeffrey Isaac, David Jones, Robert Keohane, Markus Kreuzer, Julia Lynch, Philip Martin, Nina McMurry, Ben Morse, Dawn Teele, Yang-Yang Zhou, and contributors to this volume for helpful comments and suggestions.

Specifically, I highlight the need for the type of research cycles and division of labor[2] one sees in other scientific fields, including the biomedical sciences. The notion of a research cycle that I have in mind is one that is constituted as a scholarly conversation through peer reviewed publications, and includes a mix of inductive and deductive theorizing and observation. It explicitly recognizes differences in the state of research within a substantively delimited cycle, such that we might expect a move from more tentative to more definitive claims about causal relationships. It is a cycle because we rarely expect research to "end," but merely to generate new observations and surprises that will spur new inquiries.

I should be clear that I intend the notion of a research cycle to serve primarily as a heuristic for the production of knowledge. That is, I do not envision research to proceed in a pre-ordained or mechanistic manner. Nonetheless, I believe it is useful, as specified in Figure 3.1, to envision a model of research in which contributions to understanding a particular question or problem *generally proceed* from more inductively discovered "surprises," which demand good descriptive research and a detailing of the theories such information disrupts, to more inductive theorizing based on retrospective analyses of prior sequences of events and associational relationships; to testing of hypotheses with retrospective analyses of observational research; to more design-driven prospective studies, especially those in which treatment conditions are assigned experimentally; to additional replication, verification, and consideration of hypotheses among new subject populations, or explicitly within and across particular subgroups.

Within a discipline that takes the notion of research cycles seriously, the criteria for what would constitute a contribution to knowledge depends on where in the research cycle an author was attempting to publish. More exploratory research could be recognized as "cutting-edge" if it were breaking open new questions through identification of novel patterns or processes. Large-scale randomized controlled trials (RCTs) would be more appropriate as a cycle matures, and could provide definitive evidence about more narrowly defined questions about specific causal relationships.

My point is not to eschew interest in causal questions or causal relationships, or to challenge the potential value of experimental research in political science. On the contrary, I raise the analogy to biomedical science as a science that – given its immediate practical search for knowledge to improve human

---

[2] In a complementary manner, Gehlbach 2015 argues for a methodological division of labor in political science.

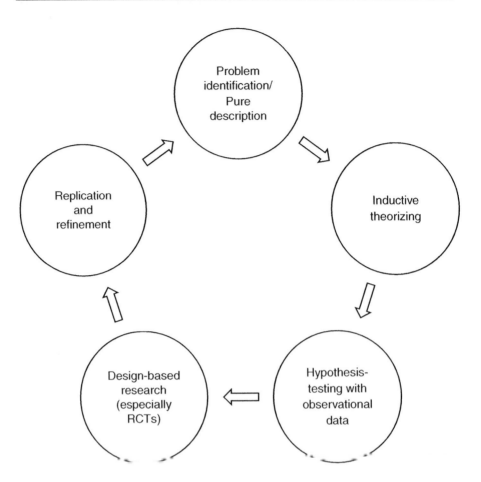

Figure 3.1 A research cycle heuristic

well-being, and recognition of the harms associated with faulty inference – is seriously concerned with establishing clear cause-and-effect relationships. But, as I will illustrate, causal analysis is just one part of the division of research-oriented labor.

In the remainder of this chapter, I begin by describing the manifestation of the research cycle in the publication of biomedical research, and highlight the extent to which an analogous cycle seems far more limited in political science, at least within leading publication outlets.[3] Subsequently, I propose

---

[3] To be sure, the very notion of a research cycle is not new, including within the discipline of political science. For example, Munck (1998) usefully reframed the central lessons of King, Keohane, and Verba's (1994) *Designing Social Inquiry* in terms of a research cycle that moves from more inductive

a framework for developing such a research cycle in the discipline, detailing some standards of excellence for evaluation and publication.

The Biomedical Research Cycle

Biomedical research and political science differ along many key dimensions such that one might question the utility of using the former as a model for the latter. A great deal of biomedical research is rooted in a clear and focused mandate to try to develop best practices and new technologies for improving the health of humans, and much research drives product and protocol development. By contrast, a much smaller share of political science research is intended for "practical" ends, as most scholars search simply for deeper understanding of the socio-political world in which we live, and generally have more modest expectations about how research might be used for practical purposes.

In terms of occupation, many biomedical researchers have responsibilities as clinicians, which complement and inform their research, whereas only a limited number of political scientists simultaneously work in the political or policy arena – though increasingly, many collaborate with "implementing partners." In turn, the resources associated with biomedical research are exponentially larger than what is available for social science. While the findings from much biomedical research are embargoed until published (in a timely manner) by a journal, most political science research has been discussed and widely circulated long before it is published in journal form (and very rarely in a timely manner).

Nonetheless, I believe that the biomedical research cycle offers insights for social scientists that are worth considering, particularly for those who seek to make greater progress in gathering evidence that can contribute to knowledge accumulation and, in some cases, practical knowledge that might have policy-related or other relevance. I recognize that not all political science research is advanced with such aims, nor with great optimism about knowledge accumulation, and the intended lessons of this chapter simply do not apply to such work.

While the leading scholarly journals of any scientific discipline are not democratic reflections of the interests and priorities of all who participate

observation to hypothesis testing. My point is that there is little evidence that important steps in such cycles are thoughtfully considered, especially through publication.

in the field, they are intended to be the most important outlets for scholarly research. Publication in such journals is rewarded through likely impact on the field and individual professional promotion, and thus, what is published in such journals helps shape the research agenda of many in the field. Arguably, the most important scientific journals of clinical medicine are the *New England Journal of Medicine* (NEJM), the *Journal of the American Medical Association* (JAMA), the *British Medical Journal* (BMJ), and the *Lancet*. These outlets provide a lens onto what is considered the most substantively significant research in that field.

For example, consider the arbitrarily selected July 30, 2015 issue of the NEJM. Not surprisingly, it includes an article on a large-scale RCT: The authors report the findings from a study of the effect of hypothermia on organ donors. And the article demonstrates exactly why randomized studies are so valued: We would be extremely unsatisfied with a study that simply reported a correlation between hypothermia and health outcomes following transplants because we would always wonder, what was it that caused some doctors or hospitals to implement this protocol and not others? Deliberate randomization does a great job of addressing potential confounders (selection effects and omitted variables that might affect health outcomes) and, at the moment, we lack a better strategy. The article reports that an interim analysis revealed that the differences in health outcomes were so profound that the experiment was "discontinued early owing to overwhelming efficacy." Treatment was associated with much better health outcomes and, given the research design, it is quite reasonable for us to infer that those outcomes were caused by the fact that they received the experimentally assigned treatment.

Political scientists could understandably envy the clarity and significance of such results. Just imagine running a field experiment on foreign aid and development and finding that a deliberative discussion led by village elders helped to produce a 30-percent decrease in funds leakage, and the World Bank and USAID insisted that the experiment be terminated early because of the demonstrated efficacy of the intervention! Indeed, this is the type of solid scientific evidence that many modern social scientists aspire to produce, and I believe it fuels the enthusiasm around impact evaluation research.

For many of us who read only the big headline stories about new medical breakthroughs and who speak frequently about treatment and control groups, it would be tempting to imagine that the leading biomedical journals are themselves outlets for just this singular (experimental) type of research, and if we want to accumulate knowledge that this is all we should be doing. But in fact, if one reads on, one quickly sees that many other types of contributions reach the peak of this scientific community.

For example, in the same issue of the aforementioned article, we find purely descriptive articles. One epidemiological study (an important sub-field that routinely provides explicitly descriptive and associational analyses) reports on the incidence of pneumonia in two American cities; another reports on the characteristics of a previously undocumented cancer variant. In neither case do the authors advance any real causal claims, but they do provide a rich set of analyses of important outcomes of interest, using their scientific expertise to accurately describe these phenomena.

Also of note, the journal reports not simply "definitive" RCTs, but early-stage research findings. Following well-institutionalized principles, biomedical researchers classify "phase-1" studies as proof-of-concept exercises in which a new drug or regimen is tested in a very small group of people, and "phase-2" studies as experiments conducted with larger groups of people to test efficacy and to further evaluate safety before risking the cost and expense to many more people. "Phase-3" trials – large-sample experiments on patients – are conducted only once prior research has demonstrated safety and efficacy. Because of stringent ethical rules around biomedical experimental research, large-scale RCTs are frequently not possible without clearing preliminary hurdles. But the results of earlier studies are still considered important scientific contributions in their own right: The aforementioned NEJM issue included a phase-1 study of a new tumor treatment with 41 patients and a randomized, double-blind study of 57 patients in a phase-2 trial of a drug to reduce triglyceride levels.

Finally, there was a very short article with an image of strawberry tongue in a child that provides a clinical observation. That article was just one paragraph long, and highlighted that this observable symptom was used to make a clinical diagnosis of Kawasaki's disease.

What makes this disparate set of articles evidence that a research cycle is at work? and what is the relevance for political science? In this one issue of a leading medical journal, we learn about a range of very different discoveries from problem identification all the way to the test of an intervention that would modify the outcome of interest in a predicted manner. Each is novel, but with different levels of uncertainty about the nature of patterns and causal relationships. At one level, we read of the most basic description – presentation of a visual image to aid in a diagnosis or classification – to some correlations, to some tentative theories about the effects of a new experimental protocol, to a late-stage RCT. Each is deemed a sufficiently important advance in thinking about substantively important problems. While no one would claim that a very brief case report would provide any deep answers to broader scientific questions of interest, as Ankeny (2011:254) argues, clinical studies published in journals have provided an important foundation for the development of diagnostic (conceptual) categories, and the formulation of key research questions and hypotheses.

Moreover, when reading the late-stage experimental study, we see that it makes reference to a retrospective study. And the very differentiation of phased trials implies a step-wise but cumulative path toward discovery.

Turning to other clinical journals, such as JAMA, BMJ, or the *Lancet*, a similar pattern is clear. And this applies also to other high-impact multidisciplinary journals such as *Nature* and *Science*. To be certain, not all biomedical research journals are as eclectic in the types of research published, and many scholars would assign very different weights to the importance of different types of research, making particular distinctions between RCTs and other types of studies. Moreover, I have not established here the actual influence of different types of scholarship on particular research efforts within a scientific community. Nonetheless, what is clear is that leading scientific outlets clearly publish across the research cycle, and causal research is frequently strongly rooted in prior published studies documenting important discoveries.

And while the focus of this chapter is empirical research, it is worth highlighting that within the leading biomedical journals, normatively oriented scholars frequently play an important role in various steps of such cycles, by commenting on the implications of particular sets of research findings, or by highlighting the need to focus more on particular questions. For example, following the publication of research demonstrating the effectiveness of HPV vaccines, and the subsequent approval of the vaccine by the US Food and Drug Administration (FDA), an ethicist from a school of public health published a brief analysis of the ethics and politics of compulsory HPV vaccination in the NEJM (Colgrove 2006). That article shed light on a range of important considerations that would strongly mediate how scientific discovery actually affects human health and well-being, but in ways that were surely not explicitly discussed in most or all of the earlier stages of the research cycle. Normative analyses routinely appear in leading medical journals through editorials and "perspectives" pieces, which help to address the ethical dimensions of research practice as well as clinical- and policy-related developments. In short, normative work is tightly linked to the empirical research cycle.

A single snapshot of a journal cannot demonstrate the full development of a research cycle, so it should be useful to consider an example of how one such cycle evolved over time. To this end, I provide a stylized discussion of biomedical research around the human immunodeficiency virus (HIV) and the associated acquired immune-deficiency syndrome (AIDS).[4] I believe that published research in this area over the past 35 years lends some support to the argument I am presenting here, and demonstrates an implicit division of labor, and associated accumulation of knowledge. Of course, many within the biomedical community would point to various flaws in the pace and flow of research; on the other hand, this is an example of a truly problem-oriented research agenda that moved from surprise to the eventual development of important pharmaceutical treatments, and the current stage of testing vaccines aimed to immunize humans.

Although HIV and what came to be known as AIDS existed for at least several decades prior to 1980, from a scientific perspective, there was no explicit research on either topic (the virus or the syndrome) before the 1981 documentation of the surprising occurrence of Kaposi's sarcoma in homosexual men, both in the CDC's Morbidity and Mortality Weekly Report as well as in the *Lancet* and the *New England Journal of Medicine*. The conclusion in the *Lancet*: "This unusual occurrence of Kaposi's sarcoma in a population much exposed to sexually transmissible diseases suggests that such exposure *may play a role in its pathogenesis* [emphasis mine]" (Hymes et al. 1981). This represented an initial documentation of an important outcome, with little data, and the expression of some tentative hypotheses.

The move from initial inductive theorizing to hypothesis testing proceeded as the epidemic progressed, and researchers and clinicians continued to publish observations of the clinical manifestations of infection and analyses of behavioral and demographic correlates of people with AIDS-related symptoms. Numerous studies from around the world would come to demonstrate that there existed certain high-risk groups – in particular, male homosexuals, injecting-drug users, and hemophiliacs receiving blood transfusions – but also that individuals who did not meet any of these criteria could also get sick with AIDS.

In 1984, the journal *Science* published an article that summed up the state of research, pointing out that researchers had isolated a virus that was associated with AIDS. The article recognized that one could not, with such a deadly disease,

---

[4] I am particularly grateful to David Jones for helpful feedback on this section. Remaining errors are my own.

inject a host with the agent to test whether the disease would subsequently develop, establishing a true cause-and-effect relationship (Marx 1984:477), but the presence of particular antibodies in the blood of AIDS patients was highly suggestive of the link. That year, various scientific agencies announced the availability of a blood test to screen for the virus that caused AIDS.

By the mid-1980s, as the scale of the epidemic intensified, a few important research programs advanced, and scientific knowledge began to accumulate, which helped to dispel some initial false hunches and claims. With a foundation of research about what almost surely was *causing* people to contract AIDS, even without any experimental evidence to support those claims, researchers moved forward in developing various drugs that would be used to treat AIDS, including the first antiretroviral drug, zidovudine or AZT, the effectiveness and risks of which would be tested through double-blind random control trials (RCTs). And in the years to come, other pharmaceuticals and prevention modalities would be tested in various experiments, and those are ongoing. Given the high stakes, the stigmatized nature of AIDS, and the high prevalence among particularly vulnerable populations, much of this research was controversial, but the RCTs eventually provided strong evidence concerning efficacy.

Along the way, important observational research would continue to inspire theorizing about the modes of transmission, including, for example, the observation that circumcised men tended to contract HIV in much lower proportions than men who had not been circumcised. Of course, no one would claim that the prevalence of male circumcision was a "random" phenomenon because it is a practice that is clearly correlated with other cultural traditions that might have been the actual cause of differential rates of infection. But the association was striking, and the link plausible, and the findings compelled additional research about the benefits of circumcision for reducing the risk of infection. In a 1994 meta-review of 30 studies, the authors concluded, "Potential sources of error, assessment of causality, implications of the findings, and future research needs are discussed. Because a substantial body of evidence links noncircumcision in men with risk for HIV infection, consideration should be given to male circumcision as an intervention to reduce HIV transmission" (Moses et al. 1994).

In turn, these findings would inspire the development of experimental studies on the effects of circumcision, leading to more definitive research and policy recommendations.[5] One could not imagine such experimental

---

[5] To be clear, I am not taking a position here on whether the findings reported prior to the RCTs were sufficiently definitive to form the basis for strong policy recommendations, and if so, whether a

research being initiated without strong correlational research appearing first. And again, the authors of one important such randomized study of 5,000 men in Uganda explicitly credited earlier stages of the research cycle as inspiration for their work, which would confirm those earlier claims: "[Prior] ecological and observational studies suggest that male circumcision reduces the risk of HIV acquisition in men ... [and in this experimental study] Male circumcision reduced HIV incidence in men without behavioural disinhibition. Circumcision can be recommended for HIV prevention in men" (Gray et al. 2007).

And while questions about the origins of HIV and AIDS and how it came to spread around the world may never be answered in a fully satisfactory manner from a strict causal identification standpoint, such research – like research on the origins of democracy or of revolution – has proven to be an important source of insight for developing additional theories about the virus and its effects on the human immune system. Despite the lack of strong counter-factual evidence, it is difficult to imagine a group of AIDS researchers from any sub-specialty *discouraging* research in this vain because of the lack of potential for causal identification! Ultimately, the larger biomedical research community would like to know how this epidemic unfolded, and the best available historical/"process-tracing" evidence is clearly preferable over no research at all.

While I have provided an extremely condensed and stylized account of a long history of scientific research, what is clear, and what is relevant for political science, is the degree to which critical discoveries were made at various stages of the research cycle. It is unimaginable how different the history of AIDS would have been if that scientific community had shown disdain for "mere description," or for studies that demonstrated statistical associations without a clear causal identification strategy. What we see is that research proceeded in steps, sometimes with reversals, but that discoveries were made through recognition of surprise, careful inductive observation, and systematic testing of evolving insights and knowledge.

And the point is not that biomedical researchers are "loose" with their views about causal inference – in fact, that research community is certainly more conservative than political science, and extremely hesitant to assign causal attribution to any observational study. Rather than dismissing such

---

potential over-reliance on RCT-based research may have inadvertently delayed the roll-out of life-saving circumcision programs. That is an important question that must be resolved by biomedical researchers and medical professionals.

work, findings are published as "associational" relationships. And in turn, policy-makers and clinicians are made aware of such findings, but are repeatedly reminded to apply such findings with great caution as healthy skepticism about causation remains.[6]

The (Near-)Absence of a Research Cycle in Contemporary Political Science

In practice, political science research already proceeds as a mix of inductive and deductive research. That is, scholars (often in their everyday clothing as civilian observers of the political world, sometimes as consultants or research partners, or as part of the early stages of their research) come to observe new phenomena that disrupt their view of the status quo, sometimes against prior theoretical expectations. In turn, scholars describe what happened, come to theorize about the causes or consequences of such phenomena, often through observation of patterns studied formally or informally, develop causal propositions, and provide evidence testing those propositions with various types of data and analyses.

And yet, what is very distinct in political science from the biomedical model I described above is that most of those steps are very rarely publicly recorded as distinct scientific enterprises. In fact, increasingly, only the last set of studies – those that test causal relationships, especially using evidence from research designs that explicitly avoid or address threats to causal inference from confounders, and designed to accurately detect null relationships[7] – are the ones that get published in top political science journals. Many of the other steps are described in a cursory manner and barely find their way into the appendices of published work. Surprise findings and explicitly tentative conclusions are almost entirely absent.

For example, if one looks at the eight empirically oriented articles of the May 2015 issue of the political science flagship journal, the *American Political Science Review*, all eight sought to provide a fully worked-out theory; most were explicitly testing causal models. Only one was an

---

[6] Within certain circles of the biomedical research community, one can find similar types of methodological debates to those we engage in political science. For example, one pair of nephrologists has recently written of their frustrations with a research paradigm that does not allow for causal attribution except in the context of an RCT, and they argue for an instrumental variables approach (Kovesdy and Kalantar-Zadeh 2012).

[7] That is, avoiding "Type-2" errors, the false failure to reject the null hypothesis.

experiment, while six used statistical analyses to analyze large datasets, and one used case studies. But in virtually all of these articles, the authors largely say or imply that they are providing the best answer to a causal question with causal evidence. My point here is not that they were all quantitative or all experimental, because there was actually a bit of diversity on those dimensions.

The vast majority of political science articles at virtually all of the top journals and the papers presented by ambitious graduate students in search of academic jobs are increasingly of a single type: they claim to provide a new theory, specify some hypotheses, test it with analysis of a large dataset, frequently associated with an experimental or quasi-experimental research design, and, on occasion, explore with a few case studies; they present the findings as tests of hypotheses and with research designs that were specified *ex ante*. A great deal of this work is excellent and, in many ways, has provided much more reliable knowledge than what was published in prior generations. More and more political scientists have turned toward design-based experimental and quasi-experimental research, and the bar for what should be trusted as causal evidence has certainly been raised. As a discipline, we have developed a heightened appreciation for the range of confounders that limit our ability to imply causal relationships even when presented with strong statistical associations. And in turn, more applied researchers have focused on implementing "well-identified" designs, lest they be challenged for over-claiming the fit between evidence and theory. Excitement over a range of new strategies for making causal inferences has implied greater attention to such work in leading political science journals and in the profession more generally. Clearly, these are largely positive developments.

But alongside this trend, Gerring documents the virtual disappearance of descriptive studies from the leading political science publication outlet and, indeed, part of the problem is that scholars are not particularly interested in carrying out "mere" description.[8] Moreover, the unspoken presumption that the best work ought to be confirmatory or a test of an *ex ante* specified hypothesis, rules out the honest publication of findings of surprise patterns. While increasing calls for the public registration of pre-analysis plans are aimed to keep professionals "honest" by limiting *post hoc* findings being reported as if they were confirmatory, such efforts may inadvertently devalue

---

[8] Gerring (2012a). Top journals do sometimes publish purely descriptive articles, but these works almost always make a significant methodological contribution as well as a substantive one.

the potential importance of strong and surprising inductive, accidental, or *post hoc* findings that shed light on big questions.

Moreover, the explicitly normative portion of the discipline – what is generally referred to within departments and the discipline as "Political Theory" – with some notable exceptions, largely operates and publishes in isolation from its more empirically oriented counterparts. While the topics of democracy, violence, public goods provision, identity formation, and the like do largely overlap, true integration within research cycles is largely absent. One rarely finds theorists citing or commenting on the latest empirical research, and one almost never finds empirical researchers discussing more contemporary normative research.

And finally, the research that seems to be disappearing most quickly from the heights of the discipline are those studies that fall in between pure description and very strong causal inference. What biomedical researchers would describe as correlational studies, such as retrospective cohort studies, are like kryptonite to aspiring young political scientists who have a good sense of how such work will be judged – irrespective of the potential substantive or theoretical importance of some such studies. We provide very little space for "tentative" or "suggestive" findings, insisting that research ought to be definitive, and provide evidence of a clear causal relationship.

In many ways, I share the view that the focus on improving the quality of causal inferences marks an important and positive development in the discipline for both quantitative and qualitative research. We should not go back to the times of interpreting any old significant regression coefficient as evidence of a causal effect. But it is also worth taking a step back to consider what it might mean for disciplinary practice and output if the only studies that are highly valued are the ones that can unambiguously demonstrate random assignment to treatment, allowing for more certain identification of causal effects. What are the implications for the types of questions that might (not) get asked? What does this imply about the efficient allocation of resources, and transparency in research? Are there lessons to be learned from the biomedical paradigm described above?

Costs: The Crowding-Out of Discovery – Premature Experimentation

If we are ultimately interested in causal questions and causal evidence, shouldn't we focus our attention on research that identifies causal effects? If, as a discipline, we lack a large body of definitive scientific findings, shouldn't we play "catch-up" by gatekeeping out the types of more tentative and ambiguous research that simply leads to endless debate about model specification and the like?

In fact, I believe that there are several important costs in terms of the potential discoveries that are not incentivized because they are not appreciated, and the potential misallocation of our human and financial resources toward experimental and quasi-experimental research, not all of which is as promising as it could be. What we might call "late-stage" RCTs are (generally) extremely expensive in multiple ways: They often involve substantial burdens on human subjects in terms of time for participation or enumeration, they can be very expensive to administer from a data collection standpoint, and if there are ethical implications these tend to be multiplied on a large scale, all because experimental analyses require analytic power, which for most social science experiments (which tend to have relatively small treatment effects) implies large sample sizes.

In the biomedical sciences, owing to the very clear threat to human life and well-being of ill-conceived treatments and protocols, phased research is generally required for research with human subjects. As discussed earlier, early-stage studies tend to be smaller in scale, and look more holistically at possible secondary and unanticipated interactive effects. For example, an adverse outcome within a subset of treated subjects would demand a retrospective analysis of differences, and an inductive, *post hoc* analysis of the predictors of heterogeneous treatment effects. Such exploratory study can be usefully carried out within the context of a smaller-scale experiment such that the findings, if deemed relevant, can be implemented in the design of subsequent, larger-scale studies.

But political scientists generally lack the equivalent opportunities to publish phase-I or phase-II trials. At the very least, we lack a shared understanding of the role that such work might play in a larger research cycle. Nonetheless, most ambitious field experiments ought to begin with some degree of piloting and qualitative research, including, for example, more open-ended focus group discussions and interviews with subjects (Glennerster 2013; Paluck 2010). Owing to costs and uncertainties, such pilot experiments are, by definition, not at a scale that allows sufficient statistical power to reach definitive answers to causal questions. The question is, should such studies form part of the "official" research cycle, in the sense of being published? Or should they remain part of the internal analytic support that largely remains hidden until the "full" study is completed? I advocate the former. At the moment, political scientists might exercise the option of writing a blog entry about their findings, but this clearly winds up being a temporary, insiders' outlet, and particularly for young scholars provides little professional reward. The lack of a peer reviewed outlet reflects the low value such findings are currently ascribed.

Absent any obvious outlet to publish such studies in political science, most political scientists will find little incentive to conduct such work or to take it as seriously as they should. Rather, they are more likely to "go big or go home," in pursuit of results that limbo their way under the conventional $p = 0.05$ level of statistical significance.

Even before conducting early-stage experimental research, good scientific practice would demand that we at least try to establish plausible connections between variables with existing or non-obtrusive data. And yet, in the leading political science journals, it is increasingly rare to find an observational analysis that simply reports important and robust associations unless the author claims to have identified some "as-if random" natural experiment and can use some type of naturally occurring discontinuity to infer causation. Now, of course, we would rather find an interesting natural experiment if the costs in terms of external validity are not too great. But sometimes, this is not possible, especially for analyses of large-scale, macro-level processes. And why are retrospective observational studies not still valuable if scholars are honest about what they can infer, demonstrating that they have made the best attempts to answer their research questions with available evidence (or all evidence that could be reasonably gathered)? Shouldn't predictive patterns provide some initial confidence that a causal relationship may exist? Correlation does not mean causation ... but it certainly can be suggestive of an important piece of evidence in support of a causal relationship. If we consider again the biomedical model, the first studies that found an association between smoking and lung cancer were hardly definitive, and we still would not run a randomized study to test the direct causal relationship. But the significance of the finding cannot be overestimated, particularly as scientists have concluded with mechanistic evidence (and without experimentation on human subjects) that smoking causes cancer.

And yet, for young social scientists – the ones most likely to be making new and creative discoveries, and perhaps the least well-positioned to be raising vast sums of money for large-scale experiments – increasingly "causal identification strategy" is the only name of the game. And if they are not implementing proper experiments, they are seeking out causal research projects through "natural experiments."[9] That

---

[9] Dunning (2012) provides a thoughtful treatment of how more inductive field research can establish a foundation for recognizing "as-if" randomly assigned treatments in natural settings.

is, they search for the perfect "plausibly exogenous" instrumental variables such as rainfall or other arbitrary cutpoints and decision-making rules. And, *de rigeur*, they are expected to proclaim that their particular strategy is "novel," and/or a rare "exploitation" of an untapped inferential resource.

To be sure, many such studies are exceptionally creative and valuable. And the sometimes quite clever identification of naturally occurring experiments is a feat that deserves proper accolades and professional rewards ... But if the proverbial tail is wagging the dog – that is, if researchers wind up looking for outcomes to study because they finally stumbled upon an exogenous source of variation of "something" that ought to be consequential, well, that seems not to be the basis for a promising or coherent research agenda. There may be undue temptations for false discovery – i.e., "I've found something exogenous, now let me try to find some plausible outcome that it can predict," in which case we may wind up with the same types of spurious associations that experimentalists have been trying to avoid. (I discuss the potential use of pre-analysis plans later in this chapter.) Moreover, I think that many will agree that way too many recent social science papers are making overly heroic claims that particular choices or events are plausible instruments and that they meet the necessary claims to make causal inferences.[10] I suspect that if our vision of good science explicitly allowed for "tentative," "suggestive," or "predictive" findings, we would see less over-claiming about the strength of causal evidence.

The increasing focus of talents, energies, and professional rewards on causal research *per se* poses several additional costs.

First, it likely obscures timely documentation of potentially important new descriptive discoveries, at least by political scientists, with the skills and insights they could bring to such research. Such descriptive analysis ought to be both an end in itself, and also a gateway to other types of observational and experimental studies (Gerring 2012a). Along these lines, the discipline has turned away from a legacy of description at potentially great cost. Of course, it is not possible to account for the studies that might have been written and published had they been properly incentivized, but, at the very least, we can say that much has happened in the political world in recent years ... and political scientists have documented very, very little of it, at least in our leading journals!

Perceptions of disciplinary norms and expectations weigh heavily and are self-reinforcing. For example, today, if I had a graduate student who was working in rural Zimbabwe and identified some new form of interest

---

[10] For example, the exclusion restriction is rarely plausibly met in political science applications of instrumental variable analysis.

articulation or deliberation that we had never seen before – let's say that they had developed a pattern of decision-making in which they decided that all of the children in the village got to determine how to manage the local budget – I am fairly sure that the only way in which that graduate student could get that observation published in a top journal would be to figure out some way to observe tons of variation in the manifestation of that institution, and then to develop a theory of its causes or consequences, and then test that theory by identifying natural randomness in the causal variable, or to run an experiment in which the institution itself was randomly assigned. And if that graduate student, who found this extremely interesting new aspect of political life that we had never seen before, could not do all of these other things, I would need to, in good conscience with respect to that student's professional prospects, advise dropping this project immediately. Maybe the student could publish in some obscure area-studies journal, but definitely not in a political science journal.

In a similar manner, if a political scientist had been able to rapidly conduct a survey of social and political attitudes of Cubans just after the thaw in US–Cuban relations, it strikes me that we would want to document such attitudes, to do it with the best social science skills available, even if the research had no ambitions of being able to detect specific causal effects. Whether Cubans favored political reform or not, the answer, particularly the distribution of responses, would be intrinsically interesting – and that piece of research could generate deeper inquiry about the causes or consequences of such sentiment. But in the near-term it would be a truly significant contribution to knowledge, simply as a piece of descriptive inference.

The point is not that political scientists should be reporting the news. They should be using their conceptual, analytical, and measurement skills to describe patterns and phenomena about contemporary and historical political life that would otherwise go unrecognized.

At the moment, however, scholars are not incentivized to use their sophisticated tools to describe what is going on because, again, we do not reward those contributions with our central currency: Publication in peer-reviewed journals. Moreover, non-peer reviewed blogs are not intended for in-depth scholarly studies, and they do not provide an opportunity for disclosure of research methodologies, uncertainty of estimates, etc.

By contrast, in the biomedical sciences, when a new set of life-threatening or otherwise critical symptoms present themselves, particularly in a patterned manner, one can be certain that such discoveries will be reported in a top journal with the expectation that future research will be needed to understand the causes and consequences of such discovery, and to develop interventions to prevent or to treat those symptoms. As discussed earlier, the *New England Journal of Medicine* published an article describing a strawberry tongue, in effect communicating, "Hey, this is important, take a look. More later."

I believe this state of affairs dis-incentivizes novel discovery, and incentivizes work within a narrow band of research in which processes and measures are already well understood. It is true that much of "normal science" involves small and marginal revisions and even just replications of prior studies. Such work deserves an important place in the discipline. But there also needs to be a place for discussion of previously unexamined phenomena even if the causal connections are not fully worked out. In recent years, many graduate students – including those who have been extremely well trained in the best methods of causal inference – have confided in me that they feel "paralyzed" by the emphasis on causal identification and close out certain types of research questions very quickly because they don't believe that they will eventually be able to estimate a causal effect in the manner that they perceive the discipline now expects.

Toward a Framework for a Research Cycle

If the concerns about the need for a publication and professional opportunity-incentivized research cycle in political science are valid, what is to be done? Importantly, I think we need to distinguish and to label the different types of contributions scholars might make, and to establish standards of excellence for each. (Although in the discussion provided earlier I identify an important place for normative research in the cycle, I do not include here a discussion of standards for such pieces. Normative contributions might be made at any stage of the cycle.) Not all journals will want to publish pieces from all stages, and the specific contributions of any piece are likely to be unique and subject to scholarly tastes and concerns. Nonetheless, authors, reviewers, editors, and readers should identify quite explicitly where in the research cycle any given study is likely to fit, and thus how to evaluate the nature of the contribution. Our expectation should not be that every paper would tackle every concern within a substantive research agenda, but that it will take its proper place within a larger division of labor.

I follow Gerring's (2012b) "criterial approach" and an appreciation of tradeoffs in research as a framework for making distinctions between types of studies (refer to Table 3.1), but with a focus on the research cycle. A key

Table 3.1 A criterial framework for assessing contributions in a political science research cycle

Study Type		Importance of Criteria for Evaluation				
		Claims/Strategies for Making Contribution	Novelty of Phenomenon/Theory being Studied within Research Cycle	Strength of Association; Statistical Significance	Quality of Measurement?	Value of ex-ante Public Registration of Propositions (i.e., Pre-analysis Plan)?
Observational	Descriptive	To describe novel or unexpected phenomena, including variation within a population	Critical	N/A	Critical	Very limited
	Associational/ predictive	To demonstrate a novel and robust pattern potentially consistent with a new or existing theoretical proposition	More important	Critical	Critical	Very limited
	Natural experiment	To estimate a specific, predicted causal effect, using a naturally occurring, but plausibly randomly assigned treatment	Less important	Important	Critical	Limited
Experimental	Early-stage experiment	To assess the plausibility of a specific causal effect and other possible (adverse) effects, using investigator randomization as identification strategy	Less important	Less important	Critical	Necessary
	Late-stage experiment	To estimate a specific, predicted causal effect, using investigator randomization as identification strategy	Least important	Least important	Critical	Critical

tenet of good social science research is to avoid "over-claiming." That is, do not attempt to draw conclusions that your data cannot support. But if we are going to provide a framework for honest research, we need a greater diversity of the types of claims that we might make, and associated standards for excellence and importance. What is critical about the notion of a research cycle is that we ought to value new contributions based on what has come previously within that substantive area of research. This, of course, places a particular burden on scholars and reviewers to be cognizant of what has and has not been learned in an area of research, and to properly frame contributions with respect to such a background. While this might seem obvious, I think it is a point worth emphasizing in order to guard against the simple application of a single set of standards (i.e., what is the strength of the causal identification strategy?) to all scholarly work.

I will describe several broad types of studies and contrast them in terms of the nature of the claims they make and how they might be evaluated based on the novelty of the descriptive or causal theories associated with the claims, the strength of association or effect size, the additional credibility associated with a publicly registered pre-analysis plan, and other considerations for evaluation. In all cases, high-quality measurement of constructs is a prerequisite for excellence: If constructs are not properly measured, no results can be considered trustworthy.

In each case, our criteria for a "significant" study should be to disrupt some aspect of prior knowledge. Critically, however, not all studies can or should contribute along every dimension.

A descriptive study in political science ought to use the best available conceptual, measurement, and sampling tools to depict a phenomenon of interest. What are citizens' political attitudes? How have certain institutions evolved over time? In order to be considered important, such studies generally need to focus on a subject that is truly novel or that disrupts conventional wisdom about a particular state of affairs; for example, documenting either a new type of institution or set of political attitudes or behaviors, describing some aspect of political life in the wake of an important historical moment, or showing that a particular way of understanding some existing phenomenon is no longer correct, given superior data or measurement techniques, which in turn might cast some existing causal theories in doubt. These are akin to the biomedical case studies or studies that simply describe the prevalence of a particular disease in different locations, perhaps reporting on associations, with no claims of estimates of causal relationships. The field of epidemiology provides critical insights for the biomedical sciences more generally by offering careful description of the pathogenesis of disease. In a similar manner, political scientists could and should be making important and methodologically sophisticated contributions by describing the prevalence and variance of key political phenomena. And with the advent of "big data," I expect that many such contributions will be advanced along these lines. In their seminal work, King, Keohane, and Verba (1994) discuss descriptive inference at length, but that part of the methodological treatise is routinely ignored. An important descriptive study must demonstrate an outcome or pattern of interest that was not previously observed or expected, and such findings should open up new areas of inquiry within a research cycle. Descriptive studies may be retrospective (tapping existing observational data) or prospective (for example, planned surveys). Fundamentally, these studies must be judged in terms of whether they demonstrate something that is truly new and if they are carefully measured or implemented.

Beyond description, analysis of observational data of naturally occurring phenomena can be used to detect patterns across or within cases and the strength of relationships among variables. Within such studies, political scientists will make claims about the extent to which relationships might be interpreted as truly causal, providing not simply statistical or qualitative assessments of uncertainty in the strength of relationships, but additional discussions of the credibility of the research design, and the ability to address rival explanations. All studies, of course, face the "fundamental problem of causal inference," which is that we cannot know for sure what the counter factual outcome would have been if particular units had received different values on the explanatory or treatment variable (Rubin 1974). Most non-experimental studies exhibit a set of hallmark limitations in this regard: We do not know for certain the process by which treatments were assigned and if the selection criteria were potentially biased in a manner that is correlated with the outcome of interest. Thus, the onus on retrospective studies trying to advance causal claims is to show that a wide range of other rival explanations are not driving the results. In turn, much scholarly attention focuses on the credibility of causal inference depending on the "identification strategy" or "identifying assumptions."

Indeed, some research designs based on observational (non-experimental) data do, in practice, appear to provide more credible estimates of causal effects because they have found a way of leveraging some phenomenon that is "plausibly" random. For other studies, more questions remain at the conclusion of the study concerning whether the key treatment or explanatory variable was truly exogenously assigned and, given that uncertainty, it is difficult to conclude that any estimated relationship reflects a causal process. In Table 3.1, I distinguish those studies that can credibly claim to be leveraging a true natural experiment from those that do not, labeling the latter "associational/predictive" studies.

And here is the fundamental rub: If we cannot be convinced that the treatment variable is truly exogenous – if we are always left wondering whether some omitted variable has confounded the results – can we really believe that the research output is significant and worthy of publication in a top journal or is the basis for professional recognition?

My answer is that strength of causal identification strategy should be considered as just one criterion among several. And again, this is where I think the notion of a research cycle sheds important light on how to evaluate a contribution. In the early stages of a research cycle, we might heavily weight the extent to which the estimated relationship between variables represents a novel and theoretically innovative association, and the extent to which the demonstrated strength of that relationship is substantively significant. Such associations might be demonstrated through careful model-based statistical analyses or (comparative) case studies, and their robustness evaluated based on the sensitivity of those findings to slight.

By contrast, in the latter stages of a cycle, particularly if a strong predictive pattern has already been empirically demonstrated, we should hold studies to standards that more credibly detect causal relationships with less tolerance for potential confounding. Specifically, here we should expect research that does a better job of approximating a "natural experiment," and we would expect to see, for example, regression discontinuity designs, effective use of instrumental variables, or difference-in-differences designs, which might more directly address the threat of confounders to causal inference as compared with a more straightforward regression or matching approach to analysis.[11] In an analogous manner, qualitative research at this stage in the research cycle would need to reach a very high bar of addressing potential confounders with explicit evidence. To the extent that researchers develop strong and credible causal research designs for testing well-motivated causal claims, we should be less concerned with the extent to which effect sizes are small or large as a criterion for publication or for professional merit more generally. We will need to depend on scholars to adequately frame the nature of the contribution and for expert evaluators to assess the particular contribution relative to prior work.

---

[11] For example, see Angrist and Pischke (2014).

Moreover, at the earlier stages of the cycle, a correlational study or its qualitative analog ought to be theory-motivating. In turn, if observed correlations are weak, or if the case study research finds no clear pattern or logic, the contribution is ambiguous and almost certainly not worthy of publication. On the other hand, at the latter stages of a research cycle, when expectations about a theory are greater, a research design that more credibly isolates the effect of X on Y ought to contribute to knowledge irrespective of the actual findings. The better the test (i.e., the less likely the research design is to report a null result when a causal relationship actually exists), the less we should be concerned about the specific results as a criterion of scholarly review. Of course, substantively large findings will always be more likely to gain more attention – unless a convincing null result is overturning an established wisdom of a positive relationship – but that is a separate issue from scientific merit.

Finally, there are experimental studies in which assignment to treatment is randomized by the investigator. Building on the biomedical paradigm, I propose that political scientists would be well served to distinguish between early-stage and late-stage experiments.

Early-stage experiments should be designed explicitly as way stations for larger-scale, costlier experiments, particularly when little experimental research has been previously conducted in this research area. While social scientists are currently not expected to adhere to phased research standards akin to clinical trials, in many circumstances there would be great value to such practice. Because early-stage studies are, almost by definition, underpowered (there are not enough subjects or observations to confidently "fail to reject the null hypothesis"), the criteria for publication or contribution to knowledge should not be the magnitude or statistical significance of estimated effects. Rather, an article reporting on an early-stage experiment ought to provide deeper insights into the fit between treatment and real-world or theoretical constructs, to discuss ethical implications of the experiment, to highlight qualitatively observed processes that link (or impede) the relationship between treatment and outcome, and to offer the specifics of an innovative experimental protocol. The criteria for publishing articles that document such studies is the extent to which the analyst provides strong evidence to motivate or to discourage large-scale experiments with the same or a related protocol. Through description of preliminary results, description of focus-group or other interviews, and description of other observations, such articles can more definitively assess the promise of carrying out potentially difficult and costly research, even if the estimates of causal effects are more tentative.

By contrast, late-stage experiments should be judged to a much greater extent in terms of the extent to which they provide unambiguous tests of the effects of X on Y. By definition, they should not be underpowered, which makes them uniquely suited for drawing conclusions about null relationships. But beyond that, experiments can be judged on the extent to which they are implemented in a manner that fully addresses potential confounders in as efficient a manner as possible. Articles reporting on large-scale, late-stage experiments should not be judged primarily on theoretical innovation or novelty of association. Such novelty ought to be established in less costly ways, earlier in a research cycle. Instead, late-stage experiments ought to be clean and definitive tests of well-motivated hypotheses. If social scientists (and funders) were to take the notion of a research cycle seriously, they would not carry out expensive or potentially unethical experiments in the absence of one of the earlier studies providing strong suggestive evidence of the merits of the hypothesis under examination.

What Role for Registration/Pre-Analysis Plans?

A welcome trend that has already been imported from the biomedical sciences to the social sciences is the practice of public pre-registration of design protocols and analysis plans prior to the fielding of experiments. In the biomedical sciences, this has been an important corrective to the burying of null results and *post hoc* finding of "positive" results obtained from "creative" re-analysis of data.

Although a full discussion of the merits of pre-analysis plans is beyond the scope of this chapter, it is worth reflecting on their potential role within the context of a research cycle. The goal of pre-analysis plans is to keep scholars "honest" and to avoid "p-hacking" – the search for results that accord with conventional thresholds for statistical significance through some combination of variables in a *post hoc* manner, after predicted findings were not attained. This is a worthy goal, and for a great deal of research I fully support the use of such plans.[12] Not only should such planning and public registration deter false discovery, but it ought to provide a public tool for justifying prospective

---

[12] See, for example, Humphreys, Sanchez de la Sierra, and van der Windt (2013), and discussion and guidelines at the Evidence in Governance and Politics (EGAP) website, http://egap.org/content/registration.

research in the first place. As I highlight in Table 3.1, for late-stage RCTs, such registration is critical and it is difficult to imagine a strong counter-argument against their use for that type of research. Even for early-stage RCTs, scholars ought to pre-register their research designs and pre-analysis plans, but our criteria for the significance of the contribution of a paper should not be as closely tied to those plans as would be the case with a late-stage RCT.

A more difficult question concerns the value of pre-registration of retrospective and non-experimental studies. On the one hand, for observational research taking place late in a research cycle, pre-registration may indeed provide great value. If scholars publicly registered that they were going to investigate a particular set of archives in a particular way, and predicted a set of patterns with a pre-specified analysis, of course, it would be very convincing and impressive to find those patterns observed in analyses conducted after the data were collected (assuming, of course, a logical theory, sensible data collection, and sound analysis). All else equal, such a study would be more credible than one that did not pre-register hypotheses and analytic strategies.

But again, if we take the idea of pre-registration too far, particularly if we develop norms in which scholars perceive that their "hands are tied" to report only those analyses that have been pre-specified, we will surely crowd out the important inductive work (some call it fishing) upon which scientific discovery depends.[13] Let me return to the (biomedical) example of HIV and AIDS. On the one hand, in the later stages of understanding this disease, science – and frankly humanity – clearly benefits from scientific practice that insists on pre-registration of trials around the efficacy of drug treatment. We would not want the practitioner community to be confused about what actually works because the only studies available to them were the ones that demonstrated positive results. Drug trial registries help to solve this problem.

On the other hand, let's consider the process of discovery around the important question of what causes the transmission of HIV. This research clearly involved a great deal of inductive pattern-detection, particularly in the early stages of the epidemic. I recognize that early recognition of the association between sexual orientation and AIDS symptoms generated some awful inductive theories (famously, the Rev. Jerry Falwell declared AIDS was a punishment from God), but also was a necessary prerequisite for valid scientific discovery of the pathways for transmission. It is difficult to reasonably

---

[13] Thoughtful advocates of pre-analysis plan registers have explained that we ought to simply make distinctions between analyses that were pre-registered and those that were not, but to feel free to report both.

imagine that such relationships could have been predicted *ex ante*, or, for that matter, hypotheses about the protective benefits of circumcision, but these have proven to be unimaginably consequential discoveries for curbing the epidemic. If gatekeepers in the biomedical community had restricted such knowledge because the research designs were not "causally well identified" or a pre-analysis plan was not on file, one can only imagine how many more lives would have been lost to the epidemic.

Recognizing that registration of studies is not a prerequisite for all forms of important research in the biomedical sciences, political science should avoid being overly restrictive and we should not necessarily value a study more than another on the sole criteria that one was pre-registered. To be more precise, the value of pre-registration depends on the type of study and place in the research cycle. In fact, because social and political phenomena are surely much less predictable and mutate more rapidly than bio-physical phenomena, I would argue that much less of our research ought to be constrained in this manner. Specifically, as I outline in Table 3.1, I find only limited value for registration of studies other than prospective RCTs. Where scholars are able to pre-specify research plans with some confidence, they should by all means do so. At the extreme, of course, purposive research is better practice than "barefoot empiricism." But particularly at the early stages of a research cycle, we should not expect that scholars will know exactly what they are looking for before they have looked. (That said, they should not claim *ex post* that they knew what they were looking for when their findings were actually a surprise.) Problem-oriented research starts with puzzles about outcomes, and the search for plausible predictors of those outcomes is necessarily inductive. It is not always easy to judge whether findings from such studies are trivial or spurious or the advancement of real knowledge, but if other scientific programs are any guide, we should not restrict such inquiry wholesale.

For retrospective studies that advance a causal identification strategy involving a "natural experiment," public pre-registration plans could be a useful disciplining device, but their use should not give readers false confidence in the results should they be consistent with predictions. By definition, a retrospective study implies that the events of interest have already occurred, and it is often difficult to imagine that a researcher proposing to study causal relationships in a particular context will not have some prior knowledge of patterns in the data. As such, the finding of consistency between actual results and pre-registered hypotheses may not be as powerful as they appear. At the very least, pre-registration of analysis plans for observational data ought to welcome discussion of what has already been observed and analyzed.

Conclusions and Recommendations

The notion of a research cycle as described here allows for the fact that intellectual progress requires many different types of contributions, and the quality of those contributions ought to be judged in terms of distinct criteria. Good research designs that allow for strong causal identification are critical for ultimately arriving at credible answers to causal questions, and these are most likely to generate knowledge that could be usable for advancing normatively attractive goals, including for designing new public policies and practices. Notwithstanding, well-executed descriptive or correlational studies also have very important roles to play in advancing such knowledge, particularly at early stages in a research cycle. Not all research questions are immediately amenable to the most definitive strategies for causal inference, but this alone should not be a barrier to pursuing substantively important research at the earlier, more tentative stages. Biomedical research has shown the way in this regard.

While there are certainly important differences between political science and biomedical science, I believe that what they do share is a concern for real-world problems. And while fundamental questions and "basic science" pursuits are important to both enterprises, the medical community *must* respond to massive epidemics such as HIV/AIDS, Ebola, and the Zika virus, and the political science community has similarly responded to waves of authoritarian rule and democratization, the fall of Communism, new forms of interest articulation, and so on. The overlap is not perfect, but I believe the analogy could be useful for how we produce knowledge within certain segments of the discipline.

Good science should be public. It should be honest. And it should be cumulative. Right now, our structure of publication, reward, etc. does not provide the right incentives for all of these goals or a good division of labor in the form of a research cycle. Political scientists could collectively make greater contributions to knowledge if we built stronger scientific foundations with a greater diversity of research techniques and allowance for recognition of different types of claims.

How could research cycles, as described earlier, play a greater role in the discipline? The most important agents in this regard should be the editors and editorial boards of our leading scholarly journals in promoting the scholarly dialogue I have proposed here.

First, editors could more explicitly recognize a larger range of research contributions within their journals and label them as such, perhaps incorporating some of the language I have used here. And they could encourage/require that contributors locate their work in such cycles.

Second, they could provide guidelines for reviewers concerning the appropriate criteria to use when reviewing articles with particular aims.

Third, we must figure out ways to incentivize a more rapid timeline from submission to publication. It simply will not be possible to use scholarly journals as serious anchors for the accumulation of knowledge if it continues to take well over a year, sometimes longer, between submission and publication for successful pieces. This might be the single greatest barrier to implementing the framework I have proposed here, but academic publishing needs to evolve more rapidly in a fast-moving, online environment, or it stands to be completely marginalized as a source of valued information and credible knowledge.

Fourth, as Gerring describes (Chapter 14, this volume), we require more essays that explicitly assess the state of knowledge in a given field. They might use the framework proposed here to describe exactly what we have learned at various stages of the research cycle, and to identify what is still uncertain.

And beyond the journals, academic departments will need to make explicit how they value different contributions in the research cycle as a basis for promotion and tenure. If younger scholars knew that they could advance their careers with different types of contributions, they would be more likely to focus on a wider set of concerns than an almost single-minded focus on strategies for causal identification. In fact, some of the self-monitoring that occurs within academic conferences and workshops might shift to dissuasion from premature experimentation on the grounds I have described. Many younger scholars might be better positioned to open new areas of inquiry in the earlier stages of a research cycle than to be the ones directing a "definitive" test in the latter stages.

To be clear, my point here is not that political science should try to look just like biomedicine. Rather, I think that there are some surprising lessons to learn that are worth considering. Academic disciplines evolve according to tastes and norms, and some appreciation of how other disciplines operate may widen our scholarly palates. At the moment, it certainly feels as if we could do a lot better in leveraging the collective research talents that exist throughout the discipline to answer serious questions about the political world.

Part II

Publishing

"Publish or perish" is the oft-repeated slogan of *academe*. Gaining access to top journals and presses is therefore a key element in an academic career, and changes in the rules of the game, as administered by editors and reviewers, can have a major impact on who survives and who perishes.

For this reason, attempts to reform the production of knowledge often center on publishing. Since these are the most immediate incentives lying before scholars, the latter ought to respond with alacrity to changes in the incentive structure. Accordingly, several of the reforms vetted in later sections of the book – e.g., transparency, pre-registration and results-blind review – envisage changes to the publication process, usually focused on journals. There, publishing is regarded as a tool for achieving broader reforms in the way in which social science is practiced.

In this section, we focus on several core features of publishing rather than on embellishments or adjunct features that are not inherent in the enterprise. Core features include peer review, the topic of Chapter 4, and length limits to articles, the topic of Chapter 5.

4 Peer Review

Tim F. Liao

This chapter critically evaluates the system-wide practice of the peer review process, the bedrock of scholarly publishing in the social sciences. In particular, the focus of the chapter is on the peer review system for scholarly journal publications, and the implications of this practice for knowledge production. In the chapter, I entertain several proposals that may serve as alternatives to the current practice of the peer review system, ranging from modifying the practice with minor revisions to abolishing the system altogether, and discuss the potential advantages and disadvantages of these alternative models and their implications for knowledge production wherever relevant.

The production of knowledge in the social sciences is about the creation of social science knowledge, also known as "social knowledge," which is defined by Camic, Gross, and Lamont (2011:3) as *descriptive information and analytical statements* about the actions, behaviors, subjective states, and capacities of human beings and/or about the properties and processes of the aggregate or collective units – the groups, networks, markets, organizations, and so on – where human agents are situated." For these authors, "social knowledge" must be knowledge claims about the past, the present, or the future that are empirically based and empirically verifiable, and these claims are of two kinds: normative statements drawing on descriptive information on the social world and the methods and tools of knowledge making with which normative and descriptive statements about the social world are produced.

How are these knowledge claims made? The mechanisms of making legitimate knowledge claims vary from discipline to discipline. At one extreme of the disciplinary spectrum, where the natural sciences are situated, knowledge claims about the natural and physical world are made almost entirely through publication in peer reviewed journals. At the other extreme, where the humanities are located, knowledge claims are produced more often than not in books. The social sciences are located between the two extremes. Whereas some scholars make their knowledge claims with books, many others do so with research papers published in peer reviewed academic journals. While both books/book chapters and journals are important outlet for knowledge production, few would dispute the critical importance of journal publications for knowledge production in the social sciences, a key reason for Franco, Malhotra, and Simonovits (2014) to focus on journals when they analyzed publication bias in the social sciences. Consequently, by centering the attention on peer reviewed journals, I recognize the centrality of journal publications for advancing social scientific knowledge without ignoring the importance of other kinds of outlets for social science scholarship, such as books and book chapters.

The peer review process provides the ex-ante assessment of journal publications by relying on the expertise of peer reviewers who take on the responsibility for assuring high-quality standards, serving as gatekeepers (Bornmann, Marx, and Haunschild 2016). Whereas the typical peer review process is rather standardized in terms of the process and how the editor uses the reviews to reach an editorial decision, the number of reviewers consulted, the expertise of reviewers, and the level of editing applied to accepted papers can be quite diverse (Shashok 2005). In this chapter, I focus on this relatively standard review process, and I use the two terms of "reviewer" and "referee" interchangeably, as both are commonly used to refer to the gatekeepers in the peer review system. As typical of social science journals, the review process is double blind, where authors and reviewers do not know each other's identity. Such double-blind peer review ensures that only high-quality papers are published (Bush 2016). While focusing our attention on the double-blind peer review system, I acknowledge alternative practices, which will be briefly discussed in the next section.

In writing this chapter, I draw on my personal experiences as an author, reviewer, and editor in the last three decades. During this period, I served two terms (2009 to 2015) as the editor of a major sociology journal published by the American Sociological Association and one term (2004 to 2009) as the editor of a major social science book series that relies on a rigorous two-stage single-blind review process where reviewers know the identity of the author, albeit not vice versa, for reviewing the book prospectus and the complete manuscript. In addition, I was a deputy editor of a regional sociology journal for two terms (eight years) in the 1990s and am currently a deputy editor of a flagship demography journal. I also regularly teach a graduate seminar for PhD students where we not only thoroughly discuss the review process but also review all participants' papers for real even though we know the identity of the author and the reviewers.

In the four main sections to follow, I first present the standard practice in manuscript reviewing in the social sciences, namely the double-blind peer review, and critically assess the practice in the next section. I then offer six models as alternatives to the standard review mechanism currently in use by social science journals, drawing on the discussions from the previous section wherever possible before offering some concluding remarks in the final section. As the reader will see, there is no perfect model when it comes to reviewing manuscripts. The reader is advised to view these proposals in a fashion not dissimilar from assessing statistical models for analyzing social data. That is, all models are wrong, but some models are better than others.

The Standard Practice

The practice of reviewing manuscripts for publication has been around since close to three centuries ago, when the Royal Societies of Edinburgh and London sought advice from their members for selecting articles for publication (Hames 2007). Today, the way we process manuscripts submitted to scholarly journals in the social sciences differs little from how papers are handled by journals in the natural and physical sciences, and it has changed little since the mid-twentieth century. Typically, an author submits a manuscript to one and only one scholarly journal. Many journals today require a statement of single submission. That is, the journal is the sole recipient of the submission. Upon receiving the submission, the editor reserves the right of rejecting the paper outright, often known as a "desk rejection," when the paper is deemed either inappropriate for the journal in terms of its scope or subject matter or in terms of its quality (i.e., lower than the standard of the journal). When a manuscript is not rejected outright, the editor sends out review requests to a number of potential reviewers, hoping at least two to three referees will eventually produce useful reviews. Because all potential referees may not agree to review, and because some of those who have agreed may not provide a review in time, if at all, editors often send out requests to a larger number of potential reviewers, even as many as eight or nine for some journals. The manuscript is officially considered under review once the editor has initiated review requests. While practices vary, once the editor has received two or more reviews, the deliberation on an editorial decision on the manuscript may begin. The outcome may range from a "rejection" to some type of "revise and resubmit" to a "conditional acceptance" to a downright "acceptance" of the paper, which is extremely rare. Journals differ in how they treat the "revise and resubmit" category. Some further divide it into two subcategories (such as encouraged revise and resubmit and permitted revise and resubmit) often related to the extent of the required revisions and the potential success of such revisions, while others do not. There are also journals that do not use the term "revise and resubmit" at all, preferring to ask a reviewer to distinguish between major revisions versus minor revisions required of the paper. When the author receives a "conditional acceptance," it most often means the manuscript requires only some minor revisions that can be taken care of quite easily. A conditionally accepted paper, once revised, does not have to go back to the original reviewers, and is often reviewed in-house (i.e., by the editorial team). However, the editor may at times decide to send the paper back to one or more of the original reviewers from the previous round of reviews to ascertain that the revisions are satisfactory.

One of the readings that I require of my graduate students in the publication seminar is a classic three-page essay titled, "Rules for Referees," by Bernard Forscher, published in the journal *Science* in 1965, in the wake of expanding volume of the scientific literature and the raised concern over how to handle such an expansion. Amazingly, almost all the points made by Forscher are still relevant today, for the social sciences to boot, especially in light of another expansion of the scientific and social scientific literatures in the digital age. I review below the highlights in the Forscher (1965) essay in the following three subsections, "Purpose of a Scientific Journal," "Role of the Journal Editor," and "Role of/Rules for Referees." To assist the flow of the presentation, I do not necessarily include further references to Forscher unless absolutely necessary, although references to other authors will be made wherever relevant and appropriate. As we see, others may share Forscher's view even though their terminologies may vary. Parenthetical comments are inserted to bring the presentation up to date.

Purpose of a Scientific Journal

Journals constitute a depository of knowledge and an official record of the transactions of science, as they are kept in libraries[1] (and increasingly online in the twenty-first century). They are a medium of communication. This mode of communication is not limited by time because journals are stored in libraries

---

[1] Here we focus on the function the library plays as a repository of scientific knowledge as opposed to a depository of data for researchers from the humanities and humanistic social sciences as studied by Abbott (2011).

(and online today). Forscher (1965) foresaw the danger of the archival aspect of scientific journals overshadowing the communication purpose, even as early as in the 1960s, when it might be possible to transmit research findings directly from laboratory computers to the library memory banks, and when that happens, it would deter progress in science. He of course did not foresee the rise of the Internet and the important dual functions the Internet plays – as a medium of archival and for communication.

Forscher (1965) valued the communication aspect of scientific journals for the reason of knowledge production, though he did not use these words. It is because the journal communicates three vitally important kinds of message: 1) new facts or data, 2) new ideas, and 3) intelligent reviews of old data and ideas. For our concern in this volume, what the journal communicates is new knowledge produced by authors whose papers grace the papers of a journal.

Role of the Journal Editor

The editor of a scientific journal takes the responsibility for accepting or rejecting manuscripts, taking into account the referees' advice, and should apply one set of rules to all manuscripts considered by the journal. The editorial decision on a paper rests with the editor, who weighs the comments made by the reviewers the editor has consulted. In the editor's communication to the author, the editor may paraphrase or quotes the parts of a referee's comments that the editor believes will help the author in making the required revisions. Alternatively or additionally, the editor may pass on the entire sets of the referees' comments verbatim (and that is the most common practice today).

When two reviewers provide conflicting reviews or when they comment on entirely different aspects of the manuscript, the editor may wish to summarize the comments instead of forwarding the referees' reports, to prevent the author from taking advantage of the reviews. (We rarely see this done, if at all. Instead, responsible editors may give summary guidance to the author to provide further directions beyond the reviewers' comments.) Regardless, the author is entitled to a clear exposition about the editorial expectations for revisions (when a revise and resubmit outcome resulted from the editorial decision).

Role of/Rules for Referees

The editor solicits the input of referees because of their expertise, while avoiding any conflicts of interest on the part of these referees. The referees review a manuscript by raising two kinds of questions, specific and general (Forscher 1965).

Specific questions. These are called specific questions because the referee makes available certain, specific kind of expertise the editor may not have.

1. Newness. Are the findings and ideas reported in the paper new, or does the paper simply rehash things previously reported by the same or other authors? If there are new findings, are they enough to warrant a full paper, or should they be condensed to a research note?[2] This question is central because, after all, the production of knowledge is about the creation of *new* knowledge or the making of *new* knowledge claims. Newness is judged on what is currently known in the literature.
2. Bibliography. Does the paper contain a complete or at least a representative coverage of the extant literature on the subject matter? If certain references are omitted, they should be cited in the review by the referee. For the sake of knowledge production, a complete account and a fair description of the relevant existing knowledge are obviously also paramount.
3. Reliability of methods. Are the methods used in the paper adequate or appropriate for the analysis that produced the conclusion? If the referee disagrees with the author, evidence must be provided. (Often extensive revisions are required precisely because the reviewer asks the author to redo the analysis using improved or more adequate methods.)
4. Internal contradictions. Based on the data reported in the paper, are there computational errors or internal inconsistencies?
5. Illustrations and tables. Are the tables informative and clear? Do the figures show what they are claimed to show? Are there too many figures and tables (or do they duplicate the text)? Are there things in the text that can be better presented in a table or a figure?

General questions.

1. Clarity. Is the paper relatively easy to follow and to understand? Are there places where one would have to read multiple times to understand? Finney (1997) made a similar point, though more from a future reader's perspective, on the need for the referee to bear in mind that a future reader may

---

[2] Note that for social scientific journals, the category of "research note" has gradually disappeared over the past three decades, while there was a time shorter papers even bore the term "research notes" in their titles.

expect to find out what the author has done, precisely and comprehensively, so that the reader could adopt similar procedures in one's own research.
2. Validity of logic. Is the reasoning applied to deriving the conclusions from the findings sound? If it is not, the reviewer must point out why it is faulty.
3. Alternative interpretations. In addition to the interpretation offered by the author, are there other, alternative interpretations that may make sense? Such alternative interpretations may not invalidate the author's interpretation, though they should be recognized.
4. Loopholes. In the set of observations and findings in the paper, are there loopholes? If there are, is it 1) essential, 2) desirable, or 3) interesting to close them? A loophole can be of the three types with a varying degree of seriousness. (When there are loopholes in findings, these findings often lack adequate explanations or the steps through which they are arrived are unclear. Negative findings can be new findings rather than loopholes.)

Finally, when preparing a review of the paper, the referee must prepare a precisely written report describing all relevant comments and recommendations (Finney 1997). These comments and recommendations must reflect the nine types of issues discussed above in the two categories of questions.

An interesting question is who gets selected as a reviewer. Needless to say, a reviewer must have some expertise in at least one key area covered by the paper under review, be it theoretical, methodological, or substantive. The reviewer selection process tends to favor more senior scholars, though junior scholars may receive a review request if their publications are cited in the paper or they are recommended by a senior scholar who may have declined the review request. It goes without saying that senior scholars receive review requests more often, and they must decline at least some of the time.

What the Reviewer Focuses On

Needless to say, reviewing for a journal is a thankless job that competes with the reviewer's own work and research priorities. While there are some reviewers who are irresponsible, sometimes a junior reviewer who is reviewing for a journal for the first few times may assume the responsibility of making sure every line in the paper should be checked to ascertain that the entire paper is free of error. This, in fact, is not necessarily what the editor expects a referee to do. In summarizing the role of the referee for statistics journals,

Gleser (1986:310–311) suggested that the referee give a quick once-over, in particular as the expert in the area of the contributions in the paper and, in so doing, the referee should focus on the following questions.

1. Are the problems discussed in the paper of substantial interest? Would solutions of these problems materially advance theoretical or methodological knowledge?
2. Does the author either solve these problems or else make a contribution toward a solution that improves substantially upon previous work?
3. Are the methods of solution novel? Do they hold promise of being of used to solve other unsolved problems of interest?
4. Does the exposition in the paper help clarify our understanding of this area of research? Does it hold our interest and make us want to give the paper the careful rereading that we give to important papers in our area of research?
5. Do the topic and nature of this paper seem appropriate for this journal? Could typical readers of this journal who are less expert than we are in the given area of research read the paper with profit and interest?

The referee is advised to think along the lines of these five questions while reviewing for a statistics journal, in particular the merits or the demerits of a paper under review in light of these questions. Whereas the last question is more for the reviewer to consider when engaged in reviewing a journal submission, all the other questions are likely the major questions we ask ourselves when skimming a new paper that has just grabbed our attention. It is true that Questions 2 and 3 are more unique to the discipline of statistics (or similarly, to quantitative methodology in the social sciences) as we are interested in whether a newly proposed method could solve other problems not focused on in the paper or at least could improve upon existing methods for the problem currently in focus. Nevertheless, all the first three questions are essentially about the production of *new* knowledge, as is Forscher's (1965) first specific question, be it an advance on theoretical or methodological knowledge, an improvement upon existing methodological knowledge, or a promise for solving other problems in a new way. It is paramount to distinguish two kinds of new knowledge, knowledge that heralds revolutions and knowledge that is built piecemeal. The first kind relates to paradigm shifts that we consider a little later. For a typical reviewer, however, a piecemeal kind of new knowledge built within the same research tradition should be – and in fact often is – given a chance to publish. It is also this emphasis on new, piecemeal knowledge that puts a premium on "new" studies instead of replication studies.

Interestingly, because major journals receive more manuscripts than they can publish and consequently have a high rejection rate (notable the *Journal of the American Statistical Association* in the discipline of statistics), according to Gleser (1986), many papers containing no serious errors are rejected, and looking for errors "puts the cart before the horse." Thus, if a paper does not measure up to the five screening questions above, it should be rejected even if the paper contains no error at all. Once again, what is emphasized is the importance of creating new knowledge because that is the only way in which a discipline can be advanced.

An Evaluation of the Standard Peer Review Practice

For assessing the function of the peer review system in the production of social scientific knowledge, I consider two types of knowledge advancement – scientific revolutions with paradigm shifts and building of knowledge in normal science (Kuhn 1962). In Kuhn's (1962) terminology, *normal science* progresses by building upon one or more past scientific achievements, which certain scientific community acknowledges as supplying the foundation for its further practice, and which can form paradigms. These paradigms help scientific communities bound their disciplines and help the scientist create avenues of inquiry, formulate questions, select methods of inquiry, define areas of research relevant, and, if I may add, establish a set of rules for screening and publish research. The normal science-based paradigm, once established, transforms a group of researchers into a profession or at least a discipline, which in turn further encourages the foundation of professional societies, the formation of scholarly journals, and the promotion of scholarly publications written for consumption by professional colleagues. In a nutshell, this normal science paradigm guides an entire scientific community's research. Note that the definition of a discipline is arbitrary and fluid. New disciplines may form from an old subdiscipline or from several subdisciplines of rather distinct old disciplines, and a paradigm may sometimes be shared by researchers only in a subdiscpline.

Such paradigms involve cumulative development of disciplinary knowledge. Paradigm shifts or scientific revolutions occur when a change in professional commitments to shared assumptions takes place and when tradition-shattering activities arise to replace tradition-bound activities that tend to suppress fundamental novelties subversive to the basic tenets of normal science. Paradigm shifts often result from discoveries brought about by encounters with anomaly, which appears only against the background provided by the very paradigm. Normal science-based professionalization restricts the scientist's vision and, through its established professional practices including professional societies and journals, resists paradigm changes. Because paradigmatic differences cannot be reconciled in the sense that the two paradigms involved are incommensurable, the assimilation of a new paradigm spells the rejection of the old. In that sense, scientific progress or knowledge production is noncumulative, while typical knowledge production in normal science is cumulative.

Paradigm shifts occur when one paradigm replaces another after a period of paradigm testing. The length of the period means that the current paradigm's persistent failure to solve a noteworthy puzzle may give rise to a crisis. Paradigm testing may involve either of the two modes of scientific theory verification: that is, theory testing via probabilistic verification and theory testing via falsification. Sometimes a generation is required to complete a paradigm shift. This length is interesting and relevant to note, considering the typically relevantly short attention span in the empirical social sciences (a point to which we will return later).

However, scientific revolutions may appear to be invisible in normal science textbooks because paradigm shifts are typically viewed, instead of as scientific revolutions, as subsequent additions to the exercise of scientific knowledge building and because the history of the field is written by scientists who are adherents of a new paradigm. In that sense, the old paradigm is somehow reshaped and built into the new paradigm, or at least in how the old is presented and described in the textbooks of the new paradigm that has established a new normal science that has replaced the old.

Therefore, for a critical assessment of the peer review system in the social sciences in the following pages, I consider how such a system functions in both the phase of normal science and that of a scientific revolution or during a paradigm shift. In doing so, I ask the following two questions: Can the current peer review system assist the production of knowledge accompanying a paradigm shift? Can the existing peer review system promote cumulative normal science knowledge building? If so, to what degree can the current peer review system help the accumulation of social scientific knowledge? These questions are of vital importance because, to advance our knowledge of the social world, we must pursue both kinds of knowledge building, that is, knowledge building in the framework of a normal science and knowledge advancement in the form of scientific revolutions and paradigm shifts.

Does Peer Review Encourage Paradigm Shifts?

We may wish to entertain two versions of the question: does the current peer review system encourage paradigm shifts? If it does not, does it permit paradigm shifts? Our review of the current practice reveals that the author of a scholarly paper is expected to provide a complete account, or at least a representative enough account, of the extant literature on the subject matter under examination. Such an account of the literature means two things for the author: it means that the author is expected to build the research under review upon the existing normal science literature; it also means the editor is likely to call upon the service of some key authors of the existing literature as referees of the submitted manuscript. These reviewers will make sure that the author has covered all the bases in the dominant practice of normal science, and, as a rule, any new knowledge proposed must be based on the existing knowledge in the dominant paradigm. Therefore, the answer to the first question is that the current review system does not encourage paradigm shifts.

Does Peer Review Permit Paradigm Shifts?

If the peer review system does not encourage fundamental changes, does it at least permit such changes or shifts? Whereas we cannot, and should not, give an absolute "no" to this second question, the answer is not very promising either. It is because typically reviewers will want to make sure that the author uses normal science terminology, applies normal science logic and methodology, and performs normal science analysis. Such usages, applications, and performances, after all, are indicative of whether the quality of the manuscript under review is up to the standard of normal science. Thus, the current peer review system tends to exercise control that guides authors back to normal science instead of toward the risky enterprise of making a scientific revolution.

Does Peer Review Encourage Developments in Normal Science?

Upon first glance, the answer to this question must be an affirmative "yes," based on the previous discussions. Given the way the current peer review system works, namely, the encouragement of taking stocks of the literature by identifying possible gaps in the literature and places where it could be improved, it goes without saying that the system must promote the cumulative development of knowledge based on the existing literature. Therefore, at least in principle, the current peer review system does indeed appear to encourage and promote knowledge building and accumulation in normal science in a piecemeal fashion. Because the creation of some new, albeit piecemeal, knowledge is rewarded with publications, replication studies are thus implicitly discouraged as it would at best confirm what another (researcher or research group) had already established.

With the answer in principle being so, the final remaining question then is the degree to which the review system actually helps the development of cumulative knowledge advancement. This version of the question seeks to find an answer in practice, namely, has the current review system in effect helped cumulative knowledge building in normal science? Unfortunately, Gans (1992), who studied a key social science – sociology – found that knowledge accumulation had not really happened because sociologists oftentimes had a rather short attention span by citing references primarily from the past decade or so,[3] resulting in a sociological amnesia. The problem tends to be more prevalent in empirical sociological research than theoretical writings (Gans 1992). Almost tongue-in-cheek, Gans (1992:707) further reasoned that knowledge noncumulation may be occupationally useful since "[s]ociology, like much of the rest of the academic piecework industry, puts a high value on originality; forgetting the past is functional for increasing (artificially to be sure) the number of original findings, and the number of articles and books that can be produced."

This pattern of noncumulative research does fit what Mannheim (1927/1952) succinctly pointed out that memory, or rather consciousness, is generational. Later, younger generations seem reluctant to recognize and acknowledge the contributions by earlier, past generations. The reason, for Mannheim (1927/1952), can be explained by the way in which social consciousness and perspectives are formed, that is, how a generation matures in a particular time and place. When it comes to social science research, generational knowledge hinges on our graduate school training and perhaps the immediately

---

[3] Once a well-established sociology colleague told me, while considering references in papers, that she applied this ten-year rule. That is, anything older than a decade could and should be considered to be omitted (perhaps with the exceptions of the classics). While the practice increases the appearance of updatedness of a paper, it at the same time echoes the findings on empirical research (as opposed to theoretical research) that Gans (1992) reported.

following years following graduate school. Furthermore, there is a tendency in our scientific practice to prize so-called up-to-date knowledge.

In summary, there exists another important reason for the difficulty the current peer review system has in playing the gatekeeper's role for both normal science research and scientific revolutions. Typical normal science empirical research relies on the mechanisms of confirmation and (Popperian) falsification while Kuhnian paradigm shifts go beyond such mechanisms in a different research dimension (Liao 1990). Using normal science means can rarely solve persistent puzzles for normal science. The current peer review system is one of such normal science means.

Whereas there is no doubt that the piecemeal normal science type of knowledge accumulation is a proper way of producing knowledge, embraced and supported by the current peer review system, knowledge production by paradigm shifts is as important a way of advancing our understanding of the social world, if not more. The current peer review system does not support such mode of knowledge production, which can be facilitated by some of the proposals in the next section.

Additional Issues

As we discussed earlier, peer review plays an important role in the production of knowledge by providing a *quality* control and relying on peer reviewers as gatekeepers. At the same time, however, the review process can also be viewed in its particular social mechanism as a form of *social* control, as reviewed by Zuckerman and Merton (1971:66, 88).

The referee system in science involves systematic use of judges to assess the acceptability of manuscripts submitted for publication. The referee is thus an example of status judges who are charged with evaluating the quality of role-performance in a social system. They are found in every institutional sphere ... Status judges are integral to any system of social control through their evaluation of role-performance and their allocation of rewards for that performance. They influence the motivation to maintain or to raise standards of performance. In the case of scientific and scholarly journals, the significant status judges are the editors and referees. Like the official readers of manuscripts of books submitted to publishers, or the presumed experts who appraise proposals for research grants, the referees ordinarily make their judgements confidentially, these being available only to the editor and usually to the author ... The composite portrait of referees is clear enough. Whether gauged by their own prestige, institutional affiliations or research accomplishments, they are largely drawn from the scientific elite, as would be expected from the principle of expertise.

Because referees as gatekeepers tend to be ones with more prestige, more reputable institutional affiliations, and greater research accomplishments, they are part of the scientific elite that form the normal science establishment. As gatekeepers, they exercise both quality control of submitted manuscripts and social control of admitting members into the normal science establishment, perhaps as an unintended consequence. The review system, then, is one of hierarchy in which the elite exercise social control over the masses.

Along these lines, rational consensus is at the same time the goal and the process of peer review (Berkenknotter 1995). It is obvious that consensus building is the enemy of moving beyond the current paradigm. Consensus or a lack thereof can present another problem for scholars in the humanities and the branch of the social sciences that practices qualitative research where multiple discourses, methodologies, and epistemologies coexist even though their data or raw materials can be identical. As Berkenknotter (1995:246) summarized, "With such diverse and competing intellectual frameworks and agendas, sending one's manuscript off for referee scrutiny can indeed be a traumatic experience" because such differences and their concomitant lines of reasoning and rhetoric conventions "can make for widely varying referee responses." The situation summarized suggests the kind of multiple paradigms coexisting in some of the social sciences (Liao 1990).

When the double-blind peer review system is fairly practiced, all may be well, to a degree, for knowledge building in normal science. However, "as resources become even scarcer … peer review as a system faces severe stresses" when "the temptation for some referees to abuse their position as gatekeepers become even greater" (Berkenknotter 1995:248). This final potential pitfall of the peer review system cannot be really empirically assessed, in part because few referees would admit unfair treatment of manuscripts they have reviewed.

Finally, the current peer review model is time-consuming and inefficient. When I became editor of a major association journal, editor colleagues of another association journal shared with me tips passed on by their predecessors, namely, the three-six-nine rule. That is, you begin with nine review requests, hoping six will agree to assist in the refereeing process, and in the end three will deliver. As editors, we all know that oftentimes we must continue our efforts in finding new referees to replace nonresponding or severely delinquent referees. As an author, I have found more than a couple of times that a manuscript of mine spent over a year with a journal in the review process. According to Nosek and Bar-Anan (2012), the average published paper did not appear in print until almost two years after it had been initially written. All these indicate a process that is rather inefficient, especially in this digital age.

The Proposed Alternatives

The critical review of the current peer review system above highlights some fundamental issues that interfere with not just paradigm shifts but also knowledge accumulation. In the space below, I describe seven proposals that have the potential to increase efficiency and knowledge accumulation and possibly even encourage publishing pieces with the potential of making paradigm shifts, notably the proposal of abolishing journals altogether.

Proposal 1

This proposal modifies the current peer review system by incorporating two kinds of reviews: 1) brief reviews that comment on the importance of the subject and the findings but do not get into the nitty-gritties of the manuscript and do not attempt to appraise the truth-value of the findings; and 2) traditional reviews where the reviewer reads the entire manuscript, along with appendices if there are any, and provides a fairly detailed report to the editor. By assuming all the findings in the manuscript true and all the analysis correct, the first set of reviewers would simply comment on the significance of the overall research and the potential contributions of the research to knowledge production and accumulation or perhaps even the potential of making a scientific revolution.

The first sort of brief review may involve at least four or five reviewers and the second may be limited to just two reviewers. The first type of reviews would involve a broad base of scholars, making the review process less stochastic and allowing for a more balanced judgment of the importance of a subject matter within a broader field or discipline or possibly multiple disciplines. The current practice more often than not relies on judgments on a paper made by specialists of the subject matter of the paper, who are often convinced of the importance of a subject because it is their specialty as well. Furthermore, too often a reviewer begins with the reference list in a paper by finding faults in things like the incomplete coverage of the bibliography. This brief first review is meant to correct that tendency as well since a paper may not necessarily have covered all the important literature but still possesses the potential of making important contributions. The proposed review system may also avoid the "putting the cart before the horse" problem that Gleser (1986) discussed.

In terms of the timing of the two kinds of reviews, it would be advantageous to begin with the first type of brief reviews, aiming to complete this first phase of reviewing in two weeks' time. When all the brief reviews are in, the editor makes a quick up-or-down decision to decide whether the manuscript would be worth the effort of going into the second phase of the detailed reviewing. If so, two additional detailed reviews on the procedures, methods, analyses, and findings, whether or not from some of the same reviewers, are to be sought.

A major shortcoming of this proposal is that sometimes it can be difficult to assess the significance of the research reported in a paper without reading carefully the details in the paper. One reason of this difficulty is that most of us have been trained to regard all components of a research project as part and parcel of the project, when in fact the significance of the overall research can be evaluated separately. The proposal has two potential advantages: it would likely increase efficiency and shorten turnaround time, and it would encourage authors to think big when it comes to knowledge production and contributions to the literature.

Proposal 2

The review system can be revised from double-blind to open reviews. This model is known as "open peer review." Currently, only a small minority of editorial offices practice single-blind reviewing where referees know the identity of the author but not vice versa, and an even smaller number use some modified version of non-blind review. I recently served as a referee for a health journal whose policy includes automatic revealing of the author's identity and optional revealing of the referee's identity. Thinking it over, I decided against keeping my review anonymous. Sure enough, I quickly received an email from the first author, asking me how to take care of a certain issue. This exchange did speed up the revisions of the paper, and the paper was published not long afterwards online. Had my overall recommendation been to reject the paper, I probably would have kept my review anonymous.

My recent experience with the health journal in late 2016 represents a recent effort by life science journals to open up the review process. In fact, as early as 1999, the *British Medical Journal* started revealing reviewers' names to authors, and since then several life science journals have adopted the practice of including reviewers' names, prepublication history, and reviewers' reports with published articles (Amsen 2014). Two major problems of the conventional practice cited by Amsen (2014) include the problem that anonymous reviewers tend to bias toward rejection or acceptance for unscientific reasons because often closest peers can turned out to be direct competitors, and the issues that the referee reports are only accessible to the editor and the authors but not to the public. Because an open peer review model makes review materials public, the model is also known as "public peer review." In addition, open peer review may facilitate direct contact between author and reviewer (useful for clarifying points of ambiguity and thereby enhancing the speed and efficiency of the review process), as my recent experience shows. A variant of this kind of communication can actually be provided by making a rather minor modification of the current peer review system by allowing direct communication between the author and the reviewer via anonymous emails or an online discussion space provided by the journal.

There are a variety of ways that open peer review can be implemented and practiced. According to Shema (2014), open peer review may take on these variants below that are not mutually exclusive to one other.

1. Signed – when reviewers' names appear alongside the published article or the reviews that are passed to the authors have the reviewers' names on them.
2. Disclosed – the author and the reviewer are aware of each other's identity and engage in discussion during the review process.
3. Editor-mediated – when an editor facilitates a part of the peer review process, either by pre-selecting articles for review and/or making the final decision regarding an article.
4. Transparent – the entire review process is "out in the open," including the original manuscripts, the reviewers' comments, and the authors' replies.
5. Crowdsourced – anyone can comment on the article (before its official publication).
6. Pre-publication – any public review occurring before the article's publication (say an article submitted to a preprint server).
7. Synchronous – the review process is supposed to happen exactly in the time of an article's publication. In reality, it doesn't exist.
8. Post-publication – review happens after an article's publication (e.g., a blog post, an F1000Prime review).

As one can see, the open peer review system is a broad concept that encompasses many aspect of the review process, from the author's and the reviewer's identity (at the time of the review vs when the paper is published), to publication of the review materials, to open-sourced commenting and reviewing, to post-publication reviews. Publication of peer reviews is considered one of the modified stages of the current system by Nosek and Bar-Anan (2012). The open peer review system can be a complex one if a journal is to adopt every aspect of the open peer review system.

There can be potential pitfalls of this proposal: 1) open peer review (i.e., without anonymity) could slightly reduce the chance of finding reviewers (Amsen 2014), leading to fewer potential reviewers to accept review invitations; 2) authors and reviewers can be unequal in status, introducing a power differential that may affect the review process; 3) reviewers may not express themselves in a candid fashion; and 4) an open review system increases the likelihood of accumulating "enemies" who may later torpedo a referee's own manuscripts or grant proposals, a serious future risk for the reviewer (DeCoursey 2006).

On the other hand, major advantages of an open peer review system include the following (DeCoursey 2006): 1) reviewers would be more constructive and tactful; 2) reviewers with a mean spirit could be more easily unmasked by authors; and 3) the publication of reviewers' name would encourage future reviewers to do a more thorough job. DeCoursey (2006), however, doubted the possibility of implementing a full-blown model of the open peer review in this competitive world and believed a half-way house would be more realistic in which reviewers only begin to make open constructive comments when a paper is conditionally accepted.

Proposal 3

The establishment of a central data storage as a form of "publication" where reviews garnered from various journals where the original publications have initially appeared and made public at some point, even after rejection, together with the original papers, so that they can bear on an editor's decisions and reviewers' deliberations, and on end-users' evaluation of a manuscript. This storage or repository can be discipline or association/society-based.

There are two major benefits of this proposal. By browsing the review storage, authors would be able to get a sense of the operation of a particular journal (in comparison with other journals) before they consider submitting a manuscript to the journal. The information provided would be much richer than the simple publication statistics (i.e., number of manuscripts received, acceptance rate, mean review time, etc.). More importantly, with the knowledge of their comments becoming public, reviewers may likely refrain from frowning upon negative or null findings, and consequently the proposal may also help alleviate the publication bias that Franco, Malhotra, and Simonovits (2014) reported due to the fact that positive findings are rewarded with publications while papers with negative or null findings most likely ended up in file drawers (also see Nosek, Spies, and Motyl 2012). This practice should be combined with a system of collating any (verification) replications that may have been conducted on the study, that is, related studies will be clustered with the original publication. As a result, research replications may be encouraged, thus avoiding the short attention span problem and facilitating knowledge accumulation. A major problem would be an ethical one. That is, whether authors and reviewers alike would be comfortable with revealing identities, not to mention making all their comments public. If the whole operation is anonymous, then the scientific replication benefit would no longer be possible.

Proposal 4

Post-publication review was listed above by Shema (2014) as one feature of an open peer review system. However, we separate it out here to highlight its uniqueness because post-publication review can also be conducted with the current blind review system, the focus in this subsection. The main goal of post-publication review is to recognize that review is an ongoing process, continuing into the future as long as a study is relevant. Who would be responsible for organizing post-publication reviews? Naturally, most scholarly journals today house websites not just for submissions but also presentations of a chosen set, if not the entire set, of published articles. It has been increasingly popular to publish online extensive appendices, data, and other additional materials that accompany published articles which may have a traditional print form. Some, especially certain online journals that I am familiar with, also allow follow-ups to published articles, including but not restricted to errata, additional research on the topic, and further expositions. Therefore, it is only reasonable for journals to set up online space for post-publication reviews.

Who would be authors of such reviews? Journal editors can surely invite scholars with expertise in the subject matter of a published article, or perhaps scholars outside of the topical area, to further reflect on the implications of the published piece, after determining the import of the paper. Another model will be an open commentary system where anyone with an interest in the paper can make comment by directly submitting a review online. Such reviews will not go through the peer review process but be checked by the editorial office for their language and writing style (including a tone of civility, for example).

The most obvious benefit of a post-publication review will be a great likelihood of knowledge accumulation. Another possible related advantage will be the encouragement of research replications, currently sorely missing in the social sciences. A potential disadvantage will be the increase in inequality among scholars. Publications by those scholars with greater reputation and based in more prestigious institutions will likely get more post-publication reviews than the papers by unknown scholars and newcomers. The editor is the only person who may have some control over this issue by ensuring the choice of papers that get post-publication reviews is made on their merits and significance and nothing else.

Proposal 5

A centralized review process – managed by a discipline-wide organizations such as the American Political Science Association (APSA), the American Psychological Association (APA), or the American Sociological Association (ASA) – in which the primary job of reviewers is to determine where (not whether) a paper is published. Along these lines, Nosek and Bar-Anan (2012) proposed a separation of the link between peer review and specific journals by setting up centralized review services that handle peer reviews. Instead of making a decision on whether a paper meets the "accept" standard of a particular journal, the review service gives a manuscript a grade. In this model, while journals could retain their own review process, they may drop the review process entirely by relying on the review service.

This proposal could change the role of the editor in a significant way. Editorial infrastructures in specific disciplines get consolidated into review services, such as all APA journal boards may be combined into a single editorial service for psychology (Nosek and Bar-Anan 2012). In their proposal, journals take on only a curator's role by selecting certain articles to promote in a specific journals.

One reason that the separation of reviewing and publication is doable lies in another proposal that Nosek and Bar-Anan (2012) made: the establishment of an open-access central repository for research, something like the current NIH repository of research conducted with NIH funding. In that sense, articles are already "published" or at least made public and the selection of them into journals serves only the purpose of further promotion. Even if we keep the current function of journals (i.e., without an open-access central repository), a centralized review process will still be beneficial in ways more than one. It may increase efficiency by consolidating expertise in a discipline; it may increase transparency by avoiding any possible double or multiple submissions. It may also improve the control of publication pace, without having to worry about too many or too few papers being in the pipeline of a given journal. Journal editors may use the grades provided by the central review service to select papers to publish in their journals, having total control over how many and which papers to publish in a given issue of a journal.

The difficulties of the proposal are also multiple. To begin with, determining the territory of a central review service can turn out to be an impossible task. There is the issue of discipline boundary, both within a given discipline, such as political science, psychology, and sociology, because there are established subdisciplines with diehard adherents, and between disciplines because sometimes the subject focus of a manuscript is not so clear-cut and can be said to be interdisciplinary, transdisciplinary, or multidisciplinary. Furthermore, even though there are international members (the APA, the APSA, and the ASA are all based in the United States), would a centralized review service of the ASA cover international journals that are based in other countries? If not, would we need to establish a global review service? Then there is the difficulty of allocating manuscripts to reviewers by the central board. Presumably, the centralized review service results from the consolidation of multiple editorial boards, with possible additions to broaden the reviewer base. When assigning reviewers, there is the unavoidable tendency of, for a manuscript of a given topic, assigning reviewers mostly related to a particular journal as far as their specialties go. All these difficulties are practical issues, and we must already assume the centralized review service can indeed play the role of grading the quality of research fairly and adequately.

Proposal 6

This proposal is related to a variant of Proposal 5 but should be consider separately. All journals are to be abolished in their present form. That also means the abolishment of the current peer review system. There are two alternatives to conventional journals as the means for disseminating research results. One is an online public repository, as discussed by Nosek and Bar-Anan (2012), and the field of physics provides a good example where arXiv, operated by Cornell University and supported by over 50 universities (as of 2012), makes preprints available to all. Most physicists rely on arXiv, which is organized in topical areas, by posting their manuscripts and by keeping up-to-date on new research in their research areas. However, arXiv as yet does not replace conventional journals because most physicists still submit their manuscripts to peer reviewed journals. Nevertheless, arXiv does publicize research by bypassing peer review. In that sense, authors self-publish and exercise self-quality control.

The number of public or open-access repositories has increased tremendously over the past decade-and-a-half. The Registry of Open Access Repositories was officially launched at the University of Southampton in 2003, and as of the beginning of 2017, it boasts of over 4,300 repositories from around the globe. When Google Scholar started to rank journals based on their impacts by using a variant of the h-index in 2012, three archiving repositories made the top-ten-ranked journal list, RePEc, arXiv, and SSRN (Nosek and Bar-Avan 2012). The final repository, SSRN (Social Science Research Networks), features a research paper subrepository where about a dozen disciplines (as of the beginning of 2017) are found, including political science but not psychology or sociology. For political science, the subrepository contains only six research centers/institutes and one department (MIT), each of which offers an open-access working paper series. The MIT political science research paper series, for example, posted 16 working papers during the second half of 2016, with the number of downloads ranging from 0 to 165 (as of January 6, 2017). There has also been a recent effort in the social sciences since July 2016 that mirrors arXiv, called SocArXiv, which has been developing steadily (as of September 2019, more than 1,600 preprints have been deposited there), which echoes but has surpassed a similar, though not quite active, endeavor in psychology, PsyArXiv. Compared with physics, it is obvious that the social science as a broad discipline still has a long way to go.

How do we exercise quality control over self-publishing in public repositories, if we assume that conventional journals will eventually go away? For quality control, we could rely on an evaluation of research impact (such as citation based) and online commentary (Nosek and Bar-Anan 2012). However, there are several potential problems and challenges: First and foremost, poor-quality research will still get "published" even though it may not generate high impact and it may eventually draw negative commentary. Second, the reputation of authors and their affiliated institutions may unnecessarily drive citation counts, the so-called the richer-get-richer conundrum. If we are to rely on impact as the means of assessment, it means novel findings will be valued and that the old file drawer problem generated by the current practice will remain. Additionally, the current practice of using publications as the chief means for the evaluation of promotion cases will have to be altered and moved more toward an impact-based mechanism.

For this author, the single biggest challenge for relying on a public repository for publication without at the same time using a central review system is the potential of lack of improvement of research papers. My years of experiences as an author, an editor, and a reviewer suggest that the quality of our papers has unquestionably improved by the formal peer review despite the downside of the current peer review system, such as inefficiency and the file drawer effect. Therefore, if we are to abolish peer review by conventional journals as well as the journals themselves, to improve our research, some form of self-policing becomes necessary, be it by a team of colleagues from our own institutions or a group of users of a repository where one's paper is downloaded (perhaps even by asking for comments as a requirement of downloading a paper). This final proposal, however, holds the promise of encouraging research with paradigmatic changing potentials because conventional journals are steeped in normal science conventions and rules.

Table 4.1 provides a summary of the chief features of the six proposals above, their main strengths and weaknesses, and their feasibilities for implementation. All things considered, Proposals 1, 2, and 4 are fairly easy to implement, while Proposals 3, 5, and 6 present a challenge for implementation. It may be beneficial for us to begin with the easier proposals first and conduct assessments prior to moving to the more difficult alternatives that would have to involve concerted action of an entire discipline or subdiscipline.

Conclusion

The afore-discussed potential problems for the six proposals notwithstanding, a major change in how scholars publish and disseminate researching findings is afoot. The transformation of the mode of publication and knowledge diffusion spells a need to change the way in which peer review is conducted. In the age of the Internet, the digital revolution is significantly changing the way of teaching, scholarly publication, and knowledge dissemination (Smith 2014). Will a revolution of the peer review system be next?

Table 4.1 A summary of the six proposals

	Main Features	Strengths	Weaknesses	Feasibility
1	Two steps: general and specific	Fast first-stage reviews to give ups or downs on papers	Difficult for some papers to assess importance without reading into the details	Readily feasible; occasionally practiced by some editors, though not necessarily in order
2	Open peer review	Transparency; reviews more constructive; fewer mean reviews	Difficulty in finding reviewers; reviewers may not be as candid; accumulation of potential enemies	The current system can be modified to an open system without changing the setup of the system
3	A repository of reviews	Rich publication information; reduction of publication bias toward positive findings	A potential ethical complication	It would take much work to transform a journal-based review system to an association or discipline-based repository
4	Post-publication reviews as an ongoing process	Enhanced knowledge accumulation; encouragement of research replications	Potential increase of inequality among authors	Relative ease of implementation by a journal editor
5	Centralized discipline-wide review; separation of review and publication	Increased efficiency; increased transparency; increased publication pace	Disciplinary boundaries difficult to define; centralized allocation of papers to reviewers difficult	It would involve an entire restructuring of the current journal-based practice to a discipline-based practice
6	Open-access repositories like arXiv, SocArXiv, PsyArXiv	Increased "publication" pace; easier "publication" of controversial research	Lack of quality control; lack of improvement in papers; reputation-based bias	The system is already there, though making papers in repositories acceptable as real publications is a challenge

The digital revolution has already changed the function of libraries. In the print age, the library was responsible for subscribing to all the important scientific and scholarly journals. Users would have to visit the library to access scientific publications. Today, however, virtually all scholarly publications are accessible at the fingertips of the researcher because publications are now web-based. Even those journals that still print paper issues all publish an online version first. As a result, few scholars still visit the library to gain access to research findings, and the library has taken on two new functions: as the institutional subscriber to the Internet access to scholarly journals and as the public space for students who prefer a large and quiet study room.

Given all these changes, it is not difficult to imagine, even if none of the proposals made in the earlier section will materialize and disciplinary and subdisciplinary journals will still rely on peer review for gate-keeping, a feasible transformation of the peer review system should be conducted. We have seen an increase in efficiency in the communication between the editor and the reviewer and between the editor and the author. However, the method of performing the review process largely remains the same – sending out requests to potential referees, obtaining referees' reports, asking the author to revise if the referees collectively deem the manuscript worthwhile, and so on. We can, to say the least, and should consider a scaled-down version of Proposal 2, by opening up the review process to all researchers with potential interest in the topic, say, all subscribers of the journal and/or all members of a scholarly association. The commentaries must conform to the journal's guidelines and be posted on the journal's internal website. Once the manuscript is accepted, it will, together with all the commentaries and reviews, be published on the journal's official website. Whereas this final proposal is less revolutionary than some of the earlier proposals, it will nonetheless render our peer review process more consistent with the ongoing digital revolution.

5 Length Limits

John Gerring and Lee Cojocaru

Journals in most social science disciplines (excepting economics) set stringent word or page limits, a fact of which every author is keenly aware.[1] Limits on the length of journal articles affect scholarly research in all sorts of ways, some more visible than others.

Some researchers, we presume, avoid projects entirely if they seem intractable in a journal format. Some researchers relinquish the goal of journal publication in preference for the more relaxed format of an academic monograph. This option, however, is decreasingly viable as university presses trim their lists and reorient priorities toward books with a popular theme and a potential crossover audience.

Our contention is that current journal policies that impose arbitrary word or page limits on published articles are not serving their discipline well. They contort the academic process in ways that are not helpful to the conduct or dissemination of scholarly research. And they waste everyone's valuable time.

We begin by surveying the policies of top political science and sociology journals. In the second section, we lay out a proposal that we suppose will not be very controversial: journals should clearly state their policies vis-à-vis length requirements and adhere to those policies. In the third section, we lay out our more controversial proposal, that journals should abolish – or at least greatly loosen – length limits.

The rest of the chapter elaborates and defends that proposal. We discuss (a) the time and hassle of adjusting manuscript length to fit journal requirements, (b) heterogeneity across venues (different journals offering different policies), (c) supplementary material posted online, (d) references (often the first aspect of an article to be cut down in order to meet a length requirement), (e) the role of length limitations in structuring the work of political science, (f) word limits in economics (where we find journal policies to be considerably more permissive), (g) the correlation between article

---

[1] Comments and suggestions on various drafts were provided by Taylor Boas, Colin Elman, Alan M. Jacobs, Carl Henrik Knutsen, and Evan Lieberman.

length and impact, and (h) the business ramifications of a relaxation of length limits.

Survey

Despite its importance, no comprehensive survey of word or page limits has ever been conducted. To remedy this omission, and to set the stage for our argument, policies and practices across top journals in political science and sociology are summarized in Tables 5.1 and 5.2. Information is drawn directly from journal web pages (instructions to authors) – supplemented, in some cases, by direct communication with editors. Journal policies are quoted verbatim in appendices to this chapter (posted online on John Gerring's homepage[2]).

Comparisons across journals are inexact inasmuch as they follow different protocols. Some count words and others pages. Some count abstracts, references, tables, figures, and footnotes, while others do not (or only count some of them). Some apply limits at the submission stage and others wait for final approval.

Here, we adopt a few standard criteria in order to provide a (more or less) systematic comparison of journal policies based on stated guidelines posted on journal web pages. Length is counted with words, as this is the usual practice in political science and is more exact than pagination. Where limits are counted in pages, we list the journal policy (in pages) and then convert pagination to word counts following journal guidelines with respect to margins and font, as noted in column 2 of Table 5.1. We assume that *online* materials (generally in the form of appendices) are not considered in the word count. However, some journals exempt references and/or appendices in the word count even if they appear as part of the published article, as noted in columns 3–4. We also note whether the word count is applied at submission or later (column 5) and whether, according to the stated policy of the journal, editors are allowed some discretion in applying the rules (column 6).

Twenty of the most influential journals from each discipline are included in this survey. For gauges of impact in political science we rely on two sources: SCImago journal rank (Elsevier) and Science Watch (Thomsen Reuters).[3] Chosen journals include *American Journal of Political Science*,

---

[2] https://utexas.app.box.com/s/6izfiz35ta2y6eyesfrm9p1i9p63dfg6.
[3] See www.scimagojr.com/journalrank.php?category=3312 and http://archive.sciencewatch.com/dr/sci/09/mar29-09_1/.

Table 5.1 Political science journals

Journal	Limit	Policies: Including References	Policies: Including Appendices	Policies: At Submission	Policies: Editors' Discretion	Practices: Mean	Practices: Minimum	Practices: Maximum	Consistency: Actual Maximum	Consistency: Column 10−Column 2
1	2	3	4	5	6	7	8	9	10	11
American Journal of Political Science	10,000	Yes	No	Yes	Yes	10,156	7,558	14,294	14,294	4,294
American Political Science Review	12,000	Yes	Yes	Yes	Yes	13,361	10,990	16,593	16,593	4,593
Annual Review of Political Science	7,800 (24)	No	No	Yes	Yes	8,522	5,799	14,467	12,525	4,725
British Journal of Political Science	12,000	Yes	Yes	No	Yes	12,048	7,830	23,596	23,596	11,596
Comparative Political Studies	12,000	Yes	Yes	Yes	Yes	11,597	8,320	15,890	15,890	3,890
Conflict Management and Peace Science	10,000	Yes	No	No	Yes	10,239	4,574	13,155	13,155	3,155
European Journal of Political Research	8,000	Yes	No	Yes	Yes	8,789	5,916	11,039	10,127	2,127
International Security	20,000	Yes	No	No	Yes	17,123	10,803	20,215	20,215	215
International Studies Quarterly	12,000	Yes	Yes	Yes	Yes	11,934	8,440	15,840	15,840	3,840
Journal of Conflict Resolution	11,000	Yes	Yes	Yes	Yes	10,570	6,870	14,201	14,201	3,201
Journal of Peace Research	10,000	Yes	Yes	Yes	No	9,382	7,445	10,417	10,417	417
Journal of Politics	10,250 (35)	Yes	No	Yes	Yes	9,948	6,917	17,754	12,720	2,470

Journal								
Journal of Public Administration Research and Theory**	12,000	Yes	No	Yes	11,610	5,298	16,091	15,284	3,284
Party Politics	8,000	Yes	Yes	Yes	8,103	4,553	14,788	14,788	6,788
Political Analysis	8,750 (30)	Yes	No	No	8,570	5,766	15,371	14,706	5,956
Political Communication	8,750 (30)	Yes	No	No	8,684	5,039	15,890	14,654	5,904
Political Geography	11,000	Yes	Yes	Yes	10,821	9,372	14,891	14,891	3,891
Political Psychology	9,000	Yes	Yes	Yes	9,253	7,776	13,014	13,014	4,014
Public Opinion Quarterly	6,500	No	No	Yes	8,520	4,160	17,775	15,451	8,951
World Politics	12,500	Yes	No	Yes	13,324	11,282	18,531	18,531	6,031
Mean or Distribution (Yes/No)	10,578	17/3	9/11	15/5	10,628	7,235	15,691	15,045	4,467

Note: **Journal** = top 20 political science journals by impact (www.scimagojr.com/journalrank.php; www.scimagojr.com/journalrank.php?category=3312; http://archive.sciencewatch.com/dr/sci/09/mar29-09_1/). **Limit** = ceiling on number of words (pages) allowed in research articles, as specified on journal web page. Where the limit is specified in pages we list the projected word limit based on the specified page limit with double-spaced lines and standard 12-point font. **At submission** = limits apply at submission. **Editor's discretion** = longer versions may be accepted with editor's approval. For further clarification of journal policies see Appendix A. **Practices** = mean, minimum, maximum word counts across all research articles and including all published material (footnotes, references, appendices, et al.). **Actual maximum** = maximum word count, including or excluding references and appendices as specified by the journal's policies. All journals observed in the calendar year 2015 except those marked with a double asterisk (**), which are observed in 2014.

American Political Science Review, Annual Review of Political Science, British Journal of Political Science, Comparative Political Studies, Conflict Management and Peace Science, European Journal of Political Research, International Security, International Studies Quarterly, Journal of Conflict Resolution, Journal of Peace Research, Journal of Politics, Journal of Public Administration Research and Theory, Party Politics, Political Analysis, Political Communication, Political Geography, Political Psychology, Public Opinion Quarterly, and *World Politics*.

For a gauge of impact in sociology we rely on the Google Scholar (scholar.google.com) H5 index. Chosen journals include *American Journal of Sociology, American Sociological Review, Annual Review of Sociology, Antipode, British Journal of Criminology, British Journal of Sociology, Criminology, Demography, Ethnic and Racial Studies, European Sociological Review, Journal of Ethnic and Migration Studies, Journal of European Social Policy, Journal of Marriage and Family, Journal of Population Economics, Population and Development Review, Qualitative Research, Social Science Research, Social Forces, Sociology, Theory,* and *Culture and Society*.

All top political science journals (by our definition) in existence in 2015 imposed space limits, as shown in Table 5.1. The tightest limit – 6,500 words (not including references or appendices) – is imposed by *Public Opinion Quarterly*. The most capacious limit – 20,000 words – is allowed by *International Security*. Most hover between 8,000 and 12,000 words, with a mean of just over 10,500. All journals except the *Journal of Peace Research* allow editorial discretion in the application of word limits.

In sociology, journal practices are somewhat more relaxed. Six journals – *American Journal of Sociology, Criminology, Journal of European Social Policy, Journal of Population Economics, Population and Development Review, Social Science Research* – impose no formal limits. Among those that impose limits, the range extends from about 8,000 to 15,000, with a mean of about 9,000. Most journals allow editorial discretion in the policing of these limits.

The second section of Tables 5.1–5.2 focuses on journal *practices*, i.e., how these length limits are administered. We report mean, minimum, and maximum word counts of all articles published in 2015 (or where unavailable, in 2014), as noted in columns 7–9. Here, we include only regular, full-length articles, as defined by the journal. For example, if a journal has a separate section for research notes, methodology notes, or reviews, these publications are excluded. To determine

Table 5.2 Sociology journals

Journal	Policies					Practices			Consistency	
	Limit	Including References	Including Appendices	At Submission	Editor's Discretion	Mean	Minimum	Maximum	Actual maximum	Column 10– Column 2
1	2	3	4	5	6	7	8	9	10	11
American Journal of Sociology	[none]					19,718	12,457	28,482	–	–
American Sociological Review	15,000	Yes	No	Yes	Yes	13,761	10,073	18,972	18,972	3,972
Annual Review of Sociology	7,800 (24)	No	No	Yes	Yes	12,395	9,455	17,634	11,729	3,929
Antipode	9,500	Yes	No	Yes	Yes	9,982	7,923	12,597	12,597	3,097
British Journal of Criminology	10,000	Yes	Yes	Yes	Yes	10,080	7,511	12,160	12,160	2,160
British Journal of Sociology	8,000	Yes	No	Yes	Yes	9,423	8,018	11,810	11,810	3,810
Criminology	[none]					13,125	9,296	19,063	–	–
Demography	8,000	No	No	Yes	Yes	11,036	4,258	15,612	12,034	4,034
Ethnic and Racial Studies	8,000	Yes	No	Yes	No	7,626	6,272	8,247	8,247	247
European Sociological Review	7,000	Yes	No	Yes	No	6,694	5,278	9,254	7,392	392
Journal of Ethnic and Migration Studies	9,000	Yes	No	Yes	Yes	9,606	7,189	12,589	10,467	1,467
Journal of European Social Policy	[none]					8,741	3,635	12,331	–	–

(*continued*)

Table 5.2 (cont.)

Journal	Policies					Practices			Consistency	
	Limit	Including References	Including Appendices	At Submission	Editor's Discretion	Mean	Minimum	Maximum	Actual maximum	Column 10-Column 2
1	2	3	4	5	6	7	8	9	10	11
Journal of Marriage and Family	10,250 (35)	Yes	Yes	Yes	Yes	9,853	4,127	14,534	14,534	2,034
Journal of Population Economics	[none]					12,356	5,975	18,214	–	–
Population and Development Review	[none]					9,547	6,026	15,907	–	–
Qualitative Research	8,000	Yes	Yes	Yes	Yes	8,747	6,742	12,946	12,946	4,946
Social Science Research	[none]					13,376	4,364	19,921	–	–
Social Forces	10,000	Yes	No	Yes	Yes	10,160	7,107	12,899	12,793	2,793
Sociology	8,000	Yes	Yes	Yes	No	8,166	7,431	8,504	8,504	504
Theory, Culture and Society	8,000	Yes	Yes	Yes	Yes	9,613	5,531	14,203	14,203	6,203
Mean or Distribution (Yes/No)	9,039	12/2	5/9	14/0	11/3	10,700	6,933	14,794	12,028	2,828

Note: **Journal** = top 20 sociology journals by impact (https://schola..google.com/citations?view_op=top_venues&hl=en&vq=soc_sociology). **Limit** = ceiling on number of words (pages) allowed in research articles, as specified on journal web page. Where the limit is specified in pages we list the projected word limit based on the specified page limit with double-spaced lines and standard 12-point font. **At submission** = limits apply at submission. **Editor's discretion** = longer versions may be accepted with editor's approval. For further clarification of journal policies see Appendix B. **Practices** = mean, minimum, maximum word counts across all research articles and including all published material (footnotes, references, appendices, et al.). **Actual maximum** = maximum word count, including or excluding references and appendices as specified by the journal's policies. All journals observed in calendar year 2015.

mean length, we record page lengths for all articles published in a year, calculate the mean (in pages), locate an article with that (approximate) length, place the contents of that article (all aspects of the article – text, abstract, footnotes, references, appendices, tables, figures – so long as it appears in the journal itself rather than in an online appendix) into a Word document, and record the number of words. To calculate minimum and maximum length we use page length to identify the longest and shortest articles and then place the contents of those articles (all aspects, as published) into a Word file to record the number of words.

We find that the mean length of articles is close to the stated word limit for most journals in political science and sociology (~10,000), and there is considerable spread from minimum (~7,000) to maximum (~15,000). Recorded word counts in practice are remarkably similar across the two disciplines.

The final section of Tables 5.1 and 5.2 focuses on consistency between policies and practices for those journals with an official limitation on length. Column 10 records the "actual maximum," the highest word count of any article published by that journal within the year, including only those elements of an article that are considered relevant to calculating length according to the journal's policies. For example, if the journal excludes references from the limit, the actual maximum does so as well. Column 11 compares the actual maximum with the official word limit, subtracting one from the other. Results are explored in the following section.

Proposal 1: Clarity and Consistency

In comparing policies with practices, we find strong correspondence between the stated limits and the mean length of articles. Comparing columns 1 and 7, only a few journals – notably *International Security* and *Public Opinion Quarterly* in political science and *Annual Review of Sociology* and *Demography* in sociology – have mean lengths that greatly surpass their official word limits, and this could be partly accounted for by our method of counting, which includes all article content (even that which is not included in a journal's assessment of word limits).

However, when comparing maximum (applicable) lengths with stated limits we find considerable divergence, at least for certain journals, as shown in the final column of Tables 5.1 and 5.2. The average difference is nearly 5,000 words in political science. That is, across the 20 top political science journals, the longest article published in a year in that journal surpassed these journals' formal limits by an average of just under 5,000 words. One journal, the *British Journal of Political Science*, published an article that is more than 11,000 words over the stated limit. And only one journal, the *Journal of Peace Research*, appears to strictly abide by its word limits (not coincidentally, it is the only journal that does not allow editorial discretion). Differences between stated policies and practices are noticeable in sociology as well, though they are not as glaring.

To be sure, most journals allow editorial discretion in the application of length limits. In this sense, they are not violating their own policies. However, length limits are described on journal web pages as if they were strictly applied. Authors without experience with a specific journal – or prior correspondence with the editor – would have no way of knowing that they might publish an article of 15,000 words in a journal with a 10,000-word limit. Strikingly, Card and DellaVigna (2014:162) find that the imposition of page limits at the *American Economic Review* had a strong effect on the length of papers submitted to the journal but no effect on the length of papers published by that journal, suggesting that the editors were not taking their formal policies very seriously.

This inconsistency between de jure and de facto policies is problematic in several respects. Authors are unsure about how to craft their work in order to meet the journal's guidelines. They do not know whether the word limit will be observed and, if not, how much leeway might be allowed. Likewise, senior faculty, who have greater experience, and perhaps know the editors personally, can muster inside information to successfully walk this tightrope.

Our first proposal will surprise no one. If wide discretion in word limits is allowed then this policy should be clearly stated on the journal's web page. Authors should not be required to second-guess this important issue. Our analysis suggests that most journal word limits in political science should be understood as *targets*, not ceilings. Note that the mean number of words in published articles aligns closely with journal word limits, with considerable dispersion about the mean. A simple change of terminology would solve this problem. Editors could change word (or page) *limit* to word (or page) *target* and disable web pages (e.g., for the *American Political Science Review*) that automatically disqualify submissions that violate the target.

While a great deal of effort has gone into enhancing the transparency of journal content (i.e., articles) in recent years, it is equally important that journal policies be transparent. This should be an easy reform because all it proposes is to bring journal policies in line with journal practices.

Proposal 2: No (Tight) Limits

Our more controversial proposal is that journals should abolish arbitrary, one-size-fits-all word limits, or greatly expand those limits. The argument for this proposal may be concisely stated. *An article, like a book or any other written product, should be as long as it needs to be – no longer, and no shorter.*

Some articles are *over*-written. There is only one basic point and it is repeated ad infinitum. Or there is a set of empirical tests that so closely resemble each other as to be redundant; they belong in an appendix or perhaps are entirely unnecessary. Nonetheless, the author feels compelled to fill up the allocated space.

Articles in top natural science journals (e.g., *Nature*, *Science*) are typically much shorter than those that appear in social science journals. While we do not think this format generally serves social science well, some points can be made with brevity, and this should not take away from their importance or their impact. In political science and sociology, short papers are often relegated to "research notes," simply because of their brevity. As a consequence of this classification, they are not taken very seriously and do not count for very much (re: promotion and tenure). This sort of classification by size seems just as arbitrary as the exclusion of longer papers that surpass word limits. Why should a paper receive less attention, and bring the author less credit, because it is short? (One might just as well propose to devote more attention and credit to longer books than to shorter books.)

Some articles are *under*-written. The author has a very large and complex argument to make or an extended set of (non-redundant) empirical exercises. We note that studies enlisting qualitative or multimethod evidence are often lengthier than studies based on a single quantitative analysis. However, under the rigid word limits assigned by most journals all that appears in the main text is the outline of a story. Here, word limits constitute a Procrustean bed.

To clarify, our argument is not for longer journal articles. Our argument is for the removal of arbitrary space constraints that have nothing to do with the content of a submission. Length should be adapted to the paper under review. Some topics can be dispensed with in 2,000 words. Others may require 20,000, or even 30,000. As such, length should be a minor feature of the review process, along with other stylistic concerns (not to mention content!). Journals do not mandate that authors present three tables and one figure. This would be patently absurd. We should not mandate that they present 10,000 words.

Thus, we are not making an argument for endless babble. Some authors need to be restrained from diarrhea of the keyboard. Other authors are terse to the point of obscurantism, and need to be drawn out ("please give a few examples of what you are talking about"). But one argument about length that does not seem admissible, if we are concerned with such things as truth and its dissemination, is that an article fit within an arbitrary (short) word limit. Journals ought not reduce academic research to a formulaic wordcount because articles are not all alike.

We are reminded of the first question we always get from students after distributing a writing assignment. "How many pages?" they ask. Most students are concerned with the minimal number of pages they will need to generate in order to pass the assignment. A few are concerned with the maximum. To both concerns we always reply with a set of bounds intended to be advisory – e.g., "10–20 pages" – followed by the admonition not to get caught up in the number of pages but rather to focus on the quality of the work they are producing. The number of pages or words is the *least* important aspect of your paper, we tell them. Unfortunately, we do not follow this advice in academic publishing.

In the remaining sections of this chapter we elaborate on why the imposition of arbitrary word limits is damaging, and why eliminating this restriction makes sense.

Time and Trouble

By all reports, researchers expend a good deal of effort trying to work within the arbitrary word limits imposed by various journals. This might involve revising successive drafts until the final version slips just under the ceiling, moving sections of a paper into online appendices, splitting up a subject into "minimal publishing units," shopping around for a publication venue with less stringent limits, or trying to negotiate special terms with an editor. A particularly vexing problem is that because different journals in a field or subfield impose different limits – or take them more/less seriously – a paper may have to be tailored to a particular journal. As such, a rejection by one journal may involve a substantial re-write in order to meet another journal's more stringent (or more relaxed) word limit.

In economics, where manuscript length is generally determined by pages rather than words, Card and Della Vigna (2014) find evidence that authors fiddle with fonts, spacing, margins, and material relegated to online appendices in order to beat the thresholds imposed by various journals. As a result of all this fiddling, the introduction of manuscript length limits at the

American Economic Review "led to an immediate drop in the number of longer submissions and the emergence of a spike in the distribution of page lengths centered around the 40-page limit" (Card and Della Vigna 2014:150–151).

Evidently, economists are playing the same game that our students play. Of course, neither should be blamed for following incentives. The problem is with the incentives. Card and Della Vigna (2014:166) conclude: "Arguably, a policy that forces hundreds of authors each year to spend time shortening papers without any obvious benefits should be reconsidered." This conclusion is especially noteworthy in light of the fact – laid out below – that economics journals impose much less stringent limits on manuscript length than other social science disciplines, suggesting that the time and trouble spent "fiddling" with fonts and phrases is even worse in political science and sociology.

Heterogeneity across Venues

A few political science journals that did not make it onto our list look favorably upon longer submissions. This includes *International Security* (20,000 words), *Studies in American Political Development* (no official limit), and the *Quarterly Journal of Political Science* (no official limit). There may be others of which we are not aware. By the same token, some journals have even tighter space restrictions than those listed in Table 5.1. For example, the newly founded *Journal of Experimental Political Science* requests papers of "approximately 2,500 words."

Evidently, there is some degree of heterogeneity across journals, and even more so in sociology, as noted in Table 5.2. This heterogeneity may increase over time if divergence rather than convergence is the overall trend within the discipline. Authors can thus shop around for an appropriate forum for their paper, as, to some extent, they do now. Supply and demand would then intersect. This seems like it might offer a happy resolution of our problem, with flexibility provided across journals (rather than across articles within the same journal).

This model of diversity fits the consumer-driven model of the commercial publishing business. Readers looking for a discursive treatment of a contemporary subject can turn to the *New York Review of Books* (*NYRB*) or the *New Yorker*. Readers looking for the quick-and-dirty might turn to a newspaper, a blog, or a publication known for terseness such as the *Economist*. Fiction readers may look for long books, short books, or short stories. They are free to choose. By all accounts, length is an important consideration in consumer choice in the commercial marketplace.

Likewise, in the world of social science the choice to read a journal article rather than a book is, to some extent, a choice about length. So, one might argue that journal heterogeneity in length requirements is merely a continuation of a spectrum that stretches from academic monographs, to short books (such as the recently inaugurated series *Cambridge Elements*), to blog entries, or even Tweets.

Unfortunately, specialization by length is inappropriate for academic journals. The reason, in brief, is that journals do not have overlapping purviews and functions. Because mass-market publications like *NYRB*, *New Yorker*, the *Economist*, and book publishers cater to the same sort of readers and cover (pretty much) the same ground, readers may choose the format they wish – short, medium, or long. This does not obviate the tradeoff – conciseness versus depth – but it means that readers can make informed choices based on their priorities.

However, journals do not offer multiple options. Indeed, they are in the business of avoiding redundancy. Unoriginal content is strictly excluded from consideration. Moreover, journals tend to specialize in a particular field or subfield. There is no space in the academic journal market for two journals focused on the same topic – one of which publishes long articles and the other of which publishes short articles.

Only general-interest journals have overlapping purviews. Here, one might envision a division of labor in which some specialize in long articles and others in short articles. This would be productive in all respects except one: differentiation by space allotment would interfere with an important function of top journals – differentiation by quality. Insofar as scholars wish to maintain a clear ranking of journals (and, all protests to the contrary, it seems that they do) space-constraints should not obstruct that goal. It seems silly to have one journal in a discipline devoted to the "best short papers," another to "best long papers," and a perhaps a third to "best medium-length papers."

Thus, heterogeneity in length limits across journals does not solve the problem. Publication decisions should hinge on topicality and quality, not quantity.

Online Supplementary Material

In recent years, the practice of posting supplementary material online has become more common, and readers may wonder if this solves the problem we are posing. Unfortunately, while online appendices are surely an improvement over the pre-Internet era, they are not ideal.

Appendices often contain information that is vital to the review process. Sometimes, they appear at the insistence of reviewers or editors. This suggests that anyone seeking to make sense of an argument (once published) would also need to access the appendix – and that it should therefore remain in stable form, post-publication. Yet, if an appendix is posted in a separate location, those who read or cite an article are likely to feel under no compunction to read it. Such material is not part of the formal record, occupying a nebulous zone. A citation to "Sullivan (1998)" does not imply "and online appendices." Separating the location of articles and appendices means that most readers will look only at the published text, ignoring any material that appears elsewhere.

Adding to the difficulty, online material is often hard to locate. Gertler and Bullock (2017) find that more than one-fourth of the links published in the *American Political Science Review* (the leading journal of political science) in 2013 were broken by the end of 2014. The phenomenon known as "reference rot" is also common in law journals (Zittrain, Albert, and Lessig 2014), communication journals (Dimitrova and Bugeja 2007), public health journals (Wagner et al. 2009), and is in fact ubiquitous (Lepore 2015). Studies focused on various fields in the natural sciences conclude that online supplementary material is a poorly curated graveyard for data, and consequently rarely visited (Evangelou, Trikalinos, and Ioannidis 2005; Moore and Beckerman 2016; Williams 2016).

Because of their low profile and general inaccessibility, online appendices may serve as a place to stow away evidence that does not fit neatly with the author's main argument. Note also that if the online appendix is under the author's control it is susceptible to post-publication manipulation.

For all these reasons it seems essential that appendices be published and stored along with the main text of an article, and under the supervision of the journal. Moreover, decisions about what material to place within the main text and what to place in appendices should be driven by matters other than arbitrary space constraints. There is nothing sillier than moving text from one place to another simply to get under a 10,000-word limit. This sort of shenanigan damages the stylistic coherence of an article, not to mention the time it imposes on the author. Note also that when an appendix appears online the distinction between main text and appendix is highly consequential – something that editors need to scrutinize closely. By contrast, if an appendix is easily accessible and part of the published version of an article, this decision is not so fundamental.

The same general point applies to other decisions that are often made under pressure from arbitrary word limits, e.g., whether to cite additional work, to address counterarguments, to provide examples, or to provide clarification of a theory or method. Authors face many decisions about content and composition, and each deserves careful consideration. Writing social science is not a paint-by-numbers exercise. In searching for the right resolution of these questions one consideration that does not seem relevant is an arbitrary word limit. And one must not lose sight of the time required to re-shuffle words and ideas until the proper quantity is obtained. Researchers' time is valuable and should not be wasted in a trivial quest for magic word counts.

References

A few journals (e.g., the *Annual Review of Political Science* and *Public Opinion Quarterly*) do not include references in their wordcount. But most do (see Table 5.1). Because references are of little concern to most authors and reviewers (unless it is their work that is being cited, naturally), and because references consume a lot of words (for each citation there is usually a two-line reference), this is usually the first lamb to be sacrificed when an author has to shorten a piece to satisfy a length limit. For this reason, it is worth pondering the value of references.

The first and perhaps most important function of citations is to frame a study within the literature on a topic. Anyone attempting to come to grips with a new area of study must be able to follow a trail of citations in order to piece together who has done what on a given subject. The intellectual history of that subject is located in the citations.

Recent work by Patrick Dunleavy (2014; see also Bastow, Dunleavy, and Tinkler 2014) suggests that citations to the literature on a subject are also essential for providing a basis for evaluation, showing how the present study fits in with an existing body of work. If that body of work is not fully represented, cumulation is impeded. A study must be understood within a context, and that context is provided by the citations. If past findings on a subject are not cited, or are only partially cited, cumulation is impeded (Gans 1992).

Third, we must consider the problem of academic honesty. We are acutely aware of plagiarism, when someone's ideas (uncited) are stolen. A problem that receives less attention – but, arguably, is much more prevalent – is when prior studies of a subject are not cited, or only briefly and ambiguously cited, leaving readers unaware of how novel the author's theory and findings really are.

Fourth, we might want to consider whether dropped citations are chosen in a biased fashion. Studies suggest that citations are often biased toward prestige journals (Callaham, Wears, and Weber 2002; Nosek and Bar-Anan

2012:219) and toward authors who are well established, senior, male (Larivière et al. 2013; Maliniak, Powers, and Walter 2013), or at top universities and departments located in the United States and Europe (Basu 2006). Common sense suggests that these biases may be exacerbated in situations where space is in short supply.[4] Here, authors are likely to favor the most prominent writer or work on a subject – the "obligatory" reference.

Fifth, we should consider the role of citations in measuring impact (see Chapter 15). Nowadays, citation counts are critical for the evaluation of scholarship at all levels. An article's impact is understood by the number of citations it receives. Journal impact is measured by the number of citations all the articles published in that journal receive. Author impact is measured by the number of citations all their publications receive. And the impact of fields and disciplines is understood according to how many citations they receive. It follows that when articles are incompletely referenced our ability to properly assess impact – of articles, journals, authors, subfields, or disciplines (at large) – is impaired. We may be able to trace the impact of "obligatory" references, but we cannot trace the impact of other work that may have affected the development of thinking on a subject.

Finally, we might consider the impact of references on impact. A number of studies have looked at the relationship between references and citation counts, with the general finding that articles with a longer list of references are more highly cited (Ale Ebrahim, Ebrahimian, Mousavi, and Tahriri 2015; Alimohammadi and Sajjadi 2009; Bornmann, Schier, Haustein et al. 2015; Mingers and Xu 2010; Rao 2011; Robson and Mousquès 2014; Webster et al. 2009). It would seem to be in the author's interest – as well as the journal's interest – to offer a full set of references. And this, in turn, may require additional space.

Right-Sizing the Discipline

The most serious cost imposed by word limits is not the author's time. Nor is it the published articles that are too long or too short, those that make use of online appendices to get around arbitrary word limits, those that omit important citations, or those that are stylistically flawed because the text is playing limbo with the journal's word count. These are fairly trivial costs. The most serious cost arises from the way in which the length limits structure the work of social science.

---

[4] We regard these selection factors as elements of potential bias since none of them – with the possible exception of journal ranking – is directly indicative of the quality and relevance of the cited work.

We assume that in our highly professionalized discipline researchers are sensitive to incentives. Since the main incentive is to publish, and since journals are increasingly the most prestigious outlets for publication (surpassing books, at least for most fields), we must consider what sort of research this regime encourages, or discourages. Substance is inevitably structured by form. And when the form is rigidly fixed, the substance must accommodate.

Smart academics choose topics and research designs that fit the space-constrained format of the journals they wish to publish in. Since most journals impose word limits, and there is not a great deal of variation in these limits – leaving aside a few journals, as noted above – shopping around does not afford much leeway.

Under the circumstances, success in the business of academic publishing involves finding bite-sized topics that can be dispatched in 8,000 to 12,000 words. Qualitative work is at a disadvantage since evidence drawn from archival, ethnographic, or interview-based research normally requires a good deal of verbiage to adequately convey the nuances of the argument and the evidence. Multimethod work is at an even more severe disadvantage since it must practice two trades – two or more separate research designs – in order to fulfill its mission. Work that embraces a large theoretical framework, with many empirical implications, is at a disadvantage. Work that applies a theory to multiple contexts is at a disadvantage. Historical work, which often involves both qualitative and quantitative evidence, is at a disadvantage. Research designs that fall far from the experimental ideal, and therefore involve a great deal of supporting argumentation and robustness tests, are at a disadvantage.[5]

Insofar as scholars are rational they will pause before undertaking such ventures, or will divide them up into separate pieces – "minimal publishing units" – that fit the space-constrained format of journal publication at the cost of some redundancy (since the evidence for a large argument is divided up across multiple publications). But our biggest concern should be about articles that never get written, or, if written (in a fit of vainglory), never get published.

Economics Journals

At this point, it may be appropriate to consider political science and sociology in relation to our social science cousins on the "hard" (naturalist) end

---

[5] We recognize that experimental research may also involve a good deal of supporting argumentation and robustness tests. But we assume that the burden carried by this sort of theoretical and empirical work is even greater when the data are observational, thus requiring more space for elaboration and demonstration.

of the spectrum. To that end, we survey the space limitation policies of 20 top journals in economics, following the procedures described previously for Tables 5.1 and 5.2.

For estimations of scholarly impact we rely on SCImago.[6] Chosen journals include *American Economic Journal (AEJ): Applied Economics, AEJ: Economic Policy, AEJ: Macroeconomics, AEJ: Microeconomics, American Economic Review, Annual Review of Economics, Brookings Papers on Economic Activity, Econometrica, Economic Journal, Journal of Economic Literature, Journal of European Economic Association, Journal of Finance, Journal of Management, Journal of Marketing, Journal of Political Economy, Quarterly Journal of Economics, Review of Economic Studies, Review of Economics and Statistics, Review of Financial Economics,* and *Review of Financial Studies.*

Table 5.3 reveals that economics journals have a considerably more relaxed set of policies with respect to article length than political science and sociology journals. This is signaled by the calculation of length in pages rather than words, for most journals. Six journals have no official limit on article length. Among the remainder, the average limit is just over 15,000 words. Only one, the *Economic Journal*, has a tight limit – in this case 7,500 words. However, we find that the average length of an article in that journal is well over 12,000 words and one article published in 2015 included over 21,000 words. So this does not constitute much of an exception from the economics norm of overall permissiveness with respect to article length.

As with political science and sociology journals, practices often depart from policies. The actual maximum length is 7,000+ over the stated limit. This means that in economics, as in other fields, limits are not strictly applied. And this, in turn, suggests a problem of transparency. But the more important point is that the journal page limits are generous, and loosely applied. Content, rather than arbitrary length limits, determines the length of articles written for economics journals.

The Impact of Length

Thus far, the gist of our argument is that by removing an arbitrary component of the publication process – article length – we will improve efficiency (spending less time worrying about limits and strategizing about how to get around them) and also arrive at higher-quality articles. Can the latter proposition be tested?

---

[6] See www.scimagojr.com/journalrank.php?area=2000.

Table 5.3 Economics journals

Journal	Limit	Policies: Including References	Policies: Including Appendices	Policies: At Submission	Policies: Editors' Discretion	Practices: Mean	Practices: Minimum	Practices: Maximum	Consistency: Actual Maximum	Consistency: Column 10− Column 2
1	2	3	4	5	6	7	8	9	10	11
AEJ: Applied Economics	15,750 (50)	Yes	No	Yes	Yes	12,989	5,581	20,125	17,293	1,543
AEJ: Economic Policy	15,750 (50)	Yes	No	Yes	Yes	14,923	8,978	25,318	20,026	4,276
AEJ: Macroeconomics	15,750 (50)	Yes	No	Yes	Yes	16,267	8,877	28,263	27,000	11,250
AEJ: Microeconomics	15,750 (50)	Yes	No	Yes	Yes	16,595	5,218	26,791	22,499	6,749
American Economic Review	15,750 (50)	Yes	No	Yes	Yes	17,183	8,305	24,099	23,545	7,795
Annual Review of Economics	[none]					13,836	7,897	19,560		
Brookings Papers on Economic Activity**	[none]					18,084	15,723	21,846		
Econometrica	17,000	Yes	No	Yes	Yes	15,998	6,589	25,139	21,042	4,042
Economic Journal	7,500	Yes	Yes	Yes	No	12,697	4,157	21,894	21,894	14,394
Journal of Economic Literature	25,000 (100)†	Yes	Yes	No	Yes	15,492	4,625	35,347	35,347	10,347
Journal of European Economic Association	[none]					13,690	4,633	28,919		
Journal of Finance	22,000 (60*)	Yes	No	Yes	Yes	14,834	7,253	23,650	23,650	1,650
Journal of Management	15,750 (50)	Yes	No	Yes	Yes	13,178	8,670	19,661	19,661	3,911
Journal of Marketing	15,750 (50)	Yes	No	Yes	No	14,247	6,490	18,718	18,718	2,968
Journal of Political Economy**	12,000 (40)	Yes	Yes	No	Yes	17,872	8,649	28,892	28,892	16,892
Quarterly Journal of Economics	15,750 (50)†	Yes	Yes	No	Yes	15,587	11,403	23,893	23,893	8,143

Journal	Limit	At submission	Editors' discretion	Minimum	Mean	Maximum	Actual maximum
Review of Economic Studies	[none]			17,104	8,661	23,514	
Review of Economics and Statistics	12,500 (45)†	Yes	No	13,053	6,753	21,609	20,114	7,614
Review of Financial Economics	[none]			13,972	7,324	19,787	
Review of Financial Studies	[none]			14,936	9,218	24,878	
Mean or Distribution (Yes/No)	15,386	14/0	4/10	10/4	12/2	15,127	7,750	24,095	23,112	7,255

Note: **Journal** = top 20 economics journals by impact (www.scimagojr.com/journalrank.php?area=2000). **Limit** = ceiling on number of words (pages) allowed in research articles, as specified on journal web page. Where the limit is specified in pages, we list the projected word count based on the specified page limit (in parentheses) with double-spaced lines or 1.5-spaced lines (*) and standard 12-point font. † = there is no official limit but the editors have communicated (to us) the unofficial limit. **At submission** = limits apply at submission. **Editors' discretion** = longer versions may be accepted with editors' approval. For further clarification of journal policies see Appendix C. **Practices** = mean, minimum, maximum word counts across all research articles and including all published material (footnotes, references, appendices, et al.). **Actual maximum** = maximum word count, including or excluding references and appendices as specified by the journal's policies. All journals observed in the calendar year 2015 except those marked with a double asterisk (**), which are observed in 2014.

In one sort of hypothetical experiment, article length would be arbitrarily assigned. Conceivably, one might enlist a journal that takes a relaxed attitude toward word limits. Submissions that surpass a given threshold (e.g., 15,000 words) and pass the review process (in that form) would then be randomized into a control group (no change) and a treatment group (subjected to a word limit of 10,000 words). Compliance (not to mention ethics) would be difficult. Authors would need to comply with the imposed limits and reviewers would also need to be brought on board. Results could then be compared by standard metrics of influence such as citations – though some confounding might result as the nature of the experiment became known throughout a discipline and authors posted "full" versions on their web sites.

Natural experiments can also be imagined. For example, one might regard length limits as an instrument for actual length (columns 1 and 7 are indeed highly correlated). Citation counts for articles could then be regressed against the instrumented values for article length. However, this research design cannot disentangle journal fixed effects (some journals are more cited than others, even among the top 20 journals in Table 5.1).

Even so, we may learn something from the simple expedient of comparing articles published in the same journal that are shorter and longer. Because we are interested in *relative* length within the same journal, it is sufficient to rely on page counts rather than word counts. The loss of precision entailed by this aggregation – from words to pages – need not concern us here since we are not striving for a precise point estimate. In any case, page counts take into account the space consumed by tables, which are not properly estimated by word counts (and perhaps should be).

As a measure of scholarly impact we rely on citation counts tallied by Web of Science, transformed by the natural logarithm (to accommodate a right-skewed distribution). To eliminate variations based on year of publication we focus on a single year located in the past (so that the article has time to be digested by the academic community) but not the distant past (since we wish to generalize about contemporary policies and contemporary academic work). Balancing these goals, we decided to focus on articles published in 2005.

Citations may be influenced by the journal so we can only reliably compare articles published by the same journal. Fortunately, a good deal of variation can be found in most economics journals, and in one political science journal, as revealed by the range (minimum/maximum) of actual word counts in Tables 5.1–5.3. Our analysis therefore focuses on those economics and political science journals with the greatest range (in 2015), provided they were published in 2005 (thus excluding journals founded after that date). This includes *British Journal of Political Science, American Economic Review, Brookings Papers on Economic Activity, Econometrica, Economic Journal, Journal of Economic Literature, Journal of European Economic Association, Journal of Finance, Journal of Management, Journal of Marketing, Journal of Political Economy, Quarterly Journal of Economics, Review of Economic Studies, Review of Economics and Statistics, Review of Financial Economics,* and *Review of Financial Studies.*

Note that our selection criterion allows us to focus on journals that do not make a fetish of length, and thus follow policies that are closer to those that we advocate. The regression analysis takes the following form: $Y = X + Z + \varepsilon$, where Y is citation count, X is article length, Z is a vector of journal fixed effects, and ε is the error term. Estimation is by ordinary least squares with standard errors clustered by journal.

The resulting model, presented in Table 5.4, suggests that there is a robust relationship between length and citations. Indeed, the relationship appears to exist in every journal in our sample. (When regression analysis is conducted upon the sample provided by each journal, separately, we invariably find a positive – though not always statistically significant – relationship between length and impact.)

A plot of marginal effects is displayed in Figure 5.1. We preserve the logged scale of citation count on the Y axis; however, tick marks on the Y axis correspond to raw (unlogged) values in order to render the exercise more understandable.

It is tempting to focus on the – apparently huge – impact of article length on citations as one approaches the right end of the X axis. However, this is not where most of our data fall, as suggested by the wide confidence bounds in Figure 5.1. The mean number of pages in our sample is about 25, with a standard deviation of about 12, so generalizations near the center of the distribution are apt to be most meaningful.

Consider an increase in article length from 25 to 35 (a little less than one standard deviation), which translates into an increase of about 6,000 words.[7] This hypothetical change is associated with a substantial increase in citations, from (roughly) 35 to 55.

The meaning of this estimate may be debated. Let us assume for a moment that a rational selection bias is at work, namely more important articles are

---

[7] We derive this wordcount estimate by drawing one normal-sized (full-text) page from each journal in our 2005 sample, counting the words on those pages, and calculating the mean across those 16 journals.

Table 5.4 Impact, marginal effects

	1
Length (pages)	0.028***
	(.005)
Journal fixed effects	✓
Journals (N)	16
Observations (N)	675
R^2	0.3050

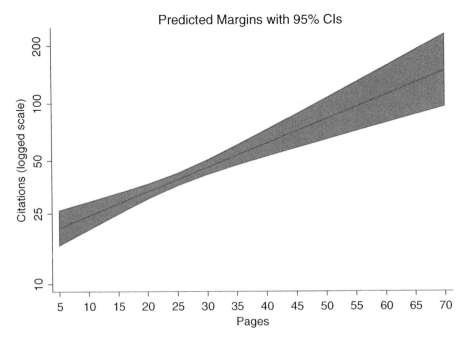

Figure 5.1 Impact, marginal effects

Marginal effect of length (pages) on impact (citations, logged), based on benchmark model in Table 5.4, with 95-percent confidence intervals

granted greater space in a journal's pages. Articles deemed less significant are granted less space, as a product of the considered judgments of authors, reviewers, and editors. In this circumstance, it should be no surprise that longer articles garner more attention, as measured by citation counts.

Of course, we cannot rule out the possibility that researchers are influenced by length in their estimation of an article's importance. Length may be regarded (implicitly) as a proxy for significance, and hence may influence citation counts. If so, these norms would reinforce our basic point that, in the considered opinion of the scholarly community, length is correlated with importance.

Citations may also be driven by the number of authors on a paper (Borsuk et al. 2009; Didegah and Thelwall 2013; Gazni and Didegah 2011; Haustein et al. 2015; Larivière et al. 2014; Leimu and Koricheva 2005a, b; Robson and Mousquès 2014; Schwarz and Kennicutt 2004; Webster, Jonason, and Schember 2009) or the number of references in a paper (as noted above). Insofar as the number of authors or references is correlated with the length of a paper – longer papers presumably having more coauthors (Fox et al. 2016) and a longer list of references (Abt and Garfield 2002) – omitting these factors from our model may confound the relationship of theoretical interest. Or not. Note that the importance of a paper may affect the number of authors (since the subject is attractive to potential authors and requires a diverse set of skills) and the number of references (since the subject engages a large field of study). If so, conditioning on these factors would block the front-door path from X to Y, introducing post-treatment confounding.

Helpfully, similar analyses have been conducted with journals in various natural science disciplines (Ball 2008; Falagas et al. 2013; Fox, Paine, and Sauterey 2016; Haustein et al. 2015; Leimu and Koricheva 2005b; Perneger 2004; Robson and Mousquès 2014; Schwarz and Kennicutt 2004; Vanclay 2013; Xiao, Yuan, and Wu 2009). Most show a robust relationship between the length of a paper and its scholarly impact, measured by citations, even when controlling for the potential confounders noted above.

Card and DellaVigna (2014) look not at citations but rather at the review process itself in economics. They find that 20 percent of long papers (those longer than the suggested page limit) submitted to the *American Economic Review* received an initial revise-and-resubmit decision, while only 6.9 percent of the short papers got past the first stage of review, suggesting that longer papers were of higher quality.

Reflecting on this body of work, Fox, Paine, and Sauterey (2016:7718) conclude, "many research projects produce complex data that does not lend itself to concise presentation of a single or simple message. It is thus likely that longer papers contain more ideas and a greater diversity of results, which provides more opportunity for citation, and thus have more diverse and possibly greater impact on the scientific community." We endorse this conclusion, with the usual caveats pertaining to problems of causal identification in observational data.

Note that we have not arbitrarily assigned the length of papers under study. Thus, we cannot say with assurance that if long papers in our sample had been assigned a "short" treatment and short papers had been assigned a "long" treatment, the former would have received fewer citations and the latter more citations. The counterfactuals are unobserved. Arguably, the directionality of the effect is more convincing in the first scenario than the second. Consider the pressures for authors, editors, and reviewers to generate shorter papers. Under the circumstances, it is plausible to regard the published papers in our sample as being biased toward the left end of the spectrum if they are *over* a journal's usual size limit or norm, i.e., "as short as possible without sacrificing something of extreme importance to the argument." For these papers, any further cut in size is likely to involve a substantial sacrifice in meaning, and hence in impact. By contrast, short papers – those that fall *below* a journal's size limit or norm – are probably not biased away from what the author regards as their appropriate length, for the author is unconstrained (s/he may add words without fear of rejection). Under this circumstance, there is no reason to suppose that a longer length would result in greater impact. But there is good reason to suppose that articles that fall at the length limit for a journal where they are published would benefit from a longer length.

Our expectation, in any case, is that if a journal – or, better, an entire discipline – that currently imposes low (e.g., 10,000 or 12,000) wordcount limits drops those limits in favor of a concision criterion that is applied in a flexible manner to account for the varying demands of the subject matter, we would find a relationship very much like that reported for those journals that currently follow that policy, as reported in the analysis in Table 5.4. In a well-designed publication system, article length should be correlated with impact because both outcomes are registering the importance, complexity, and novelty of an article's content.

Ordinary least squares regression of article citations (Web of Science), logged, on article length (pages), including journal fixed effects and clustered standard errors. *p < 0.10 ** p < 0.05 ***p < 0.01 Journals: 0 = BJPS, 1 = JEEA, 2 = JEL, 3 = AER, 4 = Brookings, 5 = Econometrica, 6 = Econ J, 7 = Finance, 8 = Management, 9 = Marketing, 10 = Pol Econ, 11 = QJE, 12 = Rw Econ Studies, 13 = Rw Econ and Stats, 14 = Rw Financial Studies, 15 = Rw Financial Econ.

	Obs.	Mean	Std. Dev.	Min.	Max.
Length (pages)	675	25.42	11.71	3.00	71.00
Cites (ln)	675	3.68	1.16	0.00	6.97

Costs

We have argued that length limits should be abolished, or at least considerably relaxed. A consequence of this change in policy is that some articles would increase in length. A few might decrease, as we have suggested, if quality rather than quantity becomes the principal metric of evaluation. But it is safe to assume that increases would be more common than decreases.

Journals might deal with this by decreasing the number of articles that they publish. We would not advise this course of action, which seems about as arbitrary as length limits (unless the journal feels it is justified for other reasons, e.g., a paucity of good submissions). We shall assume, therefore, that the size of the issues published each year by a journal that removes or increases length limits grows, relative to what it was previously. In this section, we consider the potential costs – both time and money – of this growth.

In economics, many journals charge a publication fee, which no doubt helps to support production costs and may account for the greater latitude granted to authors by journals in that discipline. This does not seem like a viable approach for other disciplines, however, as it would place authors from poorer institutions (without research budgets and with low salaries) at a distinct disadvantage. One might institute a form of differential pricing, but we shall not consider that option here. Instead, we want to consider the time/cost issue in more detail.

A longer article imposes a cost on editors and reviewers who must read the manuscript. However, if one considers the lengthy "supplementary material" that now accompanies virtually every submission – usually regarded as essential for the evaluation – there may be no increase in time-demands placed upon readers of the manuscript. All that is changed is that text and tables formerly labeled as supplementary are now integrated into the manuscript – either in the main text or the appendices. Indeed, Card and DellaVigna (2014:162) find that the imposition of page limits at the *American Economic Review* had no impact on the length of time required to complete the review process at that journal.

Another cost is associated with proofreading and typesetting additional pages of prose and tables/figures. We assume that this cost is fairly minimal. (One can envision a scenario in which long appendices are submitted in "copy-ready" form, as is the case now with online material.)

An extra cost is associated with printing and mailing the "hard-copy" version of the journal, assuming the latter increases in length. Note that under the current business model journals are sold to individuals and institutions (primarily university libraries). Some elect to receive a paper copy, which may then be bound prior to shelving (yet another cost, though one that libraries bear).

However, the hard-copy format seems increasingly anachronistic in an age when most journal output is accessed online and when many journals are adopting online-only publication formats. If this is the wave of the future, there may be good reasons to hasten its arrival. Our proposal presumes that this is possible, and desirable.

The day of its arrival would be hastened if top journals would lead the way. Currently, online-only publications are a signal of a journal's peripheral status in social science, as it offers a cheap solution to the otherwise expensive business proposition of forming a new journal. If leading journals were to adopt the format it would no longer carry a stigma and mid- and lower-tier journals that are currently bearing the cost of paper publishing would surely follow suit. This would bring a positive externality to the entire academic publishing business, relieving journals – and the university and individual subscribers who underwrite their costs – of a substantial logistical burden.

Several additional ramifications of relaxing manuscript length limitations may be attractive to publishers. We have already shown that longer articles are likely to more widely cited. Since journal rankings depend upon citation counts (Chapter 15), this should be a spur to editors and publishers to take seriously our call for reform.

Likewise, Card and DellaVigna (2014) find that when a mid-ranked economics journal, the *Journal of the European Economic Association*, imposed a short page-limit policy, submissions plunged, with authors diverting their papers to alternate journals.[8] This led the journal's editors to reverse their policy after several months. We surmise that the same consideration affects journals in other fields, where – all things equal – authors will prefer journals that allow greater leeway. This, too, should encourage editors and publishers to consider reforming current policies.

Conclusions

The expansive policies adopted by many top economics journals dovetail with a move within the field to prize quality over quantity. Economists lay their

---

[8] The same plunge in submissions was not observed at the top-ranked *American Economic Review*. Here, the prestige of the journal – and the lack of similarly ranked journals – seems to have outweighed authors' considerations of where to submit.

claim to fame on a small number of high-impact publications rather than a larger number of less-cited ones. H-index scores matter more than the length of a CV. This may have something to do with the not-so-secret desire of every economist: to obtain a Nobel prize.

While no such holy grail exists for political science and sociology, it may still be possible to adjust incentives so that the time-consuming search for fundamental discoveries and/or comprehensive analyses of a large topic is facilitated. One small but important step in this direction involves loosening the noose around authors' necks so they can focus on the task at hand, rather than the space they must fill.

Part III

Transparency and Reproducibility

If science is to progress, studies must be carried out in a transparent fashion and they must be reproducible. These core goals of science have a long history; indeed, they are truisms. However, they are not easy maxims to satisfy, as recent research on replication has shown.

Some scientists and social scientists – and many outside observers – perceive a crisis of epic proportions, one that threatens the foundation of science. Others see an issue that is somewhat overblown, due to ambiguities about what it means to be fully transparent and reproducible and the skewed incentives of replicators. However, it seems fair to say that virtually all observers perceive a problem and believe that we must raise our game.

This section of the book explores the controversy from a number of angles. Chapter 6 focuses on diagnosis. How should we conceptualize the problem and what are its dimensions? Chapter 7 focuses on potential solutions, surveying an array of options. These chapters are comprehensive in scope, but somewhat thinner on detail.

The next chapters hone in on particular aspects of the problem of transparency and reproducibility, treating them in greater detail. Chapter 8 focuses on data accessibility and the technological infrastructure that enables it. Chapter 9 focuses on pre-registration and results-blind review.

6 Transparency and Reproducibility: Conceptualizing the Problem

Garret Christensen and Edward Miguel*

Openness and transparency have long been considered key pillars of the scientific ethos (Merton 1973b). Yet there is growing awareness that current research practices often deviate from this ideal, and can sometimes produce misleading bodies of evidence (Miguel et al. 2014). As we survey in this chapter, there is growing evidence documenting the prevalence of publication bias in economics and other scientific fields, as well as specification searching, and widespread inability to replicate empirical findings. Though peer review and robustness checks aim to reduce these problems, they appear unable to solve the problem entirely. While some of these issues have been widely discussed for some time (for instance, in economics see Leamer 1983; Dewald, Thursby, and anderson 1986; DeLong and Lang 1992), there has been a notable recent flurry of activity documenting these problems, and also generating new ideas for how to address them.

The goal of this chapter is to survey this emerging literature on research transparency and reproducibility and synthesize the evidence of the problems. Awareness of these issues has come to the fore in economics (Brodeur et al. 2016), political science (Gerber, Green, and Nickerson 2001; Franco, Malhotra, and Simonovits 2014), psychology (Simmons, Nelson, and Simonsohn 2011; Open Science Collaboration 2015), sociology (Gerber and Malhotra 2008a), finance (Harvey, Liu, and Zhu 2015), and other research disciplines as well, including medicine (Ioannidis 2005). In our next chapter (Chapter 7) we discuss productive avenues for future work and potential solutions.

With the vastly greater computing power of recent decades and the ability to run a nearly infinite number of regressions (Sala-i-Martin 1997), there is renewed concern that null-hypothesis statistical testing is subject to both conscious and unconscious manipulation. At the same time, technological

---

* Work similar to Chapters 6 and 7 was previously published by the authors as "Transparency, Reproducibility, and the Credibility of Economics Research" in the *Journal of Economic Literature*, 2018, 56(3), 920–980. Any opinions and conclusions expressed herein are those of the authors and do not necessarily reflect the views of the US Census Bureau.

progress has also facilitated various new tools and potential solutions, including by streamlining the online sharing of data, statistical code, and other research materials, as well as the creation of easily accessible online study registries, data repositories, and tools for synthesizing research results across studies. Data-sharing and replication activities are certainly becoming more common within social science research. Yet, as we discuss below, the progress to date is partial, with some journals and fields in the social sciences adopting new practices to promote transparency and reproducibility and many others not (yet) doing so.

Multiple problems have been identified within the body of published research results in the social sciences. Before describing them, it is useful to frame some key issues with a simple model. We then focus on three problems that have come under greater focus in the recent push for transparency: publication bias, specification searching, and an inability to replicate results.

A Model for Understanding the Issues

A helpful model to frame some of the issues discussed below was developed in the provocatively titled "Why Most Published Research Findings Are False" by Ioannidis (2005), which is among the most highly cited medical research articles from recent years. Ioannidis develops a simple model that demonstrates how greater flexibility in data analysis may lead to an increased rate of false positives and thus incorrect inference.

Specifically, the model estimates the positive predictive value (PPV) of research, or the likelihood that a claimed empirical relationship is actually true, under various assumptions. A high PPV means that most claimed findings in a literature are reliable; a low PPV means the body of evidence is riddled with false positives. The model is similar to that of Wacholder et al. (2004), which estimates the closely related false positive report probability (FPRP).[1]

For simplicity, consider the case in which a relationship or hypothesis can be classified in a binary fashion as either a "true relationship" or "no relationship." Define R_i as the ratio of true relationships to no relationships commonly

---

[1] We should note that there is also a relatively small amount of theoretical economic research modeling the researcher and publication process, including Henry (2009), which predicts that, under certain conditions, more research effort is undertaken when not all research is observable, if such costs can be incurred to demonstrate investigator honesty. See also Henry and Ottaviani (2014) and Libgober (2015).

tested in a research field i (e.g., development economics). Prior to a study being undertaken, the probability that a true relationship exists is thus $R_i/(R_i+1)$. Using the usual notation for statistical power of the test $(1 - \beta)$ and statistical significance level (α), the PPV in research field i is given by:

$$PPV_i = (1-\beta)R_i/((1-\beta)R_i + \alpha) \qquad \text{(eqn. 1)}$$

Clearly, the better powered the study, and the stricter the statistical significance level, the closer the PPV is to 1, in which case false positives are largely eliminated. At the usual significance level of $\alpha = 0.05$ and in the case of a well-powered study $(1 - \beta = 0.80)$ in a literature in which one-third of all hypotheses are thought to be true ex ante ($R_i = 0.5$), the PPV is relatively high at 89 percent, a level that would not seem likely to threaten the validity of research in a particular subfield.

However, reality is considerably messier than this best-case scenario and, as Ioannidis describes, this could lead to much higher rates of false positives in practice due to the presence of underpowered studies, specification searching and researcher bias, and the possibility that only a subset of the analysis in a research literature is published. We discuss these extensions in turn.

We start with the issue of statistical power. Doucouliagos and Stanley (2013), Doucouliagos, Ioannidis, and Stanley (2017), and others have documented that many empirical economics studies are actually quite underpowered. With a more realistic level of statistical power for many studies, say at 0.50, but maintaining the other assumptions above, the PPV falls to 83 percent, which is beginning to potentially look like more of a concern. For power = 0.20, fully 33 percent of statistically significant findings are false positives.

This concern, and those discussed next, are all exacerbated by bias in the publication process. If all estimates in a literature were available to the scientific community, researchers could begin to undo the concerns over a low PPV by combining data across studies, effectively achieving greater statistical power and more reliable inference, for instance, using meta-analysis methods. However, as we discuss below, there is growing evidence of a pervasive bias in favor of significant results, in both economics and other fields. If only significant findings are ever seen by the researcher community, then the PPV is the relevant quantity for assessing how credible an individual result is likely to be.

Ioannidis extends the basic model to account for the possibility of what he calls researcher bias. Denoted by u, researcher bias is defined as the probability that a researcher presents a non-finding as a true finding, for reasons other than chance variation in the data. This researcher bias could take many forms, including any combination of specification searching, data manipulation, selective reporting, and even outright fraud; below, we attempt to quantify the prevalence of these behaviors among researchers. There are many checks in place that attempt to limit this bias, and through the lens of empirical economics research, we might hope that the robustness checks typically demanded of scholars in seminar presentations and during journal review manage to keep the most extreme forms of bias in check. Yet we believe most economists would agree that there remains considerable wiggle room in the presentation of results in practice, in most cases due to behaviors that fall far short of outright fraud.

Extending the above framework to incorporate the researcher bias term (u_i) in field i leads to the following expression:

$$PPV_i = ((1 - \beta)R_i + u_i\beta R_i)/((1 - \beta)R_i + \alpha + u_i\beta R_i + u_i(1-\alpha)) \qquad \text{(eqn. 2)}$$

Here the actual number of true relationships (the numerator) is almost unchanged, though there is an additional term that captures the true effects that are correctly reported as significant only due to author bias. The total number of reported significant effects could be much larger due to both sampling variation and author bias. If we go back to the case of 50-percent power, $R_i = 0.5$, and the usual 5-percent significance level, but now assume that author bias is low at 10 percent, the PPV falls from 83 to 65 percent. If 30 percent of authors are biased in their presentation of results, the PPV drops dramatically to 49 percent, meaning that nearly half of reported significant effects are actually false positives.

In a further extension, Ioannidis examines the case where there are n_i different research teams in a field i generating estimates to test a research hypothesis. Once again, if only the statistically significant findings are published, so there is no ability to pool all estimates, then the likelihood that any published estimate is truly statistically significant can again fall dramatically.

In Table 6.1 (a reproduction of Table 4 from Ioannidis (2005)), we present a range of parameter values and the resulting PPV. Different research fields may have inherently different levels of the R_i term, where presumably literatures that are at an earlier stage and thus more exploratory presumably have lower likelihoods of true relationships.

This simple framework brings a number of the issues we deal with in this article into sharper relief and contains a number of lessons. Ioannidis (2005) himself concludes that the majority of published findings in medicine are likely to be false, and while we are not prepared to make a similar claim for

Table 6.1 Predictive value of research findings

1−β	R	u	Practical Example	PPV
0.80	1:1	0.10	Adequately powered RCT with little bias and 1:1 pre-study odds	0.85
0.95	2:1	0.30	Confirmatory meta-analysis of good-quality RCTs	0.85
0.80	1:3	0.40	Meta-analysis of small inconclusive studies	0.41
0.20	1:5	0.20	Underpowered, but well-performed phase I/II RCT	0.23
0.20	1:5	0.80	Underpowered, poorly performed phase I/II RCT	0.17
0.80	1:10	0.30	Adequately powered exploratory epidemiological study	0.20
0.20	1:10	0.30	Underpowered exploratory epidemiological study	0.12
0.20	1:1,000	0.80	Discovery-oriented exploratory research with massive testing	0.0010
0.20	1:1,000	0.20	As in previous example, but with more limited bias (more standardized)	0.0015

Note: Positive predictive value (PPV) of research findings for various combinations of power (1 − ß), ratio of true to not-true relationships (R), and researcher bias (u). The estimated PPVs are derived assuming α = 0.05 for a single study. RCT: randomized controlled trial.
Source: Reproduced from table 4 of Ioannidis (2005).

empirical economics research – in part because it is difficult to quantify some of the key parameters in the model – we do feel that this exercise does raise important concerns about the reliability of findings in many literatures across the social sciences.

First off, literatures characterized by statistically underpowered (i.e., small 1 − β) studies are likely to have many false positives. A study may be underpowered both because of small sample sizes, and if the underlying effect sizes are relatively small. A possible approach to address this concern is to employ larger datasets or estimators that are more powerful.

Second, the hotter a research field, with more teams (n_i) actively running tests and higher stakes around the findings, the more likely it is that findings are false positives. This is due to both the fact that multiple testing generates more false positives (in absolute numbers) and also because author bias (u_i) may be greater when the stakes are higher. Author bias is also a concern when there are widespread prejudices in a research field, for instance, against publishing findings that contradict core theoretical concepts or assumptions.

Third, the greater the flexibility in research design, definitions, outcome measures, and analytical approaches in a field, the less likely the research findings are to be true, again due to a combination of multiple testing concerns and author bias. One possible approach to address this concern is to mandate greater data sharing so that other scholars can assess the robustness of results to alternative models. Another is through approaches such as pre-analysis plans that effectively force scholars to present a certain core set of analytical specifications, regardless of the results.

With this framework in mind, we next present empirical evidence from economics and other social science fields regarding the extent of some of the problems and biases we have been discussing, and then in Chapter 7 turn to potential ways to address them.

Publication Bias

Publication bias arises if certain types of statistical results are more likely to be published than other results, conditional on the research design and data used. This is usually thought to be most relevant in the case of studies that fail to reject the null hypothesis, which are thought to generate less support for publication among referees and journal editors. If the research community is unable to track the complete body of statistical tests that have been run, including those that fail to reject the null (and thus are less likely to be published), then we cannot determine the true proportion of tests in a literature that reject the null. Thus, it is critically important to understand how many tests have been run. The term "file drawer problem" was coined decades ago (Rosenthal 1979) to describe this problem of results that are missing from a body of research evidence. The issue was a concern even earlier; see, for example, Sterling (1959), which warned of "embarrassing and unanticipated results" from Type-1 errors if not significant results went unpublished.

Important recent research by Franco, Malhotra, and Simonovits (2014) affirms the importance of this issue in practice in contemporary social science research. They document that a large share of empirical analyses in the social sciences are never published or even written up, and the likelihood that a finding is shared with the broader research community falls sharply for "null" findings, i.e., that are not statistically significant (Franco, Malhotra, and Simonovits 2014).

Cleverly, the authors are able to look inside the file drawer through their access to the universe of studies that passed peer review and were included in a nationally representative social science survey, namely, the NSF-funded Time-sharing Experiments in the Social Sciences, or TESS.[2] TESS funded studies across research fields, including in economics, e.g., Walsh, Dolfin, and DiNardo (2009) and Allcott and Taubinsky (2015), as well as political science, sociology and other fields. Franco, Malhotra, and Simonovits successfully tracked nearly all of the original studies over time, keeping track of the nature of the empirical results as well as the ultimate publication of the study, across the dozens of studies that participated in the original project.

They find a striking empirical pattern: studies where the main hypothesis test yielded null results are 40 percentage points less likely to be published in a journal than a strongly statistically significant result, and a full 60 percentage points less likely to be written up in any form. This finding has potentially severe implications for our understanding of findings in whole bodies of social science research, if "zeros" are never seen by other scholars, even in working paper form. It implies that the PPV of research is likely to be lower than it would be otherwise, and also has negative implications for the validity of meta-analyses, if null results are not known to the scholars attempting to draw broader conclusions about a body of evidence.

Consistent with these findings, other recent analyses have documented how widespread publication bias appears to be in economics research. Brodeur et al. (2016) collected a large sample of test statistics from papers in three top journals that publish largely empirical results (the *American Economic Review*, *Quarterly Journal of Economics*, and *Journal of Political Economy*) from 2005 to 2011. They propose a method to differentiate between the journal's selection of papers with statistically stronger results and inflation of significance levels by the authors themselves. They begin by pointing out that a distribution of Z-statistics under the null hypothesis would have a monotonically decreasing probability density. Next, if journals prefer results with stronger significance levels, this selection could explain an increasing density, at least on part of the distribution. However, Brodeur et al. hypothesize that observing a local minimum density before a local maximum is unlikely if only this selection process by journals is present. They argue that a local minimum is consistent with the additional presence of inflation of significance levels by the authors.

---

[2] See http://tessexperiments.org.

Brodeur et al. (2016) document a rather disturbing two-humped density function of test statistics, with a relative dearth of reported *p*-values just above the standard 0.05 level (i.e., below a *t*-statistic of 1.96) cutoff for statistical significance, and greater density just below 0.05 (i.e., above 1.96 for *t*-statistics). This is a strong indication that some combination of author bias and publication bias is fairly common. Using a variety of possible underlying distributions of test statistics, and estimating how selection would affect these distributions, they estimate the residual ("the valley and the echoing bump") and conclude that between 10 and 20 percent of marginally significant empirical results in these journals are likely to be unreliable. They also document that the proportion of misreporting appears to be lower in articles without "eye-catchers" (such as asterisks in tables that denote statistical significance), as well as in papers written by more senior authors, including those with tenured authors.

A similar pattern strongly suggestive of publication bias also appears in other social science fields including political science, sociology, psychology, as well as in clinical medical research. Gerber and Malhotra (2008a) have used the caliper test, which compares the frequency of test statistics just above and below the key statistical significance cutoff, which is similar in spirit to a regression discontinuity design. Specifically, they compare the number of Z-scores lying in the interval $(1.96-X\%, 1.96]$ to the number in $(1.96, 1.96+X\%]$, where X is the size of the caliper, and they examine these differences at 5-, 10-, 15-, and 20-percent critical values.[3]

These caliper tests are used to examine reported empirical results in leading sociology journals (the *American Sociological Review*, *American Journal of Sociology*, and *The Sociological Quarterly*) and reject the hypothesis of no publication bias at the 1-in-10-million level (Gerber and Malhotra 2008b). Data from two leading political science journals (the *American Political Science Review* and *American Journal of Political Science*) reject the hypothesis of no publication bias at the 1-in-32-billion level (Gerber and Malhotra 2008a).

Psychologists have recently developed a related tool called the "p-curve," describing the density of reported p-values in a literature, which again takes advantage of the fact that if the null hypothesis were true (i.e., no effect), p-values should be uniformly distributed between 0 and 1 (Simonsohn,

---

[3] Note that when constructing Z-scores from regression coefficients and standard errors, rounding may lead to an artificially large number of round or even integer Z-scores. Brodeur et al. (2016) reconstruct original estimates by randomly redrawing numbers from a uniform interval, i.e., a standard error of 0.02 could actually be anything in the interval [0.015, 0.025].

Nelson, and Simmons 2014a). Intuitively, under the null of no effect, a p-value < 0.08 should occur 8 percent of the time, a *p*-value < 0.07 occurs 7 percent of the time, etc., meaning a *p*-value between 0.07 and 0.08, or between any other 0.01-wide interval, should occur 1 percent of the time. In the case of true non-zero effects, the distribution of *p*-values should be right-skewed (with a decreasing density), with more low values (0.01) than higher values (0.04) (Hung et al. 1997).[4] In contrast, in bodies of empirical literature suffering from publication bias, or "p-hacking" in their terminology, in which researchers evaluate significance as they collect data and only report results with statistically significant effects, the distribution of *p*-values would be left-skewed (assuming that researchers stop searching across specifications or collecting data once the desired level of significance is achieved).

To test whether a p-curve is right- or left-skewed, one can construct what the authors call a "*pp*-value," or *p*-value of the *p*-value – the probability of observing a significant *p*-value at least as extreme if the null were true – and then aggregate the *pp*-values in a literature with Fisher's method and test for skew with a χ^2 test. The authors also suggest a test of comparing whether a p-curve is flatter than the curve that would result if studies were (somewhat arbitrarily) powered at 33 percent, and interpret a p-curve that is significantly flatter or left-skewed than this as lacking in evidentiary value. The p-curve can also potentially be used to correct effect size estimates in literatures suffering from publication bias; corrected estimates of the "choice overload" literature exhibit a change in direction from standard published estimates (Simonsohn, Nelson, and Simmons 2014b).[5]

Thanks to the existence of study registries and ethical review boards in clinical medical research, it is increasingly possible to survey nearly the universe of studies that have been undertaken, along the lines of Franco, Malhotra, and Simonovits (2014). Easterbrook et al. (1991) reviewed the universe of protocols submitted to the Central Oxford Research Ethics Committee, and both Turner et al. (2008) and Kirsch et al. (2008) employ the universe of tests of certain anti-depressant drugs submitted to the FDA, and all found significantly higher publication rates when tests yield statistically significant results. Turner et al. found that 37 of 38 (97 percent) of trials with positive, i.e., statistically significant, results were published, while only 8 of 24 (33 percent)

---

[4] Unlike economics journals, which often use asterisks or other notation to separately indicate *p*-values (0,.01),[0.01, .05), and [.05,.1), psychology journals often indicate only whether a *p*-value is < 0.05, and this is the standard used throughout (Simonsohn, Nelson, and Simmons 2014a).

[5] For an online implementation of the p-curve, see http://p-curve.com. Also see a discussion of the robustness of the test in Ulrich and Miller (2015) and Simonsohn, Simmons, and Nelson (2015a).

with null (or negative) results were published; for a meta-meta-analysis of the latter two studies, see Ioannidis (2008).

A simple model of publication bias described in McCrary, Christensen, and Fanelli (2016) suggests that, under some relatively strong assumptions regarding the rate of non-publication of statistically non-significant results, readers of research studies could potentially adjust their significance threshold to "undo" the distortion by using a more stringent t-test statistic higher than 3 (rather than 1.96) to infer statistical significance at 95-percent confidence. They note that approximately 30 percent of published test statistics in the social sciences fall between these two cutoffs. It is also possible that this method would break down and result in a "t-ratio arms race" if all researchers were to use it, so it is mostly intended for illustrative purposes.

As an aside, it is also possible that publication bias could work *against* rejection of the null hypothesis in some cases. For instance, within economics in cases where there is a strong theoretical presumption among some scholars that the null hypothesis of no effect is likely to hold (e.g., in certain tests of market efficiency) the publication process could be biased by a preference among editors and referees for non-rejection of the null hypothesis of no effect. This complicates efforts to neatly characterize the nature of publication bias, and may limit the application of the method in McCrary, Christensen, and Fanelli (2016).

Taken together, a growing body of evidence indicates that publication bias is widespread in economics and many other scientific fields. Stepping back, these patterns do not appear to occur by chance, but are likely to indicate some combination of selective editor (and referee) decision-making, the file drawer problem alluded to above, and/or widespread specification searching (discussed in more detail below), which is closely related to what the Ioannidis (2005) model calls author bias.

Publication Bias in Several Empirical Economics Literatures

Scholars in economics have argued that there is considerable publication bias in several specific literatures including labor economics research on minimum-wage impacts and on the value of a statistical life. We discuss both briefly here, as well as several other bodies of evidence in economics.

Card and Krueger (1995) conducted a meta-analysis of the minimum-wage and unemployment literature, and test for the "inverse-square-root" relationship between sample size and t-ratio that one would expect if there was a true effect and no publication bias, since larger samples should generally produce more precise estimates (for a given research design).[6] They find that t-statistics from the 15 studies using quarterly data available at the time of writing are actually *negatively* correlated with sample sizes. A possible explanation is that a structural change in the effect of the minimum wage (a decline over time) has taken place, but the authors consider publication bias and specification searching a more likely explanation. Neumark and Wascher (1998) construct an alternative test for publication bias, which produces an attenuation of the effect size with larger sample sizes (as sample sizes increased over time) that is qualitatively similar to that in Card and Krueger (1995), but Neumark and Wascher thus place more emphasis on the structural change explanation (i.e., actual effects declined over time) and discount the possibility of publication bias. Another explanation has been proposed for Card and Krueger's findings: the simple lack of a true effect of the minimum wage on unemployment. If the null hypothesis of no effect is true, the t-statistic would have no relationship with the sample size. Studies that advance this alternative explanation (Stanley 2005; Doucouliagos and Stanley 2009) argue that the minimum-wage literature does likely suffer from some publication bias, since many studies' t-statistics hover around 2, near the standard 95-percent confidence level, and other tests, described in Chapter 7, indicate as much.

Several studies have also documented the presence of publication bias in the literature estimating the value of a statistical life (VSL). As government regulations in health, environment, and transportation are frequently based on this value, accurate estimation is of great public importance, but there is growing consensus that there is substantial publication bias in this literature, leading to a strong upward bias in reported estimates (Ashenfelter and Greenstone 2004). Using the collection of 37 studies in Bellavance, Dionne, and Lebeau (2009), Doucouliagos, Stanley, and Giles (2012) find that correcting for publication bias reduces the estimates of VSL by 70–80 percent from that produced by a standard meta-analysis regression. Similar analysis shows that, correcting for publication bias, the VSL also appears largely inelastic to individual income

---

[6] Card and Krueger explain: "A doubling of the sample size should lower the standard error of the estimated employment effect and raise the absolute t ratio by about 40 percent if the additional data are independent and the statistical model is stable. More generally, the absolute value of the t ratio should vary proportionally with the square root of the number of degrees of freedom, and a regression of the log of the t ratio on the log of the square root of the degrees of freedom should yield a coefficient of 1." In a similar test in political science, Gerber, Green, and Nickerson (2001) document likely publication bias in the voter mobilization campaign literature, showing that studies with larger sample sizes tend to produce smaller effect size estimates.

(Doucouliagos, Stanley, and Viscusi 2014). An updated analysis of publication bias in the VSL literature (Viscusi 2015) shows that although publication bias is large and leads to meaningfully inflated estimates, he argues much of it may stem from early studies in the literature that used voluntary reporting of occupational fatalities, while more recent studies estimates employing the Census of Fatal Occupational Injuries (CFOI) suffer from less measurement error and tend to produce larger estimates.

Evidence for publication bias has been documented in many other economics research literatures, although not in all. See Longhi, Nijkamp, and Poot (2005) and Knell and Stix (2005) for notable examples. Table 6.2 describes a number of related publication bias studies that might be of interest to readers, but for reasons of space they are not discussed in detail here. In the most systematic approach to date (to our knowledge), Doucouliagos and Stanley (2013) carry out a meta-meta-analysis of 87 meta-analysis papers (many of which are reported in Table 6.2), and find that over half of the literatures suffer from "substantial" or "severe" publication bias, with particularly large degrees of bias in empirical macroeconomics and in empirical research based on demand theory, and somewhat less publication bias in subfields with multiple contested economic theories.

The *Journal of Economic Surveys* has published many meta-regression papers, including a special issue devoted to meta-regression and publication bias (Roberts 2005). The statistical techniques for assessing publication bias are summarized in Stanley (2005), and many of these are applied in the articles listed in Table 6.2. One common data visualization approach is the use of funnel graphs; see Stanley and Doucouliagos (2010), Light and Pillemer (1984), and our discussion in Chapter 7.

Publication Bias and Effect Size

Another important issue related to publication bias and null hypothesis testing is the reporting of the magnitude of effect sizes. Although it appears that economics may fare somewhat better than other social science disciplines in this regard, since economics studies typically report regression coefficients and standard errors while articles in some other disciplines (e.g., psychology) have historically only reported p-values, there is some evidence that underreporting of effect magnitudes is still a concern. In a review in the *Journal of Economic Literature*, McCloskey and Ziliak (1996) find that 70 percent of full-length *American Economic Review* articles did not distinguish between statistical and practical significance. Follow-up reviews in 2004 and 2008 conclude

Table 6.2 Examples of recent meta-analyses in economics

Paper	Topic	Publication Bias?	Papers (Estimates) Used	Notes
Brodeur et al. (2016)	Wide collection of top publications	+	641 (50,078)	Finds that 10–20 percent of significant results are misplaced, and should not be considered statistically significant.
Vivalt (2015)	Developing-country impact evaluation	+	589 (26,170)	Finds publication bias/specification search is more prevalent in non-experimental work.
Viscusi (2015)	Value of a statistical life (VSL)	+	17 (550)	Use of better and more recent fatality data indicates publication bias exists, but that accepted VSL are correct.
Doucouliagos, Stanley, and Viscusi (2014)	VSL and income elasticity	+	14 (101)	Previous evidence was mixed, but controlling for publication bias shows the income elasticity of VSL is clearly inelastic.
Doucouliagos and Stanley (2013)	Meta-meta-analysis	+	87/3,599 (19,528)	87 meta-analyses with 3,599 original articles and 19,528 estimates show that 60 percent of research areas feature substantial or severe publication bias.
Havranek and Irsova (2012)	Foreign direct investment spillovers	~	57 (3,626)	Find publication bias only in published papers and only in the estimates authors consider most important.
Mookerjee (2006)	Exports and economic growth	+	76 (95)	Relationship between exports and growth remains significant, but is significantly smaller when corrected for publication bias.
Nijkamp and Poot (2005)	Wage curve literature	+	17 (208)	Evidence of publication bias in the wage curve literature (the relationship between wages and local unemployment); adjusting for it gives an elasticity estimate of −0.07 instead of the previous consensus of −0.1.
Abreu, de Groot, and Florax (2005)	Growth rate convergence	−	48 (619)	Adjusting for publication bias in the growth literature on convergence does not change estimates significantly.

(*continued*)

Table 6.2 (cont.)

Paper	Topic	Publication Bias?	Papers (Estimates) Used	Notes
Doucouliagos (2005)	Economic freedom and economic growth	+	52 (148)	Literature is tainted, but relationship persists despite publication bias.
Rose and Stanley (2005)	Trade and currency unions	+	34 (754)	Relationship persists despite publication bias. Currency union increases trade 30–90 percent.
Longhi, Nijkamp, and Poot (2005)	Immigration and wages	-	18 (348)	Publication bias is not found to be a major factor. The negative effect of immigration is quite small (0.1 percent) and varies by country.
Knell and Stix (2005)	Income elasticity of money demand	-	50 (381)	Publication bias does not significantly affect the literature. Income elasticities for narrow money range from 0.4 to 0.5 for the US and 1.0 to 1.3 for other countries.
Doucouliagos and Laroche (2003)	Union productivity effects	+	73 (73)	Publication bias is not considered a major issue. Negative productivity associations are found in the UK, with positive associations in the US.
Gorg and Strobl (2001)	Multi-national corporations and productivity spillovers	+	21 (25)	Study design affects results, with cross-sectional studies reporting higher coefficients than panel data studies. There is also some evidence of publication bias.
Ashenfelter, Harmon, and Oosterbeek (1999)	Returns to education	+	27 (96)	Publication bias is found, and controlling for it significantly reduces the differences between types of estimates of returns to education.

Note: Table shows a sample of recent papers conducting meta-analysis and testing for publication bias in certain literatures in economics. Positive evidence for publication bias is indicated by "+," evidence for no publication bias with "-," and mixed evidence with "~." The number of papers and total estimates used in the meta-analysis are also shown.

that the situation had not meaningfully improved (Ziliak and McCloskey 2004, 2008).

DeLong and Lang (1992) is an early contribution that addresses the issue of publication of null findings and effect sizes. They show that only 78 of 276 null hypotheses tested in empirical papers published in leading economics journals at the time were not rejected. However, using the uniform distribution of p-values under a true-null hypothesis, and the startling lack of published p-values close to 1, they conclude it is likely that practically all economic hypotheses are indeed false. They also conclude that the null results that actually are published in journals may also result from publication bias: a null result is arguably more interesting if it contradicts previous statistically significant results. DeLong and Lang go on to suggest that since almost all economic hypotheses are false, empirical evidence should pay more attention to practical significance and effect size rather than statistical significance alone, as is too often the case.

Specification Searching

While publication bias implies a distortion of a body of multiple research studies, bias is also possible within any given study (for instance, as captured in the author bias term u in Ioannidis (2005)). In the 1980s and 1990s, expanded access to computing power led to rising concerns that some researchers were carrying out growing numbers of analyses and selectively reporting econometric analysis that supported pre-conceived notions – or notions that were seen as particularly interesting within the research community – and ignoring, whether consciously or not, other specifications that did not.

One the most widely cited articles from this period is Leamer's (1983), "Let's Take the Con Out of Econometrics," which discusses the promise of improved research design (namely, randomized trials) and argues that in observational research, researchers ought to transparently report the entire range of estimates that result from alternative analytical decisions. Leamer's illustrative application employs data from a student's research project, namely, US data from 44 states, to test for the existence of a deterrent effect of the death penalty on the murder rate. (These data are also used in McManus (1985).) Leamer classifies variables in the data as either "important" or "doubtful" determinants of the murder rate, and then runs regressions with all possible combinations of the doubtful variables, producing a range of different estimates. Depending on which set of control variables, or covariates, were included (among state median income, unemployment, percent population non-white, percent population 15–24 years old, percent male, percent urban, percent of two-parent households, and several others), the main coefficient of interest – the number of murders estimated to be prevented by each execution – ranges widely on both sides of zero, from 29 lives saved to 12 lives lost. Of the five ways of classifying variables as important or doubtful that Leamer evaluated, three produced a range of estimates that included zero, suggesting that inference was quite fragile in this case.

Leamer's recommendation that observational studies employ greater sensitivity checks, or extreme bounds analysis (EBA), was not limited to testing the effect of including different combinations of covariates, as in Leamer (1983). More detailed descriptions of EBA in Leamer (1978) and Leamer and Leonard (1983) explain that, if provided two "doubtful" control variables z_1 and z_2, and an original regression $y_t = \beta x_t + \gamma_1 z_{1t} + \gamma_2 z_{2t} + u_t$, researchers should define a composite control variable $w_t(\theta) = z_{1t} + \theta z_{2t}$, should allow θ to vary, and then report the range of estimates produced by the regression $y_t = \beta x_t + \eta w_t(\theta) + u_t$. The recommendations that flowed from Leamer's EBA were controversial, at least partly because they exposed widespread weaknesses in the practice of applied economics research at the time, and perhaps partly due to Leamer's often pointed (or humorous, we think) writing style. Few seemed eager to defend the state of applied economics, but many remained unconvinced that sensitivity analysis, as implemented with EBA, was the right solution. In "What Will Take the Con out of Econometrics" (McAleer, Pagan, and Volker 1985), critics of EBA sensibly considered the choice of which variables to deem important and which doubtful just as open to abuse by researchers as the original issue of covariate inclusion.

Echoing some of Leamer's (1983) recommendations, a parallel approach to bolstering applied econometric inference focused on improved research design instead of sensitivity analysis. LaLonde (1986) applied widely used techniques from observational research to data from a randomized trial and showed that none of the methods reproduced the experimentally identified, and thus presumably closer to true, estimate.[7]

Since the 1980s, empirical research practices in economics have changed significantly, especially with regards to improvements in research design.

---

[7] In a similar spirit, researchers have more recently called attention to the lack of robustness in some estimates from random-coefficient demand models, where problems with certain numerical maximization algorithms may produce misleading estimates (Knittel and Metaxoglou 2011, 2013); McCullough and Vinod (2003) contains a more general discussion of robustness and replication failures in nonlinear maximization methods.

Angrist and Pischke (2010) make the point that improved experimental and quasi-experimental research designs have made much econometric inference more credible. However, Leamer (2010) argues that researchers retain a significant degree of flexibility in how they choose to analyze data, and that this leeway could introduce bias into their results.

This flexibility was highlighted in Lovell (1983), which shows that with a few assumptions regarding the variance of the error terms, searching for the best k of c explanatory variables means that a coefficient that appears to be significant at the level $\hat{\alpha}$ is actually only significant at the level $1-(1-\hat{\alpha})^{c/k}$. In the case of $k = 2$ and 5 candidate variables, this risks greatly overstating significance levels, and the risk is massive if there are, say, 100 candidate variables. Lovell (1983) goes on to argue for the same sort of transparency in analysis as Leamer (1983). Denton (1985) expands on Lovell's work and shows that data mining can occur as a collective phenomenon even if each individual researcher tests only one pre-stated hypothesis, if there is selective reporting of statistically significant results, an argument closely related to the file drawer publication bias discussion above (Rosenthal 1979).

Related points have been made in other social science fields in recent years. In psychology, Simmons, Nelson, and Simonsohn "prove" that listening to the Beatles' song "When I'm Sixty-Four" made listeners a year-and-a-half younger (Simmons, Nelson, and Simonsohn 2011). The extent and ease of this "fishing" in analysis is also described in political science by Humphreys, Sierra, and Windt (2013), who use simulations to show how a multiplicity of outcome measures and of heterogeneous treatment effects (subgroup analyses) can be used to generate a false positive, even with large sample sizes. In statistics, Gelman and Loken (2013) agree that "[a] dataset can be analyzed in so many different ways (with the choices being not just what statistical test to perform but also decisions on what data to [include] or exclude, what measures to study, what interactions to consider, etc.), that very little information is provided by the statement that a study came up with a $p<.05$ result."

The greater use of extra robustness checks in applied economics is designed to limit the extent of specification search and is a shift in the direction proposed by Leamer (1983), but it is unclear how effective these changes are in reducing bias in practice. As noted above, the analysis of 641 articles from three top economics journals in recent years presented in Brodeur et al. (2016) still shows a disturbing two-humped distribution of p-values, with relatively few p-values between 0.10 and 0.25 and far more just below 0.05. Their analysis also explores the correlates behind this pattern, and finds that this apparent misallocation of p-values just below the accepted statistical significance level was less pronounced for articles written by tenured authors, and tentatively find it less pronounced among studies based on randomized controlled trials (suggesting that improved research design itself may partially constrain data mining), but they did not detect any discernible differences in the pattern based on whether the authors had publicly posted the study's replication data in the journal's public archive.

Subgroup Analysis

One area of analytical flexibility that appears particularly important in practice is subgroup analysis. In many cases, there are multiple distinct interaction effects that could plausibly be justified by economic theory, and current datasets have a growing richness of potential covariates. Yet it is rare for applied economics studies to mention how many different interaction effects were tested, increasing the risk that only statistically significant false positives are reported.

While there are few systematic treatments of this issue in economics, there has been extensive discussion of this issue within medical research, where the use of non-prespecified subgroup analysis is strongly frowned upon. The FDA does not use subgroup analysis in its drug approval decisions (Maggioni et al. 2007). An oft-repeated, and humorous, case comes from a trial of aspirin and streptokinase use after heart attacks conducted in a large number of patients ($N = 17,187$). Aspirin and streptokinase were found to be beneficial, except for patients born under Libra and Gemini, for whom there was a harmful (but not statistically significant) effect (ISIS-2 COLLABORATIVE GROUP 1988). The authors included the zodiac subgroup analysis because journal editors had suggested that 40 subgroups be analyzed, and the authors relented under the condition that they could include a few subgroups of their own choosing to demonstrate the unreliability of such analysis (Schulz and Grimes 2005).

Inability to Replicate Results

Data Availability

There have been longstanding concerns within economics and the social sciences over the inability to replicate the results of specific published papers. The pioneering example is a project undertaken by the *Journal of Money, Credit, and Banking* (JMCB) (Dewald, Thursby, and Anderson 1986). The journal launched the JMCB Data Storage and Evaluation Project with NSF funding in 1982, which requested data and code from authors who published papers in the journal.[8] Despite the adoption of an explicit policy of data sharing by the JMCB during the project, only 78 percent of authors provided data within six months after multiple requests, although this was certainly an improvement over the 34-percent data sharing rate in the control group, namely, those who published before the new journal policy went into effect. Of the papers that were still under review by the JMCB at the time of the requests for data, one-quarter did not even respond to the request, despite the request coming from the same journal considering their paper. The data that was submitted was often an unlabeled and undocumented mess, a problem that has persisted with recent data sharing policies, as discussed below. Dewald, Thursby, and anderson (1986) attempted to replicate nine empirical papers, and despite extensive assistance from the original authors, they were often unable to reproduce the papers' published results.

The call to share data was echoed in sociology (Hauser 1987), but little changed for a long time after the publication of this landmark article. A decade later, in a follow-up piece to the JMCB Project published in the *Federal Reserve Bank of St. Louis Review*, anderson and Dewald (1994) note that only two economics journals other than the *Review* itself, namely, the *Journal of Applied Econometrics* and the *Journal of Business and Economic Statistics*, systematically requested replication data from authors, though neither requested the associated statistical code. The JMCB itself had discontinued its policy of requesting replication data in 1993 (though it reinstated it in 1996). The authors repeated their experiment with papers presented at the St. Louis Federal Reserve Bank conference in 1992 and obtained similarly discouraging response rates as in the original JMCB Project.

The first "top-five" general interest economics journal to systematically request replication data was the *American Economic Review* (AER), which began requesting data in 2003. After a 2003 article (McCullough and Vinod 2003) showed that nonlinear maximization methods from different software packages often produced wildly different estimates, that not a single *AER* article had tested their solution across different software packages, and

---

[8] Note that the NSF has long had an explicit policy of expecting researchers to share their primary data, though there seems to be minimal enforcement. "Investigators are expected to share with other researchers, at no more than incremental cost and within a reasonable time, the primary data, samples, physical collections and other supporting materials created or gathered in the course of work under NSF grants. Grantees are expected to encourage and facilitate such sharing"; see www.nsf.gov/bfa/dias/policy/dmp.jsp.

that fully half of queried authors from a chosen issue of the *AER*, including a then-editor of the journal, had failed to comply with the policy of providing data and code, editor Ben Bernanke made the data and code sharing policy mandatory in 2004 (Bernanke 2004; McCullough 2007). The current *AER* data policy states:

It is the policy of the *American Economic Review* to publish papers only if the data used in the analysis are clearly and precisely documented and are readily available to any researcher for purposes of replication. Authors of accepted papers that contain empirical work, simulations, or experimental work must provide to the *Review*, prior to publication, the data, programs, and other details of the computations sufficient to permit replication. These will be posted on the *AER* Web site. The Editor should be notified at the time of submission if the data used in a paper are proprietary or if, for some other reason, the requirements above cannot be met.[9]

In addition to all the journals published by the American Economic Association (including the *American Economic Review*, the *American Economic Journals*, and the *Journal of Economic Perspectives*), several other leading journals, including *Econometrica*, the *Journal of Applied Econometrics*, the *Journal of Money Credit and Banking*, the *Journal of Political Economy*, the *Review of Economics and Statistics*, and the *Review of Economic Studies*, now explicitly require data and code to be submitted at the time of article publication. The last of what are typically considered the leading general interest journals in the profession, the *Quarterly Journal of Economics*, finally adopted a data sharing requirement (that of the American Economic Association Journals) in April 2016.[10]

Table 6.3 summarizes journal policies regarding data sharing, publication of replications or comments, and funding or conflict-of-interest disclosures at 12 of the top economics and finance journals (according to Scientific Journal Rankings). There has clearly been considerable progress along all of these dimensions over the past decade, but journal policies remain a mixed bag. Among these leading journals, most but not all now have some data sharing requirements, and are officially open to publishing papers that could be considered "replications."[11] There is also greater use of disclosure statements. A similar, if dated, review of journal policies in political science is available in Bueno de Mesquita et al. (2003).

---

[9] www.aeaweb.org/aer/data.php.
[10] www.oxfordjournals.org/our_journals/qje/for_authors/data_policy.html.
[11] Though leading journals are officially open to publishing replications, they appear to publish few replication studies in practice.

Table 6.3 Transparency policies at selected top economics and finance journals

Journal	Data Sharing Policy?	Notes	Replication/ Comment Publication?	Notes	Funding/ Conflict-of-Interest Disclosure?	Notes
American Economic Review	Yes	Current policy was announced in 2004, becoming effective in 2005. It is in effect for all AEA journals.	Yes		Yes	Implemented in July 2012 for all AEA journals.
American Economic Journals (Applied Economics; Economic Policy; Macroeconomics)	Yes	Same as AER. Since journal inception in 2009.	Yes	Allow post-publication peer review on website.	Yes	Same as AER.
Econometrica	Yes	Began in 2004. See Dekel et al. (2006).	Yes		Yes	Peer review conflict-of-interest statement printed January 2009. Current financial disclosure policy adopted May 2014.
Journal of Finance	No		Yes		Yes	Current policy adopted August 2015.
Journal of Financial Economics	No	Some data are available on the journal webpage, but there appears to be no official policy.	No		Yes	Current policy adopted November 2015.

(continued)

Table 6.3 (cont.)

Journal	Data Sharing Policy?	Notes	Replication/ Comment Publication?	Notes	Funding/ Conflict-of-Interest Disclosure?	Notes
Journal of Political Economy	Yes	Uses the same policy as the *AER*. Announced in 2005, effective in 2006.	Yes	Submission instructions state that authors of comments must correspond with original authors.	No	
Quarterly Journal of Economics	Yes	Uses the same policy as the *AER*, adopted 2016.	Yes		Yes	
Review of Economic Studies	Yes	Start date unclear.	No		No	
Review of Financial Studies	No		Yes		Yes	Adopted August 2006. Updated June 2016.

Note: These 11 journals are at the top of the Scientific Journal Rankings (SJR), excluding the *Journal of Economic Literature*, since its publications are generally reviews; see www.scimagojr.com/journalrank.php?area=2000. The *American Economic Journal: Microeconomics* has the same policies as the other AEJ journals, but is lower ranked. Data sharing policy indicates whether the journal has a policy requiring authors to submit data that produce final results. Information obtained from journal websites and instructions for authors as well as via email to journal staff through October 2016. Replication/comment publication indicates whether the journal has published a replication, as per Duvendack, Palmer-Jones, and Reed (2015) or The Replication Network list (http://replicationnetwork.com/replication-studies/) as well as journal websites. Since "replication" is an imprecise term, this categorization is perhaps subject to some debate.

The *AER* conducted a self-review and found relatively good, though still incomplete, compliance with its data sharing policy (Glandon 2010). Despite this positive self-assessment, other observers believe that much work remains to ensure greater access to replication data in economics. Recent studies document that fewer than 15 of over 150 articles in the JMCB archive could be replicated; there is typically little to no verification that the data and code submitted to journals actually generate the published results; the majority of economics journals still have no explicit data sharing requirements (McCullough, McGeary, and Harrison 2006; anderson et al. 2008; McCullough 2009).

The uneven nature of progress along these dimensions across economics journals is mirrored in the patterns observed in other research disciplines. Medical research tends to have relatively little public data sharing, partly due to the stringency of the Health Insurance Portability and Accountability Act of 1996 (HIPAA), although it is thought that some researchers may use the law as a pretext for avoiding greater transparency (Annas 2003; Malin, Benitez, and Masys 2011). An increasing number of political science journals are now requiring data sharing (Gherghina and Katsanidou 2013), with a few journals (e.g., *International Interactions*, *Political Science Research and Methods*) doing at least some degree of in-house verification of results, and the *American Journal of Political Science* contracting out the verification to a third party.[12] A leading group of political scientists created the Data Access and Research Transparency (DART) statement, which includes data sharing requirements. That statement has been incorporated into the ethics guidelines of the American Political Science Association, and has since been adopted by nearly 30 political science journals.[13] In psychology, one leading journal, *Psychological Science*, undertook drastic policy changes in early 2014 to increase transparency and reproducibility under editor Eric Eich (Eich 2014) and these have continued under the current editor (Lindsay 2015). The changes include the introduction of "badges" included in the article itself signifying open data, open materials, and pre-registration of hypotheses, which has helped spawn an increase in data availability.[14] In sociology, Freese (2007a, b) issued a call for American Sociological Association journals to take

---

[12] The Odum Institute for Research in Social Science, University of North Carolina, Chapel Hill; see https://ajpsblogging.files.wordpress.com/2015/03/ajps-guide-for-replic-materials-1-0.pdf.

[13] See www.dartstatement.org/.

[14] More information on badges can be found here: www.psychologicalscience.org/index.php/publications/journals/psychological_science/badges or here: https://osf.io/tvyxz/wiki/home/, and information on their influence on *Psychological Science* here: www.psychologicalscience.org/index.php/publications/observer/obsonline/open-practice-badges-in-psychological-science-18-months-out.html.

advantage of new technology (the Internet) and require data sharing at the time of publication, as well as a defense against objections concerning subject confidentiality and incentives for original data gathering, among others.

Proprietary data. The American Economic Association's journal data sharing policy – which has been adopted by several other journals and organizations nearly verbatim, as shown in Table 6.3 – allows for some exceptions, importantly, for proprietary data. In particular, the policy reads: "The Editor should be notified at the time of submission if the data used in a paper are proprietary or if, for some other reason, the requirements above cannot be met."

In practice, this exemption is requested fairly often by empirical researchers, and the rate is increasing over time. During the past decade, the May *American Economic Review Papers and Proceedings* issue has featured a "Report of the Editor," which details the number of submissions to the journal, as well the number of papers published, those with data, and those that were granted exemptions. Figure 6.1 presents the percentage of papers in each issue of the *AER* since 2005 (when information became available) through 2017. A few patterns are noteworthy. First, the proportion of papers that include data has risen over time, starting at roughly 60 percent and since increasing into the 70–80 percent range, capturing the shift toward empirical research in the discipline as a whole. During this period, the proportion of papers using data that received exemptions from the data-sharing policy has risen rapidly, from roughly 10 to 40 percent over time. Thus, replication data are not available in practice for nearly half of all empirical papers published in the *AER* in recent years.

There are many common sources of proprietary or otherwise non-sharable data driving this trend. One of the most common are US government data. There are currently 29 Federal Statistical Research Data Centers (RDC), which provide researchers access to sensitive federal government data that cannot simply be shared publicly on a journal website, typically due to individual or corporate privacy concerns (e.g., IRS tax records).[15] We do not believe that research conducted with this data should be penalized in any way, and, in fact, studies employing administrative data may be particularly valuable both intellectually and in terms of public policy decisions. However, despite the exemption from data sharing, it would still be useful for researchers (and journals) to make their work as reproducible as possible given the

---

[15] For more information on researcher access to, and National Science Foundation (NSF) funding for, US administrative data, see Card et al. (2010); Mervis (2014a); Moffitt (2016) and Cowen and Tabarrok (2016), the latter of which also calls for NSF funding of replications, open data, and greater dissemination of economics research.

Conceptualizing the Problem

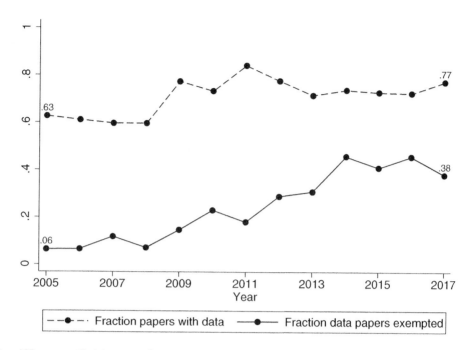

Figure 6.1 AER papers with data exempt from the data-sharing requirement

Figure shows annual data on the fraction of American Economic Review papers that use data, and the fraction of those data-using papers that were exempted from the data-sharing policy. Data are taken from the Annual Report of the Editors, which appears annually in the Papers and Proceedings issue of the AER. Figure available in public domain: http://dx.doi.org/10.7910/DVN/FUO7FC.

circumstances, for instance, by at least posting the associated statistical code and providing details about how other scholars could gain similar access to the data. Beyond government data, there are, of course, also an increasing number of proprietary datasets created by corporations or other entities that are willing to share sensitive commercial data with researchers, but not with the public at large where similar issues arise.

Beyond commercially proprietary or legally restricted government data, there is also the important issue of norms regarding the sharing of original data collected by scholars themselves. Given the years of effort and funding that goes into creating an original dataset, what special intellectual property rights (if any) do scholars involved in generating data have?

Economists should be aware of the incentives created by temporary monopoly rights to intellectual property, and in many ways the issues regarding original data collection are closely linked to traditional arguments around granting private patents. Such monopoly rights, even if temporary, could be socially beneficial if they help to drive the creation of innovative new data sources, such as the explosion of original new survey datasets in development economics over the past two decades. Yet we know of no empirical research that discusses the optimal length of such "research dataset" patents; this is an area that demands further attention, especially around the optimal length of exclusive access afforded to originators of new data.[16]

The increasingly common requirement to share data at the time of journal publication is a cause for concern in some fields. For example, in response to a proposal from the International Committee of Medical Journal Editors to require data sharing within six months of the publication of an article (Taichman et al. 2016) an editorial in the leading *New England Journal of Medicine* caused an outcry when the editors responded by describing those who do secondary analysis without the co-authorship and cooperation of the original data collecting author as "research parasites" (Longo and Drazen 2016). The journal re-affirmed its commitment to data sharing (Drazen 2016) and published a supporting piece by Senator Elizabeth Warren (Warren 2016), but also a separate piece calling for a longer embargo period after publication: "2 years after publication of the primary trial results and an additional 6 months for every year it took to complete the trial, with a maximum of 5 years before trial data are made available to those who were not involved in the trial" (The International Consortium of Investigators for Fairness in Trial Data Sharing 2016). Presumably the increasing "patent length" here for each additional year it took to complete data collection is an attempt to reward research effort in collecting unusually rich longitudinal data. Yet these sorts of rules regarding timeframes seem quite ad hoc (to us, at least), further highlighting the need for a more serious examination of how best to balance the research community's right to replicate and extend existing research with scholars' incentives to invest in valuable original data.

In political science, many journals have recently adopted policies similar to the AEA policy described above. For example, the current policy of the *American Journal of Political Science* states: "In some limited circumstances, an author may request an exemption from the replication and verification policy. This exemption would allow the author to withhold or limit public access to some or all of the data used in an analysis. All other replication materials (e.g., software commands, etc.) still must be provided. The primary reasons for such exemptions are restricted access datasets and human subjects

---

[16] Unlike a long line of empirical research on the optimal patent length for research and design such as Mansfield, Schwartz, and Wagner (1981).

protection."[17] We lack data on how often this exemption is granted, however. Additionally, this journal goes much further than economics journals in one important way: instead of simply collecting and publishing data and code from authors, the editors use a third-party research center (namely, the Odum Institute for Research in Social Science, at the University of North Carolina, Chapel Hill for quantitative analysis and the Qualitative Data Repository (QDR), at Syracuse University for qualitative analyses) to verify that the data and statistical code produce the published results.

Types of Replication Failures and Examples

There have been multiple high-profile examples in economics of cases where replication authors have claimed they are unable to replicate published results, including on topics of intense public policy interest.

It is unclear (to us, at least) exactly how pervasive the issues of lack of replicability are in economics, and thus how much confidence we should have in the body of published findings, and this is a topic on which future research should aim to gather more systematic evidence. It could certainly be the case that researchers – as well as graduate students in their courses, in a growing number of PhD training programs – usually are able to successfully replicate published results, but that this unremarkable exercise of successfully verifying published results escapes our notice because researchers do not seek to publish their work (or that editors choose not to publish it). Yet in the absence of systematic standards regarding data sharing and replication, and given examples such as those discussed below in which there are discrepancies between the original published findings and later replication results, it remains possible that the high-profile cases of failed replication may simply be the tip of the iceberg. Thankfully, a few recent papers have begun to provide some evidence on this question, which we highlight below.

We ourselves are no strangers to replication and re-analysis debates: papers by one of the authors of this article, described below, have been part of lively debates on replication and re-analysis using data that we shared publicly. These debates have led us to appreciate the great promise of replication research, as well as its potential pitfalls: exactly like original research studies, replication studies have their own particular strengths and weaknesses, and may serve to either advance the intellectual debate or could obscure particular issues. Yet there is no doubt in our minds that an overall increase in replication research

---

[17] See https://ajps.org/ajps-replication-policy/.

will serve a critical role in establishing the credibility of empirical findings in economics and, in equilibrium, will create stronger incentives for scholars to generate more reliable results.

Further complicating matters, an imprecise definition of the term "replication" itself often leads to confusion. A taxonomic proposal in Hamermesh (2007) distinguished between "pure," "statistical," and "scientific" replications, while a more recent effort (Clemens 2017) uses the terms "verification," "reproduction," "reanalysis," and "extension" to distinguish between replications (the first two) and robustness exercises (the latter two). We first present some existing evidence on the replicability of economics and social science research in the next subsection, and then provide examples of each of Clemens' categories.

Evidence on replication in economics. The articles in the 1986 *Journal of Money Credit and Banking* project and the 1994 St. Louis Federal Reserve Bank conference follow-up mentioned above provided some of the first attempts at systematic replication in economics, with fairly discouraging results. Have things improved in the last few decades?

New evidence is emerging about the reliability of empirical economics research. One of the most important recent studies is Camerer et al. (2016), which repeated 18 behavioral economics lab experiments originally published between 2011 and 2014 in the *American Economic Review* and the *Quarterly Journal of Economics* to assess their replicability. Their approach is similar in design to a large-scale replication of 100 studies in psychology known as the "Replication Project: Psychology," which we discuss in detail below. The replication studies were designed with sample sizes that aimed to have 90-percent power to detect the original effect size at the 5-percent significance level. In all, the estimated effects were statistically significant with the same sign in 11 of the 18 replication studies (61.1 percent). This is a moderate, though perhaps not entirely demoralizing, rate of replicability. Yet there is still no single accepted standard of what it means for a study to successfully replicate another, and different definitions provide somewhat more positive assessments of replicability. For instance, in 15 of the 18 replication studies (83.3 percent), estimated effects lie within a 95-percent "prediction interval" (which acknowledges sampling error in both the original study and the replication); one further replication estimate was far larger in magnitude than the original estimate, arguably raising the replication rate to 89 percent.[18] Overall,

---

[18] See Patil, Peng, and Leek (2016) and the discussion below regarding prediction intervals. An interesting, if sad, detail of the difficulties of replication is highlighted in the *Science* news article covering the results of the Camerer et al. study (Bohannon 2016). One of the replicated studies

it is reasonable to conclude from this study that the body of recent experimental economics lab studies (at least in the leading journals) is unlikely to be riddled with spurious findings.

Camerer et al. (2016) also included both a survey and a novel prediction market to assess observers' (mostly PhD students and post-doctoral researchers, as well as professors, recruited via email) priors on whether the studies would in fact successfully replicate. Both the survey and market measures were somewhat more optimistic about replicability than the actual outcomes (described above), and the prediction market did not significantly outperform the survey beliefs. Statistical tests of the correlation of a successful replication outcome with the p-value and sample size of the original study reveal significant relationships in the expected directions, namely, a negative correlation with the p-value (in other words, studies with smaller p-values were more likely to replicate) and a positive correlation with sample size, where the latter result presumably implies that original results based on larger samples were less likely to have been spuriously driven by sampling variation.

Beyond experimental economics, a recent working paper by andrew Chang and Phillip Li systematically tested the reproducibility of 67 macroeconomics papers (Chang and Li 2015). Chang and Li deliberately sampled a wider variety of journals, choosing 13 journals and articles from July 2008 to October 2013 and for comparability all papers that have an empirical component, model estimation with only US data, and have a key result based on US GDP figures. Of the 67 papers, 6 use proprietary data and are thus excluded from consideration; 35 articles are published in journals with data and code sharing requirements, but Chang and Li could obtain data for only 28 of these (80 percent) from the journal archives, suggesting limited enforcement of this requirement in many cases. Web search and emails to authors netted only one of the remaining seven missing datasets. Of the 26 papers in journals without data sharing requirements, Chang and Li were unable to obtain 15 datasets (58 percent).

With these data in hand, the overall replication success rate is 29 of 67 (43 percent) overall, or 29 of 61 (48 percent) among those using non-proprietary datasets, so roughly half. Though missing data is the largest source of replication failures, "incorrect data or code" accounts for the inability to replicate 9 papers. It should be noted that Chang and Li use a qualitative definition of replication, and test only key results of the paper,

---

(Ifcher and Zarghamee 2011) originally showed subjects a clip of comedian Robin Williams to test if happiness (positive affect) impacts time preference. The replication took place after William's tragic suicide, so the video could easily induce a different emotional state in the replication.

and this appears to lead to a fairly generous interpretation of replicability. They write: "For example, if the paper estimates a fiscal multiplier for GDP of 2.0, then any multiplier greater than 1.0 would produce the same qualitative result (i.e., there is a positive multiplier effect and that government spending is not merely a transfer or crowding out private investment)." To our minds, this is evidence that even when data are available (which they sometimes are not) a non-negligible fraction of empirical economics research cannot be reproduced, even when using the original data and a relatively non-stringent conceptual understanding of what constitutes replication success.

Other examples of replication failures abound. Clemens (2017) provides a useful taxonomy, and we provide an example of from each of the categories there to help distinguish between them, namely the two types of replication he discusses (verification and reproduction), and the two types of robustness exercises (reanalysis and extension). Of course, not all papers fit easily into one of these categories as most tend to include elements from multiple categories.

Verification. Perhaps the most straightforward type of replication in economics involves using the same specification, the same sample, and the same population. Essentially, this is running the same code on the same data and testing if you get the same results. Hamermesh (2007) referred to this as a "pure replication." We believe this basic standard should be expected of all published economics research, and hope this expectation is universal among researchers. One tiny tweak to the definition of verification is that it also includes errors in coding. If an author describes a statistical test in the paper, but the code indisputably does not correctly carry out the test as described, this is also considered a verification failure.

One of the earliest cases of quantitative economics research failing a verification test comes from an investigation of the effect of Social Security on private savings. Feldstein (1974) estimates a life cycle model showing that Social Security reduces private savings by as much as 50 percent. There were significant theoretical challenges to carrying out this exercise related to assumptions about the intergenerational transfer of wealth, but Leimer and Lesnoy (1982) discovered that a flaw in Feldstein's computer program that overestimated the growth rate of Social Security wealth for widows led to larger effects of Social Security wealth than when the mistake was corrected.

Feldstein replied to the critique saying he was grateful for having the error corrected, but that the central conclusion of the study remains largely unchanged (namely, that Social Security decreased private savings by

44 percent) (Feldstein 1982). Much of the change in coefficients in the replication exercise resulted from Leimer and Lesnoy including an expanded time series of data – this is not a failure of verification, but rather an extension, which we discuss below. Feldstein asserted that this was unwise because of an important 1972 change in Social Security law that bookended the original sample period. When including post-1972 data and modifying the Social Security wealth variable in a way to account for the change, Feldstein estimated a slightly larger deterrent effect of Social Security on private savings.

Clemens (2017) contains a larger selection of examples (see his Table 3).[19] In many (but not all) cases discussed in Clemens, the original authors clearly admit to the failure of verification, but there is vigorous and, we think, healthy scholarly debate about how important those mistakes are and whether the results are still significant – statistically and/or practically – when the code or data are corrected. Of course, authors whose papers are subject to replication debates should be commended for providing other scholars with access to their data and code in the first place, especially for these earlier articles published before journal data sharing requirements were established.

Reproduction. The other type of replication in Clemens' taxonomy is a reproduction. This approach uses the same analytical specification and the same population, but a different sample. Hamermesh (2007) refers to this as a statistical replication.

In economics, this approach would be exhibited in a study that generated a certain set of results using a 5-percent sample of the census, while a different 5-percent census sample produced different results, or an experimental economics lab study that produced one set of results with a certain sample while the reproduction study analyzed a different sample from broadly the same population (e.g., US university students).

There is, of course, some gray area and room to debate as to the definition of what constitutes a given population. If we consider US college undergraduates the population (and do not differentiate by campus), or Amazon MTurk-ers,

---

[19] Other well-known recent examples of verification debates in empirical economics include Donohue and Levitt (2001), Foote and Goetz (2008) and Donohue and Levitt (2008) on legalized abortion and crime rates; and Reinhart and Rogoff (2010) and Herndon, Ash, and Pollin (2014) on growth rates and national debt. In the debate over Hoxby's (2000) results regarding school competition in Rothstein (2007) and Hoxby (2007), the possibility is discussed that one factor contributing to lack of verification is that intermediary datasets constructed from raw data were over-written when the raw data were updated, as sometimes happens with US government data. The work of one of the authors of this chapter could be included on this list; see Miguel and Kremer (2004), Aiken et al. (2015), and Hicks, Kremer, and Miguel (2015) on the impact of school-based deworming in Kenya.

some of the failures of replication in Camerer et al. (2016) could be better classified as failures of reproduction, as long as the samples were in fact collected in broadly the same manner (i.e., in person versus online).

Reproduction failures are perhaps more precisely defined in the hard sciences where experimenters routinely attempt to do the exact same physical process as another lab, albeit with a different sample of molecules, or in the biological sciences where experiments may employ a different sample of animal subjects. For instance, in defining reproduction, Clemens mentions the infamous case of the "discovery" of cold fusion by Fleischmann and Pons (1989), which failed to reproduce in Lewis et al. (1989).

Reanalysis. Robustness exercises come in two varieties, reanalysis and extensions.

Reanalysis uses a different analytical specification on the same population (with either the same or a different sample). Many economics replication studies include both a verification aspect as well as some re-analysis. For instance, Davis (2013) conducts a successful verification of Sachs and Warner (1997), but concludes that reanalysis shows the estimates are somewhat sensitive to different statistical estimation techniques. Other well-known recent reanalysis debates in empirical economics include Miguel, Satyanath, and Sergenti (2004), Ciccone (2011), and Miguel and Satyanath (2011) on civil conflict and GDP growth using rainfall as an instrumental variable; and Acemoglu, Johnson, and Robinson (2001, 2002), Albouy (2012), on institutions and GDP growth with settler mortality as an instrumental variable. In sociological research related to the evolutionary psychological theory of parental investment (the Trivers-Willard hypothesis), a similar back-and-forth can be seen in Kanazawa (2001) and Freese and Powell (2001). In sociological work on the returns to education in urban China, Jann (2005) reanalyzes Wu and Xie (2003) with what he considers a better statistical test, showing that the earlier conclusions are premature.[20]

The debates over these and other studies makes it clear that reanalysis does not typically settle all key research questions, and the exercise often reveals that empirical economists have considerable flexibility in their analytical choices. This insight makes the development of methods to account for – and possibly constrain – this flexibility, which we discuss below in Chapter 7, all the more important.

---

[20] Additional examples from sociology include Roth and Kroll (2007), which reanalyzes earlier work by Miller and Stark (2002) on risk preference explanations for gender differences in religiosity.

Extension. Under Clemens' classification system, an extension uses the same analytical specification as an original study but a different population and a different sample. Most often this would be conducting the same analysis carried out in a different time or place.

A well-known example of an extension involves Burnside and Dollar (2000), which showed that foreign aid seemed to be effective in increasing GDP if the recipient country was well-governed. However, using the exact same regression specification but including additional countries and years to the dataset, Easterly, Levine, and Roodman (2004) do not obtain the same result. Burnside and Dollar (2004) discuss the differences between the findings and conclude that they occur largely because of the additional countries, rather than lengthening the time series.

One widely debated topic in economics that has features of both replication and robustness exercises is the topic of minimum-wage impacts on unemployment. In early work, Welch (1974) concluded that early minimum-wage legislation decreased teenage employment, increased the cyclicality of teenage employment with respect to the business cycle, and shifted teenage employment toward sectors not covered by the law. However, in the course of using Welch's data, Siskind (1977) discovered that Welch had used data for teenagers 16–19 years old instead of 14–19 years old for certain years, and once this was corrected, the minimum wage did not appear to reduce teenage employment. This was a fairly easy mistake to understand since the Current Population Survey was undergoing changes at the time, and table headings for unpublished data had not even been updated. Welch graciously acknowledged the error, and used the corrected data to extend the analysis to probe impacts by industry sector (Welch 1977).

Scholars working on this important topic have, for several decades now, continued to find significant room for disagreement on key issues of sampling, data sources, and statistical analysis methods,[21] matters on which well-intended researchers may well disagree. In this and other similarly contentious debates, we believe that the use of pre-specified research designs and analysis plans could be useful for advancing scientific progress, a point we return to in the next chapter.

---

[21] See, for instance, Card and Krueger (1994), Neumark and Wascher (2000), and Card and Krueger (2000), the latter two of which extend the analysis by using new datasets with the original specifications, as well as new econometric specifications. The Pennsylvania/New Jersey comparison from these papers was extended to the set of all cross-state minimum-wage differences in Dube, Lester, and Reich (2010), and Neumark, Salas, and Wascher (2014).

Fraud and Retractions

Though we believe (or at least, would prefer to believe) that most instances in which social science studies cannot be replicated are due to inadvertent human error or analytical judgment calls, fraud cannot be completely discounted.

Popular books such as Broad and Wade's *Betrayers of the Truth* (1983) make it clear that scientists are not always saints. A survey of 234 economists at the 1998 ASSA/AEA meeting investigated falsification of research, inappropriate inclusion or omission of co-authors, and exchange of grades for gifts, money, or sexual favors (List et al. 2001). Both a randomization coin-toss technique to elicit true responses to sensitive questions, as well as a more standard question design, indicate that 4 percent of respondents admit to having at some time falsified research data, 7–10 percent of respondents admit to having committed one of four relatively minor research infractions, while up to 0.4 percent admitted to exchange of grades for gifts, money, or sexual favors. Given the seriousness of some of these offenses, an obvious concern is that these figures understate the actual incidence of fraudulent research practices.

A more recent survey of members of the European Economics Association described in Necker (2014) asks individuals about the justifiability of certain practices as well as their behavior regarding those practices. Necker shows that 2.6 percent of researchers admit to having falsified data, while 94 percent admit to at least one instance of a practice considered inappropriate by the majority of the survey, and there is a clear positive correlation between justifiability and behavior, as well as between perceived professional publication pressures and questionable research practices.

Similar surveys in other fields such as anderson, Martinson, and Vries (2007), which surveyed researchers across disciplines funded by the US National Institutes of Health, and John, Loewenstein, and Prelec (2012) in psychology, as well as a meta-analysis of 18 surveys of academic misbehavior, do not paint a very rosy picture, with 2 percent of respondents admitting to data fabrication, and 34 percent admitting to lesser forms of academic misconduct (Fanelli 2009).

We are not aware of a recent case in economics or sociology that received media attention similar to the Michael Lacour fraud scandal uncovered by Broockman, Kalla, and Aranow (2015) in political science, or the case of Diedrick Stapel (see Carey 2011; Bhattacharjee 2013) in psychology. However, there is considerable evidence of plagiarism and other forms of research malpractice in economics. The *Journal of Economic Literature* published the results of a survey sent to 470 economics journal editors, which revealed significant problems (Enders and Hoover 2004). Among the 127 editors who responded, only 19 percent claimed that their journal had a formal policy on plagiarism, and 42 cases of plagiarism were discovered in an average year, with nearly 24 percent of editors encountering at least one case. A follow-up survey of rank-and-file economists revealed a general lack of consensus on how to respond to cases of alleged plagiarism (Enders and Hoover 2006).[22]

Article retraction is another useful indicator of research misconduct. A search of four popular article databases for terms related to article retractions identified by Karabag and Berggren (2012) found six retractions: ("Retraction Statement and Authors' Apology" 2009; Berger 2009; Nofsinger 2009; "Statement of Retraction" 2010; "Redundant Publishing – Australasian Journal of Regional Studies" 2011; "Statement of Retraction" 2012) which all occurred in the last few years. The volunteer network Research Papers in Economics (RePEc) maintains a plagiarism committee, which, as of August 2016, had documented 52 cases of plagiarism, 12 cases of self-plagiarism, and 4 cases of fraud involving 96 authors.[23]

Some institutional journal policies in economics lag behind those of other disciplines. For instance, as documented by Karabag and Berggren (2012), many economics and business journals appear not to even have explicit policies regarding ethics, plagiarism, or retraction,[24] and in many cases articles that have been retracted continue to be available on the journal's website without any indication that it has been retracted. For example, though Gerking and Morgan (2007) features "Retraction" in the title, the relevant earlier paper (Kunce, Gerking, and Morgan 2002) is still available and appears unchanged.

---

[22] Well-known plagiarism cases involve an article published in 1984 in the *Quarterly Journal of Economics* (see Chenault 1984; "Notice to Our Readers" 1984) and a case of plagiarism of an original article from *Economics Innovation and New Technology* for re-publication in *Kyklos* (Frey, Frey, and Eichenberger 1999). The most recent incident that seemed to attract significant attention was the submission of a substantively identical article to multiple journals within economics, which is also a serious lapse ("Correspondence: David H. Autor and Bruno S. Frey" 2011). Even if plagiarism of this manner would seem significantly easier to catch in the Internet age, the proliferation of journals partially counteracts this ease.

[23] https://plagiarism.repec.org/index.html.

[24] Although note that journals may present these policies online as opposed to formally publishing them in the journal; for instance, see the *Quarterly Journal of Economics*' formal ethics policy: www.oxfordjournals.org/our_journals/qje/for_authors/journal_policies.html.

If one happened to discover the webpage of the original[25] first (note that the original appears first in Google Scholar searches), one would have no reason to suspect that it had been retracted. For comparison, the webpage[26] for Maringer and Stapel (2009), which was retracted in 2015,[27] clearly reads "THIS PAPER HAS BEEN RETRACTED," the title has been altered to begin with "Retracted:" and the pdf features an obvious RETRACTED watermark on every page. This is also the case with all six of the retractions in Karabag and Berggren (2012), as well as other notable recent retractions such as LaCour and Green (2014), which was retracted by Marcia McNutt (2015).

The bottom line is that there is little reason to believe that economists are inherently more ethical than other social scientists or researchers in other disciplines, so policies regarding fraud and retraction from other disciplines might potentially be beneficially applied to economics.

Conclusion

In conclusion, we believe that the problems of publication bias, specification searching, and an inability to replicate are widespread throughout the social sciences. However, we remain optimistic, as there are numerous potential partial solutions to these problems, including study registration, pre-analysis plans, improved statistical practices such as multiple hypothesis testing adjustments, and better data sharing that we believe can help with these issues. We review these items in Chapter 7.

---

[25] www.aeaweb.org/articles.php?doi=10.1257/000282802762024656.
[26] http://onlinelibrary.wiley.com/doi/10.1002/ejsp.569/abstract.
[27] See "Retraction Statement: 'Correction or Comparison? The Effects of Prime Awareness on Social Judgments', by M. Maringer and D. Stapel" (2015).

7 Transparency and Reproducibility: Potential Solutions

Garret Christensen and Edward Miguel

There is overwhelming evidence that the problems of publication bias, p-hacking, and a lack of reproducibility are real. The previous chapter summarizes this evidence. The published literature in sociology, political science, and economics all suffer from these problems, to varying degrees. In this chapter, we focus on several new methods and tools that have emerged in social science research over the past two decades – and more forcefully over the past ten years – to address these concerns.

These approaches have in common a focus on greater transparency and openness in the research process. They include improved research design (including experimental designs and meta-analysis approaches), study registration and pre-analysis plans, strengthened disclosure and reporting practices, and new norms regarding open data and materials.

It should be clear that these potential solutions are not panaceas, and they have not yet been adopted widely enough in the social sciences to be considered proven. Nonetheless, we strongly believe that experimenting with these new practices is worthwhile.

Improved Analytical Methods: Research Designs and Meta-Analysis

There have been a number of different responses within social sciences to the view that pervasive specification searching and publication bias was affecting the credibility of empirical literatures. As mentioned in the previous chapter, there has been a shift toward a greater focus on prospective research design in several fields of applied economics and political science work. Experimental (Duflo, Glennerster, and Kremer 2007) and quasi-experimental (Angrist and Pischke 2010) research designs arguably place more constraints on researchers relative to earlier empirical approaches, since there are natural ways to present data using these designs that researchers are typically compelled to present by colleagues in seminars and by journal referees and editors. Prospective experimental studies also tend to place greater emphasis on adequately powering an analysis statistically, which may help to reduce the likelihood of publishing only false positives (Duflo, Glennerster, and Kremer 2007).

There is also suggestive evidence that the adoption of experimental and quasi-experimental empirical approaches is beginning to address some concerns about specification search and publication bias. Brodeur et al. (2016) present tentative evidence that the familiar spike in *p*-values just below the 0.05 level is less pronounced in randomized control trial studies than in studies utilizing non-experimental methods. Yet improved research design alone may not solve several other key threats to the credibility of empirical social science research, including the possibility that null or "uninteresting" findings never become known within the research community.

Understanding Statistical Model Uncertainty

In addition to improvements in research design, Leamer (1983) argued for greater disclosure of the decisions made in analysis, in what became known as "extreme bounds analysis" (described in Chapter 6). Research along these lines has dealt with model uncertainty by employing combinations of multiple models and specifications, as well as comparisons between them. Leamer himself has continued to advance this agenda (see Leamer 2016). We describe several related approaches here.

Model averaging. A natural way to deal with statistical model uncertainty is through Bayesian model averaging. In this approach, each model in the space of plausible models is assigned a probability of being true based on researcher priors and goodness of fit criteria. Averaging the resulting estimates generates a statistic incorporating model uncertainty:

$$\hat{\delta}_M = \sum_m \mu(m|D) \hat{\delta}_m, \qquad \text{(eqn. 1)}$$

where m refers to a particular statistical model, M is the space of plausible models, $\mu(m|D)$ is the posterior probability of a model being the true model given the data D, and $\hat{\delta}_m$ is the estimated statistic from model $m \in M$.

These weights must, of course, be chosen somehow. Cohen-Cole et al. (2009), from whom we borrow the above notation, study the deterrent effect of the death penalty with a model averaging exercise combining evidence from Donohue and Wolfers (2005) and Dezhbakhsh, Rubin, and Shepherd (2003) and use the Bayesian Information Criterion (BIC) (Schwarz 1978). The weighted average they generate implies a large but imprecisely estimated deterrent effect of executions on homicides in the United States. Of course, even without employing explicit probability weights, simply visualizing the distribution of estimates across the entire space of statistical models can also be quite informative on its own.

Two well-cited examples of model averaging engage in a thorough investigation of the determinants of cross-country economic growth. Sala-i-Martin's (1997) famous "I Just Ran Two Million Regressions" article uses model weights proportional to the integrated likelihoods of each model, picks all possible three-variable combinations out of 60 covariates that have been reported as being significantly related to economic growth, and finds that only about one-third of the 60 variables can be considered robustly positively correlated with economic growth across models. Sala-i-Martin, Doppelhofer, and Miller (2004) conduct what they call Bayesian Averaging of Classical Estimates (BACE), weighting estimates using an approach analogous to Schwarz's BIC, and find that just 18 of 67 variables are significantly and robustly partially correlated with economic growth, once suggesting that many findings reported in the existing empirical literature may be spuriously generated by specification searching and selective reporting.

A discussion of model uncertainty from sociology that touches on model averaging is Young (2009), which reanalyzes the question of religiosity and economic growth from McCleary and Barro (2003) and McCleary and Barro (2006). Bayesian model averaging in sociology is also discussed in Raftery (1995) and Western (1996). Young and Holsteen (2017) develop a more formalized conception of model averaging that develops a modeling standard error as well as a measure of the size of the influence of certain covariates on the model space. Applications include estimates of the union wage premium (Hirsch 2004), mortgage lending by gender (Munnell et al. 1996), and tax-induced cross-state migration in the United States (Young and Varner 2011). Bayesian model averaging is applied to political science with examples of comparative political economy and American public opinion and policy in Bartels (1997).

Specification curve. Simonsohn, Simmons, and Nelson (2015b) propose a method, which they call the "specification curve," that is similar in spirit to Leamer's extreme-bounds analysis, but recommends researchers test the exhaustive combination of analytical decisions, not just decisions about which covariates to include in the model. If the full exhaustive set is too large to be practical, a random subset can be used. After plotting the effect size from each of the specifications, researchers can assess how much the estimated effect size varies, and which combinations of decisions lead to which outcomes.

Using permutation tests (for treatment with random assignment) or bootstrapping (for treatment without random assignment), researchers can generate shuffled samples with no true effect by construction, and compare the specification curves from these placebo samples to the specification curve from the actual data. Many comparisons are possible, but the authors suggest comparing the median effect size, the share of results with predicted sign, and share of statistically significant results with predicted sign. A key comparison, which is analogous to the traditional p-value, is the percent of the shuffled samples with as many or more extreme results.

The paper builds specification curves for two examples: Jung et al. (2014), which tested the effect of the gender of hurricane names on human fatalities, and Bertrand and Mullainathan (2004), which tested job application callback rates based on the likely ethnicity of applicant names included in job resumes. Jung et al. (2014) elicited four critical responses taking issue with the analytical decisions (Christensen and Christensen 2014; Maley 2014; Malter 2014; Bakkensen and Larson 2014). The specification curve shows that 46 percent of curves from permuted data show at least as large a median effect size as the original, 16 percent show at least as many results with the predicted sign, and 85 percent show at least as many significant results with the predicted sign. This indicates that the results are likely to have been generated by chance. The Bertrand and Mullainathan (2004) specification curve, on the other hand, shows that fewer than 0.2 percent of the permuted curves generate as large a median effect, 12.5 percent of permuted curves show at least as many results with the predicted sign, and less than 0.2 percent of permuted curves show at least as many significant results with the predicted sign, providing evidence that the results are very unlikely to have been generated by chance.

Improved Publication Bias Tests

There have been significant advances in the methodological literature on quantifying the extent of publication bias in a given body of literature. Early methods mentioned above include Rosenthal's (1979) method (the "fail-safe N"), while Galbraith (1988) advocated for radial plots of log odds ratios, and Card and Krueger (1995) tested for relationships between study sample sizes and t-statistics.

Statisticians have developed methods to estimate effect sizes in meta-analyses that control for publication bias (Hedges 1992; Hedges and Vevea 1996). The tools most widely used by economists tend to be simpler, including the widely used funnel plot, which is a scatter plot of some measure of statistical precision (typically the inverse of the standard error), versus the estimated effect size. Estimates generated from smaller samples should usually form the wider base of an inverted funnel, which should be symmetric around more precise estimates in the absence of publication bias. The method is illustrated with several economics examples in Stanley and Doucouliagos (2010). In addition to scrutinizing the visual plot, a formal test of the symmetry of this plot can be conducted using data from multiple studies and regressing the relevant *t*-statistics on inverse standard errors:

$$t_i = \frac{\text{Estimated effect}_i}{SE_i} = \beta_0 + \beta_1\left(\frac{1}{SE_i}\right) + v_i. \qquad \text{(eqn. 2)}$$

The resulting *t*-test on β_0, referred to as the Funnel Asymmetry Test (FAT) (Stanley 2008), captures the correlation between estimated effect size and precision, and thus tests for publication bias.

Using the FAT, Doucouliagos and Stanley (2009) find evidence of publication bias in Card and Krueger's (1995) sample of minimum-wage studies ($\beta_0 \neq 0$), consistent with their own interpretation of the published literature at that time. β_1 here can also be interpreted as the true effect (called the precision effect test, PET) free of publication bias, and Doucouliagos and Stanley (2009) find no evidence of a true effect of the minimum wage on unemployment. The authors also conduct the FAT-PET tests with 49 additional more recent studies in this literature and find the same results: evidence of significant publication bias and no evidence of an effect of the minimum wage on unemployment. Additional meta-analysis methods, including this "FAT-PET" approach, are summarized in Stanley and Doucouliagos (2012).

Multiple Testing Corrections

Other applied econometricians have recently called for increasing the use of multiple testing corrections in order to generate more meaningful inference in study settings with many research hypotheses (Anderson 2008; Fink, McConnell, and Vollmer 2014). The practice of correcting for multiple tests is already widespread in certain scientific fields (e.g., genetics) but has yet to become the norm in the social sciences. Simply put, since we know that *p*-values fall below traditional significance thresholds (e.g., 0.05) purely by chance a certain proportion of the time, it makes sense to report adjusted *p*-values that account for the fact that we are running multiple tests, since this makes it more likely that at least one of our test statistics has a significant *p*-value simply by chance.

There are several multiple testing approaches, some of which are used and explained by anderson (2008), namely, reporting index tests, controlling the family-wise error rate (FWER), and controlling the false discovery rate (FDR). These are each discussed in turn below.

Reporting index tests. One option for scholars in cases where there are multiple related outcome measures is to forego reporting the outcomes of numerous tests, and instead standardize the related outcomes and combine them into a smaller number of indices, sometimes referred to as a mean effect. This can be implemented for a family of related outcomes by making all signs agree (i.e., allowing positive values to denote beneficial outcomes), demeaning and dividing by the control group standard deviation, and constructing a weighted average (possibly using the inverse of the covariance matrix to weight each standardized outcome). This new index can be used as a single outcome in a regression model and evaluated with a standard *t* test. Kling, Liebman, and Katz (2007) implement an early index test in the Moving to Opportunity field experiment using methods developed in biomedicine by O'Brien (1984).

This method addresses some concerns regarding the multiplicity of statistical tests by simply reducing the number of tests. A potential drawback is that the index may combine outcomes that are only weakly related, and may obscure impacts on specific outcomes that are of interest to particular scholars, although note that these specific outcomes could also be separately reported for completeness.

Controlling the family-wise error rate. The family-wise error rate (FWER) is the probability that at least one true hypothesis in a group is rejected (a Type-1 error, or false positive). This approach is considered most useful when the "damage" from incorrectly claiming *any* hypothesis is false is high. There are several ways to implement this approach, with the simplest method being the Bonferroni correction of simply multiplying every original *p*-value by the number of tests carried out (Bland and Altman 1995), although this is extremely conservative, and improved methods have also been developed.

Holm's sequential method involves ordering *p*-values by class and multiplying the lower *p*-values by higher discount factors (Holm 1979). A related and more efficient recent method is the free step-down resampling method, developed by Westfall and Young (1993), which when implemented by anderson (2008) implies that several highly cited experimental pre-school interventions (namely, the Abecedarian, Perry, and Early Training Project studies) exhibit few positive long-run impacts for males.

Another recent method improves on Holm by incorporating the dependent structure of multiple tests. Lee and Shaikh (2014) apply it to reevaluate the Mexican PROGRESA conditional cash transfer program and find that overall program impacts remain positive and significant, but are statistically significant for fewer subgroups (e.g., by gender, education) when controlling for multiple testing. List, Shaikh, and Xu (2016) propose a method of controlling the FWER for three common situations in experimental economics, namely, testing multiple outcomes, testing for heterogeneous treatment effects in multiple subgroups, and testing with multiple treatment conditions.[1]

Controlling the false discovery rate. In situations where a single Type-1 error is not considered very costly, researchers may be willing to use a somewhat less conservative method than the FWER approached discussed above, and trade off some incorrect hypothesis rejections in exchange for greater statistical power. This is made possible by controlling the false discovery rate (FDR), or the percentage of rejections that are Type-1 errors. Benjamini and Hochberg (1995) detail a simple algorithm to control this rate at a chosen level under the assumption that the *p*-values from the multiple tests are independent, though the same method was later shown to also be valid under weaker assumptions (Benjamini and Yekutieli 2001). Benjamini, Krieger, and Yekutieli (2006) describes a two-step procedure with greater statistical power, while Romano, Shaikh, and Wolf (2008) propose the first methods to incorporate information about the dependence structure of the test statistics.

Multiple hypothesis testing adjustments have recently been used in finance (Harvey, Liu, and Zhu 2015) to re-evaluate 316 factors from 313 different papers that explain the cross-section of expected stock returns. The authors employ the Bonferroni; Holm (1979); and Benjamini, Krieger, and Yekutieli (2006) methods to account for multiple testing, and conclude that *t*-statistics greater than 3.0, and possibly as high as 3.9, should be used instead of the standard 1.96, to actually conclude that a factor explains stock returns with 95-percent confidence. Index tests and both the FWER and FDR multiple testing corrections are also employed in Casey, Glennerster,

---

[1] Most methods are meant only to deal with the first and/or second of these cases. Statistical code to implement the adjustments in List, Shaikh, and Xu (2016) in Stata and Matlab is available at: https://github.com/seidelj/mht.

and Miguel (2012) to estimate the impacts of a community-driven development program in Sierra Leone using a dataset with hundreds of potentially relevant outcome variables.

Study Registration

A leading proposed solution to the problem of publication bias is the registration of empirical studies in a public registry. This would ideally be a centralized database of all attempts to conduct research on a certain question, irrespective of the nature of the results, and such that even null (not statistically significant) findings are not lost to the research community. Top medical journals have adopted a clear standard of publishing only medical trials that are registered (De Angelis et al. 2004). The largest clinical trial registry is clinicaltrials.gov, which helped to inspire the most high-profile study registry within economics, the AEA Randomized Controlled Trial Registry (Katz et al. 2013), which was launched in May 2013.[2]

While recent research in medicine finds that the clinical trial registry has not eliminated all under-reporting of null results or other forms of publication bias and specification searching (Laine et al. 2007; Mathieu et al. 2009), they do allow the research community to quantify the extent of these problems and over time may help to constrain inappropriate practices. It also helps scholars locate studies that are delayed in publication, or are never published, helping to fill in gaps in the literature and thus resolving some of the problems identified in Franco, Malhotra, and Simonovits (2014).

Though it is too soon after the adoption of the AEA's trial registry to measure its impact on research practices and the robustness of empirical results, it is worth noting that the registry is already being used by many empirical researchers – since inception in 2013, over 2,060 studies conducted in over 100 countries have been registered, and the pace of registrations continues to rise rapidly. Panel A of Figure 7.1 presents the total number of registrations over time in the AEA registry (through October 2018), and Panel B shows the number of new registrations per month. A review of the projects currently included in the registry suggests that there are a particularly large number of development economics studies, which is perhaps not surprising given the widespread use of field experimental methods in contemporary development economics.

[2] The registry can be found online at: www.socialscienceregistry.org/.

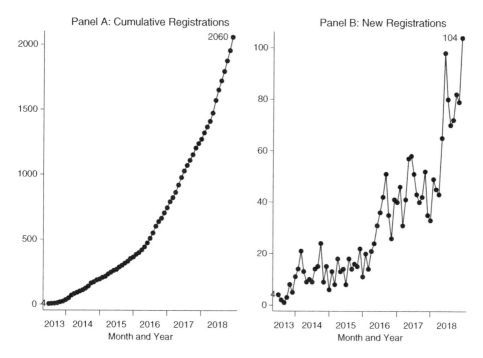

Figure 7.1 Studies in the AEA trial registry, May 2013 to October 2018

Figure shows the cumulative (Panel A) and new (Panel B) trial registrations in the American Economics Association Trial Registry (http://socialscienceregistry.org). Figure available in public domain: http://dx.doi.org/10.7910/DVN/FU07FC.

In addition to the AEA registry, several other social science registries have recently been created, including by the International Initiative for Impact Evaluation's (3ie) Registry for International Development Impact Evaluations (RIDIE, http://ridie.3ieimpact.org), launched in September 2013 (Dahl Rasmussen, Malchow-Møller, and Barnebeck andersen 2011), and the Evidence in Governance and Politics (EGAP) registry (http://egap.org/content/registration), also created in 2013. The Center for Open Science's Open Science Framework (OSF, http://osf.io) accommodates the registration of essentially any study or research document by allowing users to create a frozen time-stamped web URL with associated digital object identifier (DOI) for any materials uploaded to OSF. Several popular data storage options (including Dropbox, Dataverse, and GitHub) can also be synced with the OSF and its storage, creating a flexible way for researchers to register their research and materials. As of December 2018, researchers have posted over 281,000 searchable registrations on the OSF since the service launched in 2013.

Pre-Analysis Plans

In addition to serving as a useful way to search for research findings on a particular topic, most supporters of study registration also promote the pre-registration of studies, including pre-analysis plans (PAPs) that can be posted and time stamped even before analysis data are collected or otherwise available (Miguel et al. 2014). Registration is now the norm in medical research for randomized trials, and registrations often include (or link to) prospective statistical analysis plans as part of the project protocol. Official guidance from the US Food and Drug Administration's Center for Drug Evaluation and Research (CDER) from 1998 describes what should be included in a statistical analysis plan, and discusses eight broad categories: pre-specification of the analysis; analysis sets; missing values and outliers; data transformation; estimation, confidence intervals, and hypothesis testing; adjustment of significance and confidence levels; subgroups, interactions, and covariates; and integrity of data and computer software validity (Food and Drug Administration 1998).

While there were scattered early cases of pre-analysis plans being used in economics (most notably by Neumark 2001), the quantity of published papers employing pre-specified analysis has grown rapidly in the past few years, mirroring the rise of studies posted on the AEA registry.

There is ongoing discussion of what one should include in a PAP; detailed discussions include Glennerster and Takavarasha (2013), David McKenzie's World Bank Research Group blog post,[3] and a template for pre-analysis plans by Alejandro Ganimian (2014). Ganimian's template may be particularly useful to researchers themselves when developing their own pre-analysis plans, and instructors may find it useful in their courses. Building on, and modifying, the FDA's 1998 checklist with insights from these other recent treatments of pre-analysis plans, there appears to be a growing consensus that pre-analysis plans in the social sciences should consider discussing at least the following list of ten issues:

1. study design
2. study sample
3. outcome measures
4. mean effects family groupings
5. multiple hypothesis testing adjustments
6. subgroup analyses
7. direction of effect for one-tailed tests

[3] http://blogs.worldbank.org/impactevaluations/a-pre-analysis-plan-checklist.

8. statistical specification and method
9. structural model
10. timestamp for verification

Pre-analysis plans are relatively new to the social sciences, and this list is likely to evolve in the coming years as researchers explore the potential, and possible limitations, of this new tool.

For those concerned about the possibility of "scooping" of new research designs and questions based upon a publicly posted pre-analysis plan or project description, several of the social science registries allow temporary embargoing of project details. For instance, the AEA registry allows an embargo until a specific date or project completion. At the time of writing, the OSF allows a four-year embargo until the information is made public.[4]

Examples of Pre-Analysis Plans (PAPs)

Recent examples of social science papers based on experiments with PAPs include Casey, Glennerster, and Miguel (2012) and Finkelstein et al. (2012), among others. Casey, Glennerster, and Miguel (2012) discuss evidence from a large-scale field experiment on community-driven development (CDD) projects in Sierra Leone. The project, called GoBifo, was intended to make local institutions in post-war Sierra Leone more democratic and egalitarian. GoBifo funds were spent on a variety of local public goods infrastructure (e.g., community centers, schools, latrines, roads), agriculture, and business training projects, and were closely monitored to limit leakage. The analysis finds significant short-run benefits in terms of the "hardware" aspects of infrastructure and economic well-being; the latrines were indeed built. However, a larger goal of the project, reshaping local institutions, making them more egalitarian, increasing trust, improving local collective action, and strengthening community groups, which the researchers call the "software effects," largely failed. There are a large number of plausible outcome measures along these dimensions, hundreds in total, which the authors analyze using a mean effects index approach for nine different families of outcomes (with multiple testing adjustments). The null hypothesis of no impact cannot be rejected at 95-percent confidence for any of the nine families of outcomes.

Yet Casey et al. (2012) go on to show that, given the large numbers of outcomes in their dataset, and the multiplicity of ways to define outcome measures, finding some statistically significant results would have been relatively easy. In

---

[4] See http://help.osf.io/m/registrations/l/524207-embargoes.

Table 7.1 Erroneous interpretations under "cherry-picking"

Outcome Variable	Mean in Control Group	Treatment Effect	Standard Error
Panel A: GoBifo "weakened institutions"			
Attended meeting to decide what to do with the tarp	0.81	−0.04+	(0.02)
Everybody had equal say in deciding how to use the tarp	0.51	−0.11+	(0.06)
Community used the tarp (verified by physical assessment)	0.90	−0.08+	(0.04)
Community can show research team the tarp	0.84	−0.12*	(0.05)
Respondent would like to be a member of the VDC	0.36	−0.04*	(0.02)
Respondent voted in the local government election (2008)	0.85	−0.04*	(0.02)
Panel B: GoBifo "strengthened institutions"			
Community teachers have been trained	0.47	0.12+	(0.07)
Respondent is a member of a women's group	0.24	0.06**	(0.02)
Someone took minutes at the most recent community meeting	0.30	0.14*	(0.06)
Building materials stored in a public place when not in use	0.13	0.25*	(0.10)
Chiefdom official did not have the most influence over tarp use	0.54	0.06*	(0.03)
Respondent agrees with "Responsible young people can be good leaders"	0.76	0.04*	(0.02)
Correctly able to name the year of the next general elections	0.19	0.04*	(0.02)

Note: Reproduced from Casey et al. (2012, Table VI). i) Significance levels (per comparison p-value) indicated by + $p < 0.10$, * $p < 0.05$, ** $p < 0.01$; ii) robust standard errors; iii) treatment effects estimated on follow-up data; and iv) includes fixed effects for the district council wards (the unit of stratification) and the two balancing variables from the randomization (total households and distance to road) as controls.

fact, the paper includes an example of how, if they had had the latitude to define outcomes without a pre-analysis plan, as has been standard practice in most empirical economics studies (and in other social science fields), the authors could have reported either statistically significant and positive effects, or significantly negative effects, depending on the nature of the "cherry-picking" of results. We reproduce their results here as Table 7.1, where Panel A presents the statistically significant positive impacts identified in the GoBifo data and Panel B highlights negative effects. This finding begs the question: how many empirical social science papers with statistically significant results are, unbeknownst to us, really just some version of either Panel A or Panel B?

Finkelstein et al. (2012) study the politically charged question of the impacts of health insurance expansion, using the case of Oregon's Medicaid program, called Oregon Health Plan (OHP). In 2008, Oregon determined it could afford to enroll 10,000 additional adults, and it opted to do so by random lottery. Most of the analyses in the impact evaluation were laid out in a detailed pre-analysis plan, which was publicly posted on the National Bureau of Economic Research's website in 2010, before the researchers had access to the data.

This is important because, as in Casey et al. (2012), the researchers tested a large number of outcomes: hospital admissions through the emergency room (ER) and not through the ER; hospital days; procedures; financial strain (bankruptcy, judgments, liens, delinquency, medical debt, and non-medical debt, measured by credit report data); self-reported health from survey data, and so on. When running such a large number of tests, the researchers again could have discovered some "significant" effects simply by chance. The pre-analysis plan, in conjunction with multiple hypothesis testing adjustments, give us more confidence in the main results of the study: that recipients did not improve significantly in terms of physical health measurements, but they were more likely to have health insurance, had better self-reported health outcomes, utilized emergency rooms more, and had better detection and management of diabetes.

Additional studies that have resulted from the experiment have also employed pre-analysis plans, and they show that health insurance increased emergency department use (Taubman et al. 2014), had no effect on measured physical health outcomes after two years, but did increase health care use and diabetes management, as well as leading to lower rates of depression and financial strain (Baicker et al. 2013). The health care expansion had no significant effect on employment or earnings (Baicker et al. 2014).

Other prominent early examples of economics studies that have employed pre-analysis plans include poverty targeting programs in Indonesia, an evaluation of the Toms shoe company donation program, and a job training program in Turkey, among many others (Olken, Onishi, and Wong 2012; Alatas et al. 2012; Wydick, Katz, and Janet 2014; Hirshleifer et al. 2015). The PAP tool is also spreading to other social sciences beyond economics. For instance, in psychology, a pre-specified replication of an earlier paper that had found a link between female conception risk and racial prejudice failed to find a similar effect (Hawkins, Fitzgerald, and Nosek 2015). In political science the Election Research Preacceptance Competition ran a competition for work with pre-analysis plans based on the 2016 American National

Election Studies (ANES) data; eligible papers were required to register their analysis plan prior to the public release of the data.[5]

One issue that arises for studies that did register a pre-analysis plan is the question of characterizing the extent to which the analysis conforms to the original plan, or if it deviates in important ways from the plan. To appreciate these differences, scholars will need to compare the analysis to the plan, a step that could be seen as adding to the burden of journal editors and referees. Even if the analysis does conform exactly to the PAP, there is still the possibility that authors are consciously or unconsciously emphasizing a subset of the pre-specified analyses in the final study. Berge et al. (2015) develop an approach to comparing the distribution of p-values in the paper's main tables versus those in the PAP in order to quantify the extent of possibly selective reporting between the plan and the paper.

The Finkelstein et al. (2012) study is a model of transparency regarding the presentation of results. To the authors' credit, all analyses presented in the published paper that were not pre-specified are clearly labeled as such; in fact, the exact phrase "This analysis was not prespecified" appears in the paper six times. Tables in the main text and appendix that report analyses that were not pre-specified are labeled with a "^" character to set them apart.

Strengths, Limitations, and Other Issues Regarding Pre-Analysis Plans

There remain many open questions about whether, when, and how pre-analysis plans could and should be used in social science research, with open debates about how useful they are in different subfields of the discipline. Olken (2015), for example, highlights both their "promises and perils." On the positive side, pre-analysis plans bind the hands of researchers and greatly limit specification searching, allowing them to take full advantage of the power of their statistical tests (even making one-sided tests reasonable).

A further advantage of the use of pre-analysis plans is that they are likely to help shield researchers from pressures to affirm the policy agenda of donors and policymakers, in cases where they have a vested interest in the outcome, or when research focuses on politically controversial topics (such as health care reform). This is especially the case if researchers and their institutional partners can agree on the pre-analysis plan, as a sort of evaluation contract.

On the negative side, PAPs are often complex and take valuable time to write. Scientific breakthroughs often come at unexpected times and places,

---

[5] See www.erpc2016.com/.

often as a result of exploratory analysis, and the time spent writing PAPs may thus lead less time to spend on less-structured data exploration.

Coffman and Niederle (2015) argue that there is limited upside from PAPs when replication (in conjunction with hypothesis registries) is possible. In experimental and behavioral economics, where lab experiments utilize samples of locally recruited students and the costs of replicating an experiment are relatively low, they argue that replication could be a viable substitute for pre-analysis plans. Yet there does appear to be a growing consensus, endorsed by Coffman and Niederle, that pre-analysis plans can significantly increase the credibility of reporting and analysis in large-scale randomized trials that are expensive or difficult to repeat, or when a study that relies on a particular contextual factor makes it impossible to replicate. For instance, Berge et al. (2015) carry out a series of lab experiments timed to take place just before the 2013 Kenya elections. Replication of this lab research is clearly impossible due to the unique context, and thus use of a pre-analysis plan is valuable.

Olken (2015) as well as Coffman and Niederle (2015) discuss another potential way to address publication bias and specification search: results-blind review. Scholars in psychology have championed this method; studies that are submitted to such review are often referred to as "registered reports" in that discipline. Authors write a detailed study protocol and pre-analysis plan, and before the experiment is actually run and data are collected, submit the plan to a journal. Journals review the plan for the quality of the design and the scientific value of the research question, and may choose to give "in-principle acceptance." This can be thought of as a kind of revise and resubmit that is contingent on the data being collected and analyzed as planned. If the author follows through on the proposed design, and the data are of sufficiently high quality (e.g., with sufficiently low sample attrition rates in a longitudinal study, etc.), the results are to be published regardless of whether or not they are statistically significant, and whether they conform to the expectations of the editor or referees, or to the conventional wisdom in the discipline.

Dozens of journals currently have begun using results-blind review, either regularly or in special issues (Chambers 2013; Chambers et al. 2014; Nosek and Lakens 2014).[6] An issue of *Comparative Political Studies* was the first to feature results-blind review in political science (Findley et al. 2016), and it included both experimental and observational research studies.

---

[6] A list of journals that have adopted registered reports is available at: https://osf.io/8mpji/wiki/home/.

In our view, it would also be useful to experiment with results-blind review and registered reports in economics journals. *The Journal of Development Economics* announced a pilot of this type of submission in March 2018.[7] The rise in experimental studies and pre-analysis plans in economics, as evidenced by the rapid growth of the AEA registry, is likely to facilitate the eventual acceptance of this approach.

Observational Studies

An important open question is how widely the approach of study registration and hypothesis pre-specification could be usefully applied in non-prospective and non-experimental studies.

This issue has been extensively discussed in recent years within medical research but consensus has not yet been reached in that community. It actually appears that some of the most prestigious medical research journals, which typically publish randomized trials, are even more in favor of the registration of observational studies than the editors of journals that publish primarily non-experimental research (see the dueling editorial statements in *Epidemiology* 2010; *The Lancet* 2010; Loder, Groves, and MacAuley 2010; Dal-Ré et al. 2014).

A major logical concern with the pre-registration of non-prospective observational studies using pre-existing data is that there is often no credible way to verify that pre-registration took place before analysis was completed, which is different than the case of prospective studies in which the data have not yet been collected or accessed. In our view, proponents of the pre-registration of observational work have not formulated a convincing response to this obvious concern.

The earliest economics study of which we are aware that used a pre-analysis plan on non-experimental data was undertaken in Neumark (2001). Based on conversations with David Levine, Alan Krueger appears to have suggested to Levine, who was the editor of the *Industrial Relations* journal at the time, that multiple researchers could analyze the employment effects of an upcoming change in the federal minimum wage with pre-specified research designs, in a bid to eliminate "author effects," and that this could create a productive "adversarial collaboration" between authors with starkly different prior views on the likely impacts of the policy change (Levine 2001).

---

[7] See https://blogs.worldbank.org/impactevaluations/registered-reports-piloting-pre-results-review-process-journal-development-economics.

(The concept of adversarial collaboration – two sets of researchers with opposing theories coming together and agreeing on a way to test hypotheses before observing the data – is often associated with Daniel Kahneman; see, for example Bateman et al. 2005).

The US federal minimum wage increased in October 1996 and September 1997. Although Krueger ultimately decided not to participate, Neumark submitted a pre-specified research design consisting of the exact estimating equations, variable definitions, and subgroups that would be used to analyze the effect of the minimum wage on the unemployment of younger workers using October, November, and December Current Population Survey (CPS) data from 1995 through 1998. This detailed plan was submitted to journal editors and reviewers prior to the end of May 1997; the October 1996 data started to become available at the end of May 1997, and Neumark assures readers he had not looked at any published data at the state level prior to submitting his analysis plan.

The verifiable "time stamp" of the federal government's release of data indeed makes this approach possible, but the situation also benefits from the depth and intensity of the minimum wage debate prior to this study. Neumark had an extensive literature to draw upon when choosing specific regression functional forms and subgroup analyses. He tests two definitions of the minimum wage, the ratio of the minimum wage to the average wage (common in Neumark's previous work) as well as the fraction of workers who benefit from the newly raised minimum wage (used in David Card's earlier work, Card 1992a and Card 1992b), and tests both models with and without controls for the employment rate of higher-skilled prime-age adults (as recommended by Deere, Murphy, and Welch 1995). The results mostly fail to reject the null hypothesis of no effect of the minimum wage increase: only 18 of the 80 specifications result in statistically significant decreases in employment (at the 90-percent confidence level), with estimated elasticities ranging from –0.14 to –0.3 for the significant estimates and others closer to zero.

A more recent study bases its analysis on Neumark's exact pre-specified tests to estimate the effect of minimum wages in Canada and found larger unemployment effects, but they had access to the data before estimating their models and did not have an agreement with the journal, so the value of this "pre-specification" is perhaps less clear (Campolieti, Gunderson, and Riddell 2006). In political science, a pre-specified observational analysis measured the effect of the immigration stances of Republican representatives on their 2010 election outcomes (Monogan 2013).

It is difficult to see how a researcher could reach Neumark's level of pre-specified detail with a research question with which they were not already intimately familiar. It seems more likely that in a case where the researcher was less knowledgeable they might either pre-specify with an inadequate level of detail, or choose an inappropriate specification; this risk makes it important that researchers should not be punished for deviating from their pre-analysis plan in cases where the plan omits important details or contains errors, as argued in Casey et al. (2012) .

It seems likely to us that the majority of observational empirical work in economics will continue largely as is for the foreseeable future. However, for important, intensely debated, and well-defined questions, it would be desirable in our view for more prospective observational research to be conducted in a pre-specified fashion, following the example in Neumark (2001). Although pre-specification will not always be possible, the fact that large amounts of government data are released to the public on regular schedules, and that many policy changes are known to occur well in advance (such as in the case of the anticipated federal minimum-wage changes discussed above, with similar arguments for future elections), will make it possible for the verifiable pre-specification of research analysis to be carried out in many settings.

Comparisons to other research fields. Another frontier topic in this realm is the use of pre-specified algorithms, including machine learning approaches, rather than exact pre-analysis plans for prospective studies. For instance, the exact procedure to be used to determine which covariates should be included in order to generate the most statistically precise estimates can be laid out in advance, even if those covariates are unknown (and unknowable) before the data have been collected. This approach has not yet been widely adopted in economics (to our knowledge), but has begun to be used in medical trials and biostatistics (van der Laan et al. 2007; Sinisi et al. 2007).

A proposal related to, but slightly different than, pre-analysis plans is Nobel Prize-winning physicist Saul Perlmutter's suggestion for the social sciences to use "blind analysis" (MacCoun and Perlmutter 2015). In blind analysis, researchers add noise to the data while working with it and running the analysis, thus preventing them from knowing which way the results are turning out, and thus either consciously or unconsciously biasing their analysis, until the very end, when the noise is removed and the final results are produced. This technique is apparently quite common in experimental physics (Klein and Roodman 2005), but we are not aware of its use in economics or other social sciences.

Major differences are also beginning to emerge in the use of pre-analysis plans, and in the design and interpretation of experimental evidence more broadly, among economists versus scholars in other fields, especially health researchers, with a much greater role of theory in the design of economics experiments. Economists often design experiments to shed light on underlying theoretical mechanisms, to inform ongoing theoretical debates, and measure and estimate endogenous behavioral responses. These behavioral responses may shed light on broader issues beyond the experimental intervention at hand, and thus could contribute to greater external validity of the results. As a result, pre-analysis plans in economics are often very detailed, and make explicit reference to theoretical models. For example, Bai et al. (2015) pre-registered the theoretical microeconomic model and detailed structural econometric approach that they planned to apply to a study of commitment contracts in the Indian health sector.

This distinction between the types of studies carried out by medical researchers versus economists (including those working on health topics) has a number of important implications for assessing the reliability of evidence. One has to do with the quality standards and perceptions of the risk of bias in a particular design. For medical trialists accustomed to the CONSORT standards or other medical efficacy trial reporting guidelines (described below), studies that do not feature double-blinding, and thus run the risk of endogenous behavioral responses to the medical intervention, are considered less reliable than those studies that employ double-blinding (for a detailed discussion, see Eble, Boone, and Elbourne 2014). While a few studies conducted by economists do feature double-blinding (e.g., Thomas et al. 2003, 2006), in nearly all settings blinding participants to their status is either logistically difficult (for instance, if government partners are unwilling to distribute placebo treatments to some of their population) or even impossible.

To illustrate, how would you provide a placebo treatment in a study investigating the impact of the distribution of cash transfers on household consumption patterns? Even in settings that might seem promising for placebo treatments, such as the community-level deworming treatments discussed in Miguel and Kremer (2004), blinding participants to their status is basically impossible: deworming generates side effects (mainly gastrointestinal discomfort) in roughly 10 percent of those who take the pills, so community members in a placebo community would quickly deduce that they were in fact not receiving real deworming drugs if there are few or no local cases of side effects.

As noted above, endogenous behavioral responses are often exactly what we economists (and other social scientists) set out to measure and estimate in our field experiments, as described in our pre-analysis plans, and thus are to be embraced rather than rejected as symptomatic of a "low-quality" research design that is at "high risk of bias." Taken together, it is clear to us that the experimental literature in economics (and increasingly in other social sciences such as political science) often has very different objectives than medical, public health, and epidemiological research, and thus different research methodologies are often called for. Despite the value of learning from recent experience in biomedical research, and the inspiration that the experience of medical research has played to the rise of new experimental research methods in the social sciences, economists have not simply been able to import existing medical trial methods wholesale, but are developing new and tailored approaches to pre-registration, pre-analysis plans, reporting standards, and transparency more broadly.

Disclosure and Reporting Standards

Another approach to promoting transparency is to establish detailed standards for the disclosure of information regarding study design, data, and analysis. These could serve to limit at least some forms of data mining and specification searching, or at least might make them more apparent to the reader.

Detailed reporting standards have become widespread in medical research for both experimental and observational research. Most notably for clinical trials, the Consolidated Standards of Reporting Trials (CONSORT) was developed (Begg et al. 1996). A before-and-after comparison showed improvement in some measures of study reliability (Moher et al. 2001), and the standards have been twice revised (Moher, Schulz, and Altman 2001; Schulz et al. 2010) and since extended to at least ten specific types of research designs, interventions, or data. Among others, and possibly particularly relevant for some types of economics research, these include cluster randomized trials (Campbell, Elbourne, and Altman 2004; Campbell et al. 2012), non-pharmacological treatment interventions (Boutron et al. 2008), and patient-reported outcomes (Calvert et al. 2013). In addition to the requirement by the International Committee of Medical Journal Editors (ICMJE, a group comprised of editors of top medical journals such as the *British Medical Journal, The Lancet, JAMA*, etc.) that randomized trials be registered in a registry such as clinicaltrials.gov, it is now standard that these journals require authors to include a completed CONSORT checklist at the time of article submission.[8]

Observational research in epidemiology is increasingly subject to its own set of guidelines, the so-called Strengthening the Reporting of Observational Studies in Epidemiology, or STROBE, standards (von Elm et al. 2007). In fact, developing reporting guidelines is a growth industry in medical research: at least 284 sets of guidelines have been developed for different types of health research. To deal with the proliferation of reporting standards, the Equator Network has been established to organize these guidelines and help researchers identify the most appropriate set of guidelines for their research.[9]

There are obviously very strong, and well understood, norms regarding how to report empirical results in economics studies, but there are far fewer formal guidelines or reporting checklists than in medical research. One exception is the AEA policy, announced in January 2012,[10] that its journals would require disclosure statements from authors regarding potential conflicts of interest. The AEA journals enforced the policy in July 2012, and the NBER working paper series has since adopted a similar set of required disclosures.[11] It appears the economics discipline may have been shamed into adopting these conflict-of-interest policies, at least in part, by the scathing Academy Award-winning documentary "Inside Job," which argued that some leading economists with strong (and often undisclosed) ties to the financial services industry were at least somewhat complicit in promoting policy choices that contributed to the 2008 global financial crisis (Casselman 2012).

Despite recent progress on conflict-of-interest disclosure, there has been less change within economics regarding other forms of disclosure or reporting guidelines. The only set of disclosure guideline specific to economics that we are aware of is the Consolidated Health Economic Evaluation Reporting Standards (CHEERS), although these appear to be more widely followed in health than in economics (Husereau et al. 2013). In this regard, there has been less movement within economics than in other social sciences, including political science, where a section of the American Political Science Association

---

[8] See, for example, www.icmje.org/recommendations/browse/manuscript-preparation/preparing-for-submission.html#two and http://jama.jamanetwork.com/public/instructionsForAuthors.aspx#Clinical Trials.

[9] Equator: Enhancing the Quality and Transparency of Health Research; see www.equator-network.org/.

[10] See www.aeaweb.org/PDF_files/PR/AEA_Adopts_Extensions_to_Principles_for_Author_Disclosure_01-05-12.pdf.

[11] See www.aeaweb.org/aea_journals/AEA_Disclosure_Policy.pdf and www.nber.org/researchdisclosurepolicy.html.

has developed guidelines for reporting of experimental research (Gerber et al. 2014). The American Political Science Association has formed committees that resulted in the Data Access and Research Transparency (DART) statement, which APSA adopted in both its Ethics Guide and Journal Editors' Transparency Statement, with 27 journals choosing to enact data sharing, data citation, and analytical methods sharing standards starting January 15, 2016.[12]

In psychology, researchers have created an extension of CONSORT for social and psychological interventions (CONSORT-SPI) (Montgomery et al. 2013; Grant et al. 2013). Others psychologists have proposed that an effective way to reform reporting and disclosure norms within their discipline is for referees to enforce desirable practices when reviewing articles (Simmons, Nelson, and Simonsohn 2011). These authors recommended six conditions for referees to consider.

1. Authors must decide the rule for terminating data collection before data collection begins and report this rule in the article.
2. Authors must collect at least 20 observations per cell or else provide a compelling cost-of-data-collection justification.[13]
3. Authors must list all variables collected in a study.
4. Authors must report all experimental conditions, including failed manipulations.
5. If observations are eliminated, authors must also report what the statistical results are if those observations are included.
6. If an analysis includes a covariate, authors must report the statistical results of the analysis without the covariate.

These disclosure rules are further simplified into a simple 21-word solution to be used by authors: "We report how we determined our sample size, all data exclusions (if any), all manipulations, and all measures in the study" (Simmons, Nelson, and Simonsohn 2012). There is a corresponding statement to be used by reviewers: "I request that the authors add a statement to the paper confirming whether, for all experiments, they have reported all measures, conditions, data exclusions, and how they determined their sample sizes. The authors should, of course, add any additional text to ensure

---

[12] See www.dartstatement.org.
[13] It is now widely acknowledged, including by the authors themselves, that 20 is typically far too few. More generally, this sort of ad hoc sample size guideline seems difficult to justify as a blanket rule across all settings.

the statement is accurate. This is the standard reviewer disclosure request endorsed by the Center for Open Science (see http://osf.io/project/hadz3). I include it in every review."[14]

Recently, we, the authors of this article, were part of an interdisciplinary group of researchers that developed a detailed set of journal guidelines called the Transparency and Openness Promotion (TOP) Guidelines (Nosek et al. 2015). This modular set of guidelines for journals features eight categories, namely: citation standards, data transparency, analytic methods (code) transparency, research materials transparency, design and analysis transparency, preregistration of studies, preregistration of analysis plans, and replication – with four levels (0–3) of transparency that journals could choose to endorse or require. For example, with regards to data transparency, the level-0 standard is that the journal either encourages data sharing or says nothing, while the level-3 standard is that "data must be posted to a trusted repository, and reported analyses will be reproduced independently prior to publication"; levels 1 and 2 fall somewhere in between. Journals could choose to adopt higher standards in some categories than others, as they feel most appropriate for their research community.

In the six months after the guidelines were published in *Science*, 538 journals and 57 organizations across a wide variety of scientific disciplines, including many in the social sciences, expressed their support for the standards and agreed to evaluate them for potential adoption. *Science* has now announced that it will be implementing the standards, effective January 1, 2017 (McNutt 2016). However, none of the leading economics journals have yet chosen to endorse or implement the guidelines; we encourage economics and other social science journal editors to review the guidelines and seriously consider adopting high transparency and reproducibility standards for their journals, keeping in mind that the TOP standards are meant to be modular rather than one-size-fits-all.

One last issue is worth a brief mention. Another important dimension of research transparency related to disclosure has to do with the presentation of data and results in tables, figures, and other display items. There is a flourishing literature on effective data visualization approaches, much of it inspired by the seminal work of political scientist Edward Tufte (2001). While beyond the scope of this survey article, we refer interested readers to Gelman, Pasarica, and Dodhia (2002) and Schwabish (2014) for detailed discussions.

---

[14] See http://centerforopenscience.github.io/osc/2013/12/09/reviewer-statement-initiative/.

Fraud and Retractions

Building on the discussion from Chapter 6, it appears that the formulation of explicit social science journal standards for article retraction, and clearer communication on journal websites stating when an article is retracted, could also be beneficial. The RePEC tracking of offenses, mentioned in Chapter 6, is a helpful but only partial start. In political science, Laitin and Reich (2017) published a call to action, arguing for a more proactive approach of strong disciplinary norms and internal policing with improved graduate education, journal practices, and disciplinary practices, in the hopes that this could avoid future situations like the "Inside Job" documentary or the fraud uncovered in (Broockman, Kalla, and Aranow 2015).

There is mounting evidence from other research fields that could help inform the creation of new standards in economics. Evidence from article retractions catalogued in PubMed show that the rate of retractions in medical research is on the rise. Articles appear to be retracted sooner after publication, and it is not the case that fraud represents an increasing proportion of reasons for retractions (Steen 2010; Steen, Casadevall, and Fang 2013).With tracking of offenses, researchers can use the Retraction Index (simply the fraction of retracted articles per 1000 papers published in a journal) which Fang and Casadevall (2011) show to be positively correlated with journal impact factor.

Optimistically, perhaps, Fanelli (2013) argues that the evidence of an increasing rate of retractions points toward a stronger system, rather than an increasing rate of fraud. This claim is based on the fact that, though the rate of retractions is increasing, the rate of article corrections has not; that despite the increasing proportion of journals issuing retractions, the rate of retractions per-retracting journal has not increased; and that despite an increase in allegations made to the US Office of Research Integrity, the rate of misconduct findings has not increased.

Researchers have also developed novel statistical tools that one can use to detect fraud, using the fact that humans tend to drastically underestimate how noisy real data are when they are making up fraudulent data. Simonsohn (2013) used this forensic technique after observing summary statistics that were disturbingly similar across treatment arms to successfully combat fraud in psychology, resulting in the retraction of several papers by two prominent scholars.

Another potentially useful tool is post-publication peer review. Formalizing post-publication peer review puts us in relatively uncharted waters. Yet it is worth noting that all four of the AEA's *American Economic Journals* allow for comments to appear on every article's official webpage post-publication (anonymous comments are not allowed). The feature does not appear to be widely used, but in one case, Lundqvist, Dahlberg, and Mörk (2014), comments placed on the website have actually resulted in changes to the article between its initial online pre-publication and the final published version, suggesting that this could be a useful tool for the research community to improve the quality of published work in the future.[15]

Open Data and Materials, and Their Use for Replication

There has clearly been considerable progress on the sharing of the data and materials necessary for replication since the famous 1980s *Journal of Money, Credit, and Banking* project mentioned above. Today, all American Economic Association journals require sharing of data and code to at least make replication theoretically possible (Glandon 2010). The Data Access and Research Transparency (DART) Statement (www.dartstatement.org) was also widely adopted in political science. However, many leading journals in economics only recently introduced similar requirements, most notably the *Quarterly Journal of Economics*, and even when journal data sharing policies exist, they are rarely enforced in a serious way (McCullough, McGeary, and Harrison 2008; anderson et al. 2008). Authors can share the bare minimal final dataset necessary to generate the tables in the paper – all merging, cleaning, and removal of outliers or observations with missing data already done. Stripping this dataset of any additional variables not used in the final analysis would meet journal sharing requirements, and is certainly a big step forward relative to sharing no data at all, but it does limit the usefulness of the dataset for other researchers hoping to probe the robustness of the published results, extend the analysis, or utilize the data for other purposes.

This means that in practice, we economists as a discipline are still in a situation in which replication attempts for most empirical studies are still relatively costly in terms of time and effort. Despite improved (if still imperfect) data availability, we also know of no mainstream journal in economics that systematically tests that submitted data and code to actually produce the claimed results as a pre-condition of publication. An interesting new movement hoping to change this is the Peer Reviewer's Openness Initiative, whereby researchers can pledge that after a certain date (January 1, 2017) they

---

[15] www.aeaweb.org/articles.php?doi=10.1257/pol.6.1.167.

will begin to require data sharing in the articles they referee (Morey et al. 2015).[16] If journal reviewers demand en masse to have access to the code and data that generated the results, and new norms develop around this expectation, this might lead to rapid changes in data sharing practices, given the central role that journal publication plays in scholars' individual professional success and standing.

As discussed above, the imprecise definition of the term "replication" itself often leads to confusion (Clemens 2017). Clarification of what authors mean when they say a replication "failed" (can the data not even produce the published results, are they not robust to additional specifications, or does a new sample or extended dataset produce different results?) may be an important first step to mainstreaming replication research within the social sciences.

Some economists have advocated for a *Journal of Replication* (and as many have called for a *Journal of Null Results*), including recently Coffman and Niederle (2015) and Zimmermann (2015), but the low status that would likely accompany these journals could limit submission rates and doom them to failure. In lieu of this, several alternative solutions have been proposed. Hamermesh (2007) urges top journals to commission a few replications per year from top researchers, on a paper of the authors' choice, with acceptance guaranteed but subject to peer review (not by the original author, though they would be allowed to respond).

In psychology, Nosek, Spies, and Motyl (2012) are also skeptical of creating new journals devoted to replications or null results, and instead suggest crowdsourcing replication efforts. This seems have to been extremely successful, with two large-scale replication efforts in which many researchers worked together to repeat classic experiments in psychology with new samples, the Many Labs project (Klein et al. 2014) and the Replication Project: Psychology (Open Science Collaboration 2012, 2015). Both were published in prominent journals and widely covered in the popular media. A similar project in cancer biology is ongoing.[17]

The Many Labs project sought to reproduce 13 effects found in the literature, testing them in 36 samples with a total sample size of 6344, and determining whether online samples produced different effects than lab samples, and also comparing international to US samples. They find that two types of

---

[16] For more information, see http://opennessinitiative.org.
[17] http://elifesciences.org/collections/reproducibility-project-cancer-biology.

interventions failed to replicate entirely, while results for other replications relative to the original studies were more nuanced.

The Replication Project: Psychology (RPP) team repeated the experiments of 100 previous effects, finding that only 47 percent of the replications produced results in the original 95-percent confidence interval, and subjectively considered 39 percent of the original findings to have successfully been "reproduced."

Some in psychology have taken issue with the claims of the RPP, most notably Gilbert et al. (2016), which argues that differences in implementation between original and replication experiments were inappropriate and introduces noise in addition to the expected sampling error. When taking this into account, one should actually expect the relatively low reported replication rate, and they thus argue there is no replication crisis. Some of the original RPP authors respond that differences between original and replication studies were in fact often endorsed by original study authors and take issue with the statistical analysis in Gilbert et al. (Anderson et al. 2016).

Simonsohn (2015) engages in further discussion of how one should evaluate replication results, suggesting that powering a replication based on the effect size of the original study is problematic, and to distinguish the effect size from zero, replications (at least in psychology, with their typically small sample and effect sizes) should have a sample at least 2.5 times as large as the original. An optimistic take by Patil, Peng, and Leek (2016) suggests that researchers should compare the effect in the replication study to a "prediction interval" defined as $\hat{r}_{orig} \pm z_{0.975} \sqrt{\frac{1}{n_{orig}-3} + \frac{1}{n_{rep}-3}}$ where $\hat{r}_{orig}$ is the correlation estimate in the original study, n_{orig} and n_{rep} are the sample sizes in the original and replication studies, respectively, and $z_{0.975}$ is the 97.5-percent quantile of the normal distribution, which incorporates uncertainty in the estimates from both the original and replication study. Applying this approach leads to much higher estimates of study replication (75 percent) for the RPP.

Economists may be interested to know that the researchers behind the RPP also included a prediction market in their project, and the market did a fairly good job of predicting which of the effects studies would ultimately be reproduced (Dreber et al. 2015). Unlike the prediction market in Camerer et al. (2016), the RPP prediction market outperformed a survey of researcher beliefs.[18]

---

[18] For related research on expert predictions, see DellaVigna and Pope (2016). Other psychology researchers have tried another way to crowdsource replication: instead of bringing different research

Despite the inability to replicate so many prominent empirical papers in economics (discussed above), there have been few systematic effort to replicate findings, with one exception in addition to Camerer et al. (2016) being the new 3ie replication program for development economics studies, which has replicated a handful papers to date, including one by an author of this article.[19] Few economics journal editors specifically seek to publish replications, and even fewer are willing to publish "successful" replications, i.e., papers that demonstrate that earlier findings are indeed robust, with the *Journal of Applied Econometrics* being a notable exception (Pesaran 2003). Despite the value to the research enterprise of more systematic evidence on which empirical results are actually reliable, and the fact that many scholars have advocated for changes in this practice over the years with a near-constant stream of editorials (see among others Kane 1984; Mittelstaedt and Zorn 1984; Fuess 1996; Hunter 2001; Camfield and Palmer-Jones 2013; Duvendack and Palmer-Jones 2013; Duvendack, Palmer-Jones, and Reed 2015; Zimmermann 2015), as yet there has been little progress within the economics profession toward actually publishing replication studies on a more general basis (Andreoli-Versbach and Mueller-Langer 2014). In many ways, the patterns in economics are similar to those in the other social sciences, particularly in political science, where prominent voices have long spoken out in favor of replication, but their publication remains rare (King 1995; Gherghina and Katsanidou 2013).

Computational Issues

Scholars' ability to carry out replications and share data has been facilitated by new software and computational improvements. Some of these advances are described in Koenker and Zeileis (2009). They discuss what has come to be called Claerbout's principle: "An article about computational science in a scientific publication is not the scholarship itself, it is merely advertising of the scholarship. The actual scholarship is the complete software development environment and the complete set of instructions which generated the figures." Koenker and Zeileis recommend version control, using open-source

---

groups together to all independently run the same classic experiment, other researchers have independently analyzed the same observational dataset and attempted to answer the same question, in this case, the question of whether darker skin-toned soccer players receive more red cards as a result of their race, conditional on other factors (Silberzahn and Uhlmann 2015).

[19] www.3ieimpact.org/evaluation/impact-evaluation-replication-programme/.

programming environments when possible (including for document preparation), and literate programming, which is defined below.

Version control software makes it easier to maintain detailed record-keeping of changes to statistical code even among multiple collaborators. Koenker and Zeileis discuss one such centralized system, Subversion (SVN, http://subversion.apache.org), but in recent years distributed forms of version control such as Git have become more widely used, and are well supported by a user community.[20]

For document preparation, Koenker and Zeleis discuss LaTeX, which has a steep learning curve but has the advantage of being open-source, and has the ability to intermix, or "weave" text, code, and output. Even more recently, dynamic documents (which Koenker and Zeileis refer to as literate programming; see also Knuth 1992) can be used to write statistical analysis code and the final paper all in a single master document, making it less likely that copying and pasting between programs will lead to errors, and making it possible in some cases to reproduce an entire project with a single mouse click. The knitr package for R, incorporated into R Studio, makes this relatively easy to implement (Xie 2013, 2014). Jupyter notebooks (http://jupyter.org) also simplifies interactive sharing of computational code with over 40 popular open-source programming languages (Shen 2014). Many programs that accommodate these approaches, including R, Python, and Julia, are open-source, making it easier for members of the research community to look under the hood and possibly reduce the risk of the software computational errors documented in McCullough and Vinod (2003).[21] Computational aspects of reproducibility are discussed at length in Stodden, Leisch, and Peng (2014).

The Limits of Open Data

While we believe that the social sciences as a whole would benefit from stronger data sharing requirements and more widespread publication of

---

[20] For a how-to manual on version control and other reproducibility tools, see Matthew Gentzkow and Jesse Shapiro's Practioner's Guide at http://web.stanford.edu/~gentzkow/research/CodeAndData.pdf or the Best Practices Manual by Garret Christensen at https://github.com/garretchristensen/BestPracticesManual.

[21] The recommendations regarding checking the conditions of Hessians for non-linear solving methods proposed by McCullough and Vinod (2003) are quite detailed, and were modified after omissions were brought to light. See Shachar and Nalebuff (2004); Drukker and Wiggins (2004); McCullough and Vinod (2004).

replication research, there are also potential downsides to data sharing that cannot be ignored. Technological innovations, and in particular the explosion in Internet access over the past 20 years, have made the sharing of data and materials much less costly than was the case in earlier periods. However, the rise of "big data," and in particular the massive amounts of personal information that are now publicly available and simple to locate online, also mean that open data sharing raises new concerns regarding individual confidentiality and privacy.

For instance, it has been shown in multiple instances that it is often trivially easy to identify individuals in purportedly "de-identified" and anonymous datasets using publicly available information. In one dramatic illustration, MIT computer science PhD student Latanya Sweeney sent then-Massachusetts Governor William Weld his own complete personal health records only days after anonymized state health records were released to researchers (Sweeney 2002). A new focus of computer science theorists has been developing algorithms for "differential privacy" that simultaneously protect individual privacy while allowing for robust analysis of datasets. They have established that there is inherently a trade-off between these two objectives (Dwork and Smith 2010; Heffetz and Ligett 2014), though few actionable approaches to squaring this circle are currently available to applied researchers, to our knowledge.

Future Directions and Conclusion

The rising interest in transparency and reproducibility in the social sciences reflects broader global trends regarding these issues, both among academics and beyond. As such, we argue that "this time" really may be different than earlier bursts of interest in research transparency within economics (such as the surge of interest in the mid-1980s following Leamer's 1983 article) that later lost momentum and mostly died down.

The increased institutionalization of new practices – including through the AEA RCT registry, which has rapidly attracted thousands of studies, many employing pre-analysis plans, something unheard of in economics until a few years ago – is evidence that new norms are emerging. The rise in the use of pre-analysis plans has been particularly rapid in certain subfields, especially development economics, pushed forward by policy changes promoting pre-analysis plans in the Jameel Poverty Action Lab, Innovations for Poverty Action, and the Center for Effective Global Action. Interest in pre-analysis plans, and more broadly in issues of research transparency and openness, appears to be particularly high among PhD students and younger faculty (at least anecdotally), suggesting that there may be a generational shift at work.

The Berkeley Initiative for Transparency in the Social Sciences (BITSS) is another institution that has emerged in recent years to promote dialogue and build consensus around transparency practices. BITSS has established an active training program for the next generation of economists and other social scientists, as well as an award to recognize emerging leaders in this area, the Leamer-Rosenthal Prize for Open Social Science.[22] Other specialized organizations have also emerged in economics: the Replication Network aims promote the publication of replication studies, Project TIER has developed a curriculum to teach computational reproducibility to economics undergraduates, and MAER-NET has developed guidelines for meta-analysis (Stanley et al. 2013). Similar organizations play analogous roles in other disciplines, including the Center for Open Science (COS), which is most active within psychology (although it spans other fields), and the Evidence in Governance and Politics (EGAP) group.[23]

At the same time, we have highlighted many open questions. The role that pre-analysis plans and study registration could or should play in observational empirical research – which comprises the vast majority of empirical economics work, even a couple of decades into the well-known shift toward experimental designs – as well as in structural econometric work, macroeconomics, and economic theory remains largely unexplored. There is also a question about the impact that the adoption of these new practices will ultimately have on the reliability of empirical research in economics. Will the use of study registries, pre-analysis plans, disclosure statements, and open data and materials lead to improved research quality in a way that can be credibly measured and assessed? To this point, the presumption among advocates (including ourselves, admittedly) is that these changes will indeed lead to improvements, but rigorous evidence on these effects, using meta-analytic approaches or other methods, will be important in determining which practices are in fact most effective, and possibly in building further support for their adoption in the profession.

There are many potential avenues for promoting the adoption of new and arguably preferable practices, such as the data sharing, disclosure, and

---

[22] www.bitss.org. In the interest of full disclosure, Miguel is one of the founders of BITSS and currently its faculty director, and Christensen worked as a post-doctoral research fellow at BITSS. BITSS is an initiative of the Center for Effective Global Action at UC Berkeley.

[23] http://cos.io; www.egap.org.

pre-registration approaches described at length in this chapter. One issue that this chapter does not directly address is how to most effectively – and rapidly – shift professional norms and practices within the empirical social science research community. Shifts in graduate training curricula,[24] journal standards (such as the Transparency and Openness Promotion Guidelines), and research funder policies might also contribute to the faster adoption of new practices, but their relative importance remains an open question. The study of how social norms among economists have shifted, and continue to evolve, in this area is an exciting social science research topic in its own right, and one that we hope is also the object of greater scholarly inquiry in the coming years.

---

[24] See http://emiguel.econ.berkeley.edu/teaching/12 for an example of a recent PhD-level course on research transparency methods at UC Berkeley taught by the authors.

8 Making Research Data Accessible

Diana Kapiszewski and Sebastian Karcher*

One of the key themes in this volume is that social science takes place in a community setting. As social scientists develop and answer their questions, they adhere to the norms and practices of their respective research communities. Over time, understandings of what being a responsible community member entails change. Today, members of social science communities are increasingly expected to provide access to the data they generate and use in their research (within ethical and legal constraints). Of course, discussions about openness in social science research have deep roots. In 1985, for example, statisticians Fienberg, Martin and Straf (1985:25) called for sharing data to become a regular practice. A decade later, political scientist King (1995) highlighted the importance of making available replication data and associated materials underpinning quantitative and qualitative research publications.

The last few years, however, have seen a marked acceleration in discussions about expanding access to research data across the social sciences – spurred on by broader technological and societal changes, as well as policy interventions by the White House, National Science Foundation, National Institutes of Health, and others. There is currently increasing momentum towards making openness the default position in social science research, and towards requiring that exceptions be based on established grounds. A key motivation for these discussions and this momentum is the belief that making data accessible impacts social science's ability to produce more credible and legitimate knowledge, and catalyzes scientific progress.

Data access delivers these benefits in at least three ways: by allowing for secondary analysis of data, by enhancing pedagogy and by supporting research transparency. Data that are accessible can be used for different analyses. Indeed, for some large-scale data collection projects (e.g., the American National Elections Studies (ANES) and the Varieties of Democracy (V-Dem)

---

* An earlier version of the chapter was co-authored with Colin Elman; his foundational ideas made a significant contribution to the final piece.

project), it is only the prospect of the data that are produced being shared that allows for the considerable investment of resources that data generation requires. Further, shared data can be used to enhance training in the types of techniques and methods that were used to generate and analyze the data. Practicing methods on actual research data or on stylized datasets produced for pedagogical purposes has long been the norm in teaching quantitative research methods, and the same practice can and should be used to teach qualitative methods.

Finally, authors can use data they make accessible to more fully show the basis for the claims and conclusions in their work, thus making their research more easily understood. Making available the data that underpin scholarship also facilitates evaluation of that work (e.g., through reproduction, replication, verification, confirmation, and other processes – see Freese and Peterson, Chapter 10, and Fairfield and Charman, Chapter 12, this volume). Such assessment increases the legitimacy and credibility of research publications (and thus the social scientific enterprise), and informs decisions about whether findings and conclusions offer a solid foundation on which subsequent inquiry, and potentially policy making, can be built. Put differently, the evaluation that access to research data facilitates can catalyze the accumulation of knowledge and the emergence of conversations and dialectics around scholarly work, linking innovation to confirmation, and discovery to appraisal.

This chapter argues that these benefits will accrue more quickly, and will be more significant and more enduring, if researchers make their data "meaningfully accessible." Data are meaningfully accessible when they can be interpreted and analyzed by scholars far beyond those who generated them. Making data meaningfully accessible requires that scholars take the appropriate steps to prepare their data for sharing, and avail themselves of the increasingly sophisticated infrastructure for publishing and preserving research data. The better other researchers can understand shared data and the more researchers who can access them, the more those data will be reused for secondary analysis, producing knowledge. Likewise, the richer an understanding an instructor and her students can gain of the shared data being used to teach and learn a particular research method, the more useful those data are for that pedagogical purpose. And the more a scholar who is evaluating the work of another can learn about the evidence that underpins its claims and conclusions, the better their ability to identify problems and biases in data generation and analysis, and the better informed and thus stronger an endorsement of the work they can offer.

We advance this argument in several steps. We begin by clarifying what we mean by "social science data" and briefly considering the contrast between qualitative and quantitative data. In the chapter's third section, we discuss – and seek to de-mystify – the preparatory steps scholars should take so their shared data are meaningfully accessible. We emphasize the utility of careful documentation for those who generate data and for those who reuse them, and highlight that few of the preparatory steps we discuss require work beyond what many would consider good scholarly practice. Next, we demonstrate the importance of utilizing emerging data infrastructure, offering a brief introduction to some recent innovations, and to the institutions and individuals responsible for these remarkable developments. Of course, the significant benefits that can accrue from making data meaningfully accessible will only materialize if large swaths of scientists do so. Thus, in the chapter's penultimate section we consider some institutional initiatives that could encourage more scholars to make their data accessible. We offer concluding thoughts in the final section.

What are "Data"?

Definitions of "data" or "research data" are plentiful. Some definitions point to content, such as the following widely cited definition by the National Research Council (1999): "Data are facts, numbers, letters, and symbols that describe an object, idea, condition, situation, or other factors." Alternatively, data can be defined by their use, e.g., as "information used in scientific, engineering, and medical research as inputs to generate research conclusions" (National Academy of Science et al. 2009). Given that almost any piece of information can be employed as data for some research project, we believe the latter definition is more useful. For the purpose of this chapter we define data as *any representations of the social world relevant to a particular type of inquiry and rendered in a form suited to the analysis to be undertaken.*[1] In short, data are the empirical building blocks of knowledge production. Data are thought of differently across academic disciplines, and depending upon research substance, goals and methods. Nonetheless, we believe this definition aptly describes the kinds of data considered in this chapter: those used in social science inquiry.

---

[1] Our definition is similar to that referenced by Borgman: "A reinterpretable representation of information in a formalized manner suitable for communication, interpretation, or processing" (2009:paragraph 25).

The second part of this definition serves, in the context of research, to distinguish data from information, and from data sources. Information in multiple undifferentiated forms is all around us constantly. For instance, it is trivially easy for laypersons to both contribute and receive information about the social world, whether on YouTube, Twitter, Facebook or on their personal webpages. This more general flow of information could certainly be *converted* into data for use in a particular research project. What differentiates data from information is that data have characteristics that make them useful for the generation of knowledge. Scholars gather or create data sources (an archival document, a focus group transcript) that contain information; that information becomes *data* when a researcher transforms it into something they can use to measure or analyze, for instance.

Perhaps the most common way to distinguish *types* of data is to differentiate between qualitative and quantitative data. Rather than entailing precise categories, this distinction is based on loose family resemblance and general bundles of characteristics. Quantitative data tend to be numeric, organized into a matrix and analyzed holistically using algorithmic/computational methods with the results represented in tabular form. Such data can also correspond directly to different levels of measurement (nominal, ordinal, interval and ratio). Qualitative data tend to be non-numeric, and are often analyzed individually (e.g., a particular interview quote or passage from an archival document) or in small groupings to underpin particular claims or conclusions that form part of arguments; they are thus often deployed across the span of a book or article.

Qualitative and quantitative data also have different evidentiary strengths and present different analytic opportunities. Consider, for instance, a freeform answer to the interview question "How do you feel about presidential candidate XY?" (qualitative) versus the numerical score recorded in response to a survey question such as, "I'd like you to rate how you feel about presidential candidate XY on a feeling thermometer using a scale of 0 to 100." The qualitative data offer a richer depiction of the respondent's attitude and can be used to bring alive or nuance the description of a political context. The quantitative response includes measurement of an underlying concept into a one-dimensional score that can be more easily compared across time and respondents.

Of course, "quantitative" and "qualitative" are not perfect categories.[2] After all, quantitative data are sometimes generated by quantifying qualitative

---

[2] One example of a more precise typology commonly used in the context of cyberinfrastructure categorizes data by origin: observational, experimental (resulting from lab or field experiments), computational (generated through executing a computer model or simulation), and records of public or private life (trace data) (National Science Board 2005).

(non-numeric) information. Likewise, "big" data are often "born" textual (qualitative), but converted to machine-analyzable form and made susceptible to algorithmic and computational organization and analysis. Nonetheless, given the familiarity and ubiquity in the social sciences of the quantitative/ qualitative distinction, we employ it here.

Making Data *Meaningfully* Accessible

Making research data accessible in a meaningful sense involves ensuring that they are understandable and interpretable by scholars other than those who generated them. Consensus is beginning to develop on a set of core attributes that well-provisioned social and natural (e.g., physical, biological) science data should have and on the kinds of information that should supplement them. Ensuring that research data are marked by these characteristics augments the value, quality, and usability of the data *for the scholar who generated them* as they use and reuse them over time. It also helps that scholar to decide what information to provide with their data to make them meaningfully accessible to others, and facilitates the provision of those materials – thereby increasing others' comprehension of, and thus ability to employ, shared data.

Creating detailed documentation is an indispensable part of making data accessible.[3] One key type of documentation is the data management plan (DMP), generally associated with a particular research project. A DMP, which scholars should begin to write as they start to design a project, is a formal document discussing how the data generated through the project will be handled (e.g., cleaned, verified, formatted and organized) as they are generated and analyzed, and once the project has concluded. Developing and following a DMP helps scholars to make the data they generate both a stronger empirical base for their own work, *and* more interpretable by others. DMPs are most useful when they are "living documents" – updated regularly to reflect changing needs and to record important decisions as a research project develops (see, e.g., Michener 2015). Ongoing work also aims to make DMPs machine-actionable (see Simms 2018). Machine-actionable DMPs would automate

---

[3] Creating documentation is also a critical aspect of data management. As discussed in the next section, data repositories can aid scholars in creating documentation; repositories also extract "metadata" (information about data creation and content) from that documentation and generate additional types of metadata (e.g., structural and administrative) that augment the accessibility of the data.

communication among key stakeholders such as researchers, research support staff, ethics boards, funders and repositories, facilitating alignment between IRB documents and without the quotes, and allowing researchers to more easily notify funders of compliance with funders' data sharing requirements, for instance. By automating information flow, machine-actionable DMPs can also augment efficiency by helping researchers to avoid duplicate metadata entry and reporting requirements.

More broadly, documenting data entails outlining various types of descriptive metadata (geography, time period, etc.) to characterize the data, detailing and justifying the multiple steps taken to generate the data, and assembling all relevant research tools (e.g., interview protocols, survey questionnaires). Discussing data generation entails clearly describing and rationalizing how information encountered in the social world was selected and collected (e.g., how the scholar decided where to focus, what to ignore, and what information to record and how); how collected information was interpreted and transformed; and what each step in the data-generation process implied for subsequent steps, and the project as a whole.[4]

Documentation almost always includes certain types of information (for example, date of collection). Yet how data are documented depends heavily on the nature of the data and how they were generated. For instance, there is consensus that scholars who produce survey data should provide details such as response rates, relevant patterns of non-response, and detailed description of the sampling framework (AAPOR 2017). Likewise, there is agreement that experimental researchers should offer information about the context of the experiment, all protocols, and the sampling framework (see, e.g., Druckman, Green, Kuklinski and Lupia 2011).

Beyond these baselines, however, there are few hard-and-fast rules; researchers should produce documentation that they believe will best bring their data alive for other scholars, and for their "future selves" as they re-use their data over time. We hasten to highlight again that many of the processes entailed in preparing data so they can be meaningfully accessible to others simply represent good data management practices, and basic aspects of conducting systematic social science research, in which many scholars *already* engage.

---

[4] To mention just a few suggestive ideas, scholars might discuss why particular secondary sources (and certain parts of those sources) were read; why particular political actors were interviewed and asked certain questions; or why the contents of certain boxes and folders were explored in an archive, certain documents perused, and certain passages identified as relevant – and whether information was collected by recording it in full (e.g., via audio taping or taking digital pictures), via paraphrasing, or some other way.

Exactly which data (and accompanying documentation) a scholar will make accessible depends on the goals of the research, the objective of data sharing, and attributes of the data. In large-scale, multi-researcher projects like ANES and V-Dem, the goal of making data accessible is inherent: such projects were intended from their inception to produce data for secondary analysis, i.e., to create a public good. These endeavors almost invariably require substantial external funding, which is often contingent on the data produced through the project being accessible to the social science community at large. In such projects, producing the documentation needed for others to effectively interpret and use the data is a central aspect of the project from the outset.

Much social science research data are not generated in the context of large-scale projects, however. Instead, individual scholars or small groups of scholars generate data with the primary goal of answering their own research question. The data produced through such efforts are often referred to as the "long tail" of science (e.g., Wallis, Rolando and Borgman 2013). In these scenarios, what data and documentation scholars will make accessible depends in part on the purposes for which they are doing so. The two most common purposes are to allow for secondary analysis of the data, and to increase the transparency of research.

Scholars who share data to allow for their secondary analysis make meaningfully accessible a coherent set or collection of data relevant to a particular project or theme. The data need not be tightly tied to any particular research publication. Sharing data so they can be analyzed by others represents an invaluable contribution to the production of knowledge. Nonetheless, this objective is sometimes underemphasized in the scholarly debate (particularly discussion about sharing qualitative data), which tends to focus on the feasibility and utility of making data accessible for the purpose of research transparency. Meaningfully accessible data serve as a multiplier for knowledge generation, and are of particular benefit to scholars in the United States and other countries who lack the resources to generate their own data; for many, meaningfully accessible data generated by others *are a prerequisite* for conducting research. Happily (if anecdotally), sharing data for secondary analysis seems to be occurring more frequently, perhaps due to increasing disciplinary recognition that data represent distinct products of value, to scholars' complying with funders' data-sharing mandates and to changing norms about best practices.

Scholars who make the data they generated accessible for the purposes of increasing the openness of publications based on those data aim instead to surface the scaffolding supporting the conclusions offered in those publications, making the analysis understandable and evaluable. In this scenario, the author provides just the data that underlie the published analysis. This may be the full dataset that they created or a subset thereof sufficient to evaluate the publication (called a "replication dataset" in quantitative analysis). If the two are different and the former is not publicly available, the author must provide complete documentation about the replication dataset and its creation – *in addition to* providing the supplemental analytic materials that are typically required for analytic transparency.

Which data scholars make accessible, and how accessible those data can be made, also depends on certain characteristics of the data, as discussed in more detail in the next section. Not all shared data are freely accessible. "Open data" are entirely unrestricted, i.e., accessible by anyone and with no or minimal restrictions on their reuse. The benefits for knowledge production of open data notwithstanding, legitimate limits on data access exist. For instance, data that are under copyright cannot be shared without permission from the copyright holder. Access to data may also be limited by the commercial arrangement under which they were obtained. Alternatively, data may only be available to scholars affiliated with institutional members of the particular repository at which they are housed. Here the restrictions are part of a business model, helping to cover the provider's costs. Removing such limitations, without providing alternative revenue streams, could undermine the sustainability of repositories that rely on a paywall model (Ember and Hanisch 2013; Hodson 2016). Further, the scholar who shared the data may have requested that access controls be imposed. This could occur, for instance, when the data were generated through interaction with human participants, are sensitive, and cannot be fully de-identified, meaning open access to the data could pose a risk to participants. While access controls appear to reduce data availability, in fact they allow data sharing when it would otherwise be impossible.

In sum, no matter for what purpose data are shared, or what limits ethics and the law may place on sharing, making data meaningfully accessible requires thorough and informative documentation of the type we have described. Yet a sobering caveat on the relationship between data accessibility and the production of knowledge bears noting. Research data can only be used to produce knowledge (understood as comprising truth claims) if the data accurately capture/reflect empirical reality. Absent repeating the data generation process (i.e., without comparing the data to the empirical reality a scholar claims they reflect), the only way to gauge data's validity is by assessing the quality of the processes through which they were generated. But given the particularities of research, objectively evaluating data generation is difficult; moreover, people can describe data generation processes in ways that makes them appear more systematic than they were. Indeed, notorious cases of fraud, such as LaCour and Stapel, involved detailed descriptions of how data were (supposedly) collected. Moreover, even if data generation seems to have been systematic and robust, without seeking to re-generate the data, we cannot be sure that they reflect empirical reality. We return to this point later in the chapter.

Evolving Infrastructure for Data Accessibility

Making data meaningfully accessible requires that scholars avail themselves of the increasingly sophisticated technology and infrastructure that have been developing over the last decade to facilitate the uploading, storing, indexing, browsing and searching, and downloading of data and associated scholarly materials. Using that infrastructure also benefits scholars themselves, as storing data in institutionalized venues helps protect the data from damage and loss, increases the visibility of the data and thus their creators, and integrates them in credit-awarding systems through citation and other metrics. How the complex web of institutions and technicians who build the infrastructure for storing and transmitting data do so has a profound impact on how "FAIR" data can be (findable, accessible, interoperable and reusable; Wilkinson et al. 2016), and on how social science is undertaken, represented, and evaluated. The better scholars understand how that infrastructure looks and works, the more effectively they can use it to make their data meaningfully accessible, and the more quickly data sharing will become routine.

Venues for Sharing Data

Until recently, by far the most common way for scholars to make their data accessible was to indicate that the data and analysis code associated with a particular publication were available "by request." A popular blog chronicles corresponding requests to authors, many of them unsuccessful (https://politicalsciencereplication.wordpress.com/category/replication-correspondence/).[5] Another common method was and is for scholars to post

---

[5] Of course, "on request" arrangements can sometimes make data accessible. While an individual and potentially unrepresentative example, in Karcher and Steinberg (2013), one of us requested replication materials from six then recent studies and received data and code (which successfully replicated the papers' results) in every case. Nevertheless, even when they work as hoped, such ad hoc arrangements

data and code for their studies on their personal website. Such posting does initially allow easy access to data. However, this mode of sharing exposes data availability to "linkrot" (i.e., hyperlinks pointing to web resources that have become unavailable). For instance, more than half of the reproducibility links in articles published in the *American Political Science Review* between 2000 and 2013 could not be accessed in 2016 (Gertler and Bullock 2017:167). In part, this is due to individual researchers lacking the technical knowledge and resources to guarantee the accessibility and long-term preservation of their data when, for instance, their institutions change technologies or they change institutions.

Another option is to include data as supplementary material to journal articles, to be stored by the journal's publisher. While publishers have significant experience in preserving digital publications, they rarely extend their preservation promises and practices to supplementary material (see, e.g., Smit et al. 2011:43–44 for the broader landscape, and Butler and Currier 2017 for data in economics journals). They also exert greater effort to make the articles that appear in their journals easy to find and to cite than they do to make supplementary materials accessible. Given that data shared as supplementary materials can often be useful to other scholars, publishers handling those data without due attention to their careful preservation and indexing may do a disservice to the scientific enterprise.[6]

Dedicated repositories for publishing and preserving digital data are designed to avoid these pitfalls, and are multiplying. Broadly speaking, we can distinguish among three types of repositories: self-service repositories, which are typically open to all research data (and in some cases other materials); institutional repositories, which are operated by universities or other research institutions and accept pre-prints, working papers and, increasingly, research data generated by affiliates of that institution; and domain repositories, which focus on a specific discipline or group of disciplines (e.g., "social science" or "earth science") and provide specialized services for data commonly used in those disciplines.

---

cannot provide the benefits of data sharing via institutional venues with robust routines and systems for making data available.

[6] This is not as controversial a statement as it may seem. In 2010, the *Journal of Neuroscience* stopped accepting supplementary materials, declaring data repositories "vastly superior to supplemental material as a mechanism for disseminating data" (Maunsell 2010). Most large journal publishers, including Elsevier, Springer, Wiley, and PLoS, appear to agree, and now recommend data publication in repositories across all their journals (see Kratz and Strasser 2014 for a general discussion of this).

Self-Service Repositories

Self-service repositories are the newest type of venue; most were founded after 2000. Well-known examples include figshare (a for-profit company), Zenodo (run by CERN, the European Organization for Nuclear Research, and funded by the European Union) and Harvard Dataverse (run by the Institute for Quantitative Social Science at Harvard University). While hard to assess precisely,[7] the holdings of such venues probably comprise the largest number of individual datasets worldwide. For example, as of December 2018, figshare has more than 80,000 datasets, Harvard Dataverse holds 30,251 and Zenodo has 33,794.[8] Self-service repositories allow easy upload of data of any kind for all researchers. Both deposit and download are free of charge. While convenient and inexpensive, self-service repositories rely heavily on the expertise and efforts of depositors. Typically, deposits are either not reviewed/curated or are only minimally reviewed/curated by staff, and depositors are responsible for supplying cataloging information. Self-service repositories are commonly dedicated to "bit-level" preservation of data files, i.e., they guarantee that any deposited file can be accessed "as is" in the long-term, using multiple, geographically dispersed back-up copies. Generally, they neither check that files are valid (i.e., open correctly in the specified software) nor protect against file-format obsolescence (the inability to open old files with currently available software).

Institutional Repositories

Institutional repositories, most run by college and university libraries, have traditionally been more concerned with holding and making available the publications of their institutions' researchers than with facilitating access to the data underlying those scholars' research. However, recently many institutional repositories have begun to accept research data. Such repositories' proximity to the researchers depositing the data may increase researchers' trust, and allow for immediate contact. Moreover, as data librarians are likely to be a first point of contact for scholars with questions about DMPs, such venues can and do often provide researcher-repository contact across the lifecycle. Furthermore, libraries have significant expertise in the preservation of digital formats. Even at large research institutions, however, libraries (and thus institutional repositories) often lack the information technology and subject-specific capabilities

---

[7] Most venues host materials other than data, making it difficult to discern what exactly should be counted and how multiple versions are counted.

[8] Both Zenodo and figshare also hold figures, presentations, pre-prints, and other materials, so the total number of items in these repositories is significantly higher, e.g., around 3 million in figshare.

to provide curation, preservation, and dissemination guidance and services on par with domain repositories (see Johnston et al. 2017).

Domain Repositories

Domain repositories, which focus on a specific discipline or subject area, have the longest history of the venues considered here. With regard to the social sciences, the Inter-university Consortium for Political and Social Research (ICPSR), which began operations in 1962, is probably the most prominent domain repository of its type in the United States. Other examples include the Roper Center's public opinion archive (Cornell University), which dates to 1957, the Odum Institute's Data Archive (University of North Carolina, Chapel Hill), and the more recently established Qualitative Data Repository (QDR, Syracuse University) with which the co-authors of this chapter are affiliated. Some domain repositories are "trusted data repositories," a status conferred through a certification process. The most common certification among social science data repositories is the CoreTrustSeal (www.coretrustseal.org/).[9]

Domain repositories offer the broadest set of services and guidance to depositors, including data curation and preservation, and promoting deposited data and monitoring their use. One considerable strength of domain repositories is their curation services. Curation is a multi-stage process potentially entailing appraising and selecting certain data for publication from a large deposit, processing and storing the data, describing them with metadata, providing access, preserving and assessing reuse (Johnston 2017, vol. 2:xiii). Curation is facilitated by researchers engaging in proper data management, on which domain repositories often advise them. Curators may also assist researchers during the deposit process. Upon receiving files, curators perform a variety of checks and ensure that the files are in, or convert them to, a format that is suitable for long-term storage; files are then stored, together with information about the curation steps taken. In addition, to make data easy to find (encouraging reuse and citation), curators optimize the metadata associated with the data. In the social sciences, the most sophisticated metadata format, Data Documentation Initiative (DDI,

---

[9] To obtain CoreTrustSeal (CTS) certification, repositories provide in-depth documentation about their compliance with best practices in 16 areas under three broad headings: organization infrastructure, handling of digital objects, and technology. Their answers are peer reviewed; if they are approved, the repository is awarded certification. Currently, 39 data repositories hold CTS certification, 39 repositories hold Data Seal of Approval (DSA) certification (the pre-cursor to CTS), and 61 hold World Data System (WDS) certification. Among US social science repositories, ICPSR and the Odum Institute Data Archive hold the DSA certification; QDR and the Roper Center hold CTS certification. Other, more demanding certifications exist (e.g., the International Standardization Organization's standard 16363) but are rarely used.

http://ddialliance.org/), holds information about every variable in a quantitative dataset, allowing domain repository users to search for datasets by the text of individual variables.

Domain repositories are also commonly best equipped to store, preserve and provide access to sensitive data. Making research data accessible can be legitimately constrained by the need to respect the rights and protect the safety of the people who participated in the research (and, more broadly, sites of investigation) when participants have offered sensitive information or when they request that the information they conveyed remain confidential. Fortunately, information scientists are developing strategies, tools and technologies to facilitate making the information garnered through encounters with human participants more accessible in an ethical way, and domain repositories are capitalizing on these developments. Such repositories can aid researchers in assessing the risk involved in sharing that human participants have agreed to share. Repositories can also help researchers to develop a strategy to de-identify interview or focus group transcripts, field notes or other data sources resulting from human interaction, which can help to maintain confidentiality.[10]

Domain repositories also have (to differing degrees) the technological capacity to provide secure access to sensitive data. As mentioned previously, repositories generally allow depositors to place "access controls" on particular data files that limit who may view or download them and how they may do so. For instance, dedicated data security training or secondary IRB approval may be required before access is granted, or access may only be permitted from secure terminals or through dedicated secure connections. Domain repositories worldwide, in particular those overseeing large national studies with detailed observations on participants, also provide secure modes of remote access to sensitive materials.[11] Some offer tools that allows scholars to analyze quantitative data without fully accessing them, e.g., by allowing code execution on a remote server and screening output for potential privacy issues such as low cell counts in cross-tabs.[12]

---

[10] De-identification refers to removing from data and documentation direct identifiers (i.e., information that is sufficient, on its own, to disclose identify) and indirect identifiers (information that in combination with other available information may disclose identity). Some hold that it may be difficult, if not impossible, to fully de-identify some data; there are also clear tensions between de-identifying data and maintaining their analytic utility.

[11] An interesting development in this regard is the DataTags project (Bar-Sinai et al. 2016), which automates the handling of sensitive data, in particular the assessment of sensitivity and required protections of a given dataset. However, access requests and monitoring of compliance with usage restrictions still require human oversight.

[12] Scholars should begin considering ways to address ethical challenges to data accessibility – as well as legal constraints and proprietary obligations that may limit the amount of research data they can share – when they first begin to design the research projects, and should discuss them in their DMP.

Finally, domain repositories also play important roles in promoting the research data they hold, making them searchable (and findable), monitoring how they are used, and facilitating the awarding of credit to scholars who generate data (and whose data are used by others). Domain repositories link data to publications in which they are used and/or cited and showcase data holdings via blogposts, press releases and infographics.[13]

Hybrids

Other repositories – e.g., Dryad, UK Data's ReShare and OpenICPSR – assume a hybrid position. Dryad, which started out as a domain repository for biomedical data, now accepts data across disciplines, and performs curation services including metadata improvements and file reviews. Dryad curators are generalists, rather than domain specialists, so curation focuses more on the formal elements of data publication such as file integrity and de-identification. Re-Share and OpenICPSR are social science self-publishing repositories run by and alongside fully curated domain repositories. OpenICPSR is minimally curated, performing a metadata review after publication. Data published on ReShare benefit from reduced but still significant curation work, including several project-level checks and checks on a subset of submitted files.

Common Features

Despite these distinctions, all repositories perform a series of critical functions that aid scholars in making their data meaningfully accessible, establishing repositories as superior venues for storing and publishing data. For instance, most repositories can assign persistent identifiers such as Digital Object Identifiers (DOIs) to their data assets, enabling long-term access to digital resources and facilitating searchability.[14] The broader DOI system, i.e., the technical and social infrastructure for the registration and use of DOIs, provides metasearch functionality for repositories that issue DOIs. Using Datacite's metadata catalogue (search.datacite.org), researchers can search across all datasets that have a DOI. Once fully employed, the DOI system will greatly facilitate data generators receiving credit for the citation and reuse of

---

[13] For instance, users of ICPSR's "virtual enclave" can analyze data housed in the enclave but not retrieve data files (and ICPSR staff can review users' analysis outputs for disclosure risk).

[14] Outlets that publish data and other research products "register" the DOIs they assign, and deposit standardized metadata, with a registration agency. The oldest and largest such agency, CrossRef, mainly registers journal articles, books, and book chapters. DataCite focuses on datasets, and its metadata catalog (search.datacite.org) thus provides a powerful metacatalog of research data.

the data they generated and shared, and also significantly enhance scholars' ability to find data relevant to their work. CrossRef and DataCite are already collaborating to collect data on data citation in scholarly literature (www.scholix.org). Each time a dataset is cited in a work registered with CrossRef, the event is cataloged, establishing an automated citation count; a similar count system is used to catalog mentions of datasets on blogs or social media. Such "altmetrics" increasingly complement more traditional measures such as citation counts to assess the influence of data and the scholarly impact of work more generally (Costas, Zahedi and Wouters 2015).

Most repositories also allow the "harvesting" of their metadata through a dedicated protocol (Open Archives Initiative Protocol for Metadata Harvesting, OAI-PMH), facilitating the development of search interfaces covering many data repositories – so called meta-catalogs (similar to what Open Worldcat represents for books and Web of Science for journal articles). For example, the metadata of several social science repositories are included in the Dataverse Catalog, where users can find entries for all of ICPSR's, the Odum Institute's, Roper's and QDR's holdings.[15]

All repositories have staff, technical, and material costs that need to be covered in order for data to be curated and preserved (Ember and Hanisch 2013; Hodson 2016). Institutional repositories are obviously funded by the institution with which they are associated. Domain and hybrid repositories, as more independent entities, can face significant sustainability challenges. In many European countries such entities are considered fundamental to scientific infrastructure, and social science domain repositories (e.g., the UK Data Archive, GESIS in Germany and DANS in the Netherlands) are financed by permanent government support. Because government funding is more ad hoc in the United States, repositories must seek out other sources of support. Figshare, for instance, sells technical services to universities (i.e., it functions as a service provider for institutional repositories). The most common model, however, is for repositories to charge users (directly, or indirectly through establishing institutional memberships). As noted above, some repositories restrict *access* to data based on paid membership (e.g., ICPSR) while others charge depositors for the *curation* of data (e.g., Dryad, the Odum Institute Data Archive and QDR). Neither option is unproblematic. Charging for access violates increasingly strong norms of "open science" and "open data" by

---

[15] On perhaps the largest scale, Share (share.osf.io) harvests metadata on any research output from (as of this writing) 159 different sources and presents it in a metacatalog (where searches can be restricted to datasets).

making access contingent on the ability of a researcher's institution to afford membership (thus disadvantaging citizen scientists and researchers from less well-resourced institutions). Charging for curation may deter deposits and reinforce the same inequities.

Organizations that Support Data Infrastructure

The data infrastructure just described is embedded in a complex set of interlocking and overlapping stakeholder organizations that seek to develop and promulgate policy consensus on the handling of research data. Perhaps most directly relevant to and useful for social scientists (although less likely to set policy), IASSIST (the International Association for Social Science Information Services and Technology) provides a venue for exchange among social science data specialists, mainly from research libraries and repositories. Via an active listserv, IASSIST members discuss ongoing developments related to data infrastructure and help each other to answer data-related questions posed by members of their respective communities, thus putting an international network of data experts at the service of social science researchers.

A host of other organizations set policies and guidelines for the venues through which scholars make their data accessible, and are therefore also important for social science and social scientists, if indirectly so. The most influential research-data organization is the Research Data Alliance (RDA). Founded in 2013, today RDA has over 5,000 members and holds two well-attended meetings annually. In a sprawling net of interest groups and working groups, RDA is shaping policies that will have a significant impact on the management and sharing of research data. For example, two of the above-mentioned initiatives – the recent revision of the CoreTrustSeal guidelines and the Scholix project for collecting citation count data for DOIs – were developed under the auspices of RDA. Other working groups are currently finalizing recommendations for citation of complex data objects and licensing of data for cross-border exchange.

Another group that warrants mentioning is FORCE 11. Founded in 2011, FORCE 11 is dedicated to advancing scholarly communication – improving how "knowledge is created and shared," in the words of the organization's mission statement. Many of FORCE 11's activities are data related. It coordinated an influential declaration of data citation principles (www.force11.org/group/joint-declaration-data-citation-principles-final), which has since been endorsed by most scientific publishers, and is shaping requirements for data citation in scientific journals. Elsevier, Springer and Wiley – the world's three largest academic publishers – are pushing their journals to adapt data citation guidelines based on these recommendations.

Finally, Data-PASS (the Data Preservation Alliance for the Social Sciences) is a voluntary partnership of major US social science domain repositories. The principle goal of the alliance is a mutual guarantee of holdings: if a Data-PASS member ceases operations, other members agree to assume stewardship of its data. To facilitate this process, Harvard Dataverse contains a metadata catalog of the data holdings of most Data-PASS members. Data-PASS members also provide expertise and advocacy around data-related issues for social scientists and their organizations.

Data infrastructure helps researchers make and keep their data meaningfully accessible, and helps researchers find data. It helps scholars receive credit when their data are employed by others, and helps prevent data from being used inappropriately. Familiarity with the contours and function of that infrastructure and with the institutions that underpin it allows scholars to more effectively share and search for data. Built under the leadership of, and through cooperation among, scientist of all stripes – applied, behavioral, natural and social – that infrastructure is constantly adapting as the requirements of contemporary research evolve.

Catalyzing Access to Research Data

Over the last four decades – and during the last ten years in particular – significant progress has been made towards establishing data accessibility as a scholarly norm in the social sciences. Nonetheless, the substantial benefits that could potentially flow from greater data accessibility will only begin to accrue if more social scientists – and more scholars who generate and analyze qualitative data in particular – make their data meaningfully accessible. In this section we consider some steps that could be taken to support further movement towards that goal.

Multi-Stakeholder Conversation and Coordination

Continuing and accelerating the increasingly inclusive conversations that have emerged since 2010 about making research data accessible are critical.[16]

[16] Earlier literature from multiple scientific disciplines is a rich resource for such conversations, e.g., Mauthner, Parry and Backett-Milburn (1998); Bishop (2005, 2009, 2014); Parry and Mauthner (2004, 2005); Fielding (2004); Heaton (2008); Mauthner and Parry (2009); Corti et al. (2014); Yardley et al. (2014); Broom, Cheshire and Emmison (2009).

The more scholars engage each other in conversations about the challenges of sharing research data, the more quickly creative solutions to those challenges can be developed. Data access has been a crucial part of the groundbreaking Qualitative Transparency Deliberations (www.qualtd.net) in political science, for instance, and these discussions could form the basis of continuing debate. Engaging all of the research traditions that comprise each social science discipline will make it possible to develop solutions and standards that are appropriate for the very different styles of research that comprise each one, and to create guidance materials and other resources to aid scholars in meeting those standards.

These conversations should include leadership from social science's multiple academic associations, as well as its main gatekeepers – funders and publishers. Associations are uniquely positioned to reach scholars on all sides of each discipline's various divides from a relatively neutral standpoint. They could capitalize on that position to play a leading role in encouraging greater data access and catalyzing thoughtful discussion about how scholars can be motivated to make their data available. Funders and publishers are also well-positioned to encourage data access given their influence over the resources that support our research and the ways in which our results are disseminated (and scholarly work is rewarded).

Outreach to and partnership with the Institutional Review Board (IRB) community will also be decisive,[17] in particular given recent changes in the Common Rule.[18] Scholars from the social science community can help those involved in designing and implementing research review – members of university leadership, faculty who sit on such boards and administrators alike – to visualize the differences between medical research, hard science research and social science research. Such partnerships can also help IRB personnel to see the value of making research data meaningfully accessible. Discussions around providing template informed-consent protocols that offer varied options for handling and sharing the information conveyed through interactions with human participants, and around when and how the risks of

---

[17] One avenue to do so is through interacting with the PRIM&R (Public Responsibility in Medicine and Research) organization; founded in 1974, PRIM&R seeks to strengthen the community of research administration and oversight personnel, and offers opportunities for education and professional development (www.primr.org/).

[18] The Common Rule (1981) concerns ethics in biomedical and behavioral research involving human participants. It has been undergoing revision, and an amended version came into effect in January 2019.

sharing data can be mitigated, could be important first steps towards generating a culture of data sharing.

As they take on these challenges, stakeholders will benefit greatly from partnering with data repositories (and, through them, connecting with other stakeholders in the data management and infrastructure community). Repositories specialize in storing, publishing and preserving shared data and can thus offer invaluable assistance as stakeholders consider where and how they should encourage scholars to make their data accessible. Moreover, as repositories are experienced at interacting with scholars over their research data, association members, grantees and authors can benefit greatly from consulting with data repositories for advice about making data accessible.

The most fruitful conversations may result from all of these stakeholders working together – and with researchers – listening to each other's concerns, appreciating each other's ideas and developing shared standards and guidelines. There is undeniable value to stakeholders harmonizing their standards, for instance, by coordinating on a pre-existing solution such as the Center for Open Science's (COS) Transparency and Openness Promotion (TOP) Guidelines (https://cos.io/our-services/top-guidelines/). This sort of harmonization reduces the developmental burden on stakeholders, allows them to learn about implementation from each other, curtails inequities with the potential to skew researchers' incentives in unhealthy ways and makes it easier for scholars to develop practices to meet those consensual standards.

Shifting Incentives: Awarding Credit for Making Original Data Products Accessible

While these multi-stakeholder conversations will be wide-ranging, one key topic should be how disciplinary incentive structures can be shifted to revalue the processes of generating data and making them accessible. In most social science disciplines, textual publications (articles, chapters, books etc.) remain the coin of the realm. Acts of data generation, by contrast, are (implicitly) undervalued – perhaps due to a generalized bias towards appraisal over innovation. Certainly datasets (in particular quantitative datasets) that scholars develop can be and are listed on their CVs. However, datasets and research publications are not valued equally in merit review and promotion processes; in fact, datasets are sometimes simply included in the assessment of the publication they underlie rather than being considered a separate scholarly product.

As such, for many scholars, investing time and money in making the data they have generated meaningfully accessible may seem to simply syphon resources away from career-advancing activities.[19] More broadly, sharing research data may seem to introduce inefficiencies into the research process that disproportionately handicap some scholars, and put a drag on the collective production of knowledge (in the form of textual publications). In short, the perceived imbalance between the professional pay-off from, and the practical demands of, making data accessible may discourage scholars from sharing their research data.

Social science should take steps to foment greater appreciation for data generation activities (and their fruits). Data form the fuel that powers our research – they are the lifeblood of our scholarship. Considerable resources (both time and money), expertise and effort are required to generate data, and doing so represents an immense contribution (Lupia and Alter 2014). Shifting disciplinary reward and credit structures to revalue data generation will encourage individual scholars and teams of researchers to generate more data, and organically incentivize providing greater access to data (i.e., showcasing data generation). The greater availability of more research data could, in turn, lead to maximizing data's reuse potential becoming standard practice. Additional credit could then be awarded to those scholars who render their original data products meaningfully accessible.[20]

Since the possibility of measurement is a prerequisite for reward, perhaps the easiest transition would involve creating mechanisms for data-related activities and achievements to register on familiar accomplishment scales. For instance, published datasets (quantitative and qualitative) could be counted in review and evaluation processes as stand-alone research products rewarded independently from any related published articles, chapters and books. Further, bibliometrics (see Gerring, Karcher and Apfeld, Chapter 15, this volume) for datasets – systematic counts of how many times they are cited, downloaded and used – are being developed (e.g., www.scholix.org, makedatacount.org). There are also promising initiatives for recognizing when scholars share data in tandem with a publication; for instance, COS has created "badges" to acknowledge practices such as making the research data underlying a publication accessible in a persistent location.[21]

---

[19] This is particularly concerning when scholars fear that by sharing their data they will be "scooped" – that is, that another researcher will use those data as the basis of their own scholarship before the person who collected them has time to develop all of the scholarly products she wished to produce using the data.

[20] Data access could be encouraged via punishment (sticks) rather than incentives (carrots). We doubt the former would be salutary or effective: sticks often yield high levels of poor-quality compliance. We thus focus here on incentives.

[21] For those skeptical of the utility of using badges to signal open scholarship, COS references two studies that argue that such a system augments rates of data sharing; see Kidwell et al. (2016) and Rowhani-Farid et al. (2017).

Incentivizing scholars to make their data meaningfully accessible, however, requires more than simple counts. It entails establishing clear processes and flexible metrics to evaluate the quality of shared data and datasets and their documentation. Establishing clear criteria for distinguishing between high- and low-quality datasets and developing ways to fairly and systematically evaluate data quality – while undoubtedly complicated and challenging – could have multiple positive effects. For instance, doing so could help scholars to understand how to, and incentivize them to, produce robust data; it could also allow for the establishment of new awards and prizes for the generation and sharing of quantitative and qualitative datasets.[22]

Another way to draw attention to shared data would be to establish more "data journals" (such as Brill's *Research Data Journal for the Humanities and Social Sciences*) featuring short sophisticated essays discussing the generation and analysis of particular kinds of data or particular datasets, or critiques thereof. Journals publishing more replications (or venues specifically designated to do so) could also incentivize the generation and sharing of high-quality data.

Surfacing Data Reuse through Citation and Co-Authorship

If a key reason to make data meaningfully accessible is to facilitate their reuse by other scholars, another way to encourage researchers to share their data is to make that reuse patent. When authors use shared data to produce conclusions in a research publication, they should provide a full citation to the data they analyzed (and to the scholars who generated those data). This practice is the analogue of authors referencing the papers, articles and books on whose theories and conclusions their research builds. Citing research data generated by others acknowledges that data are a product of value themselves, linked to but distinct from publications that draw on them. Alternatively, data reusers might offer data generators co-authorship on research publication based on secondary data analysis (a practice more prevalent in the natural sciences). An intriguing compromise proposal that recently emerged in the medical field is to list "data authors" (Bierer, Crosas and Pierce 2017) on publications – a special category of contributors who receive credit for data generation but who did not collaborate on the publication nor necessarily agree with its conclusions.

---

[22] For instance, the APSA comparative politics section has been awarding the "Lijphart/Przeworski/Verba Data Set Award" since 1999.

Community standards are also evolving with regard to what *additional* steps authors who use data generated by others in their published work need to take. Scholars whose work draws on large-scale data projects typically use just a subset of the data produced by the project. Generally, in addition to the complete citation to the original data,[23] authors need to describe in full what elements they extracted for analysis (the analysis dataset) and the process of extraction (typically as software code). Some journals require that authors provide detailed instructions for reconstructing the analysis dataset from the original data; others call for a copy of the author's analysis dataset (a replication dataset) to be deposited in a place specified by the journal, regardless of whether the original dataset is available elsewhere. We believe the first of these options is preferable as it simplifies giving credit to the creators of the original data, avoids partial and incomplete data duplication in multiple venues and militates against a replication dataset becoming obsolete as updates are made to (or errors found in) the original dataset.

New Initiatives: Infrastructure and Instruction

Significant progress has been made in building the tools and infrastructure that scholars need to make their data accessible, and more can be done. One major set of efforts seeks ways to integrate data management into researchers' regular workflows. In some areas, such integration already exists and is used by a growing number of researchers. Employing tools such as knitr and R-Markdown, for example, researchers can combine statistical code and academic writing in a single, "reproducible" document (see Xie 2014). Similar tools exist for other popular languages such as python and Stata. COS's Open Science Framework (osf.io) is designed to integrate different types of tools – storage like Dropbox and Google Drive, code repositories like GitHub or bitbucket and data repositories such as Dataverse – into the scientific workflow, mainstreaming good data and document management.

Several other initiatives also hold promise. One of the most anticipated developments is the "Roadmap" project (Simms et al. 2016), spearheaded by the California Digital Library and the Digital Curation Center. Both centers currently offer popular tools for writing DMPs, the DMP Tool (https://dmptool.org/) and DMP Online (https://dmponline.dcc.ac.uk/), respectively. "Roadmap" is a next-generation tool that provides significantly more

---

[23] Journals rarely require authors to provide information about how the original dataset was generated.

guidance to researchers on data management and automates components of DMPs (see above).

Some efforts seek to bring similar benefits to qualitative researchers. As qualitative researchers increasingly use Qualitative Data Analysis (QDA) software such as NVivo or atlas.ti, repositories, developers and expert users are collaborating to develop ways to facilitate the sharing of projects organized in such software in data repositories (Karcher and Pagé 2017; cf. Corti and Gregory 2011 for UK Data's groundbreaking work on the topic). Also, building on Moravcsik's (2010) "active citation," QDR has developed an approach to making qualitative research more transparent that anticipates the sharing of relevant research data – "Annotation for Transparent Inquiry" or ATI (see Karcher et al. 2016).

Finally, integrating the teaching of data management skills – and an understanding of the technologies that are available to store and preserve data and keep them safe – into graduate training will be critical. Topics might include how to interact with IRBs, how to conduct research in a way that does not preclude sharing research data or make doing so prohibitively difficult, and how to manage data with sharing in mind from the start of a research project. Instructing young scholars on these topics will empower them to engage in and shape ongoing disciplinary debates, and will ensure that the next generation of researchers is well-equipped to share their data as new standards are introduced that call on them to do so.

Conclusion

Access to research data is expanding across the social sciences as more scholars become aware and convinced of the benefits of sharing the data that scholarly inquiries generate. The very real benefits that this trend can produce are augmented and multiplied when scholars make their data *meaningfully* accessible: when they render them interpretable and useable for multiple purposes by other scholars, and take advantage of ongoing ground breaking institutional and technical developments in data infrastructure. The achievement of these benefits will likewise accelerate as more scholars make their data accessible to others, and we considered various initiatives that scholarly communities might undertake to catalyze their doing so.

Making such changes will be challenging. Academic disciplines have deeply embedded practices that are difficult to amend. Stasis dominates due in part to human nature, yet there is also a path-dependent aspect to the stickiness of academic praxis: scholarly norms, expectations and infrastructure have been erected around existing practices and procedures, serving to lock them in place. Moreover, movement towards sharing data will engender unintended consequences that will be important – and hard – to address. To offer just one example, social science disciplines will need to reconsider how they interpret mistakes and error. The assessment of data, replication of findings and other forms of evaluation that greater data accessibility facilitates will almost certainly bring more errors to light – not because more mistakes are being made but because greater transparency raises the likelihood of error discovery. Such errors should not and cannot be interpreted as research failures, but precisely how *should* they be considered, and what *should* be done on the basis of their discovery?

The challenges associated with making data accessible notwithstanding, doing so is in line with, if not an implicit or explicit prerequisite for, many of the other proposals made throughout this volume. Reproducibility (Christensen and Miguel, Chapters 6 and 7, this volume) relies on open data, as does appraisal/re-appraisal (Gerring, Chapters 13 and 14, this volume). "Same-data replication" (Freese and Petersen, Chapter 10, this volume) clearly requires access to data, and "new-data replication" also benefits from the ability to compare newly collected data with the data used in a study being replicated to understand differences in findings and their potential causes. Carefully evaluating measurement (Reiter Chapter 11, this volume) and reliability of inference (Fairfield and Charman, Chapter 12, this volume) perhaps most crucially rely on what we call *meaningful* access to data; without careful documentation of data collection, transformation and analysis, it is all but impossible to evaluate measurement or investigate details of inferential claims. Finally, generating improved metrics for evaluating research (Gerring, Karcher and Apfeld, Chapter 15, this volume) will require the use of the data infrastructure we discuss here and should increase the incentives for data sharing.

The centrality of data access to so many of the proposals mentioned in this volume is no accident: data are the building blocks of knowledge. The fact that so many stakeholders invested in improving the production of knowledge rely on the accessibility of these building blocks bodes well for more data being made meaningfully accessible in the future.

9 Pre-registration and Results-Free Review in Observational and Qualitative Research

Alan M. Jacobs

Can published results be believed? As the editors of this volume note in their introductory chapter, there is good reason to worry that the body of empirical findings appearing in social scientific journals represents a heavily biased draw from the population of results that have in fact been realized, or could be realized, by researchers. This bias is widely understood to derive both from a preference among reviewers and editors for strong over weak or null results and from strategic efforts by authors to generate and report the kinds of results mostly likely to be published (Ioannidis 2005; Gerber and Malhotra 2008b, a; Gerber, Malhotra, Dowling, and Doherty 2010; Humphreys, Sanchez de la Sierra, and van der Windt 2013; Franco, Malhotra, and Simonovits 2014; Nyhan 2015; Dunning 2016). This bias is increasingly considered to be a serious obstacle to the production of reliable social knowledge.

What to do? Social scientists have in recent years devoted increasing attention to two promising responses to publication bias: the pre-registration of study designs and analysis plans and results-blind review.[1] These responses, while different in important respects, both rely on a logic of what we might call *blind selection*. In the case of pre-registration, researchers choose their tests blind to those tests' results; in the case of results-blind review, reviewers and editors consider manuscripts that describe study procedures but are silent about outcomes. These mechanisms address the problem of post hoc selection for positive or "strong" results by occluding information about test results from the actor making the selection. Blind-selection procedures thus reduce opportunities for the cherry-picking of results and provide researchers with a credible means of distinguishing *testing* from unconstrained exploration. The case for pre-registration and results-blind review has been made extensively across the social sciences (see, e.g., Gerber and Malhotra 2008a; Wagenmakers, Wetzels, Borsboom, Maas, and Kievit 2012; Humphreys, Sanchez de la Sierra, and van

---

[1] A third response, replication, is dealt with at length in Part IV.

der Windt 2013; Monogan III 2013; Miguel, Camerer, Casey, Cohen, Esterling, Gerber, Glennerster, Green, Humphreys, and Imbens 2014; Nyhan 2015; Findley, Jensen, Malesky, and Pepinsky 2016).

To date, however, investigation of both the problem of publication bias and the promise of possible solutions has been methodologically bounded. The examination of publication bias has been limited to the scrutiny of quantitative results, via, for instance, the search for discontinuities around the critical values associated with the 0.05 significance level (as in, e.g., Gerber and Malhotra 2008a; Gerber, Malhotra, Dowling, and Doherty 2010), and the problem is frequently conceptualized as selection for studies and analytic choices that yield statistically significant results. We thus have little sense of the degree to which published *qualitative* research represents a cherry-picked collection of findings. Likewise, pre-registration and results-blind review have until very recently been discussed and practiced almost exclusively in connection with experimental or otherwise prospective analysis. Advocates of these approaches have devoted little attention to thinking through whether or how they might be used outside the worlds of experimental or otherwise prospective research, domains where their logic operates most simply. Yet, the vast majority of empirical (including quantitative) work in the social sciences falls outside these categories: we social scientists are mostly observationalists studying events that have occurred outside our control, in the past. There has been little sustained effort, however, to examine whether or how blind-selection procedures might operate for retrospective hypothesis-testing work, whether qualitative or quantitative.

The aim of this chapter is to extend the consideration of publication bias and its potential fixes onto new methodological terrain. It does so by examining the extent of publication bias in qualitative research and by exploring the promise of pre-registration and results-blind review for enhancing the validity and credibility of non-experimental research more broadly. Recently, arguments for pre-registration of qualitative (Kern and Gleditsch 2017; Piñeiro and Rosenblatt 2016) and, more broadly, observational research (e.g., Burlig 2018) in the social sciences have been slowly emerging. The present chapter seeks to contribute to this discussion in three distinctive ways: (1) through an empirical assessment of the degree of publication bias in qualitative political science research; (2) by elaborating an analytic framework for evaluating the feasibility and utility of pre-registration and results-blind review for any form of confirmatory empirical inquiry; and (3) by marshalling evidence on the practicability of these tools for qualitative and quantitative observational political science research, given the forms of data currently in use.

The analysis proceeds in several steps. The second section of this chapter begins with a general account of the problem of publication bias, including a conceptual disaggregation of the phenomenon into two components: gatekeeping bias (the biased selection of studies by editors and reviewers) and analysis bias (the biased selection of tests for reporting by researchers). While the two processes are related, the distinction is key to understanding the different ways in which results-blind review and pre-registration might enhance the production of knowledge: the first by reducing gatekeeping bias and the second by limiting the scope for analysis bias. Gatekeeping bias itself also bears disaggregation; it seems that editors and reviewers do not just prefer positive or strong over null or weak results, but they also appear to prefer confirmatory over exploratory analysis. Researchers thus face incentives not merely to report strong results but to report *test* results, rather than inductively generated insights.

Following a brief review of evidence of publication bias in quantitative research, the chapter hones in on the nature and scope of the problem in qualitative scholarship. The first question, in such an examination, is whether qualitative research is a potential site of such bias. Publication bias refers to a skew in the set of reported empirical assessments of truth propositions about the world; it is a concept that is thus typically applied to confirmatory, as opposed to exploratory, research. Given the important role of exploration in much qualitative inquiry, we might wonder whether the concept of publication bias is a meaningful one in this domain. It is clear that key developments in process-tracing methodology over the last 15 years have involved the elaboration of the logic of empirical testing in qualitative inference. But how much qualitative research in fact seeks to test hypotheses, as opposed to generating inductive theoretical insights from case evidence? I report the results of a detailed review of the stated intellectual goals of a large set of recent qualitative journal publications, which reveals that a large share of qualitative researchers set out with the explicit intention of assessing the validity of empirical propositions. The chapter, further, illustrates why it is that the opportunities for selective reporting of results – in essence, qualitative "p-hacking" – are just as great for case-oriented as for statistical analysis.

Do we have reason to believe, then, that published qualitative test results in fact represent a biased draw from the population of realizable results? The chapter provides systematic evidence – the first reported, to my knowledge – of strong publication bias in qualitative research. Across 58 qualitative and multi-method articles published in a set of leading journals in 2015, not a single study reports a null finding on a primary hypothesis, only one draws attention to an observation that cuts against the study's conclusions, and not a single mixed-method study finds discrepancies between the statistical results and the case evidence.

Reflecting on these results, I argue that the powerful biases affecting the body of reported empirical findings – for qualitative and quantitative research alike – both arise from and reinforce a breakdown in scholarly communication. The current state of affairs is one in which researchers are free to claim to be reporting the results of structured empirical tests, but in which few can *credibly* claim to be doing so. This is, moreover, not just a problem for hypothesis-testing – it also a communicative equilibrium in which the pervasiveness and intellectual contributions of exploratory analysis are likely to be massively understated.

In the next three sections, the chapter turns to a consideration of solutions grounded in the logic of blind selection, examining their promise beyond the realm of quantitative prospective research. The third section, drawing on large existing literatures on these mechanisms, provides an overview of how pre-registration and results-blind review can enhance the credibility of empirical claims. The fourth section then examines to what kinds of research these mechanisms can be effectively applied. I argue that there is nothing intrinsic to the logic of either pre-registration or results-blind review that limits their applicability to experimental, prospective, or even quantitative inquiry. Rather than thinking about these devices in connection to broad methodological categories, we must identify the *features of the data* that allow for the credible pre-specification of tests.

I argue that the credibility gains that can be reaped from blind-selection are a function of three features of the empirical situation:

1. the *prior unobservability* of the test evidence,
2. the *independence* of new evidence from old, and
3. the *precision* with which tests can be pre-specified.

Through a further systematic review of recent observational studies – qualitative and quantitative – appearing in leading journals, I then show that much of the observational quantitative and, even more so, qualitative evidence underpinning published work displays features that would enable credible pre-specification of tests. Pre-registration and results-blind review, I contend, thus have the potential to enhance the strength and credibility of confirmatory research across a broad range of empirical methods. Further, while bolstering the integrity of test results, mechanisms of blind selection can help raise the profile and status of empirical exploration by making it harder for researchers to cloak exploratory work – a critical component of any progressive research agenda – in the mantle of testing.

The chapter's final substantive section considers a curious difficulty posed by results-blind review: in removing from reviewers the information they would need to choose with bias, it may make it difficult for them to choose at all. How exactly does one evaluate a study's contribution to knowledge without knowing what it has uncovered? I argue that this challenge is largely surmountable if reviewers assess submissions by asking *how much we should expect to learn* from a given empirical procedure. To illustrate the concept of expected learning, I propose a Bayesian operationalization that offers clear guidance in a results-free situation using the same belief sets that are required for a conventional, ex post assessment of results.

Running through this discussion is the notion that we should conceptualize the threat of publication bias and the effectiveness of solutions in continuous, rather than dichotomous, terms. Pre-registration and results-blind review may generally contribute less to the credibility of retrospective and qualitative research, where the opportunities for "peeking" at the data or adjusting analytical procedures ex post are greater. These tools undoubtedly operate most cleanly for quantitative experimental research. Even under less-than-perfect conditions, however, mechanisms of blind selection can substantially reduce the scope for cherry-picking, by both researchers and gatekeepers. They can also go a long way toward extracting the observational social sciences from an unhappy equilibrium in which many claim to be testing but few really are.

Skewed Social Knowledge

Social inquiry can generate new social knowledge only if its results are made public and widely disseminated. We have good reason to think, however, that the body of published social scientific results represent a skewed sample from the population of results in fact realized, or realizable, by researchers. The problem commonly termed "publication bias" can in fact best be separated into two distinct, if related, steps in the process of knowledge dissemination at which actors have the opportunity to select empirical analyses based on their results, rather than on how much is learned. What I will term *gatekeeping* bias is the tendency of editors and reviewers to select stronger over weaker test results for publication. *Analysis* bias refers to the tendency of researchers to select stronger over weaker results for reporting.

Gatekeeping Bias

Gatekeeping bias arises from the combination of two tendencies, one more commonly noted than the other.

Preferences for strong results. As commonly noted, editors and reviewers appear to favor strong results, which tends to mean results that are statistically significant. Franco et al. (2014) provide striking evidence of gatekeeping bias by taking advantage of a known population of studies: those survey experiments conducted via Time-Sharing Experiments in the Social Sciences (TESS). Franco et al. find that those studies that uncovered statistically significant treatment effects were considerably more likely to be published than those yielding insignificant effects.

Preferences for testing. This bias toward strong results operates jointly with an equally powerful, if less often noted, orientation toward *hypothesis testing* as the dominant form of empirical analysis. In quantitative analysis, hypothesis testing tends to mean null hypothesis significance testing – in which the focus lies on the *p*-value, or the probability of having estimated a given non-zero parameter value if the true value were zero – at the expense of other modes of analysis, such as the estimation of effect sizes. More importantly, confirmatory analysis appears to be preferred over *exploration*, or the generation of theoretical insights or hypotheses through inductive engagement with the data. This situation creates incentives for scholars to claim to have subjected propositions to tests, even when they have arrived at their findings through relatively unstructured exploration.

Analysis Bias

If gatekeeping bias describes a filter applied to manuscripts by reviewers and editors, analysis bias describes a filter applied to analytic strategies by researchers; given a choice of analytic strategies (e.g., statistical models, process-tracing tests), researchers seem to favor specifications of their tests that generate stronger, rather than weaker, results.

Analysis bias may in part derive from cognitive sources, such as confirmation bias or researchers' political or normative commitments to the hypotheses they are testing.

Yet it is likely that gatekeeping bias itself plays a large role – that, in the face of strong professional pressures to publish widely and well, researchers' analytic choices are shaped by strategic anticipation of editors' and reviewers' preferences for strong results.

The behavior we are concerned about is sometimes called "fishing": researchers choosing their empirical strategies in light of those strategies' results (Humphreys, Sanchez de la Sierra, and van der Windt 2013). These researcher-induced biases are given free rein by the broad range of choices that must be made in the course of empirical analysis: how to code variables or generate indices; which functional form to assume for the relationship of interest; what to assume about the probability structure of the errors; which variables to enter as covariates in a regression model; which interactions to include or exclude; which cases to include or drop. Researchers thus have the option of choosing the estimation strategies that yield the results they, or publication gatekeepers, want. Note that the problem applies even when researchers do not in fact carry out multiple analyses – that is, if they *stop* trying additional tests and if that decision to stop is conditional on the results of initial tests (i.e., stop if you find a significant result; see Gelman and Loken 2014).

The problem, as Humphreys et al. (2013) explain, is that the probability of "finding" a relationship where none in fact exists (Type-1 error) rises with the number of attempts if these attempts are treated in isolation from one another. In particular, with k attempts, the probability of finding at least one significant result at the 95-percent level, even if there is no true systematic relationship, is $1 - 0.95^k$. Put differently, unless the number of attempts conducted by the researcher is reported and appropriately adjusted for, the reported p-value for a "significant" result is not in fact meaningful. In this situation, what may be reported as a test result is better understood as an insight drawn from empirical exploration.

Gerber and colleagues have provided the most striking evidence to date of bias in the results published in top political science journals. Among results appearing in the *American Political Science Review* and the *American Journal of Political Science*, Gerber and Malhotra (2008a) find a massive discontinuity in reported Z scores at the critical value required to achieve a p-value below 0.05 – a pattern strongly suggestive of either analysis bias or biased selection by editors and reviews. Gerber et al. (2010) report parallel findings across a large number of political science journals in the literatures on economic voting and the effect of negative campaign advertising, while Gerber and Malhotra (2008b) find a similar pattern in top sociology journals. Christensen and Miguel (Chapter 6, this volume) provide an extensive review of evidence of publication bias in several literatures in the field of economics.

Qualitative Publication Bias

While issues of gatekeeping and analysis bias have received the greatest attention in quantitative research communities, there is good reason to think that they strike qualitative research with equal force. First, as I demonstrate through a review of recent publications, much qualitative research is – like much quantitative research – purportedly oriented toward establishing the validity of empirical propositions, and is thus potentially susceptible to gatekeeping and analysis bias. Second, opportunities for "fishing" for positive or strong findings are just as available to qualitative as to quantitative researchers. Third, a systematic review of reported findings yields strong evidence of skew in the set of qualitative results appearing in major political science journals.

The confirmatory orientation of qualitative research. First, note that testing can be central to qualitative research. Indeed, over the last decade, there has been a broad move toward the conceptualization of case-study methods as procedures for testing explanations and theoretical claims. The literature on qualitative process tracing has developed increasingly sophisticated ways of thinking about different types of qualitative tests. Many qualitative methodologists have advocated the use of, and elaborated upon, Van Evera's (1997) typology of tests, which classifies empirical predictions according to the "uniqueness" and "certainty" of the implications being examined (see also Bennett 2010; Collier 2011; Mahoney 2012). This schema yields test types known as "hoop tests," "smoking-gun tests," "doubly decisive tests," and "straw-in-the-wind tests," with differing consequences for inferences when passed or failed. More recently, a number of qualitative methodologists have reformulated process tracing tests in terms of Bayesian updating, an approach that involves the formation of beliefs about the probability that a hypothesis is true, conditional on the evidence (Beach and Pederson 2013; Bennett 2015; Humphreys and Jacobs 2015; Fairfield and Charman 2017).

We might wonder, of course, whether qualitative researchers in practice seek to carry out confirmatory analysis. Perhaps the typical qualitative study seeks to empirically induce theoretical insights rather than to test – in which case any concerns about selective reporting of qualitative results would be largely moot. I examine this question through a systematic review of a sample of 94 qualitative and multi-method articles appearing in 2015 and/or 2016 in eight highly ranked political science journals.[2] Articles were categorized

---

[2] The journals searched were: *American Political Science Review* (2015–2016), *British Journal of Political Science* (2015–2016), *Comparative Politics* (2015), *International Organization* (2015–2016), *International*

based on the purposes to which the qualitative evidence was put. In the process of classifying the articles, it became clear that the standard dichotomy of theory-testing versus theory-generating would be insufficient for capturing the range of modes of analysis on display. Many qualitative studies, for instance, do not explicitly set up their analyses as testing a hypothesis, yet deploy a body of evidence to establish the validity of a theory or an explanation. Moreover, a good deal of qualitative work claims to be using case evidence to illustrate the workings of a theory, rather than to generate the theory or probe its validity. In total, I distinguish among four potential uses of qualitative evidence.

Testing. I categorize as "testing" those articles that either (a) explicitly claim to be using the qualitative evidence presented to test or evaluate the truth value of an explanation, theory, or other claim or (b) are structured as a test in that they explicitly identify criteria of evidentiary assessment for a theory or explanation, such as its empirical predictions or its observable implications.

Substantiating. Some articles mobilize evidence to confirm or establish the validity of a proposition about the world without explicitly describing their analysis as a test. I code as "substantiating" those articles that deploy the qualitative evidence as backing for the truth value of a proposition without explicitly describing or unambiguously structuring the analysis as a test.

Illustrative. "Illustrative" articles are those that do not involve explicit test-oriented features and that clearly characterize their use of the qualitative evidence as illustrating or applying a proposition, rather than establishing its truth value.[3]

Theory-generating. A "theory-generating" article is one that explicitly frames the empirical analysis as serving to generate a set of conceptual or theoretical insights.

Note that *testing* and *substantiating* articles share an important feature in that both ask the reader to buy into a truth claim about the world on the basis of the evidence presented. While the former group is explicitly confirmatory, the latter group is implicitly so. In that key sense, concerns about

---

Security (2015), *Perspectives on Politics* (2015), *Studies in Comparative International Development* (2015), *World Politics* (2015–2016). Both the 2015 and 2016 volumes were searched for those journals that had five or fewer qualitative or multi-method articles in 2015. To be included in the sample, the article must had made substantive use of qualitative evidence, amounting minimally to a full section devoted to qualitative analysis. Abstracts of these 94 articles were then read further to determine the use to which the article put the evidence. Where abstracts were unclear, the article text was inspected. Coding rules and the dataset with articles codings are available in the paper's online appendix.

[3] The terms "elucidate" or "plausibility probe" also triggered a classification as "illustrative," as long as the empirical analysis was not otherwise structured as a test (e.g., with the assessment of empirical predictions).

Table 9.1 Use of qualitative evidence in 94 articles in 8 highly ranked political science journals (2015 and 2016)

Category	Articles	%
Testing	39	41.5
Substantiating	33	35.1
Illustrative	20	21.3
Theory-generating	2	2.1

Note: Raw codings can be found in the chapter's online appendix at https://politics.sites.olt.ubc.ca/files/2018/11/Appendix-to-Tables-1-and-2-Qualitative-Testing-and-Publication-Bias.xlsx.

selective use or interpretation of evidence arguably apply with equal force to both categories.

The results of the classification exercise are presented in Table 9.1. In this sample, 41.5 percent of articles explicitly claimed to have used the qualitative evidence presented to test the veracity of an explanation, theory, or other claim. An additional 35 percent use the qualitative evidence to substantiate a claim about the world without describing the analytic procedure as a test. Meanwhile, notwithstanding common characterizations of qualitative research as oriented toward theory-generation or illustrative analysis, fewer than a quarter of the articles in the sample use qualitative data for these purposes. Thus, while exploration and a back-and-forth between theory and evidence remains an important focus of the qualitative tradition, it is clear that the vast majority of qualitative political science research involves the use of evidence to establish the empirical validity of a proposition about the world. The question of whether evidence and analyses have been presented in a full and unbiased fashion thus arises for a large share of qualitative scholarship.

Opportunities for fishing in qualitative research. The opportunities for fishing are just as great with qualitative as with quantitative work. The problem of fishing in case study analysis can be illustrated by conceptualizing process-tracing tests in probabilistic terms (as is increasingly common; see, e.g., Beach and Pederson 2013; Bennett 2015; Humphreys and Jacobs 2015). Consider, for instance, the dynamic as it might play out in relation to what the process-tracing literature refers to as "smoking-gun" tests (Van Evera 1997). Smoking-gun tests are tests for which passage strongly strengthens a hypothesis, but failing only minimally weakens the hypothesis. Imagine the following procedure.

- We seek to test a primary hypothesis, H.

- We can do so by going looking for some number, k, of clues, K_i, $i \in [1, 2, \ldots k]$
- Suppose each of these clues would represent "smoking-gun" evidence for H. In particular, for each K_i, $p(K_i|H)=0.2$, while $p(K_i|\sim H)=0.05$.
- Assume that each of these tests is independent of the others: observing the result of one test does not change the probability of observing the other clues conditional on H.[4]
- Suppose that we allow ourselves to search for k = 5 such smoking-gun clues.

Given this procedure, there's a nearly 1-in-4 chance $(1-0.95^5 = 0.23)$ that the hypothesis will pass one of the "smoking-gun" tests even if H is false. Thus, the search for these five smoking guns is not nearly as demanding a test of the hypothesis as each test is individually.

Now, suppose that we allow our decision to report a test result to depend on what we find: we report only those tests that are passed. Unless we come clean about how many tests we have conducted, we run a considerable chance of reporting evidence for our hypothesis that is much less probative than it would appear.

While we cannot know for sure (absent a faithful record of all tests conducted by researchers), this sketch plausibly describes common practice in process-tracing research. Because failing a smoking-gun test is generally understood to have minimal impact on the validity of a hypothesis, researchers likely tend to think of it as inconsequential if they neglect to report such a failure. As we can see, however, the cumulative impact of failing multiple smoking-gun tests can in fact be quite large. Selective reporting of such test results can, thus, seriously undermine the integrity of qualitative findings. And, of course, the non-reporting of failed smoking-gun tests is a "best-case" form of fishing. Far more problematic would be the non-reporting of hoop-test results that run counter to the favored hypothesis.

One potential defense against fishing – the demands of the skeptical reviewer – is also less likely to be effective against qualitative than quantitative analysis bias. When assessing quantitative manuscripts, reviewers can usually readily imagine and ask for a set of robustness tests involving the study dataset or readily obtainable measures, allowing a direct empirical assessment of the sensitivity of results to test-specification. For qualitative work, unless a reviewer is deeply familiar with the case(s) being examined, it may be much

---

[4] Of course, the *unconditional* probability of observing a clue will change as we observe the results of prior tests since *p(H)* will be updated. But, as discussed further below, the independence of evidence hinges on the independence of the *conditional* probabilities, $p(K_i|H)$.

more difficult to imagine the evidence that might have been collected but was not reported. Reviewers of qualitative manuscripts based on intensive fieldwork are also less likely to demand to see evidence not already reported in the manuscript, given the hurdles to new data collection for such work and the difficulty of knowing what the universe of readily available clues would have looked like.

Further, to the extent that editors and reviewers prefer evidence of effects over non-effects, there is no reason to believe that gatekeeping bias would operate with any less force for qualitative than for quantitative journal submissions.

Empirical evidence of qualitative publication bias. The empirical question nonetheless arises: how comprehensively do qualitative scholars in fact report the results of the tests that they conduct? To address this question, I examined in greater depth the evidence and inferences presented in the same sample of articles analyzed above, summarizing the patterns of findings in Table 9.2. Like Table 9.1, Table 9.2 disaggregates the sample by mode of analysis, separating those articles that explicitly test from those that mobilize evidence to establish the truth value of a proposition, those that employ the evidence illustratively, and those that use the evidence to generate new theoretical insights. Consider the following three features of the pattern in Table 9.2.

1. *An absence of null findings.* Across the 94 articles examined, there is not a single example of a null finding: of conclusions that directly undermine the primary explanatory or theoretical claim that the article develops.

It is possible, outside this sample, to identify prominent instances of published qualitative null findings. These include, for instance, Snyder and Borghard (2011)'s process-tracing test of audience-costs theory and McKeown's (1983) process-tracing test of hegemonic stability theory. Yet it is telling that these studies are not tests of theories devised or otherwise advanced by the study authors. Rather, they are tests of highly influential existing theories, a situation in which clear null findings were likely to be considered novel and important. The publication of these studies shows that null qualitative findings can be published, at least when they generate surprising insights. Yet the within-sample pattern – in which we find not a single null – suggests that these prominent examples are rare exceptions.

2. *A near-absence of weak findings or mixed evidence.* Not only are all findings positive, but nearly all of the evidence *points in the same direction*, at least as interpreted by the authors. A close reading of these publications revealed only

Table 9.2 Patterns of results in 94 qualitative and mixed-method articles in 8 highly ranked political science journals (2015–2016)

Category	Articles (N = 94)	Null Result[a]	Undermining Evidence[b]	Cross-method Difference[c]
Testing	52[d] (30)	0	3	3
Substantiating	30 (0)	0	1	–
Illustrative	10 (0)	0	0	–
Theory-generating	2 (0)	0	0	–

Note: Number of mixed-method articles within each category noted in parentheses. Cross-method-consistency examined only for mixed-method articles. See text for details on sample-construction. Raw codings can be found in the chapter's online appendix at https://politics.sites.olt.ubc.ca/files/2018/11/Appendix-to-Tables-1-and-2-Qualitative-Testing-and-Publication-Bias.xlsx.

[a] An article is coded as having a null result where there is no significant evidence presented for the central theoretical proposition of interest. Where an article tests multiple competing claims, not all advanced by the author, then a null result is coded only if there is no significant evidence presented for any of the claims (other than a null hypothesis) or if there is no significant evidence for any hypothesis advanced by the author. An article that focuses on testing a prior, well-established theory and finds no evidence for this theory does not qualify as a null result since the authors' incentives are to present evidence against this theory.

[b] Undermining evidence was evidence that cut against the article's main finding(s) or conclusion. This could have included the failure to find supporting evidence when such evidence was sought. Undermining evidence must have been noted in at least one of the following locations, indicating that the author acknowledges the undermining effect on the findings: the article's abstract, introduction, any passages summarizing the empirical analysis (e.g., at the beginning or end of the empirical section(s)), discussion section, or conclusion.

[c] Cross-method inconsistency meant some significant difference – between the qualitative and quantitative evidence presented – in the degree of support lent to the article's main argument or finding. Any difference between the quantitative and qualitative findings must have been noted in at least one of the following locations, indicating that the author acknowledges the inconsistency: the article's abstract, introduction, any passages summarizing the empirical analysis (e.g., at the beginning or end of the empirical section(s)), discussion section, or conclusion.

[d] For the present analysis, an article is classified as "testing" if any major component was set up as a test. Since all multi-method articles in the sample contain statistical tests, all multi-method articles are here coded as "testing."

four articles, across 94 cases, in which the authors explicitly drew attention to evidence that diverged from or represented weak support for their primary argument or result.[5] Even if we limit the analysis to articles that use the evidence in confirmatory fashion – via explicit testing or substantiating – just

---

[5] Cross-method differences, in multi-method articles, were also counted as undermining evidence where the author explicitly points to the findings of one method as undercutting the findings of the other.

over 5 percent of articles point to a single piece of evidence that cuts against the main argument. It is worth pausing to reflect on this pattern: the presentation of qualitative evidence that all points in one direction is arguably tantamount to the presentation of a statistical result with little or no residual error – with *all* data points lying very close to or on the regression line.[6]

3. *Very high consistency of findings across analytic approaches.* We often find divergence between the quantitative and the qualitative findings generated by different researchers. This is not surprising: different bases of evidence and forms of analysis should be expected to commonly generate different findings. We might then ask to what degree researchers report divergent results across analyses when presenting *their own* multi-method inquiry. Across the 30 multi-method articles examined, all of which involved explicit testing, only three reported any substantive difference between the statistical and the qualitative findings.[7] Greater variance in *between*-study than *within*-study findings should be a cause for concern: it suggests either that the qualitative and quantitative results reported jointly in mixed-method work are commonly not arrived at independently of one another or that the editorial process is selecting for high levels of consistency.

The problems of gatekeeping and analysis bias should equally concern qualitative scholars and consumers of regression coefficients. It is important, moreover, to note that the observed pattern of published qualitative and quantitative results is not consistent with a world in which researchers, reviewers, and editors are simply attaching greater weight to novel or surprising findings, whether positive or null. If tests were being selected for the new insight or learning that their results generated, then we would expect to see a far higher proportion of null and weak results (unless, that is, we are prepared to believe that the set of hypotheses being tested is largely composed of low-plausibility claims). In sum, across empirical political science, there is strong evidence that published results represent a highly skewed sample from the population of potential findings.

---

[6] As with null results, it is possible to think of examples of mixed findings outside the sample, such as Haggard and Kaufman's (2012) test of the link between inequality and regime change. Again, however, the authors are testing a prominent existing claim in the literature, rather than finding mixed evidence for their own claim. And, as for null results, this out-of-sample instance appears to be a rare exception.

[7] An expansive definition of "difference in findings" was employed, encompassing any noted difference in the substantive meaning of the qualitative and quantitative results. For instance, in one of the three articles, Hanson (2015), the cross-method difference involved the identification in the qualitative analysis of factors not considered in the quantitative analysis, but no suggestion that this discovery undermined the quantitative results themselves.

An Impediment to Scholarly Communication

Bias in the publication of empirical test results poses a serious threat to the production of knowledge. The principal problem is not one of individual-level motives – i.e., there is no reason to believe that it is driven by researchers' desires to mislead their audiences – but of misaligned incentives and skewed selection processes. An important knock-on effect of gatekeeping and analysis bias is a weakening of scholars' ability to communicate to one another what kind of empirical enterprise they are engaged in. Consider for instance a researcher, quantitative or qualitative, who has *in fact* designed her test procedures prior to examining the evidence. In a world of frequent fishing, that researcher currently has no clear way to credibly distinguish her results – particularly when those results are strong – from the selectively reported findings of her colleagues.

Down that path lies a deeply troubling equilibrium. Where research audiences can no longer distinguish real from apparent tests, the likely result is a predicament much like the well-known "market for lemons." In what we might call the "market for fish," research consumers have little reason to believe scholars' claims to have tested; and research producers in turn have little incentive to do anything other than fish. Indeed, all scholars face mounting pressures to fish as fishing becomes increasingly common practice, raising the "strength" of the average published result. The market for principled testing disappears.

Equally worrying, moreover, are the consequences for exploratory and theory-generating work. As social scientists, we often arrive at our empirical investigations with weak theoretical priors and with weak commitments to any given test as particularly decisive. And so we frequently let the evidence suggest to us or guide us toward a set of plausible propositions; we examine a wide range of model specifications, try out multiple measures of key concepts, or comb through case study evidence for insight into how a process unfolded. Our answers often emerge from, rather than precede, our encounter with the data. Exploratory analysis is broadly understood to be a critical step in the unfolding of a progressive research agenda, a key source of theoretical insight and conceptual innovation. While both quantitative and qualitative research are often undertaken in exploratory modes, in-depth qualitative analysis is frequently considered an especially fertile source of theoretical inspiration.

Yet the current situation obscures, and thus serves to delegitimize, exploratory and theory-generating empirical work. The strong pro-testing tilt in publishing and professional norms incentivizes scholars to present results as confirmatory even when they were arrived at through a process of exploration. And critically, because editors, reviewers, and readers are poorly positioned to distinguish testing from exploration, there is little or no penalty for labeling the latter as the former. The consequence is, very likely, substantial over-claiming to have "tested" rather than explored. This outcome is undesirable not just because it distorts the corpus of test results. Equally problematic, it serves to further elevate testing above other, equally valuable stages in the research process. Despite its central role in the production of knowledge, exploratory empirical analysis has become a form of inquiry that dare not speak its name.

Two Institutional Responses

With mounting concern about gatekeeping and analysis bias in the social sciences, recent years have seen greatly increased attention to and experimentation with possible institutional responses. Two potential solutions have been at the center of debate about, and of efforts to counter, the problem: study pre-registration and results-blind peer review (see, e.g., Gerber and Malhotra 2008a; Wagenmakers, Wetzels, Borsboom, Maas, and Kievit 2012; Monogan III 2013; Miguel, Camerer, Casey, Cohen, Esterling, Gerber, Glennerster, Green, Humphreys, Imbens 2014; Nyhan 2015; Humphreys, de la Sierra, and van der Windt 2013; Findley, Jensen, Malesky, and Pepinsky 2016). While their logics are different, each of these devices operates *by concealing information about empirical results* from decision-makers at the point at which tests are selected for implementation and/or reporting: under pre-registration *researchers* select tests prior to seeing results, while under results-blind review *reviewers* and *editors* select manuscripts for publication prior to seeing results. Moreover, the two can be readily combined.

These two blind-selection devices are seen by many as promising responses to problems of publication and analysis bias.[8] Yet they are typically seen as applicable to a fairly narrow slice of empirical social scientific research. The domain of application has been defined in different ways by different advocates. Most frequently, though, pre-registration and results-blind review are associated with *experimental* or otherwise *prospective* research, in which the events or outcomes to be analyzed have not yet occurred. Study pre-registration originated in the medical sciences as a system for posting

---

[8] Though certainly not by all: for critiques, see, e.g., Tucker (2014), Laitin (2013), and Coffman and Niederle (2015).

protocols for randomized controlled trials (RCTs). As the framework has spread across disciplines, the tight link to experimentation and prospection has remained intact. One of the most prominent study registries in the social sciences – that operated by the American Economic Association – is open strictly to RCTs. The Election Research Preacceptance Competition, tied to the 2016 US elections, while focused on the ANES's observational data, was purely prospective in character, accepting design submissions only prior to the outcome of interest (the election). Broadly speaking, discussion of pre-registration and results-blind review tends to assume that these devices have little or no relevance to retrospective observational research – a category that comprises the large majority of empirical research in political science. Moreover, the use and discussion of pre-registration and results-blind review have been almost entirely limited to *quantitative* research. Just as the examination of publication and analysis bias have been largely limited to statistical work, there has been virtually no discussion of pre-registration or preacceptance of qualitative work.[9]

In the remainder of this chapter, I will argue that the methodological categories within which discussions of pre-registration and results-blind review have largely been contained are a poor or only partial fit to the problem. Rather than thinking of these devices as constrained by general methodological category – whether experimental, prospective, or quantitative – we should think of their scope of application as being defined by those features of data and of tests that logically relate to the challenge of blind selection. In particular, we can assess the potential gains from pre-registration and/or results-blind review by asking three questions of a research design.

1. *Prior unobservability*. How easily could the study data have been observed (by researchers or reviewers/editors) prior to test-selection?
2. *Independence*. How independent are the new (study) data of old data?
3. *Precision*. How precisely can a test be specified prior to seeing the data?

---

[9] Nyhan (2015), for instance, refers to results-blind review as a tool for "quantitative studies" (79). Findley et al. (2016), editors of the special results-blind-review issue of *Comparative Political Studies*, note that they were open to qualitative submissions but received none. As of January 2017, I was able to identify only one qualitative study on the EGAP registry. The only explicit treatment of qualitative study pre-registration that I am aware of are Piñeiro and Rosenblatt (2016), Kern and Gleditsch (2017), Hartman, Kern, and Mellor (2018), and the report of an ad hoc Committee on Study Registration (on which I sat), formed in 2014 by three methods sections of the American Political Science Association: Experimental Political Science, Political Methodology, and Qualitative and Multi-Method Research (Bowers, Nagler, Gerring, Jacobs, Green and Humphreys 2015).

There is no doubt that most experimental or otherwise prospective quantitative research readily meets the criteria of prior unobservability, independence, and precision; the common association of pre-registration and results-blind review with these forms of inquiry is perfectly reasonable. As I aim to demonstrate, however, other forms of test-oriented research – *especially qualitative research that focuses on testing hypotheses* – also frequently display qualities that make them promising candidates for blind selection.[10] As I will also contend, it is unproductive to conceptualize the plausibility of pre-registration and results-blind review in dichotomous terms: to think that a researcher either has or has not credibly and fully pre-specified her tests. Rather, we should conceive of these two devices as instruments for reducing bias, with the answers to the three questions above and the attendant gains to knowledge lying along a continuum. The question, then, is not whether blind selection can be applied to retrospective or qualitative research; the task, rather, is to assess, for a given study, how much the pre-specification of tests might enhance the credibility of findings, given the nature of the research design.

The remainder of this section briefly outlines the basic logic of pre-registration and results-blind review. Part IV of this volume elaborates the principles of prior unobservability, independence, and precision and examines how non-experimental qualitative and quantitative research are likely to fare against these criteria.

Pre-Registration

With its origins in the medical sciences, study registration developed as a way of preventing selective reporting of results of trials testing the efficacy and safety of pharmaceuticals and other medical treatments. Pre-registration has, more recently, gained significant traction in psychology, economics, and political science, with registries hosted by the Center for Open Science (COS), the American Economic Association, and EGAP among the most advanced initiatives in the social sciences to date.[11]

Here, in broad outline, is how pre-registration works. Prior to observing the data (or, at least, the realization of the outcomes of interest), the researcher

---

[10] In the medical field, the advocacy and use of registries for observational research, both prospective and retrospective, has also been growing (e.g., Williams, Tse, Harlan, and Zarin 2010; Swaen, Carmichael, and Doe 2011). Burlig (2018) makes a case for the pre-registration of observational studies in economics.

[11] See, respectively, https://osf.io/registries/; www.socialscienceregistry.org/; and http://egap.org/content/registration.

archives a time-stamped description of the research plan. In the most rudimentary form of registration, the researcher merely registers a study design. Registration advocates in the social sciences generally call for a more comprehensive form of archiving in which the researcher additionally pre-specifies how the analysis will be conducted in what is called a "pre-analysis plan" (PAP). In an illustration provided by Humphreys et al. (2013), the PAP involves the specification of the measures to be collected, the general model specifications to be employed, the analysis code to be used for estimation, and mock tables showing how the results will be reported. In principle, a PAP could specify a procedure for estimating a quantity, such as an effect size, as well as for testing a point hypothesis.

Importantly, pre-registration does not bind the researchers' hands by blocking the implementation of unregistered analyses; rather, it precludes researchers from reporting *as tests* those analyses that were not specified in advance. The chief advantage of comprehensive registration is thus communicative: it provides a mechanism for researchers to credibly claim not to have fished their results, and for readers to distinguish testing or estimation from exploration (Humphreys, Sanchez de la Sierra, and van der Windt 2013). Once the data are available, the researcher can conduct and report analyses precisely as specified. Reviewers and readers can, in turn, be confident that tests or estimation procedures were selected in a manner blind to the results. Where researchers conduct analyses that deviate from those that were pre-specified – and, indeed, they may explore to any extent that they please – exploration is then easy for research audiences to identify as such.

By having researchers choose their tests blind to (i.e., prior to seeing) the results, pre-registration offers powerful protection against analysis bias: researchers' post hoc choices about which tests or estimations to report. In addition, by making it easier for research audiences to identify true tests, pre-registration makes it more difficult for researchers to disguise exploration as testing, forcing scholars to call exploratory analysis by its proper name.

While the problem of "fishing" has often been associated with frequentist work (consider the term "p-hacking"), the logic of pre-registration bears no particular relationship to frequentism as compared to Bayesianism. As illustrated above, Bayesian logic of the sort often employed in process-tracing research is highly sensitive the problem of selective reporting. Fairfield and Charman (2015 and Chapter 12, this volume) nonetheless argue that Bayesian reasoning renders pre-registration redundant. They contend that this is so because it is always possible, using the rules of Bayesian probability, to "assess the reasonable degree of belief in a hypothesis" (2015:10) given the data at hand and background knowledge, regardless of the sequence in which data were gathered and the hypothesis formulated. They conclude that the time-stamping of hypotheses is thus "not relevant to the logic of scientific inference" (10).

It is, of course, true that one can arrive at the same posterior beliefs, regardless of sequencing, as long as one applies Bayes' rule in a principled fashion to all of the evidence collected, taking fully into account data that support and data that undermine the hypothesis. This is, in fact, not a feature unique to Bayesianism: in a frequentist mode, the principled analyst can conduct multiple tests and then adjust the calculation of standard errors accordingly (see Christensen and Miguel, Chapter 6, this volume, for a discussion of corrective procedures).

Yet the availability of principled analytic solutions in no way resolves the basic incentive and informational problems that generate analysis bias. Whether Bayesian or frequentist, the researcher *can* undertake appropriate analytic steps to incorporate all relevant information in assessing post hoc or multiple hypotheses. The problem is that, under prevailing publication norms, she may have strong incentives not to. In the absence of some form of pre-specification of analytic procedures, moreover, it is difficult for readers to know if they have been shown the full set of empirical results or for the researcher to credibly claim that she has presented them. The problem that pre-registration seeks to solve, in other words, is not *per se* a problem of sequencing. It is, rather, a problem of credible signaling in a context of asymmetric information and skewed incentives, and sequencing serves as a means of generating that credible signal.

Importantly, pre-registration does not by itself counter *publication* bias (Nyhan 2015). A world in which all studies are pre-registered could still be a world in which those studies that are published represent a biased sample, as long as reviewers and editors continue to prefer strong over weak or null results. In principle, however, study registration offers the possibility of compensating for publication bias. The more widely used registration becomes the more comprehensive record it represents of the analyses that researchers at some point planned to undertake, enhancing knowledge of the population of tests from which published studies are drawn. Moreover, if researchers additionally post-register the results of all pre-registered analyses regardless of publication outcome,[12] an unbiased record of the population of test or estimation results would emerge.[13]

---

[12] This would include indicating when a study was not completed or when data were not collected or analyzed as planned.

[13] As this complete record would also make publication bias more readily apparent, editors and reviewers might in turn begin to place greater value on weak or null findings.

Results-Blind Review

A second device for generating a less-biased body of knowledge about the world is results-blind review (see, e.g., Greve, Bröder, and Erdfelder 2013; Smulders 2013; Nyhan 2015; Dunning 2016; Findley, Jensen, Malesky, and Pepinsky 2016). Under results-blind review, reviewers and editors evaluate a manuscript and make a publication decision in the absence of information about the study's results. The submitted manuscript typically contains a framing of the research question, a review of the relevant literature, a statement of key hypotheses to be tested or quantities to be estimated, and a specification of the empirical strategy, including a specification of study protocols and analytic procedures. The study's results may or may not in fact be known to the authors at the time of submission; in either case, the results are not included in the submission or made publicly available prior to an editorial decision.

While registration forces authors to choose test procedures before observing the results, results-blind review forces publication gatekeepers to choose studies before observing their results. Thus, while registration principally operates to minimize analysis bias, results-blind review attacks gatekeeping bias head-on. Moreover, if we believe that analysis bias principally derives from publication incentives, widespread use of results-blind review should also substantially reduce researchers' motivation to fish for strong results, and thus additionally cut powerfully against analysis bias.

For these reasons, political science journals have begun to experiment with results-blind review. A recent special issue of *Comparative Political Studies* contained three articles selected through a purely results-blind review process (Findley, Jensen, Malesky, and Pepinsky 2016). Additionally, via the Election Research Preacceptance Competition (ERPC), tied to the 2016 US general election, nine leading political science journals agreed to review and provisionally accept manuscripts using American National Election Study data based on a pre-registered study design.[14]

The ERPC illustrates one important feature of blind-selection mechanisms: that they can be employed in combination. In principle, results-blind review can be implemented in the absence of pre-registration: authors might have analyzed the data at the time of submission but omit the results from the manuscript. In practice, the availability of this option may encourage a form of adverse selection in which researchers over-submit studies with null findings

---

[14] See program announcement at www.erpc2016.com.

for results-blind review, where they stand a better chance of acceptance than if evaluated with results. If reviewers in turn come to expect a disproportionate share of null findings among the results-blind manuscripts they are assessing, the purpose of results-blind assessment is defeated. Moreover, the integrity of the process may be undermined if the findings have been previously presented at conferences or posted online. For these reasons, some have advocated for the use of results-blind review in tandem with pre-registration, as in the COS's Registered Reports model (Nosek and Lakens 2014; see also Nyhan 2015).

Criteria for Blind Selection

Under what conditions can study pre-registration and results-blind review reduce bias? At the most basic level, these devices are oriented toward enhancing the credibility of tests and estimates. They are thus not applicable to research that seeks to inductively uncover empirical regularities or to derive theoretical inspiration from the data.

However, to what kind of test- or estimation-oriented research can blind-selection methods be usefully applied? The core logic of both pre-registration and results-blind review is one in which the test (or estimation) procedures are specified and selected without knowledge of their results so that positive or strong results cannot be favored. For pre-registration, it is the researcher who selects tests before knowing their results; for results-blind review, reviewers and editors evaluate proposed tests in ignorance of their outcomes. It is from this core logic that we can derive the criteria of prior unobservability, independence, and precision. Prior unobservability and independence minimize knowledge of test outcomes at the time of test-selection. Test-precision maximizes the visibility of any after-the-fact adjustments to data-collection or analytic procedures, helping audiences readily distinguish the test component of a study from its exploratory components. Let us examine each criterion in turn.

Prior Unobservability[15]

The credibility of study pre-registration hinges on the credibility of the researcher's claim not to have observed a test's result prior to the registration of the pre-analysis plan. For this reason, study registration has been seen as

---

[15] The discussion in this section draws conceptually on my contributions to Bowers et al. (2015).

a natural fit with experimental research. Experimental tests are purely prospective: by definition, they hinge on outcome data that *could not* have been observed at the start of the study, prior to the experimental manipulation. The experimental method thus allows researchers to demonstrably pre-specify test procedures prior to having knowledge of the results of those procedures. Study registration in the biomedical field was initially applied to randomized controlled trials; the AEA registry is strictly available to experimentalists; and the EGAP registry has been almost entirely used for experimental work. Somewhat less commonly, registration advocates have pointed to its uses for observational prospective research, in which the events to be analyzed have not yet occurred at the time of registration (for a prominent application, see Monogan III 2013).

Results-blind review, technically speaking, does not depend on researchers not having seen test results when submitting study designs for review; it merely requires that reviewers and editors be ignorant of those results. Yet, any results-blind review process will be more credible to the extent that the data required to implement the tests are not readily available at the time of review; it is less likely that reviewers could have seen, or could readily download and take a peek at, the data themselves in evaluating the results-free manuscript.

Thus, especially for pre-registration, timing is critical to bias-reduction. Yet the timing of relevance here is not in fact the timing of *outcomes* relative to registration – whether the research is experimental/prospective or retrospective – but the timing of *observation* relative to registration. Let us define the concept of *prior unobservability* as the credibility of the researcher's claim not to have seen the test data at the time of registration. In experimental and other prospective work (say, a study of an election that has not yet occurred), establishing prior unobservability is relatively straightforward, assuming it can be verified that registration occurred prior to the start of the study or outcome being observed.

What about observational work that is retrospective? Much observational analysis involves, for instance, the use of readily accessible data about past events, e.g.: election studies or other surveys that have already been carried out and their data archived; cross-national indicators that have already been compiled and posted online; or historical cases that have already been well documented in the secondary literature. Where the data to be analyzed come from a dataset that already existed in analyzable form prior to registration, establishing the prior of unobservability of the evidence may effectively be impossible, and registration will be a weak tool for credibly minimizing the scope for fishing.

However, a credible case for prior unobservability can be made for retrospective research wherever the data themselves are newly collected, newly published, or otherwise newly available, and hence (prior to that point) inaccessible to the researcher. Opportunities of this sort arise prior to the implementation or release of a new survey, the conducting of elite interviews with new subjects, the opening of a new archive or release of a new collection of historical records, or the discovery of new sources (e.g., from an archeological site). For instance, the researcher who plans to conduct a survey of civic activity may effectively be measuring behavior that has already occurred; but it will be relatively straightforward to document that the data could not have been observed before the survey was fielded.

A degree of prior unobservability also obtains for research involving the use of existing data that are costly or difficult to access, especially where the date of access can be established. This will often be the case, for instance, with documentary evidence that exists only in original form at a specific research site (e.g., an archive), access to which must be applied for, or with existing data whose use is restricted (e.g., by a private company or government agency that holds the data) or the release of which occurs at a specific point in time. It is worth noting that much qualitative research involves original data collection that requires the researcher to undertake a discrete activity – e.g., a visit to the archives or an elite interview – with a specific start date prior to which the evidence could not have been observed.

Prior unobservability in practice. To what extent does the kind of data that observational researchers, quantitative and qualitative, use in practice have features that lend themselves to plausible claims of prior unobservability? To examine this question empirically, I conducted a survey of the forms of evidence used in non-experimental articles appearing in 2015 in nine top political science journals. I examined all non-experimental articles, both qualitative and quantitative, in the *American Political Science Review*, *World Politics*, and *International Organization*. Since the numbers of qualitative articles in these journals was low, I further examined all qualitative articles appearing in 2015 in six journals that more commonly publish qualitative work: *British Journal of Political Science*, *Comparative Politics*, *International Security*, *Studies in American Political Development*, and *Studies in Comparative Political Development*. This search resulted in a sample of 61 observational quantitative and mixed-method articles and 52 purely qualitative articles.

In each article, each form of evidence (e.g., variable measure, cited source, etc.)[16] was coded into a category designed to distinguish among types of data

---

[16] For mixed-method articles, only the quantitative evidence was coded as, in most cases, this represented the majority of the empirical analysis.

according to the *barriers to observation*. The rationale is that higher barriers to observation offer firmer ground on which researchers can rest a claim that the relevant evidence was effectively unobservable at the time of study registration. All data used to measure outcome and explanatory variables or to observe features of a causal process (as in process-tracing studies) were coded. The types of barriers coded for were:

- a need to code data or place them in analyzable form;
- restrictions on access to the data imposed by third parties;
- a need to create the data from scratch, whether with or without interactions with human subjects;
- the fact that the events being studied had not yet occurred at the time that data-collection procedures were devised (i.e., that the study is fully prospective).[17]

In mapping from barriers to the credibility of prior unobservability claims, the highest credibility was assigned to data derived from events that had not yet occurred at the time of a project's conception; these are data to which the researcher could not possibly have had access prior to registration (had the study been registered). The second-highest level of credibility was assigned to data that were freshly created by the researcher, yet I distinguish between data that had to be created via interactions with human subjects (who could, in principle, independently confirm the date of that interaction) and data that were created without such interactions. Finally, I attribute moderate credibility to pre-existing data that can be accessed only with the permission of a gatekeeper (e.g., an archive or a government bureaucracy). On the one hand, a data-gatekeeper could verify a date of access; on the other hand, because the data were pre-existing, the researcher could have acquired them through an alternate route (e.g., from a fellow researcher). This is, of course, not the only plausible ranking of the evidentiary categories by potential prior unobservability; the reader is invited to adjust the labels in the second column of Table 9.3 to see how results are affected.

None of the studies reported in the sample of articles were in fact registered. Nor do we know whether any of these data were in fact observed by study authors prior to the choice of analytic procedures. The exercise is thus a purely counterfactual one, asking: if a study employing these data were

---

[17] Burlig (2018) similarly identifies observational studies that involve new data-creation, restricted data, or prospective analysis as ripe for pre-registration.

Table 9.3 Potential prior unobservability in all observational empirical articles published in nine leading journals in 2015

Data Form	Potential Credibility of a Claim to Prior Unobservability	Quantitative Articles Employing Data form (%) ($N = 61$)	Qualitative Articles Employing Data Form (%) ($N = 52$)	All Articles Employing Data Form (%) ($N = 113$)
a: Pre-existing, analyzable form				
a1: **Readily accessible** (e.g., downloadable digital file)	Low	90.2	17.3	56.6
a2: **Restricted** (e.g., by govt. agency, corporation, another scholar)	Moderate	26.2	1.9	15.0
b: Qualitative secondary evidence (e.g., books or articles)	Low	18.0	76.9	45.1
c: Pre-existing, not in analyzable form (e.g., require coding)				
c1: **Readily accessible** (e.g., newspaper articles, public official documents)	Low–moderate	16.4	69.2	40.7
c2: **Restricted** (e.g., archival and unpublished)	Moderate–high	1.6	26.9	13.3
d: Newly created				
d1: **Via human subjects** (e.g., interviews, ethnography)	High	4.9	46.1	23.9
d2: **Without human subjects** (e.g., mapping)	Moderate	0	0	0
e: Collected via a procedure devised prior to occurrence of phenomenon of interest (e.g., an election study)	Very high	0	0	0

Note: Data forms with moderate, high, or very high potential credibility shaded for ease of reading. Percentages do not add to 100 because a single article could contain multiple forms of data. Qualitative data forms that were used only minimally or peripherally to key claims were excluded. In 16.4 percent of quantitative articles, there was some variable for which the data source could not be determined from the text or supplementary materials. Raw article codings are available in the chapter's online appendix at https://politics.sites.olt.ubc.ca/files/2018/11/Appendix-to-Table-3-Prior-Unobservability.xlsx.

pre-registered, how credible would we find the claim of prior unobservability? The results are reported in Table 9.3.

A number of interesting conclusions emerge from this analysis.

1. The data reveal the likely limits of credible pre-registration of observational work. Not a single study examined involved data offering the greatest potential claim to prior unobservability (*e*): in which the event being analyzed had not yet occurred when data-collection procedures were devised (i.e., purely prospective analysis). Just below a quarter, in total, involved the collection of brand-new data via interaction with human subjects (*d1*). For three-quarters of these studies, then, claims to prior unobservability would be of moderate credibility at best.
2. There is nonetheless considerable scope for *at least* moderately credible claims of prior unobservability in quantitative observational research. Among quantitative articles, the opportunity lies mostly in the use of restricted data (*a2, c2*), either analyzable or requiring coding.[18] A small percentage involved fresh data-creation, generally via survey methods (*d1*). Nonetheless, about a third of quantitative articles used at least one form of data that would lend itself to a moderately or highly credible claim of prior unobservability.[19]
3. There is far greater scope for establishing prior unobservability for commonly used forms of *qualitative* data. A little over a quarter of qualitative articles used restricted data not yet in analyzable form (*c2*), while just under half draw on fresh data-collection from human subjects (*d1*). Moreover, examining the joint distribution of these data forms across articles (not shown in table) reveals that *63 percent of qualitative articles used a form of data that was either restricted or freshly created through engagement with human subjects (a2, c2, or d1)*. These are forms of data for which some third party – such as an archivist, an elite interview subject, or a survey research firm – was likely involved in making the data available and thus could, in principle, verify researchers' claims about when data were collected. This analysis thus suggests a widely unacknowledged and (to date) unexploited comparative advantage of the typical qualitative study over the typical quantitative, observational study: the greater opportunity,

---

[18] For an example of a study that, in effect, rests on the restricted form of quantitative data to make claims to prior unobservability credible, see Neumark (2001).

[19] This calculation cannot, of course, be derived directly from Table 9.1; it comes from the joint distribution of data forms across articles.

given the nature of the data, for making credible claims to having executed a principled test.

It is also worth noting a further, non-trivial feature of pre-registration, regardless of data form: it puts the researcher on the public record making a claim not to have observed the data yet. This feature alone is likely to be constraining for most scholars, as it turns what is now implicitly condoned as common practice (examining the data first, then claiming to have tested) into outright fraud.

As this analysis makes clear, however, researchers' claims to the prior unobservability of their data will in many cases be less than ironclad. Importantly, *this is true even for experimental research*: readers ultimately need to trust or verify researchers' claims about when treatments were administered. Researchers pre-registering retrospective observational studies need to make arguments for and present evidence of the prior unobservability of their test data; and reviewers and other audiences will need to evaluate these arguments and evidence. Like most other forms of empirical uncertainty – such as a standard error – prior unobservability is thus a matter of degree, rather than a binary condition. A researcher's claims to having carried out a true test will be more credible to the extent that they can persuasively establish that they could not have seen the data prior to registration. There may always remain some doubt about this claim, and thus about the potential for analysis bias in reported findings. Yet a world in which some forms of retrospective research were pre-registered would undoubtedly be a world of more interpretable empirical findings than the world in which we are currently operating.

Independence

That observations have not yet been made does not mean that they are new. A second criterion for blind selection relates to the degree to which the test data are *independent* of observations that the researcher could have made prior to registration or that are generally available in the literature or historical record. If the test observations are unseen but could be largely predicted based on prior observations, then "pre-registered" or "results-blind" tests have in effect already been conducted, and researchers, reviewers, and editors know the results.

Let us use the term *observational independence* to refer to the novelty of the "new" data on which hypotheses are to be tested. One way to think about observational independence is to consider the difference between independent and dependent pieces of evidence. Suppose that I plan two tests of a hypothesis, each of which involves the search for a piece of evidence, respectively E_1 and E_2. Each test is of moderately high probative value: e.g., $p(E_i|H) = 0.7$ and $p(E_i|\sim H) = 0.3$. Assume, further, that E_1 and E_2 are fully independent of one another, conditional on our confidence in the hypothesis. Suppose that we carry out the first test and observe E_1. Then the search for E_2 has no less probative value than it did before we conducted the first test. It remains the case that $p(E_2|H) = 0.7$ and $p(E_2|\sim H) = 0.3$. Finding E_2 could still have a substantial upward effect on our confidence in the hypothesis.

On the other hand, suppose that E_1 and E_2 are highly correlated with one another such that seeing E_1 greatly increases our confidence that, when we look, we will also see E_2 (independently of the first observation's effect on our confidence in H). In that situation, once we have seen E_1, the search for E_2 no longer carries the probative value that it did before. One intuitive way to think about this is that we are now much more likely to see E_2 if H is false. Were we to ignore the dependence of the second piece of evidence on the first, we would thus be greatly overstating the power of the second test. Likewise, the strength of a pre-specified test hinges on the independence of the yet-to-be observed test data from those observations that have previously been made.

Importantly, the dependence of the two pieces of evidence that we are concerned about here is their correlation conditional on $p(H)$. In the above example, seeing E_1 increases our confidence in H, and through an increase in $p(H)$, also increases the probability of observing E_2. Yet the effect of prior evidence that runs via our updated confidence in the hypothesis does not weaken the probative value of the second test. The dependence of concern, rather, is the portion of the effect of seeing E_1 on the probability of seeing E_2 that is not explained by E_1's effect on $p(H)$.

The concept of observational independence also underlines a further sense in which broad methodological categories (e.g., prospective versus retrospective) can be misleading when thinking about the plausibility of blind selection. In particular, observational independence is not established by the fact of prospectiveness. The fact that the outcomes to be observed may not yet have occurred at the time of test-specification does not imply that those outcomes are independent of data that have already been seen. Past and future events often form an autocorrelated time-series. Consider, for instance, the prospective Election Research Preacceptance Competition involving designs submitted prior to the 2016 US elections. Many patterns of political behavior that persisted through November and shape the election result were likely already observable (e.g., in polls or media coverage) prior to the election.[20] The "prospective" study and analysis plans submitted may thus, in effect, have been grounded in considerable information about the outcomes on which the tests were based. To put the point differently, retrospective analysis will sometimes involve "newer" evidence than prospective analysis. A scholar seeking to test a hypothesis against data from an upcoming election may in principle be using "older" (more observationally dependent) observations than a scholar seeking to test a retrospective hypothesis about, say, the rise of English democracy through a text-analysis of candidates' campaign speeches from the nineteenth century.

Observational independence is not a simple concept to operationalize precisely. However, I want to suggest that researchers can likely make interpretable claims about the approximate novelty of the tests that they register – claims that research audiences can reason through and scrutinize. Consider the possibility of an ordinal classification scheme, roughly as follows.

- *Low independence.* The researcher has seen evidence that (conditional on a given level of confidence in the hypothesis) is highly predictive of the evidence being sought. Low independence would hold where, for instance, old and new evidence consist of:
  - reports deriving from a common source;
  - interviews with different individuals known to have common interests and common knowledge;
  - variables known from external cases to be highly correlated with one another.
- *Moderate independence.* The researcher has seen evidence that provides a clue to the shape of the test evidence. For instance:
  - the researcher knows what arguments politicians made in public; will go looking to see what arguments they made in private;
  - the researcher knows the ethnicity of warring groups' leadership; will go looking for data on the ethnic composition of their rank-and-file;
  - variables of interest are known from external cases to be moderately correlated with one another;

---

[20] Again, the concern here is not with persistent patterns that reflect systematic features of the phenomena of interest, but rather random processes that shape observed patterns in a manner that persists over time. Thus, hypotheses could be "fit" around random patterns observed before the election and then confirmed by future election data that are partly a function of the same random disturbances.

o the test data come from observation of events that have not yet occurred (but that will plausibly be correlated with events that *have* occurred).
- *High independence.* The researcher has seen no evidence that is significantly predictive of the test evidence. The highest level of observational independence is generated by random assignment, which breaks any link between ex ante patterns across cases and the patterns against which the hypotheses are to be tested. For retrospective observational research, plausible situations of high observational independence might include:
  o the researcher goes looking to see if a particular consideration was raised in private meetings on an issue that was the topic of little public debate;
  o the researcher conducts interviews to find out which business executives attended a private meeting with ministers;
  o the researcher collects data on variables that are known from external cases to be largely orthogonal to those measures already collected;
  o the researcher collects observational data prospectively, following an exogenous shock that was likely to have disrupted random patterns in the data.

More can certainly be said about how one might establish or demonstrate the independence of new from old evidence. As with prior unobservability, researchers will need to make a logical and empirical case for the novelty of their pre-specified tests, and research audiences will evaluate the persuasiveness of that case.

It is also worth noting that the difficulties of establishing or characterizing the prior unobservability and novelty of test evidence are not problems with pre-registration or results-blind review in particular. As the E_1/E_2 example above makes clear, these two issues are fundamental, under any circumstances, to interpreting the results of an empirical test. To describe what can be or has been learned from evidence always requires taking proper account of what has already been observed and how old evidence relates to new. What registration and results-blind review can do, however, is to force claims about learning from tests to be made explicit and their justification open to scrutiny by readers.

Further, it is likely that the challenges of prior unobservability and observational independence are in part endogenous to the institutional environment in which knowledge is produced. In a world in which blind selection of non-experimental tests was a live option, researchers would be motivated to creatively address these challenges. In an effort to make their tests more credible, researchers undertaking hypothesis-testing work would have incentives to develop novel and increasingly credible procedures for establishing the prior unobservability and independence of their test data.

What about the iterative nature of much empirical research, both qualitative and quantitative? The fact that investigators often move back-and-forth, between testing and inductive discovery, presents no fundamental barrier to blind selection. Registration or results-blind submission need not take place prior to all empirical work on a project. Rather, tests can be registered or submitted for results-free review at any point in a project's development – as long as there is some discrete set of evidence bearing on rival theories that has not yet been observed and that cannot be readily predicted from that which has been observed.

Precision

Finally, the gains to pre-registration and results-blind review hinge on how precisely tests can be specified prior to seeing the data. What is at stake in precision is the amount of post hoc discretion available to the researcher, that is, the "wiggle room" available for defining details of a test or its interpretation *after* having seen the evidence. The greater the precision, the more effectively a pre-analysis plan can reduce bias and aid credible communication.

At one extreme – purely exploratory work, whether quantitative or qualitative – the researcher has little preconception of what will be found, and so meaningful tests cannot be stated in advance. At the other extreme – for quantitative confirmatory research – it will often be possible for the researcher to indicate in advance the exact measures and model specifications to be employed, including the code to be used for the analyses and mockups of the tables in which results will be presented (see, e.g., the example in Humphreys, Sanchez de la Sierra, and van der Windt 2013). Notably, the distinctions between experimental and observational (or between prospective and retrospective) research do not map well onto the precision criterion. Precision is primarily a function of the degree to which measurement and analytic procedures take, or can be reduced to, algorithmic form. Precise test pre-specification should generally be as feasible for observational (or retrospective) quantitative research as for experimental (or otherwise prospective) quantitative research.

Most confirmatory qualitative research is likely to occupy a middle ground when it comes to precision. Qualitative researchers generally cannot specify their tests as precisely as quantitative researchers; there is no qualitative equivalent to Stata code. One reason is that the analytic procedures applied to qualitative evidence in case-study work are usually non-algorithmic;[21] they typically involve some element of researcher interpretation. Related to this is the wide diversity of forms of evidence that researchers typically encounter in the course of undertaking a case study: documents of many kinds, statements of many kinds from different sorts of interview subjects, a motley collection of secondary sources and news reports. It will often, therefore, be difficult or impossible for qualitative scholars to anticipate in advance the precise form that observations relevant to their hypotheses might take. Given the variety of ways in which the particulars of qualitative observations might vary, it will be difficult in turn to specify in advance how those particulars may affect inferences drawn from the evidence. Qualitative data-search procedures may also be harder to specify in advance than quantitative sampling procedures, especially given the common difficulty in identifying an ex ante "sampling frame" for common forms of qualitative evidence-collection, such as archival research and elite interviewing. It is, in part, the high degree of prior unobservability of much qualitative evidence – the degree to which qualitative research involves going "deep" into a case – that makes precise pre-specification of tests more difficult.

A high degree of precision in test-specification will thus likely be out of reach for much qualitative work. Yet there is still quite a lot of scope for qualitative scholars to indicate in advance how they plan to evaluate their hypotheses. In a pre-analysis plan, qualitative scholars seeking to test explanations or theories should usually be able to state in advance:

- *Test propositions*: the proposition(s) to be examined.
- *Empirical predictions*: a set of empirical predictions, deriving from the test proposition(s), to be tested in the case.
- *Cases*: the case(s) being studied.
- *Search procedure*: a description of where in the case(s) she will look for evidence (e.g., which archives, interviews with what kinds of subjects).
- *Criteria*: a characterization of the kinds of evidence or observations that, if found in those places, would be consistent or inconsistent with each prediction.[22]
- *Approximate mappings from results to inferences*: some account of how satisfying or not satisfying each prediction would affect inferences. The

---

[21] An important exception is, of course, forms of qualitative research that are algorithmic, such as Qualitative Comparative Analysis.

[22] This might include an indication of multiple kinds of evidence that could speak to the same prediction (i.e., via a logic of triangulation), allowing for the possibility of uncovering mixed evidence and thus the partial satisfaction of a prediction.

degree of precision with which scholars would be able to derive these implications in advance is likely to vary. For many qualitative projects, it may not be possible to pre-specify meaningful numerical likelihoods given the wide variety of unanticipated ways in which the details of qualitative observations and their context may vary. In most situations, however, qualitative researchers should be able to provide a broad indication of how test results will affect findings. Researchers should be able to state in advance, in a general way, whether the satisfaction of a prediction would substantially or only minimally boost confidence in an explanation, and whether the non-satisfaction of that prediction would severely or only modestly discredit the explanation. Van Evera's (1997) four test types (e.g., hoop, smoking-gun, straw-in-the-wind, doubly decisive) may provide a useful set of categories for expressing these mappings.

These are little more than the elements of a research design that we routinely require our graduate students to specify in qualitative dissertation prospectuses prior to beginning fieldwork. And, of course, there are many different ways in which PAPs for qualitative studies might be structured. Piñeiro and Rosenblatt (2016), Kern and Gleditsch (2017), and Hartman, Kern, and Mellor (2018) each propose detailed templates for qualitative PAPs. Piñeiro, Perez, and Rosenblatt (2016) represent the earliest qualitative pre-registered PAP of which I am aware, while Christensen, Hartman, and Samii (2018) is, to my knowledge, the first completed study containing a pre-registered qualitative analysis.[23]

Imagine, for the sake of illustration, a qualitative scholar who seeks to test a theory explaining tax cuts by British governments in the twentieth century. The researcher might specify in advance the primary explanation that tax cuts are motivated by Keynesian aims. The scholar might then derive from this proposition the prediction that we should observe prominent mentions of the logic of Keynesian demand-management in records of deliberations over the tax cut. Having selected and specified a set of tax-policy episodes to be examined, the researcher might further indicate that she will look for mentions of Keynesian logic in all public statements by ministers reported in the daily press, records of cabinet meetings and correspondence between senior officials available in the National Archives, and statements by majority-party members of parliament recorded in Hansard. Further, the researcher

---

[23] Hartman, Samii, and Christensen's pre-registration was gated at the time of writing but located on the Open Science Framework registry at osf.io/46r87.

could specify that a failure to find prominent mentions of a Keynesian logic would severely undermine the explanation, making the search for this evidence a "hoop test."

A specification of this kind would, of course, still leave some significant features of the test ambiguous. Just how prominent do mentions of Keynesian logic have to be for the test to be passed? How many actors have to mention it? What forms of words will count as the use of Keynesian logic? There would inevitably be some wiggle room. Yet, compared with current practice – involving no public pre-declaration of research plans – this basic specification would in fact pin down a great deal about what will count as a positive or a null finding. Moreover, pre-specification is useful even in the face of unanticipated observations or unexpected features of the evidence that affect its interpretation. The provision of a pre-analysis plan allows the reader to compare the researcher's interpretation of unexpected observations to the pre-announced tests and to arrive at her own judgment about the extent to which the interpretation of the evidence is consistent with the analysis plan's broad logic.

As with prior unobservability and independence, precision will be a matter of degree, with higher credibility attaching to more crisply defined tests. And, as with the other two criteria, precision is likely itself to be shaped by the presence of blind-selection opportunities. In a world in which registration and results-blind review are options, the equilibrium outcome is likely to be one that substantially mitigates the problem of precision in qualitative testing. Audiences will be free to judge how much "wiggle room" the researcher has given herself in her pre-analysis plan, and to assess the credibility of the test result accordingly. In turn, qualitative scholars interested in hypothesis-testing will be incentivized to bind their own hands with clear pre-analysis plans. However, researchers will have incentives to *optimize*, rather than maximize, the level of precision in their PAPs: a vague plan will reduce the credibility of the test, while excessive precision raises the risk of error by excluding relevant evidence from consideration.

As Findley et al. (2016) point out, there remains the danger of "hypothesis trolling" (12): the pre-registration of a large number of empirical predictions, thus allowing ample room for "fishing" for supporting evidence. Yet pre-registration – combined with a reasonable degree of reviewer vigilance – can itself serve as a powerful check against the strategic multiplication of hypotheses. Reviewers can compare a set of reported results with the predictions specified in the pre-analysis plan, ensuring that results are presented on all predictions (or that an explanation is provided for missing results). Reviewers can additionally check that conclusions take into account the multiplicity of tests conducted. In a quantitative context, researchers can be expected to correct standard errors for the number of hypotheses tested, a procedure that imposes a "penalty" for each additional test. (For detail on multiple-comparisons corrections, see Christensen and Miguel, Chapter 6, this volume.) Assessors of qualitative work can similarly ensure that authors have given due weight to failed tests and/or that supporting evidence is suitably discounted for the number of predictions that were pre-specified. While the appropriate norms of assessment will take time to develop, limited experience to date with blind selection in political science is at least somewhat encouraging. Reflecting on the review process for their special issue of *CPS*, Findley et al. report that "hypothesis trolling was specifically targeted and rejected by reviewers" (17). To the extent that assessors penalize the proliferation of predictions, researchers will face clear incentives to specify their tests judiciously.

The Test-Credibility Space

If we imagine a three-dimensional space defined by our three credibility criteria – prior unobservability, independence, precision – individual studies are likely to be located at different points in this space. Tests to be carried out using evidence from highly restricted archives, which are expected to reveal details of decisions about which little is known, may have moderate-to-high levels of prior unobservability and independence, but relatively low precision because so little is known about what might be found. A project that will administer a structured interview protocol to elite decision-makers might display high prior unobservability and high precision (given the closed-ended nature of the questionnaire, we know what form the data will take), but middling independence (as the interview subjects may have made numerous public statements about the decisions being studied). And a quantitative social-network study using Facebook data that can be accessed only on the company's Menlo Park campus may display high test-precision (as the statistical models can be specified in advance), high observational independence (if there are no other ways of observing the network patterns being studied), and high prior unobservability (since dates of access can be independently confirmed).

The overall credibility of a claim that a set of tests were selected blind, then, depends jointly on these three qualities. We might think of credible blind-selection as a product of the level of prior unobservability, the level of independence, and the precision of the test-specification.[24] Under current practice for observational studies (no pre-registration and results-based review), we have little reason to attribute a level of prior unosbervability above 0. The overall credibility of current observational tests (and of unregistered or results-based-reviewed experimental tests) should thus itself be understood to be 0.[25] Blind-selection has the potential to enhance credibility relative to the status quo whenever levels of prior unobservability, independence, and precision are all in positive territory.

Can Studies without Results be Evaluated?

Results-blind review, in one sense, seems the perfect antidote to both publication and analysis biases: it takes the results – whether strong, weak, or null – entirely out of the equation. Results-blind review is also logistically simpler than pre-registration as it does not require the researcher to demonstrate the prior unobservability of the data. Yet results-blind review is also difficult precisely because it hides results from editors and reviewers.

Reviewers and editors are practiced at judging the strength and importance of empirical findings once they see them. But how are they to judge the value of a study *absent* any empirical claims at all? Perhaps a strong result of a planned test would be enormously informative, but how can the submission be judged without knowing whether that outcome will be realized? Reviewers might well worry about how interesting a null outcome will be, given that it might be an indication that there is in fact no true effect or merely of a weakness in the research design. Findley et al. (2016), in reviewing their experience with editing the results-blind issue of *CPS*, identify this quandary as a key stumbling block to the success of results-blind review.

Moreover, how should reviewers think about the plausibility of the proposed hypotheses? Should authors be penalized for testing hypotheses that already have a great deal of backing? Should they be rewarded for proposing novel hypotheses that have yet to be tested?

---

[24] Visually, in our three-dimensional space, this product would correspond to the volume of the rectangular cuboid defined by the origin and the point marking the levels taken on for each of the three qualities.

[25] To be clear, this does not mean that the results presented are not the true results of the specified tests; it is that we have no reason to believe that the tests were selected without reference to the strength of the results.

For results-blind review to work, those assessing study designs and analysis plans for publication must have a metric by which to judge the ex ante knowledge-generating potential of a study. I want to suggest that this problem is soluble. The relevant question, I would argue, is *how much we expect to learn from a study*: how much, in either direction, do we expect our beliefs to shift as a result of carrying out the proposed test? There are a number of ways in which we might operationalize this expectation, but any measure of expected belief change must take into account at least three features of a proposed test.

1. *Probative value*. The metric should take into account the probative value of the proposed test. Whether statistical or qualitative, proposed tests will vary in their sensitivity (how likely is the test to be passed if the theorized phenomenon is present?) and in their specificity (how likely is the test to be failed if the theorized phenomenon is absent?). We are likely to learn more from empirical tests with greater than with lesser ability to accurately distinguish among rival hypotheses. Judging the probative value of a proposed test involves an assessment of the core features of a research design, such as: the quality of the proposed measures; the relationship between sample and theoretical scope; and the relationship between theory and empirical predictions, including the appropriateness of a statistical model, the credibility of a claim of exogeneity, or the probability of observing a clue under a hypotheses or its negation.
2. *Scope for belief change*. Hypotheses vary according to how much scope there is for a change in beliefs in either direction as a result of an empirical test. For hypotheses in which we have very high confidence, there is some scope for downward movement, but little for upward movement; and vice-versa for hypotheses in which we have little confidence. As Humphreys and Jacobs (2015) demonstrate, moreover, with Bayesian updating the scope for upward revision in confidence is greatest not for very implausible hypotheses but for those of moderately low prior probability; the scope for downward revision is, likewise, greatest for hypotheses of moderately high prior probability. Any assessment of expected value of a study must thus take into account how the plausibility of the hypothesis being tested affects the scope for learning.
3. *Likelihood of an impactful result*. Empirical tests often have an asymmetrical character, in which the finding of a relationship or a clue may have a greater or lesser impact on our beliefs than the failure to find the relationship or the clue. For instance, with a hoop test of a hypothesis, not

finding the clue has a greater impact than finding it. Our measure of expected learning thus should in some way capture which of these two outcomes – the higher- or the lower-impact one – is more likely. And this, too, will be function of our prior confidence in the hypothesis. For instance, consider a hoop test of a theory in which we are highly confident. Failure of the hoop test would a substantial effect on our beliefs; however, the very fact that the hypothesis is very likely true makes it relatively *unlikely* that the hoop test will be failed and that significant learning will occur.

By way of illustration, consider a simple Bayesian operationalization of expected learning. This operationalization takes the above three considerations into account by employing the same beliefs that we routinely use for assessing the impact of test results. Assume, for the sake of exposition, a relatively simple situation in which a study can be understood as generating a single test of a hypothesis. The function is itself a simple operationalization of expected belief change: it takes the average of (1) the absolute value of the shift in confidence in the hypothesis that would result from the passage of the test and (2) the absolute value of the shift in confidence that would result from the failure of the test, weighting each potential shift by the probability of each outcome, given our prior beliefs. The inputs into this calculation are:

1. the prior plausibility of the hypothesis ($p(H)$);
2. the likelihood of a positive result if the hypothesis is true ($p(E|H)$);
3. the likelihood of a positive result if the hypothesis is false ($p(E|{\sim}H)$).

Assume, further, that we have labeled H and ${\sim}H$ such that $p(E|H) > p(E|{\sim}H)$, and so finding the evidence will always increase our confidence in H. We then get the following expression for expected learning (*EL*).

$$EL = p(E) \times \left(\frac{(p(E|H) \times p(H))}{p(E)} - p(H) \right) + (1 - p(E)) \times \left(p(H) - \frac{(1 - p(E|H)) \times p(H)}{1 - p(E)} \right)$$

The first set of terms represents the absolute belief change resulting from a positive result (finding *E*), weighted by the probability of finding *E*, and the second set of terms represents the absolute belief change resulting from a null result (not finding *E*), weighted by the probability of not finding *E*. This simplifies to:

$$EL = 2 \times p(H) \times (p(E|H) - p(E))$$

where

$$p(E) = p(H) \times p(E|H) + (1 - p(H)) \times p(E|\sim H).$$

In Figure 9.1, we graph expected learning for four different kinds of tests to examine how this quantity depends on the probative value of a test and on the prior plausibility of the hypothesis.[26] I use Van Evera's (1997) four test types, with illustrative probabilities. While these test types are generally associated with process tracing, we can readily conceive of statistical results as having similar qualities. For instance, we might believe that a particular statistically significant correlation is very likely to be observed with a given sample size if a causal effect is present, while it may also be observed even if the effect is absent – rendering this statistical test, in effect, a hoop test. Similarly, we might believe a statistical test to be sufficiently specific that we are unlikely to observe a significant correlation if the effect is absent, though the test might well miss the effect even if it is present – generating a smoking-gun test.

As can be seen here, a metric of expected learning of this kind has the potential to provide reviewers relatively straightforward guidance to the evaluation of manuscripts in the absence of results. Two principles of expected learning are readily apparent. First, unsurprisingly, the higher the probative value of the proposed test, the greater the expected learning. Better tests, more learning.

Second, and less obvious, it is for hypotheses of *middling* prior plausibility that the expected belief shift is greatest, regardless of the type of test. At first glance, this result may seem counterintuitive: shouldn't a hoop test, for instance, generate greater learning for *more* plausible hypotheses since a hoop test is most impactful on the downside? and, by the same reasoning, shouldn't a smoking-gun test be most valuable for a less likely hypothesis? It is true that a hoop test has the greatest impact on beliefs *if* it is failed, and such a result would be more impactful for a hypothesis of higher probability.[27] Countervailing this effect, however, is the effect of $p(H)$ on how likely the hoop test is to be failed in the first place. The stronger the hypothesis, the less

---

[26] Alternative conceptualizations of learning are, of course, possible. For instance, we might think of learning as a reduction in posterior variance rather than as a shift in beliefs.

[27] Though, as noted above, the maximum learning from a failed hoop test occurs at moderately high levels of $p(H)$, not at the highest level.

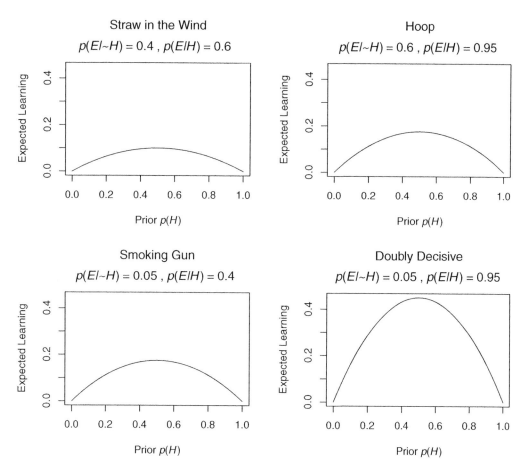

Figure 9.1 Expected learning conditional on $p(H)$, $p(E|H)$, and $p(E|\sim H)$

Note: Figure shows how the expected learning for different types of tests depends on priors regarding the proposition

likely the hypothesis is to fail the hoop test, and thus the less likely we are to learn from the test. The same goes for the smoking-gun test and the unlikely hypothesis: the most impactful result, a passed test, is highly unlikely for a weak hypothesis.

There are other possible ways of conceptualizing and operationalizing the expected intellectual value of a study absent access to its results. The key point is that we can assess the likely contribution using the very same beliefs that reviewers and editors regularly use to evaluate studies *with* results. Assessing the substantive meaning of a test result requires us to form a view of the strength of the test: was it a hard (specific) test for the hypothesis or an easy (sensitive) one? and when evaluating manuscripts with results, we routinely use judgments about the plausibility of the hypothesis being tested, given prior knowledge – whether to judge the paper's novelty and contribution to the literature or to assess the plausibility of the findings.[28] These same beliefs simply need to be mobilized in a somewhat different way for judging manuscripts without results.

A standard like expected learning can also cut against a common concern about results-blind review: that it will lead to the publication of a large number of "failed" studies with uninteresting, null findings. Results-blind review would almost certainly generate a significant increase in the publication of studies that find little or no support for the main test proposition. And these findings would indeed be uninteresting to the extent that the hypotheses being tested were never plausible to begin with. However, if reviewers judge study designs based on how much we expect to learn from them, then studies with a substantial probability of generating null results will only pass muster to the extent that a null result would be *informative*, that is, to the extent that a null finding would undermine a hypothesis in which we had some prior confidence. Similarly, and just as importantly, an expected-learning standard would weed out studies likely to produce *positive* findings for hypotheses in which we already have strong confidence. If an "interesting" result is one that shifts our beliefs closer to the truth, then results-blind review arguably has a far greater prospect of delivering interesting findings by focusing assessors' attention on the core issue of what can be learned, rather than on the distraction of whether a study happened to be "successful."

Conclusion

The *status quo* is a world in which we are almost entirely unconstrained in our ability to choose "tests" conditional on their outcomes. And yet, for many forms of observational inquiry, we are capable of articulating what we are looking for before we know what we will find. This moment of empirical

---

[28] Interestingly, reviewers may be using their beliefs about the prior plausibility of the hypothesis to judge a paper's contribution in rather counter-Bayesian ways. When they judge a paper with a highly surprising finding as making a greater contribution than a paper with less surprising findings, they are of course ignoring the role of the prior in Bayesian updating. Bayes' rule tells us that a positive result for a very unlikely hypothesis should make us only marginally more confident in the hypothesis, even if the test is a highly discriminating one.

anticipation creates an opportunity for tying our own hands – whether as authors or publication gatekeepers – forcing ourselves to choose hypotheses and study procedures on their intellectual merits, rather than on the realization of favorable results.

Neither pre-registration nor results-blind review represents a panacea for the deep selection problems that plague confirmatory social scientific research. As we move outside the realm of random assignment, assessing the contribution of blind-selection mechanisms to reducing bias requires a careful, complex assessment of the types of data and forms of tests being employed. In this assessment, there is room for subjective judgment and potentially divergent interpretations. I have sought to show, however, that these two devices can plausibly enhance the credibility of findings for a wide range of test-oriented research designs.

In closing, it is worth considering one possible interpretation of the argument that I have made. A common objection to pre-registration is that it will tend to stifle exploratory analysis and creativity in the generation of theory (e.g., Laitin 2013; Tucker 2014). Results-blind review might likewise be seen as a mechanism that favors confirmatory over exploratory research since it requires the clear specification of procedures in advance. More generally, the advocacy of the use of these mechanisms for a wide range of empirical methods could be read as a claim that the main thing that we should be doing as empirical researchers is implementing tests that have been specified prior to observation – that the scope for undisciplined exploration should be sharply limited. And even if it is not the intention of those advocating blind-selection mechanisms, the practical effect could be to constrain researchers to studying questions for which ex ante tests can be specified.

In fact, the case for expanding the use of pre-registration and results-blind submission runs precisely in the opposite direction. If the pre-specification of study procedures were to be widely *required* and imposed as a *binding constraint* – such that authors would always or usually be required to pre-announce tests and would be constrained to report *only* those analyses that were pre-announced – the result would indeed be to stifle empirical discovery and the conceptual and theoretical inspiration that it yields.

The likely effects of voluntary pre-registration and results-blind review are very different. As voluntary forms of hand-binding, these mechanisms allow for more credible communication between researcher and audience (Humphreys, Sanchez de la Sierra, and van der Windt 2013). They represent a powerful tool for the scholar who finds herself in a particular kind of research situation: one in which they seek to test a proposition and know how they want to go about that test before they implement it. Registration and results-blind review provide her with the means to credibly signal it is indeed a *test* that she has conducted. At the same time, scholars seeking to derive theoretical insights from their data or to examine questions for which the pre-specification of tests is impossible will be free to explore without constraint. The greatest benefit would accrue to research consumers, who will be much better positioned to tell the difference between the two.

Moreover, even when test procedures have been pre-specified, this specification need not be treated as constraining: in a non-binding model, researchers remain free to conduct and report analyses that were not announced in advance. What registration and results-free submission make possible is the credible distinction of the confirmatory from the exploratory elements of a set of research findings.

Rather than elevating the status of test-oriented work, wider use of blind-selection mechanisms would make it more difficult for researchers – doing quantitative or qualitative work – to claim to be testing or substantiating a claim when they are not. We would, then, all face greater pressure to identify the inductive sources of our insights and to give exploratory work its due in the process of producing knowledge.

Part IV

Appraisal

Throughout this volume, we have discussed the problem of replication – but without much detail. What does replication mean and how might it be accomplished? More generally, how are the myriad studies addressing a research question integrated into an evolving – and hopefully progressing – body of research?

Chapter 10 focuses on replication, with a primary focus on quantitative research. The authors outline a number of ways of understanding this process, and gauging its success. They also discuss why replication is rarely undertaken, and when undertaken often unnoticed (because unpublished).

Chapter 11 focuses on the problem of measurement in replication studies, with a focus on both quantitative and qualitative contexts. The author finds that follow-up studies of a topic often find measurement errors in the original work, errors that can be corrected in subsequent scholarship – if duly recorded and preserved.

Chapter 12 shifts focus to qualitative studies, examining the role of repeated studies in cumulating knowledge about a subject – understood within a Bayesian framework.

Chapter 13 discusses ways in which reappraisals of previous scholarship – including explicit replications and also follow-up studies whose primary purpose is not replication – might be encouraged, coordinated and preserved. To achieve these goals, the author envisions a reappraisal institute, a central directory of reappraisals, a reappraisal scorecard and additional support infrastructure.

Chapter 14 broadens the focus further to consider how a field of work can integrate disparate findings in an ongoing fashion. The author proposes a comprehensive approach to appraisal that goes beyond the traditional literature review (as found, for example, in the *Annual Review* series). It involves examining previous work on a subject, empirical tests that seek to resolve – or at least shed light on – ongoing controversies, and explicit attention to theoretical development.

Chapter 15 explores the role of impact metrics in the task of evaluation. If we wish to take stock of an individual scholar, a study, a field, a journal or press, a department, a discipline or any other group or organization we are in need of a metric that will allow us to systematically compare across units (whatever those units might be). Impact metrics offer an approach grounded in citation counts to particular studies, which can be aggregated up to provide metrics for larger units (individuals, journals et al.). Resort to impact metrics is increasingly common in judging performance in the social sciences, and this general approach seems destined to grow further in the coming years, so it is important to understand current shortcomings, the potential for misuse, but also the positive impact that impact metrics might have on the production of knowledge.

10 Replication for Quantitative Research

Jeremy Freese and David Peterson

In 2012, Nobel laureate Daniel Kahneman sent an open email to researchers in a psychology subfield warning of a "trainwreck looming" regarding the replicability of their findings. "Your subfield is now a poster child for the integrity of psychological research," he warned. Today, depending on which psychologist you ask, psychology is either beset by a "crisis of replication" (Pashler and Harris 2012) or by an overblown panic as to whether a crisis exists (Stroebe and Strack 2014).

Social psychology, especially, has taken a beating. A specter of radical doubt now looms over the field, with many widely reported findings regarded far more skeptically than they once were. One social psychologist writes that "no one knows what to believe anymore" (Jussim 2016), while another says the field has become vulnerable to "accusations of pervasive wrongness" (Baumeister 2016).

Yet, even as social psychology has been at the forefront of reported concerns about replicability, it has also been extremely fertile in advancing innovative proposals for improving the replicability of research. The causal direction here is complicated. Many of the same psychologists who have been particularly active in pursuing changes in research practice have also been responsible for work that called attention to the field's problems. While these "replication activists," as we will call them here, consider themselves to be pursuing the ideals of good science, others have taken a more negative view. Acrimonious exchanges have spilled into public view, including comparisons of the activists to bullies, witch-hunters, McCarthyites, and jihadists.[1]

In this chapter, we use the crisis in social psychology as a case study to articulate some of the challenges surrounding replication that bedevil efforts to improve replicability more broadly in the social sciences. We think extensive consideration of recent developments in social psychology is useful for

---

[1] Actually, all these comparisons have been made by prominent Harvard psychologist Dan Gilbert, but similar sentiments have been stated, if not always as colorfully, by various other psychologists.

two reasons. First, social psychology's crisis has prompted an outpouring of reflection and debate among active researchers about basic epistemological issues that is unusual – maybe even unprecedented – in its volume and frankness. Second, social science has also recently shown increasing interest in experiments and other strong causal-inference research designs (Jackson and Cox 2013). Notable for our purposes here is that experimentation has long been the dominant methodology of social psychology, and yet plainly this did not indemnify the field from the possibility of radical doubts being raised regarding the ultimate quality of its research results.

As for lessons to be drawn, social sciences are extremely diverse in their methods and epistemological orientations, and we warn that our response to that diversity may be frustrating for those looking to this chapter for bottom-line practical recommendations. We see replication matters as involving a welter of complications and tradeoffs that will likely prompt different paths for different parts of social science. We believe concerns about replicability pose problems that are intractable without institution-level solutions, but we think differences across and within social science make it unlikely that any single set of policy recommendations are optimal throughout.

Instead this chapter highlights what we regard as key challenges of replication for social science, with an eye toward their implication for policy. In the first half of the chapter, we consider what replication is, what grounds there might be for saying a replication problem exists, and what causes the replication problems that do exist. We then consider a number of policy changes that have been advanced to improve the replicability of studies.

Before we begin, we need to clarify two things about how we use social science here. First, as we consider the lessons of social psychology for other social sciences, we refer to the latter as "social science." This is just a terminological convenience. Second, we will mostly talk about social science as if qualitative research does not exist. We do so because the issues involved are, frankly, so different. In writing the chapter, we found that trying to consider qualitative research along the way led to detours at nearly every turn, with an ultimate unwieldiness that would not serve anyone well. Elman and Kapiszewski (2014) contend that qualitative scholars in the social sciences "remain only partially committed to replication." We agree with their ultimate assessment that many issues surrounding replication in qualitative social science are more satisfactorily considered under the broader heading of "transparency."

The Meanings of Replication

New Data or the Same Data?

Challenge 1: "Replication" means different things to different scientists.
Social psychology is dominated by experimental research, often using subject pools selected for their convenience (Henrich et al. 2010). Statistical analyses are usually straightforward. In fact, complicated analyses might even be taken as reason to worry that the researcher may have been "p-hacking" to obtain a desired result. Accordingly, questions about the stability of experimental results are conventionally viewed as best resolved by additional experiments. The term "replication" is usually taken for granted as implying *the collection of new data from new subjects*.

In contrast to sciences organized around experiments, the methodological center of social sciences has traditionally been observational data that are often subjected to complicated analyses involving many discrete steps and decisions by researchers. Even the recent enthusiasm among social scientists for experiments has focused predominantly on large, intensive experiments that may be very costly. Here, there is a much stronger sense that stability of reported results ought to be first interrogated by *looking at the same data again*. For social sciences, use of "replication" has referred less to collecting new data than it has to re-examination of the same data used in the original study.

We have seen interdisciplinary conversations about "replication" in which parties have gone on for a disconcertingly long time before realizing they were using the term to mean different things. Past papers on replication that have noted the terminological tangle have themselves come to incommensurate resolutions. To be as plain as possible, we will here just use the admittedly ungraceful terms "new-data replication" and "same-data replication" as needed.

Result-Focused or Conclusion-Focused?

Challenge 2: Replications can either emphasize similarity or difference from the original study, but which approach is interpreted as better often depends on how the replication turns out.
Replication studies may either seek to reproduce procedures used in the original study as closely as possible, or they may deliberately depart from those procedures. That distinction, in turn, maps onto what the replication study

is trying to evaluate: the specific results of the original study or more general conclusions that may be inferred from those results.

To see what we mean, consider first same-data replication. Replication in the narrowest sense here is simple *verification* of the original results (Freese and Peterson 2017): work that confirms that reported results can be generated from the data used, which may involve simply executing the same code in the same statistical package. For some, this would not be considered replication at all, but something more mundane, like merely "checking" (Collins 1991). But what is clear is that such "checking" reveals problems, as was the recent experience of the *American Journal of Political Science* when it began independently verifying that statistical results can be reproduced using the authors' code.

Verification adds confidence in the results as such, but does not add any new information about the relationship between the results and the conclusions. This can be contrasted with re-analyzing data to explore how conclusions are affected by alternative decisions the researcher could have made but did not. Brenzau (2015), for example, finds that results about public opinion and social welfare spending reported by Brooks and Manza (2006) depend on how the model is specified, and argues that his specification involves weaker and more plausible assumptions. Weakliem (2016) agrees with Brenzau's critique but argues his analyses are still not ideal and that better analyses of the same data supports Brooks and Manza's original conclusion. Here, researchers are no longer trying to verify the findings of the original study as such, but instead are deliberately juxtaposing different procedures with those of the original study and then evaluating whether and how different decisions affect the substantive conclusions drawn.

More theoretical ambiguities are raised when the replication involves new data. Researchers attempting replication in the narrowest sense seek to follow the methods of the original study as closely as practicality allows. Such work has been called "exact replication," "direct replication," or "close replication" (e.g., Simons 2014).[2] The different terms manifest diverging views of how well original studies might, in all possibly relevant details, ultimately be repeated. Important in such work, however, is that researchers deliberately try to subordinate their own independent judgment and creativity as much as possible in the effort to remain faithful to the original study.

---

[2] Elsewhere we refer to this as mechanical replication, as a nod to the concept of "mechanical objectivity" in science studies (Freese and Peterson 2017).

Repeating the methods of the original study provides the most leverage for evaluating the stability of the findings reported in the original study. At the same time, it provides the least leverage for speaking to any more general inference that might be drawn from the original study. Instead, it would seem that we learn more about whatever theoretical conclusions are at stake from work that deliberately introduces differences to the original study design. As Lucas et al. (2013:223) argue for sociology: "Replications that test theoretical propositions in new settings ... have the capacity to build and extend theory that strict replications do not." Eden (2002:842) says simply, "The less similar a replication is to an original study, the greater its potential contribution."

This reasoning in social psychology is exemplified by what is sometimes called "conceptual replication," in which researchers conduct an experiment that considers the same hypothesis as the original study, but with deliberately dissimilar methods. To borrow an example from Stroebe and Strack (2012), a famous social psychological study found that students primed with stereotypes about the elderly subsequently walked more slowly as they left the experiment (Bargh et al. 1996). One conceptual replication of this study found that students also walked more slowly after being shown a photo of old people and asked to imagine a typical day in their life (Ku et al. 2010). The idea is that successful conceptual replications provide stronger evidence for the underlying theory than simply showing that the particular result of a specific experiment can be repeatedly observed.

But conceptual replications have become controversial in social psychology. Chambers argues that, while seeking "converging evidence" using different procedures is important, "this isn't replication, and it should never be regarded as a substitute for replication." The concern is that, when conceptual replications fail to obtain results consistent with the original study, a fundamental interpretive ambiguity arises (Collins 1985). Does the failure actually speak against the original theory, to problems in a researchers' understanding of the theory, or to problems in the execution or design of the replication? The practical consequence is that conceptual replications almost only appear in print when they support a theory, since the meaning of failures is unclear and potentially controversial. Given that replication is regularly presented as essential for science to operate as a self-correcting enterprise, it is hard to see how any form of "replication" that is only publishable when successful could be part of self-correcting anything.

As a result, whether the "distance" between a replication and an original study prospectively seems like a virtue or detriment depends on how one expects it will turn out. When one believes the original findings are true, pursuing the generalizability of the finding or sturdiness of its connection to theoretical conclusions may seem to be the most fruitful course. However, when one is skeptical of the original findings, it is not. Investigating the generalizability of results that are suspect may seem like wasting effort and inviting confusion. The relative importance that social scientists place in verification or in direct new-data replications can be expected to be strongly influenced by their confidence in original studies.

Is there a Replication Problem?

Challenge 3: Whether a scientific field in general has a replication problem may be unknowable.
The perceived value of verification and direct replication depends on the perceived likelihood that such studies will fail. Social psychology's disagreement regarding whether a replication crisis exists is partly a disagreement about the prevalence of "false positives." Replication activists trying to rouse broader support for initiatives confront the same immediate questions as would-be reformers of all kinds: *Is there really a problem? How do you know?*

The compelling lesson from social psychology in this regard is how challenging it is to establish agreement even to seemingly empirical questions regarding the frequency of false positives. The implication for social science may be particularly daunting, as social psychology may have much better overall conditions for evaluating its (new-data) replicability than non-experimental social sciences.

For example, one line of evidence used to diagnose literatures as problematic has been studies of publication bias: whether properties of scientific literature diverge from what one would expect if the results of studies had no bearing on whether they were published. The potential strength of techniques for interrogating publication bias depend on features of the literature to which they are applied. The large sets of experimental results that characterize social psychology, with standard measures of effect sizes and relatively standardized reporting of test statistics, provides a best-case scenario for this work. By comparison, the quantitative observational studies that predominate most social sciences involve far more diverse statistical approaches and parameterizations that limit the potential power of meta-analysis. In other words, social psychology has much more leverage for assessing its publication bias than other social sciences, and even there one does not see consensus in what findings about publication bias mean.

More than this, social psychology's heavy reliance on relatively low-cost laboratory (or, increasingly, online) experiments allows the possibility of more extensive efforts to broadly assess the field's replicability. Replication activists organized an effort to replicate one experiment from 100 articles sampled from three psychology journals. Their finding, published in *Science*, was that only 39 percent of effects were successfully replicated. Yet, for all this work, researchers were left concluding only that "There is room to improve reproducibility in psychology" (Open Science Collaboration 2015). They write, "How many of the effects have we established are true? Zero. And how many of the effects have we established are false? Zero" (7).

More tellingly, however, is that even this weak conclusion was not enough for critics. A different team published their own re-analysis of the same data, from which they claimed "the evidence is consistent with the opposite conclusion – that the reproducibility of psychological science is quite high and, in fact, statistically indistinguishable from 100%" (Gilbert et al. 2016). Ironically, some of their criticisms invoked the fundamental interpretive ambiguities described above. How close do the methods of a replication study need to be to original work to count as a replication? How different do results need to be to say that a replication failed? Additionally, the critics pointed out that even using systematic sampling methods from specific journals still leaves an unknowable relationship between the resulting sample and the field as a whole.

The dreary conclusion for social scientists to be drawn from this episode is that replication efforts may produce an unbridgeable interpretive gap. Rather than simple tests of truth, replications may produce enough ambiguity that prospects are dim for any feasible effort to overcome inclinations to believe or deny that a problem exists. Case studies of replication controversies suggest obtaining agreement about single findings may be difficult and protracted enough (Collins 1985). As a result, however, scientists' sense of whether a broad problem exists can instead be expected to rely on less formal and systematic evidence.

What does sway support for replication initiatives? Put simply, reforms often follow scandals. In social psychology, a succession of episodes included revelation of massive fraud by a prominent Dutch researcher, embarrassment over the publication in a top journal of findings purporting to provide evidence of paranormal abilities, and publicity from an online outburst by a Yale psychologist over claimed failures to replicate his most famous experiment.

Nowhere else in social science has had quite such a run of bad press, but one can point to lesser examples. In economics, for example, the leading journal began demanding authors provide data upon publication after a study revealed conventions regarding data sharing were widely unfollowed (Bernanke 2004). Concerns about encroaching laxity were again raised when a graduate student discovered that an extremely influential finding was actually an artifact of a spreadsheet error. In sum, while social scientists would widely agree that scandals are inferior to systematic inquiry as a basis for policy, we suspect they are nevertheless not surprised that, in practice, policy changes regarding research practice are often reactions to particular scandals.

How Do Replication Crises Happen?

From a case study of high-energy physicists, Collins (1998) draws a useful distinction between "open" and "closed" cultures of evidence in science. Scientists in relatively closed cultures are risk-averse about the conclusions they draw from empirical results and are reluctant to publish results before a high evidentiary threshold is reached. In more open cultures, scientists are more willing to speculate in papers about the potential significance of results and are willing to publish more tentative findings. Closed cultures are characterized by "evidentiary individualism," meaning that scientists consider it "the job of [individual researchers] to take responsibility for the validity and meaning of scientific results." Open cultures reflect evidentiary collectivism, where the scientific collective is relied upon to "assess results from an early stage."

Either type of culture can effectively produce knowledge. In a closed culture, the community has high trust in original published findings because expectations are that their publication means that they have been rigorously demonstrated. In an open culture, more speculative findings are published but the community recognizes that further assessment of these findings is necessary for them to be considered true.

Replication activists in social psychology have diagnosed the cause of their field's putative crisis as an improper mixing of elements from the two cultures. The field is faulted for having too low a barrier for publishing findings while, at the same time, supporting too little work to replicate existing studies (Figure 10.1). We briefly describe each part of the problem here, and use the distinction to structure our discussion of policy recommendations later in the chapter.

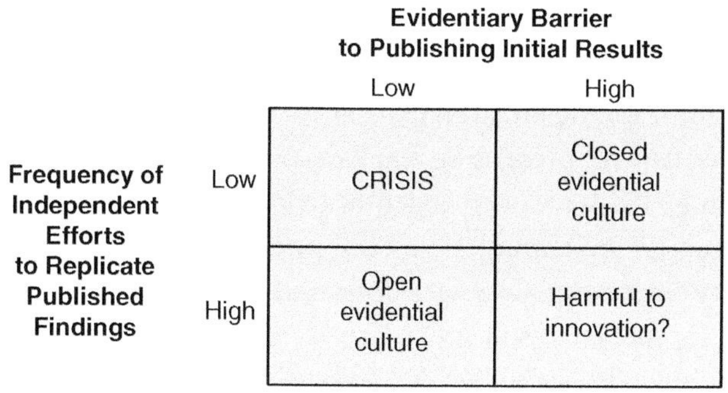

	Evidentiary Barrier to Publishing Initial Results	
Frequency of Independent Efforts to Replicate Published Findings	Low	High
Low	CRISIS	Closed evidential culture
High	Open evidential culture	Harmful to innovation?

Figure 10.1 Publishing barriers and replication frequency

Excessive Publication of False Positives

Challenge 4: The ideas that are most strongly rewarded are those that are least likely to be true.

Social psychology has been criticized for overvaluing highly counterintuitive findings, which is linked to false positives because counterintuitive results are less likely to be true. Social psychologists are rewarded for popular interest in their work in many ways, and indeed the popular attention the field receives is often cited as a key attraction of young scientists to it (Faye 2012). Counterintuitive hypotheses have particular popular appeal, which promotes the pursuit of counterintuitive findings by authors and a preference for them among editors (Nosek et al. 2012). This push to pursue unlikely hypotheses has also been criticized for reducing incentives for "normal science," that is, work that extends existing paradigms in ways that are less surprising and more incremental.

Of course, a bias toward novelty is only one type of motivation that may press researchers toward ideas with suboptimal prospects of being true. In social science, ideological biases remain a perennial source of concern (Gieryn 1999), especially to the extent that biases are shared among reviewers or editors and, thus, temper criticism. Concerns about financial conflicts promoting false positives have a long history in medical and program evaluation research. These concerns have more recently also become prominent elsewhere; controversy over financial guidelines recently prompted the American Economics Association to adopt the first official ethics guidelines in its history.

In any event, taking the pursuit of counterintuitive findings as a problem per se is problematic insofar as innovation and intellectual risk are viewed as essential to good science. Instead, one may note that false ideas only result in false positives to whatever extent the methods for testing ideas are vulnerable to generating spurious evidence. Here, much criticism has targeted null hypothesis significance testing (NHST), and specifically a strong reliance on a threshold of $p < 0.05$ for presenting results as positive support for a hypothesis. Problems with NHST have been cogently articulated for decades (e.g., Cohen 1994; Rosenthal 1979; Schmidt 1996). For purposes here, the core problem is that "flexibility" in how analyses are done and reported provide the potential to produce a significant result much greater than "$p < 0.05$" would suggest. The result is a prevailing standard for being able to present results as positive evidence for a hypothesis that is much lower than what would permit high confidence that the theory was true.

Insufficient Work to Discover and Correct Published False Positives

Challenge 5: There are few incentives to conduct replications.
In his classic depiction of science as a uniquely functional enterprise, Merton (1973b:276) describes scientists as "subject to rigorous policing, to a degree perhaps unparalleled in any other field of activity." In contrast, social psychologist Diederik Stapel (2014), revealed to have fabricated data in nearly 60 articles, describes the incentives and oversight of his field very differently: "It was very, very easy … Nobody ever checked my work; everyone trusted me … I did it all myself, with a big cookie jar right next to me … and nobody watching … I could take whatever I wanted." A long-voiced complaint in social psychology – and social science, more broadly – is that the types of replication work that might challenge existing studies are infrequently undertaken and even more rarely published (Brandt et al. 2014).

The reforms replication activists have proposed for these problems follow from their understanding of its root cause. When explaining why their field has a replication crisis, activists in psychology sound a lot like economists. That is, problematic knowledge production has been described first and fundamentally as a problem of bad systematic incentives in which the professional reward system encourages individual practices inconsistent with the collective goals of science.

Apart from its descriptive accuracy, blaming "bad incentives" decouples the diagnosis of problems from the ascription of individual blame, which may help to marshal support for proposed solutions among researchers who might otherwise react defensively. Scientists are presented as having a good-faith desire to "get it right" that is undermined by professional demands to respond to bad incentives. Social psychologist Giner-Sorolla (2012:569) puts it in academic-Darwinist terms: "anyone who stands on principle, unless very lucky in results, will fail to compete effectively."

Attributing problems to bad incentives also implies researchers are caught in a social dilemma that might only be solvable by institution-level action (Everett and Earp 2016). This is not to say that there is not encouragement of researchers to adopt practices that improve replication prospects for the sake of doing good science. However, ultimately, idealism and moral exhortation are regarded as insufficient. Instead, among replication activists, there is considerable pessimism toward any idea that raising awareness by itself is sufficient without top-down leadership and regulation by institutions (e.g., by journals, professional associations, or funding agencies).

Can We Reduce False Positives? Should We?

Challenge 6: The parties best positioned to replicate a study, the original researchers, have limited credibility in doing so.

The plainest way for a field to address problems with the reproducibility of its results might seem to be to tighten standards for publishing findings in the first place. Yet, the argument that increasing barriers to publication will reduce false positives is regularly countered by arguments that increased barriers will also keep novel and creative ideas out of the field. For example, Wilson (2014) argues that social psychology "has become preoccupied with prevention and error detection ... at the expense of exploration and discovery." Finkel et al. (2015) argue that, rather than committing fully to a strategy of "false positive reduction," the field should engage in an "error balance" approach.

If a tradeoff exists between false positives and false negatives, what tilts opinion to thinking changes must be made to reduce false positives? Important factors are the extent to which false positives are perceived as common, harmful, and difficult to subsequently correct (Peterson 2016). In social science, research directly connected to evaluation of policy may evince the strongest sense of potential harm caused by incorrect empirical conclusions. As direct policy implications recede, the relative value placed on interesting ideas versus strongly evidenced findings may shift. Social psychologist Baumeister (2016:6) warns that personality research "reduced the chances of being wrong but palpably increased the fact of being boring. [It] became more accurate but less broadly interesting." Views regarding creativity versus rigor involve values – even aesthetics – and these differences may provide another political obstacle to gaining broad support for common evidentiary principles within heterogeneous disciplines.

One way of strengthening the integrity of individual articles is to press authors to conduct their own replications prior to an article being published. Reviewers will often be more persuaded by articles that report extensive sensitivity analyses or that show that the same result can be observed across multiple datasets.

A recurring concern about "internal replications," however, is that evidence of stability might be selectively reported only when it supports the author's conclusions. In social psychology, Stroebe and colleagues claim (2012:681) that "To publish in high-impact journals, data have to provide strong, unambiguous support for the hypothesis." We suspect many social science colleagues would say the same. Consequently, there is incentive and temptation to omit results that contradict or complicate a hypothesis. Omitting information does not require deceptive motives; researchers might interpret the failure of an attempted replication to reflect a problem of conceptualization or execution, an explanation made possible by the ambiguity we outlined above.

Internal replication thus poses a problem of trust. A strategy to address the problem is to provide ways by which new data replications can be independently registered (or "preregistered") before replication data are collected. The aspiration is to create a bright line between "exploratory" and "confirmatory" work, and to provide a way for researchers to demonstrate that they are not consciously or unconsciously presenting post hoc reasoning as a priori expectations.[3]

For social science, how well the idea of internal-replication-with-registration can be extended to methodologies other than experiments is not yet established. Existing datasets predominate, and even in a situation in which one is using a dataset for the first time to do an internal replication, getting from data to results nearly always involves making numerous decisions in response to unanticipated issues, which makes it hard to envision registering in advance. As a result, even while we agree that gatekeepers can ask investigators to do more replication work themselves before publishing, we believe that ultimately what sociologist Mack (1951) wrote over six decades ago will remain true: there is something distinctly persuasive about replications conducted by personnel independent of the original study.

---

[3] Public preregistration does not resolve all potential abuses of trust, as was demonstrated by the fraudulent study by Lacour and Green (2014), which was pre-registered.

How Do We Promote More and Better Replication Work?

Anticipating Replication

Challenge 7: Research articles present findings as important, yet often evince no anticipation that others might regard them as important enough to be worthy of replication.

The promotion of independent replications is increasingly being directed toward changing decisions made before the publication of the original article. For new-data replication, these reforms emphasize providing sufficient information about materials and methods as part of initial publication, perhaps using online supplemental materials. Same-data replication, meanwhile, is only possible if the original data are available.

Traditionally, sharing data or materials so that findings can be verified has been treated an *ethical* matter. Doing so upon request was understood as something that good scientists are obliged to do. However, once a paper has been published, the incentives for authors to revisit past work are weak, especially considering the risk of a replication being used to challenge one's results. In psychology and other social sciences, spot-checking adherence to guidelines about post-publication data sharing has repeatedly found them to be ineffective (Dewald et al. 1986; Wicherts et al. 2006).

As a result – and especially given the ease of online data sharing – emphasis has moved from treating data sharing as a post-publication matter to a condition of publication (Freese 2007). One concern about doing so is that sharing data will allow researchers who have worked hard to assemble a data source to be "scooped" by others.[4] Open data activists have advocated improving data citation to increase credit for collecting data (ICPSR 2017). Beyond this, one answer is to require researchers to provide no data beyond the specific variables and observations used in a paper, thus affording verification but not much else. Replication activists in social psychology view this as inadequate, as it leaves hidden any "p-hacking" done by collecting and analyzing many measures and only using those that produced a successful result. For social science, however, this may be a necessary compromise.

A different objection to mandating data sharing is that some data cannot be shared without violating the confidentiality of research participants. While the appropriate treatment of confidential data raises many issues, what's

---

[4] A prominent medical journal published an editorial skeptical of data sharing that invoked the memorable term "research parasites" (Longo and Drazen 2016).

important for our purposes is that policy requirements regarding data sharing almost always recognize the possibility that some data cannot be shared. Instead, what is usually asked for is either the data *or* a justification for not providing it. Calls for transparency are much harder to counter than calls to regulate particular research practices. As one group of replication activists put it, "We believe there is simply no argument for authors not justifying their data and material sharing practices" (Morey et al. 2016:3–4).

Even when researchers cannot provide data, there may still be a benefit to asking them to provide the code that would reproduce the results. An oft-cited benefit of code availability is that, even if no one ever looks at it, knowing that someone *might* encourages writing clearer, more careful code. Though it often feels like a hassle in the immediate term, a public-minded approach to producing research materials minimizes problems working with collaborators and being able to reconstruct and extend one's work later (Bowers 2011).

Encouraging Replication Work

Challenge 8: Those most likely to undertake an independent effort to replicate an original finding might be interpreted as least fit to do so.
As noted, even while independent replication is regularly referred to as foundational to science, actually doing it is widely considered uninspired, grunt work. This is readily interpreted as lacking prestige, which raises an incentive problem in terms of who will actually do it.

As with many necessary but subordinate tasks in the academy, a common answer is "students." With both new-data and same-data replication, the idea that graduate students may be urged (or required) to undertake replication projects has been suggested as a twofer. First, graduate students get to build skills directly connected to the same work that has resulted in publication for others. Second, the field gets more evidence about the replicability of key findings.

While we share enthusiasm for replication as part of student training, it is worth pointing out that student-led replications are vulnerable to obvious objections around competence when replications fail. One social psychologist decried a failed replication of one of his studies because it involved "student projects" with many "beginners' mistakes" (Dijksterhuis 2013).

The weak incentives to undertake replication manifest most centrally in difficulties publishing them. A "radicalizing moment" for some replication activists in social psychology was a leading journal publishing a paper reporting evidence of paranormal abilities but then desk-rejecting a subsequent failed replication on the grounds that, as a policy, it did not accept replication studies (Yong 2012). In the ensuing years, several social psychology journals have announced or revised policies explicitly to indicate openness to publishing replication studies. Activists have advanced the idea of a "pottery barn" rule, in which those who publish findings have some responsibility for providing an outlet for efforts at replication.

Of course, the episode is more compelling because it was a replication study that failed. But this sets up its own potential perversion in which those who do replications can have an incentive for the replication to fail. Indeed, replication efforts are often motivated by a lack of belief in the original finding. These incentives can bias analytic decisions just as surely as biases produce false discoveries in the first place.

Some related solutions for these problems have been proposed. One is to offer results-blind acceptance of well-designed new-data replication studies, so that the publication prospects of the replication is demonstrably decoupled from its results. Another is to press for pre-registration; indeed, it is hard to justify why a replication study collecting new data would not be expected to be pre-registered. Advance specification also allows for the possibility of consulting in a demonstrable way with authors of the original study. This can be regarded as promoting scientific etiquette and as increasing the credibility of the replication study, especially in the case of divergence from the original results. The experience of the latter benefit should not be overstated, as there have been several episodes in which consultation beforehand still led to strong disagreement by original authors about the divergent findings could be properly considered a failed replication (Schnall 2014; Baumeister and Vohs 2016).

In general, these solutions are premised on data not yet collected. One major front for social science replication is seeing whether findings hold in datasets that already exist, like seeing whether a finding about public opinion from the General Social Survey can be replicated in the American National Election Study. Especially because measures in these cases usually do not perfectly coincide, the best way of ensuring the methodological integrity of replications here is likely to expect numerous sensitivity analyses to show whether findings depend on particular analytic decisions. But otherwise, if the worthiness of replication is appreciated, reports of results from projects like this could hopefully be very brief compared to many social science articles, as there would be no need for the lengthy literature reviews and framing exercises that papers reporting original findings often require. That brevity may decrease the cost of researchers undertaking replication projects and increase the capacity for journals to routinely accept them.

Conclusion

The "crisis" of replication in social psychology offers lessons for the rest of social science regarding the host of conceptual and motivational challenges that bedevil efforts to improve replicability. Even asking whether a problem exists can incite an acrimonious debate with limited prospects for any empirical resolution. And the term itself is used to mean such different things that discussions across fields go easily astray. The actors most interested in trying to replicate a particular result often have some stake in success or failure that can be used to discount their credibility. Overall, one sees a system beset by incentives at odds with ideals, which cries out for institution-level solutions.

Concluding that a scientific field has a problem that can only be solved by increased collective regulation generates counterarguments familiar to debates about regulation more generally (Fowler 1995). One is that regulations may be crafted and imposed to fit dominant forms of research, and may not be sensitive to unique demands posed by other types of work. For example, while experimental work may dominate social psychology, survey and other interview-based work is hardly uncommon, and researchers in these areas have expressed concern that the changes activists have sought to mandate are not sensitive to the practical realities of their research (Finkel et al. 2015). Some experimentalists have complained that some ideas – like a minimum cell size for experimental conditions – exhibit a bias toward work on convenient-to-study populations rather than studies that involve harder-to-reach populations or more intensive interventions.

Nevertheless, in social psychology, it is conspicuous how much of what has been proposed and the success of such proposals has benefitted from the domination of a particular style of research-laboratory or online experiments. The social science discipline that has made the strongest steps toward replicable practice, economics, is also noted for its strong consensus over epistemic ideals. There is so much room for potential disagreement regarding replication that similar premises among stakeholders can at least help discussion from ever-devolving back to definitions and first principles.

In political science and sociology, of course, the range of methodologies is far more diverse. This poses considerable political hurdles for achieving widespread consent of diverse groups of researchers to discipline-wide regulations. Even the idea of crafting regulations specific to particular types of research may be contested as representing some kind of value judgment about the worth of that method versus others. As a result, even while some argue that top-down policy interventions are necessary to solve replication problems, others may regard such policies as antithetical to the substantive heterogeneity of social science disciplines. In political science, for example, proposed "Data Analysis – Research Transparency" guidelines have met with the strongest resistance from groups of qualitative researchers (Isaac 2015).

Within disciplines, research areas can offer guidelines for what scholars can be expected to disclose, the way AAPOR has advanced standardized response rates and the Experimental Research section of the APSA has done for different types of experiments in political science (Gerber et al. 2014). This meso-level between individual researchers and the pluralistic confederacies of many contemporary disciplines may prove the most promising level for generating the buy-in needed for changes that stick.

Even so, we believe there are also clear paths forward despite the challenges that intradisciplinary diversity may pose. As long as the possibility of exemption is acknowledged – with transparency about when are why exemptions are granted – we hope that mandates for open data and materials continues to spread across social science journals. We are similarly bullish on expanding the verification of results by journals, especially those major social science journals that presently generate considerable revenue for professional organizations.

We hope that changes in journal policy will have spillover effects of encouraging reproducible research practices as a routine part of social science training. While we do not know of any systematic evidence on the topic, our impression is this is already the case in economics and political science. The publicity that credibility problems have generated have hopefully also sharpened some methodological sensibilities of reviewers. This may be especially useful in pressing for stronger internal replications prior to publication and heightened suspicion of obvious markers of p-hacking. For, ultimately, even as we agree with the diagnosis that institutional-level changes are needed, changes in individual practice will also be needed to restore credibility in the face of increased skepticism.

11 Measurement Replication in Qualitative and Quantitative Studies

Dan Reiter

In the physical sciences, social sciences, and the humanities, replication of empirical work is the hallmark of knowledge accumulation. In all three, claims about some element of reality are grounded in the use of a particular method, and replication demonstrates that employment of the method can generate the same conclusions as those reached by the scholar. If an empirical claim cannot be replicated, then the claim's contribution to knowledge must come into doubt.[1]

Social scientific replication can mean different things (Chapters 10, 13, and 15, this volume). For quantitative work it can mean computational replication (what Christensen and Miguel, Chapter 6, this volume, refer to as "verification"), simply ensuring that the same computer commands in a software package on the same set of data produce the same exact results. Quantitative approaches can also attempt replication through "robustness" tests, reanalyzing the data with slightly different choices in variable or model construction (what Christensen and Miguel refer to as "reanalysis"). For quantitative and qualitative methods, it can mean reproducing the demonstrated results on new data, a sample of data other than that analyzed in the original study either from the same population (what Christensen and Miguel refer to as "reproduction"), or from a different population (what Christensen and Miguel refer to as "extension").

This chapter focuses on measurement replication, the ability to replicate the original study's recorded measurements, using the study's same measurement parameters or coding rules, the same research design (such as the same quantitative estimation technique) and the original sample of the same

---

[1] As noted, replication is not a requirement of the sciences alone. Humanities scholarship also requires replication. For example, when scholars were unable through archival research to replicate the findings of an award-winning book on the history of guns in America, the findings in that book became discredited, the original publisher failed to renew the contract on the book, and its award was rescinded. See the forum in the January 2002 issue of the *William and Mary Quarterly* in Bellesile in 2000.

population (for other discussions of replication and the related issue of transparency, see Chapters 2, 12, and 13 in this volume). More specifically, this chapter seeks to accomplish two goals.

First, it further develops measurement replication as an important element of the broader mission of replication. All recognize that measurement replication is essential to knowledge accumulation. If the measurements of the original sample cannot be replicated, this introduces doubts into the internal validity of the study, and verifying internal validity is a precursor to exploring the external validity of the findings on new data. And yet, the actual practice of measurement replication deserves more extensive exposition than it generally receives in scholarship that discusses replication. John Gerring (Chapter 15) builds on Michael Clemens (2017:329), who describes replication tests as reexecuting the same research design on the same sample. This can include correcting possible measurement error, which Clemens describes only briefly as actions such as "fixing coding errors so that the code does exactly what the original paper describes ... [and] having the same sample of students take the same exam again to remedy measurement error" What Jeremy Freese and David Peterson (2017) describe as "verifiability" is conceptually similar to what Clemens means by replication, and they also describe in passing a few examples of relatively straightforward types of measurement error exposed by verifiability tests. This chapter endeavors to provide a fuller description of a wider array of possible measurement errors that measurement replication can reveal, beyond the more straightforward and shorter list of errors that other essays describe. It also provides examples in which revealing and correcting measurement error overturned important scholarly findings, demonstrating the importance of measurement replication efforts.

Second, the chapter demonstrates that measurement replication is equally important for both quantitative and qualitative work. Epistemologically it is a critical element of knowledge accumulation for both categories of methods, and because (as illustrated here) measurement replication has exposed important measurement errors in both types of work in the past, this suggests that ongoing measurement replication efforts for both types of work will be needed going forward. Somewhat relatedly, this chapter provides a single categorical framework of measurement errors exposed by replication efforts across both categories of methods.

The remainder of this chapter contains three sections. The first section discusses the importance of measurement replication in both quantitative and qualitative approaches. The second section describes three types of errors that can be exposed by measurement replication, errors in fact, errors in interpretation and context, and errors in consistency of application. The final section concludes, and offers suggestions for advancing measurement replication in scholarship and teaching.

Measurement Replication in Quantitative and Qualitative Approaches

For both quantitative and qualitative studies, measurement replication means the replication of independent and dependent variable codings using the original sample. The essence of an empirical test is evaluation of whether the relationships between independent variables and dependent variables are those predicted by the theory and hypotheses. The core of that evaluation is the values given to the independent and dependent variables, for the data being analyzed. Was Russia in 2001 a democracy? What was France's gross domestic product in 2002? What was the level of gender inequality in Tibet in 2005? If a study's original measurements can be replicated by outside scholars, then this improves confidence in the internal validity of the study, internal validity being confidence that the observed independent variable caused observed changes in the dependent variable among the data surveyed. If these values cannot be replicated by outside scholars, then this undermines faith in the internal validity of the study.

It is important to distinguish between two types of outcomes of (all types of) replication efforts, beyond the kinds of outcomes that Reappraisal Scorecards from a Reappraisal Institute (Chapter 13) might generate. The first type is replication that demonstrates fraud, plagiarism, and/or severe incompetence, sufficient to lead the journal or academic press that published the original study to issue a formal retraction. Retraction is disturbingly frequent in the natural and medical sciences; one source estimated there are 500–600 formal retractions per year in these fields, worldwide.[2] Though systematic comparative data do not exist, retraction in the social sciences may be less frequent, and among the social sciences, retractions in business and economic journals may be somewhat more frequent than in other social sciences.

---

[2] http://retractionwatch.com/help-us-heres-some-of-what-were-working-on/.

A second outcome of replication efforts is not formal retraction of a finding, but rather stimulation of scholarly debate between scholar and critics. Sometimes this leads to a consensual outcome, such as a scholar formally conceding an error exposed in a replication effort, as when James Morrow et al. (1999) conceded that a replication effort had revealed a flaw in the computer code used to generate previously published quantitative results (though the correction was not sufficiently significant to warrant the formal retraction of the entirety of the original study). Perhaps more frequently, the original authors will respond (often flatly) rebutting the original critique, such as the high-profile exchanges about measurement of deterrence success and failure between Lebow and Stein (1987) and Huth and Russett (1984, 1990). Indeed, in many of the measurement replication examples listed in the next section, the original scholar published a formal reply to the described measurement replication critique. Notably, the original scholar replies to a measurement replication critique not just out of a cynical attempt to defend her reputation or because cognitive bias prevents her from recognizing that she had made a mistake. Sometimes measurement replication efforts themselves can be flawed. Further, some measurements are genuinely difficult to make (one might call them "close-call" measurements), in the sense that reasonable arguments can be made for more than one coding decision, and the original scholar's response to a measurement replication critique can help flesh out both sides of the issue.

Though ongoing measurement debate that fails to culminate in either formal retraction or consensus between scholar and critic may be somewhat less than satisfying, it still constitutes a critical portion of the process of accumulating knowledge. Even if disagreement is not resolved, these dialogues push scholars to sharpen their arguments publicly, to the benefit of their field. Further, the prospect of experiencing a measurement replication challenge can serve the important function of encouraging scholars to raise the quality and transparency of their empirical efforts in the execution of the original study. Knowing that the field is filled with scholarly critics and graduate students hungry to publish through replication, critique motivates scholars to boost their efforts to get it right the first time.

The heading for this section begs the question, is measurement replication important for both qualitative and quantitative research? There is a temptation to view measurement replication efforts as more appropriate for quantitative as opposed to qualitative research. Measurement replication efforts in quantitative studies can produce satisfying results: exposure of measurement error leads to changing numerical entries in spreadsheet cells, and then executing computational data analysis will indicate whether those changes alter empirical inferences, specifically whether the magnitude of an independent variable's effect changes significantly, the statistical significance of a variable changes, and/or the sign on an effect changes.

Conversely, replication efforts in qualitative research might be seen to be much less satisfying. Qualitative research may draw on raw data that are difficult for outside scholars to procure and reanalyze, such as archival materials or interviews. Further, a single qualitative measurement, such as a nation's regime type, might be built on dozens of individual factual assertions. Replication that reveals flaws in a handful of these factual assertions may be unlikely to merit reconsidering the entire measurement.[3] Relatedly, much qualitative research is driven by scholarly interpretation of a set of individual facts, both with regard to measurement and process tracing, and it can be difficult to demonstrate that such interpretations are clearly wrong. Last, some make the more ambitious claim that "case study research is less prone to some kinds of measurement error because it can intensively assess a few variables along several qualitative dimensions" (George and Bennett 2005:220), perhaps implying that measurement replication is less necessary for qualitative work.

It bears stressing that replicability is equally important in qualitative research as compared with quantitative research for the accumulation of knowledge. Positivist quantitative and qualitative work both collect data on variables from a population sample to test a hypothesis, and the validity of the drawn empirical inferences for both approaches rely on valid measurement. If qualitative measures cannot be subjected to replication efforts, then our confidence in the study's findings must remain limited (King et al. 1994:26–27; Seale 1999). As discussed in the next section, qualitative replication efforts can be more likely to suggest overturning a reported finding than the above critiques portray. Sometimes, qualitative codings depend heavily on a single factual assertion, and failure to replicate that factual assertion can undermine the credibility of the entire measurement coding and in turn the study's central findings. Further, qualitative codings may sometimes be based on an inferior set of materials, such as secondary sources, and examination of primary

---

[3] Although, replication of quantitative work faces similar difficulties. A single quantitative data set can contain hundreds, thousands, or even millions of individual cell entries, and if replication efforts suggest changing only a handful of codings, then this might not change the results of the analysis (that is, changing a few variable codings might not change the sign, magnitude, or statistical significance of reported coefficient effects). That is to say, earning the payoff from a replication effort of changing a reported result is not markedly less likely for qualitative as compared with quantitative approaches, and yet both approaches need replication efforts, as described above.

materials can suggest altering several factual assertions, in turn encouraging the alteration of a reported measurement and overturning findings.

Non-hypothesis testing work using qualitative methods also demands measurement replicability. A plausibility probe that is shown to incorporate flawed measurement becomes much less plausible. Though some non-positivist social scientists are skeptical of the entire replication mission because of doubts about the assumptions of scientist objectivity, the enduring similarity of the studied phenomenon, and non-interference of the scientist with the observed subject (van der Veer et al. 1994), other non-positivists recognize the importance of measurement replication and transparency, documenting their measures and measurement rules very carefully (e.g., Hopf and Allan 2016).

The importance of qualitative replication aside, what about its difficulty? Regarding data transparency, the Internet has of course vastly facilitated the publication of archival and other primary document materials. For example, the Qualitative Data Repository (QDR) archives a variety of forms of digital data, including documents that are the basis of archival work.[4] Qualitative scholars have been discussing possible transparency standards to facilitate measurement replication, including Andrew Moravscik's (2012) support of the Active Citation standard. Further efforts such as the Reappraisal Institute would of course improve material availability.

Measurement Errors Exposed by Replication Efforts

This section describes three different types of measurement errors that have been exposed by past replication efforts of both quantitative and qualitative social science research.

Error 1: Misrepresentation of Facts

The simplest type of measurement error in any study is misrepresentation of facts, making factual claim X when in reality X is not true. Perhaps the most important task measurement replication can perform is to expose factual errors.

Unfortunately, factual errors have been shown to be present in both quantitative and qualitative empirical work. This perhaps defies the expectations

---

[4] https://qdr.syr.edu.

of some: qualitative critics of quantitative work sometimes concede the veracity of quantitative data but maintain doubts about the ability of quantitative methods to establish causation; quantitative critics of qualitative work sometimes concede the veracity of individual case studies, but argue that the small sample size of qualitative work sharply limits the external validity of their findings.

There have been a number of measurement replication efforts that have revealed factual problems in quantitative data sets, sometimes suggesting that specific reported results are flawed.

Consider one data set describing hundreds of battles since the seventeenth century. A replication effort was commissioned by the US Army. The replicators randomly selected eight battles including a total of 159 variable codings, finding that two-thirds of the variable codings were in error. Michael Desch (2008:59) used this replication effort to critique the reported finding that democratic armies are more likely to win their battles (Reiter and Stam 2002; Lieberman, Chapter 3, this volume). Fabrice Lehoucq (2017) demonstrated relatively low levels of correlation across measurements in data sets on coups d'état. He then created his own carefully researched data set on coups, essentially a replication effort of other coup data sets, and demonstrated widespread errors in existing data sets, especially false negatives (that is, he discovered coups that had been omitted in other data sets). The Alliance Treaty Organizations and Provisions data set was developed as a successor to the Correlates of War (COW) data set on alliances, and one of its many contributions was to demonstrate significant measurement error within the COW alliance data (Leeds et al. 2002). Reducing measurement error as well as making other improvements in alliance data led to different conclusions about questions such as whether or not democracies are especially likely to ally with each other (Lai and Reiter 2000).

Measurement errors affect widely used data. The COW data set on interstate war is a list of all wars between nation-states since 1816, a war being a violent conflict inflicting at least 1000 battle dead. Initially created in the 1960s, it is arguably the single most important quantitative data set in the political science subfield of international relations, having been used in hundreds of studies by students and scholars for a half-century. Version 4.0 of this data was published in 2011, and lists some 95 interstate wars.

However, replication efforts have revealed substantial factual errors within the data set (Reiter et al. 2016a, b). Specifically, in more than one-third of the cases, there was an error with regards to at least one key variable, including: whether or not the conflict event qualified as a war (mostly, were there at least 1000 battle dead); who started the war; who won the war; who participated in the war; when did the war start. Not all of these errors were factual, as in some cases they were errors emerging from inconsistent treatment across cases (see below for discussion of this topic). However, there were several errors of fact, some of which have consequences for important debates in international relations. For example, COW failed to include the Soviet Union as a participant in the Korean War, though the historical record clearly indicates that it should be included, according to COW coding rules. War-level conflict between the United States and the Soviet Union during the Cold War period is an important datum providing evidence against the long peace proposition (Gaddis 1989), and relatedly the propositions that great-power bipolarity breeds peace and that nuclear states are unlikely to fight each other (Mearsheimer 2001).

Other quantitative measurement replication efforts have also uncovered factual problems. Goran Peic (2014) sought to replicate the insurgency data set created by Jason Lyall and Isaiah Wilson (2009). However, he discovered a number of factual errors, especially in the coding of the dependent variable, insurgency outcome. For example, Lyall and Wilson coded the late-1970s Nicaraguan insurgency as ending in a draw, though the Sandinistas overthrew the Somoza government in 1979, taking power. Though Peic made only 17 changes in outcome codings across 131 cases, these changes overturn the central result from Lyall and Wilson, that counterinsurgents become less likely to win as their forces become more mechanized. Douglas Gibler et al. (2016) found widespread errors in the heavily used Militarized Interstate Dispute data set.

The above examples pertain to quantitative data collected through historical research. Measurement replication efforts are also important for exposing factual errors that emerge in other methods of quantitative data collection. For example, one psychological study of primates involved the scientist coding data by viewing a videotape of monkey behavior. That study failed measurement replication efforts when a second scientist watched the same videotape and produced different variable codings.[5]

The previous section broached the possibility that finding measurement errors might not be sufficient to overturn a finding, perhaps if the number of errors was relatively small in relation to the larger data set. However, sometimes quantitative findings can be overturned by correcting a factual error in a single variable value in a single case. Suzanne Werner and Amy Yuen

---

[5] www.nytimes.com/2010/10/26/science/26hauser.html.

(2005) studied the determinants of peace following interstate wars, and their central empirical finding that patterns of wartime combat outcomes affect postwar peace duration becomes null if a typographical error of one variable value in one case is corrected (see Lo et al. 2008). Robert Rauchhaus (2009) examined a data set of hundreds of thousands of cases, and found that nuclear weapons reduce war among dyads, but reached that conclusion by using a conflict data set that incorrectly did not classify the 1999 Kargil conflict between Pakistan and India as a war. Changing that single coding renders the nuclear weapons–peace relationship statistically insignificant (Bell and Miller 2015). Note that though these are simple factual errors, there are other studies that demonstrate that questionable (but not unambiguously wrong) codings of single outlier cases can determine whether or not there is a significant relationship between two variables, as Vipin Narang and Rebecca Nelson (2009) demonstrated with regard to the proposition that democratizing states are more conflict-prone.

Measurement replication efforts have revealed factual measurement errors in social science research using a variety of qualitative methods. Margaret Mead's landmark anthropology work on adolescence was based on field work in Samoa in the 1920s. Another scholar conducted field work in the same areas in the 1940s and 1960s, and argued that Mead factually misrepresented Samoan culture on all of the key points of her study. Another replication effort of field work of the norms and culture in a Mexican village also drew substantially different conclusions from the original author (see Seale 1999:144).

A form of qualitative research especially common to political science and sociology involves coding variables on the basis of historical information, often using primary, textual sources. Measurement replication is here more straightforward than in observational field work, as the task is essentially to track down footnotes, with the goal of verifying whether a source made the claim asserted by the author.

Measurement replication efforts have revealed factual problems in past qualitative work, in four different ways. First, and perhaps rarest, are replication efforts that are quasi-quantitative, examining the veracity of a sample or the population of footnotes of a qualitative paper, in turn reporting the frequency of footnotes that contain errors. Robert Lieshout et al. (2004) sampled some 221 footnotes from Moravscik's landmark work, *A Choice For Europe*, finding that within that sample 116 (52 percent) were not correct, and 11 more (5 percent) were only partly correct. They propose that reexamination of these sources in turn encourages different conclusions about the role of

Charles de Gaulle in European politics, a central component of the book's argument.

A second and more common type of replication effort to examine factual claims is the use of higher quality, often primary sources, to critique earlier conclusions reached using less reliable, often secondary sources. Consider the replication of Barry Posen's award-winning 1984 book, *The Sources of Military Doctrine: France, Britain and Germany Between the World Wars*, one of the most influential security studies books of the 1980s. The book's dependent variable is whether or not a country had an offensive or defensive military doctrine. Using English-language secondary sources, Posen coded France as embracing a defensive military doctrine across the entire interwar period, providing support for his balance-of-power hypothesis. Posen also coded Britain as maintaining an offensive airpower doctrine across most of the time period because an unchecked Royal Air Force was allowed to make strategy choices reflecting its organizational interests without civilian control, until the late 1930s when growing international threat pushed British civilians to intervene and impose a defensive airpower doctrine. This interpretation provides support for Posen's balance-of-power and organizational-interests hypotheses. Several years later, Elizabeth Kier (1997) attempted to replicate Posen's codings for both cases. Conducting archival work in French-language primary documents, she demonstrated that France actually engaged in an offensive military doctrine up until about 1928 when it shifted to a defensive doctrine, a shift that proves support for her theory integrating domestic politics and organizational culture, limiting the degree to which the case supports Posen's hypothesis. Regarding the British case, she provided primary evidence against Posen's interpretation, showing that the embrace of a defensive doctrine through most of the period was not a reflection of uncontrolled organizational preferences of the Royal Air Force, as Posen suggested, but rather of both civilians and the military supporting offensive doctrine during this period.

Sometimes using primary documents might only overturn a single factual claim, but that single claim is central to a broader argument. Consider the deterrence-theory hypothesis that aggressor states are more likely to attack when they doubt the resolve of status quo states (Jervis 1976). The single most important empirical episode supporting this hypothesis is from Europe in the 1930s: because France and Britain appeased Adolf Hitler at the October 1938 Munich conference regarding the political status of the Czech region of the Sudetenland, Hitler became emboldened in 1939 to annex the rest of Czechoslovakia and then to invade Poland. That interpretation in turn rests very heavily on the historical claim that at a high-level government meeting in August 1939 Hitler said, "Our enemies are worms. I saw them in Munich." The specific context was that Hitler was considering what the Anglo-French reaction might be to a German invasion of Poland. Indeed, the "worms" comment is viewed by some as the "smoking gun" for the resolve argument in the critical 1930s case. This assumption about the importance of resolve is central to international relations theory and to foreign policy-making more generally, and this interpretation of the Munich episode has itself been central to foreign policy debates. For example, in 2015, an array of prominent Republicans such as former vice president Dick Cheney and Senator Lindsay Graham critiqued the US–Iran nuclear deal as being another Munich.[6]

Daryl Press (2005) subjected the variable measurement for this episode to an intensive replication effort, to test the deterrence/resolve argument against the competing argument that deterrence credibility is driven by perceptions of military capability, and not resolve. The worms remark, the central factual assertion underpinning the coding, was recorded by Admiral Wilhelm Canaris in his notes from the August 1939 meeting. Press makes several arguments as to why this reference from Canaris' notes is not powerful evidence that Hitler's beliefs were driven primarily by perceptions about British and French resolve rather than material power. Four people at the meeting kept notes, and none of the other three recorded Hitler making the worms remark (including General Hermann Boehm, who kept the most detailed set of notes). Even Canaris' notes themselves reveal that the worms remark was more likely a tossed-off remark, rather than being at the center of Hitler's thinking. In Canaris' notes, Hitler provides more detailed explanations of seven different arguments as to why weaknesses in Anglo-French capabilities would dissuade them from intervening in Poland, including weaknesses in the British naval construction program, the imminent German-Soviet alliance, and others. The worms remark is a single sentence oddly placed in a paragraph that is mostly about Soviet interests. Last, the context suggests that the worms remark was more likely a passing remark rather than central to Hitler's beliefs, given that Hitler almost never made the same argument (inferring low British and French resolve from Munich) in other settings, whereas he much more frequently referred to military capabilities.

A third type of factual measurement error exposed by replication efforts is demonstration that the cited historical material does not support the actual claim being made, in the sense that the author argues that source X says Y,

---

[6] www.huffingtonpost.com/michael-zucker/the-iran-deal-munich-and-_b_8114206.html.

but in fact X does not say Y. For example, Jonathan Caverley (2010, 2010/ 2011) presented a theory arguing that elected leaders often prefer capital-intensive to labor-intensive military strategies in order to minimize casualties and maintain public support for the war. He applied this argument to the Vietnam War, arguing that the Lyndon Johnson administration imposed a capital-intensive military strategy on a reluctant military. James McAllister (2010/2011) examined the case study, and found that in a number of places a specific historical claim made by Caverley was not made in the cited source. For example, one specific claim is that civilians forced an unwilling military to use tanks, to reduce US casualties. However, in examining the sources that Caverley uses, McAllister failed to find anyone arguing that tanks were used to substitute for manpower during Vietnam. Caverley's sources instead suggest that tanks were used (at least in the early years of the war) because the US military believed they would boost American military effectiveness, a motivation that is outside of Caverley's theory. Measurement errors such as this one led McAllister to doubt that the Vietnam case supports Caverley's theory.

Thus far the discussion has focused on replicating variable codings. However, qualitative replication efforts sometimes focus on process tracing as well as variable coding. Process tracing is a method by which a case study endeavors to present evidence demonstrating the causal processes predicted by theories and hypotheses (see George and Bennett 2005). Specifically, a replicator may agree that a case study provides correlative evidence, that the value of the dependent variable is correctly predicted given the value of the independent variable, but the case study fails to provide evidence of process tracing, that the variation in the independent variable actually caused variation in the dependent variable. For example, Moravscik (2013) closely examined the evidence provided by Sebastian Rosato (2012) regarding the latter's empirical argument that power politics primarily and perhaps exclusively caused European integration after World War II. Moravcsik found that though Rosato coded the independent and dependent variables correctly (there was a Soviet threat to Europe and Franco-Germany rivalry, and there was European integration), Rosato failed to provide evidence of the described causal process, of power politics being the lead factors driving integration decisions.

Error 2: Interpretation and Context

A second type of measurement error that replication can reveal concerns context. Specifically, the error is not that a particular factual assertion is narrowly incorrect, but rather that the factual assertion supporting the variable coding does not justify the variable coding, as providing complete context around the single factual assertion suggests an alternative coding (the Hitler/Munich discussion above incorporates arguments about context).

Failure to account for context has led to measurement error in both quantitative and qualitative empirical research. Consider data on war initiation, who starts wars. The COW interstate war data set codes Pakistan as initiating the 1971 Bangladesh War, against India, because Pakistan launched an airstrike on Indian air fields on December 3, 1971. Narrowly, this is not a factually incorrect claim, as Pakistan did launch such an attack on India on that day. However, the larger context demonstrates that India rather than Pakistan should be coded as initiating the war. Generally, Pakistan wanted to avoid war with India, as it was in the midst of addressing a serious political crisis in East Pakistan (now, the country of Bangladesh). India wanted to go to war with Pakistan to resolve the crisis and stop the flow of refugees. More specifically, the first belligerent set of actions was taken by India, in November, when it began to send troops from India into East Pakistan, launching attacks and seizing territory. That is, describing the context in a measurement replication effort changes the coding of the initiator from Pakistan to India. In the words of one prominent history of the war, "[December 3] is usually cited for the commencement of the third Indo-Pakistani war, and because of the air strikes, Pakistan is often depicted as having taken the initiative in starting the war. In more realistic, rather than formal, terms, however, the war began on 21 November, when Indian military units occupied Pakistani territory as part of the preliminary phase of the offensive directed at capturing and liberating Dhaka" (Sisson and Rose 1990:214; see also Reiter et al. 2016a). Coding India as starting the war is important for a variety of research agendas, including whether democracies win the wars they start (India was a democracy in 1971, and went on to win the war; see Reiter and Stam 2002), and the proposition that female leaders might be less likely to initiate wars either because of biological factors related to sex or because female leaders are less likely to embrace patriarchal values (India in 1971 was led by a woman, Indira Gandhi; see Horowitz et al. 2015).

Context also matters for qualitative data measurement. Consider the hypothesis that elected leaders sometimes use deception to build popular support for war. There are few well-developed case studies of this dynamic, other than the 2003 Iraq War, the Vietnam War, and American entry into World War II. Regarding the last case, the argument is that in 1941 President

Franklin Roosevelt wanted the United States to go to war with Germany, but before the December 1941 attack on Pearl Harbor the American public was hesitant to support going to war. John Schuessler (2015) argues that in the several months before Pearl Harbor, Roosevelt secretly approved aggressive US naval activities in the Atlantic, hoping to cause a naval clash between American and German vessels. Through deception Roosevelt would cast Germany as the belligerent, thereby pushing the American public to support war with Germany, similar to how German aggression against American vessels in World War I eventually pushed the public to support war with Germany.

The key piece of evidence supporting this claim concerns a naval incident in September 1941 involving the American destroyer *Greer*. There was an exchange of fire between the *Greer* and a German submarine in the North Atlantic. A few days later, Roosevelt described the incident publicly, exaggerating the degree to which the German submarine acted aggressively. For proponents of the deception argument, this behavior seems to echo closely the actions of President Lyndon Johnson in 1964 surrounding the Gulf of Tonkin Incident.

These two facts, of the existence of the *Greer* incident and Roosevelt's initial exaggeration, are not factually incorrect. However, understanding the context discourages the conclusion that Roosevelt used deception to move public opinion in the months before Pearl Harbor. Though Roosevelt's initial description exaggerated German aggression, a few days later he directed an American admiral to provide an accurate account in Congressional testimony, which he did. Further, the *Greer* was only one of several naval incidents in 1941 involving clashes between German and American vessels. In five other incidents, both before and after the *Greer* incident, Roosevelt did not exaggerate German aggression, and in some cases went out of his way to play down the incident, in part for fear that if exaggeration were exposed, it would present severe domestic political costs. Further, Roosevelt was relatively transparent in describing the aggressiveness of US naval activities in the Atlantic in 1941, undermining the claim that Roosevelt concealed American naval belligerence (Reiter 2012, 2013). In short, accounting for context challenges the conclusion that the *Greer* incident provides powerful evidence that Roosevelt was engaged in a campaign of deception, and it challenges the dependent variable coding in this case of a president employing deception to drag his country into a war the public would otherwise rather avoid.

Error 3: Inconsistency

Scholars develop rules that provide guidance as to how to code variables. However, scholars sometimes apply these coding rules inconsistently across cases. Inconsistent application is more likely if the coding rules are more general, as the coder has more leeway in the application of these rules in specific cases. That is, it is not that any individual case is clearly coded incorrectly, but the inconsistent application of the coding rules across the cases creates a de facto measurement error. Measurement replication efforts provide the opportunity to expose such inconsistencies.

Consider the collection of data on war outcomes, classifying who wins wars. COW's rules for coding war outcomes are very general, indicating that its measurements follow "the consensus among the acknowledged specialists in deciding which side 'won' each war" (Sarkees and Wayman 2010:60). COW classifies the 1969 War of Attrition between Egypt and Israel as a draw, and the 1973 Yom Kippur War between Israel, Egypt, and Syria as an Israeli victory. The similarity across the cases is that in each case at least one Arab state attacked Israel first, the Arab attacker(s) suffered more casualties than Israel, and Israel did not end the war by making any political concessions to the Arabs (such as conceding territory). Neither of COW's decisions to code the outcomes of the 1969 and 1973 wars is in isolation factually incorrect, but they reveal an inconsistent application of COW coding rules across the two cases, producing a de facto coding error (Reiter et al. 2016a).

Another example comes from the study of terrorism. Robert Pape's (2003) widely cited work proposed that when populations perceive themselves to be under foreign occupation by democratic governments, whether foreign or domestic, then suicide terrorism becomes much more likely. Though Pape does not perform quantitative empirical tests, he does construct and present a comprehensive list of all suicide terrorist events from 1980 to 2001. However, the data contain odd inconsistencies, such as that Israel, France, and the United States are perceived as occupying Lebanon during the post-1982 multinational peacekeeping deployment, but Italy is not, though Italy also contributed peacekeeping troops to that mission. Because Italy did not experience suicide terrorism in the 1980s, the exclusion of Italy from the data set strengthens Pape's empirical claim that democracies that are perceived to be occupiers are especially likely to experience suicide terrorist attacks (Wade and Reiter 2007:338).

Going Forward

The social sciences need to continue to stress the importance of replication. The good news is that scholars continue to support and encourage efforts at transparency and replication, such as the Dataverse common repository for data, the QDR, the DA-RT replication and transparency initiative, and so on. The Reappraisal Institute would of course also advance these goals.

Here are a few further suggestions for supporting replication that have thus far received less attention. First, social scientists should also consider how they can strengthen the role of replication in undergraduate and graduate education, as a means of deepening the pro-replication norm, and in giving students hands-on replication experience. Replication is already an integral part of graduate and even undergraduate quantitative methods training. A very common class assignment will be for a student to download a publication's data set, replicate the results, and then perhaps test the robustness of the results.

Qualitative scholars should similarly consider ways of incorporating replication as part of undergraduate and graduate education. The easiest way would be to have students replicate a case study, especially the measurements of a case study's independent and dependent variables, and/or its process-tracing. Of course, such replication should be a task that can be feasibly performed as a research paper for a single course, meaning that replication should likely require acquiring only those materials that are easily available to students, such as secondary sources and those primary sources that are commonly available online and in libraries, as opposed to asking students to visit archives off campus. The exercise can be valuable even if students are simply asked to find only those sources used in the original study, rather than tasking them with also acquiring additional sources (though certainly the students' replication efforts will be richer if they have the time to consult additional sources). Personal experience has demonstrated that qualitative replication assignments highlight the importance of replication efforts, both in terms of advancing science and in terms of generating surprising results. Students are struck to discover how frequently the "emperor has no clothes," in that replication efforts sometimes reveal that even well-published and well-regarded case studies contain substantial measurement error, often because they are based on questionable or non-existent supporting evidence.

Second, scholars need to document fully the source materials from which measurement decisions are made. This means both listing all sources used for measurement, and then also using precise citation information. Though the scholarly community routinely emphasizes the need for transparency, it rarely mentions the importance of precision in transparency. Reference to exact sources including page numbers vastly facilitates measurement replication. For example, the documentation for the COW interstate war data set provides narratives and sources for each war, but does not provide page numbers or, sometimes, specific journal or newspaper issues or dates. This can create problems in measurement replication. For example, COW claims that clashes between China and Vietnam in January 1987 generated 4000 battle dead, a claim that is twice the official government estimates (Sarkees and Wayman 2010:175–176; few well-documented, non-official estimates of casualties for this clash exist). Their claim is difficult to replicate or verify, because COW refers to the *New York Times* (1987) without indicating a month or date, much less page number, and to a scholarly reference book without indicating a page number. Examination of both sources (as well as other sources on China–Vietnam relations in the 1980s) failed to turn up the 4000-battle-dead estimate.

Third, the field needs to continue to provide outlets for publication of replication efforts. Replication efforts might fall short of providing the kind of value added sufficient to merit publication as a full journal article, especially if a replication effort did not produce revolutionary new results. Journals and online sites can facilitate replication by creating venues for publishing shorter replication papers, as the promise of a publication, even a shorter one, provides professional incentive for scholars to engage in replication efforts. Many journals already do this to different degrees, publishing professional correspondence, research notes, and shorter papers. *Research and Politics* is an online political science journal that only publishes shorter papers, 4000 words or less, lending itself quite well to publishing replication efforts. The online H-Diplo International Security Studies Forum publishes qualitative replication efforts, through roundtables and reviews of journal articles as well as books.[7] The rest of the social sciences should continue to invest in these and new kinds of outlets that will incentivize replication, an effort critical to the advance of knowledge.

---

[7] https://issforum.org/.

12 Reliability of Inference: Analogs of Replication in Qualitative Research

Tasha Fairfield and Andrew Charman

How do issues related to replication translate into the context of qualitative research? As Freese and Peterson forewarn, their discussion of replication in quantitative social science cannot be directly transposed into this realm. However, we can identify analogs for the various combinations of same-versus-new-data, same-versus-different-procedures scrutiny that these authors discuss. While many of these analogs share essentially the same overarching definitions and import as their quantitative relatives, others diverge more significantly. The differences in these instances arise in large part from distinctions between frequentism, which underpins orthodox statistics, and Bayesianism, which a growing body of research identifies as the methodological foundation for inference in qualitative research.

In identifying and discussing these analogs, we will refer specifically to qualitative research that is informed by Bayesian reasoning. This approach is motivated by two considerations. First, we agree with Freese and Peterson in this volume (Chapter 10) that issues related to replication inevitably involve "a welter of complications and tradeoffs that will likely prompt different paths" for different epistemological communities, particularly when such communities espouse different understandings of inference and causation, as is the case in qualitative methods literature. Second, in our view, much of the best qualitative research that draws on process tracing and comparative historical analysis is implicitly, if not consciously, informed by Bayesian reasoning. While we recognize that a wide range of epistemological views are debated within qualitative methods, we follow Humphreys and Jacobs (2015:672), Bennett (2015:297), and Fairfield and Charman (2017) in espousing Bayesianism as the most appropriate logic of inference for qualitative research. We will therefore leave the question of how replication or analogs thereof might apply in non-Bayesian qualitative research open for other scholars to address.

By way of introduction, Bayesian inference proceeds by assigning "prior" probabilities to a set of plausible rival hypotheses given the (limited) information we possess. These prior probabilities represent our degree of confidence in (or vice versa, our degree of uncertainty about) the truth of each hypothesis taking into account salient knowledge from previous studies and/or experience. We then consider evidence obtained during the investigation at hand. We ask how likely the evidence would be if a particular hypothesis were true, and we update our beliefs in light of that evidence using Bayes' rule to derive "posterior" probabilities on our hypotheses. Bayesianism provides an especially appropriate framework for qualitative research given the following considerations: (1) Bayesianism is well-suited for explaining unique historical or sociopolitical events and allows us to conduct inference with a small number of cases and/or limited amounts of data; (2) Bayesianism can handle nonstochastic data that cannot naturally be considered to arise from a randomized sampling procedure or experiment (e.g., interviews with expert informants and evidence from archival sources); and (3) Bayesianism mandates an iterative process of theory development, data collection, and analysis, which is how qualitative research almost always proceeds in practice (Fairfield and Charman 2019).

In this chapter, we will advance two positions that we believe could help promote greater consensus and common ground among quantitative and qualitative scholars. First, we advocate restricting the use of the term *replication* to a narrowly defined set of new-data/same-procedures scrutiny that applies to orthodox statistical analysis and experimental research, both for the sake of clarity and to avoid the perception that norms from dominant subfields are being imposed inappropriately on qualitative research.[1] Second and relatedly, we argue that the overarching concern in all scientific inquiry – both quantitative and qualitative – is *reliability* of inference: how much confidence we can justifiably hold in our conclusions. Reliability encompasses but extends beyond the notions of replication and reproducibility. As Goodman, Fanelli, and Ioannidis (2016:1) observe: "The fundamental concern … is … not reproducibility per se, but whether scientific claims based on scientific results are true." Our discussion therefore focuses on practices that could help improve how we assess evidence, build consensus among scholars, and promote knowledge accumulation in qualitative research within a Bayesian framework, which provides a natural language for evaluating uncertainty about the truth of hypotheses.

The second section of this chapter presents our understanding of replication and reliability as applicable to different types of research, characterized

---

[1] Such perceptions have arisen in the debate surrounding APSA's DART initiative; see, for example, the Qualitative Transparency Deliberation blog.

by the data (quantitative versus qualitative) and the methodological framework (frequentist versus Bayesian). Here we offer some suggestions for effectively conducting new-data scrutiny of qualitative research, although our focus will be on same-data scrutiny, which we believe could have significant payoffs for improving reliability of inference. Accordingly, the third section elaborates Bayesian rules for same-data assessment and illustrates how they can be applied using published exemplars of process-tracing research and comparative historical analysis. In broad terms Bayesianism directs us to ask whether scholars have overstated the weight of evidence in support of the advocated argument by neglecting to assess how likely that evidence would be if a rival hypothesis were true, whether the hypotheses under consideration have been articulated clearly enough to assess how likely the evidence would be under a given explanation relative to rivals, and whether the background knowledge that scholars discuss justifies an initial preference for a particular hypothesis. We contend that Bayesianism provides a clear framework for scrutinizing analysis that can help build greater consensus among scholars and facilitate knowledge accumulation.

Analogs of Replication in Qualitative Research

In their elucidating discussion of different and wide-ranging understandings of replication in quantitative social science, Freese and Peterson distinguish between using (1) the same versus new data, and (2) the same versus different procedures vis-à-vis the study in question. The latter dimension in their view correlates with whether the goal entails scrutinizing the study's specific results versus the broader conclusions its draws. We likewise structure our discussion of reliability in qualitative research around these useful dimensions of data and procedures, which form the four rows in Figure 12.1.

However, rather than labeling each of the four rows as different types of replication (e.g., same-data/same-procedures replication, same-data/different-procedures replication, etc.) we use terms that are intended to reflect the specific scrutinizing and/or knowledge-accumulating activities that fall within each row. Our intent is to sidestep the confusion that has plagued debates about replication and to avoid conceptual stretching. Freese and Peterson (Chapter 10, this volume) emphasize that: "the term [replication] itself is used to mean such different things that discussions across fields go easily astray," and recount that they have observed "conversations about 'replication' in which parties have gone on for a disconcertingly long time

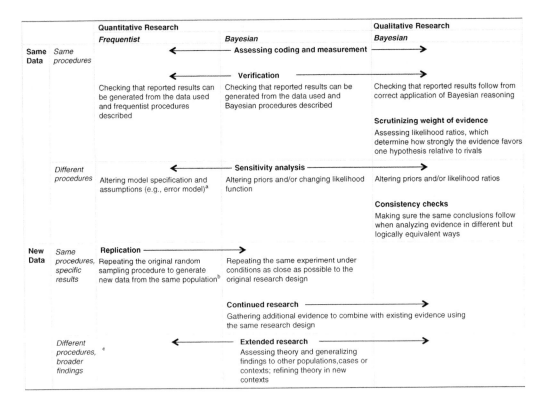

Figure 12.1 Reliability of inference

Note: (a) Clemens' (2017:327) "reanalysis tests" fit here.
(b) Our definition of replication corresponds to Clemens' (2017:327) "reproduction test," which entails "sampling precisely the same population but otherwise using identical methods to the original study."
(c) We would place Clemens' (2017:327) "extension tests" – which use data "gathered on a sample representative of a different population" – in this category. Although these tests use essentially the same statistical analysis as the original research, sampling from a different population changes the research design and aims to assess generalizability of findings.

before realizing they were using the term to mean different things." From a conceptual perspective, as Freese and Petersen point out, many scholars view the activities that fall under "same-data/same-procedures" as entailing something more trivial (although still important) compared to "new-data/same-procedures," which is the classic domain of replication in frequentist statistics.[2] Accordingly, for the former category we adopt Freese and Peterson's term *verification* – checking that "reported results can be generated from the

---

[2] As reflected in terms used to distinguish new-data/same-procedures from the other categories, which include "direct replication," "mechanical replication," and "close replication" (Freese and Peterson, Chapter 10, this volume).

data used."[3] Likewise, activities involving "new data, new procedures" in our view go beyond the scope of replication, as other scholars have also contended (see, for example, Freese and Peterson's discussion of "conceptual replication" in experiments, Chapter 10, this volume). For this row, we instead coin the term *extended research* – assessing theory and generalizing findings to other contexts. Activities entailing "same-data/different-procedures" fall closer to the realm of replication and in our view are central to the question of whether reported results reliably follow from the evidence presented. However, we prefer the term *sensitivity analysis*, which we feel more accurately captures the goal at hand.

Turning to the columns of Figure 12.1, we divide quantitative research on the left into two categories: frequentist versus Bayesian, with qualitative Bayesian research on the right. In a given row, we use the same term across columns for activities that are closely analogous in essence – for example, *verification* and *extended research* in all quantitative and qualitative research.[4] In some instances, however, there are important distinctions to be made between frequentist quantitative analysis versus Bayesian quantitative analysis, and/or quantitative Bayesian analysis versus qualitative Bayesian analysis. The former distinctions arise from the epistemological differences between frequentism and Bayesianism, which we will explicate in the section "New-Data/Same-Procedures." The latter distinctions arise from the greater degree of subjectivity inherent in analyzing the inferential import of qualitative evidence.

The most significant differences across columns arise in the new-data/same-procedures row. Here we apply a narrow definition of *replication* that is restricted to frequentist quantitative analysis and experimental research. For the more distant qualitative Bayesian analog, we devise the term *continued research* – gathering additional evidence to combine with existing evidence toward strengthening inferences within the same research design – which is also salient for quantitative research that employs a Bayesian framework. These terminological choices are again motivated by our concerns regarding conceptual stretching of "replication" beyond its natural epistemological context. As elaborated in the section on "New-Data/Same-Procedures," applying identical procedures to analyze new data makes sense for controlled experiments or observational studies where a different random sample can be taken from the same population (e.g., third-year East-Coast college

---

[3] Clemens (2017:327) uses the term verification similarly.
[4] Verification and extended research should also be directly applicable to non-Bayesian qualitative research.

students, or light from a distant galaxy – as long as salient characteristics of the data sources do not change over the intervening time period), but in qualitative research, evidence (e.g., interviews with expert informants) can rarely be treated as a random sample, and in accord with a Bayesian logic, the goal of collecting more data is to accumulate information and thereby strengthen inferences, rather than to validate findings by independently reproducing results with a new sample or a new run of the experiment. It is worth stressing that our distinction between *replication* and *continued research* is not intended in any way to downplay the importance of "new-data/same-procedures" assessment in qualitative research.

The following sub-sections explicate the qualitative analogs in each row of Figure 12.1 in more detail. The third section of this chapter will then focus on same-data scrutiny of qualitative research (the first two rows of Figure 12.1), which we find most salient to discussions of replication – or, as we prefer, reliability – in qualitative research.

Same-Data/Same-Procedures

The aim in this row entails examining existing research to ascertain whether the findings justifiably follow from the data and analytical procedures employed. Focusing first on the qualitative research column, an initial task entails assessing coding and measurement – asking whether concepts are well defined, operationalized, and scored in the study. A large body of literature provides guidelines to this end, so we will not dwell upon it here.[5] Checking that evidence has been accurately quoted or summarized from the original sources is another basic activity that we would include here (see Reiter, Chapter 11, this volume, on "measurement replication").

A second task entails verification. In a Bayesian framework, this involves checking whether the mechanics of probability theory have been correctly applied, as explicated in the third section of this chapter.[6] We view this question as an objective, technical matter, with the caveat that operationalizing Bayesian reasoning in qualitative research remains an active methodological frontier. As such, the literature contains different understandings of Bayesianism, different approaches to adopting Bayesianism in qualitative and multi-method research, and different levels of technical sophistication. For

---

[5] See, e.g., Collier and Mahon (1993); Goertz and Mahoney (2012).
[6] For example, has the author correctly defined the weight of evidence, and does Bayes' rule yield the reported posterior odds on the hypotheses given the author's stated prior odds and weight of evidence.

purely qualitative case research, we advocate the "logical Bayesian" approach presented by Fairfield and Charman (2017) (discussed further in the third section of this chapter).

For qualitative research, a third task entails scrutinizing the inferential weight of the evidence. This task inevitably involves an element of subjective judgment. In logical Bayesianism, probability represents the *rational degree of belief* we should hold in some proposition, such as a causal hypothesis, in light of all relevant background information we possess and all evidence collected as part of the study – independently of subjective opinion, personal predilections, or subconscious desires. However, logical Bayesiainism is an aspirational ideal that usually cannot be fully realized without approximations – all the more so in qualitative social science where there are no clear mathematical procedures for objectively translating complex, narrative-based, non-reproducible, highly contextual qualitative information into precise probability statements. Additional challenges arise when experts aim to independently assess the weight of evidence, as determined by the *likelihood ratio* (see the section on "Bayesian Inference in Brief," below), which entails asking how much more plausible the evidence is under a given hypothesis relative to a rival. Background information shapes how we interpret evidence, yet scholars will bring very different knowledge to the table. Authors should explicitly invoke and discuss those elements of their background information that matter most for weighing the evidence, but it is impossible to systematically list all salient background information that informs our analysis. Accordingly, the goal of scrutiny should not be to exactly reproduce numerical probabilities, but instead to promote discussion and foster a reasonable level of consensus on the inferential weight of evidence. As part of this process, elements of the author's background information that were previously used implicitly or subconsciously may come to light and help to resolve disagreements.

Turning to quantitative research, both tasks – assessing coding and measurement, and verification – are of course relevant as well. The first is an important but to our knowledge much less widely discussed issue compared to verification, which would include double-checking mathematical procedures and computer codes for errors.

Assessing measurement and coding can be fairly straightforward in some contexts – for example, running inter-coder reliability checks when datasets have been generated by coding mentions in documents or open-ended responses on surveys. In other contexts, it may be quite challenging and time consuming, particularly when large amounts of qualitative information have been condensed into quantitative scores. Mark Beissinger's comments on the Qualitative Transparency Deliberation blog are highly salient in this regard.

Having created several large-n datasets, I can attest to the enormous amount of research that necessarily must go into the coding of each individual variable for each observation and the judgments that are made by researchers in making those codings. If we are talking about real transparency in research, large-n researchers would need to provide extensive documentation on every single coding in their datasets.[7]

Despite the practical challenges, the importance of assessing measurement and coding in dataset generation should not be underestimated. For example, Haggard and Kaufman (2012:501) point out that their study on inequality and regime change:

raises serious questions about the validity of the coding of democratic transitions in these two major datasets and, as a result, casts doubt on the inferences that have been drawn in the quantitative work that employs them. Only 55.4% of the CGV [Cheibub, Ghandi, and Vreeland] transitions are also Polity [IV] cases, and 21 of the 65 CGV transitions had Polity scores of less than 6. Even where the two datasets are in agreement, moreover, our examination of the cases raises questions about the validity of the coding process.

Our point here is not only to emphasize that dataset generation should be included more centrally in discussions about reliability, replication, and research transparency, but also to emphasize that the subjective judgments that necessarily complicate qualitative research are not absent from quantitative research; they simply enter at a stage that tends to receive less attention in these debates.[8]

Same-Data/Different-Procedures

Further assessments of reliability of inference can be conducted by reanalyzing a study's data with slightly altered procedures. We refer to such endeavors as *sensitivity analysis*, whether the data are quantitative or qualitative, with an additional related but distinct task that we call *consistency checks* in qualitative Bayesian research.

---

[7] www.qualtd.net/viewtopic.php?f=13&t=157. Beissinger goes on to warn that such requirements would be infeasible: "This is simply not being asked because it is not practicable – even though the real instances of fraud that we are aware of have come from falsified codings in large-n data sets."

[8] For excellent work on assessing conceptualization and measurement in large-N datasets, see Kurtz and Schrank's (2007) critique of the World Bank Government Effectiveness Indicators and Coppedge et al.'s (2011) critique of Freedom House and other democracy indicators.

Importantly, our understanding of what "different procedures" entail necessarily changes when moving from frequentistism to Bayesianism. In the former world, different procedures might include altering model specifications or choosing different test statistics or estimators. In Bayesian analysis, "different procedures" takes on a much narrower meaning. Within a logical Bayesian framework, we must make judgments about which hypotheses to consider, where and how to acquire data, and how to interpret qualitative evidence. However, the underlying inferential procedure remains the same: apply the rules of probability to update initial beliefs regarding the plausibility of rival hypotheses in light of the evidence. As elaborated in the third section of this chapter, the analysis always involves assessing prior probabilities, assessing likelihood ratios, and updating probabilities in accord with Bayes' rule. Unlike frequentist analysis, there is no need to choose among sampling procedures, stopping rules, estimators, test statistics, or significance levels.

However, there is scope within Bayesianism for sensitivity analysis that entails assessing how much conclusions are affected by different choices of prior probabilities for the hypotheses – this is common practice in Bayesian statistics (e.g., Berger and Berry 1988:162; Greenland 2006:766). When working with qualitative information, where subjective judgment enters more strongly, additional sensitivity assessments can be carried out by varying the inferential weight attributed to the most salient pieces of evidence. This practice is particularly useful if the interpretation of key pieces of evidence is sensitive to background assumptions; for example, our level of trust in informants and/or the instrumental incentives we attribute to them.

Logical Bayesianism also provides opportunities to carry out various *consistency checks* on our inferential reasoning when we are working with qualitative evidence. Most importantly, rational reasoning requires that we must arrive at the same inference if we incorporate distinct pieces of evidence into our analysis in a different order, or if we parse the overall body of evidence into either more finely grained or more coarsely aggregated pieces of information. These consistency checks in essence entail "solving the problem" in different but logically equivalent ways. These consistency checks will be explicated in greater detail below.

New-Data/Same-Procedures

When we arrive at the new-data/same-procedures row, we find more significant differences as we move from quantitative frequentist analysis on the left-hand side of Figure 12.1 to qualitative Bayesian analysis on the right-hand side.

In quantitative frequentist research, applying identical procedures to new data is the classic realm of replication in the narrow sense. This endeavor entails using the original study's designated stochastic sampling and analysis procedures to obtain new data from the same population.[9] The centrality of repeated random sampling (in principle, if not always in practice) is built into frequentist inference on a foundational level. Probability itself is understood as the limiting proportion of some particular type of event in an infinite sequence of repeated random trials; *p*-values/significance levels, statistical power, and confidence levels are all defined in terms of long-run relative frequencies under repetition of the same experiment or sampling process, and randomization is meant to ensure balance between groups (only) in the long run – that is, under indefinite repetitions of the procedure.

Bayesianism, in contrast, focuses on making the best conclusions possible from all available data, whether generated through a stochastic process or not; repetition and long-run frequencies play much less central roles in inference, because within a Bayesian framework, what could have but did not happen, or what might but has not yet happened, is irrelevant for drawing inferences from the actual data in hand. The salient "new-data/same-procedures" endeavor is best described as *continued research* – namely, collecting more data (according to the parameters of the original research design) that will contribute to the final reported inferences, hopefully by reducing our uncertainty regarding which hypothesis is correct and/or narrowing posterior error bars for parameter estimates.

We emphasize that the key distinction between frequentist replication studies and "continued research" within a Bayesian framework is that the new data produced naturally contribute to the inferences *in combination* with the evidence that was already analyzed, not independently of the original data. Frequentist statistical theory is ill-suited for synthesizing information from multiple studies regarding the same hypotheses, in that it provides no universal rules for aggregating *p*-values from multiple null-hypothesis significance tests into an overall measure of support, nor for assessing and combining the systematic (non-random) components of estimation errors. Therefore, in frequentist-based inference, replication and meta-analysis (i.e., combining the results of many studies) traditionally have been considered as separate

---

[9] Our narrow definition of replication corresponds to Clemens' (2017:327) "reproduction test," which entails "sampling precisely the same population but otherwise using identical methods to the original study."

endeavors.[10] Alternatively, treating repetitions as intermediate steps in a so-called sequential analysis may also be problematic, since in principle all of the sampling and stopping rules must be specified in advance, and the difficulty of the analysis tends to grow with the complexities and contingencies of these rules. Given these challenges, scholars are increasingly using Bayesian tools to conduct meta-analysis of individual studies that employ orthodox statistics (e.g., Pereira and Ioannidis 2011; van Aert and van Assen 2017). However, this epistemological mismatch leads to awkwardness, as scholars must make Bayesian sense of frequentist notions such as p-values, power analysis, and estimators.

In contrast to frequentism, Bayesianism provides a unified procedure for combining evidence and learning from accumulated information. Bayesianism naturally accommodates contingent data gathering or follow-up data collection without need to distinguish preliminary from subsequent stages of analysis. And when Bayesian methods are employed at the stage of primary research and reporting, any subsequent meta-analysis simply proceeds via the same inferential framework. Probability theory itself is the mathematical expression of this updating process. Learning in the Bayesian framework occurs by virtue of the fact that (a) probability is understood as a logical concept that represents a rational degree of belief given the limited information we possess, not a long-run frequency, and (b) all probabilities within Bayesianism are necessarily *conditional* probabilities: confidence in one proposition depends on what else we know and generally changes when we make new observations. After completing an initial round of research, the posterior probabilities on our hypotheses, which take into account all evidence known so far, become the prior probabilities when we move forward to analyze additional evidence.

Stated in more concrete terms, the inferential weight of evidence in a Bayesian framework is additive. If evidence from a second round of research (or subsequent study following the same research design) runs counter to the inference drawn from a first round of research (or previous study), we would not necessarily conclude that the inference from the first round of research is "invalid" (unless scrutiny along the lines described in the sections "Same-Data/Same-Procedures" and "Same-Data/Different-Procedures" in this chapter reveals problems with the analysis). Instead, we aggregate the evidence from both rounds and examine the combined weight of evidence. Suppose the initial research concluded that hypothesis H_1 is substantially

---

[10] Some countervailing recommendations are beginning to emerge.

more plausible than rival hypothesis H_2, whereas the aggregate evidence from both rounds now leads to the conclusion that H_2 is slightly more plausible than H_1. We would not say that the findings from the first round "failed to replicate"; instead, we would assert that the tentative conclusions inferred from the earlier evidence no longer hold in light of the larger body of evidence now available. At any stage of research, our results are always conditional on the hypotheses we are comparing and the information we currently possess, and inferences are always subject to change in light of new information.

One example in which a Bayesian might conduct something more akin to a narrow-sense replication study intended to produce an independent dataset for comparison would be if there are concerns about whether an experimental apparatus is functioning correctly (e.g., Could the detector be miswired? Did the laser fire at the right intervals?). But if the new results suggest that the apparatus did indeed work properly in the original run, any data generated in the second round (conducted under conditions as close as possible to the original run) could be combined with the data from the previous round via Bayes' rule to produce a single cumulative inference, and we would hence return to the realm of "continued research" rather than multiple replications of the experiment per se. In sum, "viewed through this [Bayesian] lens, the aim of repeated experimentation is to increase the amount of evidence, measured on a continuous scale, either for or against the original claim" (Goodman et al. 2016:4).

The distinctions between frequentist replication studies and Bayesian "continued research" become more acute when we move from quantitative to qualitative research, where evidence can rarely be considered to arise from a stochastic sampling process or randomized controlled experiment. Consider interviews. In contrast to large-N survey research where random sampling is the norm, qualitative scholars purposively seek out key informants based on prior expectations of their knowledge about the topic of investigation, in accord with the Bayesian principle of research design via maximizing expected learning. In some studies those interviewed may essentially exhaust the population of expert informants.[11] Similarly, qualitative scholars often aim to scrutinize all relevant documents (e.g., legislative records, news articles, reputable historical accounts) – not some sample thereof – that might provide salient

---

[11] Fairfield's (2015) research on taxation would be an example; nearly all current and former Chilean Finance Ministry technocrats with first-hand knowledge about tax policy formulation in the 1990s and early 2000s were interviewed.

evidence.[12] Cases themselves (whether countries, policymaking episodes, or electoral campaigns) are often selected based on expectations that they will be rich in data and/or will facilitate strong tests of competing theories, which again conforms to the Bayesian principle of maximizing expected learning (Fairfield and Charman 2018).[13] Even if random sampling of cases were desirable (e.g., for lack of any better criteria), it is very often impossible to define or delineate in advance all members of the population from which the sample would be drawn. For example, scholars often discover new cases while conducting fieldwork.[14] Case selection strategies in qualitative research are sometimes presented as "replicable" (see Kapiszewski 2012:211); however, applying the designated procedures again would result in the same set of cases (or at least a very high proportion of the same cases), not an independent sample containing different cases that could be used to test the stability of the original findings.

Setting aside the issue of whether a stochastic data-generation process is fundamental to the notion of replication – our above discussion does not imply that "replication" in the literal sense of repeating exactly the same procedures to obtain new data is impossible in qualitative settings. In theory, a scholar could take a published study, follow the same case selection and data-generating procedures to the last detail described, visit (potentially the same) field sights, interview (potentially the same) informants, consult (potentially the same) archival sources, etc., and produce a separate analysis that tests the same hypotheses. We cannot imagine any scholar wanting to undertake such an endeavor, but, more importantly, we do not see much value in such an approach – indeed it strikes us as the least productive way to improve reliability of inference and foster knowledge accumulation in qualitative research. These goals are better served by scrutinizing the evidence and analysis presented in the original study – via the various activities described in the previous sections on "Same-Data/Same-Procedures" and "Same-Data/Different-Procedures" – and then seeking salient new evidence from complementary data sources through continued research, and/or extended research

---

[12] Moreover, repeated interviews with the same informant or repeated consultation of the same documents cannot sensibly be regarded as an independent random sample of statements from those sources.

[13] See also Van Evera's (1997) notions of seeking "data-rich cases" and/or "cases in which different theories make divergent predictions."

[14] See Fairfield (2015:appendix 1.3) on case selection under such circumstances.

that examines different settings and refines hypotheses in new contexts (see the section "New-Data/Different-Procedures," below).

To summarize our argument, we view "replication" in the narrow sense as largely irrelevant within a Bayesian framework – with the exception of a few specific contexts that may arise in quantitative/experimental research – because Bayesian inference follows different epistemological principles from frequentist inference. The fact that "replication" would be impractical for qualitative research is a secondary matter – the fundamental issue is that frequentist inference, with its emphasis on random sampling and stochastic data, is not appropriate for qualitative social science. Quoting Jackman and Western (1994:413): *"frequentist inference is inapplicable to the nonstochastic setting."*

As with quantitative Bayesian research, continued research in a qualitative Bayesian setting aims to gather more and different evidence that will improve inferences made from previously obtained information. Qualitative scholars regularly gather additional evidence after conducting an initial round of analysis and drawing tentative conclusions. Continued research might entail collecting new information from sources that were previously consulted – for example, following up on previous interviews by asking the informant new questions or seeking to clarify the meaning of a response from an earlier conversation. Equally well, continued research can seek new sources of information – e.g., an archive collection recently made public, an outgoing government official who now has time or political leeway to grant interviews, or an expert witness who can now comment on a recent court decision.

Continued research is typically carried out by the original author(s) in the context of refining or improving the study, either by gathering new information for the same cases or by including new cases that fall within the parameters of the original research design and the original scope of the hypotheses considered.[15] Independent scholars might conduct some work of this type, particularly if the case(s) in question are of intrinsic substantive interest and/or carry special theoretical import, and if they deem that gathering additional evidence could significantly strengthen or alter the inferences. More typically, however, independent scholars would engage in *extended research* as described in the following section.

Our recommendations for conducting productive continued research are both intuitive and practical in nature.

---

[15] It is worth noting that a "research design" in qualitative contexts tends to be much looser, more flexible, and less detailed than what one would find in experiments or in frequentist hypothesis-testing contexts, where all procedures must be specified from the outset.

- *Carry out preliminary analysis of evidence periodically.*

This practice helps us take stock of what has been learned so far and what kinds of evidence or clues would be most valuable moving forward.[16] In a Bayesian framework, the most decisive pieces of evidence are those that fit much better with a given hypothesis compared to the rival. Accordingly, we should think about where the rival hypotheses under consideration would most tend to disagree, identify divergent predictions, and seek additional evidence accordingly.

- *Revisit key informants.*

This strategy allows the scholar to gather new information as new hypotheses and new questions arise over time. For example, Fairfield (2015:23) conducted follow-up interviews with the informants who possessed the most extensive, first-hand knowledge of tax reforms over the course of both primary and follow-up fieldwork in order to pursue new lines of inquiry and to dig deeper into political processes in light of conflicting or unexpected accounts from other sources.

- *Keep an eye open for not only new sources of evidence, but also informative new cases that emerge as time progresses.*

Just as we are free to gather new evidence and combine it with previously acquired knowledge, within a Bayesian framework we can include additional cases that provide fruitful grounds for testing rival hypotheses (Fairfield and Charman 2018). Boas (2016) provides an excellent example (although he does not cast his research design in Bayesian terms). After conducting extensive research on presidential campaigns that took place from the late 1980s through 2006 in Chile, Brazil, and Peru and presenting findings based on the evidence compiled (Boas 2010). Boas (2016:29, 32–34) included three additional presidential campaigns that took place in those countries from 2009 to 2011, along with a set of elections from other countries that he deemed to fall within the scope conditions of his "success-contagion" theory.[17]

---

[16] Kapiszewski et al. (2015:chapter 10) provide useful general guidance on conducting analysis while gathering data in the field.

[17] Likewise, after conducting an initial round of research from 2006 to 2008 on tax reforms in Argentina, Bolivia, and Chile (Fairfield 2010, 2011, 2013), Fairfield (2015) added Chile's 2012 corporate tax increase. This case illustrates the phenomenon of popular mobilization counteracting business power – previously observed in Bolivia's 2005 hydrocarbons royalty – in a different context, thereby adding further support for the theory.

- *Arrange follow-up trips to field sites.*

If resources permit, this strategy allows the investigator to gain perspective over time and to seek out specific sources and clues that can best contribute to filling in gaps and strengthening the weight of evidence where needed. For example, Garay (2016) returned to Argentina after conducting primary fieldwork and successfully obtained more decisive evidence in favor of her argument that electoral competition in presidential elections is critical for expansion of social programs, as opposed to competition in legislative elections, through interviews with participants in the 2009 midterm elections, which resulted in the government's loss of its absolute majority. Similarly, Fairfield (2015) was able to secure a critical interview with a former Chilean finance minister in 2007 following primary fieldwork in 2005; the interview significantly strengthened her conclusion that business's instrumental (political) power, not structural (investment) power, explained Chile's meager progress toward increasing progressive taxation during Ricardo Lagos' presidency.

While costly, follow-up fieldwork can occasionally be strategically planned in advance. For example, Garay (2016) anticipated the need to revisit Mexico after the 2006 election, given that additional research on social policy innovations would be highly valuable regardless of which candidate prevailed; her SSRC grant allowed her to conduct several months of research prior to the elections and several months of research after the new government took power later in 2006 (Garay 2018, private communication).

By and large, we view good continued research as simply good research. Our overarching recommendation for improving continued research is to become familiar with the basic principles of Bayesian probability and to implement Bayesian-inspired best practices for assessing the inferential weight of evidence (Fairfield and Charman 2017, 2018).

New-Data/Different-Procedures

Whereas *continued research* entails gathering more data within the parameters of the original research design, *extended research* – the final row in Figure 12.1 – pushes beyond previous work by testing theories in new ways, or assessing and/or refining theory in new contexts or domains. Examples for quantitative scholarship might include asking how well findings generalize to different populations – e.g., do African voters respond to information about corruption in the same way as Brazilian voters? Do similar results hold for adults with college degrees as for third-year undergraduates? In qualitative research, scholars regularly include preliminary discussions of how findings and hypotheses might apply elsewhere – whether in different regions or countries, different time-periods, or different policy areas.[18] Literature on well-developed research agendas – for example, state-building or welfare provision – commonly assesses hypotheses from foregoing studies with new data from different contexts. Meanwhile, research on new or less-studied phenomena regularly draws on theories from other domains and adapts or extends them to address the questions at hand.[19]

Scholarship on state-building and institutional development exemplifies a long-term trajectory of extended research. Pioneering work by Tilly (1992), Ertman (1997), and others on early-modern Europe hypothesized that warfare drove the formation of strong and effective state institutions. Subsequent authors evaluated that theory and refined it to craft explanations for state-building outcomes in Africa (Herbst 2000), Latin America (Centeno 2002), and China (Hui 2005). Similarly, research on the resource curse in paradigmatic cases such as Venezuela (Karl 1997) stimulated continual reassessment and refinement of that theory in light of data on other cases, in Latin America and far beyond. New studies regularly assess the warfare hypothesis and/or the resource-curse hypothesis, proposing amendments or new explanations where they fall short (Slater 2010; Kurtz 2013; Soifer 2015).

Within this literature, we find several excellent individual illustrations of "extended research." Kurtz (2013) carefully scrutinizes assumptions underpinning previous work on the warfare and resource-curse hypotheses; for example, he argues that at their core these explanations are essentially functionalist and lack well-specified causal mechanisms (Kurtz 2009:483). The alternative theory of state-building that he develops, which focuses on labor-repressive agriculture as the key impediment to institutional development, is inspired by Barrington Moore's classic work on democratization. In essence Kurtz adapts and extends Moore's theoretical insights to a different domain. Soifer (2015) in turn aims to construct a broader theory that accounts for state weakness not just as a result of no efforts at state-building, but also as a result of failed efforts at state-building. Among other countries, Soifer reconsiders Peru. On the basis of distinct evidence about development of education and infrastructure, he argues that Kurtz mischaracterizes the period prior to the 1890s as a case in which state-building efforts never

---

[18] Excellent examples include Boas (2016:chapter 5) and Garay (2016:chapter 8).
[19] For example, Fairfield (2015) takes the classic concepts of business's instrumental and structural power from literature on regulation and welfare in the United States (Hacker and Pierson 2002; Vogel 1989), refines them, and integrates them into a unified theoretical framework for explaining tax reform politics in Latin America, which had received little previous scholarly attention.

emerged, whereas it actually exemplifies failed efforts at state-building (Soifer 2015:19). Throughout the empirical chapters Soifer reconsiders the warfare and resource-curse hypotheses and argues that his theory, which focuses on the nature of local administrative institutions, better fits the evidence.

Our main recommendation for honing "extended research" in qualitative scholarship, so that it more effectively contributes to knowledge accumulation, is once again to carefully apply Bayesian reasoning. As discussed in the section "New-Data/Same-Procedures," Bayesianism provides a natural framework for systematically aggregating inferences across multiple pieces of evidence – whether drawn from a single study, or pooled across studies. For well-established research agendas such as state-building or democratization, it would be especially useful to assess new theories against established rival arguments in light of the key pieces of evidence presented in prominent studies that originated those rival arguments – in addition to considering new and/or distinct evidence. For example, how well would Kurtz's (2009) novel labor-repressive agriculture hypothesis fare against the resource curse in light of evidence from Venezuela, a paradigmatic case that established the salience of resource wealth for institutional development (Karl 1997)? How well would Soifer's (2015) new administrative institutions hypothesis fare against Kurtz's (2009) labor-repressive agriculture hypothesis in light of the evidence that Kurtz presents to substantiate his theory? Such assessments would more consistently incorporate prior knowledge into the analysis, along with new empirical information. In the democratization literature, Collier and Mahoney (1997) informally follow this type of approach, revisiting the same case-study literature on which elite-based theories of transition were based to argue that a framework granting a more central role to labor mobilization better accounts for the political dynamics of democratization. An important related point is that knowledge accumulation depends on clearly specifying the hypotheses under consideration. New theories need to be clearly differentiated from existing theories so that we can assess how their empirical implications differ – namely, to what extent is a given piece of evidence more or less likely under the new explanation relative to the plausible extant rivals.

Same-Data Assessments of Inference in Qualitative Bayesianism

Same-data assessment of qualitative research is crucial for ascertaining to what extent reported results reliably follow from the evidence and analysis that scholars present. In this section, we aim to illustrate the different components of same-data assessment within a logical Bayesian framework and demonstrate how they could be implemented to improve the quality of inference and scholarly consensus in qualitative research. We begin by overviewing the basics of Bayesian inference and how Bayesian reasoning can be applied in qualitative research. We then elaborate rules for verification, scrutinizing weight of evidence, sensitivity analysis, and consistency checks. Throughout, we illustrate these Bayesian rules for good same-data assessment with concrete empirical examples that draw on published process-tracing research and comparative historical analysis.

Bayesian Inference in Brief

As noted previously, logical Bayesianism (Cox 1961; Jaynes 2003) views probability as the rational degree of belief we should hold in a hypothesis or some other proposition given all relevant information we possess, which will inevitably be limited. When probabilities take on the limiting values of one or zero, we are certain that the hypothesis is true or false, respectively. When probabilities take on intermediate values, we are in a situation of uncertainty regarding the truth of the proposition.

Bayes' rule, expressed in terms of conditional probabilities, states that:

$$P(H|EI) = P(H|I) P(E|HI) / P(E|I). \qquad (1)$$

The term on the left is the *posterior probability* in the truth of hypothesis H, given a body of evidence E as well as the salient background information I that we bring to bear on the problem. The first term on the right is the *prior probability* of the hypothesis given our background information alone. The second term on the right is the *likelihood* of the evidence: if we take H and I to be true, what is the probability of the evidence? The term in the denominator is the unconditional likelihood of the evidence. We can sidestep having to evaluate $P(E|I)$, which is usually very difficult, by directly comparing rival (mutually exclusive) hypotheses:

$$\frac{P(H_1|EI)}{P(H_2|EI)} = \frac{P(H_1|I)}{P(H_2|I)} \times \frac{P(E|H_1 I)}{P(E|H_2 I)}. \qquad (2)$$

This relative odds-ratio form of Bayes' rule states that the posterior relative odds on H_1 versus H_2 in light of the evidence must equal the prior odds multiplied by the *likelihood ratio*. The likelihood ratio can be thought of as the relative probability of observing the evidence E if we imagine living in a hypothetical world where

H_1 is true, compared to the probability of observing E if we imagine living in an alternative hypothetical world in which H_2 is true (Fairfield and Charman 2017).

Assessing likelihood ratios is the central inferential step in Bayesian analysis that tells us how to update our odds on the hypotheses – does the evidence increase our confidence in H_1 or does it increase our confidence in H_2? In qualitative research, we must "mentally inhabit the world" of each hypothesis (Hunter 1984) and ask how surprising (low probability) or expected (high probability) the evidence would be in each respective world. If the evidence is less surprising in the "H_j world" relative to the "H_k world," then that evidence increases the odds we place on H_j versus H_k, and vice versa. In other words, we gain confidence in one hypothesis versus another to the extent that it makes the evidence obtained more plausible.

Bayesian reasoning in qualitative research can be applied either heuristically – thinking qualitatively about probabilities without explicitly invoking the formal apparatus of Bayesian mathematics – or explicitly – by quantifying probabilities and using Bayes' rule. As an introduction to heuristic Bayesian reasoning, consider the following example that draws on Stokes' (2001) research on "neoliberalism by surprise" in Latin America during the debt crisis,[20] which is often used for explicating process tracing (Collier et. al 2004:257). Stokes assesses two hypotheses (assumed mutually exclusive) to explain why presidents who campaigned on protectionist economic platforms switched course once in office. The first is a representation hypothesis:

H_{Rep} = Presidents violated protectionist policy mandates in order to represent voters best interests.

The second is a rent-seeking hypothesis:

H_{Rent} = Presidents violated those mandates in order to seek rents associated with neoliberal reforms (e.g., privatization).

For the case of Argentina's President Menem (1989–1999), Stokes presents the following evidence:

E_M = In a 1993 interview with an Argentine journalist he [Menem] described his strategy during the 1989 campaign: "If I had said 'I will privatize the telephones, the railways, and Aerolineas Argentinas,' the whole labor movement would have been against me. There was not yet a clear consciousness of what was required" (Stokes 2001:72).

---

[20] See Fairfield and Garay (2017:appendix) for additional examples of heuristic Bayesian reasoning.

As Stokes argues, E favors H_{Rep}, but a Bayesian analysis suggests that E_M only favors that hypothesis *weakly* relative to the rival. In a world where H_{Rep} is true, E_M is unsurprising; Menem himself has sketched out the logic behind the representation explanation (although much is left implicit), and he would have every reason at this time to disclose his noble motives and foresight in choosing policies that successfully stabilized the economy. However, Menem might also tell this same story to justify his behavior if H_{Rent} is true, given that he would be highly unlikely to admit rent-seeking motives, and he would have similar incentives in this world to claim credit for fixing the economy. E_M is nevertheless somewhat less likely in the H_{Rent} world, since there are other cover stories and responses Menem could provide when interviewed about his policy decisions (e.g., "I had no choice given constraints imposed by the IMF," "I deny campaigning on an anti-neoliberal platform," "I have no comment"). In sum, even though E fits very well with H_{Rep}, this evidence is only somewhat more probable under H_{Rep} relative to H_{Rent}. Learning E_M therefore at most modestly increases the odds in favor of the representation hypothesis.

When quantifying probabilities for explicit Bayesian analysis, we advocate working with a logarithmic scale, which mirrors how the brain processes information, in conjunction with an analogy to sound, such that relative probabilities are expressed in decibels (Fairfield and Charman 2017). Equation 2 then becomes simply:

posterior log-odds *(dB)* = prior log-odds *(dB)* + weight of evidence *(dB)*, (3)

where the weight of evidence, *WoE* $(H_1 : H_2)$, is proportional to the log of the likelihood ratio.

Keeping in mind that 3 dB corresponds to the minimal difference an adult with good hearing can detect, 5 dB is clearly noticeable, 10 dB sounds about twice as loud, 20 dB sounds four times louder, and 30 dB sounds eight times louder – roughly corresponding to the difference between a normal conversation and a passing motorcycle – we can now express our assessment of weight of evidence in the above example more precisely: $WoE_M (H_{Rep} : H_{Rent}) = \sim 5$ dB.

Verification: Checking for Technical Errors

In many ways Bayesian analysis mirrors how we intuitively reason in qualitative research; however, in some regards correctly applying Bayesian reasoning changes the way we use our intuition and focuses attention to issues that might otherwise be overlooked when writing case-study narratives. We highlight here a few of the most relevant points that should be checked when scrutinizing Bayesian analysis in qualitative research, in accord with the guidelines discussed in Fairfield and Charman (2017).

As emphasized above, assessing the weight of evidence or the likelihood ratio – the key inferential step in Bayesian analysis – entails evaluating whether the evidence would be more or less likely under one hypothesis relative to a rival hypothesis. In other words, inference always involves comparing well-specified rival explanations. One common practice we have observed in the nascent Bayesian process tracing literature is to compare a working hypothesis H against its logical negation $\sim H$. This approach is best avoided, because in general, $\sim H$ will be poorly specified – there are multiple ways that a specific working hypothesis could fail to hold, each of which may correspond to a very different "world." As such, assessing the likelihood of the evidence conditional on $\sim H$ may be impossible without first asking what concrete possibilities are contained within $\sim H$. The background information I, on which we condition all probabilities, must in practice restrict our attention to a finite set of mutually exclusive hypotheses, such that we can concretely specify $\sim H$ as $\{H_1$ or H_2 or ... $H_N\}$. It is worth noting that this Bayesian approach departs sharply from frequentist null-hypothesis testing. For an example illustrating the importance of explicitly considering rival explanations rather than attempting to compare H directly against $\sim H$, see Fairfield and Charman (2017:appendix A: §A4.3).

A second and related caveat is that simply "tracing the process" corresponding to the causal mechanism of the working hypothesis is not adequate for inference.[21] The key question in Bayesian analysis is not whether the evidence fits with a hypothesis, or whether deductive predictions of a hypothesis are borne out, but whether the evidence obtained fits *better* with that hypothesis as compared to a plausible rival explanation. In the Stokes (2001) example above, if we had failed to ask how well E_M fits with the rent-seeking hypothesis, we would have significantly overestimated the degree of support that this evidence lends to the representation hypothesis. In some instances, a causal mechanism may be so unique to the working hypothesis that evidence of that mechanism may be largely incompatible with the alternative explanations; nevertheless, correctly assessing the inferential weight of evidence requires explicitly considering how plausible the evidence would

---

[21] If, however, we have already tentatively accepted a theory as correct and wish to use that theory to explain phenomena that we observe, explicit comparison of rival hypotheses becomes less salient. We suspect that most qualitative research involves a combination of theory comparison and explanation.

be under the rival explanation(s). Likewise, it is important to recognize that a given piece of evidence need not speak directly to the causal mechanism of the working hypothesis in order to boost our confidence in that hypothesis – if this evidence is less likely under the plausible alternative explanations, that evidence favors the working hypothesis.

For the same reasons, stating that a certain collection of observations fits well with the working hypothesis while another set of observations fits poorly with a rival hypothesis departs from Bayesian logic. Our preliminary readings suggest that approach may be fairly common in qualitative and multi-methods research. It is certainly possible that a few key pieces of evidence may dramatically increase the odds in favor of the working hypothesis while one or two other pieces of evidence essentially eliminate a rival explanation; again, however, correctly assessing the inferential weight of any particular piece of evidence requires explicitly asking how likely that same evidence would be in the world of the rival hypothesis. In other words, Bayesian analysis does not entail sorting the evidence into observations consistent with or supportive of one hypothesis and observations consistent with or supportive of another hypothesis. Instead, it entails assessing to what degree each piece of evidence fits with one hypothesis versus another.

Scrutinizing Weight of Evidence

Even if a study has correctly applied the Bayesian concept of weight of evidence, scholars may disagree on how strongly the evidence favors a given explanation over rivals. Bayesian analysis provides an excellent framework for scrutinizing evidence that can facilitate consensus-building or at least clarifying the locus of disagreements. Open discussion and debate on the weight of evidence can help authors to clarify and communicate their reasoning more clearly, highlight their evidence more precisely, shed light on important elements of context and background information that matter for inferential judgments, and even identify and clarify ambiguities in the hypotheses themselves.

Scrutinizing weight of evidence can be carried out in multiple settings, from informal discussions and research presentations to peer review and published commentary, as well as in the classroom. We are developing teaching exercises to encourage this practice. A first task entails explicitly identifying specific pieces of evidence that authors present, as well as the hypotheses they evaluate. A second task entails assessing and debating the weight of evidence. Students are asked to first analyze the evidence on their own and quantify their assessment of how strongly it favors one hypothesis over another using the decibel scale described above. They then discuss and debate their assessments in groups and aim to reach a consensus on the weight of evidence. The discussions we have led illustrate how widely background knowledge varies among scholars and how differently hypotheses and evidence can be evaluated unless both are very clearly specified. These exercises also illustrate that learning how to effectively "mentally inhabit the world" of each hypothesis requires significant practice.

We have already in essence illustrated the process of scrutinizing weight of evidence with the Stokes (2001) example discussed above. By way of further illustration, let us now consider additional information that she presents in her discussion of the Menem case and scrutinize her analysis of its inferential weight.

E_D = Menem's Minister of Public Works, Roberto Dromi, told Stokes in a 1994 interview: "In this country, 10% of the labor force were government employees. We knew that if we talked of privatizing Aerolíneas Argentinas, we would have the airline workers on our backs, if we talked of privatization, we would have those workers on our backs ... We knew that Argentines would disapprove of the reforms we planned, but would come to see that they were good."

Stokes (2001:74–75) characterizes this interview information as "strong evidence that policy switchers were sometimes motivated by the belief that the economy would perform much better under efficiency-oriented than under security-oriented policies" – in other words, strong evidence in favor of the representation hypothesis. Stokes' presentation of the evidence in its full and original form (which we have abridged above) and her subsequent clear and careful articulation of how and why it fits with the representation hypothesis are exemplary. Yet a Bayesian scrutiny reveals that the extent to which this evidence supports the representation hypothesis is overstated, because no similar assessment has been conducted regarding how well this evidence fits with the rival rent-seeking hypothesis. For the same reasons discussed regarding the Menem interview (E_M), while E_D fits very well with the representation hypothesis, it is also plausible under the rent-seeking hypothesis, because in that world, Dromi might tell a similar story rather than openly revealing the true ignoble motives that drove the policy switch. As with E_M, a Bayesian scrutiny reveals E_D to weakly or perhaps moderately, depending on what background information we possess regarding Dromi's probity – but not strongly – favor the representation hypothesis.[22]

---

[22] Dromi was later revealed to have been implicated in corruption scandals involving privatizations.

Sensitivity Analysis

In qualitative research, subjectivity tends to intrude most strongly at the stage of assessing priors odds on hypotheses, since it is impossible in social science to exhaustively list and carefully consider all of the background information that influences our beliefs about the plausibility of hypotheses. Assessing how much conclusions depend on the choice of priors can therefore be a useful exercise. While weight of evidence will tend to be less vulnerable to subjectivity than priors – because evidence is concrete, specific, and directly observable, whereas hypotheses are abstractions – disagreements over weight of evidence can still be substantial, as discussed above. Sensitivity checks that examine how much inferences change when key pieces of evidence are treated as more or less decisive can therefore be valuable as well.

Fairfield and Charman (2017:appendix A) include detailed illustrations of both types of sensitivity checks, drawing on Fairfield's (2013, 2015) case study of a Chilean reform that revoked a regressive tax subsidy. Fairfield argues that an "equity appeal," made during a presidential race in which inequality had assumed unusually high issue salience, drove the right-wing opposition coalition to approve the reform in congress in order to avoid electoral punishment. During the campaign, the opposition's presidential candidate blamed Chile's persistent inequality on the governing center-left coalition. The incumbent president responded by linking the tax subsidy to inequality and publicly challenging the opposition to support the reform.

Fairfield and Charman's Bayesian analysis of this case study compares the equity-appeal hypothesis against three rival explanations, which include a basic median-voter hypothesis, using three different prior probability distributions:

(1) equal odds on each hypothesis, which avoids any initial bias,

(2) a 50 dB penalty on the median-voter hypothesis, in light of extensive literature that questions its logic (e.g., Hacker and Pierson 2010; Kaufman 2009), with equal probabilities on the other three hypotheses, and

(3) a 50 dB penalty on Fairfield's explanation with equal priors for the remaining three.

The last of these prior distributions is particularly salient, given that an earlier version of Fairfield (2013) received comments from a reviewer who deemed the equity-appeal explanation implausible in light of background knowledge about the ineffectiveness of presidential appeals in US politics. The analysis in Fairfield and Charman (2017:appendix A) illustrates that even with this heavy 50 dB penalty on the equity-appeal hypothesis, it emerges as the best explanation in light of the evidence by at least 65 dB. Of course, skeptical readers might also question the assessment of the weights of evidence. The final section of Appendix A shows that even if we substantially reduce the extent to which we judge each piece of evidence to favor the equity appeal explanation over the rivals, the aggregate inference still weighs in favor of this hypothesis.

To give an example of how and when sensitivity analysis with respect to weight of evidence may be useful, consider the following piece of evidence (Fairfield 2013:49).

E_{FM} = A finance ministry official told the investigator that the tax subsidy "was a pure transfer of resources to rich people ... It was not possible for the right [coalition] to oppose the reform after making that argument about inequality."

As we will see, the weight we attribute to this evidence depends significantly on our background information. First consider the world of the equity-appeal hypothesis. E_{FM} fits well with the causal mechanism of this hypothesis in highlighting the importance of the exchange between the opposition candidate and the president that led to the equity appeal. Because E_{FM} makes the government appear savvy and effective at achieving socially desirable goals while insinuating that the opposition would otherwise have resisted redistribution, we see little reason for the government to conceal this information if the equity-appeal hypothesis is correct. Next, consider an alternative world where a basic median-voter logic operates – the opposition coalition accepted the reform because electoral competition drives politicians to converge on policies that promote the median voter's material interests,[23] and the equity appeal played no relevant causal role. While E_{FM} is less expected in this world relative to the equity-appeal world, it is not overly surprising. Government informants could have incentives to incorrectly attribute the opposition's support for the reform to the equity appeal, because this story portrays the government in a positive light and the opposition in a negative light.

---

[23] E.g., Meltzer and Richard (1981).

Yet Fairfield's background information includes significant confidence in this informant's expertise, analytical judgment, and sincerity, based on multiple interactions during fieldwork. Balancing these considerations, we judge E_{FM} to favor the equity-appeal hypothesis by 10 dB. However, a skeptical reader who possesses a very different body of background knowledge might be reluctant to share the author's confidence in the informant. To acknowledge this possibility, we can also report the overall weight of evidence presented in the case study[24] if we take E_{FM} to support the equity-appeal hypothesis over the median-voter hypothesis by a more conservative 5 dB (the same weight we attributed to Menem's interview in the section "Bayesian Inference in Brief").

Consistency Checks

As emphasized previously, the key inferential step that tells us how to update the prior odds on our hypotheses entails evaluating the weight of evidence, where E stands for all relevant information obtained over the course of the study. The mathematics of logical Bayesianism allow for a number of consistency checks on our reasoning about the overall weight of this evidence. For instance, we can directly assess the likelihood of the joint evidence E, or we can instead decompose E into any number of constituent observations. If we opt for the latter approach, we are free to incorporate the constituent observations into our analysis in any order. To see why, we need only apply the product rule of probability and the commutativity of conjunction:

$$P(E|HI) = P(E_1E_2|HI) = P(E_2E_1|HI) = P(E_1|E_2HI)\,P(E_2|HI) = P(E_2|E_1HI)\,P(E_1|HI). \quad (4)$$

Equation (4) can be easily generalized if we wish to decompose E_1 and/or E_2 into additional constituent observations. It follows that likelihood ratios can be factored into products:

$$\frac{P(E|H_i\,I)}{P(E|H_j\,I)} = \frac{P(E_1|E_2\,H_i\,I)}{P(E_1|E_2\,H_j\,I)} \times \frac{P(E_2|H_i\,I)}{P(E_2|H_j\,I)} = \frac{P(E_2|E_1\,H_i\,I)}{P(E_2|E_1\,H_j\,I)} \times \frac{P(E_1|H_i\,I)}{P(E_1|H_j\,I)}, \quad (5)$$

---

[24] The case study includes five additional key pieces of evidence.

and weights of evidence are additive:

$$\begin{aligned} WoE\ (H_j:H_k) &= WoE_1\ (H_j:H_k, E_2) + WoE_2\ (H_j:H_k) \\ &= WoE_2\ (H_j:H_k, E_1) + WoE_1\ (H_j:H_k), \end{aligned} \qquad (6)$$

with the important nuance that each piece of evidence that has already been incorporated into our analysis becomes part of the background information that we use to assess the weight of evidence for the next piece of evidence we consider.

Consistency checks that involve analyzing pieces of evidence in different orders are salient if there are potential logical dependencies among the evidence under a given hypothesis. Notice that assessing $P(E_1|E_2HI)$ entails asking: given the hypothesis and the background information, is E_1 any more or less likely given that we also know E_2? In other words, we must condition on previously incorporated information,[25] which can be a very difficult task. Given the technical subtleties and analytical challenges involved, we refer interested readers to Fairfield and Charman (2017:§3.3.3–4); appendix A (§A6) of that article provides a fully worked example.

As an example of consistency checks that entail parsing the evidence at different levels of aggregation, consider the following example based on Kurtz's (2013) research on state-building in Latin America. We wish to compare a resource-curse hypothesis H_R against a warfare hypothesis H_W (assumed mutually exclusive), in light of three salient observations $E = E_{WS}$ E_{ME} E_{IC} about the case of Peru:

H_R = Abundant mineral rents hinder institutional development. Easy money undermines administrative capacity by precluding the need to collect taxes, and public resources are directed toward inefficient industries, consumer subsidies, and patronage networks that sustain elites in power.

H_W = Absence of warfare hinders institutional development. Threat of military annihilation requires states to extract resources from society and develop strong administrative capacity in order to build and sustain armies. In the absence of external threats, state leaders lack these institution-building incentives.

E_{WS} = Peru never developed an effective state.

E_{ME} = Peru's economy has been dominated by mineral exports since colonial days.

E_{IC} = Peru was among the Latin American countries most consistently threatened by international military conflict.

---

[25] Previously incorporated information need not be collected at an earlier point in time relative to subsequently incorporated information.

One approach would be to directly assess the overall weight of evidence E. Taken together, the three observations strongly favor H_R over H_W. In a world where H_R is the correct hypothesis, mineral dependence in conjunction with weak state capacity are exactly what we would expect. Furthermore, although H_R makes no direct predictions about presence or absence of warfare, external threats are not surprising given that a weak state with mineral resources could be an easy and attractive target. In the alternative world of H_W, however, the evidence would be quite surprising; something very unusual, and hence improbable, would have to have happened for Peru to end up with a weak state if the warfare hypothesis is nevertheless correct, because weak state capacity despite military threats contradicts the expectations of the theory. Accordingly, we might assign $WoE\,(H_R : H_W) = 50$ dB, roughly corresponding to the difference between a whisper and a noisy restaurant.

A second approach could entail assessing the three pieces of evidence separately;

$$WoE\,(H_R : H_W) = WoE_{WS}\,(H_R : H_W) + WoE_{ME}\,(H_R : H_W, E_{WS}) + WoE_{IC}\,(H_R : H_W, E_{WS} E_{ME}).$$

We evaluate each term in turn. First, we have $WoE_{WS}\,(H_R : H_W) = 0$. Assuming we have no salient background information about the Peruvian case from the outset, a weak state is no more or less surprising under either hypothesis. Second, we judge $WoE_{ME}\,(H_R : H_W, E_{WS}) = 12$ dB. Mineral export dependence is exactly what we would expect under H_R given state weakness. In contrast, E_{ME} is neither surprising nor expected under H_W; the warfare hypothesis makes no predictions about Peru's economy in the absence of any relevant background information about this case. Accordingly, this evidence moderately favors the resource-curse hypothesis. Third, we deem $WoE_{IC}\,(H_R : H_W, E_{WS} E_{ME}) = 45$ dB. In a world where H_W is correct and we have a weak state, international military conflict would be highly surprising; it contradicts the expectations of the theory, which would be absence of warfare. In contrast, this evidence is moderately expected under the rival hypotheses, because a weak state with natural resources would be an easy and attractive target for invaders. The evidence therefore very strongly favors H_R over H_W. Adding the three weights of evidence, we find $WoE\,(H_R : H_W) = 57$ dB, roughly corresponding to the difference between a typical conversation and a live rock concert.

The difference between the weight of evidence we assigned via these two approaches is small, in both absolute and relative terms. However, it is a noticeable amount – 7 dB. In this case, we would judge the second approach, where we considered each of the three pieces of evidence in turn, to be more reliable. If we found a more substantial difference between the overall weight of evidence assessed through our two logically equivalent approaches, we would need to reconsider our analysis and look for the inconsistency in our reasoning.

A third type of consistency check can be relevant if we are considering three or more rival hypotheses. For three hypotheses, any two weights of evidence determine the third weight of evidence, since:

$$WoE\,(H_1 : H_2) + WoE\,(H_2 : H_3) + WoE\,(H_3 : H_1) = 0, \tag{7}$$

where our sign conventions dictate assigning negative decibels to WoE $(H_i : H_j)$ if the evidence favors H_j over H_i.[26] Equation 6 follows directly from the fact that:

$$\frac{P(E\,|\,H_1\,I)}{P(E\,|\,H_2\,I)} \times \frac{P(E\,|\,H_2\,I)}{P(E\,|\,H_3\,I)} \times \frac{P(E\,|\,H_3\,I)}{P(E\,|\,H_1\,I)} = 1. \tag{8}$$

As an illustration of the cross-checks this relationship facilitates, consider adding a third rival hypothesis to be considered alongside H_R and H_W in our previous example.

H_{LRA} = Labor-repressive agriculture hinders institutional development. Elites resist taxation and efforts to centralize authority, especially control over coercive institutions, because they anticipate that national leaders may be unable or unwilling to enforce "the strict local social control and labor coercion upon which the agrarian political economy, and potentially their physical survival, depends." Instead, elites seek to maintain their own security forces with which to repress their local labor forces (Kurtz 2013).

We will focus on E_{IC}. We have already judged that $WoE_{IC}\,(H_R : H_W, E_{WS}\,E_{ME}) = 45$ dB. By essentially identical logic, we would also judge that $WoE_{IC}\,(H_{LRA} : H_W, E_{WS}\,E_{ME}) = 45$ dB – while international conflict is highly surprising under H_W, the evidence is moderately expected under H_{LRA}, because a weak state with natural resources would be an easy and attractive target for invaders. By Equation 6, we must then have $WoE_{IC}\,(H_{LRA} : H_R, E_{WS}\,E_{ME}) = 0$ dB. As a cross-check, we can mentally inhabit the respective worlds of H_{LRA} and H_W and ask whether this last probability assignment makes intuitive

---

[26] Equation 6 is easily generalized for additional hypotheses.

sense. Indeed it does, since our same logic implies that regardless of whether labor-repressive agriculture or the resource curse gave rise to state weakness, we are not surprised that a weak state with mineral resources would experience military threats.

Suggestions for Moving Forward

How can we promote more reliable inference and better same-data scrutiny, continued research, and extended research in qualitative scholarship? In this volume, Jacobs advocates pre-registration as a useful tool for improving qualitative research (Chapter 9); we take the opposite view and argue that pre-registration is ill-suited to qualitative research that follows the principles of Bayesian inference (Fairfield and Charman 2019). Pre-registration can play an important role in frequentist inference, which requires pre-specifying sampling and analysis procedures to avoid confirmation bias, and strictly separating data used in theory-building from data used for theory-testing to prevent ad hoc hypothesizing. In contrast, logical Bayesianism imposes built-in safeguards against confirmation bias – by requiring us to consider how well the evidence fits not just with our favored working hypothesis, but also with rival hypotheses – and against ad hoc theorizing – via "Occam factors" that automatically penalize the prior probability of overly complex hypotheses if they do not add sufficient explanatory leverage relative to simpler alternatives. In lieu of pre-registration, this final section offers some suggestions for improving reliability in qualitative research that focus on disciplinary norms and training.

Disciplinary Norms

We envision two key fronts on which disciplinary norms could be usefully adjusted for the sake of promoting more reliable inference. First, altering publication norms regarding negative results and requisite levels of confidence in findings could go a long way toward mitigating incentives for falsely bolstering results. In our view, a replication crisis can arise only to the extent that scholars overestimate or mischaracterize the degree of confidence that is justified in light of the evidence. For qualitative research, embracing Bennett and Checkel's (2015:30) dictum that "conclusive process tracing is good, but not all good process tracing is conclusive" – which is firmly grounded in Bayesian reasoning – would be a major step in the right direction for reducing temptations to overstate the case in favor of a given hypothesis. An associated best practice could entail explicitly addressing the pieces of evidence that on their own run most counter to the overall inference; transparency of this type could help signal integrity and encourage critical thinking. In the messy world of social science, where causal complexity is the rule, it is implausible that a single hypothesis will outperform every considered alternative with respect to every piece of evidence. If no countervailing facts are mentioned, concern is warranted that the author has omitted or not looked hard enough for contrary evidence.

Second, we concur with others in this volume (Freese and Peterson, Chapter 10, Gerring, Mahoney, and Elman, Chapter 18) that measures should be taken to counteract publication bias toward counterintuitive findings. Within a Bayesian framework, a counterintuitive explanation should be penalized from the outset with a low prior probability; extraordinary claims require extraordinary evidence. Confirming accepted theories or validating common-sense expectations can make a positive contribution to scholarship, although editorial judgment is still required in distinguishing useful solidification of knowledge versus rehashing known facts or restating the obvious.

Bayesian Training

In reflecting on the replication crisis, Andrew Gelman has in part blamed conventional statistical discourse for fostering the misconception that the purpose of statistical testing and modeling is to somehow distill certainty from uncertainty. Instead, the goal is to confront, assess, manage, and communicate the uncertainty that inevitably remains after evidence is collected and analyzed. Bayesianism, which is becoming more widely used in quantitative as well as qualitative research, provides a natural language for talking about uncertainty in all its guises. Whenever we assess the posterior probability that a hypothesis is true in light of the evidence, we are effectively communicating how much uncertainty we believe surrounds the inference.

Accordingly, training in Bayesian probability could be highly beneficial for qualitative research. On the one hand, learning the basics of Bayesian inference can help improve and leverage intuition. Bayesianism mirrors the way we naturally approach inference in qualitative research, yet it also helps to avert cognitive biases that might unwittingly lead to faulty conclusions (Fairfield and Charman 2019). On the other hand, Bayesianism provides a clear framework for scrutinizing inference, pinpointing the sources of disagreement among scholars, building consensus on the strength of inferences, and learning from accumulated knowledge. Bayesianism highlights the importance of, and provides concrete rules for, scrutinizing the weight of evidence, assessing whether authors' (implicit) priors are well justified by the background information presented and ascertaining how sensitive conclusions are to the choice of priors, and conducting consistency checks to see if the conclusions follow when analyzing evidence in different but logically equivalent ways. Bayesian probability need not necessarily be applied explicitly and formally in qualitative research. Informal or heuristic Bayesian reasoning (especially with regard to the weight of evidence) and/or more formal Bayesian scrutiny of selected case examples or critical pieces of evidence alongside traditional case-study narratives can still have substantial beneficial effects on the quality, transparency, and reliability of inference.

13 Coordinating Reappraisals

John Gerring

The replication crisis, discussed in Chapter 10, might be summarized as follows.[1] First, there is no agreement about what replication means. Second, there is no template for how replication should be conducted. Third, too few replications are occurring, especially in the social sciences – largely because there is little payoff for conducting a replication. Fourth, there is no system for storing and retrieving replications so that they can be integrated into an ongoing stream of work. Consequently, I suspect that most replications do not see the light of day, especially if they seem to confirm published work (Berinsky et al. 2018). Fifth, replications are adversarial – *gotcha* – initiatives, conducted in an ad hoc fashion according to the whims of the reappraiser, and thus unlikely to reflect the performance of a field at large. Finally, many studies apparently fail to replicate, though it is unclear how to score success/failure (i.e., whether or to what extent a result has been successfully replicated).

A number of initiatives have arisen in recent years to address these problems. These include the Center for Open Science (focused on psychology), the Meta Research Innovation Center (medicine), the Berkeley Initiative for Transparency in the Social Sciences (economics), the Data Access and Research Transparency Initiative (DA*RT) and the Political Science Replication Initiative (political science), and the Metaketa initiative (experimental studies of politics and governance in the developing world).

Although immensely influential, these initiatives have not gone very far towards organizing and coordinating the field of replication. Note also that some of these initiatives are more about transparency (a pre-condition of replication) than about replication per se.

To coordinate the field of replications, I offer the following proposal, which encompasses all manner of follow-up studies. Whether one refers to that

---

[1] The author is grateful for comments and suggestions obtained from Colin Elman, Jeremy Freese, Mike Findley, Alan M. Jacobs, and Nate Jensen.

study as a replication, reproduction, robustness test, extension, or something else entirely is a matter of taste (and perhaps of publishing ambitions). I doubt that a uniform vocabulary will be adopted anytime soon. Nonetheless, all follow-up studies bear on the truth-value of an initial study and thus deserve to be integrated into a single initiative. I shall refer to them collectively as *reappraisals*.

I leave aside the knotty question of exactly what sort of studies are amenable to systematic reappraisal. I assume that many studies – including most quantitative studies and some qualitative studies – qualify. To keep things simple, I focus on quantitative research and causal inference in the following discussion, though most of the issues discussed here could be adapted for use with qualitative research and descriptive inference.

The proposal envisions (a) a reappraisal *institute*, (b) a central *directory* of reappraisals, (c) a reappraisal *scorecard*, and (d) additional *support infrastructure*. After laying out each of these elements, I turn to an evaluation of the proposal at-large in terms of (e) its impact on recruitment and bias, (f) incentives to replicate, and (g) overall impact.

In light of its complexity, and the considerable investments of energy and funding that are required, some may view this set of proposals as unrealistic. To be sure, it is a long-term enterprise. Even so, whatever baby-steps we can take in the near future – along with those already taken – promise a considerable return. It is hard to see how the goal of scientific cumulation could be reached without some degree of coordination among reappraisals.

Reappraisal Institute

To begin, I propose the formation of a *Reappraisal Institute* centered on one or more social science disciplines. The Institute would be small, at least initially, comprising a director and several staff (perhaps composed of graduate students or post-docs). Its governing body might include faculty from participating disciplines. A university or university-based institute (e.g., ICPR) could serve as host, providing space and perhaps underwriting some of the cost through in-kind contributions. One can hope that requisite funding would be forthcoming from private foundations (e.g., the Hewlett Foundation or the Laura and John Arnold Foundation) and the National Science Foundation.

The mandate of the Institute would be to help conceptualize and organize the massive and confusing job of reappraisal. More particularly, the Institute would be engaged in tasks outlined in the following sections.

Reappraisal Directory

Reappraisals – i.e., the written text of a reappraisal study along with associated code and data – can be stored conveniently in Dataverse (currently accomplished through the *Political Science Replication Initiative* (http://projects.iq.harvard.edu/psreplication) or in some other online storage facility such as the Qualitative Data Repository at Syracuse University.

However, in order to make full use of extant reappraisals these files need to be organized in a logical fashion. To that end, a *Reappraisal Directory* should be constructed that links each study with reappraisals of that study (and vice-versa). The Directory should include reappraisals that are published as well as those that are not, so long as they are publicly available. Comprehensiveness is important; a major purpose of the directory is to identify those studies that have been reappraised, and those that have not, as well as any background information (meta-data) about these studies. This will help to answer questions like: How many studies are reappraised? What sorts of studies are reappraised? How long after publication do these reappraisals occur? How do they continue?

Identifying reappraisals that have been conducted at some point in the past is a daunting task, precisely because such reappraisals are not located in any one place, many are unpublished, and there is no easy way to recover them from web-based searches. Nonetheless, it is a worthy task and one that the Institute might undertake, time-permitting, perhaps relying on public appeals to researchers in different areas. Once the authors of these reappraisals have been identified they can be contacted by Institute staff, and will presumably be motivated to fill out the Reappraisal Scorecard outlined in the next section.

In any case, the Directory should provide a comprehensive accounting of all reappraisals *going forward*. I imagine this will be fairly easy to achieve as authors of reappraisals have a strong incentive to log their work in the directory, where it is likely to gather citations. I imagine that the incentive is particularly strong for unpublished reappraisals. I also imagine that the authors of studies whose work has been reappraised have an incentive to make that fact known. More generally, if reappraisal becomes standard operating procedure in the social sciences, incentives to register reappraisals in the directory are likely to multiply.

If the current proposal is implemented and scholars find it useful, the Directory will grow. Which is to say, more and more reappraisals will be entered into the database and a higher share of published studies in a field will at some point be reappraised (at least once, if not multiple times). This is likely to happen first in fields where reappraisal is highly valued and fairly easy to achieve, which is to say in quantitative research and with respect to fairly narrow sorts of reappraisals (e.g., the reanalysis of existing data).

As this happens, I imagine that scholars will begin to consult the Directory regularly for a variety of purposes. It should be useful at the beginning stages of research, when a scholar is attempting to understand the lay of the land. It should be especially important when conducting a literature review or comprehensive appraisal of a field (Chapter 14). It should also be important when evaluating job candidates, candidates for promotion, and candidates for various awards and honorary positions.

To raise the profile of this initiative, one might urge journals to insert a page in each issue listing new reappraisals of articles published previously in the journal (including a link to the Directory where a summary of that reappraisal is located). Aggregators such as JSTOR could include links to the Directory for any article that has been reappraised. Authors could be encouraged to insert links on their web pages and CVs.

As references to the Directory increase (e.g., in literature reviews and blogs), one would expect web traffic to increase. At a certain point, links to the Directory may no longer be necessary insofar as the Google algorithm will display the Directory location where an article is reappraised every time that article is used as a search term. At this point, reappraisal will have become an integral part of the production of knowledge.

Reappraisal Scorecard

The impact of reappraisal on a field is enhanced if the information contained in follow-up studies can be summarized in a concise and systematic fashion. To that end, the Institute should be charged with developing a classificatory system – a *scorecard* – encompassing all reappraisals in the directory. This system should facilitate comparisons across reappraisals of the same study and across reappraisals of different studies. Of course, one must be careful about how results are portrayed. Scorecards are useful only if they bear some resemblance to the richer, more nuanced features of the studies they represent. Even so, a degree of standardization seems important, perhaps even essential, if knowledge cumulation is to occur. Several types of information may be useful as part of this scorecard, as laid out in the following sections.[2]

---

[2] In working out the details, one should strive to be faithful to standards laid out by registries for experimental studies, such as E-Gap's "Declare Design" template (https://declaredesign.org/). At the

The Original Study

A first set of issues pertains to the original study, or set of studies, chosen for reappraisal. To minimize ambiguity and human error, the Directory could be pre-populated with citations to all studies contained in Google Scholar, Scopus, Web of Science, and Microsoft Academic. When a reappraisal is registered in the Directory, the author would begin by locating that study and linking directly to it. (Citations for unpublished studies, or studies not contained in the Directory, would need to be entered by the reappraiser.)

In addition to a full citation and link to the original source and any supplementary materials, the reappraiser should specify what *hypothesis*, or hypotheses, from the original study is being tested. For ease of exposition, I shall assume that all hypotheses are formulated in a "positive" fashion, i.e., *X causes Y* (rather than *X does not cause Y*).

The reappraiser should also specify any additional hypotheses from the original study that are *not* tested in the reappraisal; otherwise, readers will have an incomplete sense of the degree to which a study has been corroborated. (Failing to reproduce one hypothesis in a study that proposes five hypotheses is quite different from failing to reproduce one hypothesis in a study that contains a single hypothesis.)

The author should also clarify the *finding(s)* of the original study with respect to the chosen hypothesis(es). We generally assume that studies claim positive findings and that the job of a reappraisal is to see whether, or to what extent, these findings hold up. But this is not always the case. Some studies claim null results (e.g., Ross 2006), and these too might be reappraised. Likewise, some studies claim weak results, or non-robust results – with explicit statements about the difficult assumptions required to reach causal inference. The reappraiser must be conscientious in stating the findings of the original study, including any caveats issued by that study. Only in this fashion can judgments about a hypothesis be distinguished from judgments about a finding.

The Reappraisal Study

A second set of issues pertain to information about the reappraisal study. The reappraiser's name, highest degree, position, institutional affiliation, and

---

same time, one should be cognizant that the research design properties of observational studies are apt to require different – and more complex – dimensions than those utilized for experimental work.

contact information should be included. This is a public activity and communication with the author of a reappraisal should be encouraged. A full citation to the reappraisal study, along with a link to that study and any supplementary materials, must be included.

Consultation

Communication with the author of the original study should be strongly encouraged, giving him/her an opportunity to offer feedback on the reappraisal plan prior to its implementation (at the pre-analysis stage) and again prior to its publication. Following Kahneman (2014:311), I propose that "the replicator [reappraiser] is not obliged to accept the author's suggestions, but is required to provide a full description of the final plan ... [in which] reasons for rejecting any of the author's suggestions must be explained in detail."

Pre-Registration

The reappraiser should state whether the reappraisal has been *pre-registered* (see Chapter 9). If so, s/he should indicate whether s/he has followed the registered design and pre-analysis plan (PAP) or deviated from that plan – and if so, in what ways, with what rationale, and with what consequences. As with any pre-registered study, there is no reason for the author to adhere to the pre-analysis plan if that plan turns out to be problematic or limiting in some respect. The point is that any such deviations should be duly noted and justified. Generally, deviations from a pre-registered plan are regarded as providing a less stringent test of a hypothesis, though sometimes the reverse may be true.

Some reappraisals are well-suited for pre-registration – specifically, those where the original plan of analysis is followed, or where a specific change or set of changes in that plan is adopted. Here, everything is scripted. Pre-registering that study should mitigate – though not entirely dispel – the bias that arises when reappraisers strive to find fault with (or vindicate) a published study, by hook or by crook. In particular, the pre-registration should make as clear as possible what would count as confirmation or disconfirmation of the original study (Nosek and Lakens 2014).

By contrast, reappraisals whose goal is to conduct an open-ended reexamination of a study – using the same or different data – may not be suited to pre-registration, as there is no pre-set plan of analysis. Nor can there be, arguably, since the purpose of this genre of reappraisal is to gauge the sensitivity of the original findings to various alterations – changes in specification, sample, estimator, and so forth. Since one can scarcely account for all the possible permutations, in advance, it would be difficult to register a highly specific PAP.

A second difficulty faced by reappraisals is that of *prior unobservability*. Because most reappraisals are undertaken on published studies, and most published studies are accompanied by full datasets and replication codes, one cannot verify that the reappraiser has not seen the data prior to conducting the reappraisal. The exception would be a reappraisal that is devised prior to the availability of the data, e.g., before the original author has posted the data, or one where new data are gathered. To facilitate this, journals might withhold replication materials for some specified time (six months?) after publication, sufficient to allow appraisers to register their pre-analysis plan.

Reappraisals

It should also be clarified what sort of reappraisal has been conducted, as this is a confusing term with many possible meanings. Let us suppose that all reappraisals of a study are focused on one hypothesis (or a set of very closely related hypotheses) drawn from that study.

Reappraisals focused on that hypothesis may differ along (at least) two dimensions: *evidence* and *measurement/analysis*. The evidence in a follow-up study may be drawn from (a) the same data, (b) the same population (re-sampled or re-measured), or (c) a different population. The measurement and analysis of that evidence may be (a) the same (scrupulously adopting the same measures and procedures, as described in the original study), or (b) different (e.g., variations in data collection, measurement, treatment level, specification, estimator, or any other feature of the research design that may be regarded as a plausible alternative to the original study).

This generates a matrix with five cells, illustrated in Table 13.1. Each may be regarded as a species of reappraisal. I do not regard a follow-up study that alters both the population *and* the analysis of an original study as a reappraisal, so cell 6 remains empty. The labels for these cells are drawn from Clemens (2017), with the exception of "Sensitivity," an option that does not appear in Clemens' typology but seems quite important nonetheless.

As emphasized in Chapter 10, there is an important distinction between follow-up studies that employ the same data and follow-up studies that employ new data (either drawn from the same or a different population). But it is not just the type of evidence that differentiates follow-up studies. Cells in Table 13.1 are numbered according to the degree of deviation from the

Table 13.1 Reappraisals

		Measurement/Analysis	
		Same	*Different*
Evidence	*Same data*	1. Verification	2. Sensitivity
	Same population	3. Reproduction	4. Reanalysis
	Different population	5. Extension	

original study, with Type 1 signifying no deviation at all (starting with the original data and continuing through the author's original analysis) and Type 5 signifying the greatest deviation.

Several caveats with respect to this typology should be noted. First, there is the question of terminology. Clemens (2017) regards options 1 (Verification) and 3 (Reproduction) as *replications*, while options 4 (Reanalysis) and 5 (Extension) are classified *robustness tests*. Freese and Peterson (Chapter 10, this volume) adopt a looser, more diffuse vision of what replication might mean, encompassing all of the options in Table 13.1. I don't take a position in this debate, except to note that authors use these terms differently, and are likely to continue doing so. To avoid potential confusion, I adopt a novel term – *reappraisal* – to encompass all such follow-up studies. (I can only hope that this neologism clarifies, rather than muddies, this crowded lexical terrain.)

A second caveat pertains to the ambiguity of "different-ness." Some populations are extremely different from the population of original study; others are fairly similar. Likewise, some analyses offer an extreme departure from the original study; others are fairly close. Since these are matters of degree, contingent upon particular research contexts, and subject to judgments about (generally untestable) assumptions, I do not force typological judgments. Within the category of "different," readers will need to judge the degree of the departure, its justification, and its ramifications.

Finally, it is important to recognize that a two-dimensional typology cannot possibly exhaust all the features of a follow-up study that are pertinent to judging that study. In the interests of parsimony and workability, it focuses on those features that appear to be the most important, and the easiest to classify. Additional features might be integrated at a later time.[3]

---

[3] My typology builds on Tsang and Kwan (1999) and Bettis, Helfat, and Shaver (2016). For alternative schemas, see Camfield and Palmer-Jones (2013), Clemens (2017), Easley, Madden, and Dunn (2000), Garcia (2016), Hamermesh (2007).

Table 13.2 Corroboration

(a) Not possible	Theory unfalsifiable, data unavailable, or procedures unclear
(b) No corroboration	Reappraisal estimate falls outside confidence interval of the original estimate
(c) Weak corroboration	Reappraisal estimate falls inside confidence interval of the original estimate in some tests
(d) Strong corroboration	Reappraisal estimate falls inside the confidence interval of the original estimate
(e) Exact corroboration	Estimate is exactly reproduced

Corroboration

A third issue concerns the degree to which the findings of the original study are *corroborated*. Conclusions may fall into one of five categories, as summarized in Table 13.2. *Not possible*: it was impossible to reproduce the original study because the theory or hypothesis was non-falsifiable, data were unobtainable or missing, or procedures were unclear or contradictory. Consequently, the attempted reappraisal was aborted. *No corroboration*: the findings stated in the original study are not corroborated by the reappraisal. In statistical terms, the estimate obtained from the reappraisal analysis falls outside the confidence interval of the estimate from the original study. *Weak corroboration*: the findings stated in the original study are weakly corroborated, or only partly corroborated, by the reappraisal. *Strong corroboration*: the findings stated in the original study are strongly corroborated by the reappraisal. *Exact corroboration*: the findings of the original study are exactly those found in the reappraisal.

The meaning of Types 1 and 5 are reasonably clear and determinate. By contrast, Types 2–4 involve degrees of corroboration – (2) *none*, (3) *weak*, (4) *strong* – that are rather difficult to define. Since these are likely to be the most common outcomes of a reappraisal that goes beyond Type 1 (same units/same analysis), one must consider carefully how to differentiate among them.

One option rests on confidence intervals (Cumming 2008; Cumming and Maillardet 2006; Cumming, Williams, and Fidler 2004). Accordingly, if a reappraisal estimate falls outside a 95-percent confidence interval (drawn from the original analysis), then there is an utter failure to corroborate. If several reappraisal tests are performed, some of which fall inside and some outside, one may say that there is weak corroboration for the original study. And if the reappraisal test, or set of tests, falls entirely inside the confidence interval, one may conclude that the original study has received strong corroboration.

To be sure, other statistical tests are possible, and each is informative in some respects (Camerer et al. 2016; Gelman and Stern 2006; Open Science Collaboration 2015; Simonsohn 2015; Verhagen and Wagenmakers 2014). I leave this issue open for further consideration.

Validation

It should be apparent that corroboration is not the same as *validation*. When judging the validity of a study one must consider not only the degree of corroboration found in a reappraisal but the degree to which the reappraisal adheres to the original data and analysis.

To gauge this issue we must compose another typology, formed from the intersection of the typology of reappraisals (Table 13.1) and the typology of corroborations (Table 13.2). This generates a matrix with 25 cells, as shown in Table 13.3. I regard this typology as providing an indication of how, and in what degrees, a study has been validated by a reappraisal.

Note that reappraisal Types 1–2 are usually regarded as reflecting on a study's "internal validity" and Type 5 reflects on its "external" validity. Types 3–4 are ambiguous in this traditional dichotomy. If one samples repeatedly from a population and is unable to replicate a result it becomes increasingly unlikely that the result is valid. These fine points need not concern us at this juncture.

Most observers would regard failures of internal validity as reflecting poorly on the author, while failures of external validity are generally regarded as beyond the purview of the claims of an author. However, if the objective of a study is to shed light on a larger population this traditional assignment of "blame" does not make a huge amount of sense. What is the point of internal validity if there is no external validity? We leave these issues behind, as they are peripheral to our concerns.

Note also that any departures from the original study – in units or data/analysis – require justification. If the justification is sound, and the original study is not corroborated, then the original study may be faulted. If the justification is faulty, or questionable, then not. These are not matters that one can pre-judge, as they depend upon contextual features of the research question and the research context.

Although the complexity of this typology may seem daunting, it is absolutely essential to clarify what sort of confirmation, or disconfirmation, has

Table 13.3 Validation Types

	Corroboration Types				
Reappraisal Types	(a) Not Possible	(b) No Corroboration	(c) Weak Corroboration	(d) Strong Corroboration	(e) Exact Corroboration
1. Same data, same measurement/ analysis	1(a)	1(b)	1(c)	1(d)	1(e)
2. Same data, different measurement/ analysis	2(a)	2(b)	2(c)	2(d)	2(e)
3. Same population, same measurement/ analysis	3(a)	3(b)	3(c)	3(d)	3(e)
4. Same population, different measurement/ analysis	4(a)	4(b)	4(c)	4(d)	4(e)
5. Different population, same measurement/ analysis	5(a)	5(b)	5(c)	5(d)	5(e)

Note: Types of validation, generated from the intersection of reappraisal types (Table 13.1) and corroboration types (Table 13.2).

been achieved by a reappraisal. Only a few redound against the credibility of the author of the original study. Most are properly regarded as reappraisals whose function is to extend our knowledge of a topic, not to excoriate (or laud) the author of an original study. Likewise, the validity of a *study* should be clearly distinguished from the validity of a *hypothesis*, addressed in the next section.

In this fashion, it is our hope that the success/failure of reappraisal, over time, loses its stigma – except in situations noted above, where the author of the original study might be culpable. By routinizing reappraisal, with the expectation that over time authors will garner a range of "hits" and "misses" across a variety of different types of reappraisal, some narrow and some broad, I expect that the activity will become less invidious.

Validity of Original Hypothesis

A separate issue concerns the validity of the hypothesis drawn from the original study, e.g., whether (or to what extent, and in what fashion) *X causes Y*.

Table 13.4 Validity of Original Hypothesis

		Validity	
		(a) Internal	(b) External
Dimensions	1. *Magnitude*	1(a)	1(b)
	2. *Robustness*	2(a)	2(b)
	3. *Plausibility*	3(a)	3(b)

Several dimensions may be distinguished. The first concerns the strength of the relationship, i.e., the magnitude of the impact of X on Y. The second concerns the robustness of the relationship, i.e., stability of an estimate when small adjustments are made to the research design, plan of analysis, or scope-conditions.

A third issue concerns the plausibility of the relationship, all things considered. Here, the reappraiser should discuss the viability of the chosen research design and analysis, i.e., the assumptions required for causal inference. This is inevitably a matter of judgment, and important to separate from the previous issues, which are largely empirical. For example, a reappraiser may believe that the specification employed in the original study is problematic, preferring a different specification of the causal model, which results in a different estimated relationship between X and Y.

In considering these issues it is vital to distinguish validity as pertains to the studied sample (*internal* validity) and to a larger population thought to be within the scope-conditions of the theory (*external* validity). Because these matters are prone to ambiguity the reappraiser should define them carefully. Note that some reappraisals are primarily focused on internal validity and others on external validity.

Dialogue

Finally, the scorecard should be engineered so as to provide ample opportunity for the original author, or other researchers unaffiliated with the original study, to comment on the reappraisals that have been conducted. This includes any *reappraisals of reappraisals* that may be undertaken. One can envision a stream of commentary, links to various published work and blogs, and so forth. Just as work on a topic is never entirely settled, one can imagine debates over reappraisals extending over many years for some contentious studies, as they have for Miguel and Kremer (2004).[4] The online system

---

[4] See http://scholar.harvard.edu/kremer/deworming-research.

established and maintained by the Institute should facilitate this, making sure that comments are preserved (and personal insults or extraneous material removed).

Summary

Putting the foregoing features together, I propose a scorecard along the lines of that sketched in Table 13.5. Naturally, many refinements might be added to this fairly simple classificatory schema.[5] In contemplating possible refinements one must balance the possible benefits of a more differentiated schema against the burdens that added complexity might place upon the reappraiser and upon end-users. The point of a scorecard is to simplify a complex reality. But not to over-simplify. I leave this as a matter for future deliberation.

In any event, I anticipate that a good deal of work will be required in order to arrive at a schema that does a good job of describing the universe of reappraisals. What I offer here is only a beginning.

One can hope that once a classification system is laid out, and a pattern of usage established, researchers will become comfortable with it and ambiguities will be resolved. Like a common-law legal system, working with a classification system requires the ability to classify objects by type. Once well-known precedents (use-cases) of each type are established, it should be fairly easy to locate new studies in the right pigeon-hole. Likewise, it should become clearer what each pigeonhole means because there are well-known paradigm-cases that help to define each cell. In this fashion, one may anticipate that the meaning of vexed words like "non-robust," "weakly robust," and "strongly robust" will gain a consistent and widely understood meaning.

Support Infrastructure

Building on the classifications in Tables 13.1–13.4, members of the Institute might develop a standard protocol for how to conduct reappraisals of various sorts. Of course, much depends upon the theory and evidence at hand, which varies by field and subfield. Nonetheless, it should be possible to draw on a growing body of extant reappraisals to illustrate various approaches that

---

[5] For a consideration of reporting options in the context of randomized control trials, see Brandt et al. (2014) and Consort (www.consort-statement.org/).

Table 13.5 Reappraisal Scorecard

Original study	
Citation	Citation and link to study and supplementary materials
Hypothesis	Brief statement of the hypothesis, along with any additional hypotheses that are *not* reappraised
Finding	Brief statement of finding, including estimate of main effect and caveats and scope-conditions
Reappraisal study	Reappraiser (name, education, position, affiliation, contact info), full citation, link to study and supplementary materials
Consultation	Indication of whether the author of the original study was consulted and whether s/he approved the reappraisal plan
Pre-registration	Link to registry if pre-registered. Indication of any deviations from the PAP
Type of reappraisal	1–5 (Table 13.1)
Corroboration of original study	a–e (Table 13.2)
Validity of original study	1a–5e (Table 13.3)
Validity of original hypothesis	1a–3b (Table 13.4)
Dialogue	Link to responses from the original author and others, reappraisals of the reappraisal, if any

reappraisers have taken or might take, including a discussion of their characteristic strengths and weaknesses.

If successful, this set of guidelines would be an important methodological contribution in its own right, and perhaps worthy of a book-length publication. It would also serve to structure the reappraisal process so that there is greater uniformity of procedure and vocabulary. Finally, by making it easier to conduct reappraisals, it might serve to stimulate more reappraisals.

The guidelines could be developed in tandem with existing graduate courses that require reappraisals as part of their coursework (Carsey 2014; Frank and Saxe 2012; Hoeffler 2013; Janz 2016; King 2006). They might be combined with a set of lectures, posted on YouTube, or a webinar or "short course" given by Institute staff at annual conventions or summer schools. Staffing permitting, the Institute might offer a help desk for those with specific questions about a reappraisal they are about to undertake, or are in the middle of.

Institute staff might also alleviate problems of data availability, transparency, and reproducibility. In her quest to replicate political science studies, Janz (2016:8) reports facing the following difficulties: "(i) The data were nowhere to be found and the original sources were not clear, (ii) the original author did not respond to queries for data, (iii) the authors did not remember where they had stored their files, (iv) the steps in the analyses were not well described, (v) it was not clear how the variables were transformed before entering the analysis, and (vi) statistical models remained opaque." Complaints of this sort have been registered many times (Lupia and Elman 2014). While the problem may be mitigated as more and more journals adopt standards for storage, transparency, and reproducibility (e.g., DA*RT in political science), it is likely to persist in some corners of the social science world. Moreover, no matter how careful an author is, or how scrupulous an editor is in vetting their work, there is a good chance that some aspect of an original study will be unclear to later scholars who attempt to replicate their work. Here, an institutional mediator may be helpful in gaining the cooperation of busy – or wary – authors. It is more difficult to refuse a request from the director of an Institute than from a graduate student, one imagines. The existence of a widely used Directory should also incentivize authors to respond to requests – otherwise the entry by their study may read "non-reproducible."

Recruitment and Bias

An important issue to consider is that of recruitment, which is intimately linked to potential errors and systematic bias. Who will conduct reappraisals, and what is their background and motivation likely to be? It is not without irony that one notes that a system designed to overcome bias in academic research is also subject to its own potential biases. (To clarify, most of these biases *already* inhabit the world of reappraisals.)

A first problem is incompetence or carelessness. Inevitably, some reappraisers will not possess the requisite methodological skills, experience, or subject knowledge to perform a competent reappraisal. Or they may have the requisite skill-set and knowledge-set but not take advantage of it, working quickly (perhaps under deadline) and making (false) judgments hastily. Either circumstance will result in a reappraisal that does not meet acceptable standards.

Second, one can anticipate that reappraisers will be drawn to studies published in top journals or studies that have received a good deal of attention, and may be disinclined to devote any time at all to unpublished studies. Perhaps this is a good bias, especially as a counterweight to publication bias. Those who publish in top journals, on hot topics, or with especially provocative results, should anticipate that a reappraisal of their work – and perhaps several – will be forthcoming. However, this means that some studies are likely to receive multiple reappraisals while others receive none at all. And this, in turn, means that those who publish in second- and third-tier journals, or who do not publish at all but post their papers somewhere on the web or in Dataverse, may have little concern for reappraisal – a problem for those who view reappraisal as a useful tonic against sloppiness and fraud.

Third, one can anticipate that reappraisers will be drawn to studies that seem problematic in some respect. These studies claim results are too good to be true, or that contradict common sense or the researcher's own sense of a subject. From the perspective of identifying bad studies – falsification – this is a beneficent selection effect. However, this will generate a misleading impression of the truthfulness of social science if these reappraisals are regarded as the basis for generalizing across the universe of published studies. Journalists, bloggers, and anyone hostile to the enterprise of social science is apt to jump to false conclusions.

Fourth, one can anticipate that some reappraisers will gravitate to studies whose results they don't like – either on programmatic or personal grounds, e.g., they dislike the author or the study contradicts their own work (Hamermesh 2007; Hoxby 2007). This is more worrisome, raising the possibility that reappraisal will be used as a venue for argumentation. "If I don't like you, or your study, I will replicate." Note that reappraisal is not a rigidly programmed activity; matters of judgment almost inevitably impinge upon the act of replicating. Thus, it seems likely that a reappraiser hostile to a study or the researcher who performed that study would be less likely to render a fair conclusion. That is one good reason for offering the original author an opportunity to respond. But an authorial response doesn't entirely solve the problem. Even more worrisome, the aggrieved author may enlist friends and colleagues to conduct further reappraisals that validate his/her study, generating "partisan" reappraisals (in the same fashion that sellers on Amazon may boost their ratings by paying others to give them high scores).

Fifth, one might worry that the sort of people who perform reappraisals are either inclined to *confirm* the chosen study (e.g., because they don't wish to offend well-established scholars in their field) or to *disconfirm* the chosen study (e.g., because they wish to interest a journal in their reappraisal and make a name for themselves).

Solutions

These are not easy problems to solve; but there are ways to mitigate them.

First, to weed out potentially incompetent reappraisals, and to assure that participants have some skin in the game, one might stipulate that reappraisals included in the Directory be conducted by researchers *with a PhD or working toward a PhD* in a relevant discipline. For those in a discipline, a strong incentive exists to provide fair and high-quality work by virtue of the public visibility of their reappraisal. Note also that the original author is likely to respond if s/he feels the judgments are unfair, and that anyone may replicate the reappraisal – a feature that becomes part of the permanent record. Note, finally, that if the Directory is limited to members of a discipline, reappraisers can anticipate that their own (original) work will be subject to reappraisal in the future. Reciprocity, the basis of norms of fairness, is thereby built in to the system.

Second, one might *randomly select studies* to be reappraised from some known universe of extant studies. This probably would demand a central body such as the Institute to put into operation. A good deal of attention would need to be devoted to defining the sampling frame – the universe of studies to be subjected to randomization. (Initially, one might focus on well-known journals. Later, pending success, one might include more obscure venues of publication as well as working papers and unpublished studies.) One would also presumably want to limit the temporal scope of the sampling frame, e.g., to recent years.

A random selection of studies would obviate cherry-picking; it would generate a random sample that could be used to generalize across populations of theoretical interest; and it would put the fear of god into all researchers (since, regardless of the prominence or provocativeness of the paper, there would be a non-trivial possibility that the study might be reappraised).

A third step would be to *randomly assign reappraisers*, stratified by specialty, to each of the chosen studies. This is not an easy matter, especially when one considers the variety of dimensions that might be relevant to a reappraisal – e.g., theoretical expertise, context expertise (linguistic, cultural, regional, etc.), methodological expertise. In many cases, no reappraiser will have the perfect profile for a given study. However, just as editors manage to find qualified reviewers for most manuscripts, it should be possible to find qualified reappraisers for each published study.

Randomly selecting studies and randomly assigning reappraisals would not obviate error. Individual reappraisers may have grudges to nurture, or flattery to dispense, and humans are prone to make mistakes. But the body of reappraisals produced by this system would presumably be unbiased. If such a system were implemented, another entry on the reappraisal scorecard could be added, indicating whether the study and/or the reappraiser was randomly chosen. And this might become an important factor in judging the veracity of the reappraisal. I hold this open as a possible course of action, if instructors and/or funders are convinced that the idea has merit.

Incentives to Replicate

Thus far, I have laid out an ideal scenario for this reappraisal initiative. But I have not discussed the problem of incentives. Arguably, the biggest obstacle in the way of reappraisal is that reappraisers receive little reward for their efforts – except, possibly, in the circumstance where a high-profile study utterly fails to replicate, and the reappraisal becomes publishable and widely cited. Duvendack, Palmer-Jones, and Reed (2015:170) write,

Would-be reappraisers reckon the time to undertake the replication and the likelihood of being published. They may be concerned about the implication of lack of originality, or of getting a reputation of having an unfavourable personality, or advancing themselves at the expense of more established authors. Months of effort may yield results which cannot be conclusive about the validity of the original study in part because failure to replicate may have arisen from errors in the original research or in the replication.

Pondering these incentives, one may wonder that anyone at all undertakes this thankless task. Even so, there is some reason for optimism.

First, Type-1 reappraisals (same sample, same analysis) are now conducted routinely by some journals as a prerequisite of acceptance. It seems likely that this practice will spread. If so, Type-1 reappraisals may become universal, or nearly so, at least in some subfields.

Second, reappraisal often occurs as a precursor to original research, and as a way to highlight the comparisons and contrasts of a piece of original research (King 2006). Indeed, reappraisal plays a key role in knowledge cumulation by providing a metric by which findings across diverse settings may be assessed. Unfortunately, these reappraisals are generally not regarded as reappraisal studies (per se) since they are focused on a novel piece of research. If, however, they could be integrated into the Directory they might another important function – verifying (or falsifying) the study that is being reappraised.

Third, reappraisal is often conducted as part of coursework for the PhD. This is widely regarded as an important exercise for those entering a discipline. (Before painting on a blank canvas, try painting by numbers.) Insofar as this classroom practice might be expanded, subject to random selection, and the resulting reappraisals preserved and organized in a systematic fashion, they would provide a good deal of fodder for the present initiative.

A problem remains for reappraisals that involve the collection of new data, which is typically time-consuming and/or expensive and beyond the means of graduate students engaged in a semester-long assignment. Costs are reduced if data can be collected on samples of students, M-Turkers, extant datasets, or sources freely available on the web (e.g., using web-crawlers). However, most new data collection is costly. Some reappraisals can be styled as "new studies," and therefore may be publishable, raising the payoffs for scholars. But for many efforts, the payoffs will be slim.

There is no easy answer to this problem, and for this reason I suspect that reappraisals will continue to be under-provided. However, in some fields there may a funder willing to underwrite the cost, which is to say, sufficient to pay for the study and offer some monetary compensation for the researcher. I imagine that this is more likely in policy fields, where government agencies, private foundations, or companies have a strong interest in determining whether a hypothesis is true, and what its generalizability might be. But it may also be achievable in fields devoted to research one or two steps removed from policies that might be implemented. The Metaketa initiative, undertaken by E-Gap, offers one example of this model of research.[6]

Anticipated Impact

What impact might this set of initiatives have on the work of scholars? My hope is that the proposed Institute, the Directory, the Scorecard, and supporting documents and courses that Institute staff might provide would help to structure the process of reappraisal so that subjective judgments on the part of reappraisers are minimized. Reappraisals should be reliable. That is, if one were to randomly assign qualified researchers to conduct reappraisals of the same study, they should reach similar conclusions (a matter that would be worthwhile testing!).

By the same token, one must not lose sight of the judgments that inevitably remain embedded in any reappraisal that goes beyond Type 1 (same sample, same analysis). These reappraisals necessarily involve a degree of researcher intervention. The researcher must determine what the population of the study

---

[6] See http://egap.org/metaketa.

is, if it is not entirely clear from the original study. S/he must determine what alterations in the original design are warranted, by way of testing the sensitivity of the original study or by way of improving that study. The choice of research design and method of analysis involves assumptions, and these assumptions are rarely amenable to decisive empirical tests. I would not want any reappraisal regime that presumes – or suggests – otherwise. This is the rationale for facilitating commentary by the author of the original study and others, as well as for additional reappraisals.

I hope that the spirit and tenor of reappraisal is changed – from "gotcha/no ya didn't" to something more like a scholarly collaboration in which the input of the original researcher is incorporated in the process of the reappraisal and in the result (by allowing space for ex post discussion and perhaps even further reappraisals). It is time, says Kahneman (2014), for "a new etiquette for replication." Kahneman points to the need for a set of norms governing the process of reappraisal, and the response to reappraisals. This initiative should help to foster, and enforce, that set of norms.

I hope, finally, that the rate of successful reappraisals will increase, i.e., that more studies are subjected to the reappraisal process. I also expect that the rate of corroboration will increase. In a world where authors can expect their work to be reappraised, one can suppose that they will be more conscientious about making their data available and stating the procedures used for the collection and analysis of the data, and less likely to engage in shenanigans – from outright fraud to subtle forms of p-hacking.

This does *not* mean that researchers should refrain from putting forth bold hypotheses that are hard to verify (e.g., the evidence is scarce or its interpretation depends upon strong assumptions). Exploratory work must continue; without it, science is unlikely to advance (Part I). But the value of exploratory work is only realized if it is, at some point, verified. Indeed, the prominence of exploratory work in the social sciences today is the strongest argument for reappraisal, for these sorts of studies are usually difficult to vet at the point of publication (note that they are not amenable to pre-registration). It is only later, and sometimes quite a bit later, that their validity can be assessed. So, I do not view reappraisal as hostile to exploratory work. Quite the contrary; I view reappraisal as a *requirement* for exploratory work.

14 Comprehensive Appraisal

John Gerring

Social scientists spend a great deal of time on the appraisal of individual studies.[1] A paper is submitted to a journal, or a book to a press, and external reviewers are asked to evaluate its truth-value and importance. Based on that review, or perhaps a series of reviews and subsequent revisions spread across several venues, a decision is made that determines whether a study will enter the pantheon of published work or languish in the subterranean basement of unpublished work, generally out of sight. If published, the review process also determines where in the pecking order of journals and presses a study will appear, a decision that affects its subsequent visibility. A published study may also be subjected to replication or reappraisal, though this is still rare in the social sciences, as discussed in preceding chapters.

In principle, knowledge on a subject accumulates as studies pass through this vetting process. True findings are corroborated and false findings are cast aside. Over time, a settled opinion on each subject should arise. Knowledge cumulates.

That's the theory. In practice, it is often difficult to tell where progress is being made, or if it is happening at all. Which studies on a subject should be regarded as authoritative? Where is a consensus developing? Where is there disagreement? What are the strengths and weaknesses of research on a topic? What is the truth of the matter, and the uncertainties (as best as we can tell)?

To answer these questions we must take a somewhat different approach than is usual to studies published in scientific journals. In the latter, the author's effort is to produce the best study, to date, of Subject X, which presumably supercedes all prior studies of X. Occasionally, this implicit claim might be justified. However, it is probably safer to proceed under the assumption that a recent study of X is simply *another study* of X. (Note that even to make an informed judgment of the topic one would have to systematically compare and contrast all extant studies of X.)

---

[1] For comments and suggestions, I am grateful to Garret Christenson, Colin Elman, and Alan M. Jacobs.

Attempting to judge a hypothesis by examining one study of that hypothesis – let's say, the most recent study, or the study appearing in the highest-quality journal – is a bit like the parable of the blind men and the elephant. One study is likely to offer one perspective on the topic, which may be quite different from others (and not necessarily superior). This is especially the case under conditions of publication bias. Thus, from time to time, we need to take stock of all the studies that have heretofore been conducted on topic X, perhaps with some complementary analysis or meta-analysis.

Granted, we do a lot of stock-taking in the normal progress of our research. Every scholarly paper begins with an attempt to review the literature on that subject. Some papers have as their sole purpose the review of extant research on a topic – referred to as a *systematic review* or *literature review* (Baumeister and Leary 1997; Feak and Swales 2009; Galvan and Galvan 2017; Gough and Elbourne 2002; Hart 2018; Mulrow 1994; Petticrew and Roberts 2006). However, I believe that these practices are incomplete and unsatisfactory as currently implemented – at least within the discipline that I am most familiar with (political science). While meta-analysis is well-defined in the context of experimental studies in psychology, it is not clear how one should appraise research in fields where research is not conducted in a standardized fashion.

In this chapter, I offer some guidelines to improve the current system of reviewing what we know (and don't know) on a topic, which I refer to as *comprehensive appraisal*. Having defined the subject, I elaborate on why it is needed – that is, why an *individualized* system of appraisal (focused on individual studies) cannot do the job.

A Different Kind of Appraisal

What does it mean to properly appraise the work that has been done in an area of scholarship? In this section I lay out what I view as the essential elements, which are considered from three angles – *product*, *process*, and *vehicle*.[2]

The Product

Comprehensive appraisal begins by paying close attention to the chosen theory or theoretical issue, in all its formulations. The research question might be fairly well developed, or it might be more open-ended. An example

---

[2] For further discussion see Petticrew and Roberts (2006).

of the latter is *modernization theory*, according to which development (variously understood) affects democracy (variously understood) through a set of mechanisms (variously understood). If there are outstanding debates or ambiguities with respect to the nature of the theory, this will require a good deal of work. Confusion notwithstanding, the writer's job is to bring diverse work on a topic together into a coherent whole. In doing so, she will need to consider the measurement of key variables, scope-conditions, as well as background factors (contextual/interaction effects) that may be at work. She will also need to consider the position of that theory within the firmament of other theories and theoretical frameworks, eliminating ad hoc and idiosyncratic elements wherever possible so that theoretical unification is enhanced. A comprehensive appraisal involves active *theorizing*. Indeed, the primary contribution of an appraisal may be theoretical rather than empirical.

Evidence to be considered as part of a comprehensive appraisal follows from the theoretical question. All relevant information, published or unpublished, should be included. Typically, some pieces of evidence are of higher quality than others; sometimes, the difference is so great as to justify the categorical exclusion of one sort of evidence. For example, on a topic where randomized control trials are numerous and observational data add little, the appraisal might be limited to a review of experimental evidence. In a more typical setting, different sorts of evidence address different parts of a question. For example, experimental evidence may demonstrate a causal link between a treatment and an outcome, but with questionable generalizability. Observational evidence may suggest a link between X and Y, but with questionable causal identification. Together, the two sorts of evidence may provide a clearer picture of a causal relationship. Likewise, quantitative evidence may shed light on causal effects while qualitative evidence sheds light on within-case causal mechanisms. And moving up and down among levels of analysis may also help to elucidate the mechanisms, and the scope-conditions, of a theory. In short, all evidence that speaks to a research question is fair game and the writer is urged to put everything on the table, so to speak. Comprehensive appraisal is an ideal venue for bringing together work conducted in different methodological traditions and different disciplines, thus realizing the ideal of multi-method research that is often discussed but rarely achieved (see Chapter 3, this volume).

The appraisal should also involve working with the data itself. This will take many different forms, depending upon the theoretical question and the state of extant research on that question.

Consider, first, a question upon which multiple quantitative studies have been conducted in different settings in a standardized fashion – e.g., measures of relevant variables are equivalent, or nearly so, units of analysis are comparable, and background features not too heterogeneous (or neutralized by experimental control. Here, a *meta-analysis* is possible, and strongly advised (Egger, Davey-Smith, and Altman 2001; Hunt 1997; O'Rourke 2007; Stanley and Doucouliagos 2012). Pooling data from extant studies allows for a more precise estimate of the effect of theoretical interest. It also, perhaps more importantly, offers the opportunity to conduct "forensic" analysis of potential biases in the data and analyses used in published studies using techniques such as the funnel plot and the p-curve. Freese and Peterson (2018:295) comment,

When the credibility of an individual claim is considered on its own, judgments of its objectivity focus on how it was produced. Once aggregated into a collection of claims, however, they may be expected to exhibit particular statistical properties if they are to appear collectively credible. When individually credible numbers do not have credible collective properties, doubt can pervade a literature. Individual credibility is threatened even if one cannot identify any specific problem in how any specific number was produced. That is, the demonstrations make possible that a collection of studies, which previously appeared impressively consistent in their findings and impeccable in methods, might be instead shown to be consistent with a "crisis of false positives," in which the true effect is either radically smaller than what had been reported or even potentially nonexistent.

To be sure, meta-analyses are impossible if extant studies of a question are insufficiently standardized to be compared directly to each other, e.g., if key variables are measured differently.

Consider, second, a question upon which multiple quantitative studies have focused on the same units or units drawn from the same population, e.g., alliances, nation-states, territories, cities, political parties, leaders, or members of the mass public. Here, the appraiser may combine data from different sources so that a theory can be tested against all the available evidence, e.g., all measures of democracy, all measures of political trust, and a combined sample of units (perhaps requiring imputation of missing data). This sort of *replication* – where no new data are collected but extant datasets are merged – is eminently feasible so long as the original datasets are publicly available. A battery of robustness tests, including alternate measures of key variables, alternate samples, alternate estimators, alternate specifications, and perhaps a version of Bayesian model averaging, may be applied in order to judge the strength of a given relationship or set of relationships.

Consider, third, a question upon which multiple qualitative studies have been conducted (in a presumably non-standardized fashion). Here, the appraiser's task may involve an attempt to summarize all studies – their research designs, findings, and possible threats to inference – in a tabular format. This might be followed by an attempt to identify key points of agreement and disagreement. It may also involve a re-consideration of disputed issues insofar as the original data are accessible, e.g., in library archives, in qualitative data archives, or elsewhere on the web.

A key issue for the appraiser to consider in reviewing a body of work on a subject is the potential biases that this body of work might represent. This includes publication bias, file-drawer bias, and researcher bias. There is no easy cure for these diseases – for reasons discussed below and elsewhere in this volume – and this should give one pause about the quality of a comprehensive appraisal. If the body of studies upon which it is based are flawed it is not going to be easy for an appraiser to uncover those flaws and overcome them. Garbage in, garbage out. However, if these biases are deeply rooted, it is all the more essential that appraisers take a hard look at the evidence – not simply what has been published but what has not been published (insofar as that can be accessed), conducting replications where possible, and considering possible biases in a field or subfield. The more biased the field of work on a subject, the greater the need for a comprehensive appraisal of that subject.

Evidently, a comprehensive appraisal must pay a great deal of attention to methodological issues that pertain to the subject under study. All substantive debates are also methodological debates, and a principal goal of the review should be to sort through the varying contributions of varying methods, and to identify new methods that might be enlisted for the task.

For each substantive conclusion reached by an appraiser there should be an implicit or explicit statement of *uncertainty*. By common assumption, where prose is unaccompanied by caveats the author is assumed to speak with authority; it is not necessary to insert "I can confidently say …" at every juncture. But where there is some non-negligible uncertainty, this should be signaled in the text by suitable qualifiers. And, where possible, it should be accompanied by a numerical estimate of uncertainty, e.g., 0–100-percent confidence. This should forestall misinterpretation or over-interpretation of results, and will allow readers to readily distinguish conclusions that are secure from those that are dubious. Note that uncertainty is something that can only be arrived at when numerous studies of the same subject are compared. One then has a distribution from which an uncertainty estimate can be derived – formally (e.g., as part of a meta-analysis) or informally (e.g., the author's sense of a field of work on a subject).

A comprehensive appraisal is apt to be lengthy, and arbitrary space limitations should be avoided – which is to say, it should be as long as it needs to be, and no longer or shorter (see Chapter 5, this volume). A comprehensive appraisal is also apt to be rather complicated. Consequently, some sort of summary – appearing at the beginning or end of the essay – seems vital in order to make the product accessible to those with limited time and attention spans.

In summary, a comprehensive appraisal should achieve several goals. It should synthesize information about a topic, reducing the ever-increasing problem of information overload presented by most fields of social science. It should work towards a theoretical synthesis, as well as an empirical synthesis of diverse findings. It should present the material in as simple and comprehensible format as possible. It should speak to the policy relevance of a topic, including policy recommendations where appropriate (and with all necessary caveats). It should identify where progress has been made in our understanding, and the studies that have contributed to that progress. It should identify false leads, dead-ends, and outright errors. It should identify areas of consensus and dissensus within a field, and possible reasons for the latter. And it should identify where further progress might be attained, pointing the way to areas for future research.

The Process

Those who conduct comprehensive appraisals must be chosen carefully. Subject expertise is of course the foremost criterion. But so, also, is an ability to review the field fairly – a characteristic that may be difficult to judge, a priori.

Comprehensive appraisal is not a lone-wolf activity. Appraisals should be carried out in direct consultation with those who have conducted the body of work that is under review. These experts may be queried or interrogated on their findings or asked to defend their general perspective on the theory. They may engage in head-to-head debates before the appraiser. If truth is the result of combat, every effort should be made to bring combatants – those with different views of a subject – together to hash out their differences and, if possible, to reach consensus. Although this is not the primary purpose of a comprehensive appraisal, it may be an important by-product.

Where consensus is impossible, appraisers should be careful to identify areas of dissensus – and, especially, areas where their own views differ from mainstream views in a field or subfield. Dissent may be also represented by brief responses to the report by experts who have conducted research in the field.

The completed appraisal should be widely reviewed prior to publication, according to the highest disciplinary standards of peer review but including more reviewers than is usual for an academic paper. It is vital that appraisals receive hard scrutiny, especially from those whose work is critically reviewed. Reviewers should include insiders (those working in the field under review) as well as knowledgeable outsiders, who can bring a broader frame of reference to bear on the subject – making sure that standards applied in one area are consistent with standards applied to other areas of research. Where disagreements among reviewers and the author(s) persist, as they are bound to in contentious areas of research, the supervising editorial board will need to make a final determination.

One might also consider an online system that allows readers to comment on various sections of a report – substantiating claims, refuting claims, adding citations to new studies that may have appeared subsequent to publication, and so forth. Readers could then read the main text and also follow a stream of commentary on that text that accumulates over time. This, too, could prove a useful tool for reaching consensus on a subject, or at least clarifying points of disagreement.

The Vehicle

In considering possible venues for a comprehensive appraisal one must bear in mind the problem of incentives. Academics are unlikely to sacrifice their scarce time to conduct wide-ranging appraisals unless the product of their labor receives due recognition. Thus, whatever vehicle is chosen must be highly regarded in academic circles, or must become so. Ideally, that venue would also be familiar to policymakers, and thus contribute to broader debates. With this as background we shall consider two potential vehicles – the *review article* and the *expert panel*.

Review article. Ostensibly, the long-established venue of a literature review accomplishes much of what is intended by a comprehensive appraisal. Many journals devote space to reviews of the literature on a topic, often under the guise of a book review, or a more discursive review of several books. Some journals have as their main mission the publication of reviews, e.g., *Contemporary Sociology*, the *Journal of Economic Literature*, and the review section of *Perspectives on Politics*. One family of journals, the *Annual Review* series, is exclusively devoted to the genre, with review journals focused on anthropology, clinical psychology, economics, environment and resources, financial economics, law and social science, linguistics, organizational psychology and organizational behavior, political science, psychology, public health, resource economics, and sociology. A few journals provide a forum for wide-ranging syntheses of work on a topic with an aim to reaching a broader audience of lay readers, e.g., *Contexts*, the *Journal of Economic Perspectives*, and *Perspectives on Politics*. Handbooks are produced by academic publishers (e.g., Cambridge, Edward Elgar, Elsevier, North Holland, Oxford, and Sage) on a wide variety of topics, each of which promises extensive reviews of the literature.

Testament to the need for evaluation and integration is the high citation count that these articles and chapters receive. Unfortunately, publishing a literature review is not highly regarded in the academy. Reviews of the literature are often not vetted to the same extent as research articles, lowering their status and presumably their quality. Reviews tend to be short, rarely involve an encounter with the data, and are often limited to an enumeration of who said what about a given subject. They may be highly opinionated, and in this sense are probably *not* the place to go to discover a discipline's settled view of a topic. Rather, they allow an author to stake out his/her position on X. (To be clear, this is a worthy goal, but it is not the same as what I am advocating under the rubric of comprehensive appraisal.) One may question whether individuals, working alone, have the capacity, or the requisite neutrality, to adequately assess a broad field of study. And even if they do, it is hard to escape the *implication* of subjectivity – that a review represents merely "the opinion of Professor X."

Expert panel. A different sort of venue that might be adopted for the task of comprehensive appraisal is the expert panel. Panels might be convened by disciplinary bodies (e.g., the American Economic Association, the American Sociological Association, or the American Political Science Association), by cross-disciplinary bodies (e.g., the National Academy of Sciences or the Social Science Research Council), or by government agencies (e.g., the US Department of Education, which commissioned the influential Equality of Educational Opportunity report, aka the "Coleman report," in 1966). Although expert panels tend to be more common in the natural sciences, there is no reason, in principle, why the format could not be exploited more fully in the social sciences.

A benefit of the panel model is that it allows cross-fertilization among those who bring together complementary areas of expertise, including both substantive knowledge and methodological skills. Another benefit is the ability to incorporate individuals with diverse views and backgrounds directly into the appraisal, which may be especially important when working on contentious subjects (where truly disinterested individuals are hard to find). A final benefit is the ability to deliberate as a group.

A disadvantage is posed by the problem of coordination and the time-demands – which tend to multiply as the number of individuals in a group increases. Committees are not the most efficient venues for academic production.

A hybrid model, incorporating both individual and group features, involves a board that supervises the work of an individual – who does most of the work and receives most of the acclaim, but must answer to the board. This is how many committees proceed, where the chair is the author and principal investigator, and the rest of the board serves an oversight and advisory function.

Individualized Appraisal versus Comprehensive Appraisal

Conducting a comprehensive appraisal is not easy, as the foregoing section has amply demonstrated. However, it is hard to see how social science can progress, and can fruitfully contribute to broader debates, without cultivating this genre.

To sharpen the argument, I will show how an individualized system of appraisal falls short and how a comprehensive approach might compensate for those deficiencies. To be clear, this is not an argument against individualized appraisal; it is an argument for supplementing it with a well-developed system of comprehensive appraisal. We need both for science to progress.

Contributions

A study is likely to be published in an academic journal if it is perceived to add to something to our knowledge of a subject. There are many ways in which a paper can make a contribution. It may develop a new concept or theory, propose a new methodology, identify new phenomena (hitherto unstudied), collect new data, develop new measures, and so forth. The collection of published studies on a subject are therefore highly heterogeneous in their goals and aspirations. Sometimes, the goal of a study is frankly exploratory. In this instance, the author proposes a new idea that has some possibility of being true or useful even though it has not been fully vetted.

(I have concluded many journal reviews with the statement – "may or may not be true, but nonetheless worthy of publishing.") Generally, new ideas (i.e., new methods, new concepts, new theories, new phenomena, new data, new measures) are less secure. Accordingly, the first publication on a topic is unlikely to resolve that topic.

In short, the purpose of a normal academic publication is varied, and some of these contributions are likely to be shaky. By contrast, the purpose of a comprehensive appraisal is focused primarily on the truth-value of theory or hypothesis. Not how novel it is, but how true it is. Because it has a narrower goal and is not conflicted by other goals, a comprehensive appraisal is more likely to achieve that goal.

This point is so obvious that it seems trite. And yet, it is vital. Our current system of individualized appraisal, as operated by most journals and presses, is designed to achieve many goals, among them *discovery* (as discussed in Part I of this book). A system of comprehensive appraisal would be designed to achieve only one goal: *appraisal.*

Separating Theory and Evidence

For accurate appraisal to occur the formation of a theory must be separated from the testing of that theory. However, there are limits to how well this may be accomplished in an individualized system of appraisal.

To begin with, there can be no separation between theory and evidence in exploratory work. Where a new idea arises from an ongoing encounter with the evidence and there is no additional evidence that can be locked away – out of the researcher's grasp – for future tests, the separation of theory and evidence is purely a narrative device. A good deal of observational work, both qualitative and quantitative, fits this description (Rueschemeyer 2009; Yom 2015).

The goal of separating moments of discovery and appraisal within the same study is *possible* in other settings – specifically, where a researcher must take an extra step to test an idea, e.g., set up an experiment, visit a research site, and so forth. However, it is *verifiable* only if the researcher is demonstrably unable to access the evidence needed to test a hypothesis when the hypothesis was developed, a situation of *prior unobservability*. In these situations, the researcher may register the hypothesis, along with a specific method of testing (a pre-analysis plan.), in advance so that the theory is falsifiable in the strongest sense of the word. In experimental work this demanding protocol is relatively straightforward and commonly practiced. In the realm of observational research, prior unobservability exists wherever data-collection has a prospective quality: where, for instance, it involves the collection of data on events that have not yet occurred or about which data are not yet available (e.g., because a survey has not been conducted or is not yet in the public domain), as discussed in Chapter 9 of this volume.

So, the ideal of separating theory and evidence is possible, and verifiable, but only in some circumstances. It follows that we must find a way to separate theory formation and theory testing in situations that fall outside the purview of a pre-registration protocol.

Comprehensive appraisal is one potential solution to this problem. To be sure, this process is subject to the same squishiness that affects any other appraisal. As the appraiser begins to work with a problem, and encounters the evidence, s/he may change her view of what constitutes an appropriate test for a theory and may develop entirely new tests. There is bound to be a back-and-forth between theory and evidence. One might seek to avoid this problem by pre-registering a comprehensive appraisal. But it is not clear what this would consist of (unless the comprehensive appraisal were to be limited to a single meta-analysis). Because the task of comprehensive appraisal is broad – taking account of all theoretical formulations of a problem and all research on that problem – it probably cannot be reduced to a pre-analysis plan.

Incentives

The current system of incentives offers rewards for discovery as well as for appraisal. The problem is that two goals often run contrary to one another (for further discussion see Chapter 18, this volume). To convince others that a discovery has occurred the scholar must emphasize the distinctiveness of her finding or her approach. As a result, the author's incentive is to dissemble, i.e., to magnify the degree of novelty of a study in light of research on that topic and to exaggerate the strength of the finding in light of the available evidence, while pretending to conduct a dispassionate, disinterested appraisal. In this fashion, full and honest appraisal may be sacrificed on the altar of discovery.

A number of reforms including pre-registration and results-blind review (discussed in previous chapters) have been proposed to overcome this problem of incentives. While these reforms are meritorious, they do not entirely resolve the conflict between contending imperatives – to discover new things about the world and to offer a full and honest appraisal of those purported discoveries. Arguably, a system of individualized appraisal *cannot* resolve this conflict.

In the field of law, prosecution and defense are vested in different persons (representing the complainant and the defendant respectively). In the field of policy evaluation, one generally looks to separate the individuals conducting a policy intervention from the individuals evaluating that intervention. If this separation of roles is important in other professional contexts there is every reason to suppose that it is important for social science. We are only human. It is ironic that social scientists, who are keen to point out the role of incentives in society, are seemingly oblivious to the role of incentives in the conduct of social science, or imagine that they can be overcome by a hyper-vigilant set of rules.

One must also bear in mind that researchers generally choose subjects that they feel passionately about, and this generally involves some a priori expectations about what is to be found "out there" in the empirical world. The longer a researcher has tilled a field the stronger his or her convictions are likely to become as s/he develops sunk costs and pre-commitments, i.e., a body of published work with which his/her career is identified. It is difficult to imagine that social scientists will become less passionate or less committed to their favored theories about the world. And it is not clear that they should do so. If passion is a structural feature of social science (Munck and Snyder 2007) one must be skeptical of a regulatory regime that seeks to suppress that feature. Even if scholarly incentives (e.g., for hiring and promotion) could be realigned there is an ongoing selection effect. Many scholars enter the academy because they wish to right wrongs, i.e., to improve some feature of society that they perceive as unjust. This sort of bias is not responsive to disciplinary incentives.

The benefit of comprehensive appraisal is that the tasks of discovery and appraisal are conducted by *different people*, each with clearly defined roles. The appraiser should have no "skin" in the game, aside from the objective of conducting a systematic and dispassionate review of the theory and evidence. And in order to pass rigorous review, the set of reviewers – and an oversight board or committee – must be convinced that the appraisal has been conducted without researcher bias. Most important, the status of the resulting appraisal, and the number of citations it is likely to garner, is dependent upon its dispassionate review of the evidence and the theory – not on the findings. This sets an appraisal apart from other genres of work in the social sciences.

Generalizability

An individualized system of appraisal focuses on the truth-claims of an individual study, claims that are usually restricted to a particular sample or population. A study based on a survey or experiment, for example, will seek to draw conclusions about study subjects as well as the population from which they were drawn. It will probably be cautious about making broader claims (re: unstudied populations), and reviewers will not expect it to do so (except in a highly speculative fashion).

And yet, it is usually the broader scope that is of greater theoretical and practical interest. We may be somewhat interested to know whether a school voucher program enhanced scholastic achievement in Cleveland from 1990 to 2000. But the success of this program is not necessarily a good guide to the likely impact of vouchers in Sacramento, or anywhere else. Indeed, when experiments are replicated in another venue or with a different sample the follow-up study often reveals a different result. This does not mean the original study was faulty (though that is one plausible explanation). It could also be that the same treatment generates a different result in different contexts due to background factors that have yet to be identified. Or it could be a product of chance (especially if the sample and the measured effect in the original study was small). We expect that observational studies are subject to even greater problems of replicability, given that they are (generally) less standardized and subject to greater contextual effects.

The point is, to gauge whether a vouchers program is likely to work in Sacramento (where it has not yet been implemented) we would want to know about the relative success of all voucher programs instituted everywhere. That means undertaking a comprehensive appraisal of all studies that bear on the hypothesis that vouchers enhance scholastic achievement. Granted, some of these studies would likely be more informative than others – based on their context, research design, the nature of the intervention, and so forth. But even to judge this question we need a bird's-eye view.

While the appraisal of an individual study rightly focuses on internal validity, with a limited understanding of external validity, a comprehensive appraisal has a much broader focus – on every context to which a hypothesis might apply. These are quite different scope-conditions, signaling a central distinction between individualized appraisal and comprehensive appraisal. To understand the generalizability of a theory or hypothesis, the latter is essential.

Assessing Progress

The current system of individualized appraisal values bite-sized chunks of knowledge, suitable for a 10,000-word journal article. Scholars respond by dividing projects into "minimally publishable units." In the textbook version of scientific progress, cumulation occurs in a semi-automatic fashion as a product of the uncoordinated activities of individual members of a research community, each producing article-length studies that demonstrate "findings," which are recognized as such by reviewers and readers, and which are then either replicated (and hence, over time, verified) or not (and hence cast aside). Findings that are replicated provide the foundation for further studies in a cumulative manner that defines scientific progress. In a purely cumulative science, one need only read the most recent study on a topic to find the discipline's considered opinion on the topic.

Perhaps this Popperian vision adequately describes the world of natural science (at least during periods of "normal" science). In the social sciences, however, we rarely encounter hypotheses that have been decisively proven or disproven. And for this reason, research guided by narrow hypotheses is unlikely to cumulate in a coherent and useful fashion (Deaton 2010; Dessler 1991; Mearsheimer and Walt 2013; Parsons 1938; Rogowski 1995; Wolpin 2013).

There are many reasons for this, which may be briefly reviewed. Outcomes of theoretical interest tend to have many potential causes, each of which is likely to be true to some extent or in some contexts. Progress is registered not by an accumulation of findings but rather by a more complex refinement of knowledge about a subject. Over time, a causal hypothesis that has been examined by a succession of scholars should render an estimate of the causal effect that is more precise, less uncertain, with more clearly specified background (scope) conditions, and a better understanding of mechanisms at work and causal heterogeneity (differential impact on units subjected to the treatment). This is the nature of scientific progress as realized in the social sciences. It is not a series of binary (yes/no) decisions but rather a long, slow, boring of hard boards, to paraphrase Max Weber (on politics).

To chart this progress, bite-sized hypotheses must be digested and synthesized in a comprehensive fashion. This includes work emanating from a diversity of fields and employing a diversity of methods. In principle, all studies that have ever been conducted on a particular topic – both published and unpublished – should be included. Active engagement in theory-building is required in order to fit a smorgasbord of disparate empirical results together into a coherent framework. Achieving progress requires *theorizing* – and not the sort of theorizing that emphasizes novelty but rather the sort that emphasizes unification, aka parsimony or "consilience" (Wilson 1998).

It should be apparent that the brief literature reviews that preface journal articles and books are not up to this demanding protocol. Indeed, they rarely do more than scratch the surface, and their objective is to demonstrate that one study – their own – says something novel about a topic, not to unify work on that topic. Duncan Watts (2017:2; see also Wallerstein 1996) concludes, "at no point does the existing system for producing social scientific knowledge either facilitate or reward the activity of reconciling disparate frameworks. As a result, facts and theories pile up in an incoherent heap."

Efficiency

There is, finally, a question of efficiency to consider (Ioannidis et al. 2014). To the extent that current reforms (e.g., pre-registration, results-free review) might work, they are burdensome and time-consuming – for authors, editors, and reviewers. And the stricter the regulatory regime, the more costs they are likely to impose. For example, registering a study is time-consuming for authors. If, in addition, it becomes necessary for reviewers to monitor the registration – assuring that the pre-analysis plan corresponds to the actual analysis and that any deviations are of minimal importance, or at least properly noted – then time-demands extend to reviewers (or to some other third party) as well. As with any principal-agency problem, assuring compliance is not easy.

Granted, setting up a system of comprehensive assessment is also costly, and conducting an assessment is time-consuming. This, too, must be appreciated. However, it might be more efficient for one person, or a small team of persons, to conduct a comprehensive appraisal of a subject every decade or so than for *all* papers on that subject (those that are eventually published as well as those that are not) to be subjected to an extensive regulatory regimen.

Conclusions

The current system of scholarly production prioritizes discovery over appraisal. This is defensible from a certain perspective. Does anyone believe that greater importance should be given to a solid appraisal than to a study that proposes something new and important about the world (assuming that the latter has a non-negligible chance of being true)? In natural science and economics, Nobel prizes are won by those who have made seminal contributions to a field – not to those who plod in their tracks with replications, syntheses, and extensions. I see no reason why political science, psychology, and sociology should be any different, even though we don't currently qualify for the Nobel. If appraisal were really to be prioritized over discovery, and incentive structures adjusted accordingly, then rewards would go to the plodders rather than the innovators. It is hard even to imagine what that sort of system would look like because it does not exist in any scholarly field of inquiry.

Yet, those who accept the "discovery" bias embedded in most scholarly activity should also accept the need to bolster the second moment of science – appraisal. Even if it comes in second place, it should be a strong second. Continual novelty is not useful unless the plausible hypotheses unearthed by exploratory work can be adequately vetted. Without cumulation there is no scientific progress, and cumulation in the social sciences is extremely difficult, demanding a great deal of self-conscious attention.

To improve the quality of appraisal, I have proposed a departure from the individualized approach that currently dominates the work of the academy. This approach takes the form of a lengthy paper or report that evaluates a scientific question in an encompassing fashion. Its goal is to evaluate accumulated findings on that subject, assigning a degree of (un)certainty to each hypothesis under review. It should encompass all work that has been conducted on a subject, published or unpublished, and should also involve a direct encounter with the evidence, e.g., meta-analysis or replication. To conduct this appraisal in a dispassionate manner one must identify experts who are conversant with the research question but not closely aligned with a particular view of the subject. The process should be overseen by a review board composed of specialists and non-specialists (those outside the subfield being assessed) and should engage those who are working on that subject, either as active participants in the appraisal or as commentators and critics of the appraisal. The resulting report should include both technical detail, with special attention to methodological issues, as well as general conclusions set forth in an accessible fashion for a lay audience. It should also seek to develop a body of theory to account for the findings at hand.

I have argued that there is much to recommend a comprehensive approach to appraisal – as a complement (not substitute) for the individualized appraisals that we already conduct.

Granted, comprehensive appraisal is not a silver bullet. Problems stemming from a lack of standardization, publication bias, the file-drawer problem, fishing/curve-fitting, and fraud, as discussed elsewhere in this volume, are still worrisome. Appraisers are not omniscient. However, experts with extensive knowledge of a subject matter, and extensive networks among those working on that area, are in the best position to judge when a single study, or a body of findings, exhibits bias – especially if they are able to conduct a forensic meta-analysis. Arguably, the more biases exist in a body of knowledge the more we need a comprehensive approach to appraisal to help us assess and digest that body of knowledge.

15 Impact Metrics

John Gerring, Sebastian Karcher and Brendan Apfeld

Virtually every evaluative task in the academy involves some sort of metric (Elkana et al. 1978; Espeland and Sauder 2016; Gingras 2016; Hix 2004; Jensenius et al. 2018; Muller 2018; Osterloh and Frey 2015; Todeschini and Baccini 2016; Van Noorden 2010; Wilsdon et al. 2015). One can decry this development, and inveigh against its abuses and its over-use (as many of the foregoing studies do). Yet, without metrics, we would be at pains to render judgments about scholars, published papers, applications (for grants, fellowships, and conferences), journals, academic presses, departments, universities, or subfields.

Of course, we also undertake to judge these issues ourselves through a deliberative process that involves reading the work under evaluation. This is the traditional approach of peer review. No one would advocate a system of evaluation that is entirely metric-driven. Even so, reading is time-consuming and inherently subjective; it is, after all, the opinion of one reader (or several readers, if there is a panel of reviewers). It is also impossible to systematically compare these judgments. To be sure, one might also read, and assess, the work of other scholars, but this does not provide a systematic basis for comparison – unless, that is, a standard metric(s) of comparison is employed. Finally, judging scholars through peer review becomes logistically intractable when the task shifts from a single scholar to a large group of scholars or a large body of work, e.g., a journal, a department, a university, a subfield, or a discipline. It is impossible to read, and assess, a library of work.

For these reasons, quantitative metrics are an unavoidable component of gatekeeping in the academy. It is not a question of whether or not to employ metrics but rather which metrics to employ. We need to think carefully about what these evaluation metrics are and how they might, in turn, establish incentives for scholars, presses, departments, and universities. The metrics that gain traction in the social sciences today will influence the production of social science knowledge tomorrow.

Traditional metrics of quality are grounded in judgments of *reputation*. Sometimes, reputation is measured in a systematic fashion through surveys of professionals in a field. Other times, they are loosely understood norms, which everyone is assumed to share. In either case, journals, presses, and departments can be ranked by considering their overall reputation. At the top of a ranking, there is likely to be a high level of agreement. Toward the middle and bottom of the scale, however, disagreement is more likely. Here, an evaluative system based on reputation breaks down, for middle- and lower-ranked units do not have clearly defined reputations. Another problem with reputational metrics is that elements under review are highly interdependent. It is difficult to separate the reputation of articles (or books) from the journals (or presses) they are published in (or by), or the reputation of scholars from the departments and universities they are employed by. The reputations of institutions tend to overshadow the reputations of studies and scholars. Moreover, these reputations are sticky, and may reflect past glories more than current performance. A pecking order based solely on reputation is likely to perpetuate itself because there is no other metric by which performance can be judged. Harvard is top not because of anything it does but because it is Harvard. Not only is this un-meritocratic, it also has a baleful effect on incentives – both for those at the top of the pecking order and for those at the bottom. No one has an incentive to improve their game if their position in the hierarchy is primarily a product of their title and institutional affiliation, especially if these factors are locked in (post-tenure).

In recent decades, another metric has come to the fore that takes a fundamentally different approach to evaluation. This approach measures *impact*, inferred from the citations accrued by a study.[1] Like reputation, impact may be measured at any level. An individual may be evaluated according to the citations accruing to her publications; a department may be evaluated according to the citations accrued by studies produced by all its faculty; a journal or press may be evaluated according to the citations accrued by all its publications; and so forth. Naturally, there is some inter-dependence among impact measures. A study's citation count is apt to be influenced by a journal's citation-count, for example. Nonetheless, there is a much greater degree of independence among the units being assessed. An implication is that impact-based metrics are more meritocratic than reputational metrics.

---

[1] For wide-ranging discussions – many of them highly critical of this development – see Bornmann and Daniel (2008), Cronin and Sugimoto (2014), Gingras (2016), Hamermesh (2018), Sugimoto and Larivière (2018), Todeschini and Baccini (2016).

We are cautiously optimistic about the increasing use of such metrics. However, this new standard of evaluation introduces several problems – as well as an entirely new set of incentives – that have not been widely appreciated. We begin by reviewing the shortcomings of current citation databases, which provide the basis for impact metrics and place limitations on the information contained in them. We view these problems as fundamental, but also temporary. In light of recent advances in information technology and library science it seems likely that these shortcomings will be overcome, perhaps in the near future. Next, we address potential objections to a citation-based system of evaluation. We argue that these objections are resolvable, for the most part. We conclude with thoughts on the possible impact of impact metrics.

Databases

Citation-based metrics have been around for a long while in the natural sciences (Garfield 1955). In the social sciences, they have come to the fore more recently – largely, it seems, because of the ready availability of citation data, which is now stored electronically and easily accessed on the web. The most widely used databases are Google Scholar (GS), Scopus, Web of Science (WoS), and, more recently, Microsoft Academic (MA)[2]. Each has its specific limitations, but all struggle to achieve three essential goals: (a) correct identification of authors, (b) complete – or at least representative – coverage, and (c) open access.

Author Identity

Publications must be linked correctly with their authors if citation metrics are to be used as an evaluative tool. A single junior faculty member with only a handful of publications may be able to track the citations of those pieces with manual searches of each one. But automation becomes essential when her publications grow in number or when one needs a systematic comparison

---

[2] A fairly recent initiative, the Open Citation Corpus (http://opencitations.net/) has the potential to provide a highly valuable and completely open alternative. Currently, its size and coverage – less than 1 percent of the number of publications in WoS – is too limited to warrant inclusion. Yet another database, dimensions.ai, published by the Digital Science group, which is co-owned with Springer/Nature, appears to provide similar services to Scopus/WoS and is currently free of charge. Its launch was too late for inclusion in this chapter, but it may be another useful source for researchers.

of scholars across a department, university, subfield, or discipline. Impact metrics are useful if citations can be quickly aggregated by author, which in turn implies that they must be able to link publications with their authors, with a minimum of error.

Several attempts have been made to standardize author identification, most notably the International Standard Name Identifier (ISNI, for any creative work) and ORCID (specifically for academic work). However, their coverage at this time is too low to be of genuine use in mapping authors to works. We are, however, optimistic about the potential for ORCID, now commonly included in citation data for new works, to help solve this issue in the future. Importantly, both Scopus and WoS collaborate with the ORCID initiative.

Given the shortcomings (in coverage) of ISNI and ORCID, each of the existing databases has been obliged to create its own method for identifying authors.

GS links documents together by author only when a researcher intentionally creates a profile on the site. Once created, GS will attempt to identify new publications to add to the profile. However, the process is not flawless and requires authors to regularly "curate" their profile, confirming correct publications, deleting incorrect publications, and combining duplicates as appropriate. The most notorious – but far from only – example of this is the world's most prolific and most widely cited author, "et al."[3] Moreover, many scholars have not created a GS profile and these absences are probably not random. As a result, GS profiles do not provide an unbiased measure of impact across groups of scholars (subfields, fields, departments, etc.).

Scopus generates scholar profiles automatically, creating a complete dataset but also one with greater opportunities for both false positives and false negatives. Scopus provides a way for authors to request corrections to their profiles. But we wonder whether any author would consider the benefits of corrections to outweigh even the minor costs of doing so – especially if the error was in the author's favor.

WoS does not create researcher profiles of the same kind as GS or Scopus. This service attempts to group publications by the same researcher together, but does not automatically create any citation statistics based on those publications. It is possible for users to generate such statistics with granular

---

[3] Their Google Scholar profile is available at https://scholar.google.nl/citations?user=qGuYgMsAAAAJ&hl=en and its backstory at http://ideophone.org/some-things-you-need-to-know-about-google-scholar/.

control over what is and is not included in these calculations, but additional steps are required and it results only in a temporary report.

MA also offers user profiles akin to those in GS. Unlike GS, however, these profiles are created automatically and researchers then have the option to "claim" and make revisions to their own profile. MA profiles are less detailed than GS ones, offering only article and total citation counts. MA offers direct access to the underlying data (discussed in greater detail below) through Microsoft Academic Graph. This provides researchers with great flexibility, but also exposes directly the core problem entailed in automatically linking documents to author identifiers.

While author identification is a particularly vexing problem for large-scale analysis, it can be solved with reasonable amounts of manual labor for medium-n analyses. Identifying false positives (i.e., studies falsely attributed to an author) is typically quick. Papers *missing* for a particular author are harder to identify, but the omission of some works is unlikely to cause significant measurement error; the citation counts of the papers for authors typically follows a power-law distribution (see, e.g., Breuer and Bowen 2014; Brzezinski 2015), so that an accurate assessment of their total citation counts depends mainly on the inclusion of their most widely cited works, which (with some notable exemptions, as noted below) is typically the case.

Coverage

In addition to linking documents to their authors, databases must also contain a large portion of the scientific record. However, "larger" is not necessarily better. The coverage needs also to be representative of the scientific record. If one portion of the record is missing from a database then all metrics generated by that database will be biased in a systematic fashion. Finally, a database needs to avoid double-counts (e.g., counting citations from a preprint and an identical journal article as if they were separately published documents).

Unfortunately, extant databases are limited in coverage and struggle with representativeness and double-counting. Moreover, there appears to be a trade-off between these goals. GS and MA have the largest corpus and do somewhat better on the inclusion of non-article items, but the quality of their data is lower. Scopus and WoS perform much better on data quality, but have poor coverage outside of traditional journal articles.

GS is the most extensive database, estimated around 140 million entries in 2014 (Sugimoto and Larivière 2018) and growing steadily. Its inclusivity with respect to contemporary sources might be regarded as a blessing – it includes working papers, papers posted on personal web sites, along with papers published in recognized journals. However, as for author identification, the quality of data in GS is so low that we do not believe it should be used without extensive manual curation. Many of these are "honest" errors, but the wide range of sources included in GS together with the lack of curation also offers an opportunity for malfeasance, as demonstrated by Delgado López-Cózar, Robinson-García, and Torres-Salinas (2014), who were able to massively boost the *h*-index of every member of their working group by uploading six fake papers to a university website.

MA is the newest citation database of the four, but its growth has been rapid. Recent estimates suggest that MA grew from 83 million records in 2015 to 140 million in 2016, with current coverage equal to or exceeding that of WoS and Scopus (Hug, Ochsner, and Brändle 2017; Wade et al. 2016). Today, the MA frontpage suggests this number has continued to increase and now stands at over 173 million publications. However, coverage by subject matter varies greatly. Estimates range from less than 10-percent coverage in the humanities to over 90 percent in engineering and technology (Hug and Brändle 2017). MA suffers from quality issues akin to GS. For example, in using MA data to identify high-impact papers, Wesley-Smith, Bergstrom, and West (2016) found that among their four highest impact articles was one duplicate, one reference to an entire journal (the *New England Journal of Medicine*) and one "In the press."

Scopus (ca. 70 million articles) and WoS (ca. 59 million articles) are significantly smaller than fully automated MA and GS, but both curate their sources, i.e., they select a subset of journals based on a specified set of standards such as peer review and ethical publication practices.[4] They argue that "the core literature for all scholarly disciplines may be concentrated in a relatively small number of journals" (Testa 2016) and that focusing on this core provides better representativeness by excluding meaningless citations. Curated indices are harder (though not impossible) to game. They also can more easily react to evidence of fraud by removing offending journals and/or authors from their indices. On the downside, the focus on formal publications introduces a significant lag. In some disciplines, the average delay between submission and acceptance can be as long as 30 months (see Ellison 2002:951 for economics), i.e., citations *to* journal articles *in* journal articles can lag as much as five years.

[4] See Testa (2016) for an in-depth discussion of the WoS journal selection process and www.elsevier.com/solutions/scopus/content for a summary of Scopus's practices.

While GS and MA cover more books than the article-focused Scopus and WoS, no database offers good coverage of books (Samuels 2013), and edited volumes constitute a particular source of confusion as editorship and authorship are often incorrectly noted in databases. Since books (including edited volumes) continue to comprise an important genre of academic production in the social sciences, this must be regarded as a major failing. Moreover, it penalizes certain sorts of work, namely, work that is broad in scope and work that employs qualitative methods, which generally require more space to articulate. Consequently, extant databases are systematically biased, giving an advantage to scholars who publish in journals, or whose work is more likely to be cited in journals.

Book production varies by subfield and by author – some subfields tend to share their scholarship in article form at greater rates than others within the same discipline and some authors tend to favor one type of publication over another. Thus, even if book missing-ness was distributed in the same way as article missing-ness, there would still be bias in the citation counts.[5]

Gingras (2016) points out that while these databases do not include citations *within* books, they do contain citations *of* books (when books are cited by articles). Unfortunately, this does not overcome the problem. Note, first, that book and book section missing-ness is extremely high. Hug and Brändle (2017) estimate that MA, Scopus, and WoS contain, respectively, 14.3, 9.7, and 6.6 percent of book sections. Coverage of edited volumes is slightly better for MA (15.6 percent) but drops to a mere 2.6 and 3.9 percent, respectively, for Scopus and WoS. These numbers are shockingly low compared with estimated coverage for articles in these databases – 73.0, 77.5, and 71.7 percent, respectively.

Book missing-ness is a problem for book authors who receive lower citation counts if their works are missing. The exclusion of citations within books affects all authors whose work is cited in these texts. This would not be a problem if citations within articles and books were highly correlated. However, books and articles do not cite the same sorts of studies. Authors' citation counts within articles is not highly correlated with their citation counts within books (Hicks 1999). The omission of book citations thus biases impact metrics in important ways.

---

[5] Note that we think it very unlikely that the distributions are the same given the different coverage rates across disciplines but that current studies have not addressed this question directly.

Access

Given the importance of metrics, it is vital that whatever database(s) becomes the basis for constructing impact metrics for a discipline be open-access. Only in this fashion will full transparency be possible. And only in this fashion will it be possible to devise a variety of metrics to suit different purposes and concerns, as discussed in the next section. It is worrisome that the databases that provide fodder for scholarly metrics are controlled by privately held companies – Alphabet (the parent company of Google), Elsevier (the parent company of Scopus), Clarivate Analytics (the parent company of WoS), and Microsoft (the parent company of MA) (Weingart 2005).

Moreover, the business of constructing metrics has been taken over by a host of private consultancies such as Academic Analytics, iFQ, Sciencemetrix, and CWTS. These companies sell their services to universities, governments, and other organizations and view their product as proprietary, which means that they make it available to administrators but not – except by special request – to researchers. It appears that these metrics are already affecting decisions about hiring, promotion, and funding without the full knowledge of stakeholders, i.e., researchers whose livelihoods and research is at issue. It is largely a behind-the-scenes operation. Equally worrisome, there are good reasons to worry about the quality of the data, and the metrics, that are driving these decisions (Basken 2018).

Of the databases considered here, access varies from completely open to both closed and behind a paywall. Scopus and WoS are both subscription services, generally subscribed to by institutional libraries.[6] The cost is non-trivial; consequently, most universities choose to purchase access to one, but not both. This means that researchers with university connections do not generally have access to the same databases. Both services provide an API for which subscribers can request a key to access the database programmatically. Scopus provides a Python module so that users with a rudimentary knowledge of that language can run searches.

MA requires no subscription and an archived version of the underlying data is, for the time being, also publicly available. For those wishing to access the current version of the data, Microsoft provides tools to access the graph in several programming languages using the Microsoft Knowledge API. Open Academic Graph provides access to the underlying data (alongside the data for a similar but smaller citation graph, AMiner). We applaud this openness

---

[6] Scopus also provides free access to a limited set of its features.

and recognize that it offers researchers opportunities unavailable with the other databases. However, we are concerned that this open-access policy could be changed at any time.

GS is also a free service. It does not, however, support any kind of programmatic or automated data access or collection. Some unofficial and unsupported tools for automatic comparisons exist (e.g., Publish or Perish (Harzing 2007)), but their functionality is limited and attempts to use them in more expansive ways will quickly hit Google's (unpublished and unknown) rate limit.[7]

Conclusions

In this section, we have discussed limitations imposed by the databases that impact metrics draw upon. These limitations are considerable. Databases have not arrived at a consistent and universal identifier for authors. They are limited in coverage, especially with respect to books. And most are not open-access. Impact metrics cannot do the job envisioned for them until these obstacles are overcome.

Our guess is that most, if not all, of these limitations will be overcome in the coming years. Citation databases are evolving quickly, and one major player – MA – has only recently entered the field and other databases like *dimensions.ai* and OCC have recently appeared. The technical barriers to solving these problems are not insuperable (though there will doubtless remain some degree of error). And the payoff to the outfit that solves these issues is vast. Since there is already competition among four leading companies – each with vast resources – we assume that one of them will see fit to provide what the academy so desperately needs. Even so, impact metrics raise other issues, which may be considered intrinsic to the enterprise and hence more fundamental in nature.

Objections

The interpretation of "impact" based on citations rests upon assumptions about why scholars cite each other. Robert Merton (1988:622) writes,

---

[7] Publish or Perish now pulls data from both GS and MA, pointing to the relatively greater openness of the newer database.

The reference serves both instrumental and symbolic functions in the transmission and enlargement of knowledge. Instrumentally, it tells us of work we may not have known before, some of which may hold further interest for us; symbolically, it registers in the enduring archives the intellectual property of the acknowledged source by providing a pellet of peer recognition of the knowledge claim, accepted or expressly rejected, that was made in that source.

Implicitly, a citation is an acknowledgment of influence.[8] Accordingly, the cumulative citation count of a study, an individual, a journal, a department, a university, or any other unit of academic production is also a measure of influence, or impact.

However, using impact metrics to evaluate research and researchers is not without problems. In this section we review a series of objections to impact metrics: (a) types of citations, (b) non-citations, (c) fake citations, gaming, and citation quality, (d) genre bias, (e) non-equivalence across contexts, and (i) gender bias.

Types of Citations

Not all citations are created equal. Some citations praise the cited paper, others point out fatal errors in it. Some citations stand alone, others engage deeply with the cited article. Some citations are a self-flattery or a courtesy to colleagues or friends, while others carry the influence of a work into an entirely new discipline. Citation counts grant all of these citations equal weight.

A promising research agenda offers to categorize every citation using an ontology; see, e.g., Shotton (2010). However, such categorizations currently rely largely on manual annotation and the chances of it reaching sufficient coverage for impact measurement in the near future are small.

"Negative" citations seem particularly troublesome. Why should an author get credited for an article criticizing their work? At a closer look, the problem may be less critical than it first appears. For one, scientific progress often occurs in a dialectical fashion, with new work criticizing old work. Sometimes, the most important study in a field is wrong in its findings but nonetheless scopes out a new area of research, perhaps by posing a new question or a new method of exploring a question. We should recognize these sorts of contributions, and impact metrics provide a convenient way of doing so. A recent study finds

---

[8] For further discussion of the various functions and motivations underlying citations, see Bornmann and Daniel (2008), Cronin (1984), Erikson and Erlandson (2014), Nicolaisen (2007).

evidence to support this optimism, noting that "negative citations concerned higher-quality papers, were focused on a study's findings rather than theories or methods" (Catalini, Lacetera, and Oettl 2015).

Similar concerns have been raised about "obligatory" citations, citations that come to dominate a topic even though other, less famous, studies are equally good. This is sometimes referred to as a bandwagon, herding, or "Matthew" effect (Hamermesh 2018:129; Merton 1968a). In some instances, the obligatory citation is to a work that is notably flawed. As with negative citations, this seems to call into question the value of a citation as a measure genuine scientific impact. Nonetheless, an important function of citations is as a placeholder, reminding the reader of a tradition of research or a particular position in a long-standing debate. Classics serve that function, even if they are no longer at the forefront of research (almost by definition, they are not). If a study has managed to formulate a position in an especially persuasive fashion, and has come to be acknowledged as a classic, then it is performing a valued function in knowledge production.

Another issue with citation-based metrics is their origin. A citation that highlights one's own work, a "self-citation" (Hudson 2007), may be regarded as a stroke of vanity rather than evidence of impact. However, it is important to recognize that authors sometimes self-cite for perfectly good reasons (Gingras 2016:24). After all, most knowledge comes from specialization, and this means that an advanced researcher will have honed a small body of knowledge over a long period of time. A recent study of citation patterns in economics seems to endorse this benign view of self-citation. Hamermesh (2018:129) reports that self-citations and other-citations are highly correlated, meaning that authors who cite themselves are also likely to be cited by others. There are some known cases of abuse[9] (more on this below), but in the case of self-citation, these are easily mitigated through a change in metric, i.e., by discarding self-citations from citation-based metrics.

A related but thornier issue concerns author networks that include significant levels of self-citation. Authors are more likely to cite work that they are familiar with, and they are more likely to be familiar with work conducted by people within their network of friends and associates (Clements and Wang 2003). Of course, everyone has a network, and if these networks are of roughly equal size and status one would expect that network effects to

---

[9] In a case that received significant attention recently, the editor of the high-impact *Perspectives on Psychological Science*, Robert Sternberg, cited his own papers 161 times (46 percent of all citations) in seven articles published in the journal *under his own editorship* (Fried 2018).

cancel each other out. A recent study of economists shows that *relative* citation counts were unaffected when stripped of citations by co-authors and those judged to be within a researcher's network (Orazbayev 2017; discussed in Hamermesh 2018:123). Networks become problematic where they are not equally available to all scholars or, worse, where they are put to strategic use as "citation cartels." We address these concerns in separate sections below.

Non-Citations

A related problem is the *non*-citation, where previous work on a topic is not acknowledged, or not fully acknowledged (i.e., with a formal citation of the sort that might be counted in a citation database). This may occur (a) if there is insufficient space in a journal article to record the provenance of an idea, (b) if an author is trying to emphasize the originality of her own work (by omitting reference to previous work on a subject), (c) if previous work is judged inferior or outdated (and hence not necessary to cite), or (d) if previous work is judged so well-established that it now counts as factual and therefore need not be cited (aka obliteration by incorporation (Merton 1968)).

Bibliometric research on this subject is not sufficiently advanced to discern the relative frequency of these four explanations for non-citations. Evidently, they have very different implications, and impact metrics do not currently provide any means of sorting them out, though it is possible that the development of artificial intelligence will provide an avenue for doing so in the not-too-distant future.

We trust that as impact metrics gain in prominence, authors, reviewers, and editors will come to regard citations as crucial aspects of a research publication, according it the space and seriousness which it deserves, subjecting non-citation to scrutiny, and thus mitigating the problem. We ought to encourage scholars to do a better job in constructing their literature reviews and a more complete job of citing relevant work. An essential component of that encouragement is granting authors sufficient space to cover the field (see Chapter 5, this volume).

Fake Citations, Gaming, and Citation Quality

A potential problem with GS and any other free-range citation database is that it does not distinguish the source of a citation. Anything defined vaguely as "scholarly" is in the catchment area, including papers posted on an author's own web site and working papers posted on other sites that may be unmonitored, or at any rate not subject to peer review. A citation is a citation is a citation.

This is unhelpful, at best, and an invitation to abuse, at worst. Note that authors can, in principle, boost their GS citation counts by posting dozens – or even hundreds – of papers that cite their work (Delgado López-Cózar, Robinson-García, and Torres-Salinas 2014; Gingras 2016: Kindle Location 1739). As noted above, databases that are open only to a curated set of formal publications (e.g., Scopus, WoS) do not face this issue. Where automated databases provide full datasets, such as MA, it is possible to restrict the citation sources included in citation counts to a subset of publications, ameliorating such problems.

As the importance of metrics to scholarly careers increases, so will attempts to "game" the system (Campbell 1979; Muller 2018). That is, scholars will try to achieve the specified target but not in a way that achieves the underlying goals that the target was intended to encourage. "Teaching to the test," is an example of this sort in primary and secondary school systems; but there are many others (Lazear 2006).

Gaming is likely to arise with respect to any metric that is used for purposes of evaluation. If the metric is quantity (number of published papers), canny scholars will divide up their publishing efforts into "minimal publishing units" or re-publish the same ideas in multiple venues (first in a peer reviewed article, then in a book, and subsequently in edited volumes).

Relative to gaming that occurs with other metrics, impact metrics are fairly transparent. We know who is citing whom and where. This means that citations leave a trail that can be investigated. Suppose one suspects that there are "citation cartels" in a field or subfield, i.e., quid-pro-quo agreements among scholars or journals to cite one another.[10] A weak cartel, one that involves just a few errant citations or a few publications, will probably be impossible to detect, but will also have little effect on anyone's impact metric. A strong cartel, by contrast, should be fairly easy to detect, and we can imagine algorithms developed explicitly for this purpose. Consider a network analysis that maps citation patterns across members of a discipline, measuring the strength of each dyadic relationship. Such an analysis can render an expected relationship for every dyad (every pair

---

[10] This flouts the intended function of a citation, i.e., to recognize important work in a field (see discussion at the outset of this section), and renders impact metrics less meaningful.

of members). This can then be evaluated against the actual strength of the relationship. Those dyads that are considerably stronger (e.g., more than one standard deviation) than predicted might be regarded as suspect, i.e., probable cartels.

In this respect, impact metrics are a bit like insider trading in the stock market. We cannot stop such behavior from occurring, but we can frequently detect it after the fact – especially if the behavior is egregious. WoS, the most influential aggregator of impact metrics to date, is already implementing such sanctions on a regular basis (see, e.g., Van Noorden 2013). However, their process is only partially transparent, focused on journals rather than individual researchers, and specific to the WoS index. An openly accessible and transparently constructed list of offenders would be invaluable.

Genre Bias

Certain types of work are more likely to be cited than others, and these patterns may not always accord with our sense of their original contributions to scientific knowledge. For example, methodological studies and reviews of the literature are apt to be more widely cited than works that attempt to make a substantive contribution (Gingras 2016: Kindle Location 1112).

Some might not be alarmed by these well-established citation patterns. If a methodological innovation, or a cogent summary of a complex method, offers useful guidance to a field this might be regarded as an important contribution. Likewise, if a summary of the literature on a subject allows scholars to mark progress, to define the current state of a field, and to point the way to future research, this is surely a valuable contribution. Both of these activities deserve to be recognized and rewarded.

For those who feel that the citation-based rewards for these kinds of contributions are too great it ought to be possible to handicap this sort of work in an impact metric. This requires a classification system that can effectively distinguish between (a) methodological studies, (b) reviews of the literature, and (c) all other work (assumed to be substantive in some fashion). Such classifications might be derived from the orientation of journals (e.g., all articles in *Annual Review* would be easy to classify as literature reviews and all articles in a methods journal would be easily classified as methodological), from the keywords and abstracts that accompany nearly all journal publications, or from discipline-specific classifications (e.g., in economics).

Non-Equivalence across Contexts

Disciplines and sub-disciplines observe different norms with respect to citation practices. Some fields encourage comprehensive citation (law journals are probably the most extreme example) while others insist upon minimal citations, presumably to improve readability or to shorten the length of the text (see Chapter 5, this volume). Additionally, some fields are larger – with more practitioners and more journals – than others. Both factors contribute to widely varying citation counts across fields and (sometimes) subfields.

The problem of non-equivalence is invidious if one is comparing across fields without correction. However, impact metrics offer the possibility of defining impact in a variety of ways. For example, one may calculate citations according to percentiles within a field or subfield. Translated into percentiles, it is then possible to compare across fields. Fields might be broadly defined ("economics") or narrowly defined ("field experiments in development economics"). One might even define specific topics, allowing one to distinguish topics that are widely studied (e.g., "economic growth") from those that are less studied ("fertility") within a discipline.

Of course, there will always be questions about how to define fields and subfields, opening the way for arbitrary manipulation. However, most of the comparisons that are drawn between individual journals, scholars, or departments are within the same field, or closely related fields. Economists are compared to other economists, and development economists to other development economists. So non-equivalence across contexts may not be a very important problem, in practice.

Gender Bias

Citations, like many other parts of academia, perpetuate existing gender biases. In what scholars have dubbed the "Matilda effect" (Rossiter 1993), the female counterpart to the "Matthew effect," women consistently receive less credit for scientific discoveries in both public discourse and among their peers. This effect has been widely demonstrated for citation patterns in the fields of communication (Knobloch-Westerwick and Glynn 2013), international relations (Malinak, Powers, and Walter 2013), and across many disciplines (Larivière et al. 2013) – though perhaps not in economics (Hammermesh 2018).

The causes of these disparate citation patterns are hard to assess, but two issues mentioned previously may contribute. First, researcher networks are not gender-neutral. For example, a study of co-authorship suggests that male political scientists are more likely to co-author with other men (Teele and Thelen 2017). And such male-dominated networks will, of course, produce male-dominated citation patterns. Self-citations are another factor contributing to gender bias in citations. Using large corpora, two different teams of researchers have found that men cite themselves more often than women do, in some disciplines as much as twice as often (Ghiasi, Larivière, and Sugimoto 2016; King et al. 2017). These patterns are troubling for impact-based metrics and there is no simple fix. With effects varying across time and disciplines, there is no single adjustment factor that can be applied, though a reasonable point of departure in a model-based impact factor is a fixed effect for author gender.

Evidently, impact metrics need to be used self-consciously, with an eye to their potential biases. These biases likely go beyond gender and may extend to researcher's race or sexual orientation (we are not aware of studies of the latter). In defense of citation metrics, we would note that there is reason to believe they are *less* biased than other commonly used measures. In a remarkable article, Weisshaar (2017) shows that gender is a strong predictor for whether researchers receive tenure, even controlling for various impact measures, including citation counts.[11] The fact that we can use such – biased – measures of impact and productivity and still detect gender discrimination in current evaluation systems indicates the magnitude of biases inherent in the status quo. This should not distract from impact metrics' weaknesses, but those who oppose them on these grounds need to reckon with the reality that current assessment methods, which are often highly subjective and personalized, may fare even worse.

Clarifications

In this section, we address two dimensions that are commonly conflated with impact metrics. The first is *productivity* and the second is *journal impact*.

Productivity

Impact metrics do not attempt to measure the quantity of scholarly production, i.e., *productivity*. A citation count of 200 might reflect citations gathered by a single study or 100 studies.

---

[11] In fact, while number of publications and publications in a "top journal" were strong predictors, accumulated citations was not.

One might take the position that the quantity of production – of an individual scholar, a journal, a department, a university, or a subfield – is irrelevant. Arguably, a single study that garners 200 citations is equivalent in impact to 100 studies that garner two citations apiece. Even so, for some purposes it is surely important to measure productivity as well as impact.

One approach is to combine these two dimensions into a single metric, such as the well-known h-index. Another approach is to regard quality (proxied by impact) and quantity as separate dimensions, to be measured independently. We generally prefer the latter approach, as there is no easy way to combine these two bits of information into a single index without considerable information loss.

The h-index has several additional flaws that have been often noted but, somehow, do not seem to discourage its proliferation in the academic world. A person's h-index can go up but not down; it is monotonic. This means that it is a poor gauge of over-time performance. A scholar who has not been cited in 30 years will have the same h-index as she did 30 years ago. Second, the h-index rewards individuals whose publication:citation ratio is close to 1, a rather arbitrary feature of academic performance. Third, and relatedly, the h-index tends to reward those who publish incessantly. By contrast, an individual with a few extremely influential publications will have a very low h-index, even if the latter are Nobel-worthy (Gingras 2016:42f.).

In any case, impact measures do not introduce any further complications into what is, at heart, a problem of multi-dimensionality. Reputation-based metrics, for example, face the same dilemma of how to combine quality and quantity.

Journal Impact

Commonly, the quality of a scholar's publications is inferred from the quality of the journals that she publishes in. Indeed, a recent experimental study discovered that the addition of "low-quality" publications to a CV downgrade the perception of a scholar's work, even when the rest of the publications on the CV are the same (Powdthavee et al. 2018).

Nowadays, the most common metric for journal quality is a journal's *impact factor*, derived from citations to articles published in that journal over a period of time (typically two years). While this may be a useful device for librarians needing to make decisions over which journals to subscribe to, it is by no means a reliable proxy for *article* impact (see Larivière et al. 2016 for an excellent summary). While there is a correlation between journal impact factor and citations received by an article in the journal, the correlation is not particularly strong and appears to be decreasing since the 1990s, presumably due to improvements in search technology that effectively separate articles from the journals they appear in (Lozano, Larivière, and Gingras, 2012). Relatedly, the distribution of articles by received citations is strongly left-skewed (the majority of articles even in highly ranked journals receive few citations) so that mean citation counts per journal is a misleading indicator, sensitive to the inclusion/exclusion of one or two widely cited articles.

Even more worrisome, there is strong evidence suggesting that journals have been attempting to "game" their impact factor (Heneberg 2016) as well as the exact criteria used in constructing such measures, in particular what counts as an "article" for the purpose of constructing the denominator of the journal impact factor.

Skepticism of journal impact factors as a tool for research assessment has become more mainstream recently. In 2012, a group of high-impact journals and funders passed the "Declaration on Research Assessment" (DORA 2012), which explicitly discourages the use of journal-level metrics to evaluate scholarship. So far as we can see, the demonstrable weakness of such aggregate measures and related heuristics such as "publication in a top journal" strengthens the case for article- and/or author-level impact metrics.

The Impact of Impact Metrics

If impact metrics are here to stay (and, by all accounts, they are growing in influence), what sort of impact are they likely to have on the production of knowledge? We must consider this matter carefully before making a recommendation in favor of a new standard of excellence, which may have unintended consequences on the activity of scholars. We shall argue that six factors need to be considered: (a) the quest for impactful work, (b) the publication process, (c) efficiency, (d) flexibility, (e) meritocracy, and (f) democracy and reliability.

Impactful Work

Insofar as citation counts drive the academic business, scholars will presumably seek to write articles and books that have broad impact. What sort of work might this be?

We presume that narrowly pitched empirical exercises are unlikely to have much impact on a field, even if published in a top venue – unless they have a surprising finding. The effect of this reorientation of scholarship is likely to further discourage replication, a problem that we have discussed at length in this section of the book. And it may prompt scholars to push their arguments further than the evidence allows or to engage in shenanigans to pass arbitrary hurdles of statistical significance. These must be counted on the negative side of the ledger, though they could be countered by other proposals discussed in this volume – to subject confirmatory studies to pre-registration (see Chapters 7 and 9), to develop mechanisms for incentivizing and publicizing replication studies (see Chapters 10–11, 13), and so forth.

On the positive side of the ledger, exploratory work (i.e., work that propounds new theories or approaches) should be more widely appreciated. Work that is synthetic – theoretically and/or empirically – ought to be more widely appreciated. Finally, work that requires enormous investments of time and/or money, perhaps involving large teams of researchers and a long time-line, is more likely to be appreciated. In these respects, we can expect that highly ambitious work will be rewarded, and perhaps undertaken with greater frequency.

Likewise, one may anticipate that work that is highly redundant – overlapping with extant work – will be avoided. Note that insofar as impact displaces quantity as a measure of academic success, one synthetic paper that receives 1,000 citations is as valuable as ten papers receiving 100 citations each. Thus, there is no incentive to reduce ideas to the smallest publishable unit or to republish work in near-identical form in multiple venues.

The Publication Process

In a world where post-publication success (judged by impact metrics) is valued over the status of the journal or press in which a manuscript is published one can imagine that the vetting process for these gatekeeping venues might be adjusted.

The current process is long (often lasting a year or more for one venue and several years if the first submission is unsuccessful), time-consuming (for authors, reviewers, and editors), stressful (for authors), and intrusive (insofar as it imposes upon the author a particular way of presenting her work, so as to please editors and reviewers). None of these features is desirable, on its face, though all might be defended if they serve to produce a better product.

However, even if the product is improved by all of this back-and-forth (a case that is by no means clear), it matters less if the ultimate arbiter of success is impact metrics rather than the status of the venue in which an article or book appears. In this scenario, the main job of journals and presses – considered as a whole – is to distinguish between work that is publishable and work that is not sufficiently worthy to be publishable. A secondary, but much less important, question is to decide upon the particular journal or press that a manuscript appears in, thus serving as an initial signal of its quality. Insofar as post-publication impact displaces journal or press reputation in the evaluation of scholarly work, the secondary goal is diminished. Scholars will care most about getting their work out, and obsess less about the imprimatur of the venue.

This, in turn, should encourage journals and presses to render up or down decisions fairly quickly about whether or not to publish a manuscript so that endless hours of precious time are not wasted in the vetting process and so that work reaches the public in a timely fashion. Authors already consider time-under-review as a criterion of journal selection; we can anticipate that this will become an even more important consideration in a world where journal prestige has less value in the academic marketplace.

Efficiency

Developing new impact metrics is a task that a few individuals (presumably well-versed in bibliometrics) can perform for the entire academy. Learning how to use them is a one-time investment that everyone will need to make. Collecting the data necessary for calculating these impact metrics (assuming a well-developed open-source citation database is developed, as discussed in the previous section) is automatic, as are periodic updates. By way of contrast, other metrics that have come to govern academic life are often extraordinarily time-consuming to collect and to maintain, feeding the growth of administrative staff that suck up university resources and faculty time (Muller 2018:chapter 7). Finally, the application of impact metrics to gatekeeping tasks is fairly easy.

Impact metrics are therefore a highly efficient mode of evaluation. This, in turn, should relieve burdens on decisionmakers – researchers, administrators, government officials – so they can get on with other tasks (e.g., research and teaching). Too often, debates about academic production are carried on without reference to opportunity costs. Evaluation, like any other activity, takes time, and the time spent on this activity is not directly productive. Insofar as impact metrics save us time, enhancing efficiencies in the production of knowledge, this should be counted as a blessing.

Flexibility

Readers should appreciate the enormous flexibility of impact measures, which can be weighted, aggregated, and denominated in various ways, providing a tool that can be adapted for a wide variety of purposes. One can discount the number of citations received by an individual, a study, or an academic institution by the quality of the source (the journal/press or publication) – which, itself, can be benchmarked by its citation count or by its network centrality (West and Vilhena 2014). One can discount the number of citations by their total, e.g., by a logarithmic transformation. (This helps to overcome the extreme skewness of citation counts (Hamermesh 2018), though it may be wondered whether, on substantive grounds, the tenth citation should be viewed as less valuable than the one-thousandth.) One can discount citations by the number of co-authors of a study. One can transform raw citations into percentiles based on overall citations for a field, subfield, discipline, country, or some other unit, generating an adjusted index that is (arguably) more equivalent across diverse contexts. On the assumption that there is a persistent gender bias in academe, one may construct model-based impact metrics that include a gender dummy.

In this fashion, many potential biases can be dealt with in statistical models. Of course, these models are only as strong as the assumptions that go into them. Nonetheless, they offer a practical recourse to problems that are widely recognized and measurable.

One can also move beyond traditional academic sources to gauge the impact of a work *outside* the academy by registering comments, ratings, re-Tweets, Facebook likes, Pinterest shares, bookmarks, and microblogging from social media or views and downloads from repositories such as Mendeley, Academia, and ResearchGate – a new area known *alternative metrics*, or *altmetrics* (Costas et al. 2014; Priem 2014).

Ultimately, one would hope to go further, to measure the impact of academic work on decision-makers. A recent report points out,

Evidence of external impacts can take a number of forms – references to, citations of or discussion of an academic or their work; in a practitioner or commercial document; in media or specialist media outlets; in the records of meetings, conferences, seminars, working groups and other interchanges; in the speeches or statements of authoritative actors; or via inclusions or referencing or weblinks to research documents in an external organisation's websites or intranets; in the funding, commissioning or contracting of research or research-based consultancy from university teams or academics; and in the direct involvement of academics in decision-making in government agencies, government or professional advisory committees, business corporations or interest groups, and trade unions, charities or other civil society organisations. (Wilsdon et al. 2015:46)

We have so far considered only a single article-level metric: the count of citations it has received. This is not for a lack of options. Looking at author impact, Wildgaard et al. (2014) identify 108 different indicators and the number has likely grown significantly since. Several of the concerns with impact measures noted above, such as the quality of citations and concerns about gaming the system, are particularly sensitive to crude measure such as absolute citation counts. Even simple corrections, such as excluding self-citations, can help to alleviate some of the problems, and more sophisticated measures can provide significant improvements.

The most promising measures, in our opinion, are *network-based*. These metrics assess the position of an article (or an author) in the network of all academic citations. In this fashion, they are able to register not just citation counts but also whether a study is cited by other influential studies and whether it is cited outside a narrow set of scholars working on a very specific topic. This methodology will be most familiar to readers from the PageRank application that underlies the Google search engine. One promising implementation, built with data from MA, is the Author Level Eigenfactor, or ALEF (Wesley-Smith, Bergstrom, and West 2016). Particularly intriguing is the suggestion in a subsequent paper from the same working group (Portenoy, Hullman, and West 2016) to graph authors' influence networks, which depict a multi-dimensional picture rather than a single score.

Granted, the flexibility of impact metrics also complicates their usage. There is no single statistic that will serve all purposes and overcome all difficulties. Instead, there are a variety of statistics – and many more that are likely to be developed in the coming years – that serve a variety of purposes. End-users must pick and choose carefully, and this opens the way for abuse. One such abuse is the over-reliance on individual metrics such as the h-index, whose flaws we have touched upon. Even so, we regard flexibility as a virtue, and we expect that, over time, a small number of metrics will come to be widely used, their strengths and weakness will be well-understood, and hence less liable to abuse.

Meritocracy

One of the flaws of reputational metrics is that evaluations of studies, individuals, departments, universities, journals, and presses bleed into one another. The reputation of one feature affects the reputation of another. For example, the reputation of a scholar is, in part, derived from her university, while the reputation of a university is, in part, derived from the scholars who teach there. The same is true for journals, presses, and subfields. Everything is endogenous to everything else. That is, the reputation of each element of a discipline is dependent on the reputations of all the other elements of a discipline.

Consequently, reputational evaluations are highly ambiguous. It is not clear what they represent, aside from an overall judgment of reputation. Additionally, because institutions are generally more well-known than individuals, institutional reputations tend to overshadow individual reputations. We are familiar with the top departments and journals in our field; we are less familiar with the individuals who work in the top departments or the articles that appear in top journals. Consequently, the latter are evaluated – reputationally – by their location. Scholar A must be top since she is in a top department; Article B must be top since it appears in a top journal. A similar logic applies to those individuals and articles who are not highly placed; they are downgraded by their association with institutions that have a lesser reputation.

Finally, these institutional reputations are sticky, for there is nothing – other than overall reputation – to cause them to rise or fall. Reputations are self-perpetuating. Harvard is top because it is Harvard, and whatever it does, and whomever is associated with it, becomes top.

Impact metrics, by contrast, allow for *independent* judgments of each unit – studies, individuals, departments, universities, journals, presses, and so forth. Each can be judged by its impact on a subfield, a discipline, or the social sciences at-large. Each varies independently, which means that a study, a scholar, a department, a university, a journal, or a press may rise or fall in impact over time and their fate is not linked (or at least not closely linked) to other institutions and individuals.

In these respects, an impact-based system of evaluation is considerably more meritocratic than a reputational system. High-performing individuals within low-performing departments receive their due. High-performing articles within low-performing journals receive their due. And so forth. It means that individuals and institutions at the top of the pecking order cannot sit on their laurels, and individuals and institutions at the bottom of the order need not remain forever in the basement.

If impact metrics are highly valued, emphasis should shift from the rank of the journal or press that a study was published in to the impact that study has achieved. Ultimately, who cares if an article (book) was published in a top journal (press) or a bottom journal (press)? Likewise, when evaluating an individual scholar we should be concerned primarily with *what* she has published and the impact that work has had – not *where* the work was published or what department or university she belongs to. Impact should trump reputation. Alternately framed, impact should drive reputation.

Of course, impact metrics do not mean that units – studies, individuals, departments, universities, journals, and presses – are *entirely* independent. The imprimatur of a publication venue and a scholar's institutional affiliation will always have some effect on the impact of a published work. Nonetheless, over time, one can hope that the arguments and evidence contained in a strong publication will outweigh the reputational effects of its venue and its author. Hamermesh (2018:151) finds that "many economists at lower-ranked faculties ... are cited more than the median faculty members at higher-ranked schools," suggesting a high degree of independence between the fate of an article and the institutional affiliation of its author. Likewise, a study of journal impact factors and the impact of articles published in those journals shows that the relationship began to weaken at the end of the twentieth century in response – one presumes – to the accessibility of articles online, which effectively removes the journal as a publishing unit, allowing readers to access articles individually (Lozano, Larivière, and Gingras 2012).

Insofar as we value meritocratic principles in the academy this ought to be pleasing. And insofar as meritocratic principles affect incentives – for those at the top as well as for those at the bottom – we should anticipate that this more meritocratic method of assessment will boost academic production overall.

Democracy and Reliability

Intertwined with the question of meritocracy is the question of democracy and reliability. In any discipline, there are a few top journals, presses, departments, and funders. These top units play a critical role in the production of knowledge, serving as gatekeepers for the most desirable positions, publications, awards, grants, and fellowships. To a remarkable extent, membership in these elite institutions overlaps, or rotates, among a small elite such that decisions affecting everyone in the academy are monopolized by a few.

To some extent, this can be justified as the product of a thoroughgoing meritocracy, where the most capable members rise to the top. Surely, no one would advocate that evaluations of manuscripts, grant and fellowship proposals, and candidates for awards, jobs, and promotion be divvied out to members chosen by lot or surveyed collectively. It is the opinions of top experts that should matter most in these determinations, and not everyone is equally informed – especially in areas of academic work that are highly specialized.

However, the current system of scholarly evaluation is top-heavy in a way that cannot be entirely justified on the basis of expertise. Positions play an important role. For example, in seeking outside reviewers for academic promotion and tenure universities will often stipulate that evaluators be situated in "peer or peer plus" institutions. Position trumps achievement, in other words. One suspects that similar considerations apply, albeit in more informal ways, to other gatekeeping tasks. On editorial boards, one finds a familiar collection of names – *eminenti* whose role is primarily to enhance the status of the journal or press, but who are nonetheless in a position to determine publication decisions of an important journal or press. Grants and fellowships are meted out to the already-famous, presumably to enhance the status of the grant or fellowship rather than to advance scientific progress. Meanwhile, the talents of scholars at lesser institutions are under-employed.

It is difficult to defend such a system as being in the long-run interests of knowledge production. It is neither efficient nor fair. Nor does it offer encouragement to scholars who are outside the top elite to improve their game, as one's position in the hierarchy is likely to be determined quite early in one's professional career, after which it is difficult to alter.

Even if the current system were entirely meritocratic, it is highly susceptible to stochastic error. When evaluating a study (e.g., for a journal or press) or a candidate (e.g., for a job, fellowship, or grant), opinions among social scientists are apt to vary. Reviews of the same manuscript are often at odds with one another; reviews of the same applicant, e.g., by members of a search committee, are often at odds with one another. This is why we often cite the "luck of the draw" when a paper, grant/fellowship proposal, or a job application is accepted or rejected.

These outcomes are stochastic not simply because there is disagreement among vetters but also, perhaps more importantly, because the pool of vetters is extremely small. Most decision-points in an academic career depend upon a small number of gatekeepers, who render a decision at a particular point in time. Decisions about hiring are made by the hiring committees of a handful of departments who have positions to fill in one's field. Decisions about publication are made by an editor along with a few reviewers. Likewise, decisions about grants and fellowships are made by a small panel, perhaps supplemented by an external review(s).

A core axiom of probability theory is that small samples produce unreliable results. We experience this unreliability at virtually every step of an academic career. In this light, a principal blessing of impact metrics is that they enlarge the pool of vetters, i.e., the number of experts who render a judgment about a given study. By enlarging the pool, impact metrics thus democratize the process of academic evaluation while enhancing its reliability.

Importantly, participants are not chosen randomly; they are restricted to those who can be presumed to know something about the work in question. They are experts, by virtue of having published on a subject. In this fashion, the fate of a study, a researcher, or any other unit of interest rests with the entire academic community – delegated to those who are experts in the relevant area – rather than with a handful of individuals who happen to control top journals, presses, and departments at a particular point in time.

Conclusions

In the first section of this chapter, we pointed out that extant citation databases – GS, Scopus, WoS, and MA – are prone to error (especially with respect to identifying authors), under-sourced (books, in particular, are often not included), and for the most part closed-source (and thus not fully transparent or fully adaptable to the many functions they might serve). We believe that these flaws are likely to be corrected in the near future as these databases (or at least one of them) expand their coverage, improve their algorithms, and shift to open-source. Until that point, we have reservations about the use of impact metrics as an evaluative tool.

In the second section, we carefully reviewed other objections to the use of impact metrics. We acknowledged that there are many problems with the way impact metrics are currently employed. For example, the two most common metrics, citation totals and h-index scores, reveal some important information but can also mislead, especially if one is comparing scholars from different fields and subfields or at different points in their career. We need a broader array of impact metrics, suitable for different purposes, and the community of end-users needs to be acquainted with the uses and possible abuses of each metric. These are not insurmountable obstacles, but they should not be taken lightly.

In the third section, we clarified the distinction between impact metrics and other subjects that are frequently conflated such as productivity (the number of studies a scholar or institution has produced). Likewise, metrics that attempt to combine impact and productivity – such as the h-index – are merging dimensions that are often poorly correlated and thus difficult to combine without bias.

In the final section of the chapter, we discussed the probable impact on scholarship of the increasing role of impact metrics. We reasoned that the rise of this new metric should enhance incentives to produce impactful work, which means that highly ambitious projects should receive their due. By the same token, scholarship that aims for incremental gains, e.g., through replications of extant work, might be given short shrift. We reasoned that the role of publishers as principal gatekeepers in the production of knowledge would be downplayed. An implication is that the publishing process might become more efficient and less stressful. We reasoned that the use of impact metrics might enhance the efficiency of judgments about scholarly achievement, freeing up time to spend on other matters such as research and teaching. We reasoned that impact metrics offer enormous flexibility in the sorts of comparisons that can be drawn and the sorts of impacts – extending, ultimately, to the "real world" – that might be measured. We reasoned, finally, that the use of impact metrics would make the academic world somewhat more meritocratic and more democratic.

Before concluding, it is important to recognize that impact metrics share the strengths and weaknesses of all statistics. A measure of democracy, of corruption, of gross domestic product, or any other concept is useful if it is used responsibly, with an understanding of its limitations. Too often, these metrics are treated as precise or are given an overly broad interpretation. Too often, statistics serve as a substitute for deliberation.

Fourcade and Healy (2017:294), argue that even "[a]mateurish or barely defensible data collection and ranking schemes turn out to have the capacity to control the status order of professional fields, partly just in virtue of their quantitative character." They also point out that such measures allow for and drive the increasing commodification of a sector; by assigning "value," they allow for "Seeing like a market" (Fourcade and Healy 2016). An oft-cited example is the effect of the *US News* ranking on the behavior of law schools, which went to considerable lengths to improve their relative ranking through activities guaranteed to be ineffectual in improving instruction or research (Espeland and Sauder 2016). Lawrence (2007) makes this argument explicitly about the incentives created by a reliance on impact factors in the evaluation of science ranging from overhyping of research results to an emphasis on networking over research. While we disagree with some of his concerns (and have addressed them throughout this chapter), we share concerns about over-reliance on metrics or their mindless application.

But to say that metrics are abused is not to say that we would be better off without them. The question to be asked of any tool is not whether it is good or bad but whether it assists in accomplishing the tasks at hand, taking into account other tools that might be used for that purpose and the overall efficiency of the enterprise.

With respect to metrics of academic performance, the principal alternatives are grounded in *reputation* (surveys of scholars about the standing of particular journals, departments, or schools), *quantity* (the number of published articles and books), or some admixture of the two. We find these metrics informative and perhaps essential for some purposes, but also limited in applicability and insight. Reputational measures may be applied to institutions but not to individuals. Measures of quantity may be applied to individuals but only to some institutions. (One cannot judge a journal by the quantity of articles published.) Neither approach offers a direct measure of scholarly impact. The other alternative is *peer review*, i.e., reading the studies produced by an individual, department, journal, or field, and reaching conclusions based on that reading. This approach, while absolutely essential in many contexts, is time-consuming, subjective, and incapable of rendering systematic comparisons. All existing methods of evaluation are prone to abuse, e.g., gaming (by researchers) or bias (of evaluators). Reputation and peer review seem especially prone to biases grounded in gender, race, or school networks.

When considered in light of the alternatives, impact metrics have much to offer. Our first proposal, therefore, is that social scientists make full use of this class of metrics. Insofar as they can assist in decisions about hiring and promotion, the allocation of resources, and other gatekeeping functions they ought to be a part of our toolkit – as a supplement, not a replacement, for other methods.

Our second proposal is to push for the development of better citation databases, and a wider class of impact metrics, so that flaws in currently available metrics can be overcome. The major technical obstacle is the database, discussed in the first section. Once that issue is solved – ideally by an open, freely available citation corpus rather than a proprietary black box – it should be possible to construct new metrics that overcome some of the oft-noted deficiencies of extant metrics.

Our third proposal is to use impact metrics appropriately. If, for example, one is interested in evaluating the impact of a journal, it is appropriate to examine journal impact metrics (aka factors). If one is interested in evaluating the impact of an article, it is appropriate to examine article impact metrics, and so forth. By contrast, it does not make sense to assume that *journal* impact factor is a proxy for *article* impact, or that a scholar's impact can be inferred from the impact of the journals she has published in.

Our fourth proposal is to make more use of network-based citation networks such as the author-level eigenfactor. These algorithms incorporate not just citation counts for a study but also the importance and breadth of the locations in which a given study is cited. This provides a deeper measure of impact and one less prone to gaming.

Part V

Diversity

Diversity has come to be regarded as a general goal applicable to all occupations, especially those with considerable power and status. For political leaders and top bureaucrats, business leaders, professionals, police and armed forces we are inclined to wonder whether these occupational groups, as a whole, represent the societies they are intended to serve. Representativeness may be judged according to demographic characteristics (e.g., race, ethnicity, religion, gender) and/or ideational characteristics (values, ideology, issue-positions).

It is a big subject, to be sure, and at first glance it may not be obvious what the goal of diversity has to do with the business of social science.

To begin, there is an issue of fairness. If certain classes of people are not well-represented in the academe that is grounds for concern that they might face some degree of discrimination. Bear in mind that the journey to a full-time academic job is a long one with many hurdles along the way. If members of a group are not reaching the finish line it could be that their progress is hindered at any stage of the educational or vocational journey. Arguably, the greatest hurdles lie prior to admission to graduate school, which means the subject lies somewhat outside the rubric of this volume (which focuses on academic disciplines rather than the societies with which they are situated). Alternatively, one might interpret under-representation for a social group as a choice. After all, academics is not the most well-remunerated occupation for those with advanced degrees.

A second issue concerns the functioning of social science. Insofar as social science is charged with the study of society, that study must be informed by society. Only by reference to society can it be determined in what an important problem, or a viable solution to a problem, might consist. The various normative goals that orient the project of social science – e.g., equality, democracy, well-being – matter because they are presumed to matter for citizens. When citizens change their views of a good society, social science must also adjust its focus to encompass those views. As an example, one might consider the rise of equality as a guiding norm for social science. A century ago, living in a less egalitarian age, most social scientists did not orient their research around this goal – or they had a more restricted view of what equality meant or should mean, limited largely to white men. Today, all this has changed, arguably in response to changing norms within society. We do not mean to suggest that social scientists merely reflect society; surely, they also shape it. The point, rather, is that social science does not exist apart from society; it gains its meaning and orientation – and importance – from society. (By contrast, the conduct of natural science is more independent of society, even if never fully independent.)

It follows that if social scientists do not represent society, at least in some respects, they are likely to be hampered in their ability to study society. They will not choose topics of interest to many members of society. They will not be able to understand certain aspects of society. And they will be unable to identify solutions that work. Their views and perspectives will be partial.

One can look back to an age when social science was monopolized by white men from privileged backgrounds, most of whom held fairly conservative views, as an example of this partiality. It is more difficult to see the blindfolds that now inhibit our work. But it seems likely that such blindfolds exist insofar as members of the academy do not represent the societies they aim to study.

Thus, diversity matters, both by reason of our commitment to fairness and by reason of our commitment to social science. In this section of the book we explore two arenas of diversity. The first concerns ideological diversity (Chapter 16) and the second gender diversity (Chapter 17). In a longer book, we would have certainly included a discussion of other dimensions – racial, ethnic, economic, and so forth. Even so, we hope that these discussions point the way to a fuller vetting of these subjects.

16 What's Wrong with Replicating the Old Boys' Networks?

Dawn Langan Teele

Things were supposed to be different for my generation. Old arguments about women not having the necessary credentials – prestigious internships, professional school degrees, and a decent amount of on-the-job experience – or about the rational economic basis of wage disparities due to time out of the labor force – have become increasingly tenuous as American women surpassed men in higher education, and as the highest ever number of women remained in the workforce even during key childbearing years.[1] And yet in every industry and most cultural domains, the old boys' network remains firmly in place.[2] The academic professions, and the social sciences in particular, are no exception. This chapter reflects on the power dynamics and everyday practices that reproduce the gender hierarchy in academia. Although women's experiences may be similar across institutions, I focus primarily on some of the major gender disparities in research universities, as the dual imperatives to publish and contribute to university life lead to a narrative that, especially for women, academia is not compatible with other pursuits like marriage and inter-generational care.[3]

---

[1] As Goldin et al. (2006) show, since 1960 women have been slightly more likely than men to receive a BA (figure 2); women born later in the century who would have been 30 around 2000 were twice as likely to be employed full-time than women earlier in the century (table 5). By 2000, women were as likely to have had high-school-level courses in math and science, and were more likely to have taken high-school-level chemistry (figure 5).

[2] For a sense of the persistence of the old boys' network in other fields, see #timesup – in film, women are dramatically under-represented among directors, and female megastars are under-paid vis-à-vis male stars. In Fortune-500 companies, women made up only 4 percent of CEOs in 2016 (Zarya 2016). In law, women are 44 percent of associates, but only 21.5 percent of income partners and 18 percent of equity partners. Notably, 100 percent of firms with both men and women report that their top-paid partner is a man (Rikleen 2015:2–3). Across occupations, pharmacy appears to be the sole exception: it has the smallest gender wage gap and also has smaller racial and ethnic wage differentials than any other field that requires a college degree (Goldin and Katz 2016:732).

[3] See Ward and Wolf-Wendel (2012) on the "narratives of constraint" in academia. Chapter 7 in their book considers work-life issues for women in non-research universities.

Anyone who has thought about power understands that people who have to constantly justify their presence in a particular setting obviously don't have much of it. When multiple people carrying similarly identifiable ascriptive characteristics find themselves in this situation, there is a sense among them and among non-group members that they do not belong.[4] Feminist and anti-racist theorists describe this phenomenon with reference to an unexamined norm about which type of person rightfully circulates through certain institutions, creating a group that is "unmarked" by difference. The flip side of this is of course the "marked" groups, those that stand out because of the obvious ways that they deviate from the standard.

With some exceptions, institutions of higher education excluded women, Jews, and people of color until the 1970s, and this history of exclusion has rendered the unmarked group in colleges and universities white men of European origin.[5] In the recent and more distant past, the cultural traditions, social services, and curricula of these institutions were designed with this group in mind. Everyone else, including white women, was understood as non-traditional students for whom it was and is necessary to make special accommodations. Special accommodations for marked groups have included, but are not limited to, separate dorms, ladies' bathrooms, the hiring of professors with similar gender/race profiles, the creation of supplementary tutoring and writing centers, and a push to teach subjects outside of the Western canon. Given the very different demographic faces of colleges and universities today, it makes sense that we should have experienced some growing pains on the path toward inclusion. But, as should be clear to anyone following stories of how campuses handle sexual assault cases (by athletes, by fraternity brothers, and by acquaintances), universities regularly shield their traditional constituents from social and legal sanctions.[6] The same is true,

---

[4] There are robust debates about whether people with similar ascriptive characteristics (like gender presentation) are actually members of a "group," but many scholars draw on Conover (1988:53), who argues that group consciousness – a politicized awareness of membership and commitment to collective action – requires a non-trivial number of people to identify with a group.

[5] For a highly readable account of coeducational reforms in the Ivy League, see Malkiel (2016). Interestingly, the Ivies were not among the first to experiment with mixed-gender education, but once they transitioned most other schools followed suit.

[6] See Sanday's (1990) book on campus sexual assault, which argues in line with her earlier work that social groups that isolate men from women produce more violence toward women, and which documents universities' turgid disciplinary structures. See too the recent documentary "The Hunting Ground." Recent investigations into campus assault at Columbia and Barnard, under the "SHIFT" program, found that by senior year, 36 percent of female undergraduates had experienced some form of sexual assault compared with almost 16 percent of male undergraduates. Mellins et al. (2017:table 2).

as we have learned recently, for faculty members, even those whose sexually predatory behavior has long been an open secret.[7] Even though women in the United States have now surpassed men in earning bachelors' degrees, the university setting is still a place where gender inequality prevails.[8]

In the following pages I describe a series of interconnected institutional practices that proscribe gender roles in the academy and cement women's inferior status. These practices include all the nuts and bolts of teaching and mentorship – from selection of readings for syllabi to the formation of collaborative research teams – as well as the implicit and explicit biases that limit the recognition of women's work – including the citation of sources in scholarly bibliographies and implicit assumptions about who contributed what to group work. Finally, I describe how practices of performance evaluation, compensation, and opportunities to engage in university leadership that are integral to the way that research universities conduct business almost guarantee the continued exploitation of women in academia.[9] Although there are some open research questions, the evidentiary body of work that I draw on is enormous, and paints a very clear picture of systematic exclusion. Readers can consult the footnotes for very detailed descriptions of the research on which I draw. In the penultimate section, I address the prospects of diversity in the social sciences moving forward and describe ways in which academics and university personnel might constructively work to upend gender domination in our disciplines. In the conclusion I argue that replicating the old boys' network is not only a problem of justice, but also one that impedes knowledge.

Women in the Academic Pipeline

Higher education first blossomed in the United States in the late nineteenth century, and in the early phases of expansion some women were present. In

---

[7] www.chronicle.com/interactives/harvard-harassment.
[8] Goldin et al. (2006:figures 2 and 3) actually argue that women were as likely to be enrolled in college and receive bachelors' degrees until after the 1915 birth cohort. The low point in women's representation in college came in 1947. Thereafter, the male-to-female ratio fell, reaching parity in the late 1960s. Today, women outnumber men in college.
[9] The term exploitation is appropriate, in its technical sense, for two reasons. First, universities' prestige comes from the research, teaching, and service activities of its faculty, but they achieve prestige by under-paying female faculty (and support staff) and by relying on a large academic precariat that is mostly female to carry many these burdens. Second, because of the gender pay gap, academic institutions contribute to the persistence of women's exploitation in the home. See Folbre (1982) for a discussion of how this operates within capitalism more generally.

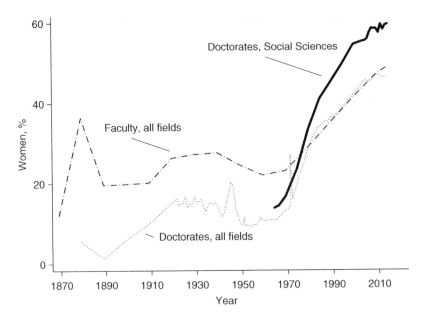

Figure 16.1 Women's representation among faculty and doctoral recipients, 1870–2015

Percent of women among all faculty in post-secondary degree-granting institutions (dash-dot), among doctoral recipients in all fields (dot), and doctoral recipients within all social science fields.

Source: author's calculations using NSF Survey of earned doctorates 2004–2007 and the Digest of Education Statistics (Snyder et al. 2016).

1869, American degree-granting post-secondary institutions employed 5,553 individual faculty, 12 percent of whom were women. A decade later, when the size of universities doubled, women made up 36.4 percent of the faculty. From 1889 until 1989 – that is, for a century – women held between 20 and 30 percent of all faculty positions; thereafter, their presence soared, reaching 49 percent by 2014. Thus, it is fair to say that women were not a major part of post-secondary institutions until the late 1970s.[10]

Figure 16.1 presents the long historical picture of women's representation in higher education, plotting the percent of women among doctoral recipients in all fields, the percent of women among faculty in all fields, and, for the 1960s onwards, women's share of social science doctorates.[11] In the early

---

[10] The Digest of Education Statistics (Snyder et al. 2016:table 301.20) provides a historical summary of faculty, enrollment, degrees conferred, and finances in degree-granting post-secondary institutions for selected years from 1869–1870 through 2014–2015. Importantly, faculty employment is recorded based on the number of individuals, not full-time equivalents (FTEs).

[11] NSF Survey of earned doctorates 2004–2007. The 2004 edition, tables 5 and 7, records doctorates by sex and major field going back to 1974.

twentieth century the number of doctorates issued was relatively small – from 54 in 1879 (women were 5.6 percent), growing to 615 in 1919 (where women were 15.1 percent). Until 1975, women held fewer than 20 percent of all new doctorates. Thereafter, with a growth of slightly less than a percentage point per year, women reached 2014 earning 46 percent of all doctorates.

The several disciplines within the social sciences have varied in their level of openness to women (see Figure 16.2, top). Among undergraduates, sociology and anthropology graduate a disproportionate number of women – something like 70 percent of all bachelors' degrees in from 2000 to 2015 were earned by women– while political science is at parity. The dismal science has, it would seem, struggled the most to recruit female undergraduates: somewhere between 33 and 30 percent of all undergraduate majors are women, with a small decline since the turn of the century. Doctoral degrees awarded to women follow a similar pattern, albeit with a downward shift in the share of women in all fields (Figure 16.2, bottom). Between 30 and 35 percent of PhDs awarded in economics are to women, in political science it is nearer 40 percent, and in sociology and anthropology around 60 percent of PhDs granted in the past 10 years have been to women. Although some disciplines do not reach parity, and others over-represent women, most of the social sciences are appealing to female undergraduates and graduate PhDs, suggesting a healthy "pipeline" for the academic social sciences.[12]

In the ranks of the professoriate there have been several significant changes in women's representation.[13] Recent data from major academic associations show that among faculty on the tenure ladder, women make up a smaller portion of full professors than associate professors, but there is a large share of women clustered at the untenured ranks. In political science as of 2016, women made up 27 percent of ladder faculty in the 20 largest PhD-granting departments, but were 38 percent of untenured faculty.[14] In economics in 2017, 126 departments with doctoral programs reported that 28.8 percent of assistant professors were women, while women make up 20 percent of all economics faculty on the ladder track.[15] In sociology, despite the fact that women

---

[12] Stock (2017:648) argues that women and minorities have increasingly chosen economics as a second major, suggesting that the pipeline for PhDs in social sciences may be larger than these numbers.

[13] Economics data from 2017 survey and report on the Committee on the Status of Women in the profession, table 1 (AEA 2018). They pertain to 126 PhD-granting departments measured in 2017.

[14] See APSA P-WAM20, and Teele and Thelen (2017:438). Alter et al. (2018) find a similar pattern of higher shares of women at lower ranks in political science for an even larger number of departments than recorded in the P-WAM data.

[15] In 1994, the economics data show that only 12.7 percent of all ladder faculty were women, but at that time women made up 24.2 percent of assistant professors. The comparison with 2017 may not be exact, however, as the 1994 data cover 80 instead of 126 departments, and no weighting is given.

408 Diversity

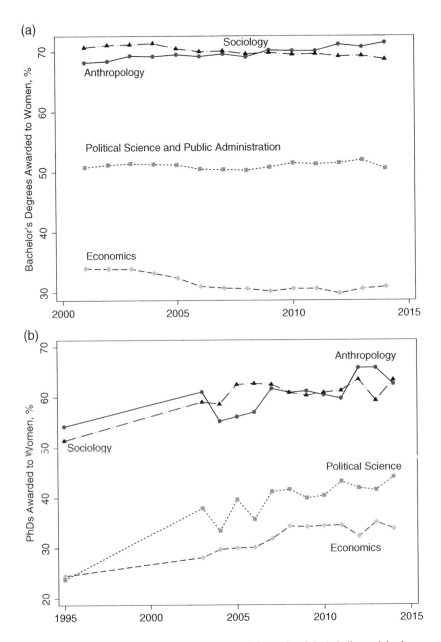

Figure 16.2 Women's representation among undergraduates and doctoral recipients in the social sciences

Percent of women among undergraduate majors (top), and doctoral recipients (bottom), by social science field.

Source: author's calculations from Stock (2017) using the IPEDS survey, and NSF (2018) data on doctorates awarded.

comprise more than 50 percent of members in the discipline, they make up less than 40 percent of most of the top 12 departments, and the 100 top universities still disproportionately hire men (Akbaritabar and Squazzoni 2018). Economics showed a similar pattern where, from 1985 to 2004, the top 50 American economics departments hired on average just four women assistant professors compared to an average of 17 men, with only a slight increase in women hires in 2005 relative to 1985 (Antecol, Bedard, and Stearns 2018).

On the whole, the growth in the share of women that enter as assistant professors is consistent with the gradual advancement of women in the academic profession. Yet there are two concerns. First, as Alter et al. (2018) point out, research universities with very high levels of research output employ the largest number of faculty overall, and, within these universities, full professors make up the largest faculty group. Since the largest gender gap in representation is at the rank of professor, and most of the prestigious positions in the profession go to members of high-output research universities, there are way fewer women in the immediate feeder group for high-status positions.

Second, even though the gender distribution looks more promising at the assistant professor rank, it is no guarantee that the future will be much different. Indeed, women face higher rates of tenure denial in the social sciences. Box-Steffensmeier et al. (2015) track the careers of 2,218 social science faculty that took positions in 19 research universities (public, private, and polytechnic) in seven social science disciplines from 1990 to 2003. Overall, they find that women were less likely to achieve tenure than men.[16] In economics, Antecol, Bedard, and Stearns (2018) present data on tenure rates for men and women in 49 of the top 50 departments in the United States. They show that for men and women who got took their first job from 1980 to 2005 – who vary from being in their 60s to being in their 40s today – average rates of tenure were much higher for men (33 percent) than women (20 percent). For those who took their first jobs in 2005, 35 percent of men earned

---

[16] Looking within academic discipline, Box-Steffensmeier et al. (2015) find that in all fields but psychology, there is a positive correlation between being male and being promoted, though these correlations are only statistically significant for economics (in one specification) and sociology (in two specifications). They do not find differences in the time to full professor for men and women, conditional on having received tenure (figure 4). This research bolsters earlier findings by Kahn (1993:54), who studied tenure differences by gender in the economics field for those who received PhDs from 1971 to 1980. Although time to tenure narrowed in later cohorts, women were more likely to remain untenured many years after receiving a PhD. The Box-Steffensmeier et al. (2015) publication does not addresses tenure differences for racial and ethnic minorities, but Kahn (1993:55) found that in economics, tenure rates were similar for black and Native American faculty as for white faculty. For

tenure compared to 23 percent of women. In the fields of sociology, computer science, and English, Weisshaar (2017:tables 1 and 3) evaluated tenure rates among faculty hired from 2000 to 2004. She randomly sampled 1,500 assistant professors from ranked research universities, over-sampling from the top 30 departments. The raw difference of means suggests that a gender tenure gap exists in all fields both in one's first job and in any position. In sociology (n = 475), 85 percent of men received tenure in any job compared with 78 percent of women. The gender tenure gap is 7.3 percentage points in general and 9.1 percentage points in the first job.[17]

Some might wonder whether gender differences in productivity, or procreative choices, may explain this outcome, but Ginther and Kahn (2004) found that even when controlling for publication, a 17-percent gender gap in tenure rates still persisted in Economics. Weisshaar (2017) finds that gender tenure gap that is unexplained by productivity, years of experience, or departmental characteristics is massive. About 45 percent of the gender tenure gap is unexplained in sociology, 40 percent unexplained in computer science, and 90 percent unexplained in English. These seem like huge differences to pin on talent or some other unobserved characteristic.

Scholars working on the "Do Babies Matter?" literature found that women who had children within five years of completing a PhD were much less likely to receive tenure than men or other women who did not have children in that period.[18] However, Wolfinger et al. (2008) contend that having children did not negatively affect tenure rates for women (table 2; n = 10,845) but rather that having children made it less likely that the female academics would get an initial tenure-track job in the first place (table 1, n = 30,568).[19] It is possible that the gender gap in tenure rates is not due to productivity differences or fertility choices, but instead is related to double standards in the assessment of scholars' work. Indeed, new research suggests that men and women's publication track records may be evaluated differently, with

---

more on racial differences in tenure rates, see the discussion in www.chronicle.com/article/Tenure-Decisions-at-Southern/135754.

[17] In computer science (n = 606) 86 percent of men and 90.5 percent of women received any tenure. There was a gap of 5.7 points in any job and 4.7 points in first job. Finally, in English (n = 478) 86 percent of men and 8 percent of women received tenure in any school. The gap was 6.2 points in the any school and 9 points in the first school. This is in spite of the fact that men in English were slightly more likely to move. Weisshaar (2017:tables 1 and 3).

[18] Mason, Goulden, and Wolfinger (2006).

[19] Wolfinger et al. (2008) studied the procurement of a tenure-track job, time to tenure, and promotion to full tenure for a large random sample from the Survey of Earned Doctorates for those who earned

women getting less credit for collaborative research during tenure decisions (Sarsons 2017).

To summarize, while women's representation among graduate students and early-career faculty in the social sciences has increased over time, most research suggests that there is a big a disparity in women's ability to advance through the career ladder.

Wolfinger et al.'s (2008) findings – that women are less likely to take tenure-track jobs than men – raise the possibility that women find more opportunities for contingent or adjunct work among the academic "precariat." In economics, 36 percent of non-ladder faculty in PhD-granting departments were female in 2017, up from 29.6 percent in 1994.[20] In political science, 33 percent of non-ladder faculty in the top 20 largest PhD-granting departments were female. The fact that women make up a larger share of faculty that are *not* on the ladder than they do of tenure-track faculty suggests that less-prestigious jobs may have fewer barriers to entry for female academics. However, as Kathy Thelen (2019:figure 1) argued in her presidential address to the American Political Science Association in 2018, this is hardly an achievement. The growth of contingent contracts in academia has far outpaced positions in tenure lines. Since these positions are often ineligible for benefits and offer little flexibility and low levels of remuneration, they undergird an academic "precariat" that mirrors the gig-economy more generally.

Departments differ in the degree to which women's representation is achieved through non-ladder faculty appointments. In political science, schools like the University of Michigan stand out, both for the high overall share of women in its academic staff (just shy of 40 percent) and because none of this representation is generated by non-ladder positions. On the other hand, there are schools like Harvard, where seemingly 40 percent of its academic staff in political science is women, but where less than 8 percent of the total are in ladder positions.[21] Both Michigan and Harvard are top departments in political science, yet they have quite distinct patterns of gender representation: one where women are found solely in the more prestigious tenure ladder positions, while the other makes up for tenure-track gender imbalances through non-ladder positions. These different strategies of diversification likely have implications for the culture of these departments

---

PhDs from 1981 to 1985. Women were 21 percent less likely to get tenure and, conditional on being tenured, women are less likely to be promoted to full professor.

[20] The 2017 economics data cover 126 departments, while the 1994 data cover 80 departments.
[21] APSA (2016), P-WAM data.

for faculty and for graduate students, and for the opportunities for women and minorities to succeed.[22]

As we saw in the figures above, the various fields of the social sciences differ in the extent of women's representation among undergraduate students, PhD recipients, and faculty members. Although there have been some notable shifts in the composition of the professoriate, the remainder of this chapter argues that there are two domains in which current academic practices reflexively reproduce white male power: the normative construction of disciplinary centrality and the market-oriented compensation structure of universities. Norms and practices produce differential visibility of scholars' work, and market-oriented compensation structures, which often reward research that fits into dominant constructions of disciplinary centrality, reinforce women's marginality in the academy and, through lower wages, in society writ large.

The Normative Construction of Disciplinary Centrality

Whose work is on the lists of great books? Whose research counts as seminal when we are writing theory sections? Which literatures are cutting-edge and which are outdated? Who is assigned in graduate survey courses? Which references are cut when we are looking to make space in our word counts? Who gets invited to panels? Who gives conference keynotes? The answers to each of these questions go a long way to explaining how men have been and are currently understood as leaders in our fields.

Before describing the construction of disciplinary centrality, it is worth establishing that women have been present and writing in the social sciences for a long time. Figure 16.3 presents data on female authorships in four social science disciplines from 1950 to 2000. It lists the number of times per decade in which a female-gendered name appears in the bylines of research articles catalogued by JSTOR. Several things stand out from this figure. First, in the 1950s, sociology boasted the largest number of female authorships, 1,140, while political science, with 32 female authorships, was the lowest.

---

[22] There is an enormous literature that looks at how descriptive representation of non-dominant groups impacts the aspirations of other non-dominant groups. Many scholars stress that role models impact peoples' sense of belonging in a particular field (e.g., Wolbrecht and Campbell 2007; Beaman et al. 2008; Gilardi 2015). Several studies examine women as role models in education: on educational attainment based on having female high school teachers (Nixon and Robinson 1999); Rask and Bailey (2002) find that when women and minorities took classes with a professor that resembled their ascriptive characteristics, they were more likely to choose that field as a major; Bettinger and Long (2005); Brajer and Gill (2010) found that female business school professors were more likely to respond to female students than male professors.

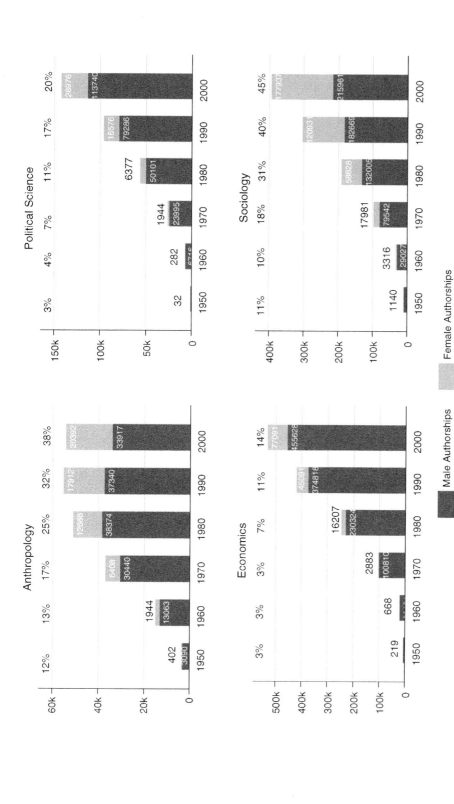

Figure 16.3 Gender and authorships in various social science disciplines, 1950–2000

The figure displays the overall number of authorships in each field by decade, and the gender breakdown of these authorships. The top number on each bar lists female authorships in that decade based on the number of times a discernable female name appears in the byline of a social science journal article as catalogued by JSTOR. The number of non-identifiable names increases over time, so these numbers likely under-state women's authorships.

Source: author's calculations using King et al. (2017)

Second, anthropology and political science experienced rapid growth in female authorships in the 1960s and 1970s, while female authorships in economics and sociology exploded in the 1970s and 1980s. Yet, the rate of growth was much faster in anthropology and in sociology. Finally, the rate at which women publish is not strictly related to market size, or to how many authorships exist in each field: sociology has the second-largest authorship pool and the highest representation of women in its bylines.[23]

Nevertheless, in spite of the fact that many women have worked and published successfully in the social sciences for more than 30 years, and that new research shows that articles written by women have the virtue of more readable prose,[24] research bylined by men populates most of the disciplines' top "generalist" journals in most social science fields,[25] it gets more disciplinary recognition, and dominates the core graduate syllabi in my own field of political science.[26]

Consider the issue of gender diversity on syllabi in political science. Political theory (which consists of political philosophy, history of political thought, critical theory, and normative theory), has the largest share of female scholars of any field in political science, yet it has been critiqued for its attachment to a white male canon.[27] Some might argue that the male (and European-origin) cast of characters that appear in core courses on the "ancients" and the "moderns" is reasonable given that women were not taught to read or write until late in history. And indeed, when we consider the known work of the ancients from Europe this appears to be more or less true (Sappho being the exception).[28] But when we get to modern European and American political thought, the

---

[23] Because Figure 16.2 is describing authorships, rather than unique authors in a discipline, high rates of co-authorship drive up the number of authorships in the y-axis of the bar graph.

[24] Hengel (2017) evaluates 9,123 abstracts from articles published in four top economics journals (AER, *Econometrica*, JPE, and QJE) finding a 1–6-percent gap in readability in favor of women. Women's prose improves in the review process, which Hengel suspects is linked to a higher level of scrutiny applied to women's work. Examining a smaller sample of 2,446 articles published in *Econometrica*, she finds that female-authored papers take six months longer in peer review, likely contributing to the publication gap between men and women (Hengel 2017:figure V).

[25] Teele and Thelen (2017) find that women comprise a much lower share of authors in most top journals than their representation in the discipline as a whole. Articles published in journals like the AJPS and APSR are bylined by women about 19 percent of the time. There is an inverse correlation between the proportion of work that is quantitative that appears in a journal's pages and the proportion of women among authors (Akbaritabar and Squazzoni 2018).

[26] There is an enormous literature on gender citation gaps cited in the footnotes of this text. Recently, Samuels and Teele (2018) find that in political science, books written by women get dramatically fewer citations ten years after publication.

[27] For an elaboration of this critique, see Charles Mills (2014:71), who calls attention to the lack of reflexivity of "white academic philosophy," and Pateman and Mills (2007), who examine social contract theory in light of both gender and racial subordination.

[28] Notably, there is now an entire field of "comparative" political theory that seeks to highlight the intellectual contributions of non-white non-European interlocutors. See Simon (2018) for a review.

absence of female thinkers is more questionable. Responding to this critique, many graduate courses contain secondary scholarship written by women, rendering theory syllabi some of the least gender-segregated in political science (Hardt et al. 2019).

Recent pushes for a more "comparative" political theory have brought non-white and non-Western thinkers into the mix, but most of these figures are great men from other cultures. In other words, there has not been a fundamental mission to re-define the canon, or re-define how canons are constructed, in political theory.[29] Great books classes at the graduate level and core courses for undergraduates do assign Mary Wollstonecraft, and they may also contain pamphlets by the Grimké sisters, or an account of a famous speech given by Sojourner Truth. But many scholars insist that most of the great thinkers or central interlocutors during the Industrial Revolution, belle époque, or Gilded Age that come to mind were men. And yet, scholars who have read the archives of those periods, who have studied the social movements and revolutions of which women formed key parts (abolition, suffrage, moral reform, temperance), now understand that, just as in the present day, women's intellectual contributions – their pamphlets, speeches, and periodicals – have been erased from our histories and political philosophies. The problem, as the renowned historian Karen Offen put it, is not lack of history; it is amnesia.[30]

Amnesia, or perhaps more insidious forces, has also been at play in erasing the contributions of black political thinkers to the field of international relations. As my colleague at the University of Pennsylvania Bob Vitalis shows in his sweeping new history of the field, much of what we now think of as IR actually emerged from the writings of a group of black male professors critiquing the interventionist policies of the early twentieth century. Here too it isn't that nothing has been written by non-white men; it's that what was written was cribbed, without attribution, and then the footprints were systematically covered over.[31] (This erasure was made easier by the exclusion of black people from the faculties of our most prestigious institutions.)

Several recent investigations into the core graduate seminars in political science reveal the prevalence of these behaviors in other political science

---

[29] Although see Simon (2019) for an account of comparative political theory's attempt to bring non-Western thinkers into the conversation.

[30] Offen (2000:17). One need not lower their standards of relevancy: Offen's 400-page magisterial book focuses solely on the writings and political arguments of women that were part of a public debate from 1700 to 1950. The prologue is an excellent and moving introduction to the burying of women's past by the academic field of history.

[31] Vitalis (2015). People also voice concerns in comparative politics and international relations that our fields are too US-centric insofar as we rely on research that emanates from US institutions and American authors. If you are studying another country, are you aware of what authors from that country have written (Robles 1993:526)?

subfields: Hardt et al. (2019) find that 18.7 percent of first authors on graduate syllabi are women, with methods courses boasting the lowest representation of women (around 10 percent of authors taught in methods classes are female). Colgan (2017) culled graduate syllabi in "core" IR courses from 42 US universities, producing a list of 3,343 required-reading assignments. In these core courses, Colgan found male authors wrote 82 percent of assigned readings (the articles were bylined either by a man working alone or an all-male team). In a secondary analysis, Colgan found that when a woman taught the class, 71.5 percent of all assigned readings were authored by men, but when men taught the class, this percentage rose to 79.1.[32]

What does it mean that we don't assign women or people of color in core classes? Several things. It means that early on, students will cite fewer works by women (insofar as they draw on writings they encountered in classes), and that the overall network of thinkers to which students are exposed will have fewer women in them overall.[33] This is because male authors tend to cite women less than do female authors, meaning that if students pursue research by using a man's bibliography as the basis for their work, they will encounter fewer female authors in the process.[34] If one does not encounter women in core courses, comprehensive exam lists, or the bibliographies of research papers and books written by men, then it is easy to assume that women have

---

[32] See also Diament et al. (2018) on syllabi in American politics. Hardt et al. (2018) study 905 PhD syllabi in political science and find that only 19 percent of required readings had female first authors but 28 percent of instructors were women.

[33] Nexon 2013.

[34] Maliniak, Powers, and Walter's (2013) network analysis in the political science sub-discipline of IR shows that women are cited less overall, but especially by men. Mitchell, Lange, and Brus (2013) find that in a top international relations Journal – ISQ – 83 percent of men's citation are to research bylined by just men, while 57 percent of women's citations are to articles bylined by just men (table 2). In ISP, another journal, they find similar citation patterns by men but, with a smaller sample, find women cite more work written by just men. Overall, women are more than twice as likely to cite research by female authors. In economics, Ferber and Brün (2011:table 1) examine the gender citation gap in economics. They differentiate between papers bylined by women (working alone or in pairs), those bylined by men (alone or in pairs), or co-ed teams. In 2008, when women worked alone or with other women, women wrote 12.7 percent of articles they cited. When men worked alone, only 5.9 percent of articles they cited were written by women. Each type of group – men alone, women alone, and co-ed teams – was about as equally likely to cite the work of coed teams (about 13.6 versus 15.6 percent). To put it another way, male authors referred to research in which women participated less than 20 percent of the time, while female authors referred to the work of women 29 percent of the time. Similar patterns emerged in bibliographies of papers in the field of labor economics. As an applied field, labor economics has been home to a high proportion of female economists, and yet men working alone refer to the work of women alone in only 9.4 percent of their citations, while women working with women cite the work of all-women bylines 17.3 percent of the time.

not made intellectual contributions to that field of knowledge. In this way, the gender bias that produced the course lists reproduces itself.

To give a sense of the magnitude of the problem, consider an extraordinary recent paper that examined 1.5 million journal articles published between 1779 and 2011. King et al. (2017) find that, across all fields, about 9.4 percent of references in research articles were self-citations, that is, they referred to previous research of one of the listed authors. But there were big gender differences in these patterns: about 31 percent of articles written by men refer to their own work versus 21 percent of articles written by women, meaning that men were more than 10 percentage points more likely to self-cite. Within the social sciences, men self-cited more in every field: men were 1.36 percent more likely to self-cite in anthropology, 1.43 percent more likely in sociology, 1.58 percent more likely in political science, 1.65 percent more likely in economics. Because women self-cite less than men, and are less likely to be cited by men, one of the key metrics of academic success is downward-biased in women's tenure files.[35]

One final issue that impacts the normative construction of disciplinary centrality has to do with methods. Speaking as a relatively young professor, I would note that amnesia is not only about systematically ignoring the work of non-white, non-male scholars, but also about downplaying the utility of knowledge that has been accumulated by our disciplinary forebears. To some degree, this forgetting is necessary. If we already knew what everyone said, the delusion of originality that is central to writing a dissertation would be impossible to maintain. And indeed, when we start to actually read it does seem like there is nothing new under the sun (or at least, in my field, something that hasn't already been said by Theda Skocpol or Maurice Duverger). But there is perhaps another reason that younger generations brashly ignore the work of the old, and that has to do with method.

So long as social scientists are hoping to uncover "objective" facts, we may be perennially unimpressed by what someone said 20 years ago. New documents, new data, and new methodologies each serve to undermine the work of earlier generations. Nevertheless, even if, methodologically, we no longer believe former scholars' assumptions, we may be likelier to give credence to work from 20 years ago that used numbers and models rather than work that

---

[35] In the political science field of IR, women are less likely to self-cite (Maliniak et al. 2013), and Colgan (2017) shows that women also assign less of their own work in classes. In non-core courses on International Relations, male professors assign 3.18 readings that they authored, on average, while women assign 1.68 readings that they authored. See Hendrix (2015) for a thoughtful analysis of citation indices in political science.

used mere words. This is because academics tend to prize sophisticated statistical and mathematical techniques. Across academic disciplines, some fields are considered to require more "innate" talent than others – in STEM fields this includes math, physics, engineering and computer science, while in the social sciences and humanities philosophy is considered to require the most innate ability (Leslie et al. 2015:figure 1). In general, those fields that require "brilliance" tend to be the most white-male-dominated, while those fields where innate ability is believed to be less important award a much higher share of PhDs to women and to African Americans (Leslie et al. 2015:figures 1 and 2). There is an additional layer of gender divisions within disciplines, where women are more frequently on the applied ends (e.g., labor and development in economics, instead of macro or micro theory), a sorting that can further contribute to the notion of the importance of specific research agendas and the centrality within disciplines.[36]

The path-dependent result of this gendered division of fields and methodology is that fewer women are clustered at the most prestigious ends of the hierarchy. In political science, fewer women run the giant laboratories that are creating multi-authored research articles, and thus the rise in co-authorship that we have witnessed across the discipline has not benefited women equally.[37] This has far-reaching implications for career trajectories, especially if there are no clear standards for how to weight collaborative work against independent research. In addition, because hiring is so competitive, junior people feel the pressure to publish at all costs more acutely than in the past. But to the extent that women have tended to populate the qualitative segments of the discipline, there may be fewer role models and mentors, and higher barriers for junior women to join research teams.

Market-Driven Compensation Structures

A second important way in which the academy reproduces gender domination is through the structure of compensation. Although there is variation in

---

[36] Although women now match men in their level of high-school exposure to math and sciences, it is clear from looking at membership in the American Political Science Association that there is a gendered division of methodology that has put women's work at the qualitative end of the spectrum. This likely influences the degree to which top journals publish work by women, as these journals publish primarily quantitative research (Teele and Thelen 2017).

[37] Teele and Thelen (2017). Rates of co-authorship for women are higher in top sociology journals (Akbaritabar and Squazzoni 2018).

how colleges and universities structure compensation, many institutions pay women less than men, with estimates between 18 and 23 percent, reduced to 5 to 7 percent when experience, rank, and field are taken into account.[38] Monroe and Chiu (2010:306) use AAUP data for all fields and show that the pay gap is worse the more prestigious the university: a 3-percent average pay gap in community colleges reaches 8 percent in Research 1 universities. The gender pay gap, which begins in entry-level assistant professor positions, is reinforced through practices that are not transparent, and can be compounded over an academic's career by biased remunerative structures.[39]

As many scholars have noted, promotion within research-based academic institutions is linked to research productivity (where the quantity, quality, and the impact of research is taken into account).[40] Although pay typically increases through different levels of promotion (from assistant to associate, associate to full), pay is also affected, in many universities, by the existence of "outside options" – job offers from different venues, including universities. Faculty in some fields appear to have a greater tendency to be on the job market and to move (economics in particular seems to be an outlier), but it is not uncommon for faculty to attempt to bid up their salaries by threatening to leave their home institution. To professionals in many fields, this practice may not be surprising or even problematic. But I submit that this practice is

---

[38] Comparable data on only the social sciences are hard to come by, but all research shows that women receive lower salaries. Monroe and Chiu (2010) use data from the American Association of University Professors and find large pay gaps across rank and institution type. In a recent economics paper, Langan (2018) finds a raw salary gap of 23 percent, which reduces to a 7-percent gap once experience, faculty rank, and field are taken into account. Toutkoushian and Conley (2005) report a wage gap of 18 percent by the late 1990s, but argue that the proportion of the wage gap that is "unexplained" by field and seniority was less than 5 percent. Looking across departments, female department heads and assistant deans earn about 85 cents on the male dollar, while for deans this is around 82 cents. The gap attenuated to 91 cents on the dollar among female university presidents, although women held less than 30 percent of these positions in 2016 (see figures 6 and 9 from Bichsel and McChesney 2017). According to McChesney (2017:figures 6 and 7), the pay gap for administrators is worse in the female-to-male comparison than in the minority-to-white pay gap, the latter of which hovers close to parity even in less-prestigious universities. A big part of the problem in the administrator pay gap for women comes from the "middle third" of institutions instead of from the "top" institutions. Note, however, that there are far fewer minority administrators (around 20 percent in 2017) than female administrators (around 50 percent in 2017). See also Carr et al. (2015) on academic medicine.

[39] Women suffer from a gender pay gap in nearly all industries and occupations (Blau and Kahn 2000). (See also footnote 2 of this chapter.) Note that the pay gap is not just about the sorting of women into specific "feminized" occupations that are low-paying, but also about pay gaps within occupations. Goldin (1992) provides the example of librarians, where most in the industry are women, but where the highest-paid librarians (e.g., in the Library of Congress) are men.

[40] The quality of teaching and service also matters, but is given different weights at liberal arts institutions versus research universities.

more problematic in the academy than in other fields due to the geographic particularities of university life – where it can be difficult if not impossible to switch jobs without physically moving to another town or city.

Acquiring an outside offer requires, at least in theory, that someone is willing to move to a new place. Discussions of "moveability" therefore crop up in conversations about hiring. As Rivera (2017) shows in a recent article on hiring practices at research universities, women's marital status and family commitments are discussed at a much higher rate on hiring committees than the marital status of male applicants. Implicit in these discussions is the idea that women's family commitments (or having an employed spouse) will make it more difficult for women to switch institutions.[41] It is an open question whether women are in fact less moveable than men, but to the extent that perceptions of moveability matter for interviewing, they also likely matter for receiving outside offers.[42] In a world where women are believed to be less moveable, they are less likely to succeed in securing a key route to pay raises. If there are gendered differences in the ability to secure leverage in the form of outside options, the damage to women's lives extends well beyond monthly paystubs. Indeed, women's lifetime savings will be lower (both because they have less money to save and because programs with "matching" benefits will contribute lower levels to women's 401Ks), and their research productivity is also likely to be lower.

Unequal access to job opportunities and lower pay can depress women's productivity for two reasons. First, faculty members are often able to use outside offers to argue for higher discretionary research budgets. These budgets allow for travel to conduct research, and enable a variety of research tasks to be carried out by others. Research budgets also allow for faculty to gain exposure by attending workshops, panels, and conferences in other locations. Since visibility is linked to citations and citations are linked to impact, lower research budgets depress women's ability to project disciplinary centrality. Note that although the idea that "women don't ask" has found currency among lean-in feminists, political science researchers found that on many dimensions of bargaining, female faculty were more likely to ask for resources

---

[41] Wolfinger et al. (2008) suggest that geographic constraints are more important for women's career decisions, and female academics are more likely to work in large cities where full-time working spouses can also find work.

[42] Some scholars argue that gender norms produce and reinforce marriages in which men are more successful or earn more than women (Bertrand, Kamenica, and Pan 2015, Schwartz and Gonalons-Pons 2016), and so highly productive women are more likely to have a spouse with a high-powered career than similarly high-powered men.

than men.[43] Persistent disparities in research funds cannot only be pinned on women's lack of chutzpah.

The second way that this market-oriented compensation structure might lower women's productivity is by reducing their ability to outsource domestic labor. With more constrained budgets, female academics likely have to spend more time on household tasks, such as shopping and cleaning, than male acdemics. Since many academics care for others, including children and aging parents, career-related events that happen outside of the normal workweek will require additional coverage. With less income, women may feel the sting of the auxiliary aspects of the academic career particularly acutely. To the extent that male and female academics have similarly demanding travel schedules, the gender pay gap, which renders women's labor in the home less replaceable, imposes higher financial burdens on families when female academics travel. In other words, when women leave the home for research trips or conferences, the family absorbs more negative shocks due to the doubly oppressive nature of the gender pay gap.

Add to this the unmistakable biological burdens of carrying and nursing children, and it is a wonder that any married woman with children can survive in the academy.[44] Although men are certainly more involved in child care than they once were (in 1965 married American men performed 2.6 hours per week of child care compared with 7.2 hours a week in 2009–2010), many women suffer a productivity loss *prior* to the birth of their children.[45] Heightened sleep requirements and increased nutritional needs during pregnancy, along with doctor's appointments, and, if there are complications, many more appointments, mean that many women invest more time in the basic human task of reproduction even if, after babies arrive, men are equal parents.

A final way that the market-oriented structure of pay negatively impacts women (and also potentially people of color) is through a lack of emphasis on "service" work (Thompson 2008). In the research university setting, teaching

---

[43] Mitchell and Hesli (2013:table 2). Using an APSA faculty survey from 2009, table 3 in the study shows that women were more likely to ask for course releases, RAs, discretionary funds, travel funds, moving expenses, and positions for their partners and spouses. There was no difference in how frequently women asked for summer salary, special tenure clock timing, housing subsidies, child care, or administrative support.

[44] On academic motherhood, see Ward and Wolf-Wendel (2012), Mason, Wolfinger, and Goulden (2013). As Courtney Jung (2015) documents in *Lactivism*, the trappings of middle-class motherhood have become more cumbersome over time. Lots of bad science and guilt reinforce the interminable years spent on breastfeeding, or, more accurately, breastpumping.

[45] Bianchi et al. (2012:table 1).

and advising, though important, are less heavily emphasized in promotion practices. Women and people of color have often alluded to experiencing higher demands for service than they perceive are made on white men. The justifications for these demands range from being the lone "role model" for students and junior faculty from minority groups, to gendered patterns of socialization where women are considered to be more caring and hence better able to perform service duties, to volunteerism among women, to universities desiring diversity on committees (Guarino and Borden 2017:676). If the university wants one woman on every committee, but there are only two women in the department, those two may do a disproportionate amount of committee work. It is also possible that due to a greater emphasis placed on women's "likeability," women may be reluctant to say no to requests for service, especially if they perceive that they will be penalized for saying no (e.g., Babcock et al. 2017a).

Recent scholarship using a large national survey of 140 American institutions with almost 19,000 faculty respondents supports the idea that women do more service than men on average; even after controlling for the type of institution, the field, and the rank of the faculty member, women do 0.6 hours more service per week.[46] Using additional data from faculty activity reports at a large Midwestern research university, Guarino and Borden (2017) further find that women are engaged in 1.4 more hours of service activities than men per year, and that the difference is driven primarily by women's heightened service in their own universities, as opposed to external service to the profession at large. As evidence that some of the added service requirements are driven by a lack of diversity in universities, Guarino and Borden find that the number of women in a given department reduces the service burden of other women in that department. Importantly, although women do more service, they volunteer more frequently for service assignments that do not affect promotion (Babcock et al. 2017b), and they do the work that requires more effort and confers lower professional status (Alter et al. 2018). As Stegmaier, Palmer, and Van Assendelft (2011:801) showed for editorships at political science journals, women are found more frequently among associate editors (23 percent) and editorial board members (26 percent), but it is quite rare that a woman gets to be the sole editor of a major journal (18 percent).

---

[46] Guarino and Borden (2017:table 1). These figures are based on self-reported activities, which are likely less accurate than time-use surveys. But time-use surveys in household settings have been found to mirror closely self-reported time allocations (Hook 2017).

These heightened service demands for women and faculty of color feeds back into the compensatory scheme in a way that likely depresses wages. To borrow vocabulary from political economy, investing more time in home institutions means that faculty from non-dominant groups develop more "firm specific" capital relative to capital that can be traded on the open academic market.[47] With university-specific capital, women's networks are likely to be more local, and, because heightened service demands likely reduce the amount of time that women and people of color have to dedicate to research activities, they will have fewer of the key academic currency: publications.

In effect, the gender pay gap in academia, less generous research budgets for women, the tendency for women to develop university-specific capital instead of more easily tradable assets, when combined with the household division of labor, and the nature of reproductive biology, all are likely to negatively affect women's research productivity. Importantly, too, there is often a perception that women with families will be less productive, and that they are less moveable, than men. Since leave time, pay, and the size of research budgets are often associated with outside offers, gendered perceptions of dedication to the academic career and the gender pay gap may produce a feedback loop in which the standards for success are not equally attainable to all people. Most likely, these concerns are reflected not only in the labor market experiences for white women, but also constrain the opportunities for people of color.

Remedies for Gender Domination

This chapter has argued that in spite of growing numerical representation of women at many stages of the career pipeline in the social sciences, current practices related to the construction of disciplinary centrality, and the structure of academic labor market in research universities, reinforce women's subordination in the academy and bolsters gender inequality in society writ large. Recent ruptures in the political sphere have ushered in a spurt of mobilization around the issue of sexual harassment in the workplace. While it is clear that universities have their fair share of problems with harassment, solving that problem will not automatically produce equal opportunities or outcomes

---

[47] I thank Kathy Thelen for formulating this analogy.

for non-dominant groups.[48] Instead, there needs to be dispositional changes among current faculty (i.e., behavioral shifts) and policy changes within academic institutions to level the playing field in the academic career. I make three recommendations: reflexive inclusivity among faculty, equalizing pay, and attending to life cycle changes.

Reflexive Inclusivity

Life can be both easier and more fun when we gravitate toward people who share our backgrounds, cultural references, and values, and yet these practices are both exclusionary to newcomers and are also potentially harmful for discovery. Individuals who want to remedy these network-type inequalities can do a few things relatively simply. First, in your own courses assign more women. If you don't know whom to assign, look at recent prizes, series lists, or hires in your subfield. If that doesn't work, find a feminist. Most of us are more than happy to make recommendations for syllabi. And of course, the "Women Also Know Stuff" website is designed specifically to help you locate women who do research in a particular area. Second, if you want to check your references in a research paper, Jane Sumner recently developed a "Gender Balance Assessment Tool" (GBAT) that can quickly scan references and produce estimates of the proportion of female authors cited in your work.[49] To use this, you will need to keep first names in your syllabi and bibliographies, and you should note that the tool often slightly over-represents the proportion of women among authors. This tool seems like it might also come in handy for journal editors, and to department or university administrators that undertake the brave initiative to systematically study the gender composition of all taught course materials. Both of these actions – assigning more women and being sure to read and cite literature written by women, will help rectify the differential rates of visibility of male and female researchers.

---

[48] The largest professional association of American political scientists, APSA, recently conducted a survey of sexual harassment at the annual meeting where 2,424 members responded (18 percent response rate). The study found that while most members had not experienced harassment in the form of belittling, unwanted sexual advances, and inappropriate touching, 11 percent of female respondents and 3 percent of male respondents had experienced inappropriate sexual advances or touching (Sapiro and Campbell 2018).

[49] Historical gendered naming conventions may make it is easier to count, and therefore observe, gender differences, which may make it easier to shine a light on gender inequities than racial disparities. Some scholars in political science are working to predict ethnic and racial heritage from names. Interested readers are pointed to Khanna and Imai (2017).

Second, each discipline has to have conversations about which types of epistemological claims deserve pride of place (and my own intuitions suggest that political science cannot survive without qualitative research), yet I maintain that to the degree that our profession counts, we have to help the women find the beans. That is, we have to provide opportunities for women to do high-quality quantitative research. There are some simple fixes here. If you are a quanty-lady, write with your female students.[50] And if you are a man, look to see what proportion of your collaborators are women.[51] If it is not near 40 percent, women are under-represented in your own network, and you should work to include women on your research teams. Finally, as institutions craft plans for hiring, think of which women can lead your core metrics sequences or formal theory courses. We don't have enough data to tell us whether women teaching methods allows more women to excel in methods, but a large literature on gender and politics tells us that role models are key to success. At the very least, it's worth a try.

Equalizing Pay

Women and men should get equal pay for equal work. There is no justification for having a gap in research budgets or pay that relies on gendered conceptions of value. If a male assistant professor threatens to leave unless his salary is increased, allow the increase to be allocated only to the point at which all other faculty at that level are afforded an equal increase. This will seem preposterous to many men, but the reality is that gendered institutional arrangements, and not only their genius, have opened the door to the opportunity. Also, men should be asked why it is so important that they get paid more than women. In other words, we should be more transparent about pay not only so women can understand that they are under-paid, but to cultivate a sense among men that they are over-paid.[52] Second, when you are chair of the faculty, a dean, or on a hiring committee, recruit women that are married and those with kids as if they are a man, i.e., without thinking at all about whether

---

[50] Initiatives in political science, like "Visions in Methodology," which create networks for women who use quantitative methods are found by most attendees to be successful. See Barnes and Beaulieu (2017).

[51] Clusters of collaborators are often single-sex (Atchison 2017). As Tudor and Yashar (2018) find in their study of submissions to a top generalist journal in political science, *World Politics*, submissions that emanate from cross-rank collaborations, where scholars are at different levels of the academic hierarchy, tend to be same-gender more frequently than within-rank collaborations. If senior scholars initiate the collaboration, this finding might suggest same-sex preferences among mentors.

[52] A recent job market paper in economics (Langan 2018) finds that three to five years after a woman replaces a man as chair, the gender pay gap in economics and sociology is reduced by about a third. This happens through relative pay increases in women's salaries, not by lowering men's wages.

they might be moveable. Who knows, maybe she wants a divorce, or maybe she wants to change the gender division of labor in her own house. Maybe she simply wants a change. There is no way to know without actually trying.

Attending to the Life Cycle

Even with demographic changes in the direction of greater diversity, persistent differences in the rates of tenure for men and women paint a mixed story for the future of women's representation in these fields. Many scholars suggest that women's representation in academic institutions is stymied by organizational cultures meant to fit the work style and time demands of the unmarked group, i.e., white men.[53] Given that 30 years ago married white women with college degrees were much less likely to work outside the home than they are today, academic institutions were adapted to suit the lifestyle of a white man with the stay-at-home spouse.[54] Transformations in family forms, and the rise of two-earner couples among the educated classes, raise new problems for university faculty. These include the need to include major life cycle events – like the birth of children and the aging of parents – into the structure of employment benefits, and to create institutions within the profession that aid scholars with diverse household arrangements. Simple changes like holding meetings and workshops during the conventional work day, syncing university breaks with public school holidays, arranging for child care options at major conferences, and supplementing research budgets to pay for dependent care travel, have already been integrated by several institutions of higher learning.[55] Yet bigger reforms that might not only reflect changing realities of family composition, but also affect the gender division of labor within households, are still wanting.

In response to a desire to utilize women's labor power along with acknowledging women's outsized contribution to reproduction, many countries

---

[53] Wolfinger et al. (2008:390). Even today, male faculty are much more likely to have an at-home spouse. Jacobs (2004) reported that 89 percent of female faculty members had partners that were employed full-time, compared with 56 percent of male faculty.

[54] Notably, Arlie Hochschild and Anne Machung pointed this out in the first preface to *The Second Shift* (1989).

[55] Some academic conferences offer child care (for a fee). And some universities, like Princeton, allow for research budgets to cover dependent care for people at all ranks who are engaging in research activities, including conference attendance. Harvard, Yale, and Cornell allow $1,000 per academic year for dependent care during academic travel for ladder faculty. Berkeley allows faculty to use existing research budgets. Other schools like Brown and Northwestern offer slightly lower amounts ($750). These data are thanks to the collective energies of the Academic Mama's Facebook group.

(excluding the United States) adopted generous leave policies for women, granting as much as a year off from work without the risk of losing one's job. But feminists and governments quickly realized that this made women much more expensive to hire, because women might take several year-long breaks from their firms.[56] Several countries have now shifted to more generous leaves for fathers (or non-bearing parents), and some even mandate use-it-or-lose-it leaves for men to try to ensure that dads are forced to engage in the process. Given the negative labor market consequences for women who take time out of the labor force, universities attempted to reduce the risk associated with hiring women, and increase incentives for men to parent, by allowing parents of any gender (bearing and non-bearing) and adoptive parents time off from teaching. Many have, moreover, adopted similar clock-"stoppage" policies that allow for a break in the tenure clock for both men and women after the arrival of a child.[57]

The research suggests that these well-meaning policies have several design flaws that may not actually be remediable. First, there is not a good model for aiding faculty whose children have out-of-the-ordinary care needs. Families where a child has a physical or mental disability, chronic health issues, or behavioral issues (something like 15–20 percent of all children) can have more intense care burdens than families with children without such issues. With special needs, the gendered patterns of care are exacerbated, and yet the even the most generous parental leave policies will be insufficient for faculty in the face of these challenges (although Columbia University, and perhaps other schools, allow for half-time work, but that would be at half-time pay).[58]

Second, in the event of children with average care needs, due to limited resources, many schools that employ two partners in a couple will only

---

[56] Goldin and Katz (2011). Morgan (2006) provides a detailed account of both the variation in leave policies across Western countries, as well as accounts of how they can influence employer incentives to hire and promote women.

[57] Parental leave policies vary widely by the type of institution. Small institutions with small departments may find it much more burdensome to allow for parental leave. See Ward and Wolf-Wendel (2012:chapter 10). Antecol et al. (2018) provide a list of changes in clock stoppage policies for 49 economics departments.

[58] Survey data show that one in five households with children has at least one child with special needs (DeRigne et al. 2017:2). Parish et al. (2004) find that mothers of children with disabilities were less consistently employed, less likely to have a full-time job later in life, and had lower lifetime savings than mothers without special-needs children. DeRigne et al. (2017) examine employment patterns in married couples. They show that both mothers' and fathers' absence from employment increases when they have a special-needs child, but that mothers are more likely to reduce work to accommodate a special-needs child. This research suggests that women with special-needs children may need special accommodations in the university setting.

provide leave for one of them. This means, most often, that women take the benefit, reinforcing women as the primary parent. In cases where both partners are allowed leave, universities often "stagger" the benefit, so that one parent doing "full-time" child care receives leave in one term while the other who does "full-time" child care can get it in another. The problem is that full-time parenting takes on a different meaning at different stages in an infant's development. In many cases, the bearing parent (the one who bore the child) will take the first leave. Recovering from labor, which increasingly involves surgery, learning how to feed a newborn (increasingly via the breast), and dealing with the most helpless of creatures means that a bearing parent's entire leave is spent in the trenches. She returns to teaching after four months out, probably still wearing early maternity clothes, and may be the child's only source of sustenance. The non-bearing parent gets his or her leave right when babies' naps become more predictable, and nighttime sleep may stretch out, leaving a bit of time for research on the side.

More egregiously, one hears many rumors around the water cooler of the man who used his entire parental leave for research, which may account for recent findings that gender-neutral clock-stopping policies increase the probability that men get tenure, but decrease the chance that women get promoted.[59] In fact, Antecol, Bedard, and Stearns (2018:table 6) find that men who start as assistant professors in departments with gender-neutral tenure clock-stoppage policies have 0.56 more top-five publications than men who start in institutions without such policies, while there is no increase in top-five publications for women under such policies. These findings are consistent with a model where men and women use parental leave in different ways, driving the growing gender gap in tenure rates. To deal with uneven reproductive burdens, but also encourage non-bearing parents to be fully involved in the early months of parenting, the easiest fix is allowing both parents, at the time of birth, to take the time off. And, in the case of stopping the clock, allow

---

[59] Antecol, Bedard, and Stearns (2018) examine the impact of "clock-stoppage" policies surrounding childbirth in 49 of the top 50 economics departments in the United States. They examine how female-only or gender-neutral policies impacted the employment history and publication patterns of more than 1,000 assistant professors hired into these departments from 1985 to 2004. Table 2 shows that men who came up under gender-neutral clock stoppage policies were 17.6 percentage points more likely to get tenure than men who came up before those policies were implemented, but that the gender gap in tenure rates grew by 37 percentage points after a neutral clock was adopted. Women who came up under gender-neutral policies were *less likely* to get tenure than women at the same university before the policy was implemented. Female-only clock-stoppage policies produced a small but imprecise gain for women. Note that the policies do not impact scholars' ability to get tenure in the profession, just at the initial institution where they were hired.

bearing parents two years off the clock as a way to account for the productivity lost during pregnancies, and to give women a genuine chance to catch up on their research.[60] (Twins, finally, should be treated like two separate children.)

Spousal hiring is another area where universities can intervene. Anecdotally, there is a perception that female academics, in addition to being more likely to have a high-powered spouse, are also more likely to be married to fellow academics.[61] To put it bluntly, gendered marital patterns mean that even when everyone is married to another academic, the woman will be more expensive to hire because her husband will need to make nearly as much as she does. Although many state schools have had success in faculty hiring and retention by addressing the spousal issue directly, the liberal arts colleges, which have fewer positions, are less able to do so. Many of the wealthiest research universities have the worst track records, perhaps because the notion of a "trailing" spouse suggests a sacrifice in quality.[62]

The remedy here is that universities should get on board with spousal hiring; it should be part of the budgeting process. Although people in other industries may balk at this notion, the geographical clustering and constraints of the academic job market make it a reality of the occupation. And just as firms want to retain talent, academic institutions should conceptualize retention in terms of the economic costs of turnover, not just in terms of salary. Just think, if you hire a couple, they will be happier, feel relatively richer (because they aren't paying for a commute) and may actually stay. To be truly great, institutions need employees who build community. Couples who are invested in the institution (who, frankly, will be harder to poach), may be excellent providers of public goods. This applies to same-sex couples as well as to different-sex couples.

---

[60] UC Berkeley, where Mary Ann Mason of "Do Babies Matter?" fame was the dean of the graduate division, adopted policies of this sort.

[61] Schiebinger, Henderson, and Gilmartin (2018); Jacobs (2004).

[62] UVA's dual-career faculty report argues that secondary spousal hires often play important roles in university life, including teaching in areas where the departments may not have had strength. At UVA, 86 percent of survey respondents reported being in a dual-career household, and a larger proportion of female faculty at all age groups reported this arrangement. Notably, at UVA, 33 percent of the dual-career spouses were employed by the university, while 13 percent were employed at a different university. http://uvacharge.virginia.edu/images/2015.12.14_FINAL_Dual_Career_Survey_Report.pdf.

Do We Need Women for Science?

For card-carrying feminists, the exclusion of women from sharing fully in the academic career is reason enough to care about gender domination in the academy. Justice itself is a worthy goal. But as a much-admired mentor of mine once barked: "What we do is science! Why do we need women for that?" This particular man was not against women – in fact, he had been an excellent mentor to many. But he balked at the notion that diversity in the academy was related to the specific mission of knowledge production. In that moment, like any self-possessed young woman might, I brushed off the comment. Which is to say I scoffed, made some argument back, and quickly changed the subject. But when I went home that night (and often since), I was struck by the absurdity of the claim. What we do is *social* science, and to do that well we absolutely need diversity.

Social science is about theorizing and documenting the regularities in human behavior, institutional formation, cooperation, and conflict that have hitherto constrained our civilizations. Society, though, is a living thing, and so a social science that is foremost concerned with predicting the future will likely fall short of its own aspirations. But just because we are not likely to become great at predicting the future, social scientists need not resign themselves to mere description. In what is perhaps the most famous statement distinguishing social science from philosophy, Karl Marx proclaimed that unlike for philosophers, our mission is not only to interpret the world, but to change it.

To my mind, the best way to change the world (fundamentally, to try to make it a better place) is to find the injustice – inequality, sexism, racism, elitism, and the like – and hammer repeatedly at the artifices that support it. But demolishing inequality does require some degree of prioritization. The Rawlsian maxim that we should look first to the improvement of the worst-off does not tell us much about how to determine what worst means. Given the sheer variety of inequalities that exist in the world, reasonable people can disagree about which ones are the most salient, about which axes of subordination are the most deserving of immediate attention. If, as Weber says, science can help you uncover facts, but it cannot tell you which questions to ask, then it is in deciding which questions to ask where lived experience proves key.

Generations of feminist, anti-racist, and anti-imperialist scholars have made this point: our positionality in the world system, our experiences of hate crime, violence, and disrespect, as well as inculcated patterns of cognitive processes, each stand to influence the normative concerns and the standpoint that people bring to the table.[63] As the moral philosophers including Adam Smith have noted, injustices that are close to home may be sensed more acutely than those that are farther afield. Problems in our own households, places of worship, schools, or workplaces may prompt us to have unique concerns for or insights into our communities. Although there is nothing in practice keeping white men from thinking about the intersectional burdens that black women face when interacting with the criminal and legal justice systems, most white men have not thought much about it.[64]

Thus we see in the subfield of gender and politics an overwhelming majority of women, and in the subfield of race and politics a disproportionate amount of people of color. It isn't that gender and race don't affect white men, it is just that as the key beneficiaries of the system, they are less likely to think of those axes of subordination as the most important thing to study. To be sure, there is no prerequisite that women and people of color study eponymous subjects, but since values determine which questions we ask, it is not surprising that people from disadvantaged groups tend to cluster. But this creates problems for minority groups insofar as these subfields are "ghettoized," the topics and the people who study them are deemed out of the mainstream, and "me studies" gets pushed to the backwaters of the intellectual and economic value hierarchy. Ultimately, the power of the unmarked group is that they have been studying themselves all along, their knowledge confined to their own concerns, and yet they have had no need to justify it.

---

[63] "Standpoint" feminists, including Sandra Harding and Nancy Hartsock, argue that women's subordination in the world gives them a unique ability to understand and critique patriarchal systems of power, that is, that people of different social locations have different kinds of knowledge. This idea finds a parallel in social psychology, where an old line of research by Taylor and Fiske (1975) argues that perceptions of causality are related to the things to which people pay attention. In other words, we attribute causation and agency based on attending to specific people or phenomena. Together, attribution theory and standpoint epistemology suggest that people may have unique knowledge that others do not have access to, but that our own perceptions may be biased. Men's lack of understanding of women's standpoints may lead to a de-emphasis on the systematic hurdles women face.

[64] To be fair, many white men have studied race, but the theorization of "Intersectionality" – the way that people that sit at intersections of gender/race/class/ethnicity/and ability may experience institutions differently – emerged among black feminists and represents a foundational shift in feminist theory, empirical social science, and social movements discourse. There is so much written in this area, but Crenshaw (1989), Brown (2014), Hancock (2007, 2015), and Choo and Ferree (2010) can get you started.

17 Ideological Diversity

Neil Gross and Christopher Robertson

Over the last fifteen years, calls have mounted to increase the political diversity of American social science. Studies of the political attitudes and party affiliations of US college and university professors have long shown academics to be disproportionately left-leaning and Democratic (Gross and Simmons 2014; Ladd and Lipset 1976; Lazarsfeld and Thielens 1958). These tendencies are especially pronounced in social science fields, and there is evidence that since the turn of the twenty-first century social scientists have become even more liberal and Democratic than they were before. For decades, conservative critics have bemoaned the liberal tilt, arguing that social scientists' political orientations seep into research and teaching, with consequences for accumulated stocks of knowledge, policy-making, student attitudes, and American political culture. These criticisms are now being supplemented by claims informed by work in social psychology and organizational behavior. The new charge is that political homogeneity – rather than a liberal orientation per se – is bad for social science because it promotes motivated reasoning, bias, and groupthink (e.g., Duarte et al. 2015; Redding 2012). Such claims, made by critics outside the academy and by a growing number of high-profile academic social scientists, are gaining traction in today's bullishly partisan political environment.

In this short chapter, we review the most credible of the current arguments made in favor of diversifying the social sciences politically. If social science fields are sites of political uniformity, is there a cost to the research and teaching function of the university? We also endeavor to move the conversation beyond applied concerns by asking whether and how discussion of political diversity and bias in academia might be reconceptualized to form the basis for meaningful empirical studies in the subfield of sociology that would seem its natural home: the sociology of ideas. To this end, we urge greater attention to the fine-grained practices of knowledge-making and knowledge-dissemination enacted by groups and networks of social scientists, and to the complex and contingent ways politics may intersect with such practices.

The Politics of American Social Scientists

That American professors tend to be more liberal politically than the US population as a whole is evident from the work of historians of higher education and from large-scale studies dating back half-a-century. Liberalism and conservatism, as coherent political ideologies, appeared on the American scene as the country underwent rapid modernization in the closing decades of the nineteenth century. These were not the same as the liberalism or conservatism of today, but bore family resemblances. Although prominent nineteenth-century academics could be found taking both recognizably liberal and conservative stances, by the time of the Progressive Era – a period of expansion for the college and university sector – a general preference for market regulation and scientifically based government action to solve social problems was becoming clear (Jewett 2012).

This preference was solidified during the Depression. Many professors lent their support and expertise to the New Deal (Camic 2007). Others flirted with radicalism. Theodore Newcomb's *Personality and Social Change* (1943), a classic book on the effects of higher education on student political attitudes, was based on a study carried out in the late 1930s at Bennington College, where the economic liberalism and New Deal sympathies of the faculty were apparent. Although the most progressive professors at the time were concerned to curb the excesses of capitalism, and sometimes held quite regressive social views, the die was cast that would make American academia a supportive environment for the left for decades to come.

Surveys of the American professoriate conducted in the 1950s and 1960s bear this out – and confirm that when it comes to liberalism, social scientists have long led the pack. Paul Lazarsfeld's 1955 study of academics amid the tumult of McCarthyism focused on social scientists because it was their political views and research most under attack from the right (Lazarsfeld and Thielens 1958). Just 16 percent of the social scientists he surveyed were Republicans, at a time when the Republican Party platform was much more centrist than it is now. Two-thirds reported that they were more liberal than the typical person in the community where they lived. In the same vein, when Everett Carll Ladd and Seymour Martin Lipset studied the politics of the American professoriate with a new survey in the late 1970s, they found not simply that professors were more liberal and Democratic on average than other Americans, but that social scientists were the most liberal of all professors (Ladd and Lipset 1976).

Recently, social scientists have become more progressive still. A 2006 survey by one of the present authors and Solon Simmons found that 58 percent of social scientists in US colleges and universities described themselves as either "very liberal" or "liberal." Humanists were the next most liberal group, at 52 percent. Only 5 percent of social scientists described themselves as either "conservative" or "very conservative." Female social scientists were more liberal than their male colleagues, at 73 versus 51 percent (Gross and Simmons 2014).

Looking at party affiliation, Gross and Simmons found that just 7 percent of social scientists were Republicans, as compared to 28 percent of all American adults. The design of their study did not allow for a breakdown of every disciplinary difference, but it did show a predictable split in the social science community: where the percentage of Republican psychologists, sociologists, and political scientists was in the single digits, in economics the number was higher, at 28 percent. Views on a range of policy and social issues went hand-in-hand with these broad markers of political identity. Gross and Simmons's findings are consistent with the findings from other studies carried out around the same time (e.g., Klein and Western 2004–2005; Rothman, Lichter, and Nevitte 2005). And surveys of the professoriate conducted since 2006 confirm that American professors remain a very liberal bloc, with far-left views gaining ground after the 2008 financial crisis and in the context of heightened public concern about inequality (Jaschik 2012).

To be sure, American professors do not look quite as left-leaning when compared to academics elsewhere. In European nations, for example, those who teach in the higher-education sector are generally more supportive of the welfare state and more critical of the market than they are here, with the gap between overall public opinion and professorial views larger than in the United States (Brooks 2014). But that does not change the fact that professors fall distinctly to the left on the American occupational politics distribution.

Calls for Political Diversification

Just as the liberal professoriate stretches back decades, so do complaints from the right about the political orientation of America's social science faculty. Anger from conservative university trustees about pro-labor economists and sociologists around the turn of the twentieth century was so intense that it generated a movement among academics in support of academic freedom protections (Hofstadter and Metzger 1955; Weinberg 1972). Likewise, one of the key texts in the history of modern conservatism, William F. Buckley's *God and Man at Yale* (1951), was a criticism directed primarily at the statist and secularizing tendencies of professors teaching in the university's departments of economics, political science, sociology, and psychology – professors who Buckley described as lecturing and assigning reading that pushed politics under the guise of science. In the 1960s and 1970s, business leaders and organizations concerned about the Keynesian proclivities of American economists counteracted by founding centers of laissez-faire economic thought (Moreton 2008). These criticisms continue in our own day, with conservative activists and organizations routinely taking aim at social scientists said to have illegitimately crossed the line into political advocacy.

The focus of this chapter, however, is not on partisan attacks, but on arguments advanced by social scientists themselves claiming that the politics of their colleagues is a problem. Two recent contributions exemplify these claims.

Political Diversity and Psychology

The first is an influential review article titled, "Political Diversity Will Improve Psychological Science," published in 2015 by a group of five psychologists – Jarret Crawford, José Duarte, Jonathan Haidt, Lee Jussim, and Philip Tetlock – and a sociologist, Charlotta Stern (Duarte et al. 2015). Zooming in on the subfield of social psychology, the authors begin by presenting evidence that the number of non-liberal social psychologists is in steep decline. In their view, the absence of conservative and Republican voices constitutes prima facie evidence that social psychology is politically homogeneous. (They are not interested in political differences among professors on the left.) The authors then make a case that political homogeneity is at odds with good science.

They open their argument by pointing to recent controversies in social psychology: instances where scientific fraud was reported, or where it proved impossible to replicate major findings. According to the authors, such problems could be minimized if conservatives entered social psychology and diversified the field. When nearly all social scientists in a discipline share political values and goals, they claim, the discipline can become a "moral community" that "blinds its members to morally or ideologically undesirable hypotheses and unanswered but important scientific questions" (4). They draw here on the work of sociologist Christian Smith (2014), who has argued that sociology is such a community, committed to progressive values such as equality in the distribution of rights and resources. Social psychology too threatens to become a moral community, the authors say, as political views get built into psychological theories and methods, leaving the field with partisan constructs and ways of knowing; as social psychologists devote their attention and resources to things they perceive to be problems, given their politics, thus neglecting other potentially important aspects of psychological life; and as liberal social psychologists produce misleading research about conservatives. They provide examples of each of these problems, such as studies presupposing that skepticism about environmental policies is equivalent to denying reality, or research claiming to show that conservatism stems from undesirable personality characteristics.

If there were more political diversity in social psychology, the authors assert, these problems could be avoided, while other benefits would flow. An enduring challenge for any social science is confirmation bias, or the tendency for researchers to interpret evidence as consistent with their prior beliefs and suppositions, even if the evidence actually points in another direction (see Nickerson 1998). In principle peer review should serve as a check on this problem, as reviewers do their due diligence as gatekeepers and refuse to allow the publication of studies that overstep their evidentiary bases. But the authors suggest that this aspect of gatekeeping breaks down when reviewers and authors share political priors, since reviewers who are politically and cognitively motivated to agree with the findings of a study may be satisfied with lower standards. Beyond this, the authors argue that having more social psychologists representing political positions in the minority in the academy would increase scientific dissent and spur creativity at the department and disciplinary levels, helping to avoid the ideological complacency that characterizes groupthink in organizations (Janis 1982).

In order to increase political diversity in social psychology, the authors urge scholarly organizations and academic departments to take formal stances in favor of it; encourage individual social psychologists to do what they can to engage colleagues whose politics differ from their own; and suggest that research practices change as well, from peer reviewers becoming more conscious of the possibility of political bias in manuscript evaluation to scholars purposefully seeking out what the authors describe as "adversarial collaborations" (42). The authors have also been involved in establishing a website, heterodoxacademy.org, that seeks to further the cause of "viewpoint diversity" on campus.

Published to great fanfare in *Behavioral and Brain Sciences*, their article generated dozens of responses. With the bulk of our evaluation to follow, here we would simply note one peculiarity of the argument: it proceeds as though its understanding of what constitutes good social science is commonsensical and uniformly held, when in fact there is serious disagreement about this in the social science community. Though the article is neither an exercise in epistemology or the sociology of science, the authors draw on the work of Robert K. Merton (1973b) to argue that at its best all science involves the norms of "universalism," "communism" (scientific knowledge is owned by the community as a whole), "disinterestedness," and "organized skepticism." Political diversity in social psychology could shore up these norms, they suggest. For example, universalism could be enhanced if "the same standards of evidence and proof" (12) were applied to conservative as to liberal social psychologists.

But Merton's ideas to this effect, brilliant though they are, were first laid down in 1942. The philosophy and sociology of social science have shifted in the ensuing three-quarters-of-a-century. Some social scientists today continue to think that Merton's norms represent an ideal to which all social science should be held. Yet others do not, and the Duarte et al. review makes no effort to connect with any of the alternative perspectives – some highly defensible – that have cropped up more recently.

One significant intellectual development to which Duarte et al. might have attended is the growing appreciation among social scientists that causal explanation requires not only the discovery of robust empirical associations among variables, but also the identification of underlying causal mechanisms (e.g., Gorski 2009; Hedström 2005). This is not at odds with Merton's own vision of social science – his "middle-range" theorizing is seen by mechanisms scholars as exemplary – but it would not be unusual to find a contemporary social scientist thinking that adequate mechanism identification is every bit as important a criterion of scientific merit as adherence to Merton's norms (even if these criteria operate at different levels). And one could imagine that this demand alone, if heeded, might go some way toward reducing whatever ideological distortions may be present in social science, since in principle it is easier to manipulate associational data than to validate the existence of mechanisms as part of an effort at discovering causal effects. Where some social scientists think of mechanisms as speculative hypotheses the researcher comes up with post hoc to account for empirical associations – which would make them subject to *greater* manipulation – the demand increasingly is that hypothesized mechanisms be subjected to rigorous empirical verification in their own right, a laborious and data-intensive task for which the most partisan of scholars are ill-suited.

Another important development is the growth of various strains of post-positivist social science. Technically speaking, research on causal mechanisms also belongs to this post-positivist moment, since positivism refers to the idea that social science seeks to identify universal laws of society, and scholars of mechanisms doubt the existence of many – or any – such laws. But we have in mind here more encompassing theoretical approaches such as pragmatism (e.g., Joas 1993), critical realism (e.g., Bhaskar 1979), or Bourdieusian sociology (e.g., Bourdieu, Chamboredon, and Passeron [1968] 1991). A key element of post-positivist social science is recognition that the fact/values distinction is philosophically blurry. (This point is recognized not only by sociological theorists but also by key conservative thinkers, such as Leo Strauss and Russell Kirk.) According to post-positivists, social research that reflects in certain respects the political values of the investigator, or the community of investigators, need not be considered unscientific, and does not necessarily become more scientific by being counterbalanced by investigations undertaken from the standpoint of other political values.

For pragmatists, for example – influenced by philosophers like Charles S. Peirce and John Dewey – investigations into social matters are scientific if they are carried out in a spirit of experimentalism where the aim is to use the best available evidence to find solutions to pressing intellectual puzzles or problems with real social import. Experimentalism and entrenched partisanship are indeed at odds: the partisan will be unwilling to relinquish cherished beliefs even if they do not find experimental support, and may also be unable to think past conventional ways of understanding a problem at hand. Yet as pragmatists understand it, social inquiry undertaken without a genuine desire to make the world a better place – with all the values that entails, political and otherwise – is *also* not properly scientific, since scientific experimentalism grows out of and gains its warrant from the general human need and capacity for problem-solving, and is empty and devoid of meaning and worth if it cannot bring about practical consequences. (The classic discussion of this is Lynd 1939). Max Weber famously argued that social scientists' personal values – except those to do with scientific integrity – should cease to play a role in research after being used to guide the selection of research topics. Pragmatists disagree, believing that moral and political commitments carefully reflected upon must also factor among those resources used to discover solutions to scientific puzzles – and especially so in the realm of the social, where finding solutions means ultimately finding better ways for humans to live together. Furthermore, while pragmatism favors vigorous dialogue within a community of investigators – not least over questions of value – to help achieve explanatory/pragmatic aims, it offers little reason for believing that dialogue would be enhanced simply by having more conservatives in social science. Pragmatists view dialogue as a practical accomplishment, not an automatic function of social composition.

Along similar lines, post-positivist epistemologies of social science note that different social science fields and subfields in different national contexts have dissimilar, shifting, and sometimes incommensurable understandings of what counts as a legitimate contribution, and insist there is little to be gained from attempts at standardization. Sociology today, for example, is a very different intellectual beast in the United States and Mexico (Abend 2006), and in America looks nothing like cultural anthropology or social history, and only some of the time like political science (see Steinmetz 2005). These are not just subject matter differences; they reflect variation in epistemological and even ontological assumptions. And on the whole they are to be celebrated. If the social world is "dappled," to use philosopher Nancy Cartwright's (1999) evocative term – governed only in limited respects by law-like regularities, with contingency, conjunction, flux, and ontological heterogeneity rampant – then in fact we need a plethora of theories, intellectual perspectives, methodologies, and philosophies to understand its many dimensions and aspects, so that the diversity of views on what counts as good social science, which accompanies and underwrites this pluralism, is a net positive. While a case might be made for political diversity in social psychology or other social science fields on just these grounds – if we could assume that people with differing politics had radically different views on how social science should be practiced – that is not the same as the positivist, reductionist grounds presented by the authors – i.e., that political diversity enhances the scientificity of social science by facilitating the accumulation of verifiable facts relevant to the discovery of general laws. ("Reductionist" here is not meant to be pejorative; the Duarte et al. approach is reductionist in the specific sense that it would reduce the biodiversity of social science to a single species, and makes an argument about how the fitness of that species could be enhanced.) Interestingly, in some of his other work Tetlock has sounded some of these same post-positivist notes (Tetlock and Mitchell 2015), drawing on research in science and technology studies (STS) to question the possibility of value-free knowledge, and arguing that since it is inevitable social science will be affected by values – including political values – we need conservatives around not to bolster objectivity, but to lend more multi-sidedness to the social science enterprise.

Conservatives in Social Science

A second set of critiques – one that dovetails with the Duarte et al. article – can be found in Jon Shields and Joshua Dunn's book, *Passing on the Right: Conservative Professors in the Progressive University* (Shields and Dunn 2016). Based on interviews with 153 conservative faculty members teaching in social sciences and humanities fields at colleges and universities around the country, the book charts the experiences of conservative academics – a stigmatized group, say Shields and Dunn – and discusses the strategies they use to manage their careers and work-related relationships. The book also argues for the value of faculty political diversity.

One of the strengths of Shields and Dunn's interview-based approach is that it allows them to describe what it feels like to be in the extreme political minority in a higher-education setting. Despite stigmatization, most of their interviewees describe relationships with colleagues as fairly cordial. Perhaps this is because, according to the authors, conservative faculty members learn early on to avoid confrontation. Libertarians report more cordial relationships than social conservatives, however – reflecting the emphasis on social liberalism in faculty political attitudes. The authors also note significant disciplinary differences. For example, conservatives in political science appear to find more acceptance than their peers in sociology. Cordial relationships turn out to be central to three arguments Shields and Dunn make for the benefits of political diversity.

First, when courses in the social sciences and humanities are taught by conservative faculty members, students may be exposed to very different readings and ideas. Although Shields and Dunn see little evidence that college students are being converted to the left by time spent with liberal professors, they contend that a beneficial broadening of intellectual horizons occurs when conservative perspectives are given a sympathetic hearing in the classroom (see Lyons 2009). Second, Shields and Dunn claim that a major problem for democratic governance in the United States presently is that people have lost the capacity for civil dialogue and disagreement with others holding opposing political views. Higher education could be a setting where such a capacity is nurtured, but this requires that students see their professors modeling dialogical and politically tolerant behavior. What better occasion is there for this than in interaction with colleagues? Without conservatives on the faculty, such interaction becomes impossible. Third, Shields and Dunn note that many conservative professors feel more comfortable in academia than in the Republican Party. Beyond a love for their fields of study, and for the routines and pleasures of an intellectual life, conservative social scientists and humanists are, on the whole, less inclined toward right-wing populism than their fellow members of the GOP. Many are traditionalists and elitists of a sort who worry about the disruptive and even irrational social changes that may be introduced by mass political movements (see Nash 1976). According to Shields and Dunn, more conservative professors might temper the populism of students from both the left and right, with stabilizing spillover effects on the polity.

Shields and Dunn also agree with the authors of the *Behavioral and Brain Sciences* article that social science research could be enhanced if there were more conservatives in these disciplines. They pay less attention to evidentiary matters and motivated reasoning than to the fact that investigators' values and interests naturally affect the questions they take up. Shields and Dunn recognize that not all researchers are guided by political concerns, but they see it as obvious that the American social sciences would look different topically and thematically if there were more conservatives doing the research. For example, they claim, there would be more work about important subjects like religion, and more research on "taboo" topics such as the genetic determinants of behavior or the relationship between family structure and poverty in the African-American community. (Here we would note in passing that the sociology of religion has actually seen an efflorescence in the last twenty years – coinciding with a *decline* in the number of conservative social scientists. Also, there is an enormous social-scientific literature on family structure and poverty, and a growing literature on behavioral genetics. We do not contest the general point that politics may render some topics taboo.)

Shields and Dunn concur with other research done by Gross that the main reason there are so few conservatives in the social sciences, and in academia generally, is self-selection: given the current intellectual and political makeup of these fields, and of the academy, few conservatives aspire to spend their lives there. For this reason, to increase faculty political diversity they advocate not giving direct preferences to conservatives in hiring – which might be appropriate if conservatives were being blocked by widespread discrimination – but instead creating special programs to recruit conservative academic talent. This might entail prioritizing hiring in areas that appeal especially to conservative scholars or funding more research centers that could become on-campus hubs for right-leaning thinkers and their ideas.

Evaluating the Claims

Do the claims of Duarte et al. and Shields and Dunn have merit? We have a number of points to make in response.

First, concerning research, we would bring up and expand upon an issue Gelman and Gross (2015) raised in a short commentary on Duarte et al. Beyond the philosophy-of-science issue, it is also the case that those who take the social sciences as their object of empirical investigation – sociologists and anthropologists of science and knowledge, intellectual historians, and others – have reached no consensus on the question of how one might treat the quality of scholarship produced in a given period, or in certain institutional settings or networks, as an outcome with causes that could be studied systematically. Instead, there are multiple possible approaches. Should we follow Randall Collins's (1998) work on philosophy, for example, and measure quality by the amount of attention that ends up being devoted to a set of ideas downstream, whether operationalized as citations, pages in textbooks, or awards? By the absence of scandal or controversy? By how much creative intellectual ferment there is versus routine, normal science? By pragmatic benefits, as seen through effects on public policy? By how well findings hold up to current epistemic ideals?

This matters, because in the absence of an agreed-upon metric of social-scientific quality, it has been impossible to carry out research assessing whether you tend to get higher-quality social science when there is more political diversity – the core assertion of Duarte et al. While one might be tempted to follow the authors by extrapolating from research on entrepreneurialism, organizational learning, and decision-making, concluding that if a diversity of viewpoints is associated with more creative solutions to problems (e.g., Stark 2009) then we should also want more political diversity in social science, there is no reason to think that a diversity of political views would be more beneficial in this regard than other forms of intellectual diversity: a diversity of educational backgrounds and academic interests, a diversity of theoretical and methodological perspectives, a diversity of social experiences, and so on. Of course, there need not be a tradeoff among these, but as a practical matter fields trying to diversify intellectually may need to prioritize. Political science, for example, could in principle decide it was becoming narrow, and make a concerted move toward intellectual diversity by favoring applicants to graduate programs who were humanities majors in college. It could be difficult to maintain a strong pool doing this, however, while also seeking to recruit non-liberal students, since conservatives are under-represented among humanities majors, and since – political theory aside – it is the rare humanities major who wants to become a political scientist. Political scientists would then need to pick which type of diversity they wanted to select. If they were looking to make an evidenced-based choice, they would find – again – that no research demonstrates directly that the quality of social science goes up when the social-scientific workforce is more politically balanced.

Second, while we lack studies on the relationship between political heterogeneity and research quality, the one well-known empirical association that speaks to the issue suggests that broad political agreement among faculty members is not, in fact, an impediment to good research, where goodness is measured by metrics commonly employed by higher-education institutions, even if they lack strong intellectual justification. We have known since Lazarsfeld's study of American social scientists that the imbalance of liberals to conservatives is greatest at elite research schools. Ladd and Lipset (1976), for their part, devoted considerable attention to this finding, arguing it shows the intrinsic connection between liberalism and creativity. Gross (2013) develops an alternative, self-selection-based explanation. But the matter can be given a different gloss. Judging by citations and research productivity, more impactful scholarship gets done at the top of the academic hierarchy than at the bottom. Although different teaching loads, access to resources, and processes of cumulative advantage are clearly a major part of the story here (Headworth and Freese 2016), can't the productivity of elite social science departments also be seen as evidence – according to this metric – that political homogeneity need not be at odds with research excellence? (We note here the irony of Duarte et al.'s invocation of Merton in support of the project of political diversification. Merton spent decades teaching in the sociology department at Columbia University, where he was surrounded by others who, like him, were on the broad political left – Paul Lazarsfeld, Robert Lynd, C. Wright Mills, etc.). It is worth considering the hypothesis that relative agreement on politics is functional for high-quality social science, not dysfunctional.

Third, though Duarte et al. and Shields and Dunn flag as a major point that there are fewer conservatives in the social sciences today than in previous decades, neither set of authors offers a compelling explanation for the trend. Duarte et al. suggest that bias or discrimination in academic employment may be involved, as liberal social scientists refuse to hire conservative colleagues, their departments become even more liberal, political bias is further ramped up, and so on in an escalating cycle. But Shields and Dunn insist that discrimination is not the main factor keeping conservatives out of the academic fold.

A more obvious explanation for the change is that highly educated Americans inside and outside academia have been abandoning the Republican Party in recent years – and conservatism along with it – as the party has veered sharply to the right, so that developments in the social sciences reflect merely amplified versions of trends affecting the electorate as a whole. (This point is consistent with the argument of Shields and Dunn about the discomfort many academic conservatives feel with the GOP.) Figure 17.1, drawn from General Social Survey data, shows over-time trends in party affiliation broken down by education level. The drop-off since the mid-1990s in Republican Party affiliation for both bachelors and graduate degree holders is notable, and consistent with other survey data showing that on numerous issues, from the need for income redistribution to environmental protection, Americans with graduate degrees have been moving to the left (Pew Research Center 2016). True, exposure to higher-education environments, and to the progressivism of the typical college town, must have some role to play in this. But that movement leftward is evident for people across entirely different fields of study, from education to medicine to law and, also – according to other data – among high school students aiming for professional careers, suggests that we are in the midst of a political realignment of the professional class driven by causes well beyond the leanings of the professoriate.

As noted elsewhere, another contributing factor to the decline of conservatives in academia is the mass entry of women into the academic profession (Gross 2013). Over the last twenty years or so, highly educated women in the United States have been a strongly Democratic and liberal group. It should come as no surprise, then, that as more women have entered the social sciences (women now comprise the majority of social science doctoral recipients), those fields have become more liberal. Looking at data from faculty surveys conducted in 1969 and 1997, Gross found that while during this time there was a 9-percentage-point increase in the number of faculty members who described themselves as liberal, among male faculty members this increase amounted to just 3 percentage points. The aggregate shift left appears to have been brought about mostly by the liberalism of female academics, and by their growing ranks.

These factors bear on the practicality of the proposals made by Duarte et al. and Shields and Dunn. For, if the highly educated are leaving the GOP and becoming more liberal, and if ever-increasing majorities of entry-level social scientists are women with progressive politics, from where exactly could we recruit the conservative social scientists who would lead the way toward political diversification? (Shields and Dunn acknowledge this point

Ideological Diversity

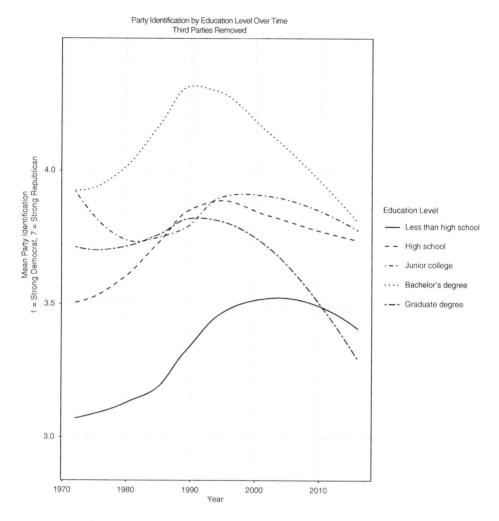

Figure 17.1 Party identification and education

in the conclusion of their book, where they note that most conservative professors in the social sciences and humanities are white men.) Yes, if there were a few more conservatives hired at leading institutions, it would probably encourage some conservative students to enter the social science pipeline. But this would be swimming against a powerful tide. To put this in different terms, for all we know based on the current literature, the small number of conservative academic social scientists presently swimming against this tide – including Shields and Dunn – comprise the total population (more or less) of credentialed, qualified conservatives eligible for and interested in these positions, and not the outlying exceptions that prove the rule of political bias in academia's hiring practices.

Fourth, if it is the case that important topics are being ignored in social science research because of the political orientation of the researchers, there is a well-established institutional mechanism for correcting this: making grant money available to professors to incentivize work in the overlooked areas. This would seem a far more direct means for correcting any politically based "knowledge gaps" (Frickel 2008) that may be plaguing the social sciences at present, and one likely to be especially powerful in an era of resource scarcity. If public and philanthropic dollars were suddenly devoted to unfettered research on topics likely to be of special interest to conservative audiences and policy-makers, a side benefit might be that it could encourage at least a few more conservatives to take up academic careers, bringing about some of the diversity advocates seek without requiring intervention into the academic recruitment process.

Fifth and finally, while it is plausible to think that undergraduate students exposed to a wider range of political viewpoints in their social science courses might become more politically tolerant, and leave college better equipped to participate in meaningful political dialogue, we are not aware of any systematic research demonstrating this. Studies of political socialization in college are not usually set up so that they can assess the impact of particular sets of readings, say, or of student interaction with politically homogeneous versus politically diverse faculty members in a department. Shields and Dunn's claims on teaching are as unproven as those of Duarte et al. concerning research.

All in all, while Duarte et al. and Shields and Dunn raise important points, we do not think they have put forward a convincing, evidence-based case for diversifying the social sciences politically. There may well be other, stronger reasons to favor injecting more political diversity into the social science faculty – for example, in order to enhance the credibility of the social sciences for conservative audiences, as a way of introducing previously neglected thinkers and theory to ongoing research, or on the philosophical grounds of rights to representation – but it is not yet established that political diversity would "improve" any of the social science fields.

Toward a Sociology of Politics and Ideas

Although we have doubts about some of the arguments for political diversity, it seems to us that such arguments have considerable merit in another respect.

In the last three decades, research has blossomed in a subfield of sociology that should in principle be very much concerned with how the political views and commitments of researchers shape the knowledge they produce and how they go about disseminating it. That subfield is the sociology of ideas, an offshoot of the broader sociology of knowledge (see Camic and Gross 2001). The fuzzy and somewhat ad hoc dividing line between the two is set at whether the focus is on people, groups, or institutions occupationally specialized in the production of ideas – scientists, intellectuals, experts of various kinds – or instead on how knowledge claims swirl about among other segments of the population, coming to form part of larger complexes like public opinion, cultural tastes, or collective memory or identity. Naturally, much research tacks back and forth between the two sets of concerns.

Thomas Medvetz's book *Think Tanks in America* (2012) is a prime example: it shows how ideas generated in the "interstitial field" of think tanks flow out to affect political debates and policy in consequential and surprising ways. Still, research on specialized knowledge producers is distinctive in its focus on the elaborate occupational worlds inhabited by producers of ideas, the institutions and formal organizations of those worlds, and the wider social, cultural, political, and economic environments that form their backdrop. Sociologists of ideas ask: to what extent are claims to knowledge dependent on these social factors, and how, if at all, should awareness of such dependence change our evaluation of those claims? Sociologists of ideas, and those in aligned areas like STS, have produced an expansive body of research centered around these questions. Much of this has been on natural scientists and humanists, but social scientists have also come under the microscope.

One might imagine that, in a politically polarized age when the objectivity of the social sciences is in question, sociologists of ideas would have closely examined the relationship between the politics of social scientists and the knowledge they produce. Yet while scholars obviously have a rough sense that certain topics – the 1960s, say – look different when examined through radical versus liberal versus conservative analytic lenses, few studies have been concerned with the basic and vital issue raised by Duarte et al. and Shields and Dunn: in what ways precisely do social scientists' partisan political commitments, values, and attitudes affect their work? This is a subject deserving of a great deal of research, and if claims like those of Duarte et al. and Shields and Dunn serve as a prod for new inquiries, they will have been worthwhile. For such research to have maximum value, however, a key development in the sociology of ideas must be heeded.

A Turn toward Practice

An important feature of the best sociological research on ideas is attention to the social practices of knowledge making and dissemination: the habits, routines, techniques, procedures, and other taken-for-granted ways of doing things employed by particular groups of knowledge producers as they go about their day-to-day intellectual lives (see Camic, Gross, and Lamont 2011). Where a previous generation of scholarship on scientists and intellectuals identified individual-, institution-, or macro-level variables thought to influence the content of ideas or their volume or spread, newer work, grounded in fine-grained historical studies and ethnographies, recognizes that the impact of variable factors is always mediated by the local and meaning-rich patterns of interaction and labor of those involved. These patterns are neither wholly idiosyncratic to individual knowledge producers nor fully interpretable by reference to abstract scientific or intellectual ideals.

On the one hand, by their nature, knowledge-making practices are shared among members of an epistemic community, their enactment a joint accomplishment that depends on effective socialization procedures, tacit understandings, cultural schemas, and widely used technologies. On the other hand, unlike abstract ideals, practices have histories: they evolve, and evolutions can be traced. And to speak of knowledge *making* practices is to treat the discoveries of natural and social scientists, the books written by philosophers, and the articles produced by journalists as objects of labor with histories of their own, infused with contingency. Research using this approach engages in explanation by tracing the connections among practices, actors, ideas, and broader social configurations.

In a sterling example of scholarship of this sort, Sarah Igo (2011) examines the techniques used by pioneers of public opinion polling to persuade skeptical Americans that answering questions about their beliefs and experiences was worthwhile. She begins by noting that social research on the physical and biological sciences has found that rendering nature amenable to analysis requires creating instruments for measurement, getting others in the scientific community to regard those instruments and their measures as legitimate, making and standardizing specimens, finagling things so that experiments will run as planned, and so on. Nature's cooperation with science must be induced.

So it is with the social sciences, Igo insists, where researchers face the additional complication that the objects of knowledge – human beings – must be persuaded of the value of the knowledge to be gained from their participation before they agree to take part in research. This is obvious from a methodological perspective, where much has been written on how psychologists should go about recruiting subjects to come in to the laboratory or how ethnographers can convince wary members of a subgroup to open their lives to observers. But sociologists of ideas had heretofore given little consideration to these and other cooperation-inducing practices. Igo uses the early-twentieth-century history of public opinion polling as a case study to move such an analysis forward.

When opinion polls were first introduced in the United States, few members of the public understood their purpose. Especially outside the circle of the highly educated, people did not grasp how talking to a small random sample of Americans could result in knowledge of the public more generally. But unless people agreed to talk to pollsters – applied social scientists – when they knocked on the door or called on the phone or sent queries through the mail, polling would have been impossible. So, while leading pollsters like George Gallup and Elmo Roper were busy working up techniques for analyzing data, they were also developing strategies of persuasion.

After some trial and error, they hit upon the idea that polls should be seen as public-service enterprises. They argued that short of elections, polls were the best way to gauge the views of the sprawling American public, and could be used to inform policy-making that was responsive to the will of the people. By taking part in polling, individual Americans would contribute to democracy. Pollsters pushed this message in a multifaceted public relations campaign. Although not wholly effective, the campaign succeeded in getting response rates high enough that polling soon became institutionalized. Igo does not deny that public opinion polling only emerged in a particular macrosocial context – a large, industrialized, democratic nation where elites were searching for technologies that would help them govern in a legitimate fashion. But she argues that the knowledge and ideas generated through polls cannot be fully understood without attention to the social practices of persuasion that made polling possible.

Building on such insights, we argue that research on political diversity and political bias in social science would benefit from greater emphasis on the practices of social scientists. Now, some scholars working on the topic already do flag practices, if not in the terms used by sociologists of ideas. On one reading, this is a major concern of Shields and Dunn: they describe how conservative social scientists and humanists developed – individually and collectively – a number of strategies for protecting their careers, including staying "in the closet" about their political views until after tenure. But the bulk of the research in the area is inattentive to practices, and because of this is at best incomplete and at worst flawed. Duarte et al., for instance, might be seen as highlighting practices when they argue, based on several studies of outcomes of the peer review process, that due to motivated cognition, reviewers favor manuscripts whose conclusions they agree with politically. Yet studies like these make no attempt to observe practices as they unfold in real time, or even to reconstruct them second-hand (through interviews, say). They assume there is a single ideal form peer review should take, and then further assume that seemingly objectionable patterns in outcome must reflect intellectual procedures that deviate from that ideal. Practices are assumed rather than studied objects.

Studies of peer review not focused on politics but instead on broader evaluative practices make clear why such an analytic distinction is important. In research on interdisciplinary panels that review grant applications in the social sciences and the humanities, Michèle Lamont (2009) finds that scholars are highly conscious of the need to avoid the appearance of impropriety in their evaluations, and to shore up the sense among committee members that the evaluation process is meritocratic and fair. This leads them to engage in behaviors that would not otherwise be evident, such as deferring to the disciplinary expertise of other panel members even when a proposal is not in line with their own intellectual tastes, what Lamont and her co-authors call "cognitive contextualism."

How do peer reviewers in the social sciences actually construct reviews when asked to evaluate studies with clear political implications? Surely some succumb to a knee-jerk, partisan response, favoring studies with which they agree politically and disfavoring those they oppose. But it is reasonable to suppose that others, after years of training and professional socialization, are far more thoughtful and measured, resorting to an assortment of techniques – some likely well-established in the social science community, some perhaps local innovations – to counter their own motivated cognition. One technique that Gross has used (and has seen other reviewers use) is to try to imagine all the reasonable objections to a claim that might be raised by people on the other side of an issue; and to insist that the evidence authors bring forth, and their interpretations of that evidence, be strong enough to withstand the scrutiny of less sympathetic readers. Unless one were to observe such practices, one would never know of their existence. How prevalent are they? What various forms do they take? How are they distributed across the social science community? What effect do they end up having on the content of knowledge? If it is generally the case that practices of knowledge-making mediate the effects of background variables on ideas, then it is worth studying how this may be so when the variables in question are social scientists' political commitments.

We can think of an enormous number of valuable studies that might be carried out around this spectrum of concerns. To give a few examples: by means of what practices do graduate students in the social sciences, with guidance from their advisors, come to select topics for dissertation research, and how do students' political involvements – their partisan identities and affiliations and the causes they may be a part of – influence their decisions? Or: in many social science fields – for example, sociology, anthropology, and political science – there is a significant split between scholars who cleave to a "professional" image of social science and others who have more of an "activist" view of the enterprise. What strategies do young social scientists use to position themselves in and around these camps as they put together dissertation committees, build publication portfolios, and navigate the academic job market? What practices of teaching do they pick up along the way? How are these inflected by politics – or how do such practices attempt to keep politics at bay? How if at all does politics thread through such mundane but important activities as selecting post-dissertation research projects, choosing cities and towns to live in, interacting informally with students, participating on the academic conference circuit, writing op-eds, signing petitions, getting involved with new scientific or intellectual movements, and so on? How does this vary across disciplines, types of institutional settings (for example, elite research universities versus religiously affiliated colleges versus think tanks), across time, and cross-nationally? And what are the consequences for the content of ideas – the ideas of individuals and of subfields or entire disciplines?

We are aware of only a handful of studies that address these matters in a sustained way. For example, Gross (2013) asked professors in economics, sociology, and other disciplines how politics factored into their research and teaching. He sought to identify a few of the practices scholars used to navigate between their commitments to science and their political commitments, such as the practice of remaining politically neutral in classroom discussions versus revealing one's own political stand and encouraging students to debate. Likewise, Medvetz (2012), whose work on think tanks we mentioned earlier, considered how think tank-based partisan social scientists go about trying to establish the credibility of their research in the absence of peer review. And in work now in progress, Robertson compares the knowledge practices of professors and political socialization of students in the natural sciences, social sciences, and humanities at two conservative liberal arts colleges. More research of this sort is called for – research that would utilize the methodologies best suited to the study of intellectual practices: ethnography, in-depth interviewing, and historical analysis, in conjunction with consideration of larger structuring forces.

Sociologists of ideas have written extensively on politics and social science in other respects. Fourcade-Gourinchas and Babb (2002), for example, show how a fit between the pro-free-market orientation of economists trained at the University of Chicago and the governance needs of a number of democratic as well as authoritarian states in the 1970s and 1980s facilitated the rise of neo-liberalism. Campbell and Pedersen (2014) discuss the institutional origins of the US "knowledge regime," explaining how partisan social knowledge generated by think tanks became an important part of the policy landscape here. The work of Steven Teles (2008) shows how the conservative legal movement became influential in American politics. Ferree, Khan, and Morimoto (2007) chart the various ways that feminism altered the trajectory of research and teaching in American sociology. Meanwhile, thinkers like Randall Collins and Robert Wuthnow have written on the historical conditions under which social science, in Europe and the United States, acquired enough autonomy and independence from politics, the state, and religion that it could develop fully. Though not about practices per se, these contributions are of great importance, not least because they make clear that "politics" is not simply a matter of people's positioning on a continuum from liberal to conservative, but rather a complex and historically malleable construct.

The Study of Political/Philosophical Worldviews

Rather than conclude our chapter with a blanket call for more research, we want to end by highlighting one specific topic we think it would be especially fruitful to explore: how a social scientist's political identity and commitments might affect scholarship via research practices that come to seem sensible in light of the deep philosophical assumptions that are often bundled together with politics. We term these political/philosophical worldviews. A few examples will help us flesh out what we mean.

In "The Political Unconscious of Social and Cultural History, or, Confessions of a Former Quantitative Historian," sociologist-historian William Sewell, Jr. (2005) uses the arc of his own career as a case study for exploring how politics can have unintended consequences for scholarship. Like many young historians of his generation, Sewell began his academic research committed to the burgeoning social history movement, as well as the left-leaning activism of the 1960s. These new social historians "tended to regard what [they] called 'traditional narrative history' as atheoretical and intellectually bankrupt" (178), and thus worked to make their field "scientific" by drawing on data and quantitative methods from their colleagues in sociology, political science, and economics. But while social history's focus on marginalized groups and social structure was consistent with their shared political convictions, a younger generation of social historians came to believe its philosophical presuppositions were not. While the radical left movements of the late 1960s critiqued America's involvement in the Vietnam War and state support of white supremacy, they also rejected the "defects of Fordist capitalism, especially corporate conformity, bureaucratic monotony, repressive morality, and stultifying forms of mass culture" (180). The Fordist mode of macrosocial and macroeconomic production that birthed the post-war order seemed to rely on the very claims to positivist epistemology, ontological objectivity, and managerial science that undergirded the methodological practices of social historical analyses.

Sewell argues that by the mid- to late 1970s, the anti-Fordist critique of many social historians pulled them away from structural accounts, social-scientific methods, and the search for objectivity and causal explanations, and into the arms of cultural anthropology, French post-structural philosophy, and feminist critical theory. In other words, politics – not liberal or conservative in the partisan sense but rather a politically informed theoretical orientation – had influenced their objects of analysis (discourses of power versus materialist social structures), data sources (textual representations versus records of lived experience), and methods (interpretations of meaning versus systematic analyses of data), by inadvertently and implicitly shifting the philosophical presuppositions of an entire subdisciplinary cohort. In Sewell's estimation, this resulted in "a form of history that, for all its impressive achievements and in spite of its continuing vitality and political relevance, nevertheless finds itself disarmed in the face of some of the most important questions posed to us by the history of our own era" (190), namely – and ironically – the collapse of the same Fordist regime that initially "turned" social historians away from macrosocial structures and to the micropolitics of culture.

The point here is not that political commitments threatened to bias research in the sense of leading scholars to misunderstand the evidence in front of them, though certainly this is a possibility. Instead, political and cultural changes within disciplines can shift the underlying philosophical assumptions of scholarship, giving researchers a worldview that leads them to embrace different practices and to produce different forms of social science than they would have otherwise. Following Mannheim's early contributions to the sociology of knowledge, which gave pride of place to worldviews, we see this as a common phenomenon.

Sewell's claims echo those found in the path-breaking work of standpoint theorists beginning in the 1970s. This group of feminist social scientists highlighted the intertwining of social position and scholarly practices. They focused especially on the naturalization of exploitation into seemingly immutable gendered and racialized categories (Harding 2005). Contrary to some of standpoint theory's critics, investigating the lived experience of academic knowledge-making aimed, in the words of Dorothy Smith, not "at a reiteration of what we already (tacitly) know, but at an exploration of what passes beyond that knowledge … *in the modes by which we enter into relations with the object of knowledge*" [emphasis added] (1990:24). The focus is placed on what relations underly taken-for-granted scholarly assumptions and practices. Continuing on with this project by identifying the politics-laden assumptions of different social science communities would be an eminently worthwhile enterprise – provided this could be done in an inductive manner, and not with the selective use of evidence to back a preconceived characterization.

Helen Longino's book *Studying Human Behavior* (2013) proceeds in the inductive fashion we have in mind, though politics is only one of several influences on deep-seated assumptions she examines. The book recasts the seemingly interminable "nature/nurture debate" as a study of social epistemology to account for the limits of what can be known empirically about human aggression and sexuality in the behavioral sciences. Though Longino is a philosopher by training and academic appointment, her empirical approach uses close analysis of primary and secondary materials.

Longino investigates the evidentiary standards and argumentative styles used by different groups of behavioral scientists – for example, behavioral geneticists and psychologists – to support claims made about aggression and sexuality. She traces these back to underlying epistemological, ontological, and theoretical assumptions. First, she argues that the various disciplinary approaches should be understood as epistemologically pluralistic rather than exclusive; this suggests tearing down many of the walls that unnecessarily presuppose knowledge from one domain is antithetical to claims in another. Second, she argues that since there is not one overarching concept of behavior that makes the different behavioral sciences incommensurable, the object of research (i.e., human behavior) ends up reflecting the folk psychologies, political leanings, and moral values of research communities through the particular ways they operationalize different behaviors. This claim further confirms the importance of studying how the findings of researchers depend in crucial respects on tacit knowledge, which is seen in practices of knowledge making and rarely talked about explicitly. Last, Longino argues that social (and political) forces shape "downstream" public beliefs about what behavioral investigation can and cannot explain. Longino's book hints at what sociologists of ideas might turn up if they set out to unpack the bedrock assumptions of different social science communities and their political anchors. (Julian Go's (2016) work on the intellectual legacy of colonialism in sociology – which also draws on Longino – traverses similar theoretical ground.)

Conclusion

Should there be more political diversity in the social sciences, to reduce bias and achieve other aims? A number of prominent scholars say yes. Although no one has made a persuasive case for keeping the political balance in the social sciences as it currently stands – with liberals massively outnumbering conservatives – neither are we compelled by the arguments made for change. Before signing on to proposals for large-scale reform, we would like to see some convincing empirical evidence that increasing the political diversity of social science departments really would yield better research or teaching.

That does not mean calls for political diversification are not worthwhile. As we have endeavored to show, such calls have the potential to seed a valuable line of research into what critics of the social sciences' liberal tilt assert but cannot yet demonstrate: that given operative practices of knowledge-making, social science research and teaching end up looking different in liberal versus conservative hands. We are hopeful that our chapter will encourage more of this work, and that it will be carried out under the auspices of the sociology of ideas.

Part VI

Conclusions

18 Proposals

John Gerring, James Mahoney and Colin Elman

Our goal in this book has been to examine the production of knowledge in the social science disciplines with an eye to improvements that might be implemented, now or in the foreseeable future. To bring this matter into view, we adopted a *systemic* (macro-level) framework – as distinguished from the micro-level framework usual to social science methodology, which focuses primarily on the production and vetting of individual studies. At a macro level, the question of interest is not so much what individual scholars could do better but what individual disciplines – and the social sciences at large – could do better. A "system," as explained in Chapter 1, includes all the institutions integral to academic production, e.g., subfields, departments, disciplines, universities, professional associations, journals, presses, and funders. It encompasses formal rules (e.g., word limits on journal articles) as well as informal norms (e.g., to make transparent all relevant aspects of data collection and analysis except those that compromise the confidentiality of subjects or compromise formal arrangements or law).

In this final chapter, we seek to bring together some of the themes of the book and point the way forward to possible reforms. We begin with a discussion of conflicting imperatives – between discovery and appraisal – that, in our view, underlie many of the difficulties encountered in setting standards for the social sciences. Next, we lay out a set of general principles that ought to guide any set of reforms. Third, we list a series of suggestions, recommendations, and exhortations, building on discussion in previous chapters. Fourth, we discuss metrics that might allow us to measure the adoption of the suggested reforms. Finally, we discuss the opportunities and challenges that face any reform initiative within the social sciences.

Conflicting Imperatives: True versus New

To some extent, the pathologies outlined in previous chapters may be understood as a product of conflicting goals. Two goals, in particular, seem to be at loggerheads.

On the one hand, science aims to represent an empirical reality "out there." It aspires to truth (aka believability, credibility, verisimilitude, authenticity, plausibility).

On the other hand, science aims for discovery. There is little profit in repeatedly studying things that we already know to be true, or are pretty sure to be true (or false). Science aims to expand the boundaries of truth – to study new things, or improve our understanding of things that have already been studied. Note that the highest honors of science – Nobel prizes and lifetime achievement awards – are reserved for those who have made fundamental contributions to a field of study. They have discovered something new.[1]

The trouble is that novel claims, by their nature, are less likely to be correct. And correct claims are less likely to be novel. *If new not true and if true not new*, goes the old saw. Of course, there are exceptions: some truisms are false, and some novelties are true. All truisms were once novelties, after all. But as a probabilistic statement the "true-versus-new" tradeoff often applies, and this suggests that these two fundamental goals of science may be in considerable tension with each another.

One might regard this as a productive conflict, establishing a dialectic of discovery and appraisal. In this vein, Karl Popper (1963) envisioned a scientific process composed of "conjectures and refutations." Yet, for this dynamic to be progressive it must move closer to the truth, which means that untrue discoveries are quickly (or at least eventually) falsified and discarded. Unfortunately, this does not always happen in the social sciences. It is not always easy to tell when something is wrong, as noted in previous chapters. The data rarely speak with a single voice, and attaining truth, in any case, is a probabilistic affair with multiple dimensions, e.g., internal validity, external validity, the strength of the effect (if causal), the precision of the effect, the mechanisms at work, and so forth. Studies are not easy to evaluate since there are multiple dimensions of adequacy (Chapter 13).

Complicating matters further, the conflict between truth and innovation generates countervailing incentives. On the one hand, researchers are urged to make an original contribution, without which they will not reach the Shangri-La of publication in a top venue, high citation counts, and occupational rewards (a good job and promotion to tenure). To make an original contribution, one must distinguish one's work from all that has come before. At the same time, the work must be true. To convince gatekeepers (editors, reviewers, hiring committees) that the argument is correct a number of hurdles must be

---

[1] Issues raised in this section are discussed in greater detail in Chapter 14.

cleared, the most familiar of which is the 95-percent confidence interval ($p < 0.05$). Because there is a good deal of flexibility in these hurdles – many ways in which scope-conditions may be established and samples from a population identified, analyzed, interpreted, and reported – authors enjoy a lot of wiggle room. This caveat also applies to qualitative styles of research, which by virtue of informality offer many opportunities for authorial intervention (Chapter 9).

"Fishing" can take many forms and this, in turn, seems to have contributed to a general devaluation of exploratory work (Chapters 2–3). While qualitative work has long faced a skeptical reception, this skeptical lens has lately turned toward quantitative work, especially that based on observational data. Terms like *creative* and *original*, formerly regarded as virtues, are now employed as terms of abuse, issued with brackets ("creative," "original") intended to suggest questionable assumptions or outright foul play.

In the face of such thoroughgoing skepticism, scholars may be reticent to engage with data (or to admit having done so) lest they fall prey to "forking paths" – the many decisions along the road to publication that may lead to false conclusions (Gelman and Loken 2013). Soaking and poking is no longer viewed as a valued skill, but rather as a dark art. Yet, it is not clear how we are to learn about the world if engagement with that world is viewed as potentially compromising.

In response to the new-versus-true dilemma, scholars may choose to prioritize one goal over the other. For some, innovation is the main calling, and since innovation sometimes requires a degree of methodological abandon (Feyerabend 1993) scholars may be prepared to publish work that is more difficult to assess. For others, truth is the main desiderata, and all measures to avoid falsity – including pre-registration (with a specific pre-analysis plan) and results-blind review – should be adopted.

Variation in preferences – for new-versus-true – can be found through time and across fields and subfields in the social sciences. At present, our impression is that sociology leans in the direction of discovery, while political science leans in the direction of appraisal. Journals, departments, and funders may also be located along this spectrum and their relative position may change over time.

However, we suspect that most social scientists prize both goals. They want new things, and they want them to be true. This suggests that a movement too far in one direction or the other may compromise the standing of an individual, department, journal, field, or discipline.

Consider a top journal that erects high barriers against false findings. Such a journal is likely to publish lots of research that is not very innovative, i.e., studies that confirm things that scholars already knew, or strongly suspected. The latter articles are unlikely to be widely cited, which will drive down the journal's impact factor. As a consequence, that journal is likely to fall in prestige. It will no longer be regarded as the most desirable place to publish one's work, and this will institute a vicious cycle in which scholars do not send their best work there.

The same tradeoff faces a journal that takes a different approach, prioritizing theory formation over theory testing and thus erecting low barriers against Type-1 error. Over time, researchers may come to regard papers in that journal skeptically, knowing that a good deal of it might not be true, or even falsifiable. As a consequence, articles from this journal are not likely to be widely cited – or they will be cited with suspicion. Again, the journal's reputation is likely to suffer.

It is telling that no journals – or, at any rate, no prominent journals – have adopted an extreme position on this spectrum. Specifically, no social science journal that we are aware of accepts only pre-registered studies or conducts reviews only through a results-blind process. Likewise, no journal that we are aware of makes no bones about theories being true.

One might still insist that the tension between truth and novelty is a healthy tension. However, we are brought to a fundamental problem. One can strive for truth and innovation, but one cannot really maximize both criteria in the same venture because the two goals call for different approaches. Discovery must be open ended, unconstrained, hopeful, and optimistic about finding new things in the world. Appraisal must be taciturn and suspicious, looking for error at every turn.[2]

Consider that for strong appraisal to occur, a hypothesis and research design (including a specific plan of analysis) must be laid out in advance. Otherwise, researchers may be inclined to cheat, e.g., reporting tests that confirm their hypothesis and slipping others under the rug. Or they may adjust the parameters of the hypothesis or research design as they go along to generate a better fit to the data. For example, if a relationship between X and Y is strong in one setting and weak in another they may decide that there are good reasons for this, i.e., differences in background factors that might affect X's impact on Y, justifying an alteration in the scope-conditions of the theory.

---

[2] A caveat: pre-registration *can* be coupled with exploratory research if researchers feel free to explore hypotheses that were not included in the pre-registered study (or were listed as subsidiary hypotheses). For experimental studies with large samples this makes a lot of sense. But for other modes of research, probably not.

From the perspective of exploratory research, this is not cheating; it is good research. But it doesn't make for a strong test of the theory since the theory is re-jiggered as the research proceeds, making it more likely that a positive result will be achieved.

In other words, the same practices that make for good exploratory research can make for bad confirmatory research, and vice-versa. Discovery is impeded if hemmed in by rules intended to facilitate testing, while appraisal is impeded if the research question or procedure is open-ended.

This might seem like a zero-sum game. However, the two goals can be reconciled, and a productive dialectic between discovery and appraisal promoted, if we can effectively *distinguish* between work that is exploratory (where the goal is to discover something new about the world) and work that is confirmatory (where the goal is to test a preconceived hypothesis).

One such mechanism is pre-registration. Research questions characterized by prior unobservability, new data independent of old, and tests of reasonable precision may be pre-registered, along with a specific pre-analysis plan (Chapter 9). This should be sufficient to qualify a piece of research as confirmatory (so long as the PAP is followed). However, it is not a viable option for research where prior unobservability does not apply. Here, it may be necessary to designate individuals and venues whose explicit goal is appraisal, so that their incentives are aligned with that task (as proposed in Chapter 14). This reinforces another central theme of this book, which is that social science is a communal activity in which different individuals play different – and hopefully complementary – roles (Chapter 3).

In any case, keeping the goals of exploration and appraisal separate increases the likelihood that each will be fully achieved. While this does not resolve the tension between these fundamental goals of science, it reduces the confusion. Exploratory work does not need to pose as confirmatory, and confirmatory work does not need to deliver something novel.

Principles

Drawing on insights from the previous chapters, we adopt five general principles to guide the process of reform.

First, we suggest that social scientists keep the twin objectives of science in view. Scientific progress depends upon both *discovery* (aka exploration, innovation) and *appraisal* (aka assessment, confirmation, falsification/verification, justification, testing), as discussed. The possibility of Type-1 errors (accepting a false hypothesis) must be balanced against the possibility of Type-2 errors (rejecting a true hypothesis). More specifically, any reform that bolsters the strength of scientific appraisal should do so without unduly constraining incentives for discovery.

Second, reforms must be synchronized with *scholarly incentives* – or those incentives must be altered in a fashion that generates the desired practice. It is not sufficient to identify "best practices" unless scholars and institutions (e.g., journals, departments, and funding agencies) are willing and able to follow them. Formulating a new norm is pointless if following that norm imposes unacceptable sacrifices of time, money, or success. Proposed reforms must be grounded in a realistic sociology of science.

Third, reforms should enhance – or at least not detract from – the overall *efficiency* of the enterprise (Gans 2017; Ioannidis et al. 2014; Stephan 2012). Social science is not a well-funded activity, at least not by comparison with the natural sciences, the medical sciences, or the private sector. Any suggested reforms of these disciplines must therefore be considered in light of the temporal and monetary costs they are likely to impose as well as the practices they might displace. It is sobering to consider that, according to a recent estimate, unpaid academic reviewing by faculty imposes a cost on universities of roughly $2.4 billion a year (Corbyn 2008). This is not to say that it is a waste; it is simply to point out that such an expenditure must be considered in light of other activities that $2.4 billion could support. Every cost involves an opportunity cost.

Fourth, reforms – as well as the process of deliberation leading up to their adoption – should be as *inclusive* as possible. Proposed changes should not systematically disadvantage scholars who bear certain ascriptive characteristics or ideological attachments. Changes should encompass all major methodological traditions in the social sciences – quantitative and qualitative, experimental and observational, descriptive and causal. Granted, this is not always possible; some reforms are more appropriate for experimental or quantitative methods, for example. However, solutions developed in one context can often be adapted to another context without sacrificing the unique contributions of each approach.

Fifth, reforms should be *feasible*, i.e., realizable in the near future and without a huge investment of funds or a major reorganization of academic life. This is not intended to dismiss reforms that involve a fundamentally different way of organizing the production of knowledge, e.g., abolishing journals and academic presses or reformulating the structure of university education. These more radical reforms are also worth considering. However, in the present context we want to maintain a focus on incremental changes that seem more or less within reach, based on existing academic organizations.

Recommendations, Exhortations, Suggestions

In this section, we enumerate, and briefly explain, a series of proposals that – in the judgment of the authors, and following the guidelines laid out above – bear serious consideration. Consistent with the structure of the book, many of these reforms are systemic in nature, targeted at institutions rather than individuals.

Some proposals take the form of specific *recommendations*. Others are diffuse *exhortations*, which we also feel committed to but which are difficult to operationalize and enforce. Still others take the form of *suggestions*, the virtues and vices of which remain unclear but which deserve further discussion and extensive pilot-testing.

Each of these proposals is discussed at greater length in preceding sections of the book, so our treatment here will be brief and does not include references to work on the subject. We follow the sequence of the book, marking chapters where various issues are discussed in greater depth.

Some of these reforms have already been adopted or experimented with, though perhaps only in a small corner of the scientific universe. Others remain on the horizon but are nonetheless feasible, in our judgment.

We do not presume that readers will agree with all of these proposals. (Indeed, there is debate among the contributing authors of this book.) Our purpose in presenting them is to recapitulate the ground covered in previous chapters and to lay out a wide-ranging agenda for the consideration of economists, political scientists, sociologists, and those in allied disciplines. Arguably, the best way to move forward is to place specific initiatives on the table. If a discipline turns toward a different solution, or resolves to continue with the status quo, at least the debate has been joined.

Discovery (Part I)

Discovery is widely praised in the abstract but largely ignored by the curriculum of social science methodology and swept under the rug in the act of publication, where authors are encouraged to present their theories as if they sprung, fully formed, from well-grounded a priori assumptions. The immaculate-conception vision of social science is misleading, in the extreme. By covering our tracks, we are removing information that could allow scholars to better judge the veracity of a theory, and also better understand the act of creation. To improve the craft of discovery and its productive employment in scholarship, we make five recommendations.

1. *Soaking and poking* (Chapter 2). Researchers should not be afraid to embark on limited tours of a topic without strong preconceptions of what they might find and how they might go about finding it (i.e., without a determinate research design). Researchers should keep their minds open for as long as possible, allowing themselves to be led by hunches and stray pieces of evidence, barking up trees, following avenues until they lead to dead-ends. Social science, like journalism, needs open-ended, investigatory work. To this end, scholars should fully exploit the potential of "soaking and poking," and funders should regard it as an important category of research to be supported.[3]

Such research might take the form of a brief case study, including selective interviews with informants or preliminary fieldwork. It might consist of analyzing a dataset, perhaps with the assistance of algorithms that search for best-fit relationships (e.g., random forests, LASSO). Virtually any sort of observational research may be conducted in an exploratory manner. Even experimental research may be approached in an exploratory fashion, e.g., by examining background covariates, interaction effects, or outcomes that were not envisioned as part of the original research. So long as exploratory research is not forced to masquerade as confirmatory research, it is likely to be recognized as a vital part of the production of knowledge.

2. *Abduction* (Chapter 2). We ought to practice abduction, the art of constructing explanations for phenomena. Granted, theoretical innovation cannot be taught in a rote fashion (there are no textbooks or software for learning how to think about things in new ways). However, abduction may be taught in a more indirect fashion, e.g., by reading about the process of discovery or by conducting exercises (generating hypotheses that might explain a given phenomenon). We can "learn to un-learn" established ways of thinking so that a topic can be re-conceptualized in new ways.

3. *High-risk/high-payoff research* (Chapter 2). Most social science research is fairly timid, conducted in a low-risk environment with theories that are

---

[3] An unusual – but highly welcome – venture in this direction is NSF's Early-Concept Grants for Exploratory Research (EAGER).

well-established or empirical territory that is well-trodden. Since one is dealing with a known universe, there are relatively few uncertainties and research investments may be minimal. However, this sort of research is unlikely to lead to fundamental breakthroughs.

We encourage researchers to make high-risk/high-payoff investments. This is understood as a piece of research that (a) requires a substantial investment in time and/or resources, (b) whose results are highly uncertain (insofar as the research design envisioned by the researcher may turn out to be impossible to implement or might not render the expected findings), and (c) for which success would constitute a substantial contribution to our knowledge of a subject.

To be sure, high-risk/high-payoff research may not be the best career advice for those in tenuous positions (e.g., graduate students and assistant professors). But it is surely an appropriate strategy for those enshrined with academic tenure. One of the presumed benefits of job security is the ability to take risks. For this to happen, scholars must fight the urge to settle into established research problems and routines. They must stretch themselves into areas of discomfort, and expose themselves to failure. In this, we have much to learn from the community of business entrepreneurs, where for every successful start-up there are multiple failures. We should view the failure of a high-risk/high-payoff venture not as a personal failure but rather as a signal of likely future success.

4. *Research cycles* (Chapter 3). In the social sciences, the convention is that a single study conducted by a single author or a small team of authors presents a fundamentally new idea and tests it in a rigorous fashion. In the medical sciences, by contrast, the production of knowledge is a group activity involving many different scholars, each of whom is likely to play a somewhat different role and whose involvement is ongoing rather than single-shot (i.e., a single study). Some conduct exploratory research, i.e., open-ended investigations (perhaps of a clinical nature) and speculative theorizing. Others conduct confirmatory research, e.g., large-scale clinical trials or epidemiological analyses focused on a large population. Given the wide range of expertise required for most social science research, and given the length of time it usually takes to develop new theories, this approach holds promise for the social sciences. To establish an honored and fruitful position for discovery in the academy we ought to consider its position within a broader research cycle.

5. *Distinguishing exploration and appraisal* (Chapters 2, 9, 14). Exploratory research gets a bad rap because publishing conventions force all research to masquerade as theory-driven, opening up the charge that researchers are engaged in curve-fitting or fishing. We need to find ways to effectively signal when research is conducted in an exploratory mode and when it is conducted in a confirmatory mode, so that confusion is minimized. Preliminary theories and weak tests should be taken for what they are. But this does not mean they should be excluded from scholarly discourse or relegated to second-tier publication venues. If innovation is essential to the progress of science scholars must be incentivized to innovate, and this means having access to top-flight journals. At the same time, scholars should be *dis*-incentivized from dressing up their novel ideas and weak tests as if they were solidly grounded in theory and empirics. If we can develop ways of distinguishing – to reviewers, editors, and readers – work that is exploratory from work that is confirmatory, we shall have a mechanism for establishing appropriate standards for each type of work while avoiding confusion about their probable truth-value.

Several options seem viable, singly or in combination.

Pre-registration (discussed below) is one approach. Arguably, if a study is not pre-registered (with a specific pre-analysis plan), it should be regarded as exploratory. In this fashion, research that meets the desiderata of pre-registration (prior unobservability, new data independent of old, and precise tests (Chapter 9)) would be encouraged to follow that regimen. Everything else, which we assume will continue to constitute the majority of work in the social sciences, would be grouped under the broad rubric of exploratory. Because the residual category is large, we assume that it will not suffer ignominy.

Granted, this way of dividing up the world of social science does a disservice to work that follows the confirmatory model but uses data that are already in the public domain, and hence cannot establish prior unobservability. However, this sacrifice is justified. In the absence of pre-registration (and prior unobservability) there is no way to verify that the researcher has not fished her results. If we leave it open to researchers to declare whether they followed the rules of confirmatory research (e.g., separating theory formation from theory testing) we are offering an incentive for them to misrepresent their work, with unfortunate downstream effects on everyone: liars will prosper and honest-brokers will lose out.

For work that does not allow for pre-registration, there is only one credible approach to confirmation. This involves a clear division of labor between "explorers" and "appraisers." The former would be tasked with developing new theories, the latter with testing those theories, e.g., with replications, meta-analyses, and extensive reviews of the literature. It is assumed that explorers would follow traditional publishing routes while the latter would be enlisted for special journals or task forces or special sections of journals reserved for the task of appraisal. As such, researchers' incentives should be aligned with the task at hand and there would be no confusion about whether the study was exploratory or confirmatory. Further discussion of such a system of appraisal is taken up below.

Publishing (Part II)

The centrality of publishing to the academic enterprise makes the gatekeepers – academic journals and presses, and their editors and reviewers – especially influential in the conduct of science. Of course, there are other avenues to putting one's work before the public, e.g., posting a paper on a public platform like SSRN, EconPapers, IDEAS, a working paper series, or a personal web site. Some have argued for a thorough overhaul of the journal-centered system of academic production (Chapter 4). At present, however, journals and presses serve as the principal gatekeepers of knowledge, and an implicit hierarchy among journals and presses serves as an important signal of quality. As long as this system persists, it is important to look closely at the standards applied by the publishing industry, and possible improvements thereto. In this spirit, we offer the following recommendations: (1) significance reviews, (2) open peer reviews, and (3) the abolition (or softening) of length limits. (Other reforms, central to transparency and reproducibility, are taken up in the following section.)

1. *Significance reviews* (Chapter 4). A key question in the review of any manuscript is its import for the discipline, as well as for ordinary citizens and policymakers. This may be distinguished from its truth-value. While specialists are well-positioned to judge the truth-value of a claim, they may be less well-positioned to judge its overall significance. Insofar as a journal or press wishes to make this a priority, editors are encouraged to seek significance reviews in addition to traditional reviews (ascertaining its truth-value). A significance review inquires about the importance of an author's chosen topic (in everyday terms) and its potential contribution to the scholarly literature

(assuming the empirical claims are true). Claims of significance are of course a matter of degrees, and this is precisely what a significance review is designed to determine. Such a review may require only a quick reading of the introductory and concluding sections of a paper or book and thus should be fairly easy to conduct and to report. The report itself might consist of answering several multiple-choice questions. One would hope to get input from several reviewers, at least some of whom are outside the subfield in which the paper falls. We anticipate that significance reviews would shift scholarly attention to broader, more theoretically significant subjects, and would also force writers to seriously consider the external validity of their findings and a broader set of potential readers. It would no longer be sufficient to appeal to a micro-audience of specialists who study the same thing, who review each others' work regularly, and who are likely to share the same substantive and methodological commitments.

2. *Open peer review* (Chapter 4). Review processes are generally double-blind, or at least single-blind (where the reviewer's identity is unknown to the author), and mediated by a rather cumbersome mechanism of staged reviews. The only opportunity for authors and reviewers to communicate is through the journal office at each stage of the review. Given the substantial time invested by reviewers (generally uncompensated) it might make sense to acknowledge their contributions, which would serve as a form of compensation and also might raise the level of effort and attention granted to this onerous task. It would also make the process more transparent.

Several options are available to open up the peer review process. These may be categorized as (a) *facilitated* – when authors and reviewers are allowed to communicate directly with one another on an ongoing basis but without revealing each other's identity, (b) *signed* – when reviewers' names appear alongside the published article or the reviews that are passed to the authors have the reviewers' names on them, (c) *disclosed* – when the author and the reviewer are aware of each other's identity and engage in discussion during the review process, (d) *transparent* – when the entire review process is "out in the open," including the original manuscripts, the reviewers' comments and the authors' replies, (e) *crowdsourced* – when anyone can comment on the article before its official publication, (f) *pre-publication* – when a public review occurs before the article's publication, or (g) *post-publication* – when review happens after an article's publication, perhaps through a blog post. These options may be employed singly, or in combination.

The first option (a) seems to impose very little cost, except for the cost of programming an interface (akin to the Craig'slist server) that will allow reviewers and authors to communicate directly with each other. Presumably, it would serve to clarify points that might otherwise lead to an incorrect assessment and would also reduce the time and burden of completing a thorough review. Just as a question during an academic talk helps to clarify what is going on, we imagine that a quick question during an initial reading of a paper would alleviate many misunderstandings. Since it is entirely optional, it would not impose a burden on reviewers who prefer to utilize the traditional approach (formal letters written to the editor).

For options that involve the revelation of a reviewer's identity, we suggest that this be voluntary. If reviewers are required to reveal their identity it might compromise the ability of editors to recruit reviewers, and the ability of reviewers to speak their minds frankly.

However, it seems like a reasonable option for reviewers to allow their names to become public at some point in the process, e.g., after an article has been accepted for publication. A possible downside is that reviewers might seek to ingratiate themselves with influential colleagues by writing flattering reviews.

For options that involve the revelation of an author's identity (prior to acceptance for publication), we are unsure. While it is true that this can usually be ascertained by reviewers – e.g., by searching the web by title in order to find a working paper or conference paper – anonymity is a useful fiction. It establishes the principle that evaluations of a manuscript should not be influenced by the identity of the author – her status in the profession, ascriptive characteristics, or personal relationship to the reviewer. This is an essential principle. Even if reviewers cheat (looking up the name of the author on the web), they are likely to feel self-conscious about letting this knowledge influence their review. By contrast, if the name of the author appears on a manuscript it may be more difficult for reviewers to separate their opinions of the paper from their opinions of the author. They may even feel that it is a legitimate consideration.

For options that involve crowdsourcing after the publication of a paper, we suggest that the identity of commentators be made public as a requirement of participation. Otherwise, the risk of nepotism, cranks or trolls is unacceptably high. Even so, we worry that the acerbic, and occasionally confrontational, nature of online discussion might discourage junior scholars, women, minorities and those who are shy by nature from participating (Bear and

Collier 2016; Vasilescu, Capiluppi, and Serebrenik 2014). Active monitoring may be required, depending upon the tone of discussion and observed rates of participation.

3. *Length limits* (Chapter 5). The arbitrary word or page limits imposed by most journals do not serve the progress of science. They contort the academic process in ways that are not conducive to the conduct or dissemination of scholarly research, and they may introduce bias that reinforces other pathologies (e.g., reluctance to publish work that relies on qualitative or multimethod research, or work that is theoretically ambitious). Accordingly, we recommend that journals should abolish – or at least loosen – length limits. The relevant standard for articles should be *as long as is necessary* – no longer, and no shorter. Of course, this is a matter of judgment. But just as reviewers judge the quality of a manuscript along other dimensions, they should be encouraged to assess whether an article is appropriately sized. Importantly, this recommendation is contingent upon the willingness of journals to move to an exclusively online publication format; otherwise, publication costs might preclude its feasibility.

Transparency and Reproducibility (Part III)

Social science research should be open and transparent, data and analytic procedures should be available to future researchers and results should be verifiable. These are fundamental principles of science. Of course, there are limits to what can be achieved in this area by reason of logistical constraints (e.g., the time and trouble it would require to track, and to store, all relevant information pertaining to a study), legal constraints (e.g., intellectual property), and ethical constraints (e.g., preserving the confidentiality of sources). But within these bounds, it is important to insist on high standards. We offer five recommendations, as follows.

1. *Data Access and Infrastructure* (Chapters 7–8). Despite widespread acceptance of the goals of transparency and reproducibility it is often difficult, or impossible, to gain access to the information used to reach inferences contained in published works of social science. Either the data have not been preserved, or they are kept private, or the author does not respond to queries about their location. We propose that researchers should record, preserve, and make public the procedures used for data collection and analysis as well as the data itself so that findings can be reproduced – so long as the confidentiality of sources is preserved, where such confidentiality is required as an ethical, legal, or practical condition of conducting the research. In the cases

where data cannot be publicly shared (for example, US Census Bureau data accessed through the Federal Statistical Research Data Centers), researchers should provide clear instructions on how an interested party would attempt to gain access to the data.

We propose that journals and presses enforce this goal by adopting standards appropriate for specific fields and types of research. For example, they might require authors to use particular reporting guidelines, such as CONSORT for clinical trials, CONSORT-SPI for psychology and STROBE for observational studies in epidemiology. They might also ask authors to follow transparency standards, such as those formulated by TOP for the sciences generally, and DA-RT for political science. A key element in developing appropriate standards for different types of research is the acknowledgment that while the general principles are universally applicable, the practices that instantiate those principles will differ according to the nature of the data and the analyses conducted using them. The computational analysis of a matrix dataset and process tracing analysis that uses heterogeneous data, for example, must both show their workings. But how that transparency is achieved, and the ways that different challenges to openness present themselves, will vary across contexts.

2. *Pre-registration* (Chapters 7, 9). For inquiries that aim to test a proposition against data, researchers should look for opportunities to enhance the credibility of their tests by publicly declaring their study design and plans for analysis prior to encountering the data. Pre-registration can help underwrite the integrity of claims to have tested, rather than fished, the hypotheses under examination. It can thus help reduce biases in favor of strong, positive results. Implemented properly, pre-registration need not limit the scope for ex post discovery or exploratory analysis. Rather, pre-registration allows researchers to credibly *distinguish* the elements of their analysis that constitute tests from those elements that are exploratory or were carried out ex post. By enabling credible communication about forms of analysis, pre-registration can help elevate the status of exploratory inquiry, making it harder for researchers to cloak discovery in the mantle of testing, as discussed.

Ideally, a study and pre-analysis plan specify in detail how data are to be collected, how they are to be analyzed, and what counts as evidence for or against the hypothesis. To facilitate this, pre-registration sites in the social sciences have been developed, including the Evidence in Governance and Politics (EGAP) registry and the American Economic Association's www.socialscienceregistry.org.

To date, pre-registration has been used primarily for randomized experiments, a prospective form of research (by definition). However, pre-registration may be applied to any study – experimental or observational, quantitative or qualitative – if (a) the data are unobservable to the researcher at the time of registration, (b) the test data are independent of prior observations and (c) tests can be precisely specified in advance. It is not clear how many social science studies qualify on all three criteria, and hence how broad the ambit of pre-registration might be.

3. *Results-blind review* (Chapter 9). Even under a system of pre-registration researchers and publishers have an incentive to select intriguing, counter-intuitive results for publication, leaving aside mundane results that confirm established wisdom. Since counterintuitive results are less likely to be true the body of published work in a field is likely to misrepresent the truth. To combat publication bias and the file-drawer problem, journals should consider reserving a significant portion of their submission stream for results-blind review.

Under results-blind review, the researcher submits for peer review a manuscript containing all standard elements of a writeup – framing of the research question; theory; methods and specification of tests – except for the empirical results. It may be that the author has not yet conducted the analysis or that the results have been removed from the paper. In either case, reviewers and editors evaluate the manuscript based on the plausibility of the hypotheses, the quality of the study design and the importance of the question being addressed. In effect, it is a proposal of research that might be conducted, and in this respect follow well-established procedures for reviewing grant proposals. Authors can then receive in-principle acceptance of their article: an editorial commitment to publish paper with the results regardless of what those results might be as long as the data collection and analysis plans are faithfully executed.

This is a very new idea and there is not much of a track record. It is difficult to say how feasible it might be in the social sciences, what sort of work it might be appropriate for, and what its impact might be. What does seem clear is that results-blind review is most effective in combating bias when combined with pre-registration, as in the "registered reports" model of publication (Nosek and Lakens 2014). However, even where research does not meet the demanding requirements of pre-registration there may important benefits from a results-blind review process.

4. *Unsurprising findings*. Studies that confirm conventional wisdom are less likely to be published by virtue of that fact. The author may choose to leave

the study unsubmitted (in the proverbial file drawer) or may submit it to a journal only to find that it is rejected on account of "uninteresting" findings. This contributes to an overall bias in which published results do not accurately represent the entire set of results that scholars have obtained. Results-blind review offers one solution to this problem, though this would probably apply only to studies that are judged to have highly interesting research questions and determinate research designs.

Recently, several journals have been founded, or reformulated, with the intention of providing an outlet for such studies. This includes the *International Journal of Negative and Null Results* and *PLoS ONE* (natural sciences), the *Journal of Negative Results in BioMedicine*, the *Journal of Articles in Support of the Null Hypothesis* (psychology) and *SURE: The Series of Unsurprising Results in Economics*. The latter imposes only two criteria for submission: (a) the article has been rejected at a journal indexed in EconLit, and (b) the rejection centered on results that were regarded by the editor or reviewers for the original journal as statistically insignificant or otherwise unsurprising.

It is too early to tell how successful these ventures will be. On the one hand, authors who have already exhausted the peer review process at other journals may find the option attractive, as it requires little extra work, offers a publication for their CV and the opportunity to gain more citations than they might with a working paper. On the other hand, if it is perceived as a low-quality publication some authors may prefer to stay unpublished. Furthermore, the presence of a low-prestige journal does little to motivate scholars to conduct studies or to complete studies (once conducted) that have un-sexy results. In any case, we are anxious to observe the track record of these journals as they develop and recommend that other disciplines consider following their lead.

Appraisal (Part IV)

Arguably, the same individual who constructs a new hypothesis should not be responsible for testing that hypothesis, even if strong safeguards (e.g., pre-registration) are in place. Only by separating the tasks of discovery and appraisal, and investing them in different people, can we be reasonably sure that each goal will be achieved. Researchers can always find ways – licit or illicit – to fool the system, which sets up an arms-race between researchers and enforcers, who must invest enormous time and energy adapting rules and enforcement mechanisms to make sure that regulations are faithfully followed. If, however, the explorer and appraiser are different people, responsive to different incentives, there is no need (or less need) for an intrusive and expensive regulatory system to oversee scholarly behavior. One can rely on incentives to govern behavior. To assist in the process of appraisal we suggest the following initiatives, centered on (1) replication, (2) comprehensive appraisal, and (3) citation-based metrics of impact.

1. *Replication* (Chapters 10–11, 13). For science to progress, results (published or unpublished) must be replicated. These replications must occur frequently (not merely on an occasional basis), they ought to be of varying types (not just "same data/same analysis"), they must be conducted in an unbiased fashion (not as "gotcha" exercises), they must conform to a standard template (one that recognizes an idiosyncratic variety of dimensions of truthfulness) and they must be preserved and collated (regardless of their outcome). Judging from current practices in the social sciences, these goals are very far off. While replication is a regular feature in the natural sciences it has only recently been recognized as an essential feature in social science research. Because social science is not well-funded, because there are no oversight bodies (e.g., the Food and Drug Administration or the Environmental Protection Agency) for most areas of social science, because some sorts of research (particularly qualitative research) is hard to replicate, and because social science does not occur in a strictly cumulative fashion (one which would require replication of previous results as a precursor to further research), it is by no means clear how to motivate and organize the conduct of replication studies.

Nonetheless, there are things we might do. This includes (a) encouraging every PhD program to make replication exercises a required part of the graduate curriculum, (b) random assignment of studies to replicate within a subfield so that replicators cannot choose their targets (alleviating one form of bias), (c) centralized funding and coordination around particular research hypotheses (along the models provided by Many Labs and The Replication Project in psychology, 3ie in development economics and Metaketa in international development), (d) journal policies that guarantee publication (online) of any replication of a paper published in that journal that meets minimum standards, (e) the development of guidelines for producing replications and for judging the validity of studies that are replicated, (f) a replications directory to organize replications in a logical fashion and provide links to the original studies, (g) a replication scorecard to record information about the original study and its replication(s) in a standardized format, including responses from the original author and other commentators, and (h) replication institutes within each discipline to coordinate the foregoing activities.

Before concluding, we want to issue a caveat. Replication studies are not blinded, and it is difficult to imagine that they could be. Consequently, replicators know the identity of the authors of the study they are attempting to replicate. This means replications are open to any biases that result from this knowledge. In particular, one must wonder whether the choice of studies, or judgments about those studies (under replication), are affected by the characteristics of the author or the replicator – sex, race, status, and so forth. The good news is that these issues can be studied in experimental and non-experimental settings. There may also be ways of randomizing the selection of studies to replicate, as suggested above. But there is no apparent solution to replicator bias in the conduct of replication studies.

2. *Comprehensive appraisal* (Chapter 14). Replications, by themselves, are unlikely to cumulate knowledge. Explicit attention must be paid to how various studies of a subject, conducted in various contexts and (quite possibly) with varying methods, can be reconciled. The pieces of this vast puzzle must be put together. We envision a comprehensive appraisal, taking the form of a lengthy paper or report that evaluates a scientific question in an encompassing fashion. Its goal is to evaluate accumulated findings on that subject, assigning a degree of (un)certainty to each hypothesis under review. It should encompass all work that has been conducted on a subject, published or unpublished, and should also involve a direct encounter with the evidence.

To conduct this appraisal in a dispassionate manner one must identify experts who are conversant with the research question but not closely aligned with a particular view of the subject. The process could be overseen by a review board composed of specialists and non-specialists (those outside the subfield being assessed) and should engage those who are working on that subject, either as active participants in the appraisal or as commentators and critics of the appraisal. The resulting report should include both technical detail, with special attention to methodological issues, as well as general conclusions set forth in an accessible fashion for a lay audience.

3. *Impact metrics* (Chapter 15). One aspect of appraisal is scholarly impact. To that end, we propose that impact metrics be improved and more widely adopted. Improvements should center initially on databases – Google Scholar, Scopus, Web of Science, and Microsoft Academic – which are currently at pains to identify authors correctly, which do not have comprehensive coverage (especially with respect to books), and most of which are not open access (MA is the exception). Impact metrics derived from these databases need to be refined so that they measure what they purport to measure and are less liable to abuse (by journals, departments, or individual scholars). With

these improvements, we believe that impact metrics offer an important tool for the evaluation of academic achievement, one that relieves pressure on an overburdened process of peer review, that enhances efficiency in the time-consuming task of evaluation, that provides flexibility in the sorts of impact that can be evaluated and the sorts of comparisons that can be made, that is more meritocratic than the current, reputation-based system of evaluation and that is more democratic, opening up the task of evaluation to entire fields of experts rather than a small cadre of gatekeepers.

Equality and Diversity (Part V)

A large volume research suggests that the institutions of the social sciences are not structured in an equitable fashion for individuals of varying race, class, gender and ideological backgrounds. Formal institutions and informal norms pose obstacles for those who are not part of the majority culture, which one might characterize as male, white, liberal and middle-class.

These inequities are unjust. They also introduce the prospect of bias. Scholars, like everyone else, are naturally drawn to areas that they imagine to be especially praiseworthy or problematic. If their views of the good society differ from views held by other citizens that is likely to show up in the work that they produce. Additionally, one's personal background often hinders, or assists, one's ability to effectively study a chosen research area. Familiarity can provide entrée and insight. People talk to those they trust, and they are more likely to trust those who share a common background or viewpoint.

Inequities in the academy are unlikely to rectify themselves. Indeed, they are self-perpetuating, as individuals who don't fit the mold are presumably less likely to choose a career in the social sciences, and less likely to leap all the hurdles along the path to a successful career. For this reason, it behoves us to consider possible interventions. Following previous chapters, we explore two areas: (1) gender and (2) ideology.

1. *Gender* (Chapter 16). Men predominate in most positions of power and status within the social sciences, though the degree of inequality varies by field and subfield and by seniority, with higher levels generally manifesting greater imbalances. To address these inequities, we offer a number of suggestions.

Employers and professional associations should regularly compile data that shed light on potential gender-based inequities. This includes leadership positions, committees and panels; hiring, attrition, and promotion at all levels; and resources and burdens (e.g., salary, retirement packages, research budgets, grant support, teaching loads, advising duties, service obligations, staff support, research assistant support, lab space, office size, and family leave). Aggregate results should be made public – hopefully, without compromising the identity of individuals.

Based on this data, special committees at various levels – university, departmental, disciplinary – should be charged with assessing problems of diversity and developing specific recommendations, which can then provide the basis for discussion in the relevant community, and from thence the adoption of specific reforms. Each of these changes should be designed to help move the social sciences toward full equality.

While particular reforms will depend on the data and the committees' subsequent discussions, several specific ideas are already well-supported. To ease the burden of childcare, which often falls disproportionately on mothers, universities and professional associations should offer free childcare or financial support to pay for childcare. Leadership positions within universities and professional associations – including admissions, hiring, and policymaking committees – should aim for gender equality. Universities and professional associations should supplement sexual harassment policies with regular anonymous survey data designed to measure and understand the forms and extent of discrimination that their members experience. Associations should consider providing an ombudsperson at meetings to provide support for individuals who experience sexual harassment. Funding agencies should develop policies on requiring grantee institutions to report harassment by principal or co-principal investigators working on funded projects, and the likely consequences for the grantee and personnel when they receive such reports (see, for example, National Science Foundation 2018).

Note that while these proposals focus on gender inequality, similar inequities plague the social sciences along other dimensions including race, ethnicity and sexual orientation. We strongly endorse parallel data-gathering efforts, consensus-building discussions and reforms in these areas.

2. *Ideology* (Chapter 17). Ideologies encapsulate different ideas about well-being as well as different theories about how to get there. An ideologically diverse academy would presumably lead to a more spirited debate among scholars about what to study and what to conclude from those studies. Insofar as debate sharpens ideas and strengthens empirical work, we may regard this as helpful – perhaps even essential – in the search for truth.

A more ideologically diverse academy would also better represent the views of the citizenry. Of course, this raises questions about who the citizenry is – citizens in the region where a university is located, citizens nationally or citizens internationally? Universities do not have clearly defined constituencies, and even if they did it is not clear that they should be territorially defined. In any case, no one is proposing that social scientists represent citizens in the way that elected officials do. Nor is it clear whether the purview of "ideological diversity" should extend to *all* ideologies (fascism?), or whether an appropriate criterion of "acceptable" could ever be devised.

Nonetheless, one may agree that the high degree of ideological uniformity that characterizes social science fields is unhelpful to the long-term goals of social science. Those who study society should not live in a liberal bubble. At the very least, opposing views allows for a healthy exchange of opinions.

There is also a problem of perceptions. Insofar as the academy is viewed as a bastion of liberalism, research emanating from the social sciences is not likely to be taken seriously by those who do not share that point of view.

Thus, we propose that ideological diversity be regarded as a worthwhile goal to be considered as part of the gatekeeping functions of social science – in the choice of colleagues, recipients of grants and fellowships, conference panels, edited volumes and the like. (We regret that we were unable to fulfill this goal in the present volume.) However, we do not recommend the adoption of firm commitments (e.g., quotas) or a strict definition of what ideological diversity might consist of. It is too ineffable, and certainly not a high priority for most academic tasks.

There is also an additional risk that a bid to include ideological diversity as a criterion of academic gatekeeping might encourage academics to define themselves in rigidly ideological terms, undermining goals such as objectivity and deliberation that are central to the scientific enterprise. Ideological diversity within the academy is a good thing, but an academy of ideologues is manifestly a bad thing.

Metrics of Reform

Having issued a set of proposals for reforming the norms and practices of social science, we face an important question about how to mark change that might – or might not – be occurring. How do we know if progress is being achieved toward the specific reforms identified above?

To measure take-up we try to identify metrics for each proposal listed in the previous section. Granted, not all proposals are easily measured. Thus, some proposals do not appear at all in the following list and others are represented by metrics that are rather fuzzy around the edges. Nonetheless, one must grapple with the challenge of operationalization; otherwise, one has no way of knowing which way the wind is blowing.

To do so in a systematic fashion requires measuring the following outcomes at regular intervals, e.g., every year, every five years or every decade. We assume that metrics would be gathered at the disciplinary level (e.g., for economics, political science, sociology, and cognate disciplines), though it could in principle be conducted at any level (e.g., subfields or the social sciences at-large). We assume, finally, that survey subjects are drawn randomly from known populations, wherever possible.

1. *Discovery: the priority assigned to exploratory research.*
   (a) *New data.* Survey published articles to see whether the data for key variables are already existing (from extant datasets) or original (collected by the author).
   (b) *New topics.* Survey published articles and books to see whether the chosen topics are novel. Of course, judgments of novelty are never automatic, as every topic is new in some ways and old in others. Nonetheless, a carefully crafted coding frame could distinguish, e.g., between studies that ask new questions and studies that focus on well-established questions.
   (c) *High-risk research.* Survey research proposals – from the National Science Foundation and/or from departments who preserve dissertation prospectuses – to see whether the research is high-risk/high-reward or not. Again, suitable coding schemes would need to be devised and some degree of error would need to be accepted.
   (d) *Cross-disciplinary research.* Examine citation patterns in published research to see whether authors cite works published in other fields or subfields. Examine authorship in published research to see whether authors cross fields or subfields.
2. *Publishing.*
   (a) *Significance reviews.* Survey journals to see whether they routinely conduct significance reviews.
   (b) *Open peer review.* Survey journals and presses to see whether any open peer review practices are in place – and if so, which ones.
   (c) *Length limits.* Survey journals to see what length limits are in place and how long published articles (which sometimes vary from journal guidelines) actually are.

3. *Transparency and reproducibility.*
   (a) *Data access and infrastructure.* Survey journals to see what standards (if any) are in place to ensure data access and reproducibility. Survey articles to see how many provide readily accessible data suitable for replication. Among those who do not, ascertain the probable reason, e.g., ethical constraints, proprietorial data, unwieldy qualitative data or non-empirical subject matter.
   (b) *Pre-registration.* Survey published articles to see how many were pre-registered. Survey registries to see how many studies are registered. Develop classifications to describe the sort of work that is pre-registered, e.g., experimental, observational/quantitative, observational/qualitative.
   (c) *Results-blind review.* Survey journals to discern their policies.
   (d) *Null results.* Survey published articles to see how many report null results.
   (e) *Conventional findings.* Survey published articles to see how many reported conventional findings (no change or little change to accepted theories).
4. *Appraisal.*
   (a) *Survey replications.* Count the number of replications, classifying them within a typology – perhaps following the guidelines laid out in Chapter 13.
   (b) *Classroom replication exercises.* Survey departments to see what graduate classes require students to conduct replications, how this exercise is constructed and where replications are stored.
   (c) *Centrally coordinated efforts.* Survey each field and subfield to see what (if any) centrally coordinated efforts of appraisal exist.
   (d) *Guaranteed publication for replications.* Survey journals to see whether they publish replications and, if so, what policies they have adopted to handle replications.
   (e) *Replications directory, scorecard, guidelines, institute.* Survey each field to see what may have developed.
   (f) *Comprehensive appraisal.* Survey each field to see whether some form of comprehensive appraisal has been developed.
   (g) *Impact metrics.* Survey departments to see what impact metrics (if any) are used to evaluate candidates for promotion. Check a sample of academics (drawn from a list of members in a professional society) to see how many have Google Scholar Profiles and, of these, how many are carefully curated. Survey academics to see what impact metrics they use routinely to evaluate their work and the work of others.

5. *Diversity*.
    (a) *Gender, race, ethnicity*. Supplement surveys conducted by professional associations with additional surveys of publishing, hiring, and promotion to gauge the success of historically under-represented groups.
    (b) *Ideology*. Survey academics to see where they fall on a right-left spectrum, their party identification and other elements of political belief and political philosophy.

A few of these metrics – especially gender, racial, and ethnic diversity – might be regarded as intrinsically valuable. But most are valuable only insofar as they promote the broader goal of scientific progress. Our assumption is that they will do so. However, this assumption will need to be carefully evaluated in the coming years, especially in light of the many caveats we have issued. No reform is costless, and some threaten spillovers or adaptive behavior that are not easy to assess. Even so, each must be evaluated in light of its total impact on social science. Here, we must be concerned with broader goals such as efficiency, discovery, rigor and consensus – as well as more specific goals that apply to a particular theory or framework, e.g., breadth, precision, coherence, parsimony, relevance (to everyday life and practical concerns), falsifiability, and, of course, truth (Gerring 2012b).

Challenges and Opportunities

Notwithstanding the granularity of the proposals vetted in this chapter it is important to recall that they are in service of the book's larger argument: namely, the production of knowledge is a communal enterprise. A great many institutions – departments, universities, journals, presses, professional associations – interact to set the formal rules by which academic work is conducted. These are accompanied by a larger set of informal norms that help shape how scholars create, consume, and evaluate the work in their respective fields.

Communalism is an inescapable element of social science. When elements of the framework are poorly configured, they have the potential to do enormous harm. No matter how brilliant the scholar, how clever the method, or how important the question, studies that are embedded in a flawed system will suffer for it. By the same token, attention to this broader framework holds out the promise of improvements in the way we do business. Although the "bureaucracy" of social science might not seem intrinsically interesting, it has crucial consequences and for that reason deserves to be carefully considered. Our foremost hope is that this book will spark greater attention to system-wide rules and conventions, topics generally consigned to the peripheries of social science – to association officers, special committees, and spasmotic reform movements.

What, then, are the prospects of reform in the disciplines of economics, political science, economics and their many associated fields? Any reform initiative intended to change the production of knowledge must be informed by a realistic sociology of knowledge. In this final section, we offer some reflections on the challenges and opportunities of reform within the social science disciplines.

On the one hand, the actions of academics, departments, journals, associations and funders are relatively unconstrained. They can choose to reward, or sanction, certain types of people or certain types of work. They can establish new standards, or revise old standards. They can change standards for employment, promotion, publishing, and virtually any other gatekeeping task. As self-governing bodies, departments, journals, and associations are free to reform themselves – within the constraints of the law and those imposed by their employers (largely, universities).

On the other hand, academic institutions often seem hide-bound. Vestigial remnants of a medieval age, they are generally slow to innovate. Life-long employment, guaranteed by tenured appointments, means that generational turnover is slow. Power generally rests with a gerontocracy of senior scholars. Moreover, certain features of academic employment – lower pay and greater security than one might expect from a similar job in the private sector – tends to attract risk-averse individuals. Scholars may praise "creative destruction" when it applies to markets, but they are likely to feel differently when it is applied to the university sector, which has come to resemble the public sector even where it is not run by government.

The administrative structure of universities is highly decentralized, which gives departments some room to maneuver, but only within constraints imposed from above. Since universities rarely go out of business, and competition between them is limited, there are few pressures for change – especially at the top. Of course, private universities without large endowments are vulnerable, and hence from a certain perspective ought to be open to reform. However, these universities are unlikely to take leadership roles in setting standards for a discipline. Harvard University matters more than Lesley University – where teaching, rather than research, is the main activity – and Harvard is relatively immune to market forces.

Another way to think about the reform enterprise centers on *reputational* factors. There is no clear way to measure the value of a university, a department, a journal, a press or a scholar. Consequently, we tend to fall back on a general sense of what others think. Harvard is top (at least on some lists) because lots of people think it is top. Harvard's position in the academic hierarchy is in some respects the product of a circular definition of status. Because it is rated first, whatever it does is regarded as first-rate. The very fact that Harvard engages in a practice imbues that practice with prestige. In this respect, reputations are sticky and reforms are difficult. Harvard has no incentive to change if whatever it does is regarded as excellent.

On the other hand, the reputational quality of academic life means that if attitudes change, e.g., with respect to what people expect and value in a university, Harvard's status may fall if it does not perform well on that dimension. From this perspective, the reputational quality of the academic game offers a hopeful scenario for would-be reformers. All they need to do is convince the audience of academics – who provide the reputational ratings that drive rankings – that a reform is desirable, and institutions will be compelled to adopt it.

Although we have used a university as our exemplar, it should be recognized that the same reputational dynamic applies to departments, journals, presses and individual scholars. All are subject to reputational effects, and these effects are sticky in some respects and malleable in other respects.

Let us imagine that the community of scholars within a discipline or sub-discipline decide that *Reform A*, pertaining to the publication process, is desirable. Journals and presses may resist the idea. However, if one journal or press breaks ranks to adopt the reform, we can imagine that it will gain in status as a result of its early adoption. And this, in turn, places pressure on other journals and presses to follow suit. Here, changing norms within a scholarly community lead to institutional changes, with potentially far-reaching effects.

In any case, reforms in the production of knowledge are already underway. Indeed, many of the suggestions, recommendations, and exhortations put forward in this volume (summarized in the previous section) have already been adopted in some respects or in some instances.

More generally, we observe that the practice of social science has undergone a remarkable transformation over the past several decades. Perhaps the relevant question is not whether further change could possibly occur but, rather, what could possibly stop it?

References

AAPOR. 2017. "AAPOR Transparency Certification Agreement." Oakbrook Terrace, IL: American Association for Public Opinion Research. www.aapor.org/AAPOR_Main/media/MainSiteFiles/AAPORTransparencyCertificationAgreement-Revised-October-2017.pdf.

Abbott, Andrew. 2001. *Chaos of Disciplines*. Chicago: University of Chicago Press.

2011. "Library Research Infrastructure for Humanistic and Social Scientific Scholarship in the Twentieth Century." Pp. 43–88 in *Social Knowledge in the Making*, edited by Charles Camic, Neil Gross and Michèle Lamont. Chicago: University of Chicago Press.

Abend, Gabriel. 2006. "Styles of Sociological Thought: Sociologies, Epistemologies, and the Mexican and U.S. Quests for Truth." *Sociological Theory* 24: 1–41.

Abreu, Maria, Henri L. F. de Groot and Raymond J. G. M. Florax. 2005. "A Meta-Analysis of β-Convergence: The Legendary 2%." *Journal of Economic Surveys* 19 (3): 389–420.

Abt, Helmut A. and Eugene Garfield. 2002. "Is the Relationship between Numbers of References and Paper Lengths the Same for All Sciences?" *Journal of the American Society for Information Science and Technology* 53 (13): 1106–1112.

Acemoglu, Daron, Simon Johnson and James A. Robinson. 2001. "The Colonial Origins of Comparative Development: An Empirical Investigation." *American Economic Review* 91 (5): 1369–1401.

2002. "Reversal of Fortune: Geography and Institutions in the Making of the Modern World Income Distribution." *Quarterly Journal of Economics* 117 (4): 1231–1294.

AEA. 2018. "Reports from the American Economics Association Committee on the Status of Women in the Profession." www.aeaweb.org/content/file?id=6388.

Aiken, Alexander M., Calum Davey, James R. Hargreaves and Richard J. Hayes. 2015. "Re-Analysis of Health and Educational Impacts of a School-Based Deworming Programme in Western Kenya: A Pure Replication." *International Journal of Epidemiology* 44 (5): 1572–1580.

Akbaritabar, Aliakbar and Flaminio Squazzoni. 2018. "Gender and Ethnic Patterns of Publication in Top Sociology Journals (Success Stories Only!)." GECS (Research Group in Experimental and Computational Sociology) seminars, January 10, 2018, University of Brescia, Brescia, Italy.

Alatas, Vivi, Abhijit Banerjee, Rema Hanna, Benjamin A. Olken and Julia Tobias. 2012. "Targeting the Poor: Evidence from a Field Experiment in Indonesia." *American Economic Review* 102 (4): 1206–1240.

Albouy, David Y. 2012. "The Colonial Origins of Comparative Development: An Empirical Investigation: Comment." *American Economic Review* 102 (6): 3059–3076.

Ale Ebrahim, Nader, Hamed Ebrahimian, Maryam Mousavi and Farzad Tahriri. 2015. "Does a Long Reference List Guarantee More Citations? Analysis of Malaysian Highly Cited and Review Papers." *International Journal of Management Science and Business* 1 (3): 6–15.

Alimohammadi, Dariush and Mahshid Sajjadi. 2009. "Correlation between References and Citations." *Webology* 6 (2): a71.

Allcott, Hunt and Dmitry Taubinsky. 2015. "Evaluating Behaviorally Motivated Policy: Experimental Evidence from the Lightbulb Market." *American Economic Review* 105 (8): 2501–2538.

Altbach, Philip G. (ed). 2000. *The Changing Academic Workplace: Comparative Perspectives*. Chestnut Hill, MA: Boston College Center for International Higher Education.

Alter, Karen J., Jean Clipperton, Emily Schraudenbach and Laura Rozier. 2018. "Gender and Status in American Political Science: Who Determines Whether a Scholar Is Noteworthy?" *SSRN Electronic Journal*. doi: 10.2139/ssrn.3235786.

American Political Science Association (APSA). 2012. *A Guide to Professional Ethics in Political Science*. 2nd ed. Washington, DC: American Political Science Association.

Amsen, Eva. 2014. "What Is Open Peer Review?" F1000Research, May 21. http://blog.f1000research.com/2014/05/21/what-is-open-peer-review/.

Anderson, Christopher J., Štěpán Bahník, Michael Barnett-Cowan, Frank A. Bosco, Jesse Chandler, Christopher R. Chartier, Felix Cheung, et al. 2016. "Response to Comment on 'Estimating the Reproducibility of Psychological Science.'" *Science* 351 (6277): 1037.

Anderson, Melissa S., Brian C. Martinson and Raymond De Vries. 2007. "Normative Dissonance in Science: Results from a National Survey of U.S. Scientists." *Journal of Empirical Research on Human Research Ethics* 2 (4): 3–14.

Anderson, Michael L. 2008. "Multiple Inference and Gender Differences in the Effects of Early Intervention: A Reevaluation of the Abecedarian, Perry Preschool, and Early Training Projects." *Journal of the American Statistical Association* 103 (484): 1481–1495.

Anderson, Richard G. and William G. Dewald. 1994. "Replication and Scientific Standards in Applied Economics a Decade after the Journal of Money, Credit and Banking Project." *Federal Reserve Bank of St. Louis Review* no. Nov: 79–83.

Anderson, Richard G., William H. Greene, Bruce D. McCullough and Hrishikesh D. Vinod. 2008. "The Role of Data/Code Archives in the Future of Economic Research." *Journal of Economic Methodology* 15 (1): 99–119.

Andreoli-Versbach, Patrick and Frank Mueller-Langer. 2014. "Open Access to Data: An Ideal Professed but Not Practised." *Research Policy*. doi:10.1016/j.respol.2014.04.008.

Angell, Robert. 1936. *The Family Encounters the Depression*. New York: Charles Scribner's Sons.

Angrist, Joshua D. and Jörn-Steffen Pischke. 2009. *Mostly Harmless Econometrics: An Empiricist's Companion*. Princeton, NJ: Princeton University Press.

    2010. "The Credibility Revolution in Empirical Economics: How Better Research Design Is Taking the Con out of Econometrics." *Journal of Economic Perspectives* 24 (2): 3–30.

    2014. *Mastering 'Metrics: The Path from Cause to Effect*. Princeton, NJ: Princeton University Press.

Ankeny, Rachel A. 2011. "Using Cases to Establish Novel Diagnoses: Creating Generic Facts by Making Particular Facts Travel Together." Pp. 252–272 in S. Morgan and P. Howlett (eds), *How Well Do Facts Travel? The Dissemination of Reliable Knowledge*. New York: Cambridge University Press.

Annas, George J. 2003. "HIPAA Regulations – A New Era of Medical-Record Privacy?" *New England Journal of Medicine* 348 (15): 1486–1490.

References

Antecol, Heather, Kelly Bedard and Jenna Stearns. 2018. "Equal but Inequitable: Who Benefits from Gender-Neutral Tenure Clock Stopping Policies?" *American Economic Review* 108 (9): 2420–2441.

APA. 2016. "Ethical Principles of Psychologists and Code of Conduct." Washington, DC: American Psychological Association. www.apa.org/ethics/code/ethics-code-2017.pdf.

APSA. 2012. A *Guide to Professional Ethics in Political Science*. 2nd ed. Washington, DC: American Political Science Association.

2016. "P- WAM20: Pipeline for Women and Minorities in the 20 Largest Departments – Data for Faculty and Students." Washington, DC: American Political Science Association.

ASA. 1997. "Code of Ethics of the ASA Committee on Professional Ethics." Washington, DC: American Sociological Association. www.asanet.org/sites/default/files/code_of_ethics_aug_2017_2_1.pdf.

Ashenfelter, Orley and Michael Greenstone. 2004. "Estimating the Value of a Statistical Life: The Importance of Omitted Variables and Publication Bias." Princeton University, Department of Economics, Center for Economic Policy Studies., Working Papers: 105, 2004. http://search.proquest.com/econlit/docview/56626726/1A493319C9B3407FPQ/4?accountid=14496.

Ashenfelter, Orley, Colm Harmon and Hessel Oosterbeek. 1999. "A Review of Estimates of the Schooling/Earnings Relationship, with Tests for Publication Bias." Princeton, Department of Economics – Industrial Relations Sections, Princeton, Department of Economics – Industrial Relations Sections, 1999. http://search.proquest.com/econlit/docview/56307618/5A788ADBA14C479EPQ/2?accountid=14496.

Atchison, Amy L. 2017. "Negating the Gender Citation Advantage in Political Science." *PS: Political Science and Politics* 50 (2): 448–455.

Atmanspacher, Harald and Sabine Maasen (eds). 2016. *Reproducibility: Principles, Problems, Practices, and Prospects*. New York: John Wiley and Sons.

Babcock, Linda, Maria P. Recalde and Lise Vesterlund. 2017a. "Gender Differences in the Allocation of Low-Promotability Tasks: The Role of Backlash." *American Economic Review*, 107 (5): 131–135.

Babcock, Linda, Maria P. Recalde, Lise Vesterlund and Laurie Weingart. 2017b. "Gender Differences in Accepting and Receiving Requests for Tasks with Low Promotability." *American Economic Review*, 107 (3): 714–747.

Backhouse, Roger E. and Mary S. Morgan. 2000. "Introduction: Is Data Mining a Methodological Problem?" *Journal of Economic Methodology* 7 (2): 171–81.

Bai, Liang, Benjamin Handel, Edward Miguel and Gautam Rao. 2015. "Self-Control and Chronic Illness: Evidence from Commitment Contracts for Doctor Visits." Unpublished manuscript. UC Berkeley.

Baicker, Katherine, Amy Finkelstein, Jae Song and Sarah Taubman. 2014. "The Impact of Medicaid on Labor Market Activity and Program Participation: Evidence from the Oregon Health Insurance Experiment." *American Economic Review* 104 (5): 322–328.

Baicker, Katherine, Sarah L. Taubman, Heidi L. Allen, Mira Bernstein, Jonathan H. Gruber, Joseph P. Newhouse, Eric C. Schneider, Bill J. Wright, Alan M. Zaslavsky and Amy N. Finkelstein. 2013. "The Oregon Experiment – Effects of Medicaid on Clinical Outcomes." *New England Journal of Medicine* 368 (18): 1713–1722.

Bakkensen, Laura A. and William Larson. 2014. "Population Matters When Modeling Hurricane Fatalities." *Proceedings of the National Academy of Sciences of the United States of America* 111 (50): E5331–E5332.

Ball, P. 2008. "A Longer Paper Gathers More Citations." *Nature* 455 (7211): 274–275.

Bandalos, Deborah L. 2018. *Measurement Theory and Applications in the Social Sciences*. New York: Guilford Press.

Bar-Sinai, Michael, Latanya Sweeney and Merce Crosas. 2016. "DataTags, Data Handling Policy Spaces and the Tags Language." In *2016 IEEE Security and Privacy Workshops (SPW)*, 1–8. doi:10.1109/SPW.2016.11.

Bargh, John A., Mark Chen and Lara Burrows. 1996. "Automaticity of Social Behavior: Direct Effects of Trait Construct and Stereotype-Activation on Action." *Journal of Personality and Social Psychology* 71: 230–244.

Barnes, Tiffany D. and Emily Beaulieu. 2017. "Engaging Women: Addressing the Gender Gap in Women's Networking and Productivity." *PS: Political Science and Politics* 50 (2): 461–466.

Barone, Tom and Elliot Eisner (eds). 2011. *Arts-Based Research*. London: Sage Publications.

Bartels, Larry M. 1997. "Specification Uncertainty and Model Averaging." *American Journal of Political Science* 41 (2): 641–674.

Barton, Allen. 1979. "Paul Lazarsfeld and Applied Social Research: Invention of the University Applied Social Research Institute." *Social Science History* 3 (3): 4–44.

Barton, Judith. 1984. *Guide to the Bureau of Applied Social Research*. New York: Clearwater Publishing Company.

Basken, Paul. 2018. "UT-Austin Professors Join Campaign Against Faculty-Productivity Company." *Chronicle of Higher Education* (January 24).

Bastow, Simon, Patrick Dunleavy and Jane Tinkler. 2014. *The Impact of the Social Sciences: How Academics and their Research Make a Difference*. London: Sage Publications.

Basu, Aparna. 2006. "Using ISI's 'Highly Cited Researchers' to Obtain a Country Level Indicator of Citation Excellence." *Scientometrics* 68(3): 361–375.

Bateman, Ian, Daniel Kahneman, Alistair Munro, Chris Starmer and Robert Sugden. 2005. "Testing Competing Models of Loss Aversion: An Adversarial Collaboration." *Journal of Public Economics, The Experimental Approaches to Public Economics* 89 (8): 1561–1580.

Baumeister, Roy F. 2016. "Charting the Future of Social Psychology on Stormy Seas: Winners, Losers, and Recommendations." *Journal of Experimental Social Psychology* 66: 153–158.

Baumeister, Roy F. and Mark R. Leary. 1997. "Writing Narrative Literature Reviews." *Review of General Psychology* 1 (3): 311.

Baumeister, Roy F. and Kathleen D. Vohs. 2016. "Misguided Effort with Elusive Implications." *Perspectives on Psychological Science* 11 (4): 574–575.

Beach, Derek and Rasmus Brun Pederson. 2013. *Process-Tracing Methods: Foundations and Guidelines*. Ann Arbor, MI: University of Michigan Press.

Beaman, Lori, Raghabendra Chattopadhyay, Ester Duflo, Rohini Pande and Petia Topalova. 2008. *Powerful Women: Does Exposure Reduce Bias?* Cambridge, MA: MIT Press.

Beaman, Lori, Esther Duflo, Rohini Pande and Petia Topalova. 2012. "Female Leadership Raises Aspirations and Educational Attainment for Girls: A Policy Experiment in India." *Science* 335 (6068): 582–586.

Bear, Julia B. and Benjamin Collier. 2016. "Where are the Women in Wikipedia? Understanding the Different Psychological Experiences of Men and Women in Wikipedia." *Sex Roles* 74 (5–6): 254–265.

References

Begg Colin, Mildred Cho, Susan Eastwood, Richard Horton, David Moher, Ingram Olkin, Roy Pitkin, Drummond Rennie, Kenneth F. Schulz, David Simel and Donna F. Stroup. 1996. "Improving the Quality of Reporting of Randomized Controlled Trials: The Consort Statement." *Journal of the American Medical Association* 276 (8): 637–639.

Bell, Mark S. and Nicholas L. Miller. 2015. "Questioning the Effect of Nuclear Weapons on Conflict." *Journal of Conflict Resolution* 59 (1): 74–92.

Bellavance, François, Georges Dionne and Martin Lebeau. 2009. "The Value of a Statistical Life: A Meta-Analysis with a Mixed Effects Regression Model." *Journal of Health Economics* 28 (2): 444–464.

Bellesiles, Michael A. 2000. *Arming America: The Origins of a National Gun Culture*. New York: Knopf.

Benjamini, Yoav and Yosef Hochberg. 1995. "Controlling the False Discovery Rate: A Practical and Powerful Approach to Multiple Testing." *Journal of the Royal Statistical Society*. Series B (Methodological) 57 (1): 289–300.

Benjamini, Yoav, Abba M. Krieger and Daniel Yekutieli. 2006. "Adaptive Linear Step-up Procedures That Control the False Discovery Rate." *Biometrika* 93 (3): 491–507.

Benjamini, Yoav and Daniel Yekutieli. 2001. "The Control of the False Discovery Rate in Multiple Testing under Dependency." *The Annals of Statistics* 29 (4): 1165–1188.

Bennet, Andrew. 2010. "Process Tracing and Casual Inference." In H. E. Brady and D. Collier (eds), *Rethinking Social Inquiry: Diverse Tools, Shared Standards*. New York: Rowman and Littlefield.

Bennett, Andrew and Jeffrey Checkel (eds). 2015. *Process Tracing in the Social Sciences: From Metaphor to Analytic Tool*. New York: Cambridge University Press.

Bennett, Andrew. 2015. "Appendix." Pp. 276–298 in Andrew Bennett and Jeffrey Checkel (eds), *Process Tracing: From Metaphor to Analytic Tool*. New York: Cambridge University Press.

Berelson, Bernard, Paul Lazarsfeld and William McPhee. 1954. *Voting: A Study of Opinion Formation in a Presidential Campaign*. Chicago: University of Chicago Press.

Berge, Lars Ivar Oppedal, Kjetil Bjorvatn, Simon Galle, Edward Miguel, Daniel N. Posner, Bertil Tungodden and Kelly Zhang. 2015. "How Strong Are Ethnic Preferences?" Working Paper 21715. National Bureau of Economic Research. www.nber.org/papers/w21715.

Berger, James and Donald Berry. 1988. "Statistical Analysis and the Illusion of Objectivity." *American Scientist* (March–April): 159–165.

Berger, Ulrich. 2009. "The Convergence of Fictitious Play in Games with Strategic Complementarities: A Comment." IDEAS Working Paper Series from RePEc. https://mpra.ub.uni-muenchen.de/20241/.

Berinsky, Adam J., James N. Druckman and Teppei Yamamoto. 2018. "Why Replications Do Not Fix the Reproducibility Crisis: A Model and Evidence from a Large-Scale Vignette Experiment." Unpublished paper, Department of Political Science, MIT.

Berkenkotter, Carol. 1995. "The Power and the Perils of Peer Review." *Rhetoric Review* 13 (2): 245–248.

Bernanke, Ben S. 2004. "Editorial Statement." *American Economic Review* 94 (1): 404–404.

Bertrand, Marianne, Emir Kamenica and Jessica Pan. 2015. "Gender Identity and Relative Income Within Households." *Quarterly Journal of Economics* 130 (2): 571–614.

Bertrand, Marianne and Sendhil Mullainathan. 2004. "Are Emily and Greg More Employable than Lakisha and Jamal? A Field Experiment on Labor Market Discrimination." *American Economic Review* 94 (4): 991–1013.

Bess, James L. 1998. "Contract Systems, Bureaucracies, and Faculty Motivation: The Probable Effects of a No-Tenure Policy." *Journal of Higher Education* 69 (1): 1–22.

Bettinger, Eric P. and Bridget Terry Long. 2005. "Do Faculty Serve as Role models? The Impact of Instructor Gender on Female Students." *American Economic Review* 95 (2): 152–157.

Bettis, Richard A., Constance E. Helfat and J. Myles Shaver. 2016. "The Necessity, Logic, and Forms of Replication." *Strategic Management Journal* 37 (11): 2193–2203.

Bhaskar, Roy. 1979. *The Possibility of Naturalism: A Philosophical Critique of the Contemporary Human Sciences*. Atlantic Highlands, NJ: Humanities Press.

Bhattacharjee, Yudhijit. 2013. "Diederik Stapel's Audacious Academic Fraud." *New York Times*, April 26, 2013, sec. Magazine. www.nytimes.com/2013/04/28/magazine/diederik-stapels-audacious-academic-fraud.html.

Bianchi, Suzanne M., Liana C. Sayer, Melissa A. Milkie and John P. Robinson. 2012. "Housework: Who Did, Does or Will Do It, and How Much Does It Matter?" *Social Forces* 91 (1): 55–63.

Bichsel, Jacqueline and McChesney, Jasper 2017. *The Gender Pay Gap and the Representation of Women in Higher Education Administrative Positions: The Century So Far*. Research report. CUPA-HR. February. www.cupahr.org/surveys/briefs.aspx.

Bierer, Barbara E., Mercè Crosas and Heather H. Pierce. 2017. "Data Authorship as an Incentive to Data Sharing." *New England Journal of Medicine* 376 (17): 1684–1687.

Bishop, Libby. 2005. "Protecting Respondents and Enabling Data Sharing: Reply to Parry and Mauthner." *Sociology* 39 (2): 333–336.

  2009. "Ethical Sharing and Reuse of Qualitative Data." *Australian Journal of Social Issues* 44 (3): 255–272.

  2014. "Re-Using Qualitative Data: A Little Evidence, on Going Issues and Modest Reflections." *Studia Socjologiczne* 3: 167.

Blackburn, Robert T. and Janet H. Lawrence. 1995. *Faculty at Work: Motivation, Expectation, Satisfaction*. Baltimore, MD: Johns Hopkins University Press.

Blackburn, Robert T. and Robert J. Havighurst. 1979. "Career Patterns of US Male Academic Social Scientists." *Higher Education* 8 (5): 553–572.

Bland, J. Martin and Douglas G. Altman. 1995. "Multiple Significance Tests: The Bonferroni Method." *BMJ: British Medical Journal* 310 (6973): 170.

Blau, Francine D. and Lawrence M. Kahn. 2000. "Gender Differences in Pay." *Journal of Economic Perspectives* 14 (4): 75–99.

Blumer, Herbert. 1933. *Movies and Conduct*. New York: The Macmillan Company.

  1969. *Symbolic Interactionism: Perspective and Method*. Berkeley, CA: University of California Press.

Boas, Taylor. 2010. "Varieties of Electioneering: Success Contagion and Presidential Campaigns in Latin America." *World Politics* 62 (4): 636–675.

  2015. "Voting for Democracy: Campaign Effects in Chile's Democratic Transition." *Latin American Politics and Society* 57 (2): 67–90.

  2016. *Presidential Campaigns in Latin America: Electoral Strategies and Success Contagion*. New York: Cambridge University Press.

References

Bohannon, John. 2016. "About 40% of Economics Experiments Fail Replication Survey." *Science*, March. doi:10.1126/science.aaf4141.

Boix, Carles. 2015. *Political Order and Inequality*. Cambridge: Cambridge University Press.

Bontemps, Christophe and Grayham E. Mizon. 2008. "Encompassing: Concepts and Implementation." *Oxford Bulletin of Economics and Statistics* 70 (December): 721–750.

Bourdieu, Pierre, Jean-Claude Chamboredon and Jean-Claude Passeron. [1968] 1991. *The Craft of Sociology: Epistemological Preliminaries*. Berlin: Walter de Gruyter.

Borgatti, Stephen P., Martin G. Everett and Jeffrey C. Johnson. 2018. *Analyzing Social Networks*. London: Sage.

Borgman, Christine L. 2009. "The Digital Future Is Now: A Call to Action for the Humanities." *Digital Humanities Quarterly* 3 (4). www.digitalhumanities.org/dhq/vol/3/4/000077/000077.html.

2012. "The Conundrum of Sharing Research Data." *Journal of the American Society for Information Science and Technology* 63 (6): 1059–1078.

Bornmann, Lutz, Hermann Schier, Werner Marx and Hans-Dieter Daniel. 2012. "What Factors Determine Citation Counts of Publications in Chemistry Besides their Quality?" *Journal of Informetrics* 6 (1): 11–18.

Bornmann, Lutz and Hans Dieter Daniel. 2008. "What Do Citation Counts Measure? A Review of Studies on Citing Behavior." *Journal of Documentation* 64 (1): 45–80.

Bornmann, Lutz, Werner Marx and Robin Haunschild. 2016. "Calculating Journal Rankings: Peer Review, Bibliometrics, and Alternative Metrics?" Pp. 42–55 in Ciaran Sugre and Serfika Mertkan (eds), *Publishing and the Academic World: Passion, Purpose, and Possible Futures*. London: Routledge.

Borsuk, Robyn M., Amber E. Budden, Roosa Leimu, Lonnie W. Aarssen and Christopher J. Lortie. 2009. "The Influence of Author Gender, National Language and Number of Authors on Citation Rate in Ecology." *Open Ecology Journal* 2: 25–28.

Bourdieu, Pierre, Jean-Claude Chamboredon and Jean Claude-Passeron. 1991. *The Craft of Sociology: Epistemological Preliminaries*. Berlin: Walter de Gruyter.

Boutron, Isabelle, David Moher, Douglas G. Altman, Kenneth F. Schulz and Philippe Ravaud. 2008. "Extending the CONSORT Statement to Randomized Trials of Nonpharmacologic Treatment: Explanation and Elaboration." *Annals of Internal Medicine* 148 (4): 295–309.

Bowers, Jake. 2011. "Six Steps to a Better Relationship with Your Future Self." *The Political Methodologist* 18 (2): 2–8.

Bowers, Jake, Jonathan Nagler, John Gerring, Alan Jacobs, Don Green and Macartan Humphreys. 2015. "A Proposal for a Political Science Registry." Available at http://blogs.bu.edu/jgerring/files/2015/09/Aproposal-foraPoliticalScienceRegistry.pdf.

Box-Steffensmeier, Janet M., Henry E. Brady and David Collier. 2008. *The Oxford Handbook of Political Methodology*. Oxford; New York: Oxford University Press.

Box-Steffensmeier, Janet M., Raphael C. Cunha, Roumen A. Varbanov, Yee Shwen Hoh, Margaret L. Knisley and Mary Alice Holmes. 2015. "Survival Analysis of Faculty Retention and Promotion in the Social Sciences by Gender." *PloS ONE*, 10, e0143093.

Box-Steffensmeier, Janet M., Henry Brady and David Collier (eds). 2008. *The Oxford Handbook of Political Methodology*. New York: Oxford University Press.

Brady, Henry E. and David Collier (eds). 2010. *Rethinking Social Inquiry: Diverse Tools, Shared Standards*. 2nd ed. Lanham, MD: Rowman and Littlefield.

References

Brajer, Victor and Andrew Gill. 2010. "Yakity-Yak: Who Talks Back? An Email Experiment." *Social Science Quarterly* 91 (4): 1007–1024.

Brandt, Mark J., Hans IJzerman, Ap Dijksterhuis, Frank J. Farach, Jason Geller, Roger Giner-Sorolla, James A. Grange, Marco Perugini, Jeffrey R. Spies and Anna van 't Veer. 2014. "The Replication Recipe: What Makes for a Convincing Replication?" *Journal of Experimental Social Psychology* 50: 217–224.

Breuer, Peter T. and Jonathan P. Bowen. 2014. "Empirical Patterns in Google Scholar Citation Counts." ArXiv:1401.1861 [Cs], April, 398–403. https://doi.org/10.1109/SOSE.2014.55.

Breznau, Nate. 2015. "The Missing Main Effect of Welfare State Regimes: A Replication of 'Social Policy Responsiveness in Developed Democracies' by Brooks and Manza." *Sociological Science* 2: 420–441.

Broad, William and Nicholas Wade. 1983. *Betrayers of the Truth*. New York: Simon and Schuster.

Brodeur, Abel, Mathias Le, Marc Sangnier and Yanos Zylberberg. 2016. "Star Wars: The Empirics Strike Back." *American Economic Journal: Applied Economics* 8 (1): 1–32.

Broockman, David, Joshua Kalla and Peter Aranow. 2015. "Irregularities in LaCour (2014)." UC Berkeley. http://stanford.edu/~dbroock/broockman_kalla_aronow_lg_irregularities.pdf.

Brooks, Clem. 2014. "Nations, Classes, and the Politics of Professors: A Comparative Perspective." Pp. 82–108 in Neil Gross and Solon Simmons (eds), *Professors and Their Politics*. Baltimore, MD: Johns Hopkins University Press.

Brooks, Clem and Jeff Manza. 2006. "Social Policy Responsiveness in Developed Democracies." *American Sociological Review* 71 (3): 474–494.

Broom, Alex, Lynda Cheshire and Michael Emmison. 2009. "Qualitative Researchers' Understandings of Their Practice and the Implications for Data Archiving and Sharing." *Sociology* 43 (6): 1163–1180.

Brown, Nadia E. 2014. *Sisters in the Statehouse: Black Women and Legislative Decision Making*. New York: Oxford University Press.

Brown, Robert. 1984. *The Nature of Social Laws: Machiavelli to Mill*. Cambridge: Cambridge University Press.

Brzezinski, Michal. 2015. "Power Laws in Citation Distributions: Evidence from Scopus." *Scientometrics* 103 (1): 213–228.

Buckley, William. 1951. *God and Man at Yale: The Superstitions of Academic Freedom*. Chicago: Regnery.

Bueno de Mesquita, Bruce, Nils Petter Gleditsch, Patrick James, Gary King, Claire Metelits, James Lee Ray, Bruce Russett, Havard Strand and Brandon Valeriano. 2003. "Symposium on Replication in International Studies Research." *International Studies Perspectives* 4 (1): 72–107.

Bueno de Mesquita, Bruce, Alastair Smith, Randolph M. Siverson and James D. Morrow. 2003. *The Logic of Political Survival*. Cambridge, MA: MIT Press.

Burlig, Fiona. 2018. "Improving Transparency in Observational Social Science Research: A Pre-Analysis Plan Approach." *Economics Letters* 168: 56–60.

Burnside, Craig and David Dollar. 2000. "Aid, Policies, and Growth." *American Economic Review* 90 (4): 847–868.

2004. "Aid, Policies, and Growth: Reply." *American Economic Review* 94 (3): 781–784.

Bush, Tony. 2016. "Understanding the Peer-Review Process: Reject, Revise, Resubmit." Pp. 90–98 in Ciaran Sugre and Serfika Mertkan (eds), *Publishing and the Academic World: Passion, Purpose, and Possible Futures*. London: Routledge.

Butler, Courtney and Brett Currier. 2017. "You Can't Replicate What You Can't Find: Data Preservation Policies in Economic Journals." presented at the IASSIST 2017, Lawrence, Kansas, May 25. http://iassist2017.org/program/s107.html.

Callaham, Michael, Robert L. Wears and Ellen Weber. 2002. "Journal Prestige, Publication Bias, and Other Characteristics Associated With Citation of Published Studies in Peer-Reviewed Journals." *Journal of the American Medical Association* 287 (21): 2847–2850.

Calvert, Melanie, Jane Blazeby, Douglas G. Altman, Dennis A. Revicki, David Moher and Michael D. Brundage. 2013. "Reporting of Patient-Reported Outcomes in Randomized Trials: The Consort pro Extension." *Journal of the American Medical Association* 309 (8): 814–822.

Camerer, Colin F., Anna Dreber, Eskil Forsell, Teck-Hua Ho, Jürgen Huber, Magnus Johannesson, Michael Kirchler et al. 2016. "Evaluating Replicability of Laboratory Experiments in Economics." *Science* 351 (6280): 1433–1436.

Camfield, Laura and Richard Palmer-Jones. 2013. "Three 'Rs' of Econometrics: Repetition, Reproduction and Replication." *Journal of Development Studies* 49 (12): 1607–1614.

Camic, Charles. 2007. "On Edge: Sociology During the Great Depression and the New Deal." Pp. 225–280 in Craig Calhoun (ed.), *Sociology in America*. Chicago: University of Chicago Press.

Camic, Charles and Neil Gross. 2001. "The New Sociology of Ideas." Pp. 236–249 in Judith Blau (ed.), *The Blackwell Companion to Sociology*. Malden, MA: Blackwell.

Camic, Charles, Neil Gross and Michèle Lamont (eds). 2011. *Social Knowledge in the Making*. Chicago: University of Chicago Press.2011. "Introduction: The Study of Social Knowledge Making." Pp. 1–40 in Charles Camic, Neil Gross and Michèle Lamont (eds), *Social Knowledge in the Making*. Chicago: University of Chicago Press.

Campbell, Donald T. 1979. "Assessing the Impact of Planned Social Change." *Evaluation and Program Planning* 2 (1): 67–90.

Campbell, John and Ove Pedersen. 2014. *The National Origins of Policy Ideas: Knowledge Regimes in the United States, France, Germany, and Denmark*. Princeton, NJ: Princeton University Press.

Campbell, Marion K., Diana R. Elbourne and Douglas G. Altman. 2004. "CONSORT Statement: Extension to Cluster Randomised Trials." *British Medical Journal* 328 (7441): 702–708.

2012. "Consort 2010 Statement: Extension to Cluster Randomised Trials." *British Medical Journal* 345: e5661.

Campolieti, Michele, Morley Gunderson and Chris Riddell. 2006. "Minimum Wage Impacts from a Prespecified Research Design: Canada 1981–1997." *Industrial Relations: A Journal of Economy and Society* 45 (2): 195–216.

Card, David. 1992a. "Do Minimum Wages Reduce Employment? A Case Study of California, 1987–89." *Industrial and Labor Relations Review* 46 (1): 38–54.

1992b. "Using Regional Variation in Wages to Measure the Effects of the Federal Minimum Wage." *Industrial and Labor Relations Review* 46 (1): 22–37.

Card, David and Alan B. Krueger. 1994. "Minimum Wages and Employment: A Case Study of the Fast-Food Industry in New Jersey and Pennsylvania." *American Economic Review* 84 (4): 772–793.
  1995. "Time-Series Minimum-Wage Studies: A Meta-Analysis." *American Economic Review* 85 (2): 238–243.
  2000. "Minimum Wages and Employment: A Case Study of the Fast-Food Industry in New Jersey and Pennsylvania: Reply." *American Economic Review* 90 (5): 1397–1420.
Card, David, Raj Chetty, Martin Feldstein and Emmanuel Saez. 2010. "Expanding Access to Administrative Data for Research in the United States." 112. NSF SBE 2020. www.nsf.gov/sbe/sbe_2020/2020_pdfs/Card_David_112.pdf.
Card, David and S. DellaVigna. 2014. "Page Limits on Economics Articles: Evidence from Two Journals." *Journal of Economic Perspectives* 28 (3): 149–167.
Carey, Benedict. 2011. "Noted Dutch Psychologist, Stapel, Accused of Research Fraud." *New York Times*, November 2, sec. Health/Research. www.nytimes.com/2011/11/03/health/research/noted-dutch-psychologist-stapel-accused-of-research-fraud.html.
Carr, Phyllis L., Gunn, Christine M., Kaplan, Samantha A., Raj, Anita and Freund, Karen M. 2015. "Inadequate Progress for Women in Academic Medicine: Findings from the National Faculty Study." *Journal of Women's Health* 24 (3): 190–199.
Carsey, Thomas M. 2014. "Making DA-RT a Reality." *PS, Political Science and Politics* 47 (1): 72–77.
Cartwright, Nancy. 1999. *The Dappled World: A Study of the Boundaries of Science*. Cambridge: Cambridge University Press.
Casey, Katherine, Rachel Glennerster and Edward Miguel. 2012. "Reshaping Institutions: Evidence on Aid Impacts Using a Preanalysis Plan." *Quarterly Journal of Economics* 127 (4): 1755–1812.
Casselman, Ben. 2012. "Economists Set Rules on Ethics." *Wall Street Journal*, January 9, sec. Careers. www.wsj.com/articles/SB10001424052970203436904577148940410667970.
Catalini, Christian, Nicola Lacetera and Alexander Oettl. 2015. "The Incidence and Role of Negative Citations in Science." *Proceedings of the National Academy of Sciences* 112 (45): 13823–13826.
Caverley, Jonathan D. 2009/2010. "The Myth of Military Myopia: Democracy, Small Wars, and Vietnam." *International Security* 34 (Winter): 119–157.
  2010/2011. "Explaining U.S. Military Strategy in Vietnam: Thinking Clearly About Causation." *International Security* 35 (Winter): 124–143.
Centeno, Miguel. 2002. *Blood and Debt: War and the Nation State in Latin America*. University Park, PA: Pennsylvania State University Press.
Chalmers, Alan F. 2013. *What is This Thing Called Science?* New York: Hackett Publishing.
Chambers, Christopher. 2013. "Registered Reports: A New Publishing Initative at Cortex." *Cortex* 49: 609–610.
Chambers, Christopher, Eva Feredoes, Suresh D. Muthukumaraswamy and Peter J. Etchells. 2014. "Instead of 'Playing the Game' It Is Time to Change the Rules: Registered Reports at AIMS Neuroscience and Beyond." *AIMS Environmental Science* 1 (1): 4–17.
Chang, Andrew C. and Phillip Li. 2015. "Is Economics Research Replicable? Sixty Published Papers from Thirteen Journals Say 'Usually Not.'" Finance and Economics Discussion Series 2015–83. Board of Governors of the Federal Reserve System (US).

Chapman, Colin D., Christian Benedict and Helgi B. Schiöth. 2018. "Experimenter Gender and Replicability in Science." *Science Advances* 4 (1): 1–7.
Chen, Jihui, Myongjin Kim and Qihong Liu. 2017. "Gender Gap in Tenure and Promotion: Evidence from the Economics Ph.D. Class of 2008." Available at SSRN: https://ssrn.com/abstract=2880240 or http://dx.doi.org/10.2139/ssrn.2880240.
Chenault, Larry A. 1984. "A Note on the Stability Limitations in 'A Stable Price Adjustment Process.'" *Quarterly Journal of Economics* 99 (2): 385.
Chernoff, Fred. 2014. *Explanation and Progress in Security Studies: Bridging Theoretical Divides in International Relations*. Stanford, CA: Stanford University Press.
Chomsky, Noam. 2009. "Opening Remarks." Pp. 13–43 in Massimo Piattelli-Palmarini et al. (eds), *Of Minds and Language*. New York: Oxford University Press.
Choo, Hae Yeon and Myra Marx Ferree. 2010. "Practicing Intersectionality in Sociological Research: A Critical Analysis of Inclusions, Interactions, and Institutions in the Study of Inequalities." *Sociological Theory* 28 (2): 129–149.
Christensen, Björn and Sören Christensen. 2014. "Are Female Hurricanes Really Deadlier than Male Hurricanes?" *Proceedings of the National Academy of Sciences* 111 (34): E3497–E3498.
Christensen, Darin, Alexandra Hartman and Cyrus Samii. 2018. "Property Rights, Investment, and Land Grabs: An Institutional Natural Experiment in Liberia." Unpublished working paper. Available online at https://darinchristensen.com/publication/liberia-tenure/.
Christensen, Garret and Edward Miguel. 2018. "Transparency, Reproducibility, and the Credibility of Economics Research." *Journal of Economic Literature* 56 (3): 920–980.
Ciccone, Antonio. 2011. "Economic Shocks and Civil Conflict: A Comment." *American Economic Journal: Applied Economics* 3 (4): 215–227.
Clemens, Michael. 2017. "The Meaning of Failed Replications: A Review and Proposal." *Journal of Economic Surveys* 31(February): 326–342.
Clements, Kenneth W. and Patricia Wang. 2003. "Who Cites What?" *Economic Record* 79 (245): 229–244.
Coffman, Lucas C. and Muriel Niederle. 2015. "Pre-Analysis Plans have Limited Upside, Especially Where Replications are Feasible." *Journal of Economic Perspectives* 29 (3): 81–97.
Cohen, Jacob. 1994. "The Earth is Round (p < .05)." *American Psychologist* 49: 997–1003.
Cohen-Cole, Ethan, Steven Durlauf, Jeffrey Fagan and Daniel Nagin. 2009. "Model Uncertainty and the Deterrent Effect of Capital Punishment." *American Law and Economics Review* 11 (2): 335–369.
Cole, Stephen. 1994. "Why Sociology Doesn't Make Progress like the Natural Sciences." *Sociological Forum* 9: 133–154.
Coleman, James. 1958. *Nigeria: Background to Nationalism*. Berkeley: University of California Press.
Coleman, James, Elihu Katz and Herbert Menzel. 1966. *Medical Innovation: A Diffusion Study*. New York: Bobbs-Merrill.
Colgan, Jeff. 2017. "Gender Bias in International Relations Graduate Education? New Evidence from Syllabi." *PS: Political Science and Politics* 50 (2): 456–460.
Colgrove, James. 2006. "The Ethics and Politics of Compulsory HPV Vaccination." *The New England Journal of Medicine* 355: 2389–2391.

Collier, David. 2011. "Understanding Process Tracing." *PS:Political Science and Politics* 44 (4): 823–830.

Collier, David, Henry Brady and Jason Seawright. 2004. "Sources of Leverage in Causal Inference: Toward an Alternative View of Methodology." Pp. 229–266 in Henry Brady and David Collier (eds), *Rethinking Social Inquiry: Diverse Tools, Shared Standards*. Lanham, MD: Rowman and Littlefield.

Collier, David and James E. Mahon, Jr. 1993. "Conceptual 'Stretching' Revisited: Adapting Categories in Comparative Analysis." *American Political Science Review* 87 (4): 845–855.

Collier, Ruth Berins and James Mahoney. 1997. "Adding Collective Actors to Collective Outcomes: Labor and Recent Democratization in South America and Southern Europe." *Comparative Politics* 29 (3): 285–303.

Collins, Harry M. 1985. *Changing Order: Replication and Induction in Scientific Practice*. London: Sage Publications.

   1991. "The Meaning of Replication and the Science of Economics." *History of Political Economy* 23: 123–142.

   1998. "The Meaning of Data: Open and Closed Evidential Cultures in the Search for Gravitational Waves." *American Journal of Sociology* 104 (2): 293–338.

Collins, Randall. 1994. "Why the Social Sciences Won't Become High-Consensus, Rapid-Discovery Science." *Sociological Forum* 9 (2): 155–177.

   1998. *The Sociology of Philosophies: A Global Theory of Intellectual Change*. Cambridge, MA: Belknap Press of Harvard University Press.

Conover, Pamela Johnston. 1988. "The Role of Social Groups in Political Thinking." *British Journal of Political Science* 51–76.

Converse, Jean. 1987. *Survey Research in the United States: Roots and Emergence 1890–1960*. Berkeley, CA: University of California Press.

Coppedge, Michael. 2012. *Democratization and Research Methods*. Cambridge: Cambridge University Press.

Coppedge, Michael, John Gerring, David Altman, Michael Bernhard, Steven Fish, Allen Hicken, Matthew Kroenig, Staffan I. Lindberg, Kelly McMann, Pamela Paxton, Holli A. Semetko, Svend-Erik Skaaning, Jeffrey Staton and Jan Teorell. 2011. "Conceptualizing and Measuring Democracy: A New Approach." *Perspectives on Politics* 9 (2, June): 247–267.

Corbyn, Zoe. 2008. "Unpaid Peer Review is worth £1.9bn." *Times Higher Education*, May 29.

"Correspondence: David H. Autor and Bruno S. Frey." 2011. *Journal of Economic Perspectives* 25 (3): 239–240.

Corti, Louise and Arofan Gregory. 2011. "CAQDAS Comparability. What About CAQDAS Data Exchange?" *Forum Qualitative Sozialforschung/Forum: Qualitative Social Research* 12 (1). www.qualitative-research.net/index.php/fqs/article/view/1634.

Corti, Louise, Veerle van den Eynden, Libby Bishop and Matthew Woollard. 2014. *Managing and Sharing Research Data: A Guide to Good Practice*. Los Angeles, CA: SAGE.

Costas, Rodrigo, Zohreh Zahedi and Paul Wouters. 2014. "How Well Developed are Altmetrics? A Cross-Disciplinary Analysis of the Presence of 'Alternative Metrics' in Scientific Publications." *Scientometrics* 101 (2): 1491–1513.

Costas, Rodrigo, Zohreh Zahedi and Paul Wouters. 2015. "Do 'Altmetrics' Correlate with Citations? *Journal of the Association for Information Science and Technology* 66: 2003–2019.

Cowen, Tyler and Alex Tabarrok. 2016. "A Skeptical View of the National Science Foundation's Role in Economic Research." *Journal of Economic Perspectives* 30 (3): 235–248.

References

Cox, Richard. 1961. *The Algebra of Probable Inference*. Baltimore, MD: Johns Hopkins University Press.

Crenshaw, Kimberlé. 1989. "Demarginalizing The Intersection of Race and Sex: A Black Feminist Critique of Antidiscrimination Doctrine, Feminist Theory, and Antiracist Politics." *University of Chicago Legal Forces*, 139–168

Cronin, Blaise. 1984. *The Citation Process. The Role and Significance of Citations in Scientific Communication*. London: Taylor Graham.

Cronin, Blaise and Cassidy R. Sugimoto (eds). 2014. *Beyond Bibliometrics: Harnessing Multidimensional Indicators of Scholarly Impact*. Cambridge, MA: MIT Press.

Cumming, Geoff. 2008. "Replication and p Intervals: P Values Predict the Future Only Vaguely, but Confidence Intervals Do Much Better." *Perspectives on Psychological Science* 3: 286–300.

Cumming, Geoff and Robert Maillardet. 2006. "Confidence Intervals and Replication: Where Will the Next Mean Fall?" *Psychological Methods* 11: 217–227.

Cumming, Geoff, Jennifer Williams and Fiona Fidler. 2004. "Replication, and Researchers' Understanding of Confidence Intervals and Standard Error Bars." *Understanding Statistics* 3: 299–311.

Dahl Rasmussen, Ole, Nikolaj Malchow-Møller and Thomas Barnebeck Andersen. 2011. "Walking the Talk: The Need for a Trial Registry for Development Interventions." *Journal of Development Effectiveness* 3 (4): 502–519.

Dal-Ré, Rafael, John P. Ioannidis, Michael B. Bracken, Patricia A. Buffler, An-Wen Chan, Eduardo L. Franco, Carlo La Vecchia and Elisabete Weiderpass. 2014. "Making Prospective Registration of Observational Research a Reality." *Science Translational Medicine* 6 (224): 224cm1–224cm1.

David, Paul A. 1985. "Clio and the Economics of QWERTY." *American Economic Review* 75 (2): 332–337.

Davis, Graham A. 2013. "Replicating Sachs and Warner's Working Papers on the Resource Curse." *Journal of Development Studies* 49 (12): 1615–1630.

Davis, James. 1958. "Review of Robert Merton et al, The Student-Physician," *American Journal of Sociology* 63 (4): 445–446.

De Angelis, Catherine, Jeffrey M. Drazen, Frank A. Frizelle, Charlotte Haug, John Hoey, Richard Horton, Sheldon Kotzin et al. 2004. "Clinical Trial Registration: A Statement from the International Committee of Medical Journal Editors." *New England Journal of Medicine* 351 (12): 1250–1251.

Deaton, Angus. 2010. "Instruments, Randomization, and Learning about Development." *Journal of Economic Literature* 48 (2): 424–455.

DeCoursey, Tom. 2006. "Perspective: The Pros and Cons of Open Peer Review." *Nature*. www.nature.com/nature/peerreview/debate/nature04991.html.

Deere, Donald, Kevin M. Murphy and Finis Welch. 1995. "Employment and the 1990–1991 Minimum-Wage Hike." *American Economic Review* 85 (2): 232–237.

Dekel, Eddie, David Levine, Costas Meghir, Whitney Newey and Andrew Postlewaite. 2006. "Report of the Editors." *Econometrica* 74 (1): 307–310.

Delgado López-Cózar, Emilio, Nicolas Robinson-García and Daniel Torres-Salinas. 2014. "The Google Scholar Experiment: How to Index False Papers and Manipulate Bibliometric Indicators." *Journal of the Association for Information Science and Technology* 65 (3): 446–454.

Della Porta, Donatella and Michael Keating (eds). 2008. *Approaches and Methodologies in the Social Sciences: A Pluralist Perspective.* Cambridge: Cambridge University Press.

DellaVigna, Stefano and Devin Pope. 2016. "Predicting Experimental Results: Who Knows What?" Working Paper 22566. National Bureau of Economic Research. www.nber.org/papers/w22566.

DeLong, J. Bradford and Kevin Lang. 1992. "Are All Economic Hypotheses False?" *Journal of Political Economy* 100 (6): 1257–1272.

Denton, Frank T. 1985. "Data Mining as an Industry." *Review of Economics and Statistics* 67 (1): 124–127.

DeRigne, LeaAnne and Shirley L. Porterfield. 2017. "Employment Change Among Married Parents of Children With Special Health Care Needs." *Journal of Family Issues* 38 (5): 579–606.

Desch, Michael C. 2008. *Power and Military Effectiveness: The Fallacy of Democratic Triumphalism.* Baltimore, MD: Johns Hopkins University Press.

Dessler, David. 1991. "Beyond Correlations: Toward a Causal Theory of War." *International Studies Quarterly* 35 (3): 337–355.

Dewald, William G., Jerry G. Thursby and Richard G. Anderson. 1986. "Replication in Empirical Economics: The Journal of Money, Credit and Banking Project." *American Economic Review* 76 (4): 587–603.

Dezhbakhsh, Hashem, Paul H. Rubin and Joanna M. Shepherd. 2003. "Does Capital Punishment Have a Deterrent Effect? New Evidence from Postmoratorium Panel Data." *American Law and Economics Review* 5 (2): 344–376.

Diament, Sean M., Adam J. Howat and Matthew J. Lacombe. 2018. "Gender Representation in the American Politics Canon: An Analysis of Core Graduate Syllabi." *PS: Political Science and Politics*: 1–6.

Didegah, Fereshteh and Mike Thelwall. 2013. "Determinants of Research Citation Impact in Nanoscience and Nanotechnology." *Journal of the American Society for Information Science and Technology* 64 (5): 1055–1064.

Dijksterhuis, Ap 2013. "Replication Crisis or Crisis in Replication A Reinterpretation of Shanks et al." Reader comment. www.plosone.org/annotation/listThread.action?root=64751.

Dijksterhuis, Ap, Russell Spears and Vincent Lepinasse. 2001. "Reflecting and Deflecting Stereotypes: Assimilation and Contrast in Impression Formation and Automatic Behavior." *Journal of Experimental Social Psychology* 37: 286–299.

DiMaggio, Paul J. and Walter W. Powell (eds). 1991. *The New Institutionalism in Organizational Analysis.* Chicago: University of Chicago Press.

Dimitrova, Daniela V. and Michael Bugeja. 2007. "The Half-Life of Internet References Cited in Communication Journals." *New Media and Society* 9 (5): 811–826.

Djupe, Paul, Amy Erica Smith and Anand Sokhey, 2018. "Explaining Gender in the Journals: How Submission Practices Affect Publication Patterns in Political Science." Paper presented at the Visions in Methodology Conference, Ohio State University, May 7–9.

Dollard, John. 1937. *Caste and Class in a Southern Town.* New edition. New York: Harper and Brothers.

Donohue, John J. and Steven D. Levitt. 2001. "The Impact of Legalized Abortion on Crime." *Quarterly Journal of Economics* 116 (2): 379.

2008. "Measurement Error, Legalized Abortion, and the Decline in Crime: A Response to Foote and Goetz (Christopher L, Foote, Christopher F. Goetz) (Report)." *Quarterly Journal of Economics* 123 (1): 425.

Donohue, John J. and Justin Wolfers. 2005. "Uses and Abuses of Empirical Evidence in the Death Penalty Debate." *Stanford Law Review* 58 (3): 791–845.

DORA. 2012. "San Francisco Declaration on Research Assessment." 2012. https://sfdora.org/read/.

Doucet, Andrea and Natasha S. Mauthner. 2008. "What Can Be Known and How? Narrated Subjects and the Listening Guide." *Qualitative Research* 8 (3): 399–409.

Doucouliagos, Chris. 2005. "Publication Bias in the Economic Freedom and Economic Growth Literature." *Journal of Economic Surveys* 19 (3): 367–387.

Doucouliagos, Chris and T. D. Stanley. 2013. "Are All Economic Facts Greatly Exaggerated? Theory Competition and Selectivity." *Journal of Economic Surveys* 27 (2): 316–339.

Doucouliagos, Chris, T. D. Stanley and Margaret Giles. 2012. "Are Estimates of the Value of a Statistical Life Exaggerated?" *Journal of Health Economics* 31 (1): 197–206.

Doucouliagos, Christos and Patrice Laroche. 2003. "What Do Unions Do to Productivity? A Meta-Analysis." *Industrial Relations: A Journal of Economy and Society* 42 (4): 650–691.

Doucouliagos, Hristos, John P. Ioannidis and Tom Stanley. 2017. "The Power of Bias in Economics." *Economic Journal* 127 (October): F236–F265.

Doucouliagos, Hristos and T. D. Stanley. 2009. "Publication Selection Bias in Minimum-Wage Research? A Meta-Regression Analysis." *British Journal of Industrial Relations* 47 (2): 406–428.

Doucouliagos, Hristos, T. D. Stanley and W. Kip Viscusi. 2014. "Publication Selection and the Income Elasticity of the Value of a Statistical Life." *Journal of Health Economics* 33 (January): 67–75.

Douven, Igor. 2011. "Abduction" and "Supplement to Abduction: Peirce on Abduction," *The Stanford Encyclopedia of Philosophy* (Spring 2011 Edition), Edward N. Zalta (ed.). http://plato.stanford.edu/archives/spr2011/entries/abduction/.

Drazen, Jeffrey M. 2016. "Data Sharing and the Journal." *New England Journal of Medicine* 374 (19): e24.

Dreber, Anna, Thomas Pfeiffer, Johan Almenberg, Siri Isaksson, Brad Wilson, Yiling Chen, Brian A. Nosek and Magnus Johannesson. 2015. "Using Prediction Markets to Estimate the Reproducibility of Scientific Research." *Proceedings of the National Academy of Sciences*, November, 201516179. doi:10.1073/pnas.1516179112.

Druckman, James N. and Donald P. Green (eds). 2011. *Cambridge Handbook of Experimental Political Science*. Cambridge: Cambridge University Press.

Druckman, James N., Donald P. Green, James H. Kuklinski and Arthur Lupia. 2006. "The Growth and Development of Experimental Research in Political Science." *American Political Science Review* 100 (4): 627–635.

Drukker, David M. and Vince Wiggins. 2004. "Verifying the Solution from a Nonlinear Solver: A Case Study: Comment." *American Economic Review* 94 (1): 397–399.

Du Bois, W. E. B. 1937. "Southern Trauma: Review of Caste and Class in a Southern Town by John Dollard." *North Georgia Review* 2: 9–10.

Duarte, José et al. 2015. "Political Diversity Will Improve Psychological Science." *Behavioral and Brain Sciences* 1–58.

Dube, Arindrajit, T. William Lester and Michael Reich. 2010. "Minimum Wage Effects Across State Borders: Estimates Using Contiguous Counties." *Review of Economics and Statistics* 92 (4): 945–964.

Duflo, Esther, Rachel Glennerster and Michael Kremer. 2007. "Chapter 61 Using Randomization in Development Economics Research: A Toolkit." Pp. 3895–3962 in T. Paul Schultz and John A. Strauss (eds), *Handbook of Development Economics*. New York: Elsevier.

Dumont, Clayton W. 2008. *The Promise of Poststructuralist Sociology: Marginalized Peoples and the Problem of Knowledge*. Albany, NY: SUNY Press.

Dunleavy, Patrick. 2014. "Poor Citation Practices are a Form of Academic Self-Harm in the Humanities and Social Sciences." Blog post. https://medium.com/advice-and-help-in-authoring-a-phd-or-non-fiction/poor-citation-practices-are-a-form-of-academic-self-harm-in-the-humanities-and-social-sciences-2cddf250b3c2#.6vnf69w17.

Dunning, Thad. 2012. *Natural Experiments in the Social Sciences: A Design-Based Approach*. Cambridge: Cambridge University Press.

  2016. "Transparency, Replication, and Cumulative Learning: What Experiments Alone Cannot Achieve." *Annual Review of Political Science* 19: 541–563.

Duvendack, Maren and Richard Palmer-Jones. 2013. "Replication of Quantitative Work in Development Studies: Experiences and Suggestions." *Progress in Development Studies* 13 (4): 307–322.

Duvendack, Maren, Richard Palmer-Jones and Robert W. Reed. 2015. "Replications in Economics: A Progress Report." *Economic Journal Watch* 12 (2): 164–191.

Dwork, Cynthia and Adam Smith. 2010. "Differential Privacy for Statistics: What We Know and What We Want to Learn." *Journal of Privacy and Confidentiality* 1 (2). http://repository.cmu.edu/jpc/vol1/iss2/2.

Easley, Richard W., Charles S. Madden and Mark G. Dunn. 2000. "Conducting Marketing Science: The Role of Replication in the Research Process." *Journal of Business Research* 48 (1): 83–92.

Easterbrook, Phillipa J., Ramana Gopalan, Jesse A. Berlin and David R. Matthews. 1991. "Publication Bias in Clinical Research." *The Lancet*, originally published as 337 (8746): 867–872.

Easterly, William, Ross Levine and David Roodman. 2004. "Aid, Policies, and Growth: Comment." *American Economic Review* 94 (3): 774–780.

Eble, Alex, Peter Boone and Diana Elbourne. 2014. "On Minimizing the Risk of Bias in Randomized Controlled Trials in Economics." SSRN Scholarly Paper ID 2272141. Rochester, NY: Social Science Research Network. http://papers.ssrn.com/abstract=2272141.

Eden, Dov. 2002. "From the Editors: Replication, Meta-Analysis, Scientific Progress, and AMJ's Publication Policy." *Academy of Management Journal* 45: 841–846.

Egger, Matthias, George Davey-Smith and Douglas G. Altman (eds). 2001. *Systematic Reviews in Health Care: Meta-Analysis in Context*. London: BMJ Publishing Group.

Eich, Eric. 2014. "Business Not as Usual." *Psychological Science* 25 (1): 3–6. https://doi.org/10.1177/0956797613512465.

Eidlin, Fred. 1983. "Area Studies and/or Social Science: Contextually-Limited Generalizations versus General Laws." Pp. 199–216 in Fred Eidlin (ed.), *Constitutional Democracy: Essays in Comparative Politics*. Boulder, CO: Westview.

Elkana, Yehuda, Joshua Lederberg, Robert K. Merton, Arnold Thackray and Harriet Zuckerman. 1978. *Towards a Metric of Science: The Advent of Science Indicators*. New York: Wiley.

Ellison, Glenn. 2002. "The Slowdown of the Economics Publishing Process." *Journal of Political Economy* 110 (5): 947–993.

Elm, Erik von, Douglas G. Altman, Matthias Egger, Stuart J. Pocock, Peter C. Gøtzsche and Jan P. Vandenbroucke. 2007. "The Strengthening the Reporting of Observational Studies in Epidemiology (STROBE) Statement: Guidelines for Reporting Observational Studies." *Preventive Medicine* 45 (4): 247–251.

Elman, Colin and Diana Kapiszewski. 2014. "Data Access and Research Transparency in the Qualitative Tradition." *PS: Political Science and Politics* 47 (1): 43–47.

Ember, Carol and Robert Hanisch. 2013. "Sustaining Domain Repositories for Digital Data: A White Paper, December 11." doi:10.3886/SustainingDomainRepositoriesDigitalData.

Enders, Walter and Gary A. Hoover. 2004. "Whose Line Is It? Plagiarism in Economics." *Journal of Economic Literature* 42 (2): 487–493.

  2006. "Plagiarism in the Economics Profession: A Survey." *Challenge* 49 (5): 92–107.

Epidemiology. 2010. "The Registration of Observational Studies – When Metaphors Go Bad." *Epidemiology*, July, 1. doi:10.1097/EDE.0b013e3181eafbcf.

Erikson, Martin G. and Peter Erlandson. 2014. "A Taxonomy of Motives to Cite." *Social Studies of Science* 44 (4): 625–637.

Ertman, Thomas. 1997. *Birth of the Leviathan: Building States and Regimes in Medieval and Early Modern Europe*. Cambridge: Cambridge University Press.

Espeland, Wendy Nelson and Michael Sauder. 2016. *Engines of Anxiety: Academic Rankings, Reputation, and Accountability*. New York: Russell Sage Foundation.

Etz, Alexander and Joachim Vandekerckhove. 2016. "A Bayesian Perspective on the Reproducibility Project: Psychology." *PLoS ONE* 11 (2): e0149794.

Evangelou, Evangelos, Thomas A. Trikalinos and John P. Ioannidis. 2005. "Unavailability of Online Supplementary Scientific Information from Articles Published in Major Journals." *The FASEB Journal* 19 (14): 1943–1944.

Everett, Jim A. C. and Brian D. Earp. 2016. "A Tragedy of the (Academic) Commons: Interpreting the Replication Crises in Psychology as a Social Dilemma for Early-Career Researchers." *Frontiers in Psychology* 6: 1152.

Fairfield, Tasha. 2010. "Business Power and Tax Reform: Taxing Income and Profits in Chile and Argentina." *Latin American Politics and Society* 52 (2): 37–71.

  2011. "Business Power and Protest: Argentina's Agricultural Producers Protest in Comparative Context." *Studies in Comparative International Development* 46 (4): 424–453.

  2013. "Going Where the Money Is: Strategies for Taxing Economic Elites in Unequal Democracies." *World Development* 47: 42–57.

  2015. *Private Wealth and Public Revenue in Latin America: Business Power and Tax Politics*. New York: Cambridge University Press.

Fairfield, Tasha and Andrew Charman. 2015. "Bayesian Probability: The Logic of (Political) Science: Opportunities, Caveats and Guidelines." Paper presented at Annual Meeting of the American Political Science Association, September 3–6, San Francisco.

  2017. "Explicit Bayesian Analysis for Process Tracing: Guidelines, Opportunities, and Caveats." *Political Analysis* 25 (3): 363–380.

2018. "A Bayesian Perspective on Case Selection." Presented at the American Political Science Association Annual Meeting, Boston, MA, August 30–September 2.

2019. "The Bayesian Foundations of Iterative Research in Qualitative Social Science: A Dialogue with the Data." *Perspectives on Politics* 17 (1): 154–167.

2020. *Social Inquiry and Bayesian Inference: Rethinking Qualitative Research*. Cambridge: Cambridge University Press.

Fairfield, Tasha and Candelaria Garay. 2017. "Redistribution under the Right in Latin America: Electoral Competition and Organized Actors in Policymaking," *Comparative Political Studies* 50 (14): 1871–1906.

Falagas, Matthew E., Angeliki Zarkali, Drosos E. Karageorgopoulos, Vangelis Bardakas and Michael N. Mavros. 2013. "The Impact of Article Length on the Number of Future Citations: A Bibliometric Analysis of General Medicine Journals." *PLoS ONE* 8 (2): e49476.

Fanelli, Daniele. 2009. "How Many Scientists Fabricate and Falsify Research? A Systematic Review and Meta-Analysis of Survey Data." *PLoS ONE* 4 (5): e5738.

2013. "Why Growing Retractions Are (Mostly) a Good Sign." *PLoS Medicine* 10 (12): e1001563.

Fang, Ferric C. and Arturo Casadevall. 2011. "Retracted Science and the Retraction Index." *Infection and Immunity* 79 (10): 3855–3859.

Fann, Kuang Tih. 1970. *Peirce's Theory of Abduction*. The Hague: Martinus Nijhoff.

Faye, Cathy. 2012. "American Social Psychology: Examining the Contours of the 1970s Crisis." *Studies in the History and Philosophy of Science Part C: Biological and Biomedical Sciences* 43 (2): 514–521.

Feak, Christine B. and John M. Swales. 2009. *Telling a Research Story: Writing a Literature Review*. Ann Arbor, MI: University of Michigan Press.

Feigenbaum, Susan and David M. Levy. 1993. "The Market for (Ir)reproducible Econometrics." *Social Epistemology* 7: 215–232.

Feldstein, Martin. 1974. "Social Security, Induced Retirement, and Aggregate Capital Accumulation." *Journal of Political Economy* 82 (5): 905–926.

"Social Security and Private Saving: Reply." *Journal of Political Economy* 90 (3): 630–642.

Ferber, Marianne A. and Michael Brün. 2011. "The Gender Gap in Citations: Does It Persist?" *Feminist Economics* 17 (1): 151–158.

Ferree, Myra Marx, Shamus Khan and Shauna Morimoto. 2007. "Assessing the Feminist Revolution: The Presence and Absence of Gender in Theory and Practice." Pp. 438–479 in Craig Calhoun (ed.), *Sociology in America*. Chicago: University of Chicago Press.

Feyerabend, Paul. 1993. *Against Method*. London: Verso.

Fielding, Nigel. 2004. "Getting the Most from Archived Qualitative Data: Epistemological, Practical and Professional Obstacles." *International Journal of Social Research Methodology* 7 (1): 97–104.

Fienberg, Stephen E., Margaret E. Martin and Miron L. Straf (eds). 1985. *Sharing Research Data*. Washington, DC: National Academy Press.

Findley, Michael G., Nathan M. Jensen, Edmund J. Malesky and Thomas B. Pepinsky. 2016. "Can Results-Free Review Reduce Publication Bias? The Results and Implications of a Pilot Study." *Comparative Political Studies* 49 (13): 1667–1703.

Fink, Günther, Margaret McConnell and Sebastian Vollmer. 2014. "Testing for Heterogeneous Treatment Effects in Experimental Data: False Discovery Risks and Correction Procedures." *Journal of Development Effectiveness* 6 (1): 44–57.

Finkel, Eli J., Paul W. Eastwick and Harry T. Reis. 2015. "Best Research Practices in Psychology: Illustrating Epistemological and Pragmatic Considerations with the Case of Relationship Science." *Journal of Personality and Social Psychology* 108 (2): 275–297.

Finkelstein, Amy, Sarah Taubman, Bill Wright, Mira Bernstein, Jonathan Gruber, Joseph P. Newhouse, Heidi Allen and Katherine Baicker. 2012. "The Oregon Health Insurance Experiment: Evidence from the First Year." *Quarterly Journal of Economics* 127 (3): 1057–1106.

Finney, David. 1997. "The Responsible Referee." *Biometrics* 53 (2): 715–719.

Fleischmann, Martin and Stanley Pons. 1989. "Electrochemically Induced Nuclear Fusion of Deuterium." *Journal of Electroanalytical Chemistry and Interfacial Electrochemistry* 261 (2): 301–308.

Folbre, Nancy 1982. "Exploitation Comes Home: A Critique of the Marxian Theory of Family Labor." *Cambridge Journal of Economics* 6 (4): 317–329.

Food and Drug Administration. 1998. "Guidance for Industry: E9 Statistical Principles for Clinical Trials." www.fda.gov/downloads/drugs/guidancecomplianceregulatoryinformation/guidances/ucm073137.pdf.n.d. "E9 Statistical Principles for Clinical Trials." Guidance for Industry. Rockville, MD: Food and Drug Administration. www.fda.gov/downloads/drugs/guidancecomplianceregulatoryinformation/guidances/ucm073137.pdf.

Foote, Christopher L. and Christopher F. Goetz. 2008. "The Impact of Legalized Abortion on Crime: Comment (Report)." *Quarterly Journal of Economics* 123 (1): 407.

Forscher, Bernard. 1965. "Rules for Referees." *Science* 150 (3694): 319–321.

Fourcade-Gourinchas, Marion and Sarah Babb. 2002. "The Rebirth of the Liberal Creed: Paths to Neoliberalism in Four Countries." *American Journal of Sociology* 108: 533–579.

Fourcade, Marion. 2009. *Economists and societies: Discipline and profession in the United States, Britain, and France, 1890s to 1990s*. Princeton, NJ: Princeton University Press.

Fourcade, Marion and Kieran Healy. 2016. "Seeing Like a Market." *Socio-Economic Review* (December): 9–29.

2017. "Categories All the Way Down." *Historical Social Research* 42 (1): 286–296.

Fowler, Linda L. 1995. "Replication as Regulation." *PS: Political Science and Politics* 28 (3): 478–481.

Fox, Charles W., C. E. Timothy Paine and Boris Sauterey. 2016. "Citations Increase with Manuscript Length, Author Number, and References Cited in Ecology Journals." *Ecology and Evolution* 6 (21): 7717–7726.

Franco, Annie, Neil Malhotra and Gabor Simonovits. 2014. "Publication Bias in the Social Sciences: Unlocking the File Drawer." *Science* 345 (6203): 1502–1505.

Frank, Michael C. and Rebecca Saxe. 2012. "Teaching Replication." *Perspectives on Psychological Science* 7 (6): 600–604.

Freese, Jeremy. 2007a. "Overcoming Objections to Open-Source Social Science." *Sociological Methods and Research* 36 (2): 220–226.

2007b. "Replication Standards for Quantitative Social Science: Why Not Sociology?" *Sociological Methods and Research* 36 (2): 153–172.

Freese, Jeremy and David Peterson. 2016. "The Emergence of Forensic Objectivity." osf.io/2ft8x.

2017. "Replication in Social Science." *Annual Review of Sociology* 43 (1): 147–165.

2018. "The Emergence of Statistical Objectivity." *Sociological Theory* 36 (3): 289–313.

Freese, Jeremy and Brian Powell. 2001. "Commentary and Debate: Making Love Out of Nothing at All? Null Findings and the Trivers-Willard Hypothesis." *American Journal of Sociology* 106 (6): 1776–1788.

Frey, René L., Bruno S. Frey and Reiner Eichenberger. 1999. "A Case of Plagiarism." *Kyklos* 52 (3): 311.

Frickel, Scott. 2008. "On Missing New Orleans: Lost Knowledge and Knowledge Gaps in an Urban Hazardscape." *Environmental History* 13: 643–650.

Frickel, Scott and Neil Gross. 2005. "A General Theory of Scientific/Intellectual Movements." *American Sociological Review* 70 (2): 204–232.

Fried, Eiko. 2018. "7 Sternberg Papers: 351 References, 161 Self-Citations." March 29, 2018. http://eiko-fried.com/sternberg-selfcitations/.

Frijters, Paul and Benno Torgler. 2016. "Improving the Peer Review Process: A Proposed Market System." Discussion paper No. 9894, IZA/The Institute for the Study of Labor, Bonn, Germany.

Fuess, Scott M., Jr. 1996. "On Replication in Business and Economics Research: The QJBE Case." *Quarterly Journal of Business and Economics* 35 (2): 3–13.

Gaddis, John Lewis. 1989. *The Long Peace: Inquiries into the History of the Cold War*. Oxford: Oxford University Press.

Galbraith, Rex F. 1988. "A Note on Graphical Presentation of Estimated Odds Ratios from Several Clinical Trials." *Statistics in Medicine* 7 (8): 889–894.

Galvan, Jose L. and Melisa C. Galvan. 2017. *Writing Literature Reviews: A guide for Students of the Social and Behavioral Sciences*. London: Routledge.

Ganimian, Alejandro. 2014. "Pre-Analysis Plan Template." Template document. Harvard University. http://scholar.harvard.edu/files/alejandro_ganimian/files/pre-analysis_plan_template_0.pdf.

Gans, Herbert J. 1992. "Sociological Amnesia: The Noncumulation of Normal Social Science." *Sociological Forum* 7: 701–710.

Gans, Joshua. 2017. *Scholarly Publishing and its Discontents: An Economist's Perspective on Dealing with Market Power and its Consequences*. Toronto: Core Economic Research.

Garay, Candelaria. 2016. *Social Policy Expansion in Latin America*. New York: Cambridge University Press.

García, Fernando Martel. 2016. "Replication and the Manufacture of Scientific Inferences: A Formal Approach." *International Studies Perspectives* 17 (4): 408–425.

Garfield, E. 1955. "Citation Indexes for Science: A New Dimension in Documentation through Association of Ideas." *Science* 122 (3159): 108–111.

Gazni, Ali and Fereshteh Didegah. 2011. "Investigating Different Types of Research Collaboration and Citation Impact: A Case Study of Harvard University's Publications." *Scientometrics* 87 (2): 251–265.

Gehlbach, Scott. 2015. "The Fallacy of Multiple Methods." *Comparative Politics Newsletter* 25 (2): 11–12.

Geller, Daniel S. and John A. Vasquez (eds). 2005. *The Construction and Cumulation of Knowledge in International Relations*. Oxford: Wiley-Blackwell.

Gelman, Andrew and Neil Gross. 2015. "Political Attitudes in Social Environments." *Behavioral and Brain Sciences* 38: E114.

Gelman, Andrew and Eric Loken. 2013. "The Garden of Forking Paths: Why Multiple Comparisons Can Be a Problem, Even When There is No 'Fishing Expedition' or 'p-Hacking' and the Research Hypothesis Was Posited ahead of Time." November. www.stat.columbia.edu/~gelman/research/unpublished/p_hacking.pdf.

2014. "The Statistical Crisis in Science: Data-dependent Analysis – A "Garden of Forking Paths" – Explains Why Many Statistically Significant Comparisons Don't Hold Up." *American Scientist* 102 (6): 460.

Gelman, Andrew, Cristian Pasarica and Rahul Dodhia. 2002. "Let's Practice What We Preach." *The American Statistician* 56 (2): 121–130.

Gelman, Andrew and Hal Stern. 2006. "The Difference between "Significant" and "Not Significant" is Not Itself Statistically Significant." *Journal of the American Statistical Association* 60: 328–331.

George, Alexander L. and Andrew Bennett. 2005. *Case Studies and Theory Development in the Social Sciences*. Cambridge, MA: MIT Press.

Gerber, Alan S. and Neil Malhotra. 2008a. "Do Statistical Reporting Standards Affect What is Published? Publication Bias in Two Leading Political Science Journals." *Quarterly Journal of Political Science* 3: 313–326.

2008b. "Publication Bias in Empirical Sociological Research: Do Arbitrary Significance Levels Distort Published Results?" *Sociological Methods and Research* 37 (1): 3–30.

Gerber, Alan S., Donald P. Green and David Nickerson. 2001. "Testing for Publication Bias in Political Science." *Political Analysis* 9 (4): 385–392.

Gerber, Alan S., Neil Malhotra, Conor Dowling and David Doherty. 2010. "Publication Bias in Two Political Behavior Literatures." *American Politics Research* 38 (4): 591–613.

Gerber, Alan, Kevin Arceneaux, Cheryl Boudreau, Conor Dowling, Sunshine Hillygus, Thomas Palfrey, Daniel R. Biggers and David J. Hendry. 2014. "Reporting Guidelines for Experimental Research: A Report from the Experimental Research Section Standards Committee." *Journal of Experimental Political Science* 1 (1): 81–98.

Gerking, Shelby and William E Morgan. 2007. "Effects of Environmental and Land Use Regulation in the Oil and Gas Industry Using the Wyoming Checkerboard as a Natural Experiment: Retraction." *American Economic Review* 97 (3): 1032.

Gerring, John. 2012a. "Mere Description." *British Journal of Political Science* 42 (04): 721–746.

2012b. *Social Science Methodology: A Unified Framework*. Cambridge: Cambridge University Press.

2017. *Case Study Research: Principles and Practices*. 2d ed. Cambridge: Cambridge University Press.

Gerring, John and Lee Cojocaru. 2016. "Arbitrary Limits to Scholarly Speech: Why (Short) Word Limits Should be Abolished." *Qualitative and Multi-Method Research: Newsletter of the American Political Science Association Organized Section on Qualitative and Multi-Method Research* 14: 1/2 (Spring/Fall): 2–13.

Gertler, Aaron L. and John G. Bullock. 2017. "Reference Rot: An Emerging Threat to Transparency in Political Science." *PS: Political Science and Politics* 50 (1): 166–171.

Gherghina, Sergiu and Alexia Katsanidou. 2013. "Data Availability in Political Science Journals." *European Political Science* 12 (3): 333–349.

Ghiasi, Gita, Vincent Larivière and Cassidy R. Sugimoto. 2016. "Gender Differences in Synchronous and Diachronous Self-Citations." In *Proceedings of the 21st International Conference on Science and Technology Indicators*. Valencia, Spain: Editorial Universitat Politecnica de Valencia.

Gibler, Douglas M., Steven M. Miller and Erin K. Little. 2016. Analysis of the Militarized Interstate Dispute (MID) Dataset, 1816–2001. *International Studies Quarterly* 60 (December): 719–730.

Gieryn, Thomas. 1999. *Cultural Boundaries of Science: Credibility on the Line.* Chicago: University of Chicago Press.

Gilardi, Fabrizio. 2015. "The Temporary Importance of Role Models for Women's Political Representation." *American Journal of Political Science* 59 (4): 957–970.

Gilbert, Christopher L. 1989. "LSE and the British Approach to Time Series Econometrics." Oxford Economic Papers, *New Series* 41 (1): 108–128.

Gilbert, Daniel T., Gary King, Stephen Pettigrew and Timothy D. Wilson. 2016. "Comment on 'Estimating the Reproducibility of Psychological Science.'" *Science* 351 (6277): 1037.

Giner-Sorolla, Roger. 2012. "Science or Art? How Aesthetic Standards Grease the Way Through the Publication Bottleneck but Undermine Science." *Perspectives on Psychological Science* 7 (6): 562–571.

Gingras, Y. 2016. *Bibliometrics and Research Evaluation: Uses and Abuses.* Cambridge, MA: MIT Press.

Ginther, Donna K. and Shulamit Kahn. 2004. "Women in Economics: Moving Up or Falling Off the Academic Career Ladder?" *Journal of Economic Perspectives* 18 (3): 193–214.

Glandon, Philip. 2010. "Report on the American Economic Review Data Availability Compliance Project." Vanderbilt University. https://aeaweb.org/aer/2011_Data_Compliance_Report.pdf.

Glaser, Barney and Anselm Strauss. 1967. *The Discovery of Grounded Theory: Strategies for Qualitative Research.* Chicago: Aldine Publishing Company.

Glass, Gene V., Mary Lee Smith and Barry McGaw. 1981. *Meta-Analysis in Social Research.* London: Sage.

Glennerster, Rachel and Kudzai Takavarasha. 2013. *Running Randomized Evaluations: A Practical Guide.* Princeton, NJ: Princeton University Press.

Gleser, Leon J. 1986. "Some Notes on Refereeing." *The American Statistician* 40 (4): 310–312.

Go, Julian. 2016. *Postcolonial Thought and Social Theory.* New York: Oxford University Press.

Goertz, Gary. 2017. "Descriptive-Causal Generalizations: 'Empirical Laws' in the Social Sciences?" Pp. 85–108 in *Oxford Handbook of the Philosophy of the Social Sciences*, Harold Kincaid (ed.). Oxford: Oxford University Press.

Goertz, Gary and Mahoney, James. 2012. "Concepts and Measurement: Ontology and Epistemology." *Social Science Information* 51 (2): 205–216.

Goffman, Erving. 1959. *The Presentation of Self in Everyday Life.* New York: Doubleday and Company.

Goldberg, Pinelopi Koujianou. 2016. "Report of the Editor: American Economic Review." *American Economic Review* 106 (5): 700–712.

Goldin, Claudia. 1992. *Understanding the Gender Gap: An Economic History of American Women.* Oxford: Oxford University Press.

  2006. "The Quiet Revolution that Transformed Women's Employment, Education, and Family." *American Economic Review* 96 (2): 1–21.

Goldin, Claudia and Larry F. Katz. 2016. "A Most Egalitarian Profession: Pharmacy and the Evolution of a Family Friendly Occupation." *Journal of Labor Economics* 34 (3): 705–745.2011. "The Cost of Workplace Flexibility for High-Powered Professionals." *The Annals of the American Academy of Political and Social Science* 638 (1): 45–67.

References

Goldin, Claudia, Lawrence F. Katz and Ilyana Kuziemko. 2006. "The Homecoming of American College Women: The Reversal of the Gender Gap in College." *Journal of Economic Perspectives* 20: 133–156.

Goodman, Steven, Daniele Fanelli and John Ioannidis. 2016. "What Does Research Reproducibility Mean?" *Science Translational Medicine* 8 (341): 1–6.

Gorg, Holger and Eric Strobl. 2001. "Multinational Companies and Productivity Spillovers: A Meta-Analysis." *Economic Journal* 111 (475): 723–739.

Gorski, Philip S. 2009. "Social 'Mechanisms' and Comparative-Historical Sociology: A Critical Realist Proposal." Pp. 147–194 in Peter Hedström and Björn Wittrock (eds), *Frontiers of Sociology*. Leiden: Brill.

Gough, David and Diana Elbourne. 2002. "Systematic Research Synthesis to Inform Policy, Practice, and Democratic Debate." *Social Policy and Society* 1: 225–236.

Gough, Ian. 2015. "The Political Economy of Prevention." *British Journal of Political Science* 45 (02): 307–327.

Gouldner, Alvin. 1954. *Patterns of Industrial Democracy*. New York: The Free Press.

Gouldner, Alvin and Richard Peterson. 1962. *Notes on Technology and the Moral Order*. New York: Bobbs-Merrill.

Grant, Sean, Evan Mayo-Wilson, Sally Hopewell, Geraldine Macdonald, David Moher and Paul Montgomery. 2013. "Developing a Reporting Guideline for Social and Psychological Intervention Trials." *Journal of Experimental Criminology* 9 (3): 355–367.

Gray, Paul et al. 2007. *The Research Imagination: An Introduction to Qualitative and Quantitative Methods*. New York: Cambridge University Press.

Gray, Ronald H. et al. 2007. "Male Circumcision for HIV Prevention in Men in Rakai, Uganda: A Randomised Trial." *Lancet* 369 (9562): 657–666.

Greenland, Sander. 2006. "Bayesian Perspectives for Epidemiological Research." *International Journal of Epidemiology* (35): 765–775.

Greenwald, Anthony G. 1975. "Consequences of Prejudice against the Null Hypothesis." *Psychological Bulletin* 82 (1): 1.

Greve, Werner, Arndt Bröder and Edgar Erdfelder. 2013. "Result-Blind Peer Reviews and Editorial Decisions." *European Psychologist* 18 (4) 286–294.

Gross, Neil. 2009. "A Pragmatist Theory of Social Mechanisms." *American Sociological Review* 74: 358–379.

2013. *Why Are Professors Liberal and Why Do Conservatives Care?* Cambridge, MA: Harvard University Press.

Gross, Neil and Solon Simmons (eds). 2014. *Professors and Their Politics*. Baltimore, MD: Johns Hopkins University Press.

Guarino, Cassandra M. and Victor M. H. Borden. 2017. "Faculty Service Loads and Gender: Are Women Taking Care of the Academic Family?" *Research in Higher Education* 58 (6): 672–694.

Gunaratnam, Yasmin. 2003. *Researching "Race" and Ethnicity: Methods, Knowledge and Power*. London: Sage.

Gutzkow, Joshua, Michèle Lamont and Grégoire Mallard. 2004. "What is Originality in the Humanities and the Social Sciences?" *American Sociological Review* 69: 190–212.

Hacker, Jacob and Paul Pierson. 2002. "Business Power and Social Policy: Employers and the Formation of the American Welfare State." *Politics and Society* 30 (2): 277–325.

2010. "Winner-Take-All-Politics: Public Policy, Political Organization, and the Precipitous Rise of Top Incomes in the United States." *Politics and Society* 38 (2): 152–204.

Hacking, Ian. 1983. *Representing and Intervening: Introductory Topics in the Philosophy of Natural Science*. Cambridge: Cambridge University Press.

1999. *The Social Construction of What?* Cambridge: Cambridge University Press.

Haggard, Stephan and Robert R. Kaufman. 2012. "Inequality and Regime Change: Democratic Transitions and the Stability of Democratic Rule." *American Political Science Review* 106 (3): 495–516.

Hall, Peter A. and Rosemary C. R. Taylor. 1996. "Political Science and the Three New Institutionalisms." *Political Studies* XLIV: 936–957.

Hamermesh, Daniel S. 2007. "Viewpoint: Replication in economics." *Canadian Journal of Economics* 40: 715–733.

2018. "Citations in Economics: Measurement, Uses and Impacts." *Journal of Economic Literature* 56 (1): 115–156.

Hames, Irene. 2007. *Peer Review and Manuscript Management in Scientific Journals: Guidelines for Good Practice*. Malden, MA: Blackwell.

Hammersley, Martyn. 2010. "Can We Re-Use Qualitative Data via Secondary Analysis? Notes on Some Terminological and Substantive Issues." *Sociological Research Online* 15 (1): 1–7.

Hancock, Ange Marie. 2007. "When Multiplication Doesn't Equal Quick Addition: Examining Intersectionality as a Research Paradigm." *Perspectives on Politics* 5 (1): 63–79.

2015. "Intersectionality's Will toward Social Transformation." *New Political Science* 37 (4): 620–627.

2016. *Intersectionality: An Intellectual History*. Oxford: Oxford University Press.

Handcock, Mark and Krista Gile. 2011. "Comment: On the Concept of Snowball Sampling." *Sociological Methodology* 41 (1): 367–371.

Hankins, Dorothy. 1929. "Current Research Projects." *American Journal of Sociology* 35 (3): 445–468.

Hansen, Peter Reinhard. 2005. "A Test for Superior Predictive Ability." *Journal of Business and Economic Statistics* 23 (4): 365–380.

Hanson, Jonathan K. 2015. "Democracy and State Capacity: Complements or Substitutes?" *Studies in Comparative International Development* 50 (3): 304–330.

Harding, Sandra. 2005. "Negotiating with the Positivist Legacy: New Social Justice Movements and a Standpoint Politics of Method." Pp. 346–365 in George Steinmetz (ed.), *The Politics of Method in the Human Sciences: Positivism and Its Epistemological Others*. Durham, NC: Duke University Press.

Hardt, Heidi, Amy Erica Smith, Hannah Kim and Philippe Meister. 2018. "The Gender Readings Gap in Political Science." Presented at the Visions in Methodology Conference.

2019. "The Gender Readings Gap in Political Science Graduate Training." *Journal of Politics* 81 (4): n. p.

Hart, Chris. 2018. *Doing a Literature Review: Releasing the Research Imagination*. London: Sage.

Hartman, Alexandra, Cyrus Samii and Darin Christensen. 2017. "A Qualitative Pre-Analysis Plan for Legible Institutions and Land Demand: The Effect of Property Rights Systems on Investment in Liberia." October 20. osf.io/46r87.

Hartman, Alexandra, Florian Kern and David T. Mellor. 2018. "Preregistration for Qualitative Research Template." OSF. osf.io/j7ghv. September 27.

Harvey, Campbell R., Yan Liu and Heqing Zhu. 2015. "And the Cross-Section of Expected Returns." *Review of Financial Studies* (October): hhv059.

Harzing, A. W. 2007. Publish or Perish, available at www.harzing.com/pop.htm.

Hauser, Robert M. 1987. "Sharing Data – It's Time for ASA Journals to Follow the Folkways of a Scientific Sociology." *American Sociological Review* 52 (6): vi–viii.

Haustein, Stefanie, Isabella Peters, Cassidy R. Sugimoto, Mike Thelwall and Vincent Larivière. 2014. "Tweeting Biomedicine: An Analysis of Tweets and Citations in the Biomedical Literature." *Journal of the Association for Information Science and Technology* 65 (4): 656–669.

Haustein, Stefanie, Rodrigo Costas and Vincent Larivière. 2015. "Characterizing Social Media Metrics of Scholarly Papers: The Effect of Document Properties and Collaboration Patterns." *PLoS ONE* 10 (3): e0120495.

Havranek, Tomas and Zuzana Irsova. 2012. "Survey Article: Publication Bias in the Literature on Foreign Direct Investment Spillovers." *Journal of Development Studies* 48 (10): 1375–1396.

Hawkins, Carlee Beth, Cailey E. Fitzgerald and Brian A. Nosek. 2015. "In Search of an Association Between Conception Risk and Prejudice." *Psychological Science* 26 (2): 249–252.

Hayes, Wayland. 1942. "An Exploratory Study of Objectives for Introductory Sociology." *Social Forces* 21 (2): 165–172.

Headworth, Spencer and Jeremy Freese. 2016. "Credential Privilege or Cumulative Advantage? Prestige, Productivity, and Placement in the Academic Sociology Job Market." *Social Forces* 94: 1257–1282.

Health Research Council (HRC). 2016. Health Research Council of New Zealand. Downloaded on September 22, 2016 from www.hrc.govt.nz/funding-opportunities/researcher-initiated-proposals/explorer-grants.

Healy, Kieran and James Moody. 2014. "Data Visualization in Sociology." *Annual Review of Sociology* 40: 105–128.

Heaton, Janet. 2008. "Secondary Analysis of Qualitative Data: An Overview." *Historical Social Research/Historische Sozialforschung* 33 (3 (125)): 33–45.

Hedges, Larry V. 1992. "Modeling Publication Selection Effects in Meta-Analysis." *Statistical Science* 7 (2): 246–255.

Hedges, Larry V. and Jack L. Vevea. 1996. "Estimating Effect Size Under Publication Bias: Small Sample Properties and Robustness of a Random Effects Selection Model." *Journal of Educational and Behavioral Statistics* 21 (4): 299–332.

Hedström, Peter. 2005. *Dissecting the Social: On the Principles of Analytical Sociology*. Cambridge: Cambridge University Press.

Heffetz, Ori and Katrina Ligett. 2014. "Privacy and Data-Based Research." *Journal of Economic Perspectives* 28 (2): 75–98.

Hendrix, Cullen. 2015. "Google Scholar Metrics and Scholarly Productivity in International Relations." Guest post on Duck of Minerva. http://duckofminerva.com/2015/08/google-scholar-metrics-and-scholarly-productivity-in-international-relations.html.

Hendry, David F. 1987. "Econometric Methodology: A Personal Perspective." Pp. 29–48 in Truman Bewley (ed.), *Advances in Econometrics: Volume 2: Fifth World Congress*. Cambridge: Cambridge University Press.

1995. *Dynamic Econometrics*. Oxford: Oxford University Press.

Heneberg, Petr. 2016. "From Excessive Journal Self-Cites to Citation Stacking: Analysis of Journal Self-Citation Kinetics in Search for Journals, Which Boost Their Scientometric Indicators." *PloS ONE* 11 (4): e0153730.

Hengel, Erin. 2017. "Publishing while Female. Are Women Held to Higher Standards? Evidence from Peer Review." Cambridge Working Papers in Economics 1753, Faculty of Economics, University of Cambridge.

Henrich, Joseph, Steven J. Heine and Ara Norensayan. 2010. "The Weirdest People in the World?" *Behavioral and Brain Sciences* 33: 61–135.

Henry, Emeric. 2009. "Strategic Disclosure of Research Results: The Cost of Proving Your Honesty." *Economic Journal* 119 (539): 1036–1064.

Henry, Emeric and Marco Ottaviani. 2014. "Research and the Approval Process: The Organization of Persuasion." *American Economic Review* 109 (3): 911–955.

Herbst, Jeffrey. 2000. *States and Power in Africa: Comparative Lessons in Authority and Control*. Princeton, NJ: Princeton University Press.

Herndon, Thomas, Michael Ash and Robert Pollin. 2014. "Does High Public Debt Consistently Stifle Economic Growth? A Critique of Reinhart and Rogoff." *Cambridge Journal of Economics* 38 (2): 257–279.

Hewitt, John K. 2012. "Editorial Policy on Candidate Gene Association and Candidate Gene-by-Environment Interaction Studies of Complex Traits." *Behavior Genetics* 42: 1–2.

Hicks, Diana. 1999. "The Difficulty of Achieving Full Coverage of International Social Science Literature and the Bibliometric Consequences." *Scientometrics* 44 (2): 193–215.

Hicks, Joan Hamory, Michael Kremer and Edward Miguel. 2015. "Commentary: Deworming Externalities and Schooling Impacts in Kenya: A Comment on Aiken Et al. (2015) and Davey Et al. (2015)." *International Journal of Epidemiology* 44 (5): 1593–1596.

Hirsch, Barry T. 2004. "Reconsidering Union Wage Effects: Surveying New Evidence on an Old Topic." *Journal of Labor Research* 25 (2): 233–266.

Hirshleifer, Sarojini, David McKenzie, Rita Almeida and Cristobal Ridao-Cano. 2015. "The Impact of Vocational Training for the Unemployed: Experimental Evidence from Turkey." *Economic Journal*, June, n/a-n/a. doi:10.1111/ecoj.12211.

Hix, Simon. 2004. "A Global Ranking of Political Science Departments." *Political Studies Review* 2 (3): 293–313.

Hochschild, Arlie. 1969. "The Ambassador's Wife: An Exploratory Study." *Journal of Marriage and the Family* 31: 73–87.

1983. *The Managed Heart: Commercialization of Human Feeling*. Berkeley, CA: University of California Press.

2016. *Strangers in Their Own Land: Anger and Mourning on the American Right*. New York: The New Press.

2017. Email on exploratory studies. February 17.

Hodson, Simon. 2016. "Sustainable Business Models for Data Repositories." RDA Plenary, Tokyo, March 3. https://rd-alliance.org/sites/default/files/attachment/S.%20Hodson%20Business%20Models%20Presentation.pdf.

Hoeffler, Jan H. 2013. "Teaching Replication in Quantitative Empirical Economics." World Economics Association (WEA), Conference on the Economics Curriculum: Towards a Radical Reformation: May 3–31.

Hofstadter, Richard and Walter Metzger. 1955. *The Development of Academic Freedom in the United States*. New York: Columbia University Press.

Holm, Sture. 1979. "A Simple Sequentially Rejective Multiple Test Procedure." *Scandinavian Journal of Statistics* 6 (2): 65–70.

Hook, Jennifer. 2017. "Women's Housework: New Tests of Time and Money." *Journal of Marriage and Family* 79 (1): 179–198.

Hopf, Ted and Bentley B. Allan (eds). 2016. *Making Identity Count: Building a National Identity Database*. Oxford: Oxford University Press.

Horowitz, Michael C., Allan C. Stam and Cali M. Ellis. 2015. *Why Leaders Fight*. Cambridge: Cambridge University Press.

Hochschild, Arlie Russell and Anne Machung. 1989. *The Second Shift: Working Parents and the Revolution at Home*. New York: Viking.

Hoxby, Caroline M. 2000. "Does Competition among Public Schools Benefit Students and Taxpayers?" *American Economic Review* 90 (5): 1209–1238.

2007. "Does Competition among Public Schools Benefit Students and Taxpayers? A Reply." *American Economic Review* 97 (5): 2038–2055.

Hudson, John. 2007. "Be Known by the Company You Keep: Citations – Quality or Chance?" *Scientometrics* 71 (2): 231–238.

Hug, Sven E. and Martin P. Brändle. 2017. "The Coverage of Microsoft Academic: Analyzing the Publication Output of a University." *Scientometrics* 113: 1551.

Hug, Sven E., Michael Ochsner and Martin P. Brändle. 2017. "Citation Analysis with Microsoft Academic." *Scientometrics* 111: 371–378.

Hughes, Everett C. 1949. "Review of John Dollard, Caste and Class in a Southern Town." *American Journal of Sociology* 55 (2): 20709.

1960. "Introduction: The Place of Field Work in Social Science". Pp. iii–xiii in Buford Junker (ed.), *Field Work: An Introduction to the Social Sciences*. Chicago: University of Chicago Press.

Hui, Victoria. 2005. *War and State Formation in Ancient China and Early Modern Europe*. New York: Cambridge University Press.

Humphreys, Macartan and Alan M. Jacobs. 2015. "Mixing Methods: A Bayesian Approach." *American Political Science Review* 109 (4): 653–673.

2021. *Integrated Inferences*. Cambridge: Cambridge University Press.

Humphreys, Macartan, Raul Sanchez de la Sierra and Peter van der Windt. 2013. "Fishing, Commitment, and Communication: A Proposal for Comprehensive Nonbinding Research Registration." *Political Analysis* 21 (1): 1–20.

Hung, H. M. James, Robert T. O'Neill, Peter Bauer and Karl Kohne. 1997. "The Behavior of the P-Value When the Alternative Hypothesis Is True." *Biometrics* 53 (1): 11–22.

Hunt, Morton. 1997. *How Science Takes Stock: The Story of Meta-Analysis*. New York: Russell Sage Foundation.

Hunter, Douglas. 1984. *Political/Military Applications of Bayesian Analysis*. Boulder, CO: Westview.

Hunter, John E. 2001. "The Desperate Need for Replications." *Journal of Consumer Research* 28 (1): 149–158.

Husereau, Don, Michael Drummond, Stavros Petrou, Chris Carswell, David Moher, Dan Greenberg, Federico Augustovski et al. 2013. "Consolidated Health Economic Evaluation

Reporting Standards (CHEERS) Statement." *Value in Health: Journal of the International Society for Pharmacoeconomics and Outcomes Research* 16 (2): e1–5.

Huth, Paul and Bruce Russett. 1984. "What Makes Deterrence Work? Cases from 1900 to 1980." *World Politics* 36 (July): 496–526.

———. 1990. "Testing Deterrence Theory: Rigor Makes a Difference." *World Politics* 42 (July): 466–501.

Hyman, Herbert. 1991. *Taking Society's Measure: A Personal History of Survey Research*. New York: Russel Sage Foundation.

Hymes, Kenneth B. et al. 1981. "Kaposi's Sarcoma in Homosexual Men – a Report of Eight Cases." *The Lancet* 318 (8247): 598–600.

Ifcher, John and Homa Zarghamee. 2011. "Happiness and Time Preference: The Effect of Positive Affect in a Random-Assignment Experiment." *American Economic Review* 101 (7): 3109–3129.

Igo, Sarah. 2011. "Subjects of Persuasion: Survey Research as a Solicitous Science, or, The Public Relations of the Polls." Pp. 285–306 in Charles Camic, Neil Gross and Michèle Lamont (eds), *Social Knowledge in the Making*. Chicago: University of Chicago Press.

Inter-University Consortium for Political and Social Research (ICPSR). 2017. "Data Citations." www.icpsr.umich.edu/icpsrweb/ICPSR/curation/citations.jsp.

International Consortium of Investigators for Fairness in Trial Data Sharing. 2016. "Toward Fairness in Data Sharing." *New England Journal of Medicine* 375 (5): 405–407.

Ioannidis, John P. A. 2005. "Why Most Published Research Findings Are False." *PLoS Medicine* 2 (8): e124.

———. 2008. "Effectiveness of Antidepressants: An Evidence Myth Constructed from a Thousand Randomized Trials?" *Philosophy, Ethics, and Humanities in Medicine* 3 (1): 14.

Ioannidis, John P., Sander Greenland, Mark A. Hlatky, Muin J. Khoury, Malcolm R. Macleod, David Moher, Kenneth F. Schulz and Robert Tibshirani. 2014. "Increasing Value and Reducing Waste in Research Design, Conduct, and Analysis." *The Lancet* 383 (9912): 166–175.

Irwin, Sarah and Mandy Winterton. 2012. "Qualitative Secondary Analysis and Social Explanation." *Sociological Research Online* 17 (2): 1–12.

Isaac, Jeffrey C. 2015. "For a More Public Political Science." *Perspectives on Politics* 13 (2): 269–283.

ISIS-2 (Second International Study of Infarct Survival) Collaborative Group. 1988. "Randomised Trial of Intravenous Streptokinase, Oral Aspirin, Both, Or Neither Among 17 187 Cases Of Suspected Acute Myocardial Infarction: ISIS-2." *The Lancet*, originally published as 2 (8607): 349–360.

Iversen, Torben and Frances Rosenbluth. 2006. "The Political Economy of Gender: Explaining Cross-National Variation in the Gender Division of Labor and the Gender Voting Gap." *American Journal of Political Science* 50 (1): 1–19.

Jackman, Simon and Bruce Western. 1994. "Bayesian Inference for Comparative Research." *American Political Science Review* 88 (2) :412–423.

Jackson, Michelle and D. R. Cox. 2013. "The Principles of Experimental Design and their Application in Sociology." *Annual Review of Sociology* 39: 27–49.

Jacobs, Jerry A. 2004. "Presidential Address: The Faculty Time Divide." *Sociological Forum* 19 (1): 3–27.

Jahoda, Marie and Stuart Cook. 1952. "Security Measures and Freedom of Thought: An Exploratory Study of the Impact of Loyalty and Security Programs." *The Yale Law Journal* 61 (3): 295–333.

Jahoda, Marie, Morton Deutsch and Stuart Cook. 1951. *Research Methods in Social Relations with Especial Reference to Prejudice*. 2 vols. New York: the Dryden Press.

Janis, Irving. 1982. *Groupthink: Psychological Studies of Policy Decisions and Fiascoes*. Boston: Houghton Mifflin.

Jann, Ben. 2005. "Comment: Earnings Returns to Education in Urban China: A Note on Testing Differences among Groups." *American Sociological Review* 70 (5): 860–864.

Janz, Nicole. 2016. "Bringing the Gold Standard into the Classroom: Replication in University Teaching." *International Studies Perspectives* 17 (4): 392–407.

Jaschik, Scott. 2012. "Moving Further to the Left." Insidehighered.com, October 24. www.insidehighered.com/news/2012/10/24/survey-finds-professors-already-liberal-have-moved-further-left.

Jaynes, Edwin T. 2003. *Probability Theory: The Logic of Science*. Cambridge: Cambridge University Press.

Jensenius, Francesca R., Mala Htun, David J. Samuels, David A. Singer, Adria Lawrence and Michael Chwe. 2018. "The Benefits and Pitfalls of Google Scholar." *PS: Political Science and Politics* 51 (4): 820–824.

Jervis, Robert. 1976. *Perception and Misperception in International Politics*. Princeton, NJ: Princeton University Press.

Jewett, Andrew. 2012. *Science, Democracy, and the American University: From the Civil War to the Cold War*. New York: Cambridge University Press.

Joas, Hans. 1993. *Pragmatism and Social Theory*. Chicago: University of Chicago Press.

John, Leslie K., George Loewenstein and Drazen Prelec. 2012. "Measuring the Prevalence of Questionable Research Practices With Incentives for Truth Telling." *Psychological Science* 23 (5): 524–532.

Johnson, James. 2003. "Conceptual Problems as Obstacles to Progress in Political Science: Four Decades of Political Culture Research." *Journal of Theoretical Politics* 15 (1): 87–115.

Johnston, Lisa R., Jake Carlson, Cynthia Hudson-Vitale, Heidi Imker, Wendy A. Kozlowski, Robert Olendorf and Claire Stewart. 2017. "Data Curation Network: A Cross-Institutional Staffing Model for Curating Research Data." http://hdl.handle.net/11299/188654.

Johnston, Lisa (ed.). 2016. *Curating Research Data*. Chicago: Association of College and Research Libraries.

Jung, Courtney. 2015. *Lactivism: How Feminists and Fundamentalists, Hippies and Yuppies, and Physicians and Politicians made Breastfeeding Big Business and Bad Policy*. New York: Basic Books.

Jung, Kiju, Sharon Shavitt, Madhu Viswanathan and Joseph M. Hilbe. 2014. "Female Hurricanes Are Deadlier than Male Hurricanes." *Proceedings of the National Academy of Sciences* 111 (24): 8782–8787.

Jussim, Lee. 2016. "Are Most Published Social Psychology Findings False?" Heterodox Academy. http://heterodoxacademy.org/2016/02/23/are-most-published-social-psychology-findings-false/.

Kagel, John H. and Alvin E. Roth (eds). 2016. *The Handbook of Experimental Economics, Volume 2: The Handbook of Experimental Economics*. Princeton, NJ: Princeton University Press.

Kahn, S. 1993. "Gender Differences in Academic Career Paths of Economists." *American Economic Review* 83 (2): 52–56.

Kahneman, Daniel. 2012. "A Proposal to Deal with Questions about Priming Effects." *Nature*. www.nature.com/polopoly_fs/7.6716.1349271308!/suppinfoFile/Kahneman%20 Letter.pdf.
    2014. "A New Etiquette for Replication." *Social Psychology* 45 (4): 310.
Kanazawa, Satoshi. 2001. "Comment: Why We Love Our Children." *American Journal of Sociology* 106 (6): 1761–1776.
Kane, Edward J. 1984. "Why Journal Editors Should Encourage the Replication of Applied Econometric Research." *Quarterly Journal of Business and Economics* 23 (1): 3–8.
Kapiszewski, Diana. 2012. *High Courts and Economic Governance in Argentina and Brazil*. New York: Cambridge University Press.
Kapiszewski, Diana, Lauren M. Maclean and Benjamin L. Read. 2015. *Field Research in Political Science: Practices and Principles*. Cambridge: Cambridge University Press.
Karabag, Solmaz Filiz and Christian Berggren. 2012. "Retraction, Dishonesty and Plagiarism: Analysis of a Crucial Issue for Academic Publishing, and the Inadequate Responses from Leading Journals in Economics and Management Disciplines." *Journal of Applied Economics and Business Research* 2 (4): 172–183.
Karcher, Sebastian and Christiane Pagé. 2017. "Workshop Report: CAQDAS Projects and Digital Repositories' Best Practices." *D-Lib Magazine* 23 (3/4). doi:10.1045/march2017-karcher.
Karcher, Sebastian and David A. Steinberg. 2013. "Assessing the Causes of Capital Account Liberalization: How Measurement Matters." *International Studies Quarterly* 57 (1): 128–137.
Karcher, Sebastian, Dessislava Kirilova and Nicholas Weber. 2016. "Beyond the Matrix: Repository Services for Qualitative Data." *IFLA Journal* 42 (4): 292–302.
Karl, Terry. 1997. *The Paradox of Plenty*. Berkeley, CA: University of California Press.
Katz, Daniel. 1955. "Review of Berelson, Lazarsfeld and McPhee, Voting." *Public Opinion Quarterly* 19: 326–328.
Katz, Larry, Esther Duflo, Pinelopi Goldberg and Duncan Thomas. 2013. "AEA E-Mail Announcement." American Economic Association. www.aeaweb.org/announcements/20131118_rct_email.php.
Kaufman, Robert. 2009. "The Political Effects of Inequality in Latin America: Some Inconvenient Facts." *Comparative Politics* 41 (3): 359–379.
Kendall, Patricia. 1957. "Appendix C: Note on Significance Tests". Pp. 301–305 in Robert K. Merton, George Reader and Patricia Kendall (eds), *The Student-Physician*. Cambridge, MA: Harvard University Press.
Kern, Florian G. and Kristian Gleditsch. 2017. "Exploring Pre-registration and Pre-analysis Plans for Qualitative Inference." Unpublished working paper. Available online at https://bit.ly/2NBXNrk.
Khanna, Kabir and Kosuke Imai. 2017. "Wru: Who are you? Bayesian Prediction of Racial Category using Surname and Geolocation." https://cran.r-project.org/web/packages/wru/index.html.
Kidwell, Mallory C., Ljiljana B. Lazarević, Erica Baranski, Tom E. Hardwicke, Sarah Piechowski, Lina-Sophia Falkenberg, Curtis Kennett et al. 2016. "Badges to Acknowledge Open Practices: A Simple, Low-Cost, Effective Method for Increasing Transparency." *PLoS Biology* 14 (5): e1002456.
Kier, Elizabeth. 1997. *Imagining War: French and British Military Doctrine Between the Wars*. Princeton, NJ: Princeton University Press.

Kincaid, Harold. 1990. "Defending Laws in the Social Sciences." *Philosophy of the Social Sciences* 20 (1): 56–83.

King, Gary. 1995. "Replication, Replication." *PS: Political Science and Politics* 28 (03): 444–452.

   2006. "Publication, Publication." *PS: Political Science and Politics* 39 (1): 119–125.

   2014. "Restructuring the Social Sciences: Reflections from Harvard's Institute for Quantitative Social Science." *PS: Political Science and Politics* 47 (1): 165–172.

King, Gary, Robert Keohane and Sidney Verba. 1994. *Designing Social Inquiry: Scientific Inference in Qualitative Research*. Princeton, NJ: Princeton University Press.

King, Molly M., Carl T. Bergstrom, Shelley J. Correll, Jennifer Jacquet and Jevin D. West. 2017. "Men Set their Own Cites High: Gender and Self-Citation across Fields and over Time." *Socius: Sociological Research for a Dynamic World* 3 (December): 237802311773890.

Kirsch, Irving, Brett J. Deacon, Tania B. Huedo-Medina, Alan Scoboria, Thomas J. Moore and Blair T. Johnson. 2008. "Initial Severity and Antidepressant Benefits: A Meta-Analysis of Data Submitted to the Food and Drug Administration." *PLoS Medicine* 5 (2). https://doi.org/10.1371/journal.pmed.0050045.

Klein, Daniel and Andrew Western. 2004–2005. "Voter Registration of Berkeley and Stanford Faculty." *Academic Questions* 18: 53–65.

Klein, Joshua R. and Aaron Roodman. 2005. "Blind Analysis in Nuclear and Particle Physics." *Annual Review of Nuclear and Particle Science* 55 (1): 141–163.

Klein, Richard A., Kate A. Ratliff, Michelangelo Vianello, Reginald B. Adams, Štěpán Bahník, Michael J. Bernstein, Konrad Bocian et al. 2014. "Investigating Variation in Replicability." *Social Psychology* 45 (3): 142–152.

Kleinberg, Jon, Himabindu Lakkaraju, Jure Leskovec, Jens Ludwig and Sendhil Mullainathan. 2015. "Human Decisions and Machine Problems." Unpublished manuscript.

Kleinberg, Jon, Jens Ludwig, Sendhil Mullainathan and Ziad Obermeyer. 2015. "Prediction Policy Problems." *American Economic Review* 105 (5): 491–495.

Kling, Jeffrey R., Jeffrey B. Liebman and Lawrence F. Katz. 2007. "Experimental Analysis of Neighborhood Effects." *Econometrica* 75 (1): 83–119.

Knell, Markus and Helmut Stix. 2005. "The Income Elasticity of Money Demand: A Meta-Analysis of Empirical Results." *Journal of Economic Surveys* 19 (3): 513–533.

Knittel, Christopher R. and Konstantinos Metaxoglou. 2011. "Challenges in Merger Simulation Analysis." *American Economic Review* 101 (3): 56–59.

   2013. "Estimation of Random-Coefficient Demand Models: Two Empiricists' Perspective." *Review of Economics and Statistics* 96 (1): 34–59.

Knobloch-Westerwick, Silvia and Carroll J. Glynn. 2013. "The Matilda Effect – Role Congruity Effects on Scholarly Communication: A Citation Analysis of Communication Research and Journal of Communication Articles." *Communication Research* 40 (1): 3–26.

Knowles, J. Gary and Ardra Cole (eds). 2008. *Handbook of the Arts in Qualitative Research*. Los Angeles, CA: SAGE.

Knuth, Donald Ervin. 1992. *Literate Programming*. Stanford: Center for the Study of Language and Information.

Koenker, Roger and Achim Zeileis. 2009. "On Reproducible Econometric Research." *Journal of Applied Econometrics* 24 (5): 833–847.

Koole, Sander L. and Daniel Lakens. 2012. "Rewarding Replications: A Sure and Simple Way to Improve Psychological Science." *Perspectives on Psychological Science* 7 (6): 608–614.

References

Kovesdy, Csaba P. and Kamyar Kalantar-Zadeh. 2012. "Observational Studies versus Randomized Controlled Trials: Avenues to Causal Inference in Nephrology." *Advances in Chronic Kidney Disease* 19 (1): 11–18.

Kratz, John and Carly Strasser. 2014. "Data Publication Consensus and Controversies." F1000Research, October. doi:10.12688/f1000research.3979.3.

Ku, G., C. S. Wang and A. D. Galinsky. 2010. "Perception through a Perspective-Taking Lens: Differential Effects on Judgments and Behavior." *Journal of Experimental Social Psychology* 46: 792–798.

Kuhn, Thomas. 1962. *The Structure of Scientific Revolutions*. Chicago: University of Chicago Press.

Kunce, Mitch, Shelby Gerking and William Morgan. 2002. "Effects of Environmental and Land Use Regulation in the Oil and Gas Industry Using the Wyoming Checkerboard as an Experimental Design." *American Economic Review* 92 (5): 1588–1593.

Kurtz, Marcus. 2009. "The Social Foundations of Institutional Order: Reconsidering War and the 'Resource Curse' in Third World State Building." *Politics and Society* 37 (4): 479–520.

2013. *Latin American State Building in Comparative Perspective*. New York: Cambridge University Press.

Kurtz, Marcus and Andrew Schrank. 2007. "Growth and Governance: Models, Measures, and Mechanisms." *Journal of Politics* 69 (2): 538–554.

Laan, van der, Mark J, Eric C. Polley and Alan E. Hubbard. 2007. "Super Learner." *Statistical Applications in Genetics and Molecular Biology* 6 (1). www.degruyter.com/view/j/sagmb.2007.6.1/sagmb.2007.6.1.1309/sagmb.2007.6.1.1309.xml.

LaCour, Michael J. and Donald P. Green. 2014. "When Contact Changes Minds: An Experiment on Transmission of Support for Gay Equality." *Science* 346 (6215): 1366.

Ladd, Everett Carll, Jr. and Seymour Martin Lipset. 1976. *The Divided Academy: Professors and Politics*. New York: Norton.

Lai, Brian and Dan Reiter. 2000. "Democracy, Political Similarity, and International Alliances, 1816–1992." *Journal of Conflict Resolution* 44 (2): 203–227.

Laine, Christine, Richard Horton, Catherine D. DeAngelis, Jeffrey M. Drazen, Frank A. Frizelle, Fiona Godlee, Charlotte Haug et al. 2007. "Clinical Trial Registration – Looking Back and Moving Ahead." *New England Journal of Medicine* 356 (26): 2734–2736.

Laitin, David D. 2013. "Fisheries Management." *Political Analysis* 21 (1): 42–47.

Laitin, David D. and Rob Reich. 2017. "Trust, Transparency, and Replication in Political Science." *PS: Political Science and Politics* 50 (1): 172–175. =

LaLonde, Robert J. 1986. "Evaluating the Econometric Evaluations of Training Programs with Experimental Data." *American Economic Review* 76 (4): 604–620.

Lamont, Michèle. 2009. *How Professors Think*. Cambridge, MA: Harvard University Press.

Langan, Andrew. 2018. "Female Managers and Gender Disparities: The Case of Academic Department Chairs." November.

"Female Managers and Gender Disparities: The Case of Academic Department Chairs." (Working Paper).

Larivière, Vincent, Yves Gingras, Cassidy R. Sugimoto and Andrew Tsou. 2014. "Team Size Matters: Collaboration and Scientific Impact since 1900." *Journal of the Association for Information Science and Technology* 66: 1323–1332.

References

Larivière, Vincent, Chaoqun Ni, Yves Gingras, Blaise Cronin and Cassidy R. Sugimoto. 2013. "Bibliometrics: Global Gender Disparities in Science." *Nature News* 504 (7479): 211.

Larivière, Vincent, Veronique Kiermer, Catriona J. MacCallum, Marcia McNutt, Mark Patterson, Bernd Pulverer, Sowmya Swaminathan, Stuart Taylor and Stephen Curry. 2016. "A Simple Proposal for the Publication of Journal Citation Distributions." *BioRxiv*, July, 062109. https://doi.org/10.1101/062109.

Laudan, Larry. 1977. *Progress and its Problems: Towards a Theory of Scientific Growth*. Berkeley, CA: University of California Press.

Lave, Charles A. and James G. March. 1993. *An Introduction to Models in the Social Sciences*. New York: University Press of America.

Lawrence, Peter A. 2007. "The Mismeasurement of Science." *Current Biology* 17 (15): R583–R585.

Lazarsfeld, Paul and Morris Rosenberg (eds). 1955. *The Language of Social Research: A Reader in the Methodology of Social Research*. 2nd ed. Glencoe, IL: The Free Press.

Lazarsfeld, Paul and Wagner Thielens. 1958. *The Academic Mind: Social Scientists in a Time of Crisis*. Glencoe, IL: Free Press.

Lazear, Edward P. 2006. "Speeding, Terrorism, and Teaching to the Test." *Quarterly Journal of Economics* 121 (3): 1029–1061.

Leamer, Edward E. 1978. *Specification Searches: Ad Hoc Inference with Nonexperimental Data*. New York: Wiley.

  1983. "Let's Take the Con Out of Econometrics." *American Economic Review* 73 (1): 31–43.

  2010. "Tantalus on the Road to Asymptopia." *Journal of Economic Perspectives* 24 (2): 31–46.

  2016. "S-Values: Conventional Context-Minimal Measures of the Sturdiness of Regression Coefficients." *Journal of Econometrics* 193 (1): 147–161.

Leamer, Edward E. and Herman Leonard. 1983. "Reporting the Fragility of Regression Estimates." *Review of Economics and Statistics* 65 (2): 306–317.

Lebow, Richard Ned and Janice Gross Stein. 1987. "Beyond Deterrence." *Journal of Social* Issues 43(Winter): 5–71.

Lee, Soohyung and Azeem M. Shaikh. 2014. "Multiple Testing and Heterogeneous Treatment Effects: Re-Evaluating the Effect of Progresa on School Enrollment." *Journal of Applied Econometrics* 29 (4): 612–626.

Leeds, Brett Ashley, Jeffrey M. Ritter, Sara McLaughlin Mitchell and Andrew G. Long. 2002. "Alliance Treaty Obligations and Provisions, 1815-1944." *International Interactions* 28: 237–260.

Lehoucq, Fabrice. 2017. "Validity is Not Conformity: Measuring Accuracy in Coup Datasets." *APSA-CD Newsletter* 15(June): 5, 13–16.

Leimer, Dean R. and Selig D. Lesnoy. 1982. "Social Security and Private Saving: New Time-Series Evidence." *Journal of Political Economy* 90 (3): 606–629.

Leimu, Roosa and Julia Koricheva. 2005a. "Does Scientific Collaboration Increase the Impact of Ecological Articles?" *BioScience* 55 (5): 438–443.

  2005b. "What Determines the Citation Frequency of Ecological Papers?" *Trends in Ecology and Evolution* 20 (1): 28–32.

Leplin, Jarrett (ed.). 1984. *Scientific Realism*. Berkeley, CA: University of California Press.

Lepore, Jill. 2015. "The Cobweb." *The New Yorker*, January 26, 33–41.

References

Leslie, Sarah-Jane, Andrei Cimpian, Meredith Meyer and Edward Freeland. 2015. "Expectations of Brilliance Underlie Gender Distributions across Academic Disciplines." *Science* 347 (6219): 262–265.

Levine, David I. 2001. "Editor's Introduction to 'The Unemployment Effects of Minimum Wages: Evidence from a Prespecified Research Design.'" *Industrial Relations: A Journal of Economy and Society* 40 (2): 161–162.

Lewis-Beck, Michael, Alan Bryman and Tim F. Liao (eds). 2004. *The SAGE Encyclopedia of Social Science Research Methods*. London: Sage.

Lewis, Janet. 2000. "Funding Social Science Research in Academia." *Social Policy and Administration* 34 (4): 365–376.

Lewis, Jenny. 2013. *Academic Governance: Disciplines and Policy*. London: Routledge.

Lewis, Nathan S., Charles A. Barnes, Michael J. Heben, Anil Kumar, Sharon R. Lunt, George E. McManis, Gordon M. Miskelly, et al. 1989. "Searches for Low-Temperature Nuclear Fusion of Deuterium in Palladium." *Nature* 340 (6234). https://sofi-northwestern.pure.elsevier.com/en/publications/searches-for-low-temperature-nuclear-fusion-of-deuterium-in-palla.

Lewis-Beck, Michael S., Alan Bryman and Tim F. Liao. 2003. *The Sage Encyclopedia of Social Science Research Methods*. Thousand Oaks, CA; London: Sage Publications.

Liao, Tim F. 1990. "A Unified Three-Dimensional Framework of Theory Development and Development in Sociology." *Sociological Theory* 8: 85–98.

Libgober, Jonathan. 2015. "False Positives in Scientific Research." SSRN Scholarly Paper ID 2617130. Rochester, NY: Social Science Research Network. http://papers.ssrn.com/abstract=2617130.

Lieberman, Evan S. 2016. "Can the Biomedical Research Cycle be a Model for Political Science." *Perspectives on Politics* 14 (4) (December): 1054–1066.

Lieshout, Robert S., Mathieu L. L. Segers and Johanna Maria van der Vleuten. 2004. "De Gaulle, Moravcsik, and the Choice for Europe: Soft Sources, Weak Evidence." *Journal of Cold War History* 6(Fall): 89–139.

Light, Richard J. and David B. Pillemer. 1984. *Summing Up: The Science of Reviewing Research*. Cambridge, MA: Harvard University Press.

Lindsay, D. Stephen. 2015. "Replication in Psychological Science." *Psychological Science*, November, 0956797615616374. https://doi.org/10.1177/0956797615616374.

Lipset, Seymour Martin. 1959. "Some Social Requisites of Democracy: Economic Development and Political Legitimacy." *American Political Science Review* 53 (March): 69–105.

　1967. "The Biography of a Research Project: Union Democracy." Pp. 111–39 in Phillip Hammond (ed.), *Sociologists at Work*. New York: Doubleday and Company.

Lipset, Seymour Martin and Reinhard Bendix. 1952. "Social Mobility and Occupational Career Patterns II. Social Mobility." *American Journal of Sociology* 57 (5): 494–504.

Lipset, Seymour Martin, Martin Trow and James Coleman. 1956. *Union Democracy: The Internal Politics of the International Typographical Union*. New York: The Free Press.

Lipsey, Mark W. and David B. Wilson. 2001. *Practical Meta-Analysis*. Thousand Oaks, CA: Sage.

List, John, Charles Bailey, Patricia Euzent and Thomas Martin. 2001. "Academic Economists Behaving Badly? A Survey on Three Areas of Unethical Behavior." *Economic Inquiry* 39 (1): 162–170.

References

List, John A., Azeem M. Shaikh and Yang Xu. 2016. "Multiple Hypothesis Testing in Experimental Economics." Working Paper 21875. *National Bureau of Economic Research*. www.nber.org/papers/w21875.

Lo, Nigel, Barry Hashimoto and Dan Reiter. 2008. "Ensuring Peace: Foreign-Imposed Regime Change and Postwar Peace Duration, 1914–2001." *International Organization* 62(October): 717–736.

Loder, Elizabeth, Trish Groves and Domhnall MacAuley. 2010. "Registration of Observational Studies: The Next Step towards Research Transparency." *British Medical Journal* 340 (February 18 2): c950.

Longhi, Simonetta, Peter Nijkamp and Jacques Poot. 2005. "A Meta-Analytic Assessment of the Effect of Immigration on Wages." *Journal of Economic Surveys* 19 (3): 451–477.

Longino, Helen. 2013. *Studying Human Behavior: How Scientists Investigate Aggression and Sexuality*. Chicago: University of Chicago Press.

Longo, Dan L. and Jeffrey M. Drazen. 2016. "Data Sharing." *New England Journal of Medicine* 374 (3): 276–277.

Lovell, Michael C. 1983. "Data Mining." *Review of Economics and Statistics* 65 (1): 1–12.

Lozano, George A., Vincent Larivière and Yves Gingras. 2012. "The Weakening Relationship between the Impact Factor and Papers' Citations in the Digital Age." *Journal of the American Society for Information Science and Technology* 63 (11): 2140–2145.

Lucas, Jeffrey W., Kevin Morrell and Marek Posard. (2013) "Considerations on the 'Replication Problem' in Sociology." *The American Sociologist* 44: 217–232.

Lundberg, Shelly and Robert Pollak. 1993. "Separate Spheres Bargaining and the Marriage Market." *Journal of Political Economy* 101 (6): 988–1010.

Lundqvist, Heléne, Matz Dahlberg and Eva Mörk. 2014. "Stimulating Local Public Employment: Do General Grants Work?" *American Economic Journal: Economic Policy* 6 (1): 167–192.

Lupia, Arthur and George Alter. 2014. "Data Access and Research Transparency in the Quantitative Tradition." *PS: Political Science and Politics* 47 (01): 54–59.

Lyall, Jason and Isaiah Wilson III. 2009. "Rage Against the Machines: Explaining Outcomes in Counterinsurgency Wars." *International Organization* 63(Winter): 67–106.

Lynd, Robert. 1939. *Knowledge for What? The Place of Social Science in American Culture*. Princeton, NJ: Princeton University Press.

Lyons, Paul. 2009. *American Conservatism: Thinking It, Teaching It*. Nashville, TN: Vanderbilt University Press.

MacCoun, Robert and Saul Perlmutter. 2015. "Blind Analysis: Hide Results to Seek the Truth." *Nature* 526 (7572): 187–189.

Mack, Raymond W. 1951. "The Need for Replication Research in Sociology." *American Sociological Review* 16 (1):93–94.

Maggioni, Aldo P., Bernadette Darne, Dan Atar, Eric Abadie, Bertram Pitt and Faiez Zannad. 2007. "FDA and CPMP Rulings on Subgroup Analyses." *Cardiology* 107 (2): 97–102.

Mahoney, James. 2012. "The Logic of Process Tracing Tests in the Social Sciences." *Sociological Methods and Research* 41(4): 570–597.

Maley, Steve. 2014. "Statistics Show No Evidence of Gender Bias in the Public's Hurricane Preparedness." *Proceedings of the National Academy of Sciences* 111 (37): E3834–E3834.

Malin, Bradley, Kathleen Benitez and Daniel Masys. 2011. "Never Too Old for Anonymity: A Statistical Standard for Demographic Data Sharing via the HIPAA Privacy Rule." *Journal of the American Medical Informatics Association* 18 (1): 3–10.

Maliniak, Daniel, Ryan Powers and Barbara Walter. 2013. "The Gender Citation Gap in International Relations." *International Organization* 67 (4): 889–922.

Malkiel, Nancy Weiss. 2016. *"Keep the Damned Women Out": The Struggle for Coeducation*. Princeton, NJ: Princeton University Press.

Malter, Daniel. 2014. "Female Hurricanes Are Not Deadlier than Male Hurricanes." *Proceedings of the National Academy of Sciences* 111 (34): E3496–E3496.

Mannheim, Karl. 1927/1952. "The Problem of Generations." Pp. 276–322 in Paul Kecskemeti (ed.), *Essays on the Sociology of Knowledge: Collected Works*. Volume 5. New York: Routledge.

Mansfield, Edwin, Mark Schwartz and Samuel Wagner. 1981. "Imitation Costs and Patents: An Empirical Study." *Economic Journal* 91 (364): 907–918.

March, James G. 1991. "Exploration and Exploitation in Organizational Learning." *Organization and Science* 2 (1):71–87.

Maringer, Marcus and Diederik A. Stapel. 2009. "Retracted: Correction or Comparison? The Effects of Prime Awareness on Social Judgments." *European Journal of Social Psychology* 39 (5): 719–733.

Marx, Jean L. 1984. "Strong New Candidate for AIDS Agent; A Newly Discovered Member of the Human T-Cell Leukemia Virus Family is Very Closely Linked to the Immunodeficiency Disease." *Science* 224: 475.

Mason, Mary Ann, Marc Goulden and Nicholas H. Wolfinger. 2006. "Babies Matter." In *The Balancing Act: Gendered Perspectives in Faculty Roles and Work Lives*. Sterling, VA: Stylus Publishing.

Mason, Mary Ann, Nicholas H. Wolfinger and Marc Goulden. 2013. *Do Babies Matter? Gender and Family in the Ivory Tower*, New Brunswick, NJ: Rutgers University Press.

Mathieu Sylvain, Isabelle Boutron, David Moher, Douglas G. Altman and Philippe Ravaud. 2009. "Comparison of Registered and Published Primary Outcomes in Randomized Controlled Trials." *Journal of the American Medical Association* 302 (9): 977–984.

Maunsell, John. 2010. "Announcement Regarding Supplemental Material." *Journal of Neuroscience* 30 (32): 10599–10600.

Mauthner, Natasha S. and Andrea Doucet. 2003. "Reflexive Accounts and Accounts of Reflexivity in Qualitative Data Analysis." *Sociology* 37 (3): 413–431.

  2009. "Qualitative Data Preservation and Sharing in the Social Sciences: On Whose Philosophical Terms?" *Australian Journal of Social Issues* 44 (3): 291–307.

Mauthner, Natasha S, Odette Parry and Kathryn Backett-Milburn. 1998. "The Data Are out There, or Are They? Implications for Archiving and Revisiting Qualitative Data." *Sociology* 32 (04): 733–745.

Maxwell, Scott E., Michael Y. Lau and George S. Howard. 2015. "Is Psychology Suffering from a Replication Crisis? What Does "Failure to Replicate" Really Mean?" *American Psychologist* 70: 487–498.

McAleer, Michael, Adrian R. Pagan and Paul A. Volker. 1985. "What Will Take the Con Out of Econometrics?" *American Economic Review* 75 (3): 293–307.

McAllister, James. 2010/11. "Who Lost Vietnam? Soldiers, Civilians, and U.S. Military Strategy." *International Security* 35 (3): 95–123.

McChesney, Jasper. 2017. "The Representation and Pay of Women and Minorities in Higher Education Administration: Institutions That Are Getting It Right." Research report. CUPA-HR. Available from: http://cupahr.org/surveys/publications/research-briefs/.

McCleary, Rachel and Robert Barro. 2003. "Religion and Economic Growth across Countries." *American Sociological Review* 68 (5): 760–781.

2006. "Religion and Economy." *Journal of Economic Perspectives* 20 (2): 49–72.

McCloskey, Deirdre N. and Stephen T. Ziliak. 1996. "The Standard Error of Regressions." *Journal of Economic Literature* 34 (1): 97–114.

McCrary, Justin, Garret Christensen and Daniele Fanelli. 2016. "Conservative Tests under Satisficing Models of Publication Bias." *PLoS ONE*. February 22. https://doi.org/10.1371/journal.pone.0149590.

McCullough, Bruce D. 2007. "Got Replicability? The Journal of Money, Credit and Banking Archive." *Economic Journal Watch* 4 (3): 326–337.

2009. "Open Access Economics Journals and the Market for Reproducible Economic Research." March. http://search.informit.com.au/documentSummary;dn=775889276720076;res=IELBUS.

McCullough, Bruce D. and Hrishikesh D. Vinod. 2003. "Verifying the Solution from a Nonlinear Solver: A Case Study." *American Economic Review* 93 (3): 873–892.

2004. "Verifying the Solution from a Nonlinear Solver: A Case Study: Reply." *American Economic Review* 94 (1): 400–403.

McCullough, Bruce D., Kerry Anne McGeary and Teresa D. Harrison. 2006. "Lessons from the JMCB Archive." *Journal of Money, Credit, and Banking* 38 (4): 1093–1107.

2008. "Do Economics Journal Archives Promote Replicable Research?" *Canadian Journal of Economics/Revue Canadienne D'économique* 41 (4): 1406–1420.

McIntyre, Lee C. 1996. *Laws and Explanation in the Social Sciences: Defending a Science of Human Behavior*. Boulder, CO: Westview.

McKeown, Timothy J. 1983. "Hegemonic Stability Theory and 19th Century Tariff Levels in Europe." *International Organization* 37 (1): 73–91.

McManus, Walter S. 1985. "Estimates of the Deterrent Effect of Capital Punishment: The Importance of the Researcher's Prior Beliefs." *Journal of Political Economy* 93 (2): 417–425.

McNutt, Marcia. 2015. "Editorial Retraction." *Science* 348 (6239): 1100.

2016. "Taking up TOP." *Science* 352 (6290): 1147.

Mearsheimer, John J. 2001. *The Tragedy of Great Power Politics*. New York: W. W. Norton.

Mearsheimer, John J. and Stephen M. Walt. 2013. "Leaving Theory Behind: Why Simplistic Hypothesis Testing is Bad for International Relations." *European Journal of International Relations* 19 (3): 427–457.

Medvetz, Thomas. 2012. *Think Tanks in America*. Chicago: University of Chicago Press.

Mellins, Claude A., Katie Walsh, Aaron Sarvet, Melanie Wall, Louisa Gilbert, John S. Santelli, Martie Thompson, Patrick Wilson, Shamus Khan, Stephanie Benson, Karimata Bah, Kathy A. Kaufman, Leigh Reardon and Jennifer S. Hirsch. 2017. "Sexual Assault Incidents among College Undergraduates: Prevalence and Factors Associated with Risk." *PLoS ONE* 12 (11): e0186471.

Meltzer, Allan and Scott Richard. 1981. "A Rational Theory of the Size of Government." *Journal of Political Economy* 89 (5): 914–927.

Merton, Robert K. 1943. "TIME-Readership and the Influence Structure of Dover, N.J." Bureau of Applied Social Research. Columbia University. B-0187.

1949. "Patterns of Influence: A Study of Interpersonal Influence and of Communication Behavior in a Local Community." Pp. 180–219 in Paul Lazarsfeld and Frank Stanton (eds), *Communications Research 1948-1949*. New York: Harper and Brothers.

1957. "Some Preliminaries to a Sociology of Medical Education." Pp. 3–79 in Robert K. Merton, George Reader and Patricia Kendall (eds), *The Student-Physician*. Cambridge, MA: Harvard University Press.

1959. "Notes on Problem-Finding in Sociology." Pp. ix–xxxiv in Robert K. Merton, Leonard Broom and Leonard Cottrell (eds), *Sociology Today*. New York: Basic Books.

1968a. "The Matthew Effect in Science." *Science* 159 (3810): 56–63.

1968b. *Social Theory and Social Structure*. Enlarged ed. New York: The Free Press.

1973a. "Age, Aging, and Age Structure in Science". Pp. 497–559 in Robert K. Merton (ed.), *The Sociology of Science: Theoretical and Empirical Investigations*. Chicago: University of Chicago Press.1973b. *The Sociology of Science: Theoretical and Empirical Investigations*. Chicago: University of Chicago Press.

"Socially Expected Durations: A Case Study of Concept Formation in Sociology". Pp. 262–83 in Walter W. Powell and Richard Robbins (eds), *Conflict and Consensus: In Honor of Lewis A. Coser*. New York: The Free Press.

1987a. "The Focussed Interview and Focus Groups: Continuities and Discontinuities." *Public Opinion Quarterly* 51 (4):550–566.

1987b. "Three Fragments from a Sociologist's Notebooks: Establishing the Phenomenon, Specified Ignorance, and Strategic Research Materials." *Annual Review of Sociology* 3: 1–29.

1988. "The Matthew Effect in Science, II: Cumulative Advantage and the Symbolism of Intellectual Property." *Isis* 79 (4): 606–623.

Merton, Robert K. and Elinor Barber. 2006. *The Travels and Adventures of Serendipity: A Study in Sociological Semantics and the Sociology of Science*. Princeton, NJ: Princeton University Press.

Merton, Robert K. and Patricia Kendall. 1946. "The Focused Interview." *American Journal of Sociology* 51: 541–557.

Merton, Robert K., Marjorie Fiske and Patricia Kendall. 1956. *The Focused Interview: A Manual of Problems and Procedures*. Glencoe, IL: The Free Press.

Mervis, Jeffrey. 2014a. "How Two Economists Got Direct Access to IRS Tax Records." *Science | AAAS*. May 20. www.sciencemag.org/news/2014/05/how-two-economists-got-direct-access-irs-tax-records.

2014b. "Why Null Results Rarely See the Light of Day." *Science* 345 (6200): 992.

Michener, William K. 2015. "Ten Simple Rules for Creating a Good Data Management Plan." *PLoS Computational Biology* 11 (10): e1004525.

Miguel, Edward, Colin Camerer, Katherine Casey, Joshua Cohen, Kevin M. Esterling, Alan Gerber, Rachel Glennerster, Don P. Green, Macartan Humphreys and Guido Impens. 2014. "Promoting Transparency in Social Science Research." *Science* 343 (6166): 30–31.

References

Miguel, Edward and Michael Kremer. 2004. "Worms: Identifying Impacts on Education and Health in the Presence of Treatment Externalities." *Econometrica* 72 (1): 159–217.

Miguel, Edward and Shanker Satyanath. 2011. "Re-Examining Economic Shocks and Civil Conflict." *American Economic Journal. Applied Economics* 3 (4): 228–232.

Miguel, Edward, Shanker Satyanath and Ernest Sergenti. 2004. "Economic Shocks and Civil Conflict: An Instrumental Variables Approach." *Journal of Political Economy* 112 (4): 725–753.

Miller, Alan S. and Rodney Stark. 2002. "Gender and Religiousness: Can Socialization Explanations Be Saved?" *American Journal of Sociology* 107 (6): 1399–1423.

Mills, Charles Wright. 1959. *The Sociological Imagination*. New York: Oxford University Press. 2014 [1997]. *The Racial Contract*. Ithaca, NY: Cornell University Press.

Mingers, John and Fang Xu. 2010. "The Drivers of Citations in Management Science Journals." *European Journal of Operational Research* 205 (2): 422–430.

Mitchell, Sara McLaughlin and Vicki L. Hesli. 2013. "Women Don't Ask? Women Don't Say No? Bargaining and Service in the Political Science Profession." *PS: Political Science and Politics* 46 (2): 355–369.

Mitchell, Sara McLaughlin, Samantha Lange and Holly Brus. 2013. "Gendered Citation Patterns in International Relations Journals." *International Studies Perspectives* 14 (4): 485–492.

Mitroff, Ian I. 1974. "Norms and Counter-Norms in a Select Group of the Apollo Moon Scientists: A Case Study of the Ambivalence of Scientists." *American Sociological Review* 39(4): 579–595.

Mittelstaedt, Robert A. and Thomas S. Zorn. 1984. "Econometric Replication: Lessons from the Experimental Sciences." *Quarterly Journal of Business and Economics* 23 (1): 9–15.

Mizon, Grayham E. and Jean-Francois Richard. 1986. "The Encompassing Principle and Its Application to Testing Non-Nested Hypotheses." *Econometrica* 54 (3): 657–678.

Moffitt, Robert A. 2016. "In Defense of the NSF Economics Program." *Journal of Economic Perspectives* 30 (3): 213–234.

Moher, David, Alison Jones and Leah Lepage, and for the CONSORT Group. 2001. "Use of the Consort Statement and Quality of Reports of Randomized Trials: A Comparative before-and-after Evaluation." *Journal of the American Medical Association* 285 (15): 1992–1995.

Moher, David, Kenneth F. Schulz and Douglas G. Altman. 2001. "The CONSORT Statement: Revised Recommendations for Improving the Quality of Reports of Parallel Group Randomized Trials." *BMC Medical Research Methodology* 1 (1): 2.

Monogan, James E. 2013. "A Case for Registering Studies of Political Outcomes: An Application in the 2010 House Elections." *Political Analysis* 21 (1): 21–37.

Monroe, Kristen Renwick and William F. Chiu. 2010. "Gender Equality in the Academy: The Pipeline Problem." *PS: Political Science and Politics* 43 (2): 303–308.

Montgomery, Paul, Sean Grant, Sally Hopewell, Geraldine Macdonald, David Moher, Susan Michie and Evan Mayo-Wilson. 2013. "Protocol for CONSORT-SPI: An Extension for Social and Psychological Interventions." *Implementation Science* 8 (1): 99.

Mookerjee, Rajen. 2006. "A Meta-Analysis of the Export Growth Hypothesis." *Economics Letters* 91 (3): 395–401.

Moore, Alan J. and Andrew Beckerman. 2016. "Ecology and Evolution in an Open World (or: Why Supplementary Data are Evil)." *Ecology and Evolution* 6 (9): 2655–2656.

Moravcsik, Andrew. 2010. "Active Citation: A Precondition for Replicable Qualitative Research." *PS: Political Science and Politics* 43 (01): 29–35.

2012. "Active Citation and Qualitative Political Science." *Qualitative and Multi-Method Research* 10 (Spring): 33–37.

2013. "Did Power Politics Cause European Integration? Realist Theory Meets Qualitative Methods." *Security Studies* 22(4): 773–790.

Moreton, Bethany. 2008. "Make Payroll, Not War: Business Culture as Youth Culture." In Bruce Schulman and Julian Zelizer (eds), *Rightward Bound: Making America Conservative in the 1970s*. Cambridge, MA: Harvard University Press.

Morey, Richard D., Christopher D. Chambers, Peter J. Etchells, Christine R. Harris, Rink Hoekstra, Daniel Lakens, Stephan Lewandowsky, et al. 2015. "The Peer Reviewers' Openness Initiative: Incentivising Open Research Practices through Peer Review." *Royal Society for Open Science* 3: 150547.

Morgan, Kimberly. 2006. *Working Mothers and the Welfare State: Religion and the Politics of Work-Family Policy in Western Europe and the United States*. Palo Alto, CA: Stanford University Press.

Morgan, Stephen L. and Christopher Winship. 2015. *Counterfactuals and Causal Inference: Methods and Principles for Social Research*, 2d 3d. Cambridge: Cambridge University Press.

Morrison, Denton and Ramon Henkel (eds). 1970. *The Significance Test Controversy*. Chicago: Aldine Publishing Company.

Morrow, James D., Randolph M. Siverson and Tressa E. Tabares. 1999. Correction to "The Political Determinants of International Trade." *American Political Science Review* 93 (December): 931–933.

Moses, Stephen, F. A. Plummer, Je Bradley, Jo Ndinyaachola, Njd Nagelkerke and Ar Ronald. 1994. "The Association between Lack of Male Circumcision and Risk for HIV Infection: A Review of the Epidemiological Data." *Sexually Transmitted Diseases* 21 (4): 201–210.

Mosley, Layna (ed.) 2013. "Introduction. 'Just Talk to People'? Interviews in Contemporary Political Science." In *Interview Research in Political Science*. Ithaca, NY: Cornell University Press.

Muller, Jerry Z. 2018. *The Tyranny of Metrics*. Princeton, NJ: Princeton University Press.

Mulrow, Cynthia D. 1994. "Systematic Reviews: Rationale for Systematic Reviews." *British Medical Journal* 309: 597–599.

Munck, Gerardo L. 1998. "Canons of Research Design in Qualitative Analysis." *Studies in Comparative International Development* 33 (3): 18–45.

Munck, Gerardo L. and Richard Snyder. 2007. *Passion, Craft, and Method in Comparative Politics*. Baltimore, MD: Johns Hopkins University Press.

Munnell, Alicia H., Geoffrey M. B. Tootell, Lynn E. Browne and James McEneaney. 1996. "Mortgage Lending in Boston: Interpreting HMDA Data." *American Economic Review* 86 (1): 25–53.

Nagendran, Myura, Tiago V. Pereira, Grace Kiew, Douglas G. Altman, Mahiben Maruthappu, John P. A. Ioannidis and Peter McCulloch. 2016. "Very Large Treatment Effects in Randomised Trials as an Empirical Marker to Indicate whether Subsequent Trials are Necessary: Meta-Epidemiological Assessment." *British Medical Journal* 355: i5432.

Narang, Vipin and Rebecca M. Nelson. 2009. "Who are these Belligerent Democratizers? Reassessing the Impact of Democratization on War." *International Organization* 63 (Spring): 357–379.

Nash, George. 1976. *The Conservative Intellectual Movement in America Since 1945*. New York: Basic Books.

National Academy of Sciences, National Academy of Engineering (US) and Institute of Medicine (US) Committee on Ensuring the Utility and Integrity of Research Data in a Digital Age, and Institute of Medicine. 2009. *Research Data in the Digital Age*. National Academies Press (US). www.ncbi.nlm.nih.gov/books/NBK215259/.

National Research Council. 1999. *A Question of Balance: Private Rights and the Public Interest in Scientific and Technical Databases*. Washington, DC: The National Academies Press. https://doi.org/10.17226/9692.

National Science Board. 2005. *Long-Lived Data Collections: Enabling Research and Education in the 20st Century*. Arlington, VA: National Science Foundation.

National Science Foundation (NSF). 2016a. "Definition of Transformative Research." Downloaded on September 22, 2016 from www.nsf.gov/about/transformative_research/definition.jsp.

2016b. "Where to Submit Potentially Transformative Research Proposals." Downloaded on September14, 2016 from http://nsf.gov/about/transformative_research/submit.jsp.

2018a. "News Release 18–082. 'NSF announces new measures to protect research community from harassment.'" Downloaded on September 22, 2018 from www.nsf.gov/news/news_summ.jsp?cntn_id=296610.

2018b. "Survey of Earned Doctorates." www.nsf.gov/statistics/2016/nsf16300/data-tables .cfm, accessed April 2018.

Necker, Sarah. 2014. "Scientific Misbehavior in Economics." *Research Policy* 43 (10): 1747–1759.

Nelson, Leif D., Simmons, Joseph P. and Uri Simonsohn. 2012. "Let's Publish Fewer Papers." *Psychological Inquiry* 23: 291–293.

Neumark, David. 2001. "The Employment Effects of Minimum Wages: Evidence from a Prespecified Research Design." *Industrial Relations: A Journal of Economy and Society* 40 (1): 121–144.

Neumark, David and William Wascher. 1998. "Is the Time-Series Evidence on Minimum Wage Effects Contaminated by Publication Bias?" *Economic Inquiry* 36 (3): 458–470.

2000. "Minimum Wages and Employment: A Case Study of the Fast-Food Industry in New Jersey and Pennsylvania: Comment." *American Economic Review* 90 (5): 1362–1396.

Neumark, David, J. M. Ian Salas and William Wascher. 2014. "Revisiting the Minimum Wage – Employment Debate: Throwing Out the Baby with the Bathwater?" *Industrial and Labor Relations Review* 67 (3 suppl): 608–648.

Newcomb, Theodore. 1943. *Personality and Social Change: Attitude Formation in a Student Community*. New York: Dryden Press.

Nexon, Daniel. 2013. "The Citation Gap: Results of a Self-Experiment." *Duck of Minerva*, August 16. http://duckofminerva.com/2013/08/the-citation-gapresults-of-a-self-experiment.html.

2013. "The Citation Gap: Results of a Self-Experiment." *Duck of Minerva*, August 16. http://duckofminerva.com/2013/08/the-citation-gapresults-of-a-self-experiment.html.

Nickerson, Raymond. 1998. "Confirmation Bias: A Ubiquitous Phenomenon in Many Guises." *Review of General Psychology* 2: 175–220.

Nicolaisen, Jeppe. 2007. "Citation Analysis." *Annual Review of Information Science and Technology* 41 (1): 609–641.

References

Nijkamp, Peter and Jacques Poot. 2005. "The Last Word on the Wage Curve?" *Journal of Economic Surveys* 19 (3): 421–450.

Nixon, Lucia A. and Michael D. Robinson. 1999. "The Educational Attainment of Young Women: Role Model Effects of Female High School Faculty." *Demography* 36(2): 185–194.

Nofsinger, John R. 2009. "Retraction Notice to 'Social Mood: The Stock Market and Political Cycles' [J. Socio-Econ. 36 (2007) 734–744]." *Journal of Socio-Economics* 38 (3): 547.

North, Douglass C. 1986. "The New Institutional Economics." *Journal of Institutional and Theoretical Economics (JITE)/Zeitschrift für die gesamte Staatswissenschaft* 142 (1): 230–237.

North, Douglass C. and Barry R. Weingast. 1989. "Constitutions and Commitment: The Evolution of Institutions Governing Public Choice in Seventeenth-Century England." *Journal of Economic History* 49 (4) (December): 803–832.

Northcott, Robert. 2017. "Partial Explanations in Social Science." Pp. 130–153 in Harold Kincaid (ed.), *Oxford Handbook of the Philosophy of the Social Sciences*. Oxford: Oxford University Press.

Nosek, Brian A., George Alter, George C. Banks, Denny Borsboom, Sara D. Bowman, Steven J. Breckler and Stuart Buck. 2015. "Promoting an Open Research Culture." *Science* 348 (6242): 1422–1425.

Nosek, Brian A. and Yoav Bar-Anan. 2012. "Scientific Utopia: I. Opening Scientific Communication." *Psychological Inquiry* 23: 217–243.

Nosek, Brian A. and Daniël Lakens. 2014. "Registered Reports: A Method to Increase the Credibility of Published Results." *Social Psychology* 45 (3): 137–141.

Nosek, Brian A., Jeffrey R. Spies and Matt Mortyl. 2012. "Scientific Utopia: II. Restructuring Incentives and Practices to Promote Truth over Publishability." *Perspectives on Psychological Science* 7: 615–637.

"Notice to Our Readers," 1984. *Quarterly Journal of Economics* 99 (2): 383–384.

Nyhan, Brendan. 2015. "Increasing the Credibility of Political Science Research: A Proposal for Journal Reforms." *PS: Political Science and Politics* 48 (Supplement S1): 78–83.

O'Brien, Peter C. 1984. "Procedures for Comparing Samples with Multiple Endpoints." *Biometrics* 40 (4): 1079–1087.

Offen, Karen M. 2000. *European Feminisms, 1700–1950: A Political History*. Stanford, CA: Stanford University Press.

O'Rourke, Keith. 2007. "An Historical Perspective on Meta-analysis: Dealing Quantitatively with Varying Study Results." *Journal of the Royal Society of Medicine* 100(12): 579–82.

Olken, Benjamin A. 2015. "Promises and Perils of Pre-Analysis Plans." *Journal of Economic Perspectives* 29 (3): 61–80.

Olken, Benjamin A., Junko Onishi and Susan Wong. 2012. "Should Aid Reward Performance? Evidence from a Field Experiment on Health and Education in Indonesia." Working Paper 17892. National Bureau of Economic Research. www.nber.org/papers/w17892.

Open Science Collaboration. 2012. "An Open, Large-Scale, Collaborative Effort to Estimate the Reproducibility of Psychological Science." *Perspectives on Psychological Science* 7 (6): 657–660.

2015. "Estimating the Reproducibility of Psychological Science." *Science* 349: aac4716.

Orazbayev, Sultan. 2017. "Diversity and Collaboration in Economics." Unpublished, UCL SSEES.

Østby, Gudrun, Håvard Strand, Ragnhild Nordås and Nils Petter Gleditsch. 2013. "Gender Gap or Gender Bias in Peace Research? Publication Patterns and Citation Rates for Journal of Peace Research, 1983–2008." *International Studies Perspectives* 14 (4): 493–506.

Osterloh, Margit and Bruno S. Frey. 2015. "Ranking Games." *Evaluation Review* 39 (1): 102–129.

Pagan, Adrian. 1987. "Three Econometric Methodologies: A Critical Appraisal." *Journal of Economic Surveys* 1 (1–2): 3–23.

Palattella, John. 2016. "Svetlana Alexievich's Voices," *The Nation*. July 6. www.thenation.com/article/svetlana-alexievichs-voices/.

Paluck, Elizabeth. 2010. "The Promising Integration of Qualitative Methods and Field Experiments." *Annals of the American Academy of Political and Social Science* 628 (1): 59.

Pampel, Fred. 2004. "Exploratory Data Analysis". Pp. 359–60 in Michael Lewis-Beck, Alan Bryman and Tim F. Liao (eds), *The SAGE Encyclopedia of Social Science Research Methods*. Volume 1. London: Sage.

Pape, Robert A. 2003. "The Strategic Logic of Suicide Terrorism." *American Political Science Review* 97(August): 343–361.

Parish, Susan L., Marsha Mailick Seltzer, Jan S. Greenberg and Frank Floyd. 2004. "Economic Implications of Caregiving at Midlife: Comparing Parents with and without Children who have Developmental Disabilities." *Mental Retardation* 42 (6) : 413–426.

Park, Robert E. 1937. "Review of John Dollard, Caste and Class in a Southern Town." *The Annals of the American Academy of Political and Social Science* 193 (September): 210–211.

Parry, Odette and Natasha Mauthner. 2005. "Back to Basics: Who Re-Uses Qualitative Data and Why?" *Sociology* 39 (2): 337–342.

　2004. "Whose Data Are They Anyway? Practical, Legal and Ethical Issues in Archiving Qualitative Research Data." *Sociology* 38 (1): 139–152.

Parsons, Talcott. 1938. "The Role of Theory in Social Research." *American Sociological Review* 3 (1) (February): 13–20.

Pashler, Harold and Christine R. Harris. 2012. "Is the Replicability Crisis Overblown? Three Arguments Examined." *Perspectives on Psychological Science* 7: 531–536.

Pateman, Carole and Charles Wade Mills. 2007. *Contract and Domination*. Cambridge: Polity.

Patil, Prasad, Roger D. Peng and Jeffrey T. Leek. 2016. "What Should Researchers Expect When They Replicate Studies? A Statistical View of Replicability in Psychological Science." *Perspectives on Psychological Science* 11 (4): 539–544.

Pearl, Judea and Dana Mackenzie. 2018. *The Book of Why: The New Science of Cause and Effect*. New York: Basic Books.

Peic, Goran. 2014. "Civilian Defense Forces, State Capacity, and Government Victory in Counterinsurgency Wars." *Studies in Conflict and Terrorism* 37 (2): 162–184.

Peirce, Charles S. 1906. "Lecture I of a Planned Course." Harvard University, Houghton Library, MS 857.

　1929. "Guessing," *The Hound and Horn* 2 (3) (Spring): 267–285.

　1934. *Vol. 5 of Collected Papers of Charles Sanders Peirce*. Cambridge, MA: Belknap Press.

　1992. "Training in Reasoning." Pp. 181–196 in Charles Sanders Peirce, Kenneth Laine Ketner and Hilary Putnam (eds), *Reasoning and the Logic of Things*. Cambridge, MA: Harvard University Press.

Pereira, Tiago and John P. A. Ioannidis 2011. "Statistically Significant Meta-Analyses of Clinical Trials have Modest Credibility and Inflated Effects." *Journal of Clinical Epidemiology* 64 (10): 1060–1069.

Perneger, Thomas V. 2004. "Relation between Online 'Hit Counts' and Subsequent Citations: Prospective Study of Research Papers in the BMJ." *British Medical Journal* 329 (7465): 546–547.

Pesaran, Hashem. 2003. "Introducing a Replication Section." *Journal of Applied Econometrics* 18 (1): 111.

Peterson, David. 2015. "All that is Solid: Bench-Building at the Frontiers of Two Experimental Sciences." *American Sociological Review* 80 (6): 1201–1225.

2016. "The Baby Factory: Difficult Research Objects, Disciplinary Standards, and the Production of Statistical Significance." *Socius* 2: 1–10.

Petticrew, Mark and Helen Roberts. 2006. *Systematic Reviews in the Social Sciences A Practical Guide*. Malden, MA: Blackwell.

Pew Research Center. 2016. "A Wider Ideological Gap Between More and Less Educated Adults." www.people-press.org/2016/04/26/a-wider-ideological-gap-between-more-and-less-educated-adults/.

Phillips, Peter C. B. 1988. "Reflections on Econometric Methodology." *Economic Record* 64 (4): 344–359.

Piñeiro, Rafael and Fernando Rosenblatt. 2016. "Pre-Analysis Plans for Qualitative Research." *Revista de Ciencia Política* 36 (3): 785–796.

Piñeiro, Rafael, Verónica Pérez and Fernando Rosenblatt. 2016. "Pre-Analysis Plan: The Broad Front: A Mass-Based Leftist Party in Latin America: History, Organization and Resilience." Posted at EGAP Registry, July 19. https://egap.org/registration/1989.

Platt, Jennifer. 1996. *A History of Sociological Research Methods in America, 1920–1960*. Cambridge: Cambridge University Press.

2002. "The History of the Interview." Pp. 33–54 in Jaber Gubrium and James Holstein (eds), *Handbook of Interview Research*. London: SAGE.

2011. *Interview by the Author on the Pilot Study*. Los Angeles, August 21.

Popper, Karl R. 1963. *Conjectures and Refutations*. New York: Harper and Row.

Portenoy, Jason, Jessica Hullman and Jevin D. West. 2016. "Leveraging Citation Networks to Visualize Scholarly Influence Over Time," November. https://doi.org/10.3389/frma.2017.00008.

Posen, Barry R. 1984. *The Sources of Military Doctrine: France, Britain, and Germany Between the World Wars*. Ithaca, NY: Cornell University Press.

Powdthavee, Nattavudh, Yohanes E. Riyanto and Jack L. Knetsch. 2018. "Lower-Rated Publications Do Lower Academics' Judgments of Publication Lists: Evidence from a Survey Experiment of Economists." *Journal of Economic Psychology* 66: 33–44.

Press, Daryl G. 2005. *Calculating Credibility: How Leaders Assess Military Threats*. Ithaca, NY: Cornell University Press.

Priem, Jason. 2014. "Altmetrics." Pp. 263–287 in Blaise Cronin and Cassidy R. Sugimoto (eds), *Beyond Bibliometrics: Harnessing Multidimensional Indicators of Scholarly Impact*. Cambridge, MA: MIT Press.

Raftery, Adrian E. 1995. "Bayesian Model Selection in Social Research." *Sociological Methodology* 25: 111–163.

Rao, Inna Kedage Ravichandra 2011. "Relations Among the Number of Citations, References and Authors: Revisited." Proceedings of the International Conference on Webometrics, Informetrics and Scientometrics (WIS) and COLLNET Meeting, September 20–23, Istanbul Bilgi University, Turkey, 55–66.

Rask, Kevin N. and Elizabeth M Bailey. 2002. "Are Faculty Role Models? Evidence from Major Choice in an Undergraduate Institution." *Journal of Economic Education* 33 (2): 99–124.

Rauchhaus, Robert. 2009. "Evaluating the Nuclear Peace Hypothesis: A Quantitative Approach." *Journal of Conflict Resolution* 53 (2): 258–277.

Redding, Richard. 2012. "Likes Attract: The Sociopolitical Groupthink of (Social) Psychologists." *Perspectives on Psychological Science* 7: 512.

"Redundant Publishing – Australasian Journal of Regional Studies." 2011. *Regional Studies* 45 (2): 282.

Reinhart, Carmen M. and Kenneth S. Rogoff. 2010. "Growth in a Time of Debt." *American Economic Review* 100 (2): n. p.

Reiter, Dan. 2012. "Democracy, Deception, and Entry into War." *Security Studies* 21 (4): 594–623.

2013. "Response to Trachtenberg, Schuessler, and Kaiser." *Democracy, Deception, and Entry into War, ISSF Roundtable* 5 (4). https://issforum.org/roundtables/5-4-democracy-deception-war.

Reiter, Dan and Allan C. Stam. 2002. *Democracies at War*. Princeton, NJ: Princeton University Press.

Reiter, Dan, Allan C. Stam and Michael C. Horowitz. 2016a. "A Revised Look at Interstate Wars." *Journal of Conflict Resolution* 60 (5): 956–976.

2016b. "A Deeper Look at Interstate War Data version 1.1." *Research and Politics* 3 (4): 1–3.

Renear, Allen H., Simone Sacchi and Karen M. Wickett. 2010. "Definitions of Dataset in the Scientific and Technical Literature." In Proceedings of the 73rd ASIS&T Annual Meeting on Navigating Streams in an Information Ecosystem. Volume 47, 81: 1–81: 4. ASIS&T '10. Silver Springs, MD: American Society for Information Science.

"Retraction Statement: 'Correction or Comparison? The Effects of Prime Awareness on Social Judgments', by M. Maringer and D. Stapel." 2015. *European Journal of Social Psychology*, January, n/a-n/a. doi:10.1002/ejsp.2173.

"Retraction Statement and Authors' Apology." 2009. *Regional Studies* 43 (1): 156.

Rikleen, Lauren Stiller. 2015. "Women Lawyers Continue to Lag Behind Male Colleagues: Report of the Ninth Annual NAWL National Survey of Retention and Promotion of Women in Law Firms." *Women Lawyers Journal* 100 (4): 25.

Rivera, Lauren A. 2017. "When Two Bodies are (Not) a Problem: Gender and Relationship Status Discrimination in Academic Hiring." *American Sociological Review* 82 (6): 1111–1138.

Roberts, Colin J. 2005. "Issues in Meta-Regression Analysis: An Overview." *Journal of Economic Surveys* 19 (3): 295–298.

Robles, Alfredo C. 1993. "How" International" Are International Relations Syllabi?" *PS: Political Science and Politics* 26 (3): 526–528.

Robson, Barbara J. and Aurélie Mousquès. 2014. "Predicting citation counts of environmental modelling papers." In Proceedings of the 7th International Congress on Environmental Modelling and Software, International Environmental Modelling and Software Society (iEMSs), San Diego.

Rogowski, Ronald. 1995. "The Role of Theory and Anomaly in Social-Scientific Inference." *American Political Science Review* 89 (2): 467–470.

Romano, Joseph P., Azeem M. Shaikh and Michael Wolf. 2008. "Control of the False Discovery Rate under Dependence Using the Bootstrap and Subsampling." *TEST* 17 (3): 417.

Rosato, Sebastian. 2012. *Europe United: Power Politics and the Making of the European Community*. Ithaca, NY: Cornell University Press.

Rose, Andrew K. and Tom D. Stanley. 2005. "A Meta-Analysis of the Effect of Common Currencies on International Trade*." *Journal of Economic Surveys* 19 (3): 347–365.

Rosenthal, Robert. 1978. "Combining Results of Independent Studies." *Psychological Bulletin* 85 (1): 185.

1979. "The File Drawer Problem and Tolerance for Null Results." *Psychological Bulletin* 86 (3): 638–641.

Ross, Michael. 2006. "Is Democracy Good for the Poor?" *American Journal of Political Science* 50 (4): 860–874.

Rossiter, Margaret W. 1993. "The Matthew Matilda Effect in Science." *Social Studies of Science* 23 (2): 325–341.

Roth, Louise Marie and Jeffrey C. Kroll. 2007. "Risky Business: Assessing Risk Preference Explanations for Gender Differences in Religiosity." *American Sociological Review* 72 (2): 205–220.

Rothenberg, Marc. 2013. "Funding High Risk Proposals at the National Science Foundation: A Brief History." July 3. http://robohub.org/funding-high-risk-proposals-at-the-national-science-foundation-a-brief-history/.

Rothman, Stanley, S. Robert Lichter and Neil Nevitte. 2005. "Politics and Professional Advancement Among College Faculty." *Forum* 3: art 2.

Rothstein, Donna S. 2007. "High School Employment and Youths' Academic Achievement." *Journal of Human Resources* 42 (1): 194–213.

Rowhani-Farid, Anisa, Michelle Allen and Adrian G. Barnett. 2017. "What Incentives Increase Data Sharing in Health and Medical Research? A Systematic Review." *Research Integrity and Peer Review* 2 (1). doi:10.1186/s41073-017-0028-9.

Rubin, Donald. B. 1974. "Estimating Causal Effects of Treatments in Randomized and Nonrandomized Studies." *Journal of Educational Psychology* 66(5): 688–701.

Rueschemeyer, Dietrich. 2009. *Usable Theory: Analytic Tools for Social and Political Research*. Cambridge: Cambridge University Press.

Rule, James B. 1997. *Theory and Progress in Social Science*. Cambridge: Cambridge University Press.

Sachs, Jeffrey and Andrew Warner. 1997. "Natural Resource Abundance and Economic Growth." Center for International Development and Harvard Institute for International Development. www.cid.harvard.edu/ciddata/warner_files/natresf5.pdf.

Sala-i-Martin, Xavier X. 1997. "I Just Ran Two Million Regressions." *American Economic Review* 87 (2): 178–183.

Sala-i-Martin, Xavier X., Gernot Doppelhofer and Ronald I. Miller. 2004. "Determinants of Long-Term Growth: A Bayesian Averaging of Classical Estimates (BACE) Approach." *American Economic Review* 94 (4): 813–835.

Samuels, David. 2013. "Book Citations Count." *PS: Political Science and Politics* 46 (4): 785–790.

Samuels, David and Dawn Langan Teele. 2018. "New Medium, Same Story: Gender Gaps in Book Publishing." Working paper. Available at https://ssrn.com/abstract=3283107.

Sanday, Peggy Reeves. 1990. *Fraternity Gang Rape: Sex, Brotherhood, and Privilege on Campus*. New York: NYU Press.

References

Sapiro, Virginia and David Campbell 2018. "American Political Science Association Committee on Professional Ethics, Rights, and Freedoms Report on the 2017 APSA Survey on Sexual Harassment at Annual Meeting." American Political Science Association mimeo.

Sarkees, Meredith Reid and Frank Whelon Wayman. 2010. *Resort to War, 1816–2007*. Washington, DC: CQ Press.

Sarsons, Heather. 2015. "Gender Differences in Recognition for Group Work." Harvard Economics Department Working Paper. December 3.

2017. "Recognition for Group Work: Gender Differences in Academia." *American Economic Review* 107 (5): 141–145.

Schiebinger, Linda L., Andrea D. Henderson and Shannon K. Gilmartin. 2008. "Dual-Career Academic Couples: What Universities Need to Know." Michelle R. Clayman Institute for Gender Research, Stanford University.

Schmidt, Frank L. 1996. "Statistical Significance Testing and Cumulative Knowledge in Psychology: Implications for Training of Researchers." *Psychological Methods* 1 (2): 115–129.

Schnall, Simone. 2014. "Social Media and the Crowd-Sourcing of Social Psychology." www.psychol.cam.ac.uk/cece/blog.

Schneider, Carsten Q. and Claudius Wagemann. 2012. "Set-Theoretic Methods for Social Sciences." In Colin Elman, John Gerring and James Mahoney (eds), *Strategies for Social Inquiry*. Cambridge: Cambridge University Press.

Schuessler, John M. 2015. *Deceit on the Road to War: Presidents, Politics, and American Democracy*. Ithaca, NY: Cornell University Press.

Schulz, Kenneth F. and David A. Grimes. 2005. "Multiplicity in Randomised Trials II: Subgroup and Interim Analyses." *The Lancet* 365 (9471): 1657–1661.

Schulz, Kenneth F., Douglas G. Altman and David Moher. 2010. "CONSORT 2010 Statement: Updated Guidelines for Reporting Parallel Group Randomised Trials." *Journal of Clinical Epidemiology* 63(8): 834–840.

Schwabish, Jonathan A. 2014. "An Economist's Guide to Visualizing Data." *Journal of Economic Perspectives* 28 (1): 209–233. doi:10.1257/jep.28.1.209.

Schwartz, Christine R. and Gonalons-Pons, Pilar 2016. "Trends in Relative Earnings and Marital Dissolution: Are Wives Who Outearn Their Husbands Still More Likely to Divorce?" *RSF: The Russell Sage Foundation Journal of the Social Sciences* 2 (4): 218–236.

Schwarz, Greg J. and Robert C. Kennicutt, Jr. 2004. "Demographic and Citation Trends in Astrophysical Journal Papers and Preprints." arXiv preprint astro-ph/0411275.

Schwarz, Gideon. 1978. "Estimating the Dimension of a Model." *The Annals of Statistics* 6 (2): 461–464.

Seale, Clive. 1999. *The Quality of Qualitative Research*. London: Sage.

Seawright, Jason. 2016. *Multi-Method Social Science: Combining Qualitative and Quantitative Tools*. Cambridge: Cambridge University Press.

Selltiz, Claire, Marie Jahoda, Morton Deutsch and Stuart Cook. 1959. *Research Methods in Social Relations*. New York: Holt, Rinehart and Winston.

Selvin, Hanan. 1957. "A Critique of Tests of Significance in Survey Research." *American Sociological Review* 22 (5): 519–527.

Sewell, William, Jr. 2005. "The Political Unconscious of Social and Cultural History, or Confessions of a Former Quantitative Historian." In George Steinmetz (ed.), *The Politics of Method in the Human Sciences: Positivism and Its Epistemological Others*. Durham, NC: Duke University Press.

Shachar, Ron and Barry Nalebuff. 2004. "Verifying the Solution from a Nonlinear Solver: A Case Study: Comment." *American Economic Review* 94 (1): 382–390.

Shames, Shauna and Tess Wise. 2017. "Gender Diversity and Methods in Political Science: A Theory of Selection and Survival Biases." *PS: Political Science and Politics* 50 (3): 811–823.

Shashok, Karen. 2005. "Standardization vs Diversity: How Can We Push Peer Review Research Forward?" *Medscape General Medicine* 7 (1): 11.

Shema, Hadas. 2014. "An Introduction to Open Peer Review." *Information Culture, Scientific American*, June 28. https://blogs.scientificamerican.com/information-culture/an-introduction-to-open-peer-review/.

Shen, Helen. 2014. "Interactive Notebooks: Sharing the Code." *Nature* 515 (7525): 151–152.

Shields, Jon and Joshua Dunn Sr. 2016. *Passing on the Right: Conservative Professors in the Progressive University*. New York: Oxford University Press.

Shotton, David. 2010. "CiTO, the Citation Typing Ontology." *Journal of Biomedical Semantics* 1 (1): S6.

Shugart, Matthew S. and Rein Taagepera. 2017. *Votes from Seats: Logical Models of Electoral Systems*. Cambridge: Cambridge University Press.

Silberzahn, Raphael and Eric L. Uhlmann. 2015. "Crowdsourced Research: Many Hands Make Tight Work." *Nature* 526 (7572): 189–191.

Simien, Evelyn M. and Ange-Marie Hancock. 2011. "Mini-Symposium: Intersectionality Research." *Political Research Quarterly* 64: 185–186.

Simmons, Joseph P., Leif D. Nelson and Uri Simonsohn. 2011. "False-Positive Psychology Undisclosed Flexibility in Data Collection and Analysis Allows Presenting Anything as Significant." *Psychological Science* 22 (11): 1359–1366.

2012. "A 21 Word Solution." *Dialogue: The Official Newsletter of the Society for Personality and Social Psychology* 26 (2): 4–7.

Simms, Stephanie. 2018. 'Scoping Machine-Actionable DMPs'. *DMPTool Blog* (blog). July 9. https://blog.dmptool.org/2018/07/09/scoping-machine-actionable-dmps/.

Simms, Stephanie, Sarah Jones, Kevin Ashley, Marta Ribeiro, John Chodacki, Stephen Abrams and Marisa Strong. 2016. "Roadmap: A Research Data Management Advisory Platform." *Research Ideas and Outcomes* 2: 1–8.

Simon, Joshua. 2018. "From the American System to the Anglo-Saxon Union: Scientific Racism and Supra-Nationalism in Nineteenth Century North America." Pp. 72–94 in Andrew J. Arato, Jean L. Cohen and Astrid von Busekist (eds), *Forms of Pluralism and Democratic Constitutionalism*. New York: Columbia University Press.

Simons, Daniel J. 2014. "The Value of Direct Replication." *Perspectives on Psychological Science* 9 (1): 76–80.

Simonsohn, Uri. 2013. "Just Post It: The Lesson From Two Cases of Fabricated Data Detected by Statistics Alone." *Psychological Science* 24 (10): 1875–1888.

2015. "Small Telescopes Detectability and the Evaluation of Replication Results." *Psychological Science* 26 (5): 559–569.

Simonsohn, Uri, Joseph P. Simmons and Leif D. Nelson. 2015a. "Better P-Curves: Making P-Curve Analysis More Robust to Errors, Fraud, and Ambitious P-Hacking, a Reply to Ulrich and Miller (2015)." *Journal of Experimental Psychology: General* 144 (6): 1146–1152.

2015b. "Specification Curve: Descriptive and Inferential Statistics on All Reasonable Specifications." SSRN Scholarly Paper ID 2694998. Rochester, NY: Social Science Research Network.

References

Simonsohn, Uri, Leif D. Nelson, and Joseph P. Simmons. 2014a. "P-Curve: A Key to the File-Drawer." *Journal of Experimental Psychology: General* 143 (2): 534–547.

2014b. "P-Curve and Effect Size Correcting for Publication Bias Using Only Significant Results." *Perspectives on Psychological Science* 9 (6): 666–681.

Simowitz, Roslyn. 1998. "Evaluating Conflict Research on the Diffusion of War." *Journal of Peace Research* 35 (2) (March): 211–230.

Sinisi, Sandra E., Eric C Polley, Maya L Petersen, Soo-Yon Rhee and der Laan Mark J. van. 2007. "Super Learning: An Application to the Prediction of HIV-1 Drug Resistance." *Statistical Applications in Genetics and Molecular Biology* 6 (1). doi:10.2202/1544-6115.1240.

Siskind, Frederic B. 1977. "Minimum Wage Legislation in the United States: Comment." *Economic Inquiry* 15 (1): 135–138.

Sisson, Richard and Leo E. Rose. 1990. *War and Secession: Pakistan, India, and the Creation of Bangladesh*. Berkeley, CA: University of California Press.

Sjöblom, Gunnar. 1977. "The Cumulation Problem in Political Science." *European Journal of Political Science* 5 (1): 1–32.

1997. "The Cumulation Problem Revisited." *European Journal of Political Research* 31 (1) (February): 78–81.

Skocpol, Theda. 1980. "Political Response to Capitalist Crisis: Neo-Marxist Theories of the State and the Case of the New Deal." *Politics and Society* 10 (2): 155–201.

Slater, Dan. 2010. *Ordering Power: Contentious Politics and Authoritarian Leviathans in Southeast Asia*. New York: Cambridge University Press.

Smit, Eefke, Jeffrey van der Hoeven and David Giaretta. 2011. "Avoiding a Digital Dark Age for Data: Why Publishers Should Care about Digital Preservation." *Learned Publishing* 24 (1): 35–49.

Smith, Christian. 2014. *The Sacred Project of American Sociology*. New York: Oxford University Press.

Smith, Dorothy. 1990. *The Conceptual Practices of Power: A Feminist Sociology of Knowledge*. Boston, MA: Northeastern University Press.

Smith, Kevin. 2005. "Data Don't Matter? Academic Research and School Choice." *Perspectives on Politics* 3 (2) (June): 285–299.

Smith, Mary Lee. 1980. "Publication Bias and Meta-Analysis." *Evaluation in Education* 4: 22–24.

Smith, Robert B. 2008. *Cumulative Social Inquiry*. New York: Guilford Press.

Smith, Steven Rathgeb. 2014. "Reflections on the Status of the Field." *PS: Political Science and Politics* 43 (3): 741–742.

Smulders, Yvo M. 2013. "A Two-Step Manuscript Submission Process Can Reduce Publication Bias." *Journal of Clinical Epidemiology* 66 (9): 946–947.

Snyder, Jack and Erica D. Borghard. 2011. "The Cost of Empty Threats: A Penny, Not a Pound." *American Political Science Review* 105 (03): 437–456.

Snyder, Thomas D., de Brey, Cristobal and Sally A. Dillow. 2016. "Digest of Education Statistics." National Center for Education Statistics. https://nces.ed.gov/pubsearch/pubsinfo.asp?pubid=2017094.

Soifer, Hillel David. 2015. *State Building in Latin America*. Cambridge: Cambridge University Press.

Somekh, Bridget and Cathy Lewin. 2005. *Research Methods in the Social Sciences*. London: SAGE.

Stanley, Tom D. 2005. "Beyond Publication Bias." *Journal of Economic Surveys* 19 (3): 309–345.

2008. "Meta-Regression Methods for Detecting and Estimating Empirical Effects in the Presence of Publication Selection." *Oxford Bulletin of Economics and Statistics* 70 (1): 103–127.

Stanley, Tom D. and Hristos Doucouliagos. 2010. "Picture This: A Simple Graph That Reveals Much Ado About Research." *Journal of Economic Surveys* 24 (1): 170–191.

2012. *Meta-Regression Analysis in Economics and Business*. London: Routledge.

Stanley, Tom D., Hristos Doucouliagos, Margaret Giles, Jost H. Heckemeyer, Robert J. Johnston, Patrice Laroche, Jon P. Nelson et al. 2013. "Meta-Analysis of Economics Research Reporting Guidelines." *Journal of Economic Surveys* 27 (2): 390–394.

Stapel, Diederik. 2014. "Faking Science: A True Story of Academic Fraud." Translated by Nicholas Brown. http://nick.brown.free.fr/stapel/FakingScience-20161115.pdf.

Stark, David. 2009. *The Sense of Dissonance: Accounts of Worth in Economic Life*. Princeton, NJ: Princeton University Press.

"Statement of Retraction." 2010. *Journal of Economic Policy Reform* 13 (4): 387.

"Statement of Retraction." 2012. *Applied Economics Letters* 19 (16): 1649.

Stebbins, Robert. 2001. *Exploratory Research in the Social Sciences*. Qualitative Research Methods Series 48. London: Sage Publications.

Steen, R. Grant. 2010. "Retractions in the Scientific Literature: Is the Incidence of Research Fraud Increasing?" *Journal of Medical Ethics*, December, jme.2010.040923. doi:10.1136/jme.2010.040923.

Steen, R. Grant, Arturo Casadevall and Ferric C. Fang. 2013. "Why Has the Number of Scientific Retractions Increased?" *PLoS ONE* 8 (7): e68397.

Stegmaier, Mary, Barbara Palmer and Laura Van Assendelft. 2011. "Getting on the Board: The Presence of Women in Political Science Journal Editorial Positions." *PS: Political Science and Politics* 44 (4): 799–804.

Steinberg, Steven J. and Sheila L. Steinberg. 2005. *Geographic Information Systems for the Social Sciences: Investigating Space and Place*. London: Sage Publications.

Steinert-Threlkeld, Zachary C. 2018. *Twitter as Data*. Cambridge: Cambridge University Press.

Steinmetz, George (ed.). 2005. *The Politics of Method in the Human Sciences: Positivism and Its Epistemological Others*. Durham, NC: Duke University Press

Stephan, Paula. 2012. "Research efficiency: Perverse incentives." *Nature* 484 (7392): 29–31.

Sterling, Theodore D. 1959. "Publication Decisions and Their Possible Effects on Inferences Drawn from Tests of Significance – or Vice Versa." *Journal of the American Statistical Association* 54 (285): 30–34.

Sterne, Jonathan. 2005. "C. Wright Mills, the Bureau for Applied Social Research, and the Meaning of Critical Scholarship." *Critical Studies Critical Methodologies* 5 (1): 86–94.

Stevens, Mitchell L., Cynthia Miller-Idriss and Seteney Shami. 2018. *Seeing the World: How US Universities Make Knowledge in a Global Era*. Princeton, NJ: Princeton University Press.

Stock, Wendy A. 2017. "Trends in Economics and Other Undergraduate Majors." *American Economic Review* 107 (5): 644–649.

Stodden, Victoria, Friedrich Leisch and Roger D Peng. 2014. *Implementing Reproducible Research*. Boca Raton, FL: CRC Press.

Stokes, Susan. 2001. *Neoliberalism by Surprise: Mandates and Democracy in Latin America*. Cambridge: Cambridge University Press.

Stouffer, Samuel and Paul Lazarsfeld. 1937. *Research Memorandum on the Family in the Depression*. New York: Social Science Research Council.

Streb, Christoph. 2010. "Exploratory Case Study." In Albert Mills, Gabrielle Durepos and Elden Wiebe (eds), *Encyclopedia of Case Study Research*. Thousand Oaks, CA: Sage Reference.

Stroebe, Wolfgang, Tom Postmes and Russell Spears. 2012. "Scientific Misconduct and the Myth of Self-Correction in Science." *Perspectives on Psychological Science* 7 (6): 670–688.

Stroebe, Wolfgang and Fritz Strack. 2014. "The Alleged Crisis and the Illusion of Exact Replication." *Perspectives on Psychological Science* 9 (1): 59–71.

Sugimoto, Cassidy R. and Vincent Larivière. 2018. *Measuring Research: What Everyone Needs to Know*. Oxford: Oxford University Press.

Sullivan, Ryan, Allan Timmermann and Halbert White. 1999. "Data-Snooping, Technical Trading Rule Performance, and the Bootstrap." *Journal of Finance* 54 (5): 1647–1691.

Sumner, Jane. 2018. "The Gender Balance Assessment Tool (GBAT): A Web-Based Tool for Estimating Gender Balance in Syllabi and Bibliographies." *PS: Political Science and Politics* 51 (2): 396–400.

Swaen, Gerald M. H., Neil Carmichael and John Doe. 2011. "Strengthening the Reliability and Credibility of Observational Epidemiology Studies by Creating an Observational Studies Register." *Journal of Clinical Epidemiology* 64: 481–486.

Swedberg, Richard. 2009. "Tocqueville as an Empirical Researcher." Pp. 279–292 in Mohammed Chaerkaouie and Peter Hamilton (eds), *Raymond Boudon: A Life in Sociology*. Volume 1. Oxford: Bardwell Press.

2014. *The Art of Social Theory*. Princeton, NJ: Princeton University Press.

2016. "Before Theory Comes Theorizing or How to Make Social Science More Interesting." *British Journal of Sociology* 67 (1): 5–70.

Sweeney, Latanya. 2002. "K-Anonymity: A Model for Protecting Privacy." *International Journal of Uncertainty, Fuzziness and Knowledge-Based Systems* 10 (05): 557–570.

Taagepera, Rein. 2008. *Making Social Sciences More Scientific: The Need for Predictive Models*. Oxford: Oxford University Press.

Taichman, Darren B., J. Backus, C. Baethge et al. 2016. "Sharing Clinical Trial Data: A Proposal from the International Committee of Medical Journal Editors." *Journal of the American Medical Association* 315 (5): 467–468.

Taubman, Sarah L., Heidi L. Allen, Bill J. Wright, Katherine Baicker and Amy N. Finkelstein. 2014. "Medicaid Increases Emergency-Department Use: Evidence from Oregon's Health Insurance Experiment." *Science* 343 (6168): 263–268.

Taylor, Shelley E. and Susan T. Fiske. 1975. "Point of View and Perceptions of Causality." *Journal of Personality and Social Psychology* 32 (3): 439.

Teele, Dawn and Kathleen Thelen. 2017. "Gender in the Journals: Methodology, Coauthorship, and Publication Patterns in Political Science's Flagship Journals." *PS: Political Science and Politics* 50 (2): 433–447.

Teles, Steven. 2008. *The Rise of the Conservative Legal Movement*. Princeton, NJ: Princeton University Press.

Testa, James. 2016. "Journal Selection Process." Clarivate Analytics. https://clarivate.com/essays/journal-selection-process/.

Tetlock, Philip and Gregory Mitchell. 2015. "Why So Few Conservatives and Should We Care?" *Society* 52: 28–34.

The Lancet. 2010. "Should Protocols for Observational Research Be Registered?" *The Lancet* 375 (9712): 348.

Thelen, Kathleen. 2019. "The American Precariat: U.S. Capitalism in Comparative Perspective" *Perspectives on Politics* 17 (1): 5–27.

Thomas, Duncan, Elizabeth Frankenberg, Jed Friedman, Jean-Pierre Habicht, Mohammed Hakimi, Nathan Jones Jaswadi, Gretel Pelto et al. 2003. "Iron Deficiency and the Well-Being of Older Adults: Early Results from a Randomized Nutrition Intervention." Paper presented at the Population Association of America Annual Meetings, April 2003, Minneapolis.

Thomas, Duncan, Elizabeth Frankenberg, Jed Friedman, Jean-Pierre Habicht, Mohammed Hakimi, Nicholas Ingwersen, Nathan Jones et al. 2006. "Causal Effect of Health on Labor Market Outcomes: Experimental Evidence." UCLA CCPR Population Working Papers. https://escholarship.org/uc/item/0g28k77w.

Thompson, Chastity Q. 2008. "Recruitment, Retention, and Mentoring Faculty of Color: The Chronicle Continues." *New Directions for Higher Education* 143: 47–54.

Tilly, Charles. 1992. *Coercion, Capital, and European States, AD 990–1992*. Oxford: Blackwell.

Todeschini, Roberto and Alberto Baccini. 2016. *Handbook of Bibliometric Indicators: Quantitative Tools for Studying and Evaluating Research*. Weinheim: Wiley-VCH.

Toutkoushian, Robert K. and Valerie M. Conley. 2005. "Progress for Women in Academe, Yet Inequities Persist: Evidence from NSOPF:99." *Research in Higher Education* 46 (1): 1–28.

Tsang, Eric W. K. and Kai-Man Kwan. 1999. "Replications and Theory Development in Organizational Science: A Critical Realist Perspective." *Academy of Management Review* 24: 759–780.

Tucker, Joshua. 2014. "Experiments, Preregistration, and Journals." On OUPblog. http://blog.oup.com/2014/09/pro-con-research-preregistration/.

Tudor, Carissa L. and Deborah J. Yashar. 2018. "Gender and the Editorial Process: World Politics, 2007–2017." *Academy of Management Review* 24 (4): 759–780.

Tufte, Edward R. 2001. *The Visual Display of Quantitative Information*. Cheshire, CT: Graphics Press.

Tukey, John Wilder. 1977. *Exploratory Data Analysis*. Reading, MA: Addison-Wesley.

Turner, Erick H., Annette M. Matthews, Eftihia Linardatos, Robert A. Tell and Robert Rosenthal. 2008. "Selective Publication of Antidepressant Trials and Its Influence on Apparent Efficacy." *New England Journal of Medicine* 358 (3): 252–260.

Ulrich, Rolf and Jeff Miller. 2015. "P-Hacking by Post Hoc Selection with Multiple Opportunities: Detectability by Skewness Test?: Comment on Simonsohn, Nelson, and Simmons (2014)." *Journal of Experimental Psychology: General* 144 (6): 1137–1145.

Van Aert RCM, Van Assen MALM. 2017. "Bayesian Evaluation of Effect Size after Replicating an Original Study." *PLoS ONE* 12 (4): e0175302.

Van der Veer, René, Marinus van IJzendoorn and Jaan Valsiner (eds). 1994. *Reconstructing the Mind: Replicability in Research on Human Development*. Norwood, NJ: Ablex.

Van Evera, Stephen. 1997. *Guide to Methods for Students of Political Science*. Ithaca, NY: Cornell University Press.

Van Noorden, Richard. 2010. "A Profusion of Measures." *Nature* 465 (7300): 864–867.

2013. "New Record: 66 Journals Banned for Boosting Impact Factor with Self-Citations : News Blog." Nature News Blog (blog). June 19. http://blogs.nature.com/news/2013/06/new-record-66-journals-banned-for-boosting-impact-factor-with-self-citations.html.

van Teijlingen, Edwin and Vanora Hundley. 2001. "The Importance of Pilot Studies." Social Research Update (University of Surrey), issue 35. http://sru.soc.surrey.ac.uk/SRU35.html.

Vanclay, Jerome K. 2013. "Factors Affecting Citation Rates in Environmental Science." *Journal of Informetrics* 7 (2): 265–271.

Vasilescu, Bogdan, Andrea Capiluppi and Alexander Serebrenik. 2014. "Gender, Representation and Online Participation: A Quantitative Study." *Interacting with Computers* 26 (5): 488–511.

Verhagen, Josine and Eric-Jan Wagenmakers. 2014. "Bayesian Tests to Quantify the Result of a Replication Attempt." *Journal of Experimental Psychology: General* 143: 1457–1475.

Viscusi, W. Kip. 2015. "The Role of Publication Selection Bias in Estimates of the Value of a Statistical Life." *American Journal of Health Economics* 1 (1): 27–52.

Vitalis, Robert. 2015. *White World Order, Black Power Politics: The Birth of American International Relations*. Ithaca, NY: Cornell University Press.

Vivalt, Eva. 2015. "The Trajectory of Specification Searching Across Methods and Disciplines." http://evavivalt.com/wp-content/uploads/2015/09/Trajectory-of-Specification-Searching.pdf.

Wacholder, Sholom, Stephen Chanock, Montserrat Garcia-Closas, Laure El Ghormli and Nathaniel Rothman. 2004. "Assessing the Probability That a Positive Report Is False: An Approach for Molecular Epidemiology Studies." *Journal of the National Cancer Institute* 96 (6): 434–442.

Wade, Alex D., Kuansan Wang, Yizhou Sun and Antonio Gulli. 2016. "WSDM Cup 2016: Entity Ranking Challenge." Pp. 593–94 in Proceedings of the Ninth Acm International Conference on Web Search and Data Mining. WSDM 2016. New York: ACM.

Wade, Sara Jackson and Dan Reiter. 2007. "Does Democracy Matter? Regime Type and Suicide Terrorism." *Journal of Conflict Resolution* 51 (2): 329–348.

Wagenmakers, Eric-Jan, Ruud Wetzels, Denny Borsboom, Han L. J. van der Maas and Rogier A. Kievit. 2012. "An Agenda for Purely Confirmatory Research." *Perspectives on Psychological Science* 7 (6): 632–638.

Wagner, Caroline and Jeffrey Alexander. 2013. "Evaluating Transformative Research Programmes: A Case Study of the NSF Small Grants for Exploratory Research Programme." *Research Evaluation* 22 (3): 187–197.

Wagner, Cassie, Meseret D. Gebremichael, Mary K. Taylor and Michael J. Soltys. 2009. "Disappearing Act: Decay of Uniform Resource Locators in Health Care Management Journals." *Journal of the Medical Library Association* 97 (2): 122–130.

Wallerstein, Immanuel. 1996. *Open the Social Sciences: Report of the Gulbenkian Commission on the Restructuring of the Social Sciences*. Stanford, CA: Stanford University Press.

Wallis Jillian C., Elizabeth Rolando and Christine L. Borgman. 2013. "If We Share Data, Will Anyone Use Them? Data Sharing and Reuse in the Long Tail of Science and Technology." *PLoS ONE* 8 (7): e67332.

Walsh, Elias, Sarah Dolfin and John DiNardo. 2009. "Lies, Damn Lies, and Pre-Election Polling." *American Economic Review* 99 (2): 316–322.

Walters, Maggie. 2010. *Social Research Methods*. 2nd ed. Oxford: Oxford University Press.

Wang, Jian, Reinhilde Veugelers and Paula Stephan. 2017. "Bias against Novelty in Science: A Cautionary Tale for Users of Bibliometric Indicators." *Research Policy* 46 (8): 1416–1436.

Ward, Kelly and Lisa Wolf-Wendel. 2012. *Academic Motherhood: How Faculty Manage Work and Family*. New Brunswick, NJ: Rutgers University Press.

Warren, Elizabeth. 2016. "Strengthening Research through Data Sharing." *New England Journal of Medicine* 375 (5): 401–403.

Watts, Duncan J. 2007. "A Twenty-First Century Science." *Nature* 445 (7127): 489.

— 2017. "Should Social Science be More Solution-Oriented?" *Nature Human Behaviour* 1 (0015): 1–5.

Weakliem, David L. 2016. "The Missing Main Effect of Welfare State Regimes: A Comment." *Sociological Science* 3: 109–115.

Weber, Max. 1946. "Science as a Vocation." Pp. 129–56 in Hans Gerth and C. Wright Mills (eds), *Max Weber: Essays in Sociology*. New York: Oxford University Press.

— 2012. *Collected Methodological Writings*. Hans Henrik Bruun and Sam Whimster (eds), Hans Henrik Bruun (trans.). London: Routledge.

Webster, Gregory D., Peter K. Jonason and Tatiana O. Schember. 2009. "Hot Topics and Popular Papers in Evolutionary Psychology: Analyses of Title Words and Citation Counts in Evolution and Human Behavior, 1979–2008." *Evolutionary Psychology* 7 (3): 348–362.

Weinberg, Julius. 1972, *Edward Alsworth Ross and the Sociology of Progressivism*. Madison, WI: State Historical Society of Wisconsin.

Weingart, Peter. 2005. "Impact of Bibliometrics upon the Science System: Inadvertent Consequences." *Scientometrics* 62 (1): 117–131.

Weisshaar, Katherine. 2017. "Publish and Perish? An Assessment of Gender Gaps in Promotion to Tenure in Academia." *Social Forces* 96 (2): 529–560.

Welch, Finis. 1974. "Minimum Wage Legislation in the United States." *Economic Inquiry* 12 (3): 285–318.

— 1977. "Minimum Wage Legislation in the United States: Reply." *Economic Inquiry* 15 (1): 139–142.

Werner, Suzanne and Amy Yuen. 2005. "Making and Keeping Peace." *International Organization* 59(April): 261–292.

Wesley-Smith, Ian, Carl T. Bergstrom and Jevin D. West. 2016. "Static Ranking of Scholarly Papers Using Article-Level Eigenfactor (ALEF)." ArXiv:1606.08534 [Cs], June. http://arxiv.org/abs/1606.08534.

West, Jevin D. and Daril A. Vilhena. 2014. "A Network Approach to Scholarly Evaluation." Pp. 151–165 in Blaise Cronin and Cassidy R. Sugimoto (eds), *Beyond Bibliometrics: Harnessing Multidimensional Indicators of Scholarly Impact*. Cambridge, MA: MIT Press.

Western, Bruce. 1996. "Vague Theory and Model Uncertainty in Macrosociology." *Sociological Methodology* 26: 165–192.

Westfall, Peter H. and S. Stanley Young. 1993. *Resampling-Based Multiple Testing: Examples and Methods for P-Value Adjustment*. New York: John Wiley and Sons.

Whicker, Marcia Lynn, Jennie Jacobs Kronenfeld and Ruth Ann Strickland. 1993. *Getting Tenure*. Newbury Park, CA: Sage Publications.

White, Halbert. 2000. "A Reality Check for Data Snooping." *Econometrica* 68 (5): 1097–1126.

Wicherts, Jelte M., Denny Borsboom, Judith Kats and Dylan Molenaar. 2006. "The Poor Availability of Psychological Data for Reanalysis." *American Psychologist* 61 (7): 726–728.

Wildgaard, Lorna, Jesper W. Schneider and Birger Larsen. 2014. "A Review of the Characteristics of 108 Author-Level Bibliometric Indicators." *Scientometrics* 101 (1): 125–158.

References

Wilkinson, Mark D., Michel Dumontier, Ijsbrand Jan Aalbersberg, Gabrielle Appleton, Myles Axton, Arie Baak, Niklas Blomberg et al. 2016. "The FAIR Guiding Principles for Scientific Data Management and Stewardship." *Scientific Data* 3 (March). doi:10.1038/sdata.2016.18.

Williams, Rebecca J., Tony Tse, William R. Harlan and Deborah A. Zarin. 2010. "Registration of Observational Studies: Is it Time?" *Canadian Medical Association Journal* 182 (15): 1638–1642.

Williams, S. C. 2016. "Practices, Policies, and Persistence: A Study of Supplementary Materials in Crop Science Journals." *Journal of Agricultural and Food Information* 17 (1): 11–22.

Wilsdon, James, Liz Allen, Eleonora Belfiore, Philip Campbell, Stephen Curry, Steven Hill, Richard Jones, Roger Kain, Simon Kerridge, Mike Thelwall, Jane Tinkler, Ian Viney, Paul Wouters, Jude Hill and Ben Johnson. 2015. *The Metric Tide: Report of the Independent Review of the Role of Metrics in Research Assessment and Management*. London: SAGE.

Wilson, Edward O. 1998. *Consilience: The Unity of Knowledge*. New York: Knopf.

Wilson, Timothy. 2014. "Is There a Crisis of False Negatives in Psychology?" https://timwilsonredirect.wordpress.com/2014/06/15/is-there-a-crisis-of-false-negatives-in-psychology/.

Wimmer, Andreas and Reinhart Kossler (eds). 2005. *Understanding Change: Models, Methodologies and Metaphors*. Basingstoke: Palgrave Macmillan.

Winch, Peter. 1958. *The Idea of a Social Science, and its Relation to Philosophy*. London: Routledge and Kegan Paul.

Wolbrecht, Christina and David E Campbell. 2007. "Leading by Example: Female Members of Parliament as Political Role Models." *American Journal of Political Science* 51 (4): 921–939.

Wolfinger, Nicholas H., Mary Ann Mason and Marc Goulden. 2008. "Problems in the Pipeline: Gender, Marriage, and Fertility in the Ivory Tower." *Journal of Higher Education* 79 (4): 388–405.

Wolpin, Kenneth I. 2013. *The Limits of Inference without Theory*. Cambridge, MA: MIT Press.

Wu, Xiaogang and Yu Xie. 2003. "Does the Market Pay Off? Earnings Returns to Education in Urban China." *American Sociological Review* 68 (3): 425–442.

Wydick, Bruce, Elizabeth Katz and Brendan Janet. 2014. "Do in-Kind Transfers Damage Local Markets? The Case of TOMS Shoe Donations in El Salvador." *Journal of Development Effectiveness* 6 (3): 249–267.

Xiao, Hong, Fei Yuan and Jian-Guo Wu. 2009. "Factors Affecting Citations: A Comparison between Chinese and English Journals in Ecology." *Chinese Journal of Applied Ecology* 20: 1253–1262.

Xie, Yihui. 2013. *Dynamic Documents with R and Knitr*. Boca Raton, FL: CRC Press.

  2014. "Knitr: A Comprehensive Tool for Reproducible Research in R." Pp. 3–32 in Victoria Stodden, Friedrich Leisch and Roger D. Peng (eds), *Implementing Reproducible Research*. Boca Raton, FL: CRC Press.

Yardley, Sarah J., Kate M. Watts, Jennifer Pearson and Jane C. Richardson. 2014. "Ethical Issues in the Reuse of Qualitative Data Perspectives From Literature, Practice, and Participants." *Qualitative Health Research* 24 (1): 102–113.

Yom, Sean. 2015. "From Methodology to Practice: Inductive Iteration in Comparative Research." *Comparative Political Studies* 48 (5): 616–644.

Yong, Ed. 2012. "Bad Copy." *Nature* 485: 298–300.

Young, Cristobal. 2009. "Model Uncertainty in Sociological Research: An Application to Religion and Economic Growth." *American Sociological Review* 74 (3): 380–397.

Young, Christobal and Katherine Holsteen. 2015. "Model Uncertainty and Robustness: A Computational Framework for Multimodal Analysis," *Sociological Methods and Research* 46 (1): 3–40.

2017. "Model Uncertainty and Robustness: A Computational Framework for Multimodel Analysis." *Sociological Methods and Research* 46 (1): 3–40.

Young, Cristobal and Charles Varner. 2011. "Millionaire Migration and State Taxation of Top Incomes: Evidence From a Natural Experiment." *National Tax Journal* 64 (2): 255–283.

Zarya, Valentina. "The Percentage of Female CEOs in the Fortune 500 Drops to 4%." Fortune. com, 7 June.

Ziliak, Stephen T. and Deirdre N. McCloskey. 2004. "Size Matters: The Standard Error of Regressions in the American Economic Review." *Journal of Socio-Economics, Statistical Significance* 33 (5): 527–546.

2008. *The Cult of Statistical Significance: How the Standard Error Costs Us Jobs, Justice, and Lives*. Ann Arbor, MI: University of Michigan Press.

Zimmermann, Christian. 2015. "On the Need for a Replication Journal." Working Paper Series, no. No. 2015–016 (August). http://research.stlouisfed.org/wp/more/2015-016/.

Zittrain, Jonathan, Kendra Albert and Lawrence Lessig. 2014. "Perma: Scoping and Addressing the Problem of Link and Reference Rot in Legal Citations." *Harvard Law Review* 127 (February): 176–199.

Zuckerman, Harriet. 1972. "Interviewing an Ultra-Elite." *Public Opinion Quarterly* 36 (2): 159–175.

Zuckerman, Harriet and Robert K. Merton. 1971. "Patterns of Evaluation in Science: Institutionalisation, Structure and Functions of the Referee System." *Minerva* 9: 66–100.

Index

Allen, Heidi, 177, 178
American Economic Association (AEA), 154, 162, 275, 361
   journals of, 148, *149t6.3*, 152, 189
   randomized controlled trials registry, 172, 194, 237, 238, 243, 473
American Political Science Association (APSA), 92, 93, 185, 217n23, 361, 411, 418n36, 424n48
   and research transparency, 151, 186, 237n9, 283, 302n1
American Sociological Association (ASA), 74, 92, 93, 151, 361
anthropology, 7, 292, 361, 407, 414, 417, 439, 453
archives, 1, 66, 202n5, 208, 378
   journals and, 77, 146, 151, 157
   as qualitative evidence, 114, 200, 243–244, 253, 288, 289, 302
   and replication, 284n1, 293, 299, 313
   and repositories, 94
   restricted access to, 245, *246t9.3*, 256

Baicker, Katherine, 177, 178
Bar-Anan, Yoav, 86, 92–95
Bayesianism, 1, 10, 228, 239–240, 262n28, *see also* epistemologies; process tracing
   and expected learning, 225, 258, 259
   and model averaging, 166–167, 357
Berkeley Initiative for Transparency in the Social Sciences, 195, 334
Bernstein, Mira, 177, 178
bias
   appraisal over novelty, 215, 275, 332
   citation, 112
   cognitive, 332
   data, 357
   file-drawer, 358
   gatekeeper, 232
   and results-blind review, 241
   gender, 405, 417
   ideological, 275
   in publication review process, 89
   in replication, 477
   in research metrics, 375–377, 397
big data, 62, 194
biomedical research, 48, 52, 61, 65, 184, 243
Blumer, Herbert, 22, 30–31, 33
Bureau of Applied Social Research, 22, 29, *see also* Columbia University

Card, David, 106, 108, 121, 123, 124, 139, 168, 169
case studies, 61, 235, 299
   comparative, 63
   example of, 267, 273, 274, 296, 325, 449, 452
   exploratory, 21, 25–26, 28–29
   and measurement error, 288, 290
   qualitative, 64
   as research strategy, 53, 253, 295, 466
   and sociological methods, *21t2.1, 21t2.2*
   and theory testing, 53, 230, 327
Casey, Katherine, 171, 175–177, 182
causal inference, 1, 42, 51–54, 57, 62, 63, 338, 345
Center for Open Science, 173, 187, 195, 215, 238, 334
Chang, Andrew, 157–158
citation, 300, 336, 360, 443, 475, *see also* data
   active citation, 219, 289
   and article length, 115–122
   and gender, 405, 417
   metrics, 266, 338, 361, 372–377, 391–393, 460
   and publication length, 112
   and reputation, 95
Clemens, Michael, 156, 159–161, 285, *304f12.1*, 340
coding, 296
   error, 158, 285, 290
   and quantitative analysis, 247
   rules, 284, 298, 481
Coffman, Lucas, 179, 190
Coleman, James, 22, 24, 25, 29, 31
Columbia University, 22, 23–24, 26, 28–32, 427, 443
comparative historical analysis, 301, 303, 319
concepts, 7, 25, 466
   and conceptual replication, 271
   generation, 36, 363
   operationalization, 28, 235, 306

concepts (*cont.*)
  and theory, 134
conferences and workshops, academic, 165, 392, 420, 426, 451, 480
  as checks for bias, 132
  and mentoring, 69
confirmation bias, 331, 436
conflict-of-interest policies, 148, *149*, 185
Crawford, Jarret, 435–439, 447

data
  availability, 151, 189, 347
  citation, 186, 279
  curation, 376
  fabrication, 162
  gathering, *see* data collection
  manipulation, 132
  mining, 145, 146, 184
  quality, 26, 375
  repositories, 130, *see also* Qualitative Data Repository
  visualization, 140, 187
data access, 243–245, 358, 472
  impact metrics databases, 375, 379
  in journals, *246*, 482
Data Access and Research Transparency (DART), 151, 186, 189, 302n1
data collection, 186, 340, 379, 474, 479
  costs, 55, 352
  incentives for, 152
  and intellectual property, 153
  and pre-registration, 66
  qualitative, 232, 244, 302, 311
  quantitative, 154, 291, 397
  tools for, 1
  transparency, 459, 472
data sharing, 164, 195, 274
  concerns with, 193
  policies, 146–154, 186, 189, 279–280
  and replication, 134, 157
  standards for, 155
  transparency, 187
deductive research, 52, 322
DellaVigna, Stefano, 106, 108, 121, 123, 124
democracy (in academia), 394–396
description
  case study, 28
descriptive research, 36, 47, 57–62, *60t3.1*, 430, 464
  and publication, 53
  qualitative, 335
desk rejection, 75
discrimination, 401, 479
  gender, 386
  ideological, 441, 443
dissertation, 18, 37, 38, 40t2.3, 254, 417, 451, 481

division of labor
  gendered, 11, 423, 426
  in knowledge production, 43, 49, 59, 68, 110, 469
Dollard, John, 20
Doucouliagos, Hristos, 131, 140, 169
Duarte, José, 435–439, 442, 443, 447, 450
Dunn, Joshua, 440–441, 443–446, 449

economics
  and citations, 381
  gender in, 411
  ideological composition, 434
  journals, 123, *141t6.2*, 187, 189, 273
    policies, 114–115, 149t6.3, 163
  pre-registration, 174, 177, 180
  publication bias, 140
  replication, 155, 156, 192, 282
  transparency, 185
editor, journal
  bias, 120, 134, 138, 221, 223, 225, 232, 275
  costs, 389
  discretion, 99, *100t5.1*, 102, *103t5.2*, 106, 116t5.3
  and gender, 422, 424
  and promotion of transparency policies, 148, 151, 186, 187
  proposals, 475
  and research cycles, 68
  and results-blind review, 241, 243, 257
  role in pre-registration, 178, 180–181, 236, 240, 368
  role in review process, 75–76, 77, 79, 396
    proposals for, 93
  survey of, 163
editorial board, 68, 93, 360, 395, 422
epistemologies, 268, 285, 425, 437, 454
  frequentism versus Bayesianism, 305, 311, 314
  positivist, 453
  post-positivist, 439
  views within qualitative research, 86, 301
ethnography, 21, *21t2.1*, *21t2.2*, 31, 32, 114, *246t9.3*, 448, 452
Evidence in Governance and Politics (EGAP), 173, 195, 237n9, 238, 243, 473
experiments, 1, *60t3.1*, 165, 438, 448, *see also* prospective studies; randomized controlled trials
  and design-based research, 53, 268
  early-stage, 64–65
  and exploratory research, 466
  and generalizability, 356, 366
  natural, 63, 67, 118
  and pre-registration, 175, 177, 179–180
  and prior unobservability, 248

replication, 156, 190, 269, 272–273, 302, 305
reporting guidelines, 186, 202
and sociological methods, 21, *21t2.1*, *21t2.2*
exploratory research, 43, 55, 132, 179, 353, 461, 469
    as theory generating, 235, 263, 389
    versus testing, 239, 242, 252, 264, 363, 369, 462–463
external validity, 56, 183, 285, 290, 343–345, 366, 460, 470

false positive, 130–134, 166, 272, 357, 374
falsifiable, 342, *342t13.2*, 363, 462
Feldstein, Martin, 158
fieldwork, 30, 232, 254, 327
    and case selection, 313
    and exploratory research, 29, 30, 33, 466
    follow-up, 315–316
    and measurement error, 292
Findley, Michael, 255, 256, 257
Finkelstein, Amy, 177, 178
focus group, 55, 200, 209
Forscher, Bernard, 76–77
fraud in research, 205, 273, 286, 308n7, 435
    checks against, 132, 248
    and impact metrics, 376
    and reappraisal, 349, 370
Freese, Jeremy, 285, 301, 303–305, 357
funding, 203, 441, 464, *see also* National Science Foundation (NSF)
    for data collection, 153
    disclosure in publications, 148, *149*
    metrics for, 378
    for replication, 335, 476
    for repositories, 211
    for pilot studies, 56, 68
    and sexual harassment policies, 479

generalizability, 272, 304f12.1, 352, 356
Glennerster, Rachel, 171, 182
Google Scholar, 94, 102, 338, 379, 482
Gouldner, Alvin, 22, 24, 25–28, 31
graduate
    seminar, 38
        on publication, 74, 76
        and replication, 155, 347
        syllabi, 412–416
    training, 84, 196
        and data management, 219
        replication, 476, 482
graduate students, 254, 412, 451
    gender composition, 407
    and incentives for causal analysis, 53, 57, 59
    intellectual diversity, 442, 444
    pre-dissertation research, 37

and replication, 280, 287, 352
Gruber, Jonathan, 177, 178

Haidt, Jonathan, 435–439
Harvard, 372, 393, 411, 426n55, 462–463
    Dataverse, 207, 213
hierarchies, academic
    junior faculty, 79, 373, 418, 422, 471
    senior faculty, 79, 106, 113, 136, 484
h-index, 94, 125, 376, 387, 392, 396
hiring, 365, 396, 460
    and gender, 404, 420, 425–429, 478, 483
    and political bias, 441, 446
    and productivity, 4, 378, 398, 418
Hochschild, Arlie, 22, 31–32
Hughes, Everett C., 20, 30
humanities, 7, 73, 86, 376, 418, 442, 450
    and ideological diversity, 440–441
    and impact metrics, 376
    and libraries, 76n1
    and publications, 73
    and replication, 284

Igo, Sarah, 448–449
impact factor, 188, 386, 387–388, 394, 398, 399, 462
impact, research, *see* citation; impact factor
    and journals, 278
incentive, 460
    for care work, 427
    and impact metrics, 371, 397, 398
    and negative results, 331
    for new research procedures, 251
    for novelty, 275
    for original data gathering, 152, 154, 215–217
    for pilot studies, 56, 68
    for publication, 109, 223, 226, 235, 240, 278, 365
    and registration, 255
    and replication, 127, 156, 276–277, 280–281, 300
    for researchers, 114, 336, 469
    structure, 5, 360, 464
inductive research, 43, 51, 66–67, 226, 454
    and discovery, 252
    and initial theorizing, 43, 49, 223
    and surprise findings, 54
Institutional Review Board (IRB), 202, 214, 219
interdisciplinary, 39, 93, 187, 269, 450
internal validity, 285, 286, 343, 345, 366, 460
Inter-university Consortium for Political and Social Research (ICPSR), 208, 211
interviews, 209, *246t9.3*, 250, 251, 316, 440
    elite, 244, 247, 253, 256
    with experts, 27, 40, 302, 306
    as exploratory method, 26, 28, 55, 64, 466
    follow-up, 314, 315

Index

interviews (*cont.*)
  in-depth, 452
  as qualitative data, 114, 200, 288, 312, 320, 324
  technique, 35
Ioannidis, John P., 130–134, 138, 143

Jensen, Nathan M., 255, 256, 257
JSTOR, 21, 21t2.2, 24, 337, 412
Jussim, Lee, 435–439

Krueger, Alan B., 139, 168, 180
Kuhn, Thomas, 81, 85

Ladd, Everett Carll, 433, 443
Lazarsfeld, Paul, 22, 23–26, 29, 433, 443
Leamer, Edward E., 143–146, 166, 167
Li, Phillip, 157–158
libraries, 76, 212, 299, 358, 419n39
  and the digital revolution, 97, 207, 218, 373
  and institutional subscriptions, 124, 378, 387
Lipset, Seymour Martin, 22, 25, 34, 433, 443
Longino, Helen, 454

machine learning, 1, 182
Malesky, Edmund J., 255, 256, 257
Mannheim, Karl, 84, 453
measurement, 27, 58, 200, 216
  and algorithms, 252
  and descriptive studies, 61
  error, 140, 375
  instruments for, 448
  quality, 60
  and reappraisals, 340, 341, 356
mechanism, causal, 13, 183, 317, 322, 326, 356, 367, 437
Merton, Robert K., 22, 23–28, 35, 37, 85, 276, 379, 437, 443
meta-analysis, 195, 272, 310, 355, 357, 369
metadata, 202, 208–213
Microsoft Academic, 338, 373–379, 477
Miguel, Edward, 171, 175–177, 182
mixed methods, 32, 224, 233t9.2, 234, 244, 306, 323, 356
multi-method, *see* mixed methods

National Institutes of Health, 162, 197
National Science Foundation, 38, 135, 147n9, 481
  data access policies, 197
  and exploratory research, 38–40
  funding, 147, 152n16, 335
natural sciences, 7, 73, 111
  comparison with, 217, 361, 373, 451, 464
  replication in, 6, 476
negative results, 331, 475
Neumark, David, 180–182

Newhouse, Joseph P., 177, 178
Niederle, Muriel, 179, 190
normative
  argument, 20, 73
  commitments, 226, 430
  goals, 401
  research, 48, 54, 59
Nosek, Brian, 86, 92–95
null hypothesis, *see* testing

Odum Institute for Research in Social Science, 151n13, 155, 208, 208n10, 211
online
  academic publishing, 69, 91, 97, 123, 124, 394, 472
  commentary, 89, 94, 360
  data access, 299
  data sharing, 130, 279
  experiments, 282
  pre-publication, 189, 242
  repository, 94, 336
  reviews, 91
  supplementary materials, 91, 98, 108, 111, 113, 279
open access, 92, 94, 204, 373, 477
open data, 152n16, 165, 194, 195, 204, 211, 220, 279
  and journals, 151, 283
Open Science Framework, 173, 218, 254n23

paradigm, 13, 39, 80, 81–83, 85, 86, 87, 275, 346
  biomedical, 54, 64
peer review, 135, 323, 478
  of appraisals, 360
  open, 470
  post-publication, 188
  and publication bias, 129, 436, 450
  publications
    and descriptive research, 42, 58
    and exploratory research, 56
    of replication, 190
  results-blind, *see* results-blind review
  as system of evaluation, 371, 398
Peirce, Charles Sanders, 34–37, 438
Pepinsky, Thomas B., 255, 256, 257
Peterson, David, 285, 301, 303–305, 357
philosophy, 453
  of science, 437, 442
plagiarism, 162–164, 286
political bias, 436, 443, 446, 449
political science, 290, 461
  conservatives in, 440, 442
  core graduate seminars, 415
  and disciplinary norms, 188
  gender composition in, 407, 411, 414

and repositories, 94
and results-blind review, 179, 241
and transparency, 214, 473
political science journals, 56, *230t9.1*, *233t9.2*, 244
and data sharing, 151, 206
policies, 99, *100t5.1*, 102
publication bias, 136, 227, 234
Popper, Karl, 85, 113, 121, 173, 180, 189, 219, 222, 241, 254, 367, 375, 376, 377, 383, 385, 386, 387, 388, 394, 437, 450, 460
pre-analysis plan, 239, 339, 340, 368, 461, 468, 473, *see also* registration
against false positives, 134
and precision, 252
and prior unobservability, 242, 363
in qualitative research, 253, 256
for reappraisals, 364
and transparency, 165, 194
versus inductive findings, 53
pre-registration, *see* registration
process tracing, 51, 288, 299, 331, 473
and Bayesian logic, 239, 301, 322
tests, 223, 230, 231, 232
productivity, research, 443, *see also* hiring; promotion
gender differences in, 410, 420, 423
promotion, 378, 460, 484, *see also* tenure
and gender, 478
and incentives, 365
practices, 69, 215, 337, 395, 398, 422, 482
and productivity, 4, 46, 95, 107, 419
proprietary data, 148, 152–153, 399
prospective studies
and data collection, 364
descriptive, 62
design-driven, 43, 165
and observational independence, 249
and pre-registration, 65, 67, 174, 180, 182, 222, 238, 474
and prior unobservability, 243
psychology, 273
journals, 92
and transparency, 151, 186
publication bias, 275, 280
replication, 156, 177, 190, 195, 267–268, 271, 276
repositories, 94
results-blind review, 179
public policy
agenda, 178
and data access, 197
debates, 294, 447
evaluation, 365
makers, 360
practice and academics, 45
relevance, 13, 152, 155, 359, 469

research effects on, 277, 442
publication bias, 141, 272, 355, 358
and article length, 122
and novel results, 2
and null findings, 91
in observational research, 224, 232
and pre-registration, 172, 243, 473
and replication, 4, 281
and results-blind review, 179, 182–184, 263, 474
and statistical significance, 134, 145, 166, 222

Qualitative Data Repository, 155, 208, 211, 219, 289, 299, 336
qualitative research and methods, 358, 377
and article length, 107, 114
and causal mechanisms, 356
and data, 197, 200–201, 213, 219
and exploratory analysis, 32, 55
and replication, 335, 476
and research cycle, 63–64
and sociologists, 29
and women, 418
quantitative research and methods, 234, *246*, 335, 357, 461
and article length, 107, 114
and Bayesianism, 314
and causal inference, 54, 356
and data, 197, 200–201, 209
and hypothesis testing, 226
and prior unobservability, 247
and publication bias, 228, 231
and replication, 158, 200–201, 252–253
versus qualitative, 252–253
and women, 425

randomized controlled trials, 46, 143, 144, 146, 166, 312, 356
and causal relationships, 56
registration, 172, 174, 179, 184, 237, 243, 474
and research cycles, 42, 43
registration, *60*, 281, 364, 474, *see also* pre-analysis plan
and data availability, 151
and observational research, 195, 278
in qualitative research, 331
and reappraisals, 339, *347*
and transparency, 187, 473–474
replication, 43, 59, *149*, 179, 334–335, 341, 353, 476–477
and data access, 146, 197, 204, 205n6, 218, 340
and knowledge accumulation, 367
difficulties of, 347, 349
feasibility, 357
inability to, 129, 130, 435

replication (*cont.*)
  incentives for, 389
  promotion of, 195
  and publication, 81, 84, 91, 217
  and publication bias, 2, 4
  results of, 3, 343, 366
  and transparency, 187
repository, *see also* data; online; Qualitative Data Repository
  affiliation, 204
  of data, 187
  of research, 92, 94
  of reviews, 90, *96t4.1*
reputation, 287, 351, 485
  of journal, 462
  as metric of quality, 372–373, 387, 390, 393–394
  of scholars, 92, 94
researcher bias, 131, 358, 365
results-blind review, 236–238, 242, 243, 248, 461, 474–475
  evaluation of, 257, 482
  and hypothesis testing, 252, 255, 264
  and negative findings, 262
  in non-experimental research, 251–252
  in psychology, 179
  and publication bias, 221, 263
  and replication, 281
  special issue in *Comparative Political Studies*, 179, 237n9, 241
retractions, 163, 188–189, 286
retrospective studies, 43, 55, 62, 225
  and results-blind review, 222, 238
  and observational independence, 250
  and pre-registration, 66, 67
  and prior unobservability, 244, 248
revise and resubmit, 75–76, 77, 179

sample size, 138–139, 145, 168, 191
  in experimental research, 55, 186
  and exploratory research, 40t2.3
  in qualitative research, 290
  and statistical power, 133, 156–157, 260
Scopus, 338, 373–378
Sewell, William, Jr., 452–454
Shields, Jon, 440–441, 443–446, 449
social media, 211, 391
Social Science Research Council (SSRC), 316, 361
Social Science Research Networks (SSRN), 94, 469
sociology, 452, 461
  exploratory studies in, 23, 32
  and gender in discipline, 102–105, 412
  journals, *21t2.1, 21t2.2*
    and data sharing, 151
    practices, *103t5.2*, 105
    publication bias, 136, 227

model averaging in, 167
of science, 7, 437, 464
Stanley, TD., 131, 140, 169
statistical
  manipulation, 129
  power, 55, 131, 171, 310
  significance, *see* bias, publication
Stouffer, Samuel, 22, 24–26
surveys, 1
  as data, 154, 202, 243–244, 247
  of economists, 162
  experiments, 226
  in exploratory research, 21, 26, 30, 40
  methods, 282, 312
  and population sample, 366
  and research firms, 247
  in sociology journals, *21t2.1, 21t2.2*
  of scholars, 398, 433–434, 444
  and variable coding, 307
syllabi, 405, 414–416, 424

Taubman, Sarah, 177, 178
teaching, 95, 397, 432, 446, 478
  data management, 219
  and gender, 405, 421, 427
  and ideological diversity, 432, 435, 440, 443, 451–452, 455
  research methods, 198, 323, 425
tenure, 449, 460, 484
  and author bias, 136
  evaluation for, 69, 107, 395
  and gender, 386, 407–412, 426
  post-tenure incentives, 372, 467
testing
  and author bias, 133
  hypothesis, 42, 52, 140, 251
    adjustment, 174, 177
    in biomedical research, 49
    in journal publications, 52, 229, *230t9.1*, 233
    and multiple testing correction, 169–172
    and novelty, 257
  null hypothesis significance, 129, 226, 276, 322
  paradigm, 82
  in qualitative research, 223, 228, 255, 289
  rival hypotheses, 315
  theory, 229, 331, 363, 462
  and verification, 158
  versus exploration, 221, 225, 235, 239, 252, 463, 473
Tetlock, Phillip, 435–439, 450
Time-Sharing Experiments in the Social Sciences, 135, 226
transparency, 2, 280
  and impact metrics, 378
  of journal policies, 106, 115, 283

Index

and journals policies of, 347
and precision in sources, 300
proposals to increase, 472–475
in qualitative research, 268, 308, 332
and replication, 287, 289, 299
and review process, 93
Trow, Martin, 22, 25

uncertainty, 248, 332, 358
   and causal relationships, 47, 62
   of estimates, 58, 191, 310
   and experiments, 62
   and modeling, 166–167
   and prior probability, 302, 319
undergraduates, 195, 415, 446
   gender composition, 407, 412
   methods training, 299
   as population, 159, 316
universities, 3, 404, 423, 434, 459, 464, 480, 483, 484
   and citation biases, 113
   and diversity, 479
   and gender disparities, 403, 407–410, 419, 422
   and hiring policies, 429
   and institutional repositories, 206, 211
   and metrics, 371, 378
   and public repository of research, 94
   reputation, 372, 393, 395

verification, 43, 156, 306, 341, 437
   and quantitative methods, 25–28
   of results, 151, 154, 272, 283
      same data, 160, 270, 279, 304, 341t13.1
   theory, 82

Web of Science, 118, 338, 373–379, 477
Weber, Max, 34, 37, 367, 430, 438
workshops, academic, *see* conferences and workshops, academic
Wright, Bill, 177, 178